Advance Praise for Yahoo! Web An

In Yahoo! Web Analytics *Dennis Mortensen manages to do the impossibl knowledge of web analytics in an already crowded market. His clear lang make this book required reading for any web analytics practitioner intere freely-available tools. Dennis is one of the best and brightest in the web a.* Web Analytics *reinforces that with every page.*

—Eric T. Peterson, author of *Web Analytics Demystified*

Dennis doesn't just know what he's talking about, he's built it, grown it, consulted on it, and sold it to Yahoo! Now—finally—he's written the book. Don't let Dennis's smile and positive attitude fool you—he has the proverbial steel-trap mind and doesn't miss a thing. You get the advantage of his insight, his wisdom, and his unerring ability to tell it like it is. He can explain the "why" of web analytics very well but is stellar at showing you the "how." Specific variable settings, actual conversion tracking, and getting the most out of your search marketing dollar—it's all here. If you want to actually derive value from these tools rather than just look at the pretty reports, Dennis lays it all out. This is a book you can count on.

—JIM STERNE, Founder, eMetrics Marketing Optimization Summit

Web analytics is complex, but Dennis prefers things to be simple. As the individual who drove the initial development of Yahoo!'s Web Analytics tool, he managed to conquer mind-numbingly complex issues by presenting them in a simple and useful way. It's no wonder that he did it again with his Yahoo! Web Analytics book. Dennis takes you behind the scenes of this robust web analytics application and explains how to implement it in just about every situation so that you get what you need out of this tool. Whether you use the Yahoo! Web Analytics or not, this book belongs on any serious web analytics professional's desk.

—BRYAN EISENBERG, *New York Times* bestselling author of *Call to Action* and *Always Be Testing*, cofounder of FutureNow, Inc.

As insightful as it is inspiring, this is the definitive book for making the most out of Yahoo! Web Analytics. It is a guiding light for navigating the solution's capabilities and detailed enough to be a step-by-step guide. And who better than Dennis to write it! It is clear that Dennis has poured his experience from uncountable numbers of client conversations into this work. It is worth the equivalent of 100 hours of consulting from the well-known figurehead behind Yahoo! Web Analytics.

—AKIN ARIKAN, *Multichannel Marketing* author and Internet marketing product strategist at Unica Corporation

In Yahoo! Web Analytics, *Mortensen does more than just give insight, tips, and tricks about the tool—he provides the details about the impact Yahoo! Web Analytics can have on your business with a laser-like focus on moving from data to true business insight and action. It's a must-read for those interested in not only web analytics, but for those interested in improving their business online!*

—JASON BURBY, Chief Analytics & Optimization Officer, ZAAZ, and coauthor of *Actionable Web Analytics*

Measurement, testing, and constant improvement are at the heart of all successful online marketing campaigns. This book is a detailed and practical guide to using Yahoo! Web Analytics to turbo-charge your business performance. Dennis is eminently qualified to be your guide—he was instrumental in building the software. Get the book before your competitors do!

—TIM ASH, CEO of SiteTuners.com and bestselling author of *Landing Page Optimization*

Yahoo!®
Web Analytics

Yahoo!® Web Analytics

Tracking, Reporting, and Analyzing for Data-Driven Insights

Dennis R. Mortensen

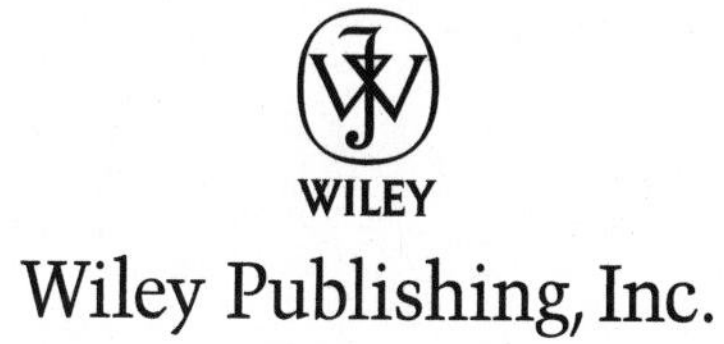

Wiley Publishing, Inc.

Senior Acquisitions Editor: Willem Knibbe
Development Editor: Susan Herman
Technical Editor: Mihaela Popa
Production Editor: Dassi Zeidel
Copy Editor: Liz Welch
Production Manager: Tim Tate
Vice President and Executive Group Publisher: Richard Swadley
Vice President and Publisher: Neil Edde
Book Designer: Franz Baumhackl
Compositor: Chris Gillespie, Happenstance Type-O-Rama
Proofreader: Kathy Pope, Word One New York
Indexer: Ted Laux
Project Coordinator, Cover: Lynsey Stanford
Cover Designer: Ryan Sneed
Cover Image: iStockPhoto

Published simultaneously in Canada

ISBN: 978-0-470-42424-7

For general information on our other products and services or to obtain technical support, please contact our Customer Care Department within the U.S. at (877) 762-2974, outside the U.S. at (317) 572-3993 or fax (317) 572-4002.

Wiley also publishes its books in a variety of electronic formats. Some content that appears in print may not be available in electronic books.

Library of Congress Cataloging-in-Publication Data

Mortensen, Dennis R., 1972-

Yahoo! Web analytics : tracking, reporting, and analyzing for data-driven insights / Dennis R. Mortensen.

p. cm.

ISBN-13: 978-0-470-42424-7 (pbk.)

ISBN-10: 0-470-42424-9 (pbk.)

1. Yahoo! Web analytics. 2. Web usage mining—Computer programs. 3. Internet users—Statistics—Data processing. 4. Web sites—Statisics—Data processing. 5. Consumer preferences—Data processing. I. Title.

TK5105.885.Y34M67 2009

006.7—dc22

2009009722

10 9 8 7 6 5 4 3 2 1

Dear Reader,

Thank you for choosing *Yahoo! Web Analytics*. This book is part of a family of premium-quality Sybex books, all of which are written by outstanding authors who combine practical experience with a gift for teaching.

Sybex was founded in 1976. More than thirty years later, we're still committed to producing consistently exceptional books. With each of our titles we're working hard to set a new standard for the industry. From the paper we print on, to the authors we work with, our goal is to bring you the best books available.

I hope you see all that reflected in these pages. I'd be very interested to hear your comments and get your feedback on how we're doing. Feel free to let me know what you think about this or any other Sybex book by sending me an email at `nedde@wiley.com`, or if you think you've found a technical error in this book, please visit `http://sybex.custhelp.com`. Customer feedback is critical to our efforts at Sybex.

Best regards,

Neil Edde
Vice President and Publisher
Sybex, an imprint of Wiley

Acknowledgments

For me, writing a book goes like this. I wake up early Saturday morning and wobble out to the kitchen. I fix bowls of cereal for the girls, who've been up for hours for some reason, hit the shower, and get ready for work—writing another chapter.

We'll put on our jeans and T-shirts, stumble out the door as soon as we can, and on most days, stop by Murray's Bagels and get some supplies—which include the obligatory Red Bull for me.

Then it's off to the Yahoo! 18th Street office, where we spend the entire Saturday working before heading home late in the evening. Lather, rinse, and repeat for 5 months.

And finally I can email the final chapter to the amazing people at Wiley!

And for this, I would like to thank Elisabeth, Victoria, and Vibeke for their lovely support.

To everybody else, and you know exactly who you are, thank you so much for your wonderful support in everything I do and in making this book a reality. I would hate to mention anybody by name in danger of actually forgetting some. That wouldn't be fair!

Cheers :-)
Dennis

About the Author

Dennis R. Mortensen is a pioneer and expert in the web analytics industry. He is an accredited associate web analytics instructor at the University of British Columbia and a frequent speaker on the subject of analytics and online marketing. Mortensen is an entrepreneur and was the COO of IndexTools until it was acquired by Yahoo! Inc. in May 2008. Today he is Director of Data Insights at Yahoo! and sits on the board of directors at the Web Analytics Association. He maintains the highly popular analytics blog, `VisualRevenue.com/blog`.

Contents

Foreword *xix*

Introduction *xxi*

Part I Advanced Web Analytics Installation 1

Chapter 1 Getting Started **3**

Competing on Analytics 4

Preinstallation Steps 6

Basic Installation 10

Data Collection Grouping 14

Adding and Managing Projects 18

Tracking Script Customization 20

Chapter 2 Content and Advanced Conversion Tracking **25**

Document Names 26

Document Groups 28

Track Downloads 28

Tracking Exit Links 30

Tracking Registered Members 31

Tracking Conversion Actions 34

Tracking Multiple Sales Actions During the Same Visit 38

Tracking Multiple Occurrences of the Same Action on a Web Page 38

Tracking Multiple Actions on the Same Web Page 41

Tracking On-click Actions 42

Visitor Conversion Count Methodology 44

Track Revenue 45

Tracking Revenue in Multiple Currencies 46

Track Order ID 48

Revenue Encryption 49

Creating Scenarios for Funnel Analysis 53

Chapter 3 Enterprise Campaign Tracking **57**

Types of Campaigns 58

Paid Search Setup 62

Creating and Managing Campaign Categories 63
Identifying Campaigns 67
Setting Up New Campaigns. 68
Single Campaign Management 72
Bulk Campaign Management 72
Setting Up a Fallback Campaign 74
Example Paid Search Deployment 75
Yahoo! Paid Search 76
Google Paid Search 77
Microsoft Paid Search 77
Paid Search Verification Opportunities 78
Internal Campaigns 79

Chapter 4 Merchandising Tracking and Reporting 83

Merchandising Basics 84
Setting Up Merchandising Tracking 86
Tracking SKU Information 86
Tracking Units and Amounts 87
Working with Multiple Currencies 89
Tracking Products Viewed. 90
Tracking Products Added to the Cart 92
Track Pending Sales and Reconciling Orders 93
Tracking Products Purchased 96
Tracking Discount, Tax, and Shipping 99
Setting Up Merchandising Categories 101
Merchandising Setup Tips 105
Avoiding Duplicate Order IDs Captured in Different Visits 105
Tracking Sales Across Secure and Nonsecure Domains 106

Chapter 5 Advanced Instrumentation 109

Tracking Custom Fields 110
Tracking Internal Searches 114
Instrumentation for Flash-Based Objects 116
Instrumentation for Ajax-Based Objects 121
Tracking Page Views vs. Actions Alone 125
Artificially Triggering Campaigns 127
Setting Up External Data Sources 128
Validating Your Code 131

Part II **Utilizing an Enterprise Web Analytics Platform** 133

Chapter 6 **Working with Report Results** **135**

What to Expect from a Report 136

A Traditional Reporting Interface 137

Using Calendars for Time Period Reporting 141
Reporting on Unique Visitors over Specific Time Periods 142
Time Comparative Reporting 144

Using Cross-Reference Filters 147
Choosing Scope of Filter 152
Using the Right Traffic Attribution Filters 153
Applying Regular Expression Filters 155
Adding and Using Metric Filters 155

Using Drill-downs and Drill-throughs. 157

Sorting Report Results 158

Color-Coding Data 160

Applying Report Notes and Reasoning 162

Exporting Data 163

Chapter 7 **Customizing Report Results** **165**

Using Metric Alerts 166
What to Monitor with an Alert 166
Alert Timing and Triggers 168

Event Management 170

Using Scheduled Reports 175

Building Custom Reports 179

Bookmarking Reports 185

Using Segments in Reporting. 188
Creating and Configuring Segments 190
Segmenting Loyal Customer Data 190
Additional Tips on Setting Up Data Segments 192

User Rights and Role Administration 193

Chapter 8 **Using Basic Reports as Templates for Customization** **195**

Visit Reports 196

Demographics Reports 203

Content Reports 207

Navigation Reports 211

Search Engines and Referrers Reports . . . 215

Conversion Reports . . . 217

System Reports . . . 219

Chapter 9 Using Dashboards **223**

Defining a Dashboard . . . 224

Adding a New Dashboard . . . 227

Adding New Dashboard Items . . . 229

Understanding Dashboard Items . . . 232
Tabular Data 233
Pie Charts 235
Bar and Row Charts 236
Key Performance Indicators (KPIs) 238
Gauge 240
Goal Charts 242
Trend Charts 243
Notes 245

Chapter 10 Distinctive Reports and Usage **249**

Understanding Path Analysis . . . 250
Standalone Path Analysis Reports 250
Path Analysis Drill-Down Examples 254

Using Scenarios for Funnel Analysis . . . 257
Setting Up a Predefined Scenario 258
Setting Up an Ad Hoc Scenario 260

Merchandising Reports . . . 263
Merchandising Summary Report 263
Cross-Sell Analysis Report 265
A Sample Custom Merchandising Report 266

Using Campaign Reports . . . 268

Using Internal Search Reports . . . 272

Part III Actionable Insights 279

Chapter 11 Paid Search Analysis and Optimization **281**

Defining Paid Search Objectives . . . 282
Tips for Clarifying Your Objectives 282
Paid Search as a Cross-Channel Optimization Tool 283

Getting Started with Paid Search Analysis . . . 283
Organizing Ad Groups 286
Matching Options 287
Search Engine Content Networks 287
Comparing Search Engine Data to Your Website Data 288

Detailed Paid Search Reporting. 288

Optimizing Paid Search for an E-commerce Site 292

Optimizing Paid Search for a Content Site 296

Balancing Paid Search with Organic Search 300

Chapter 12 Form Analysis and Optimization 303

Form Analysis and Form Actions 304

Using Funnels in Form Optimization 306

Prequalifying Traffic Sent to the Funnel 308

Form Abandonment 312

Form Page Optimization 315

Form Submit Optimization 319

Chapter 13 Content Optimization and Competitive Analysis 325

Using the Long Tail for Keyword Optimization 326

Using the Long Tail for Content Optimization 330

Determining Your Internal Search Query Box 335

Optimizing Content for Search- and Navigation-Dominant Visitors . . 340

Using Competitive Intelligence 341

Competitive Intelligence Tools 342

Comparing Metrics Appropriately 345

Finding Your Competitors in Upstream and Downstream Visits 346

Comparing Traffic from Search Engines 346

Who Owns Which Part of the Funnel? 347

Appendix Yahoo! Web Analytics Web Services API 349

Index 367

Foreword

Several years ago, when I was the director of analytics and research at Intuit, I had postulated the 10/90 rule. Simply put, it stated that if you had a budget of $100 (or dinars or rupees or pesos) for online decision making, then you should spend $10 on the web analytics tool and spend $90 on people (the "planet-sized brains" part of the equation).

The rule was derived from my own experience. I had access to a world-class (translation: expensive!) web analytics tool. It was producing 200 reports—all kinds of things were tagged and tracked and hugged. Yet there was very little to show in terms of actionable insights.

The problem, it turns out, was that the tool was simply puking data out. There were finite resources (translation: analysts) available to make sense of the data, and online marketers were simply not able to understand much from the 200 reports. The result? Not much.

Following a deliberative shift in strategy that involved purchasing a significantly cheaper tool (translation: it would not help you into your underwear each day but did give you all the data you needed) and investing in analysts—people who could take that data, make sense of it, and translate it into implementable business actions—the results were impressive.

Fast-forward to today and one important part of the 10/90 rule, the tools part, is not an issue anymore.

You can still buy and find valid productive uses for paid web analytics tools. But they are not mandatory.

You can use completely free world-class web analytics tools from Yahoo!, Google, Microsoft, and others. You can now take your precious budget and focus it all on the big planet-sized brains part.

What this translates into is your chance to be data rich *and* analysis rich as well!

Yes, yes, I see you jumping up and down saying access to tools, even free ones, is not enough. You are absolutely right.

Web analysis is not free. Your delightful people with planet-sized brains need training and coaching. You'll still have to "smartify" your online marketers.

My good friend Dennis Mortensen to the rescue!

This book is going to be your starting point and a constant companion on the journey to making sense of all that data you now have access to from your Yahoo! Web Analytics tool.

I have known Dennis for a number of years now. He is smart. He is supremely knowledgeable about online marketing and decision making. He has deep hands-on experience in the world of web analytics (not just pontificating about it but actually rolling up his sleeves and getting jiggy with the data).

He is uniquely qualified to write this book, thanks to him being at IndexTools since its inception.

This book covers the length and depth and breadth of Yahoo! Web Analytics. Chapters 1 and 2 will get you going with all the right buttons to press, and before the end of first part of the book, your website will be lit up like the glorious Christmas tree at Rockefeller Center in New York City, to produce all the data, accurately, that you'll need.

But of course that is the start of the glory. Reports, segmentation, templates, and customizable dashboards await you. Never again will you produce a dashboard that gets on the "auto delete" list!

Once there you'll want to forsake sleep completely until you finish the book because search analysis and optimization is as awesome as it sounds. Understanding the value of your content and being truly customer-centric will be well within your grasp.

This book will ensure that your web analysts get off to a flying start and stay smart as they dig deeper into the tool to leverage all the power that lies within. They'll be able to create custom segments and cross-tabulate data with unique reports (just as I have been doing for the three years that I have been using IndexTools).

I am excited that you have purchased this book. I know you are going to have a ton of fun learning about web analytics. I am positive that by the time you are done with the book, you'll agree with me that analysis is sexycool.

To infinity and beyond!

AVINASH KAUSHIK
Analytics evangelist and author
Mountain View, CA.

Introduction

My goal is to take you through how you should approach analytics, and in this book we mainly use the application Yahoo! Web Analytics. You will become a true expert in this application by the end of this book. My philosophy is that you should focus on three different but equally important tasks. I have divided the book into three parts to reflect these broad tasks.

Part I, "Advanced Web Analytics Installation," consists of Chapters 1 through 5. The focus is on data collection.

True competitive advantage in web marketing comes from collecting the right data, but also, and no less important, from configuring your web analytics tool in such a way that you can derive insight from the data. Part 1 features detailed code examples that webmasters or developers can apply directly. Marketing people and executives will learn the opportunities they can demand from this tool.

I also show you how to add reporting dimensions to the predefined report structures for fantastic filtering and segmentation opportunities.

Part II, "Utilizing an Enterprise Web Analytics Platform," encompasses Chapters 6 through 10, where we focus on reports.

Creating reports is an easy feat, but remember that reports are never better than the data you collect. You need an exceedingly good understanding of how to work with your data.

Part II is less technical than the first part. In it I'll teach you to use your reporting toolbox to provide targeted answers to specific questions, such as "How much revenue did we make from first-time organic search visitors from Canada last week?" For this and many other questions you'll encounter, there is no standard report, but you will know how to get this answer and hundreds of others when you're through with this section.

Part III, "Actionable Insights," encompasses Chapters 11 through 13 and focuses on how to take action on your data to optimize your web property. Having gone through the effort of implementing the data collection and reporting strategies in Parts 1 and 2, you will have gained enough insight to start an optimization process.

Part III introduces you to optimization using a set of actionable insights. This is merely an appetizer, and the handful of optimizations I present are not, by any means, the only ones you can pursue. But the ideas and attitude behind them can most definitely be copied and carry you down other optimization avenues. Think of this section as an idea catalog. One of the most important questions I tackle in this section is paid search optimization. Always keep your eyes on the money, eh?

Who Should Read This Book?

Anybody interested in web analytics on a detailed level should read this book, in particular if you want to use analytics for website optimization. In my world, that includes people in the following professions: website developers and engineers who are responsible for setting up web analytics; sales and marketing people who are eager to know what they can expect from analytics at this level; and finally, my fellow web analytics and optimization experts who want a fresh angle on how to optimize their websites and truly gain a competitive advantage.

You don't necessarily have to be a Yahoo! Web Analytics user or client to appreciate this book. However, general knowledge about website management and online marketing is a great benefit. This book does not cover the inner workings of analytics from an IT architectural point of view.

Book Companion Websites

While reading the book and once you have finished it, you are more than welcome to continue your web analytics journey online.

I maintain an active web analytics and online marketing blog, which I will update with features new to Yahoo! Web Analytics as they arrive, new reports as they are introduced, and optimization tips as they come along:

Blog: `http://visualrevenue.com/blog/`

Book: `http://visualrevenue.com/blog/yahoo-analytics-book`

Contacting the Author

If you have questions, feedback, or critique, I am eager to hear from you. You can reach me through the blog mentioned earlier, but also through these social media destinations:

`http://www.linkedin.com/in/dennismortensen`

`http://www.facebook.com/people/Dennis-R-Mortensen/571491680`

`http://twitter.com/dennismortensen`

And you are always welcome to email me directly at `dennis.mortensen@evcrp.com`.

Yahoo!®
Web Analytics

Advanced Web Analytics Installation

I

Yahoo! Web Analytics uses a browser-based system to identify and track visitors through your website. It is able to pinpoint details about visitors, such as where they go and what they do while on your website. Part I of this book is intended to help you identify the successful elements of your web property. You will learn to assign costs to any type of marketing campaign, allowing you to measure return on your ad spending and other metrics. You will also learn how to add reporting dimensions to the predefined report structures for fantastic filtering and segmentation opportunities later.

Chapter 1 **Getting Started**

Chapter 2 **Content and Advanced Conversion Tracking**

Chapter 3 **Enterprise Campaign Tracking**

Chapter 4 **Merchandising Tracking and Reporting**

Chapter 5 **Advanced Instrumentation**

Getting Started

True competitive advantage in web marketing comes from collecting the right data, but also, and no less important, configuring your web analytics tool in such a way that you get an opportunity to derive insight from the data. In this chapter you will learn how to install Yahoo! Web Analytics and manage projects. You will see examples of data collection grouping such as vertical and horizontal segmentation. Finally, you will learn what a tracking script is and how its data collection flexibility opens opportunities for reporting and analysis.

1

Chapter Contents

Competing on Analytics
Preinstallation Steps
Basic Installation
Data Collection Grouping
Adding and Managing Projects
Tracking Script Customization

Competing on Analytics

I am not the one to lecture you about the importance of web analytics or how it works. Since you are reading this book, I expect that you already know the importance and value of using analytics in your business. Instead, I aim to show you how to create a situation where you are able to *compete on analytics*; that is, to gain a competitive advantage using web analytics. For this to happen, you are simply forced to do more sophisticated analysis than just looking at reports about the number of page views or the number of visits on your web properties, an activity also known as report surfing.

Note: Report surfing, where one looks at reports without a clear agenda, is not only unfortunate web analytics tool-usage behavior, it is one of the greatest sins a web analytics practitioner can do. The phenomenon and a solution suggestion are debated here: `http://visualrevenue.com/blog/2007/09/web-analytics-report-surfing-and-how-to.html`.

To compete on analytics, you need a sophisticated data collection strategy, because you cannot analyze data that you have not collected. It is that simple. You cannot collect too much data on the behavior of your visitors. You can present and report on too much data, but that is a debate we will undertake in Part II of this book, "Utilizing an Enterprise Web Analytics Platform."

Yahoo! Web Analytics and other similar applications on the market have achieved a high level of sophistication only by collecting the correct data. Simpler applications that deploy what some call either plain-vanilla- or simple footer tagging offer nothing more than basic insights.

Plain-Vanilla Tagging

This is also known as *simple footer tagging*. Tagging your complete website by using the provided default tracking script and simply applying that to the footer of your website templates does not collect enough data to create the insights you need to be competitive.

If you are in doubt about the value of collecting data—and bear in mind that I am saying this with my Yahoo! hat on—why do you think that Yahoo!, Google, and Microsoft provide you with free analytics tools? Partly because even the *leftover* data (aggregated visitor data across multiple websites) provides so much value that it makes up for the cost of giving away the tool. Now imagine the value you can get out of your highly customized, nonaggregated data. Isn't this just fascinating to think about?

Yahoo! Web Analytics provides industry-standard reporting that includes pooling multiple visits into visitor profiles, differentiating new visitors from returning visitors, applying campaign attribution choices on first touch point and not necessarily last click, and so on. However, I will not be debating the accuracy of these common ways of collecting data, nor will I discuss the inherited challenges of cookie-based tracking. I suggest reading Brian Clifton's *Advanced Web Metrics with Google Analytics* (Sybex, 2008) because it has some very good chapters, including in-depth commentary on that topic, explaining the difference between log files and page tagging.

You will be required, when reading the first part of this book, to have some basic understanding of JavaScript, not on a programming level but on a simple customization level. Most of this and the next four chapters are about customizing the standard tracking script, shown here:

```
<!- IndexTools Customization Code ->
<!- Remove leading // to activate custom variables ->
<script type="text/javascript">
//var DOCUMENTGROUP='';
//var DOCUMENTNAME='';
//var ACTION='';
</script>
<!- End of Customization Code ->
<!- IndexTools Code v4.00 - All rights reserved ->
<script type="text/javascript" src="http://visualrevenue.com/indextools.
js"></script><noscript>
<div><img src="http://stats.indextools.com/p.pl?a=10001277xxxxx&amp;js=no"
width="1" height="1" alt="" /></div></noscript><!-//->
<!- End of IndexTools Code ->
```

This tracking script is what we would call a plain-vanilla tag, simply because it collects the basic information needed on a page on your website. This is also the tracking script that you will use as the foundation and the one you will mold, by applying different variables, into collecting much more interesting information than just the page title, a basic referring URL, or other simple system information.

The previous tracking code is the original tracking script Version 4, and the following is the new updated Version 5 of the tracking script:

```
<!- Yahoo! Web Analytics - All rights reserved ->
<script type="text/javascript"
src="http://d.yimg.com/mi/ywa.js"></script>
<script type="text/javascript">
var YWATracker = YWA.getTracker("1000123xxxx");
//YWATracker.setDocumentName("");
YWATracker.submit();
</script>
<noscript>
<div><img
```

```
src="http://a.analytics.yahoo.com/p.pl?a=1000123xxxx&amp;js=no"
width="1" height="1" alt="" /></div>
</noscript>
<!- End of Yahoo! Web Analytics Code ->
```

There is no difference in the type of data that you can collect with the two track script versions, but you should expect to transition to the updated version if you are not already using it. The biggest difference from a deployment point of view is that you no longer set JavaScript variables but call a JavaScript function to do the same.

Throughout the book I will reference this according to the variable and not the function, but the two concepts are interchangeable and are going to give you the same result.

So, making sure we are on the same page, the following code does the same, and I will reference both as setting the value of the variable.

```
var DOCUMENTNAME="About us"; // Version 4
YWATracker.setDocumentName("About us"); // Version 5
```

Later in this chapter there is a complete list of available custom variables, which can be combined in a number of ways. Chapters 2–5 go through various ways of applying the variables and the rationales for doing so.

Preinstallation Steps

Before I introduce the code implementation, I would like to draw your attention to two important destinations within Yahoo! in regard to analytics. `analytics.yahoo.com` is the starting point for anything analytics at Yahoo! and also the starting point for more information on Yahoo! Web Analytics (see Figure 1.1).

`web.analytics.yahoo.com` is the web analytics application domain that you should bookmark for easy access to your reporting interface.

Your first task, if you have not achieved this already, is to have a Yahoo! Web Analytics account created. There are multiple ways of getting an account, and I suggest that you follow the `analytics.yahoo.com` domain or the accompanying book blog at `visualrevenue.com/blog` to find the most up-to-date access points. However, let me list a number of places where you will be able to get access to an account:

Yahoo! Web Analytics Partner Networks This is where I suggest you start if you are not affiliated with any of the following Yahoo! offerings.

Yahoo! Small Business Merchant Solutions Included as an automated part of the offering; if you run a store, this is the way to go forward.

Yahoo! Japan For the Japanese market only, but essentially a free-for-all offering.

Yahoo! Buzz Customers If you are an advertiser, you will have the Analytics Package included.

Yahoo! Custom Customers If you are an advertiser, you will have the Analytics Package included.

Y! OS If you are a widget developer, the Dashboards are powered by Yahoo! Web Analytics, so you should in theory have a full account.

Figure 1.1 Anything Analytics at Yahoo!

Figure 1.2 shows an example of where to go to open your Yahoo! Web Analytics account.

Please bear in mind that some user interface and general semantics surrounding Yahoo! Web Analytics might be slightly different, depending on where you get the account. That said, the underlying technology and tracking is exactly the same.

Collecting the first row of data, meaning the very first page view, is fairly simple and does not take much effort. Just insert the tracking script on every page of your website and upload the general tracking script include file (`indextools.js`) to your web server. That is it, and you are done!

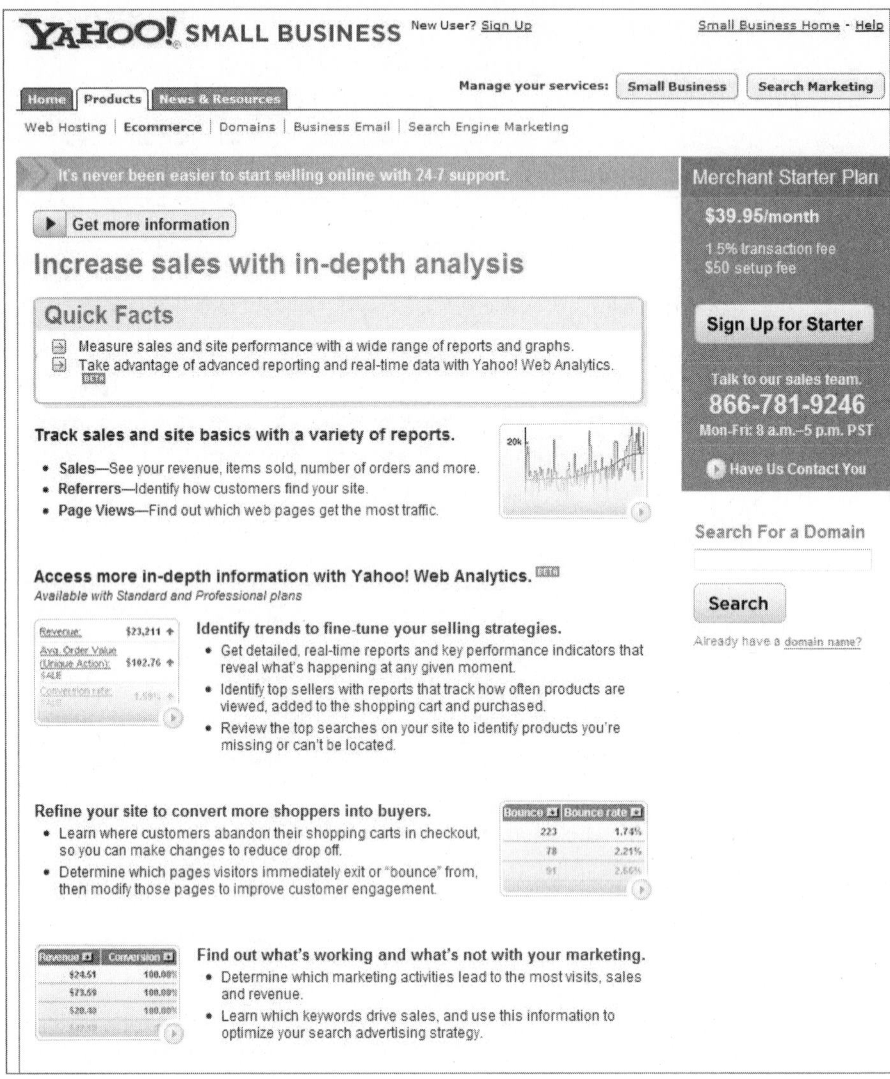

Figure 1.2 Yahoo! Small Business Merchant Solutions

Yahoo! Web Analytics collects and presents data in real time, or more precisely, there is a 7-second delay between visitors viewing your website and the visit being viewable in the reporting interface.

Each project you track is identified by a unique tracking script and a unique tracking script include file. A *project* is a website or a related group of websites, but I will discuss the idea of data collection grouping later in this chapter. You can find the tracking script template under the Installation tab in Yahoo! Web Analytics.

As I indicated earlier, some understanding of JavaScript is necessary, but for a basic installation, basic knowledge of HTML and JavaScript is useful but hardly needed. You will have to edit your web pages to add the provided tracking script.

And I am most sure that in a lot of cases your job will not consist of editing but merely sending off requirements of specific code that should be added to specific pages. Then your web department will execute! Besides adding the tracking script to all your pages, you need to upload the tracking script include file onto your web server, typically in the root folder. We will be more specific about this in a second, but to reiterate:

1. Apply the provided tracking script to *all* pages.
2. Upload the provided tracking script include file.

Yahoo! Web Analytics uses a well-defined, browser-based tracking system to identify and track visitors through your website, and it is able to identify details about your website visitors, where visitors go on your site, and what they do while on the site.

Without going into too much detail, let me explain how it works, which will be a good reference for you in understanding what is going on. Upon loading a web page, the browser processes the above-mentioned tracking script, which you applied to all your web pages. This tracking script directs the browser to retrieve a small, invisible pixel from the Yahoo! Web Analytics servers and to process the larger uploaded tracking script include file. By doing so, detailed information about your visitors' activity is sent back to the Yahoo! Web Analytics databases.

Yahoo! Web Analytics then either sets a new first-party cookie in the visitors' browser or resets the existing one. The first time a visitor comes to your website, Yahoo! Web Analytics sets a one-year, first-party, persistent cookie in their browser that includes unique visitor information. During the first visit, people are identified as first-time visitors. On subsequent visits, Yahoo! Web Analytics resets the cookie life to one year beyond the date of the visit, and identifies them as a returning visitor for the duration of that visit. If a cookie cannot be set, then the visitor is indentified as a first-time visitor. If the visitor has deleted the cookie, Yahoo! Web Analytics will again identify them as a first-time visitor and reissue a new first-party cookie.

You can define and track further information by applying variables to the tracking script, which is then sent back to the database and subsequently made available for analysis. So to conclude, during a visit, Yahoo! Web Analytics recognizes each time the browser loads a page and thus executes the script, and records yet another page view with all its accompanying metrics. All pages viewed by one visitor are grouped together as one visit, which is also called a session. A session stops after 30 minutes of inactivity. A large pool of the default metrics are collected from what is called the user agent string.

User Agent String

Very simply put, a user agent string is a text field in an HTTP request header that contains information such as name and version of the web browser and operating system.

Here is an example of what a user agent string looks like:

```
Mozilla/5.0 (Windows; U; Windows NT 6.0; en-GB; rv:1.9.0.4) Gecko/2008102920
Firefox/3.0.4
```

Yahoo! Web Analytics maintains detailed records of every visit to your website in its database, including the information in the user agent string. When you request a report, Yahoo! Web Analytics mines this database to produce real-time reports for any reporting period you selected.

Basic Installation

Now to the meat of the matter—actually installing the tracking script and recording that first page view. Go to the installation part of your account and request the tracking script. Having applied the URL visualrevenue.com when creating the account as the primary website, the tracking script comes out looking like this:

Version 4

```
<!- IndexTools Customization Code ->
<!- Remove leading // to activate custom variables ->
<script type="text/javascript">
//var DOCUMENTGROUP='';
//var DOCUMENTNAME='';
//var ACTION='';
</script>
<!- End of Customization Code ->
<!- IndexTools Code v4.00 - All rights reserved ->
<script type="text/javascript" src="http://visualrevenue.com/indextools.
js"></script><noscript>
<div><img src="http://stats.indextools.com/p.pl?a=10001277xxxxx&amp;js=no"
width="1" height="1" alt="" /></div></noscript><!-//->
<!- End of IndexTools Code ->
```

It does not mean that the tracking script is dedicated to that specific URL—all it means is that it applied the location of the tracking script include file in the tracking script. This is something you can change yourself by hand if needed. Yahoo! Web Analytics assumes by default that you locate the tracking script include file (indextools.js) in the root folder:

```
<script type="text/javascript" src="http://visualrevenue.com/indextools.
js"></script>
```

The tracking script reference to the root location is something you can modify, should you have restrictions or procedures for where to put JavaScript include files:

```
<script type="text/javascript" src="http://visualrevenue.com/includes/js/
indextools.js"></script>
```

You need to make sure that the physical placement of the file matches your reference.

Here is a summary of the steps for how to install the tracking script:

1. Go to the Yahoo! Web Analytics website and log in to your account.
2. Select the Installation tab and follow the two-page setup process. On the second page, you will receive the tracking script for your website's pages and a tracking script include file.
3. I strongly recommend that you upload the tracking script include file to the root directory of your web server.
4. Select the Yahoo! Web Analytics tracking script and copy it to the clipboard. Make sure you have selected all the code.
5. Open your HTML page in a text editor and paste the code into the body section of your page, directly above the closing body tag `</BODY>`.
6. Repeat steps 4 and 5 for every page on your website that you want Yahoo! Web Analytics to track.

Figure 1.3 shows a simple web page as an example: `http://visualrevenue.com/`.

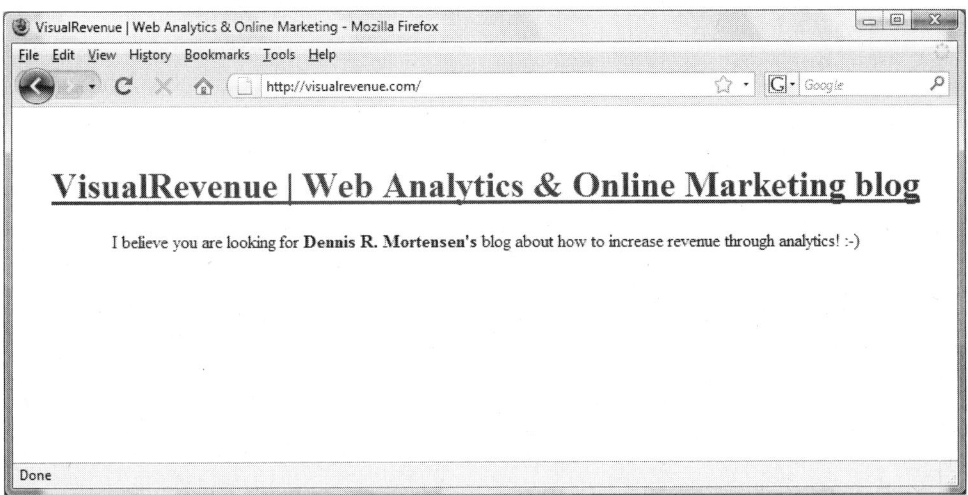

Figure 1.3 Simple HTML page

Applying these steps and viewing the HTML source for the page will give you a direct idea of where to place the tracking script and how it relates to the rest of the HTML code.

```
<!DOCTYPE HTML PUBLIC "-//W3C//DTD HTML 4.0 Transitional//EN" "http://www
.w3.org/TR/html4/loose.dtd">
<html>
<head>
```

```
<title>VisualRevenue | Web Analytics &amp; Online Marketing</title>
</head>
<body>
<center>
<BR>
<h1 id="blog-title"><a href="http://visualrevenue.com/blog/">VisualRevenue |
Web Analytics &amp; Online Marketing blog</a> </h1>
<p>I believe you are looking for <strong> Dennis R. Mortensen's</strong>
blog about how to increase revenue through analytics! :-)</p>
</center>
<!- IndexTools Customization Code ->
<!- Remove leading // to activate custom variables ->
<script type="text/javascript">
var DOCUMENTNAME='Homepage';
</script>
<!- End of Customization Code ->
<!- IndexTools Code v4.00 - All rights reserved ->
<script type="text/javascript" src="http://visualrevenue.com/indextools.
js"></script><noscript>
<div><img src="http://stats.indextools.com/p.pl?a=1000127718971&amp;js=no"
width="1" height="1" alt="" /></div></noscript><!-//->
<!- End of IndexTools Code ->
</body>
</html>
```


Upgrades to the way Yahoo! Web Analytics collects the data are rarely something that require changes to the tracking script. The upgrades are typically done in the tracking script include file, and all you need to do is upload the newest version to the web server to take advantage of newly introduced data collection features. The reporting updates are done entirely remotely without any action needed from you.

The new Version 5 of the tracking script no longer requires you to upload a tracking script include file, as this is hosted by Yahoo. So it makes the initial deployment of the code a whole lot easier.

Version 5

```
<!- Yahoo! Web Analytics - All rights reserved ->
<script type="text/javascript"
src="http://d.yimg.com/mi/ywa.js"></script>
<script type="text/javascript">
var YWATracker = YWA.getTracker("1000123xxxx");
YWATracker.setDocumentName("About us");
YWATracker.submit();
```

```
</script>
<noscript>
<div><img
src="http://a.analytics.yahoo.com/p.pl?a=1000123xxxx&amp;js=no"
width="1" height="1" alt="" /></div>
</noscript>
<!- End of Yahoo! Web Analytics Code ->
```

Note: Please note that if your website uses frames or Ajax, you are forced to take a slightly different route in applying the code. This topic is covered in later sections.

If your website is secured by SSL (Secure Sockets Layer), you have to use a special tracking script. Under the installation section of Yahoo! Web Analytics, you are given the opportunity to choose between a tracking script for standard HTTP pages including Flash websites and, in general, other normal browser applications, or a unique Yahoo! Web Analytics SSL tracking script. The complete script without any modifications looks like this:

```
<!- IndexTools Customization Code ->
<!- Remove leading // to activate custom variables ->
<script type="text/javascript">
//var DOCUMENTGROUP='';
//var DOCUMENTNAME='';
//var ACTION='';
//var AMOUNT='USD0.00';
//var ORDERID='';
</script>
<!- End of Customization Code ->
<!- IndexTools SSL Code v4.00 - All rights reserved ->
<script type="text/javascript" src="https://visualrevenue.com/indextools_
ssl.js"></script><noscript>
<div><img src="https://secure.indextools.com/p.pl?a=100012771897l&amp;js=no"
width="1" height="1" alt="" /></div></noscript><!-//->
<!- End of IndexTools Code ->
```

As you probably noticed, the set of variables included in the default tracking script is extended by AMOUNT and ORDERID—even though they are commented out. The reason for this is as noted earlier—just to give you a head start—and they indicate very nicely where you typically would have SSL pages, such as the pages where products are sold.

But more importantly, you will notice that you are required to download the `indextools_ssl.js` script and place that in your preferred folder and reference this tracking script include file instead of the regular tracking include file.

If your website contains a mixture of SSL and standard pages, then you need to tag each page with the appropriate form of the tracking script. You also need to upload both versions of the include file to the root directory of your web server.

Data Collection Grouping

It is of the utmost importance that you decide on a strategy for grouping the collected data before deploying the first tracking script—there is no opportunity for you to roll back this choice, and there is no feature to untangle unrelated data or group related data at a later stage.

Yahoo! Web Analytics works with a data collection grouping concept called *projects*. Projects are essentially just data containers that hold any collected data you choose—and you should consider that freedom before you start deploying any tracking scripts.

When you create a project, a new unique tracking script is created, with a unique project ID. Whenever that tracking script is executed, the data is collected in the same project. The tracking script is not domain dependent, and you can deploy the tracking script on completely unrelated domains and, in theory, have it deployed under domains you have no control of, such as third-party partner domains.

There is no technical right or wrong, but I strongly recommend that you replicate organizational company structures. Let's look at the following example created for ValueClick Inc., a fictional company:

- ValueClick (Company)
    - Corporate Marketing
        - `valueclick.com` (primary domain)
        - `valueclick.co.uk` (domain for the UK)
- Shopping Comparison (Division)
    - PriceRunner (Business Unit)
        - `pricerunner.com` (domain for the US)
        - `pricerunner.co.uk` (domain for the UK)
        - `pricerunner.dk` (domain for Denmark)
        - `pricerunner.se` (domain for Sweden)
        - `Etc.`

- Affiliate Marketing (Division)
    - Commission Junction (Business Unit)
        - `cj.com (primary domain)`
        - `uk.cj.com (domain for the UK)`
        - `de.cj.com (domain for Germany)`
        - `members.cj.com (domains for affiliate application)`
        - `Etc.`

And I am sure they have hundreds of domains to complement these and hundreds of vanity domains on top of that as well. As you can see, we are left with a decision as to how to group these domains (what tracking script to place on which domains) and the future reporting implications of those choices. My best advice is to replicate company structures and group not by web domains but by matching goals and thus data similarity. In our ValueClick example, that could look like this:

- Project 1: ValueClick Corporate Marketing Websites
    - `valueclick.com`
    - `valueclick.co.uk`
- Project 2: PriceRunner Shopping Comparison Websites
    - `pricerunner.com`
    - `pricerunner.co.uk`
    - `pricerunner.dk`
    - `pricerunner.se`
- Project 3: Commission Junction Public Websites
    - `cj.com` (primary domain)
    - `uk.cj.com` (domain for the UK)
    - `de.cj.com` (domain for Germany)
- Project 4: Commission Junction Affiliate Applications
    - `members.cj.com`

By grouping some 10 PriceRunner countries into one big—and at first sight, messy—pool of data, we create the opportunity to do two types of data segmentation: vertical and horizontal segmentation.

Vertical segmentation means that we can, at any point and on any of the collected data, create a segment based on, say, the dimension Entry Domain (such as entry domain = `pricerunner.co.uk` for the UK country manager). Or it could be, and probably more correctly so, a segment based on the Dimension of Visiting Countries

(Visiting Countries = United Kingdom). See Figure 1.4 to see what this looks like in the Yahoo! Web Analytics Segmentation Wizard.

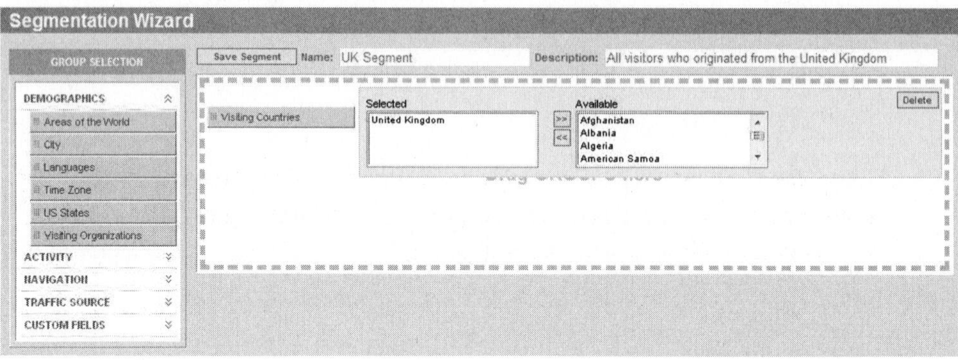

Figure 1.4 Yahoo! Web Analytics Segmentation Wizard

Horizontal segmentation means that we can create a segment across all domains (and this is one reason why data should be related in a project). For example, segmenting data on the dimension Page URL (such as Page URL = Apple-iPod-Touch-16GB-Black) will give us information about a given product across all countries/domains, allowing access to such information as the visit-to-sale conversion rate compared across countries.

These segments can be applied on all reports and, even more importantly, on dashboard items, which then creates the opportunity to have a set of similar dashboard items (on the same metric or *key performance indicator [KPI]*). This could be a look at your conversion rate—but for every single country individually, compared to the global average, thus spotting high- and low-performing teams.

Key Performance Indicators (KPIs)

KPIs are promoted metrics, such as cost per new subscriber, that function as communication and steering vehicles for management—or in plain English, the numbers that are important to you! Find a detailed explanation of the difference between a KPI and a metric here: `http://visualrevenue.com/blog/2008/02/difference-between-kpi-and-metric.html`.

Chapter 7, "Customizing Report Results," devotes an entire section to segmentation in general, and will explain how to set up and use this functionality.

Even though you might have a set of different projects, you still have the opportunity to create a high-level *project rollup*, which will create sums on basic metrics, such as page views, across all your projects and also provide a simple tree structure for visual comparison. You can find this feature under the Dashboard menu.

Domain Grouping

Your data collection project strategy is not to be confused with domain grouping. It is quite common to run matching versions of a website under different domain names or vanity domains, such as:

Domain 1: `http://visualrevenue.com/`

Domain 2: `http://visualrevenue.net/`

Multiple domains, if not set up correctly, will create suboptimal, and to some extent faulty, reporting in areas such as most popular pages, where you might have duplicates but it is in fact the same page, just served from two different domains.

To avoid this, Yahoo! Web Analytics allows you to group all your different domains under a project, and all of them are treated as the same website. You can find this option under Settings:

This procedure allows you to map each page of your secondary domain to your primary domain and thus ensure the reporting will be amalgamated correctly.

Note that this setting is a rewrite upon data collection and it takes effect immediately after saving it; it is not something that can be changed for previous collected data.

Vanity URL

A vanity URL (unique domain) is typically created by a company as part of an advertising campaign that points to a microsite (you will see this used in offline campaigns the most), with the assumption that it is easier to remember a specific domain name, such as:

Country URL: http://www.hp.com/country/dk/da/welcome.html

Vanity URL: http://www.hp.dk

The rule of thumb is that you should have a good reason to split your data collection into separate projects. Unless you are running very different web properties, you should end up with something like the setup shown in Figure 1.5.

If and when you deploy multiple Yahoo! Web Analytics projects, always make sure that you choose the correct and corresponding project tracking script.

View reports

VIEW REPORTS	BASE URL	EDITION NAME
	http://www.fourseasons.com	Enterprise Edition
	http://test.fourseasons.com	Enterprise Edition
	http://dev1.fourseasons.com	Enterprise Edition

You can manage more than one web site under your account. Please note that a distinct tracking code will be generated for each site. Add new web site (project)

Figure 1.5 Project setup example

Adding and Managing Projects

Keep in mind that in addition to serving as a container for data collected, a project holds and defines a set of properties for the data and their interpretation and reporting visualization.

Depending on your account permission, you can manage anything from one single project to an almost unlimited number of projects. You add new projects under the Settings sections, and this is also where you manage existing projects (see Figure 1.6). Whether you create a new project or edit an existing one, it is the same set of properties that you edit.

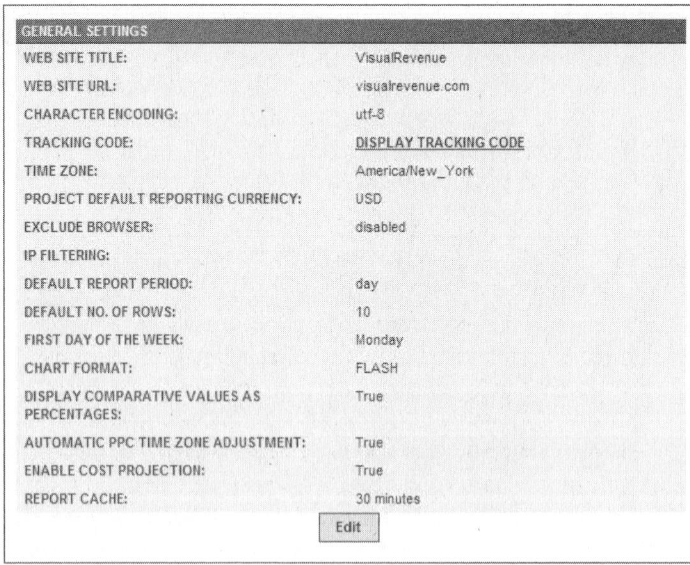

GENERAL SETTINGS	
WEB SITE TITLE:	VisualRevenue
WEB SITE URL:	visualrevenue.com
CHARACTER ENCODING:	utf-8
TRACKING CODE:	DISPLAY TRACKING CODE
TIME ZONE:	America/New_York
PROJECT DEFAULT REPORTING CURRENCY:	USD
EXCLUDE BROWSER:	disabled
IP FILTERING:	
DEFAULT REPORT PERIOD:	day
DEFAULT NO. OF ROWS:	10
FIRST DAY OF THE WEEK:	Monday
CHART FORMAT:	FLASH
DISPLAY COMPARATIVE VALUES AS PERCENTAGES:	True
AUTOMATIC PPC TIME ZONE ADJUSTMENT:	True
ENABLE COST PROJECTION:	True
REPORT CACHE:	30 minutes

Edit

Figure 1.6 Project settings

Table 1.1 is a comprehensive list of all the available project settings and their reporting implications.

► **Table 1.1** List of Available Project Properties

Setting	Implication
Web Site Title	Specifies the friendly name of the project used throughout the system, including scheduled reports.
Web Site URL	The primary domain and the one you see your data grouped around. This setting does not prevent you from using the tracking script elsewhere.
Character Encoding	Specifies how Yahoo! Web Analytics is to interpret the collected data. You can leave the default setting or consult your web development department for the encoding of your web properties.
Estimated Pageview	This setting is legacy and intended for capacity planning purposes. It has no impact on the functioning of your account.
Time Zone	This setting is used to determine how to split days when reporting. It should be set to the primary time zone of the corporation. However, any single user can set a time zone and have individual reporting on it, such as a regional manager with regional needs.
First Day of the Week	Basic calendar formatting; used for splitting week views.
Exclude Browser	To ensure that you have as accurate data as possible, I strongly suggest you choose to exclude your own visits, unless needed for testing purposes. You want real visitors with real intent in your data. You would usually enable this setting if you have a dynamic IP address and cannot be part of the IP Filtering setting. This setting is based on cookies, and you therefore need to have cookies enabled to use this function.
IP Filtering	This setting is a typical companywide exclusion of all visits from either one fixed IP address or a complete range of IPs. You can apply multiple lines of IP ranges. Note that IP Filtering affects the data stored and cannot be reversed as with other settings.
Default Report Period	You set Default Report Period to the typical reporting period (day, week, or month) as a simple setting to optimize your daily use of the system.
Default No. of Rows	You set Default No. of Rows to the typical reporting period (10, 25, 50, or 100) as a simple setting to optimize your daily use of the system.
Project Default Reporting Currency	You can choose one projectwide reporting currency, which can be independent of both cost currency and revenue currency. This setting affects all your campaign and revenue figures (except for the Sales Details report, which will still be a line item report). I will discuss the currencies supported and the currency conversion system in Chapter 4, "Merchandising Tracking and Reporting." As with time zones, any single user can set a default reporting currency and have individual reporting on it, such as a regional manager with regional needs.
Chart Format	Yahoo! Web Analytics provides Flash chart visualizations by default, but you can choose to revert the chart format back to PNG. The reason for doing so is typically either incompatibility or more often the need to copy charts for use elsewhere.
Display Comparative Values as Percentages	Leaving this option unchecked will provide you with comparative values displayed numerically.

(continues)

▶ Table 1.1 List of Available Project Properties *(continued)*

Setting	Implication
Automatic PPC Time Zone Adjustment	Adjust the time zone of your pay-per-click (PPC) campaigns to the search engine's local time zone (e.g., Google: PST, Yahoo! US: PST, Yahoo! UK: GMT, Miva UK: GMT) in order to be able to accurately match up click and cost metrics.
Enable Cost Projection	Due to the search engines' inability to report metrics (e.g., impressions, clicks, and most importantly, cost) on the same day, Cost Projection provides you with an opportunity to populate current-day averages based on those of the previous day. Otherwise, your search engine cost-associated data will be zero. More about this subject in Chapter 3, "Enterprise Campaign Tracking."
Project Go-Live Date	This is a onetime off setting that you use only when you initially deploy a project. It provides you with the opportunity to do testing and collect data in a staging phase and before rolling it out on the real site or before the campaign got started. The Project Go-Live Date setting allows you to eliminate the period for which you do not want any data to be displayed and thus provides an accurate picture of real visitors with real intent. The data you choose to eliminate from your reports is not lost, though; this is just a reporting setting.
Report Cache	If you have a high-volume website in the ten or even hundreds of millions of page views per month, the Report Cache can store your most recently accessed reports and metrics and serve them from cache to all your account users, resulting in significantly faster loading times.

If you need to delete a project, such as in the event of tracking a time-limited campaign or microsite where results and data do not need to be saved for later use, remember that you have to remove the tracking from your website as well.

Tracking Script Customization

You can customize the tracking script to your specific business needs. The tracking script includes JavaScript variables that you can activate in order to collect deeper information about your visitors or to track specific actions and data, such as a document name, a sale action, or the corresponding revenue. In the default Yahoo! Web Analytics tracking scripts is a section marked `Customization Code`, and within that section you will notice a set of inactivated variables. The leading slashes (//) are JavaScript syntax for commenting; they must be removed to activate the three suggestions. The section in question looks like this:

Version 4

```
<!- IndexTools Customization Code ->
<!- Remove leading // to activate custom variables ->
<script type="text/javascript">
//var DOCUMENTGROUP='';
//var DOCUMENTNAME='';
```

```
//var ACTION='';
</script>
<!- End of Customization Code ->
```

Version 5

```
<!- Yahoo! Web Analytics - All rights reserved ->
<script type="text/javascript">
var YWATracker = YWA.getTracker("1000123xxxx");
YWATracker.setDocumentName("");
YWATracker.submit();
</script>
```

There is no demand that you use these three customization variables (DOCUMENT-GROUP, DOCUMENTNAME, and ACTION). They are only provided by Yahoo! as examples and for ease of use in getting started.

There is a full host of variables that I will list later and that we will debate in detail throughout Part I of this book. These variables can be used to collect specific and unique data.

As a quick example of the variables needed in a sales scenario, let's pretend we want to record a sale with the Order ID of 5001 of two unique products (defined by SKU equaling DM822 and DM092), with three units sold of DM822 at EUR 100.00 a piece and 1 DM092 unit sold at EUR 50.00. The variables needed to collect this information would look like:

Version 4

```
var ACTION='01';
var _S_SKU ='DM822;DM092';
var _S_UNITS='3;1';
var _S_AMOUNTS='300.00;50.00';
var ORDERID='5001';
var AMOUNT='EUR350.00';
```

Version 5

```
YWATracker.setAction("01");
YWATracker.setSKU("DM822;DM092");
YWATracker.setUnits("3;1");
YWATracker.setAmounts("300.00;50.00");
YWATracker.setOrderId("5001");
YWATracker.setAmount("EUR350.00");
```

I would like to confirm once again that it is not an explicit demand that all variables are used, and what you will see in the following chapters are best practice advice and not necessarily technical syntax. The previous example does not, from a technical point of view, need the variables _S_SKU, _S_UNITS, and _S_AMOUNTS if you are not out to analyze individual products. (I, of course, suggest you do, but that is a different story.)

Stock Keeping Unit (SKU)

Stock keeping unit (SKU) is a unique identifier for each distinct product and service that can be ordered from a merchant. The SKU system is rooted in data management, enabling merchants to be in control of their inventory.

Note that whenever we talk about variables, I have chosen not to list the full tracking script again and again, but only focus on the actual variable you need to insert. The reason is not just to shorten the text, but also because your specific needs and use might force you to use a combination of variables, which then makes listing full tracking scripts of little use.

As a final note, you can add (depending on your account) a free-form field that can expand the reporting capabilities of Yahoo! Web Analytics immensely by applying your specific reporting categories to the predefined structures already available. You can use a free-form field to mirror critical business metrics. For example, if you are in the hospitality industry, you could collect data on travel destination, travel source, ticket type, length of stay, and member level. The collected data could then be used as dimensions in the system for when you create custom reports.

Imagine the power you have in choosing the right online campaign if you know that previous visitors typically went for business class or longer stays. This truly moves you beyond looking at clicks, page views, and visits. I will go into more detail on the power of custom fields in Chapter 5, "Advanced Instrumentation."

Table 1.2 contains a list of variables that are all extensions. The use of variables should be seen as data collected on top of the data collected out of the box without applying any variables, such as a referring URL, country of origin, or search phrase.

I uploaded an eight-page reference of all available metrics and dimensions here:

http://visualrevenue.com/blog/PDF/yahoo-analytics-metrics-groups.pdf

I would also like to note that beyond the default metrics collected, and beyond the enhancement through custom variables or even custom fields, you can further enrich the dataset by either configuring categorization within Yahoo! Web Analytics or by uploading additional data such as merchandising categorization beyond what's collected. You'll learn more about categorization later in the book.

Finally, before checking out the custom variables in Table 1.2, please note—and this will, of course, be visible in my follow-up examples later—that:

- All variable names are case sensitive. (Note that custom fields are always lowercase.)

- A variable cannot be longer than 75 characters.
- You must not use non-ASCII characters in variable names. Do not use any of the following characters in the name: '<>#&;:?-*~`´)(=%!". These and other non-ASCII characters may interfere with the operation of the tracking script.

Table 1.2 List of Available Custom Variables in Version 4

Name	Value
DOCUMENTNAME	Assign titles to your web pages for reporting purposes.
DOCUMENTGROUP	Group web pages for reporting purposes.
MEMBERID	Assign member IDs to your visitors.
ACTION	Set custom actions (goals); naming is done as a setting.
AMOUNT	Set revenue total sum.
ORDERID	Set the order ID of a purchase.
_S_TAX	Set the tax value on a visitor's purchase.
_S_SHIPPING	Set the shipping charges on a visitor's purchase.
_S_DISCOUNT	Set the potential discount on a visitor's purchase.
_S_SKU	Set the unique SKU for specific products sold. Other information is uploaded.
_S_UNITS	Set the number of units sold.
_S_AMOUNTS	Set the individual revenue if multiple items were sold in the same purchase session.
_S_RUN	If you set this variable to false, the automatic execution of the tracking script will be disabled. (Usually used on sites with frames.)
_s_cfxx (_s_cf01, _s_cf02)	This variable allows you to use custom fields and to add your specific tracking variables to the standard variables already available in the system.
_S_CMPQUERY	This variable allows you to track the URL of a referring campaign even though the website is set to remove the tracking string.
DOMAINS	This variable helps you track websites that have different subdomains and third-level domains. If you set the variable DOMAINS to equal wildcard (*) + the main domain name, e.g., var DOMAINS='*.abc.net', all the subdomains will not be counted as exit links but as part of the main domain.
FLASHURL	This variable is used for recording the location of the Flash object. This variable should be used when the location of the Flash object cannot be determined by the URL.

As noted earlier, I am referencing both the variables in Version 4 and the functions in Version 5 as variables throughout. In Table 1.3 you will find a reference list of available functions in Version 5.

► **Table 1.3** List of Available Functions in Version 5

Name	Value
`YWATracker.setDocumentName("xxx");`	Assign titles to your web pages for reporting purposes.
`YWATracker.setDocumentGroup("xxx");`	Group web pages for reporting purposes.
`YWATracker.setMemberId("xxx");`	Assign member IDs to your visitors.
`YWATracker.setAction("xxx");`	Set custom actions (goals); naming is done as a setting.
`YWATracker.setAmount("xxx");`	Set revenue total sum.
`YWATracker.setOrderId("xxx");`	Set the order ID of a purchase.
`YWATracker.setTax("xxx");`	Set the tax value on a visitor's purchase.
`YWATracker.setShipping("xxx");`	Set the shipping charges on a visitor's purchase.
`YWATracker.setDiscount("xxx");`	Set the potential discount on a visitor's purchase.
`YWATracker.setSKU("xxx");`	Set the unique SKU for specific products sold. Other information is uploaded.
`YWATracker.setUnits("xxx");`	Set the number of units sold.
`YWATracker.setAmounts("xxx");`	Set the individual revenue if multiple items were sold in the same purchase session.
`YWATracker.setCF(1, "xxx");` `YWATracker.setCF(2, "xxx");`	This variable allows you to use custom fields and to add your specific tracking variables to the standard variables already available in the system.
`YWATracker.setCmpQuery("xxx");`	This variable allows you to track the URL of a referring campaign even though the website is set to remove the tracking string.
`YWATracker.setDomains("xxx");`	This variable helps you track websites that have different subdomains and third-level domains. If you set the `setDomains` function to equal wildcard (*) + the main domain name, e.g., `YWATracker.setDomains("*.abc.net")`, all the subdomains will not be counted as exit links but as part of the main domain.
`YWATracker.setFlashUrl("xxx");`	This variable is used for recording the location of the Flash object. This variable should be used when the location of the Flash object cannot be determined by the URL.
`YWATracker.setISK("xxx");`	This variable is used to track internal search phrases and has to be inflated on the internal search results page.
`YWATracker.setISR("xxx");`	This variable is used to track the number of internal search results and has to be inflated on the internal search results page.

I expect by now that you have a clear understanding of what the tracking script is, its flexibility, and the vast opportunities for reporting and analysis, given this type of enhancement. We have yet to explain it in detail, so let's quickly move on to content and advanced conversion tracking in the next chapter.

Content and Advanced Conversion Tracking

Yahoo! Web Analytics becomes vastly more valuable after you have exploited actions such as conversion tracking. Having paired actions with intelligent and unique document naming and grouping, you are set to do advanced data analysis. In this chapter you will learn how to paint a detailed picture of your visitors by tracking the following data:

- *Where your visitors came from, including how they were referred.*
- *What they did on your website and the specific content they consumed.*
- *Whether their mission was accomplished, and if not, where did it fail?*

Executing the steps you learn in this chapter will move you far up the professional ladder.

2

Chapter Contents

Document Names
Document Groups
Track Downloads
Track Exit Links
Track Registered Members
Track Conversion Actions
Track Revenue
Creating Scenarios for Funnel Analysis

Document Names

Yahoo! Web Analytics enables you to assign each page on your website a unique name for the purposes of reporting. This is an override function; you are not forced to use it. If you do not assign unique names to each page, Yahoo! Web Analytics will apply the HTML title tag as the name of the page viewed.

Many users do not make the effort to create a naming strategy for their pages, with the result that they create errors in reporting and forego the ease of creating new reports. I will describe several examples of this problem.

First, any serious search engine optimization (SEO) activity includes optimization on the HTML title tag for the pages in question. With the title tag changing every now and then, the collected and reported-on information will show a new page for every change. So if my HTML title tag changes from:

```
<title>VisualRevenue | Web Analytics &amp; Online Marketing</title>
```

to:

```
<title>Web Analytics &amp; Online Marketing</title>
```

I will have the same page reported as two distinct pages—which is, of course, extremely bad, both for long-term reporting (yearly or more) as well as short-term reporting (for example, on the effects of SEO activity itself). This is a great example of where we need the `DOCUMENTNAME` variable. In the previous example `DOCUMENTNAME` might be set to `homepage`, which would then be the name no matter how many times we change the title tag.

Search Engine Optimization (SEO)

SEO is the process of improving the amount and quality of traffic to a website based on organic search results from search engines. Organic search results refer to those listings in search engine results pages that appear because of their relevance to the search terms, as opposed to advertisements.

In a second hypothetical situation, you could choose to keep identical HTML titles on two different pages (where *different* is defined as two distinct URLs with two different sets of content). Because they have the same HTML titles, those two pages would be grouped together as if they were one, and all views would be counted as one sum.

There are many other examples where you either end up splitting the same page into multiple pages or group different pages into one. There might even be scenarios where you would want to group different pages into one without using document grouping.

Some erroneous reporting is likely to come about unintentionally; an SEO team is not focusing on reporting, a web developer is not focused on titling, and content management systems (CMS) apply automatic templates.

I would like to note that a quick hack—not to be seen as a long-term fix—allows you to always report on URLs, which tend to be unique. Conversely, dynamic URLs are essentially worthless for reporting purposes.

So to conclude, I highly recommend you use the DCOUMENTNAME variable, or at least, that you adopt a clear naming strategy before you start. Beyond accurate data you also get reports that are easier to understand; more rapid report navigation; and optimized use of filters, custom reports, and segments.

Here is how to deploy the DOCUMENTNAME variable on your default page (e.g., yourdomain.com/index.html):

Version 4

```
var DOCUMENTNAME='Homepage';
```

Version 5

```
YWATracker.setDocumentName("Homepage");
```

Looking at the result of an implementation, you will see the most basic report output, like that shown in Figure 2.1.

Page Title	Page Views	%	Avg. Time On Page
VisualRevenue | Web Analytics & Online Marketing blog	1,651	24.71%	0m 52s
VisualRevenue | 18 most popular Web Analytics blog posts of 2007	421	6.30%	1m 35s
VisualRevenue | Web Analytics & ...arketing blog: July 2007 Archive	399	5.97%	0m 19s
VisualRevenue | What and how to measure Social Networking websites	301	4.50%	1m 6s
VisualRevenue | The Online Business Measurement Quadrant	218	3.26%	1m 46s
VisualRevenue | Tracking RSS sub...tag - a quick Web Analytics HACK	196	2.93%	0m 55s
VisualRevenue | Search Engine Be...s: Visit to sale conversion rate	191	2.86%	1m 1s
VisualRevenue | The Long Tail .....how to calculate missing Revenue	147	2.20%	0m 52s
Homepage	92	1.38%	1m 43s
VisualRevenue | Your most popula...NOT to be your most popular page	91	1.36%	0m 50s
Subtotal	**3,707**	**55.48%**	**1m 0s**
Total	**6,682**	**100.00%**	**1m 35s**
« PREVIOUS 10			NEXT 10 »

Figure 2.1 Top 10 pages by page title

Note that your DOCUMENTNAME variable must not be longer than 75 characters and that you must not use non-ASCII characters. In addition, do not use any of the following characters in the name:

```
' < > # & ; : ? - * ~ ` ´ ) ( = % ! "
```

These and other non-ASCII characters may have a negative effect on the general tracking script and the way it operates. As you remember from Chapter 1, DOCUMENTNAME is provided as an example with the default tracking code but commented out, so remember to remove the leading slashes (//) to activate the variable.

Yahoo! Web Analytics is a real-time system, so you can test your changes to the tracking script by changing the DOCUMENTNAME variable and refreshing the page. You should then see your reporting change.

Document Groups

Document grouping is very valuable, but I would not stress it as much as document naming, because data collecting and reporting can be done accurately and correctly without document grouping. Document groups do, however, create an opportunity to categorize your content for reporting purposes, and I certainly recommend it after document names have been set up.

You can group together similar pages with document groups, such as your entire checkout process, and do reporting and analysis on this group combined. You can create similar groups based on content, such as news and sports, and compare the popularity of these sections in your reports.

You cannot create hierarchical subgroups with the `DOCUMENTGROUP` variable alone; for this, custom fields are needed. For example, an online publisher might create a Products document group, followed by a subcategory called Books. Details on how to achieve this using custom fields or merchandising can be found in Chapter 4 and Chapter 5.

Use the `DOCUMENTGROUP` variable in your tracking code to identify each page that you wish to be part of a document group. For example, all your pages that provide news could be identified by the document group name News.

Version 4

```
var DOCUMENTGROUP='News';
```

Version 5

```
YWATracker.setDocumentGroup("News");
```

Note that your `DOCUMENTGROUP` variable must not be longer than 75 characters and that you must not use non-ASCII characters. In addition, do not use any of these characters in the name:

```
' < > # & ; : ? - * ~ ` ´ ) ( = % ! "
```

These and other non-ASCII characters may have a negative effect on the general tracking script and the way it operates. As you remember from Chapter 1, the `DOCUMENTGROUP` is provided as an example with the default tracking code but commented out, so remember to remove the leading slashes (//) to activate the variable.

Again, please note that there is an opportunity to create further categorization and hierarchies using custom fields. You'll learn much more about this and the other powers of custom fields in Chapter 5, "Advanced Instrumentation."

Track Downloads

There are fundamental differences in collecting data through a JavaScript tracking script and collecting data from web server logs. The reason I mention this is that, regrettably, you have to accept that not every download will be registered. The accuracy of download metrics depends heavily on site structure and marketing reference to the files in question.

I reference the file (notice the extension): `http://visualrevenue.com/blog/PDF/Best-Pratices-for-Online-Travel-and-Hospitality.pdf` on the following page: `http://visualrevenue.com/blog/2007/10/what-and-how-to-measure-online-travel.html`. If you provide the HTML web page as a reference for visitors to get the file, and if they indeed click the link provided on that page, Yahoo! Web Analytics will track the click as a download.

It is not a measurement of whether the download was actually started or whether it was completed; it is only a reference point to the fact that someone initiated it. *Initiated* means clicking the file link in question on the page that you are tracking. Tracking is not associated with the file itself as such.

On the other hand, if you reference the PDF file in your marketing material directly, as in `http://visualrevenue.com/blog/PDF/Best-Pratices-for-Online-Travel-and-Hospitality.pdf`, Yahoo! Web Analytics will not register this, and usage statistics are lost. This inaccuracy is common to all page-tagging solutions.

The ability to create a reference to the downloadable file is provided out of the box, and you need not do anything else but install the plain-vanilla tracking code.

One interesting result of tracking downloads is that you can create a trended report for a unique file, which looks like the example in Figure 2.2.

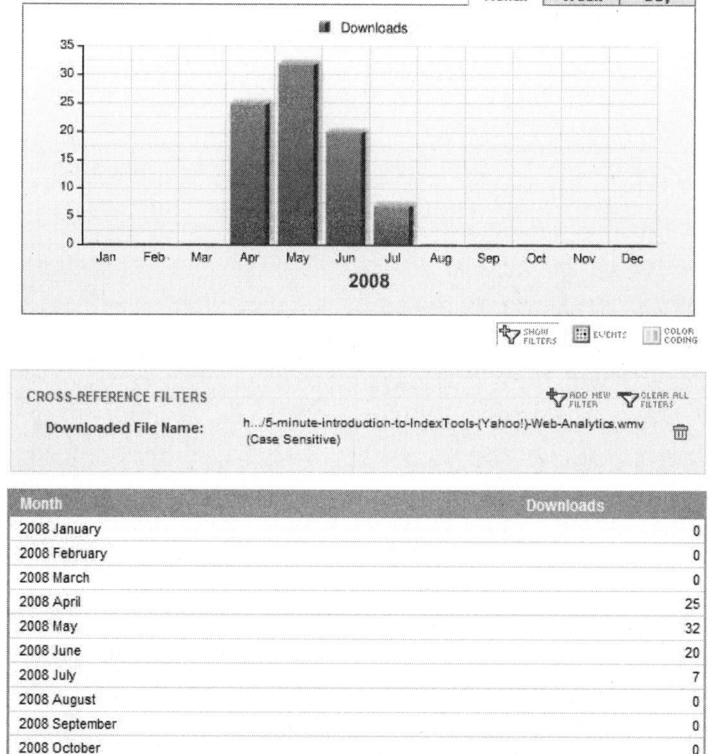

Month	Downloads
2008 January	0
2008 February	0
2008 March	0
2008 April	25
2008 May	32
2008 June	20
2008 July	7
2008 August	0
2008 September	0
2008 October	0
2008 November	0
2008 December	0
Total	84

Figure 2.2
Downloaded file trend

In this report you are also able to view which pages the files are downloaded from.

The file types in Table 2.1 are registered as page views, including any URL that contains the text `jsessionid`. All other file types are treated as downloads and presented in the download reports.

► **Table 2.1** Page View File Types

File Extension		
.html	.asp	.cfm
.jsp	.cgi	.php3
.php4	.php5	.pl
.taf	.tml	.dll
.vm	.mv	.do
.go	.wem	.tpl

However, if you want to track downloads (that is, download links) as actions, you can do this either directly within the link or as an on-click wrapper function. You'll learn more about action tracking and download extensions in the sections that follow.

Tracking Exit Links

Tracking exit links is, in nature and tracking technology, very similar to tracking downloads. Yahoo! Web Analytics attaches itself to all links. If a link outside of the domain structure is clicked, it is registered as an exit link.

This is one of the advantages of page tagging versus log file analysis, as all exit links are tracked. You are in control of when something is to be registered as an exit link.

The ability to track exit links is provided out of the box, and you need not do anything else but install the plain-vanilla tracking code.

The simplest results of an exit link tracking report look like Figure 2.3.

Domain	Clicks	%
http://www.blogger.com	238	9.91%
http://www.kaushik.net	155	6.46%
http://feeds.feedburner.com	148	6.16%
http://blog.webanalyticsdemystified.com	123	5.12%
http://www.indextools.com	110	4.58%
http://manojjasra.blogspot.com	105	4.37%
http://www.linkedin.com	102	4.25%
http://visualrevenue.com	95	3.96%
http://webanalytics.wordpress.com	79	3.29%
http://www.grokdotcom.com	65	2.71%
Subtotal	**1,220**	**50.81%**
Total	**2,401**	**100.00%**
« PREVIOUS 10		NEXT 10 »

Figure 2.3 Top 10 exit links

In Figure 2.3 you will notice that the results are grouped by domain and not specific URLs. This is a reporting choice you can make at the time of generation. Another option is to report the pages at which your exit links are located. This option helps you find your exit links and determine possible correlations between high site-traffic leakage and specific content.

As with downloads, if you want to track exit links as actions, you can do this directly within the link or as an on-click wrapper function—we'll look at action tracking and exit link extensions a bit later.

Note that should you use a redirect function to send traffic out to business partners, for example, this is not measured other than traffic to the redirect page. This is a setup where tracking the link as an action might not be a bad idea.

Tracking Registered Members

Using Yahoo! Web Analytics works especially well in an environment where visitors are required to log in or identify themselves through their usual path toward solving their problem. This could be as obvious as the last steps of a sales funnel and checkout process, but also something as innocent as capturing a person when signing up to a webinar.

I am very comfortable in tracking registered members when they are in an environment where they are fully aware that they are being registered. Examples of such environments would be websites such as LinkedIn or Facebook, where users tend to be fully aware that you know who they are. Allowing users explicit opportunities to hand over additional personal identifiable information (PII), or telling them you will be analyzing PII data, helps create a positive consumer attitude toward this type of data collection. Yahoo! has a strict, consumer-friendly attitude toward this and has incorporated that attitude into their Terms and Conditions.

Personal Identifiable Information (PII)

PII is any piece of information that can potentially be used to uniquely identify, contact, or locate a single person.

Note: Be aware that Yahoo! requires you to append to your privacy policy wording along the lines of "We use third-party web beacons from Yahoo! to help analyze where visitors go and what they do while visiting our website. Yahoo! may also use anonymous information about your visits to this and other websites in order to improve its products and services and provide advertisements about goods and services of interest to you. If you would like more information about this practice and to know your choices about not having this information used by Yahoo!, click here. (/agreement.html)."

I strongly recommend that you be absolutely up front and honest about what data you collect.

To track registered members, you need to apply the variable MEMBERID. This variable cannot be a static variable such as:

Version 4

```
var MEMBERID='dennis.mortensen@evcrp.com';
```

Version 5

```
YWATracker.setMemberId("dennis.mortensen@evcrp.com");
```

Rather, the variable has to be populated with the member's identity information at runtime. This means that you and your team are forced to do changes directly in the scripting language behind your website solution, such as PHP or ASP, to make this work. Let me provide an example of how you would populate the MEMBERID variable with the email from a commenter in the popular blogging software WordPress.

Version 4

```
<!- IndexTools Customization Code ->
<!- Remove leading // to activate custom variables ->
<script type="text/javascript">
//var DOCUMENTGROUP='';
//var DOCUMENTNAME='';
//var ACTION='';
var MEMBERID='<?php echo $comment_author_email; ?>';
</script>
<!- End of Customization Code ->
<!- IndexTools Code v4.00 - All rights reserved ->
<script type="text/javascript" src="http://visualrevenue.com/indextools.
js"></script><noscript>
<div><img src="http://stats.indextools.com/p.pl?a=10001277xxxxx&amp;js=no"
width="1" height="1" alt="" /></div></noscript><!-//->
<!- End of IndexTools Code ->
```

Deploying a code like the previous snippet will immediately give you access to information on a member level, such as the last visitor details. Figure 2.4 is a sample report showing real-time activity data on a web property.

Note that, just because the previous example and figure focus on a MEMBERID, which equals the user's email, it does not have to be an email. The MEMBERID is essentially just a unique key to identify the member. I have experienced a lot of examples where this is a customer ID number from clients' customer relationship management (CRM) systems. The reasoning for that approach is that you can pair this up with offline data in raw data exports Yahoo! Web Analytics offers.

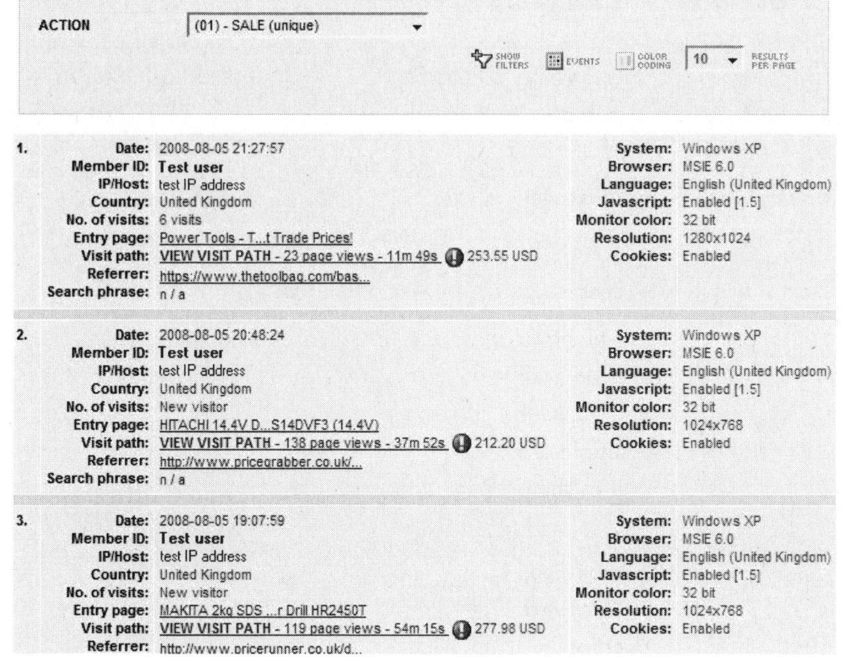

Figure 2.4 Last visitor details filtered by the Sale action

Customer Relationship Management (CRM)

CRM is a term applied to processes implemented by a company to handle contact with its customers.

As for other variables mentioned thus far in the chapter, the MEMBERID variable must not be longer than 75 characters, and you must not use non-ASCII characters. In addition, do not use any of the following characters in the variable:

' < > # & ; : ? - * ~ ` ´) (= % ! "

Part II, "Utilizing an Enterprise Web Analytics Platform," will expand on how to track product use data, but it may be useful to see an example illustrating the value of MEMBERID here. Figure 2.5 shows a custom report, where we have MEMBERID as the left-hand dimension and Revenue as one of the three metrics. You can replace Revenue with other success metrics for non-commerce-based websites. Running the report on today, and sorting the list on Revenue, you get an instant list of top customers. Remember that the system is in real time. A similar report could be run to show daily service actions, such as writing personal emails asking for product satisfaction.

Member	Visits	Avg. Time per Visit	Revenue
sell@stodec.com	1	1m 48s	$625.69
_stuff@dsl.pipex.com	1	54m 15s	$277.98
@blueyonder.co.uk	1	16m 51s	$268.25
neandonlyphilbassett2005@hotmail.com	1	11m 49s	$253.55
_tracey@ntlworld.com	1	1h 23m 26s	$245.35
juice@blueyonder.co.uk	1	37m 52s	$212.20
@hotmail.com	1	57m 53s	$165.58
martin@manx.net	1	9m 13s	$161.53
landdell@tiscali.co.uk	1	1h 44m 57s	$120.08
@cityandstone.co.uk	1	11m 3s	$99.55
Subtotal	**10**	**38m 55s**	**$2,429.76**
Total	**1,941**	**3m 43s**	**$2,937.59**

« PREVIOUS 10 NEXT 10 »

Figure 2.5 Revenue per MEMBERID

Tracking Conversion Actions

Any web property has a set of success criteria, and it is of the utmost importance that these be tracked. Yahoo! Web Analytics defines these success points as actions. These actions can include the following fixed-system actions:

- SALE
- INTERNAL_SEARCH
- PENDING_SALE
- CANCELLED_SALE
- PRODUCT_VIEW
- ADD_TO_CART

There are also custom definable actions that you not only name any way you want, but also assign to a success criterion specific for your web property. Examples of custom-definable actions are:

- RSS Subscriber Signup
- Post a Comment
- Share Content
- Print
- New Member Registration
- Lead Form Signup

Once an action is defined and populated with a value, you get an instant opportunity to run conversion reports, getting insight on behaviors in the context of successful actions. If you define a conversion as a visitor completing an action, you thereby configure a success point. And this is where the power of actions comes into play, as you are now enabled with the opportunity to determine the success of online marketing campaigns, organic traffic, and specific search phrases. Additionally, you can determine the value of user behavior, such as whether more time spent on site does indeed result in more conversions. We will talk much more about the insights derived from actions and conversions in Part II, "Utilizing an Enterprise Web Analytics Platform."

Yahoo! Web Analytics provides nine custom actions beyond the fixed ones out of the box, but technically it holds up to 255 actions, and with a little love from your account manager, you should be able to increase this if needed.

All the fixed actions are named by Yahoo! Web Analytics and will be presented by that name in the reporting system; however, you can name the custom action variables freely. Find these naming opportunities under the Settings menu, shown in Figure 2.6.

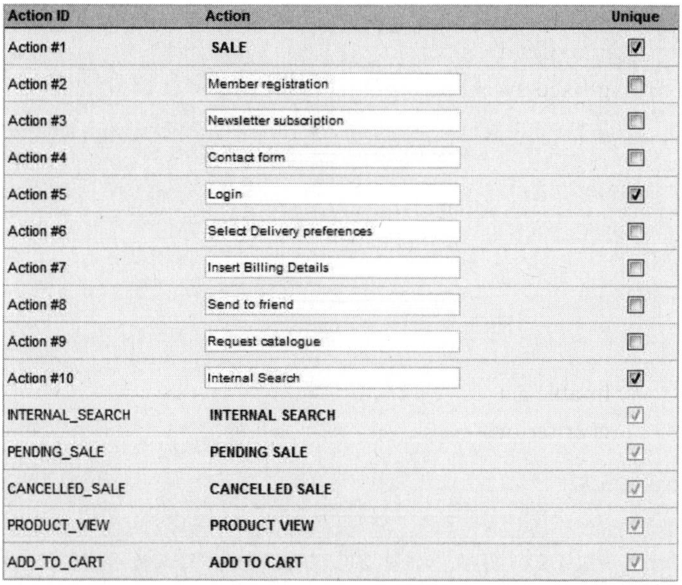

Action ID	Action	Unique
Action #1	SALE	☑
Action #2	Member registration	☐
Action #3	Newsletter subscription	☐
Action #4	Contact form	☐
Action #5	Login	☑
Action #6	Select Delivery preferences	☐
Action #7	Insert Billing Details	☐
Action #8	Send to friend	☐
Action #9	Request catalogue	☐
Action #10	Internal Search	☑
INTERNAL_SEARCH	INTERNAL SEARCH	☑
PENDING_SALE	PENDING SALE	☑
CANCELLED_SALE	CANCELLED SALE	☑
PRODUCT_VIEW	PRODUCT VIEW	☑
ADD_TO_CART	ADD TO CART	☑

Figure 2.6 Settings for naming actions

According to the naming system earlier, you would code an implementation on the Thank You for Requesting Our Catalogue page like this:

Version 4

```
var ACTION='09';
```

Version 5

```
YWATracker.setAction("09");
```

Action number 9 represents the Request Catalogue action. Wherever actions are available in the reporting system, such as the conversion summary, the action is mentioned by its name (see Figure 2.7).

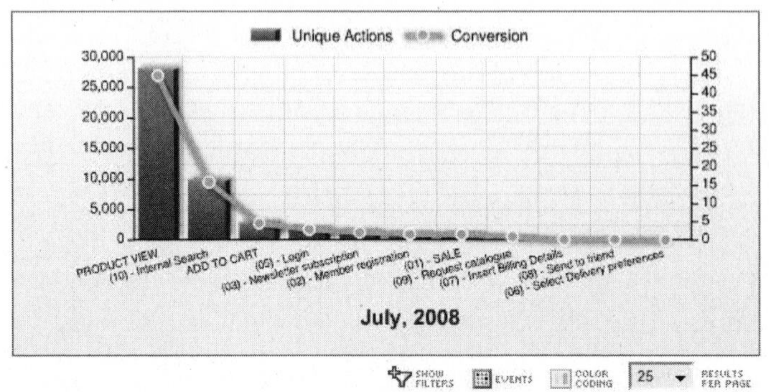

Action	Action	Unique Actions	Conversion
PRODUCT VIEW	60,828	28,155	45.01%
(10) - Internal Search	19,086	9,934	15.88%
ADD TO CART	6,983	2,904	4.64%
(05) - Login	3,054	1,758	2.81%
(03) - Newsletter subscription	1,352	1,303	2.08%
(02) - Member registration	963	963	1.54%
(01) - SALE	935	919	1.47%
(09) - Request catalogue	606	565	0.90%
(07) - Insert Billing Details	97	88	0.14%
(08) - Send to friend	69	63	0.10%
(06) - Select Delivery preferences	32	26	0.04%
Total	**94,005**	**46,678**	**74.62%**

Figure 2.7 Conversion Summary report

As I indicated in the section on tracking registered members, the goal is not just to collect the data for one unique report, but to collect data for overall use throughout the system. Put yourself in a position where you can do further analysis with yet another metric in your toolbox. Figure 2.8 is an example report showing how many people sign up for your newsletter, grouped by search engine. Each bar in the graph represents a different search engine.

Keep in mind that every time a page on which you have deployed an action is viewed, an action is recorded. This means that you should place this code on success pages and not passing pages, such as the pages toward a goal. It also means that the action typically can be static and not something that needs to be inflated with a value beyond the action number or name.

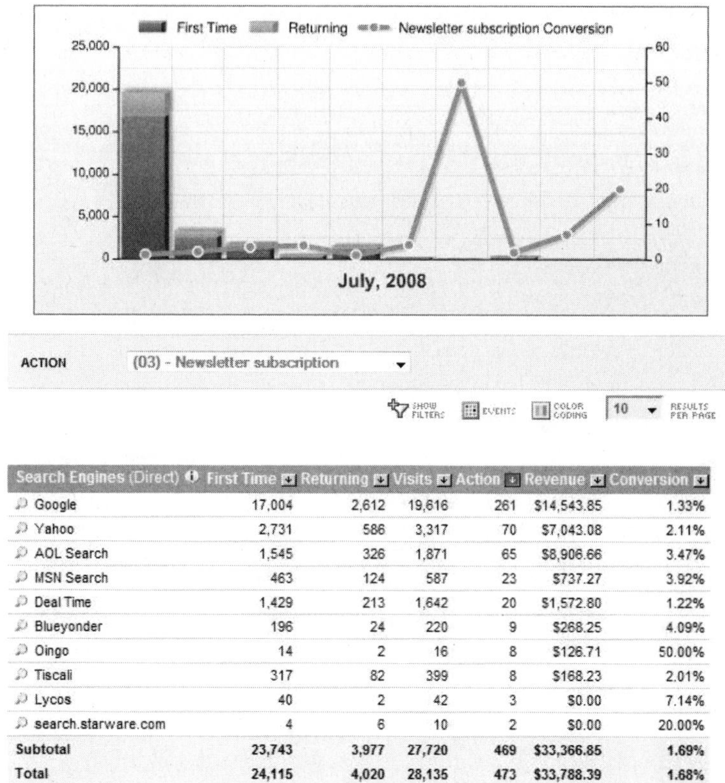

Search Engines (Direct)	First Time	Returning	Visits	Action	Revenue	Conversion
Google	17,004	2,612	19,616	261	$14,543.85	1.33%
Yahoo	2,731	586	3,317	70	$7,043.08	2.11%
AOL Search	1,545	326	1,871	65	$8,906.66	3.47%
MSN Search	463	124	587	23	$737.27	3.92%
Deal Time	1,429	213	1,642	20	$1,572.80	1.22%
Blueyonder	196	24	220	9	$268.25	4.09%
Oingo	14	2	16	8	$126.71	50.00%
Tiscali	317	82	399	8	$168.23	2.01%
Lycos	40	2	42	3	$0.00	7.14%
search.starware.com	4	6	10	2	$0.00	20.00%
Subtotal	**23,743**	**3,977**	**27,720**	**469**	**$33,366.85**	**1.69%**
Total	**24,115**	**4,020**	**28,135**	**473**	**$33,788.39**	**1.68%**

« PREVIOUS 10 NEXT 10 »

Figure 2.8 Newsletter conversions grouped by search engines

When using the fixed action SALE (action number 01), you may also include the additional variables such as `AMOUNT` or `ORDERID`, which are then connected to the action in question. I will in detail debate revenue tracking in the "Tracking Revenue" section later in this chapter. But it should be noted that the variables introduced in Chapter 1 are not excluded just because they are in a different category. Content variables can definitely enhance action tracking. Take a look at the following example, where the sale action is deployed together with a page name and a categorization:

Version 4

```
var ACTION='01';
var DOCUMENTGROUP='Checkout Pages';
var DOCUMENTNAME='Sales Confirmation';
```

Version 5

```
YWATracker.setAction("01");
YWATracker.setDocumentGroup("Checkout Pages");
YWATracker.setDocumentName("Sales Confirmation");
```

I am sure you noticed that an action can be set as unique. I will discuss action naming and visitor count methods later in this chapter.

Tracking Multiple Sales Actions During the Same Visit

This might sound like an inconceivable scenario: having a customer buy a widget, and then within the same visit, having the same customer buy another widget. I am actually quite happy to say that this happens more often than you would think, and to an extent where Yahoo! Web Analytics has developed instrumentation to take advantage of it.

If you track multiple sales on the same page during the same visit, you have to make sure that your `ORDERID` is unique. If your `ORDERID` value is fixed, you need to remove the variable altogether as it will otherwise not be recorded by the second sale action.

Keep in mind that this is closely connected to your choices and attitudes regarding how to count conversions in one visit (two sales or just one?). I will explore the topic of visitor conversion count methodology later in this chapter. But as a quick note, if you configure the sale actions on the page with multiple sale actions as Unique, then the reporting interface will display the number of unique sale actions in all the conversion reports. The only exception is the Conversion Summary report, which displays the total number of actions and the number of unique actions.

If you configure the sale actions on the page with multiple sales as not Unique, then the reporting interface will display the total number of sale actions in all the conversion reports. This will increase your conversion rate—not that this is bad, you should just be fully aware of what kind of numbers you are looking at. Therefore, in order to avoid this, I strongly suggest that you always configure the sale action as Unique if you have pages with multiple sales.

Tracking Multiple Occurrences of the Same Action on a Web Page

Now we are ready to move beyond just looking at the visit as a whole, as we've been doing, and into tracking multiple occurrences of the same action on the same page, whether a fixed or a custom action. Once you need to track multiple occurrences of the same action on a web page, you are required to move beyond the fixed tracking script introduced in Chapter 1. You are required to set up a tracking script object—which is super exciting, as you are now able to splash the code around the page as you want. And please take a mental note, as this is down the same alley as tracking more advanced Ajax elements, which we will talk about later in Chapter 5, "Advanced Instrumentation."

Ajax

Ajax, Asynchronous JavaScript and XML, is a group of interrelated web development techniques used for creating interactive web applications or rich Internet applications.

Let me show a quick example of how to set up the tracking script object and how to call it. The tracking script function created next, also sometimes called a *wrapper function*, is completely unique to your site and can be constructed any way you want. So our focus is on tracking multiple occurrences of the same action on the same page (applying two variables wouldn't work):

Version 4

```
var ACTION='01';
var AMOUNT='USD100.00';
var ACTION='01';  – ERROR, you cannot use the same variable twice
var AMOUNT='USD50.00'– ERROR, you cannot use the same variable twice
```

So to have two sales, not just in the same visit but on the same page, you could create a wrapper function like this:

Version 4

```
<script language="Javascript">
function recordsale(orderid, amount) {
        var tracking_object = createITT();
        tracking_object.ACTION = '01';
        tracking_object.ORDERID = orderid;
        tracking_object.AMOUNT = amount;
        tracking_object.submit_action();
}
</script>
```

Version 5

```
<script language="Javascript">
function recordsale(orderid, amount) {
var YWATracker = YWA.getTracker("1000123xxxx");
        YWATracker.setAction("01");
        YWATracker.setOrderId(orderid);
        YWATracker.setAmount(amount);
        YWATracker.submit_action();
}
</script>
```

Here I've created the Version 4 tracking object by writing `var tracking_object = createITT();` and then applying the variables needed. I've then executed the tracking script by submitting it: `tracking_object.submit_action();`. You can extend beyond the three variables I applied here.

Now you know how to create the tracking script object, but bear in mind that no tracking is done unless the function is called from the page itself, as in clicking a link and calling the wrapper function:

```
<a href='/thankyou.html' onclick='recordaction(23453,100)'>Buy</a>
```

Or you could choose to create a complete wrapper function including the values and call it once the customer confirms the buy (typically by clicking the Buy button). With this method, everything is included in the tracking script object and it would look like this:

Version 4

```
<script language="Javascript">
function recordsale(orderid, amount) {
        var tracking_object = createITT();
        tracking_object.ACTION = '01';
        tracking_object.ORDERID = orderid;
        tracking_object.AMOUNT = amount;
        tracking_object.submit_action();
}

recordsale ('orderid 1', 'USD100');
recordsale ('orderid 2', 'USD50');
</script>
```

Version 5

```
<script language="Javascript">
function recordsale(orderid, amount) {
var YWATracker = YWA.getTracker("1000123xxxx");
        YWATracker.setAction("01");
        YWATracker.setOrderId(orderid);
        YWATracker.setAmount(amount);
        YWATracker.submit_action();
}

recordsale ('orderid 1', 'USD100');
recordsale ('orderid 2', 'USD50');
</script>
```

Here you are forced to inflate the `ORDERID` and `AMOUNT` values into the two `recordsale` function calls in the end to use it correctly.

Tracking Multiple Actions on the Same Web Page

Finally we come to some less strict scenarios, such as the need to record both a sale action and a newsletter signup action on the same web page. This is very much a continuation of the tracking script object debate from the previous section. You could create a wrapper function that looks like this:

Version 4

```
<script language="Javascript">
function recordaction(actionnumber) {
        var tracking_object = createITT();
        tracking_object.ACTION = actionnumber;
        tracking_object.submit_action();
}
</script>
```

Version 5

```
<script language="Javascript">
function recordaction(actionnumber) {
var YWATracker = YWA.getTracker("1000123xxxx");
        YWATracker.setAction(action);
        YWATracker.submit_action();
}
</script>
```

The good news is that Yahoo! Web Analytics has a shortcut to do this as well. When you need to track multiple actions on the same web page, you can do so by simply adding multiple actions in one request. So the code for the previous example of recording both a sale and a newsletter signup on the same page could look like this:

Version 4

```
var ACTION="01;02";
var AMOUNT="USD100.00;";
```

Version 5

```
YWATracker.setAction("01;02");
YWATracker.setAmount("USD100.00;");
```

Let's see a more detailed example so you can truly understand the syntax. This example shows how to record a sale action of USD (United States dollars) 100, a newsletter signup, and finally a pending sale of USD 2.50:

Version 4

```
var ACTION="01;02;PENDING_SALE";
var AMOUNT="USD100.00;;USD2.50";
```

Version 5

```
YWATracker.setAction("01;02;PENDING_SALE");
YWATracker.setAmount("USD100.00;;USD2.50");
```

Whether you assign newsletter signup to action number 02 is up to you, and you might have a different action named for newsletter signup. As we debated in the initial section about tracking conversion actions, you can use the following variables multiple times in one request:

- ACTION
- AMOUNT
- ORDERID
- _S_TAX
- _S_SHIPPING
- _S_DISCOUNT
- All action-based custom fields. (I will discuss custom fields in Chapter 5.)

I know that we have not yet discussed merchandizing variables, such as _S_UNITS, but it is important to note that they will only refer to the very first action in the previous list.

Tracking On-click Actions

When I say *on-click*, I am talking about the onclick event registered on your web page objects. This event registers when the object has been clicked and provides you with an opportunity to execute a desired action on that click, such as record it. This is again a continuation of the tracking script object discussion from the previous sections, and you would in fact be able to use the same wrapper function from previous examples for this scenario:

Version 4

```
<script language="Javascript">
function recordaction(actionnumber) {
       var tracking_object = createITT();
       tracking_object.ACTION = actionnumber;
       tracking_object.submit_action();
}
</script>
```

Version 5

```
<script language="Javascript">
function recordaction(actionnumber) {
var YWATracker = YWA.getTracker("1000123xxxx");
YWATracker.setAction(actionnumber);
YWATracker.submit_action();
}
</script>
```

You could apply that wrapper function as the positive action to take on the onclick event, such as:

```
<a href="/leadsignup" onclick="recordaction(7) ">Submit Form<>
```

Remember that the previous wrapper functions do not record anything unless called.

The clicked-on object can be anything from an image, form dropdown, form submit, or just an ordinary web link (a download link or an exit link as well). Yahoo! Web Analytics has a great shortcut for tracking on-clicks like this using something called the s_action function.

When you use the _s_action function, only an action is recorded and not both an action and a page view, which would be collecting poor data, as you will be recording dual-page views. Using the _s_action variable is a two-step procedure.

In step 1, make sure that before positive on-click actions are called, you activate the ACTION variable. In most cases the ACTION variable will be empty.

Version 4

```
<script language="Javascript">
var ACTION='';
</script>
```

I'll provide several examples for step 2, which I am sure you can mold into a lot of good uses on your web property.

Version 4

1. Clicking an image

```
Visit my LinkedIN profile <a onclick="_s_action('06')" href=" http://
www.linkedin.com/in/dennismortensen" ><img src="/images/linkedinlogo.
gif"></a>
```

2. Clicking an ordinary link (see Figure 2.9)

```
Subscribe via <a onclick="_s_action('04')" href=" http://feeds.
feedburner.com/WebAnalyticsAffiliateMarketingBlog" > RSS </a>
```

Figure 2.9 Subscribe to RSS Link example

3. Clicking a file for download

```
Download <a onclick="_s_action('09')" href=" http://visualrevenue.com/
blog/PDF/Best-Practices-for-the-Online-Finance-Industry.pdf" > Best
Practice White Paper </a>
```

4. Clicking an image for mailto action

```
<img src="/images/dennis.gif" onClick="location.href='mailto:dennis.
mortensen@evcrp.com'; _s_action('17');">
```

5. Clicking an ordinary link, track multiple actions

```
<a href="http://visualrevenue.com/blog/about" onclick="_s_
action('17;18;19');"> onclick with multiple actions</a>
```

For Version 5, which is a whole lot more flexible, you just create a wrapper function, which you call from the `onclick`. The following example of clicking an image uses the wrapper from earlier:

Version 5

```
Visit my LinkedIN profile <a onclick="recordaction('01')" href=" http://www
.linkedin.com/in/dennismortensen" ><img src="/images/linkedinlogo.gif"></a>
```

Tracking downloads and tracking exit links sections are both done automatically by Yahoo! Web Analytics. However, there might be scenarios where you would want to collect this as distinctive actions instead, for further and more detailed analysis.

To track downloads as actions:

```
<a href=" http://visualrevenue.com/blog/PDF/Best-Pratices-for-Online-Travel-
and-Hospitality.pdf" onClick="ACTION='05'">
```

To track exit links as actions:

```
<a href="http://kaushik.net/avinash/" onClick="ACTION='09'">
```

Visitor Conversion Count Methodology

As indicated multiple places in this chapter, once you set up an action you have to decide whether it should be treated as unique or not unique in the reporting interface.

The rationale behind providing you with a choice for how you want the actions summed up is that different types of actions require different attitudes on how to sum them up. Even for similar actions, different companies might have different and legitimate reasons for summing up differently.

Envision a scenario where you would want to track downloads of a PDF whitepaper as an action. Using the on-click code example from before:

```
<a href=" http://visualrevenue.com/blog/PDF/Best-Pratices-for-Online-Travel-
and-Hospitality.pdf" onClick="ACTION='05'">
```

I suggest that you track it as a unique action by selecting the Unique checkbox when naming your actions, as shown in Figure 2.10.

Unique means that, should a visitor choose to download the whitepaper three times in the same visit, the choice is only counted once. That seems good data quality; the visitor can only read it once.

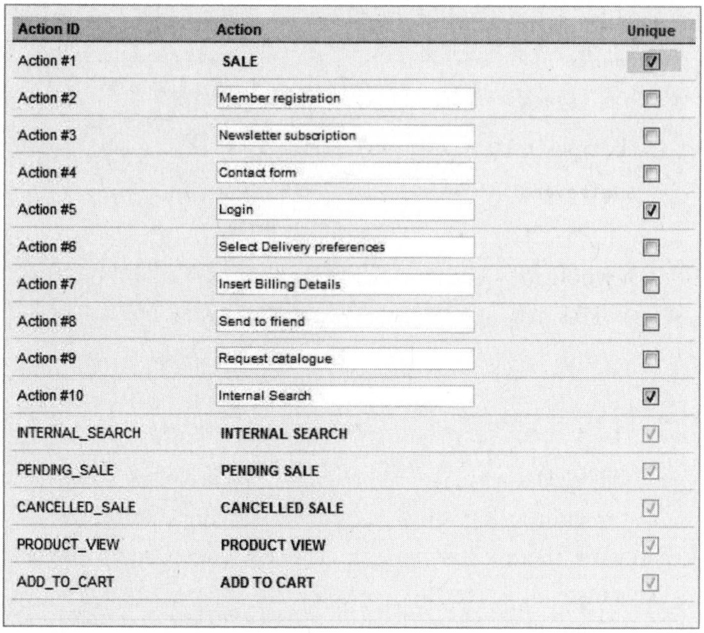

Action ID	Action	Unique
Action #1	SALE	[x]
Action #2	Member registration	[ ]
Action #3	Newsletter subscription	[ ]
Action #4	Contact form	[ ]
Action #5	Login	[x]
Action #6	Select Delivery preferences	[ ]
Action #7	Insert Billing Details	[ ]
Action #8	Send to friend	[ ]
Action #9	Request catalogue	[ ]
Action #10	Internal Search	[x]
INTERNAL_SEARCH	INTERNAL SEARCH	[x]
PENDING_SALE	PENDING SALE	[x]
CANCELLED_SALE	CANCELLED SALE	[x]
PRODUCT_VIEW	PRODUCT VIEW	[x]
ADD_TO_CART	ADD TO CART	[x]

Figure 2.10 Unique Actions Setting

Another scenario where you would want to track the action as unique might be a sales lead signup page, where once again, a lead is still just one lead, no matter how many times the visitor signs up.

You should configure an action as non-unique (by leaving the checkbox empty), if every time that a visitor performs the action in question, it is of unique value. A sale would be such a case, where a sale is something that has value every time a visitor performs the action. Another example could be a comment provided to a blog, where every new blog comment might have value and it should be summed up in the system with a number that equals the actual number of comments to the blog.

Please note that this is only a configuration of the reporting interface and does not affect the actual data collection. This means that if four actions have been collected, Yahoo! Web Analytics does indeed hold the four actions, but reports on them depending on your Unique setting, which could be 1, 2, 3, or 4.

Track Revenue

If you run a commerce web property, you would definitely want to track your revenue for a whole host of reasons, such as the ability to use a return on advertising spending (ROAS) metric for campaign performance review, figuring out average value per visit, and in general applying the opportunity to tie in money to any equation you do in the reporting interface. I love working with revenue as a metric, and if not as a metric, at least as a proxy for revenue as it makes everything crystal clear.

Return on Advertising Spending (ROAS)

ROAS represents the dollars earned per dollars spent on the corresponding advertising. Web analytics and online marketing expert Akin Arikan would pitch that it is actually *revenue* on advertising spending, and he is indeed right!

We have already seen how to collect revenue, without my explicitly spelling it out, but let's review it here. Revenue is collected as part of the sale action and provided to the AMOUNT variable. So to track \$100 in sales, you write the following:

Version 4

```
var ACTION='01';
var AMOUNT='100';
```

You probably noticed that I wrote "100" as plain text in the AMOUNT variable, which equals the currency I use to buy sushi around the corner here in Manhattan, also known as United States dollars (USD). But in a global world you will most likely be forced to track a sale in more currencies, track a cost in more currencies, and perhaps even provide a consolidated reporting view in one united currency. Yahoo! Web Analytics provides features for all of the before-mentioned needs. The first one is the quality to track your revenue in more than just USD.

Tracking Revenue in Multiple Currencies

Tracking revenue in multiple currencies is tremendously valuable and super easy to deploy. As we know, recording the revenue of a sale demands that you inflate the AMOUNT variable.

The AMOUNT variable can only be used together with the sale ACTION. In most cases the AMOUNT variable is not a fixed variable, simply due to the nature of the sales process; you do not know what the final sales sum is going to be beforehand.

To set the tracking currency, you simply place the three-letter currency abbreviation directly in front of the revenue amount (see Figure 2.11). A sale of 33.58 British pounds would look like this:

Version 4

```
var ACTION='01';
var AMOUNT='GBP33.58';
```

Version 5

```
YWATracker.setAction("01");
YWATracker.setAmount("GBP33.58");
```

Remember that just because you see the reporting in GBP, you did not have to collect the revenue in that particular currency.

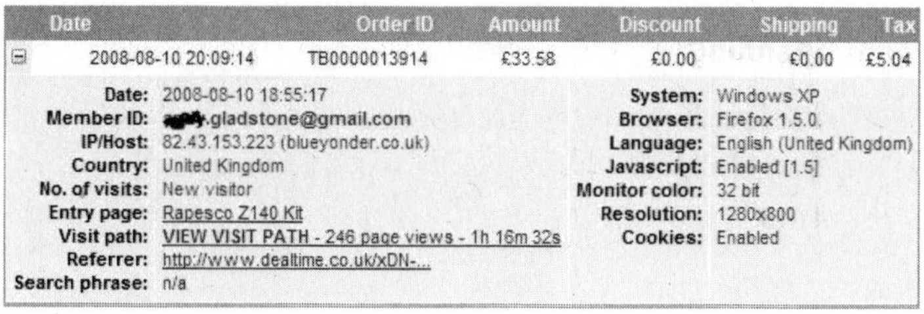

Date	Order ID	Amount	Discount	Shipping	Tax
2008-08-10 20:09:14	TB0000013914	£33.58	£0.00	£0.00	£5.04

Date:	2008-08-10 18:55:17	System:	Windows XP
Member ID:	[illegible].gladstone@gmail.com	Browser:	Firefox 1.5.0
IP/Host:	82.43.153.223 (blueyonder.co.uk)	Language:	English (United Kingdom)
Country:	United Kingdom	Javascript:	Enabled [1.5]
No. of visits:	New visitor	Monitor color:	32 bit
Entry page:	Rapesco Z140 Kit	Resolution:	1280x800
Visit path:	VIEW VISIT PATH - 246 page views - 1h 16m 32s	Cookies:	Enabled
Referrer:	http://www.dealtime.co.uk/xDN-...		
Search phrase:	n/a		

Figure 2.11 Currency tracking example

Table 2.2 is a complete list of all the supported revenue tracking currencies.

► **Table 2.2** Currencies Supported

Currency Code	Currency	Currency Code	Currency
USD	American Dollar	CAD	Canadian Dollar
BRL	Brazilian Real	AUD	Australian Dollar
LTL	Lithuanian Litas	EUR	Euro
LVL	Latvian Lats	BGN	Bulgarian Lev
MXN	Mexican Peso	GBP	British Pounds
CHF	Swiss Franc	NZD	New Zealand Dollar
JPY	Japanese Yen	CNY	Chinese Yuan Renminbi
PLN	Polish Zloty	DKK	Danish Krone
CRC	Costa Rica Colon	RON	Romanian New Leu
HUF	Hungarian Forint	EEK	Estonian Kroon
RSD	Serbian Dinar	NOK	Norwegian Kroner
HKD	Hong Kong Dollars	RUB	Russian Rouble
SEK	Swedish Krona	HRK	Croatian Kuna
SGD	Singapore Dollars	ISK	Iceland Krona
INR	India Rupees	THB	Thai Baht
CZK	Czech Koruna	ISL	New Israeli Sheqel
TRY	Turkish Lira	SKK	Slovak Koruna
KRW	South Korean Won	UAH	Ukraine Hryvnia
ZAR	South African Rand		

When using a commerce system or basic shopping cart, the value is likely to be inflated into the tracking code dynamically. The following example shows a sample tracking script with the `AMOUNT` variable inflated with two local commerce system variables named `ccode` and `saleamount`. Any local variables are unique to your commerce system.

Version 4

```
var ACTION="01";
var AMOUNT="<%ccode%><%saleamount%>" //(could equal:: VAR
AMOUNT="USD100.00");
```

Version 5

```
YWATracker.setAction("01");
YWATracker.setAmount("<%ccode%><%saleamount%>");
```

Be aware that even though your revenue is tracked in your desired currency, the currency property of the project might override this in the reporting interface. If you set your default currency for the project to USD, all your campaign figures, sales figures, and other revenue tied in figures are converted to this currency.

Yahoo! Web Analytics uses monthly average exchange rates to convert the currencies into the project default reporting currency. This is important to know when you're trying to align the numbers with offline numbers. This means that a quarterly revenue report is calculated by the three months sums by the average currency value for those three months. However, any reporting user with administrator rights can override the default reporting currency and select a specific reporting currency. You can change your default currency under Settings > Personal Setup.

Once you select a user-defined reporting currency, all your reports except the Sales Details report will be displayed in your chosen currency. The figures displayed in the user-defined reporting currency are calculated in the same way as the figures in the project default reporting currency: by multiplying the revenue numbers obtained in the tracking currency with the monthly average exchange rates.

The `AMOUNT` variable holds all the characteristics of variables in general and can therefore not be longer than 75 characters. You must not use non-ASCII characters in the variable name and refrain from using any of the following characters as part of the value:

```
' < > # & ; : ? - * ~ ` ´ ) ( = % ! "
```

As a final note and as a tradition throughout the system, you have access to the raw data collected—which for this section means the initial currency of the sale, also known as the tracking currency, no matter what the reporting interface is set to. This is to be found in the Sales Details report.

Track Order ID

You have seen `ORDERID` introduced on several occasions before this section, simply because it is so closely tied into the sale `ACTION` and the `AMOUNT` (revenue) variable.

As with the `AMOUNT` variable, `ORDERID` is simple to deploy. It provides you not only with the opportunity to put sale activity in order, but also with the ability to truly utilize your exported raw data and have this tied directly into your CRM system. But even beyond that, you are provided with other opportunities, such as multiple sales in one session.

Tracking the `ORDERID` variable for a commerce site is almost obligatory, as this can improve the accuracy of monitoring your sales in both systems, making sure that there are no duplicate orders captured during a visit. This also shows why `ORDERID` is heavily used by the Yahoo! support teams when troubleshooting issues with revenue and sales tracking in general.

Furthermore, if you become advanced enough to use the application programming interface (API), `ORDERID` is absolutely necessary as a key to that system.

As you can see in the next example, the `ORDERID` variable goes hand in hand with the sale `ACTION` from a technical point of view, and from a rational point of view, the `AMOUNT` variable.

Version 4

```
var ACTION='01';
var AMOUNT='USD19.95';
var ORDERID='10099801';
```

Version 5

```
YWATracker.setAction("01");
YWATracker.setAmount("USD19.95");
YWATracker.setOrderId("10099801");
```

I think this is my last time repeating the general note that an `ORDERID` variable must not be longer than 75 characters and that you must not use non-ASCII characters. In addition to that, do not use any of the following characters in the name:

```
' < > # & ; : ? - * ~ ` ´ ) ( = % ! "
```

These and other non-ASCII characters may have a negative effect on the general tracking script and the way it operates.

Revenue Encryption

Yahoo! Web Analytics has designed a feature that allows you to avoid passing on your revenue in clear text over the Internet, for those clients and situations that warrant such a decision. In most cases, though, having a sale of $19.95 would look like this example:

Version 4

```
var ACTION='01';
var AMOUNT='USD19.95';
```

Version 5

```
YWATracker.setAction("01");
YWATracker.setAmount("USD19.95");
```

The information was transferred freely over the Internet as part of the check-out process. Remember that just by looking at the figure in your browser, it has been sent from the web server to the client. However, there might be situations where your revenue is not public knowledge. Imagine a shopping comparison site, such as Kelkoo (shown in Figures 2.12), which provides a free service for all its users to compare prices on a given product.

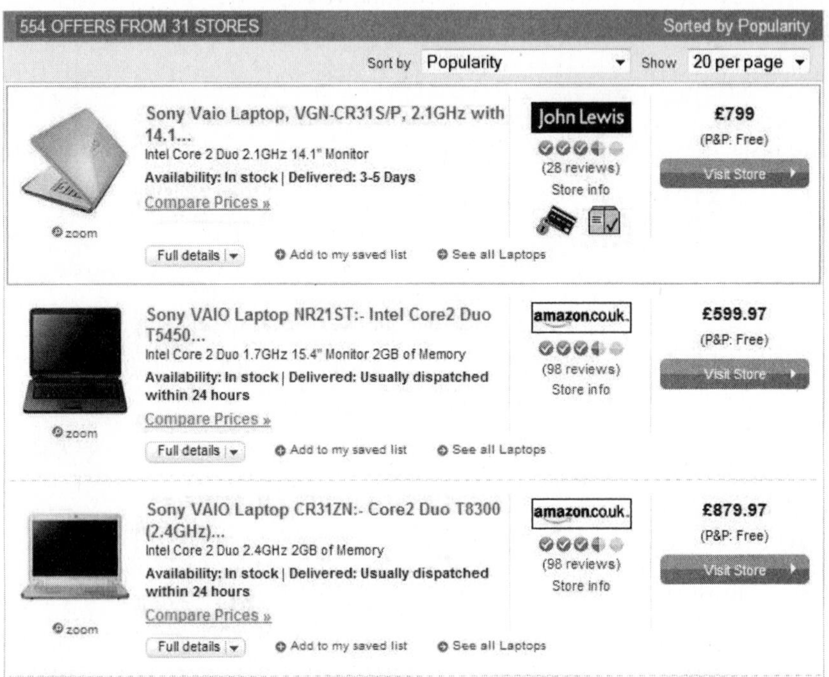

Figure 2.12 Kelkoo comparison price listing for laptops

Figure 2.12 shows prices for Sony laptops, but that does not mean that Kelkoo sells any of these products. Their business model, like any other shopping comparison site, is to charge on the click-out to the retailer, quite similar to a paid search. Therefore, the revenue Kelkoo generates by having a visitor click a retailer and go to their site is indeed confidential information. It's the same as if I go to Google and search for digital cameras—I would not know what the true cost per click is on any of the text ads.

This is not the only scenario. Many businesses offer a free service to consumers, and revenue is generated as a business-to-business activity. Here you would simply not want to pass the revenue figures in plain text through the Yahoo! Web Analytics tracking code. This technique will also prevent robots and spiders alike from gathering competitive intelligence on your website's revenue, margins, or general agreements with affiliates.

Revenue encryption is not automatically applied to all accounts, and you would have to request that it be added through the Yahoo! support organization. You are required to provide at least one encryption key, an element that I will discuss in a moment. Once the Yahoo! Web Analytics team has applied this key to the data collection service, you are ready to submit revenue in encrypted form.

I know this explanation is going to be a bit hairy, but it is unfortunately the only way to achieve what we are looking for. The first thing you should be aware of is that Yahoo! Web Analytics currently only supports encryption in the industry-standard Advanced Encryption Standard (AES) in Cipher Feedback (CFB) mode.

Advanced Encryption Standard (AES)

AES is a block cipher adopted as an encryption standard by the U.S. government.

The key length should be a minimum of 16 and a maximum of 32 characters, and it must be a multiple of 8. You may supply an arbitrary number of keys to be used during decryption, but you must select one for each given amount.

To recap, collecting a USD19.95 sale, I would apply the following variables:

Version 4

```
var ACTION='01';
var AMOUNT='USD19.95';
```

This is where the change is going to happen when we want to use revenue encryption. The first thing you have to do is start all `AMOUNT` variables with AES (which is case sensitive) and follow that by the key ID number. You are allowed to have up to 10 different keys. And finally, as the third part of the `AMOUNT` variable, apply a colon character (:) and the encrypted data. This should result in a variable looking like this:

Version 4

```
var ACTION='01';
var AMOUNT= "AES1:F8A0998CAAC1C58145828B4318EB341268300CE0AAECC55A7E9BCA59BD
243905A58F0944570D78DCA39DF6A8E74C867D"
```

Version 5

```
YWATracker.setAction("01");
YWATracker.setAmount("AES1:F8A0998CAAC1C58145828B4318EB341268300CE0AAECC55A7
E9BCA59BD243905A58F0944570D78DCA39DF6A8E74C867D");
```

Here's a direct installation manual-like example to get you started:

1. Get the revenue amount, including the currency, as you would normally.
2. Embed the prepared revenue string into a 40-character random string at a random starting position; however, the position should be at least 4.

3. Specify the starting position of the currency in the first two characters of the string and the length of the complete revenue string (including the currency code) in the third and fourth characters of the string. If you put the revenue string at position 4 and we use the previous `AMOUNT` variable of USD19.95, this would be 0408.
4. Append a hexed 32-bit cyclic redundancy check (CRC) value to the string (this would be 8 characters). Calculate the CRC for the entire 40-character string, including the prefix. The resulting string should be 48 characters.
5. Encrypt the entire string using AES in CFB mode.
6. Hex the entire encrypted data. The result should be 96 characters.

Hexing

Hexing is a form of encoding for data from a binary to a string representation, where each byte is represented by hexadecimal value in characters.

Cyclic Redundancy Check (CRC)

A CRC is a type of function that takes as input a data stream of any length and produces as output a value of a certain space, commonly a 32-bit integer. The term CRC is often used to denote either the function or the function's output. A CRC can be used as a checksum to detect alteration of data during transmission or storage.

Here's a detailed Version 4 example, applying the steps outlined earlier:

1. First you get the revenue amount and currency as usual, such as:

   ```
   var AMOUNT='USD19.95';
   ```

   This leaves us with an eight-character-long revenue and currency string value of:

   ```
   USD19.95
   ```

2. You then choose a random 40-character long string such as:

   ```
   DENNIS7890123456789012345678901234567890
   ```

3. You then position (overwrite) the revenue and currency string within the random string anywhere you want, just not in the first four characters, like this:

   ```
   DENNIS78901234567890USD19.95901234567890
   ```

   In this example, we positioned it randomly at character 20 and overwrote eight characters.

4. We then write this into the first four characters of the string:

   ```
   2008IS78901234567890USD19.95901234567890
   ```

5. Then you calculate a 32-bit CRC value for the entire 40-character-long string and hex it. The CRC value for our string is:

   ```
   C5601867
   ```

6. The CRC value is then appended to the end, to create a 48-character-long string, looking like this:

   ```
   2008IS78901234567890USD19.95901234567890C5601867
   ```

7. And this is the string that you should encrypt with AES. A 16-character-long encryption key like the following:

   ```
   DENNISRMORTENSEN
   ```

   will result in an encrypted and hexed string like this:

   ```
   8E14F3D8742B2216269F2D7CBED00819C29D3B6D99E201F0DFB0FF87451C5FEC3FEED38
   FF4327F40215EF5DA5353876B
   ```

   This is the value you would use in the `AMOUNT` variable:

   ```
   var ACTION='01';
   var AMOUNT= "AES1:8E14F3D8742B2216269F2D7CBED00819C29D3B6D99E201F0DFB0FF
   87451C5FEC3FEED38FF4327F40215EF5DA5353876B"
   ```

   Version 5

   ```
   YWATracker.setAction("01");
   YWATracker.setAmount("AES1:8E14F3D8742B2216269F2D7CBED00819C29D3B6D99E20
   1F0DFB0FF87451C5FEC3FEED38FF4327F40215EF5DA5353876B");
   ```

Long-winded, yes? Worth it? In a situation where you would not want to disclose your revenue data, surely! Now on to something a bit more down to earth: setting up fixed funnels for analysis.

Creating Scenarios for Funnel Analysis

Traditional funnel analysis is called scenario analysis within Yahoo! Web Analytics, which provides two types of scenario analysis: predefined scenarios and ad hoc scenarios.

I will discuss predefined scenarios here and leave the remainder of the discussion for Chapter 10, "Distinctive Reports and Usage," where I will be discussing how we can use scenarios for in-depth funnel analysis and what kind of insights we will be getting from it.

I bring up scenario analysis at this point because it is common to see web analytics software require you to append the tracking code with funnel step variables in order to set up the funnel.

In Yahoo! Web Analytics, you are not required to append anything to the tracking code and all setup is done within the reporting tool itself. Ad hoc scenarios are done on the fly and do not require any setup whatsoever. Creating predefined scenarios helps you increase reporting speed, and it requires that you use more than eight steps in the funnel. If you are running a web property that is anything below 10 million page views a month, predefined scenarios will not help too much, and I suggest that you just go ahead and use ad hoc scenarios when needed.

On a conceptual level, scenarios are defined as a set of steps moving toward a goal that you have in mind. The first thing you do is apply a set of simple properties to your predefined scenario, as shown in Figure 2.13.

EDIT SCENARIO
In this interface you can edit existing Scenario steps or add new steps to your already established path.
SCENARIO PROPERTIES
SCENARIO NAME:
blog post visit to subscriber funnel
Description:
A funnel created to see where new visitors fall off if they do not sign up for the blog's RSS feed.
AD-HOC SCENARIO:
Check this box if you're unsure about the event sequence you want to track and you want to try various combinations first.
Add
Cancel

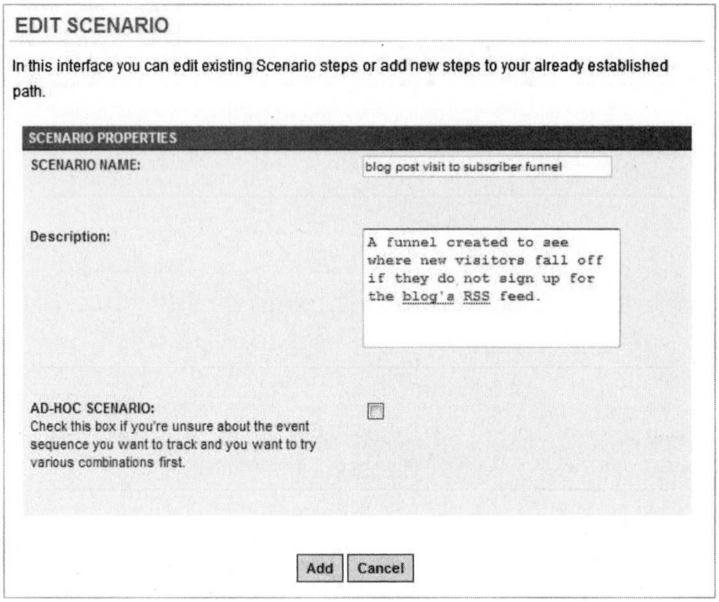

Figure 2.13 Scenario setup

Then you apply the steps as a simple set of criteria met on one of the following metrics:

- Page title
- Page URL
- `ACTION`

Continuing the example in our previous figure, which asked for a funnel visualizing the falloff from blog post visits to RSS subscribers, we could define two simple steps, as you can see in Figure 2.14.

#	NAME OF SCENARIO STEP	CONFIGURATION	VALUE	DELETE
1	Visits to the blog	URL contains	/blog/	
2	Subscribe to RSS fee	ACTION equals	(04) - Subscribe to this blog	

Figure 2.14 Defining steps for a new scenario

You would have to filter out first-time visitors before displaying the data in a report (see Figure 2.15). Also, the action defined as RSS subscribers should be evaluated to see whether it would be a good proxy for actual RSS subscribers. We'll go into more detail on scenarios and general funnel analysis in Chapter 10.

Figure 2.15 Scenario result report

You can create up to 200 different scenarios, which should be enough to satisfy even the most exacting analyst.

Enterprise Campaign Tracking

This is one web analytics setup activity where good enough just isn't good enough. For you to truly gain a complete and fair picture of all your campaigns, you are forced to have every single activity measured, to the extent where no single visitor arrives at your website without you knowing from where, whether it was a paid-for campaign activity, what the impact was, and whether you could better allocate those resources.

Keep in mind that a campaign can be anything from a nationwide TV campaign with a unique vanity URL or something as simple as a link exchange with another site in your industry. Both are examples of activities that impact your online traffic acquisition, and both should be tracked as part of your campaign-tracking efforts.

3

Chapter Contents

Types of Campaigns
Paid Search Setup
Creating and Managing Campaign Categories
Identifying Campaigns
Setting Up New Campaigns
Setting Up a Fallback Campaign
Example Paid Search Deployment
Internal Campaigns

Types of Campaigns

Yahoo! Web Analytics provides an opportunity for you to track all your commercial traffic–acquisition activities as unique and individual campaigns. You can track campaigns to the extent that you are completely in control of where all your incoming traffic is coming from. Doing this will give you insight into the impact of one campaign on another and into specific advertising metrics such as the cost per visit.

> **Traffic Acquisition**
>
> Traffic acquisition is the practice of managing the inflow of visits to your web properties through paid advertising or other efforts.

Determining a campaign's impact involves pairing campaigns with the actions described in Chapter 2, "Content and Advanced Conversion Tracking." By pairing campaigns and actions, you are able to see which actions occurred after a visit generated by a campaign or even by a visitor previously acquired by a campaign.

You can define any type of incoming traffic as a campaign. Yahoo! Web Analytics groups campaigns into these main categories:

- Banner Campaigns
- Email Campaigns
- Affiliate Campaigns
- Paid Search
- Other
- Fallback Campaigns

A fallback campaign is not a true category by itself but a safeguard against not picking up campaign activity that was overlooked when configuring it initially. You would always want campaign activity counted in your campaign reports, and this is where nonconfigured or improperly configured campaigns would fall.

One of the main differences between campaign types and online campaigns in general is the way cost is attributed to them. Yahoo! Web Analytics offers these categories for attributing costs:

- Free Campaign / Other Cost Type
- One-time Cost (Typically CPM, Cost Per Thousand Impressions)
- CPC (Fixed Cost per Click)
- CPA (Fixed Cost per Action)
- PPC (Pay per Click)

Cost per Thousand (CPM)

CPM is an online display advertising pricing model, where the advertiser pays per one thousand impressions. (The *M* in the acronym stands for *mille*, the Latin word for *thousand*.)

Cost per Click (CPC)

CPC is an online advertising pricing model typically used in search engine marketing, where the advertiser pays for every single click and site visit.

Cost per Action (CPA)

CPA is an online advertising pricing model, where the advertiser pays for each specified action, such as a purchase, a lead, etc., linked to the advertisement in question.

Pay per Click (PPC)

PPC is an Internet advertising model typically used on search engines, where advertisers only pay when a user actually clicks on an advertisement to visit the advertiser's website. Advertisers typically bid on keyword phrases and thus have a variable cost per click.

I'll give some reasons why you might choose certain cost types over others later in this chapter, in the section "Setting Up New Campaigns."

By applying the campaign cost type information to your incoming traffic and having it grouped by the campaign categories, we get a plethora of opportunities beyond just the primary campaign summary report. See Figure 3.1 for an example of a custom campaign summary.

Channel (Intelligent) / Vendor (Intelligent) / Subcategory (Intelligent) / Campaign (Intelligent)	Clicks	Unique Clicks	Returning	Bounce rate	Revenue	Action	Conversion	CPA
Paid Search	123,135	49,439	2,028	3.51%	$69,159.94	623	0.51%	$0.00
Email Campaigns	4,517	1,186	94	2.88%	$2,793.59	34	0.75%	$0.00
Banner Campaigns	1,492	565	13	6.57%	$347.56	2	0.13%	$0.00
Total	129,144	51,190	2,135	3.53%	$72,301.09	659	0.51%	$0.00

« PREVIOUS 10 NEXT 10 »

Figure 3.1 A custom campaign summary

The Campaign Summary, provided out of the box from Yahoo!, is a tad too aggressive on the number of metrics displayed, so I used the Custom Report Wizard (more on that in Chapter 7, "Customizing Report Results") and removed a few columns for a better visual display. However, even when you expand the tree and explore the categorization, as shown in Figure 3.2, you have not even touched on the full power of campaign tracking. The initial campaign summary is valuable, but definitely not the end of what you can and should do with campaign tracking.

Channel (Intelligent) / Vendor (Intelligent) / Subcategory (Intelligent) / Campaign (Intelligent)	Clicks	Unique Clicks	Returning	Bounce rate	Revenue	Action	Conversion	CPA
⊟ **Paid Search**	**123,135**	**49,439**	**2,028**	**3.51%**	**$69,159.94**	**623**	**0.51%**	**$0.00**
⊞ Shopping Comparison	46,234	10,671	426	4.97%	$20,475.36	193	0.42%	$0.00
⊟ Yahoo	40,619	13,361	575	2.48%	$20,453.88	149	0.37%	$0.00
⊟ YSM	40,619	13,361	575	2.48%	$20,453.88	149	0.37%	$0.00
Yahoo PPC	40,619	13,361	575	2.48%	$20,453.88	149	0.37%	$0.00
⊞ Google	30,996	23,609	1,001	3.51%	$26,495.37	263	0.85%	$0.00
⊞ BuyAt	5,129	1,676	24	0.86%	$1,541.10	17	0.33%	$0.00
⊞ Microsoft	147	121	2	1.48%	$194.23	1	0.68%	$0.00
⊞ Ciao	10	1	0	0.00%	$0.00	0	0.00%	$0.00
⊞ CP	0	0	0	0.00%	$0.00	0	0.00%	$0.00
⊞ Peoples Web	0	0	0	0.00%	$0.00	0	0.00%	$0.00
⊞ **Email Campaigns**	**4,517**	**1,186**	**94**	**2.88%**	**$2,793.59**	**34**	**0.75%**	**$0.00**
⊞ **Banner Campaigns**	**1,492**	**565**	**13**	**6.57%**	**$347.56**	**2**	**0.13%**	**$0.00**
Total	**129,144**	**51,190**	**2,135**	**3.53%**	**$72,301.09**	**659**	**0.51%**	**$0.00**

« PREVIOUS 10 NEXT 10 »

Figure 3.2 Expanded custom campaign summary

Once you deploy campaign tracking, a set of new metrics becomes available throughout the system, including the Custom Report Wizard and filters. Table 3.1 summarizes what each of these metrics does.

► **Table 3.1** Campaign Metrics

Metric	Definition
Campaign Clicks	Number of direct campaign clicks
Unique Campaign Clicks	Number of unique visitor campaign clicks
Returning Campaign Clicks	Number of returning visitor campaign clicks
Campaign Cost	Total amount spent on the advertising campaign during the selected time period, reported in the consolidated reporting interface currency
Campaign Conversion	The campaign conversion according to the chosen action on the interface
ROAS	Return on advertising spend: revenue divided by cost of advertising
CPA	Cost per action: cost of advertising divided by action
ACC	Average cost per click
Impressions	The number of ad views as reported back from the advertising channel in question
Average Position	The average position on the PPC search engine

It is important to note that you can track a campaign in any of the currencies mentioned in Table 2.2, "Currencies Supported." Remember that you have the ability to work with currencies on three levels. You can track cost in multiple currencies, track revenue in multiple currencies, and report on all this in a single consolidated currency in the interface. You are not limited to one single corporate currency in the interface, but you can designate a unique currency for each individual user of Yahoo! Web Analytics. Figure 3.3 shows a currency choice of Canadian dollars (CAD) as the cost per click.

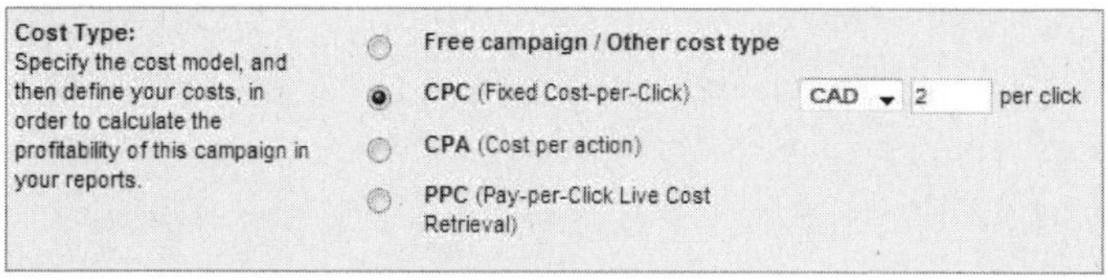

Cost Type:
Specify the cost model, and then define your costs, in order to calculate the profitability of this campaign in your reports.

Free campaign / Other cost type
CPC (Fixed Cost-per-Click) CAD 2 per click
CPA (Cost per action)
PPC (Pay-per-Click Live Cost Retrieval)

Figure 3.3 Currency choice for campaign costs

You might remember that Yahoo! Web Analytics is a web application coming from the acquisition of IndexTools in May 2008 and that one of their products was Bid Management. The Bid Management product provided extensive paid search insights and actions. By incorporating Bid Management, Yahoo! Web Analytics now offers an additional level of accuracy by consolidating the live data collected by the reporting system with data reported by the paid search engines. Yahoo! Web Analytics supports Google, Yahoo!, and Microsoft paid search as of this writing.

You will notice that I did not mention the tracking code script at all. In any normal campaign setup you are not required to apply any variables to the tracking script. Pretty much everything in regard to campaign tracking is done as a combination of campaign setups within Yahoo! Web Analytics and landing page URL setups within your ad serving system (such as Google AdWords).

I believe your biggest challenge in executing enterprise campaign tracking will not be so much the technology setups, which are fairly simple and straightforward, but creating and adhering to a set of organizational campaign procedures and standards. Having campaign procedures in place is absolutely necessary if you have multiple online advertising activities in place run by multiple people or departments. This is not the book to suggest how to build, maintain, and sell such standards in your organization, but if you are completely out of ideas, I suggest you create a one-page guideline for how your colleagues should name their landing pages and how they should communicate with you as the web analyst. Apply a warning in the campaign procedure document along the lines that if the procedures are not followed, the campaign is not tracked and no success parameters can be attached to it. Politely conclude that the money is wasted!

Paid Search Setup

Paid search, offered through Google, Yahoo!, Microsoft, and others, is for most people synonymous with running online advertising campaigns. Because paid search marketing is likely to be a big chunk of your incoming traffic, Yahoo! Web Analytics has a dedicated setup for paid search. Note that, although you can choose from dozens of paid search engines, only the three major ones mentioned here are actively supported as points from which costs can be collected. Also, note that paid search is not the only type of successful online advertising campaign; you should see this as just one channel of many that can be compared easily using web analytics.

To track a paid search campaign, your first task is to configure each campaign within the paid search engines and apply your Yahoo! Web Analytics settings. I expect that you already have a working knowledge of how to set up and manage campaigns within the search engines.

The single most important link between Yahoo! Web Analytics campaign tracking and the search engines is the destination URL, which is something you configure at the search engine. I will explain more about URL patterns in the section "Identifying Campaigns."

The first thing you need to do is go to Settings > Manage PPC Logins, which will take you to the paid search engines setup (see Figure 3.4).

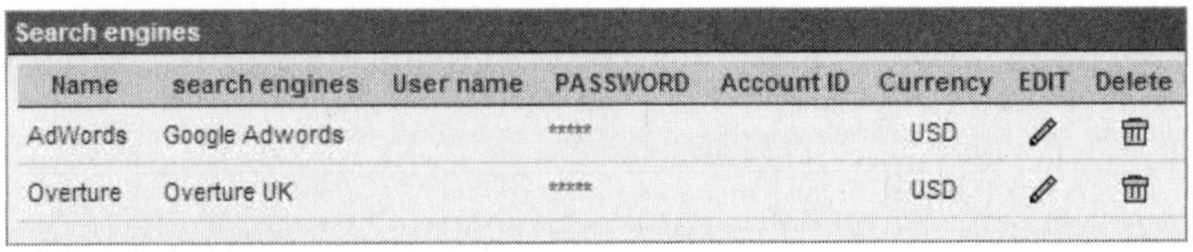

Search engines

Name	search engines	User name	PASSWORD	Account ID	Currency	EDIT	Delete
AdWords	Google Adwords		*****		USD		
Overture	Overture UK		*****		USD		

Figure 3.4 Managing paid search engines

In order for Yahoo! to retrieve your dynamic paid search cost data, you need to enter your search engine credentials when adding a new paid search engine (see Figure 3.5). Bear in mind that paid search engine refers to the Paid Search Engine account (profile); thus, if you have multiple Google AdWords or other accounts, you would have to add each one.

As you would expect, once you have set up the paid search engine, you can configure multiple campaigns using the same engine.

It is important to notice that there is a slight difference in the setup of the various paid search engines and in particular for Google AdWords. A Google AdWords account can be managed directly by your organization, and if so, you are required to connect that account to the Yahoo! Web Analytics Google MCC Account. If you want to connect using your own MCC account, this is provided as an option as well. This is, however, not a route I suggest you take because Yahoo! covers the Google AdWords API costs if you are connected to their MCC account.

PPC Engine settings

Search engine: Google Adwords

Name: AdWords

Currency: USD

Login ID*:

Password*:
*Enter the login id and password for the administration interface of the CPC engine. Please note that this information is needed to retrieve real time cost information from the search engine.

Account ID (Overture/Google/ MSN Ad Center/Adknowledge)*:
*Please note that this information is needed to retrieve real time cost information from the search engine.

(Recommended) I authorize yahoo to access my Google Account

(Advanced users only) I intend to use my own Google MCC account What's this?

Please provide the login details of the Google MCC account that is managing your Adwords account.

Save Cancel

Figure 3.5 Paid search engines setup

Google MCC

The Google My Client Center (MCC) is a placeholder for handling multiple Google AdWords accounts. MCC is typically used by larger advertisers with more than one account and for third-party agencies, such as search engine marketers (SEMs), search engine optimizers (SEOs), and automated bid managers (ABMs). You can think of MCC as an umbrella account with multiple AdWords accounts (a.k.a. managed accounts) linked to it.

Google AdWords API

The Google AdWords API lets developers build applications that interact directly with the AdWords platform. With these applications, advertisers and third parties can more efficiently and creatively manage their large or complex AdWords accounts and campaigns.

Note that it is of the utmost importance that you align the currency setup of the paid search engine account with the actual currency in the account, as you otherwise might apply discrepancy to the data collected and consolidated later.

Before thinking about collecting the actual campaign information, let's move on to another setup—creating campaign categories.

Creating and Managing Campaign Categories

Our discussion of this feature is not really of much value unless you run 50 or so campaigns or more. First of all, Yahoo! Web Analytics provides native categorization of your campaigns, as described in the earlier section "Types of Campaigns." This native categorization is more than adequate until you reach 50 or so campaigns, unless of course you have specific segmentation needs from the get-go, in which case you'll need something more than the native categorization tools.

The extended campaign categorization can help you organize the campaigns beyond one level. Keep in mind that yet again, this is not just about the ability to open up a tree of categories, as shown in Figure 3.2, but about creating an opportunity to work with multiple dimensions. Figure 3.2 reveals four levels of categorization:

- Channel
- Vendor
- Subcategory
- Campaign

These categories are set up under Settings > Manage Campaign Categories. See Figure 3.6 for an illustration of the Manage Campaign Categories screen.

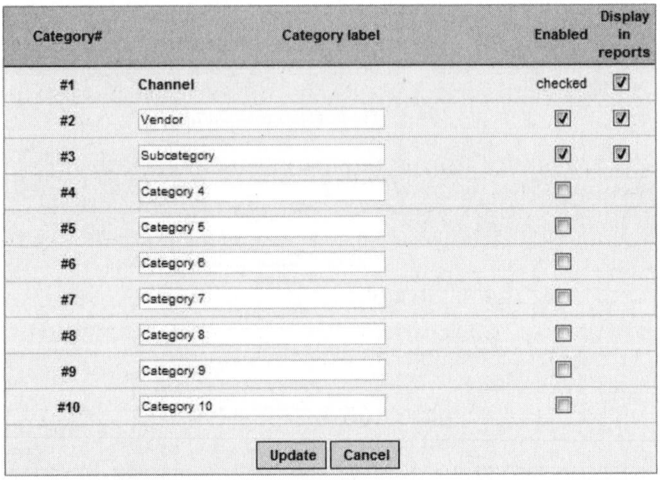

Category#	Category label	Enabled	Display in reports
#1	Channel	checked	☑
#2	Vendor	☑	☑
#3	Subcategory	☑	☑
#4	Category 4	☐	
#5	Category 5	☐	
#6	Category 6	☐	
#7	Category 7	☐	
#8	Category 8	☐	
#9	Category 9	☐	
#10	Category 10	☐	

Update Cancel

Figure 3.6 Custom campaign categories

Your imagination is your only limit when customizing your categories. However, you are more likely to use this tool to replicate your marketing channel mix and setup in your web analytics campaign categories.

As you can see in Figure 3.6, the first level, Channel, is fixed and cannot be changed. The only thing that is changeable is the choice for you to have the campaign category enabled or to have the campaign category displayed in reports.

If you choose to enable the campaign, you make the campaign visible in the Custom Report Wizard, cross-reference filters and drill-down options, and so on. Aside from user rights management, I find it difficult to name a situation where you would not want to do this. So I highly recommend you select Enable whenever adding a category.

If you choose to have the campaign category displayed in reports, this category is displayed in the fixed report called Campaign Summary, as shown in Figure 3.2. You might choose to be a tad more aggressive on campaign categorization for custom analysis later on and then want a simpler view in the Campaign Summary. However, I have to say that most clients I have been working with end up having both the Enable and the Display in Reports options selected whenever they create a new category. I have seen this done differently only when there is an agency partner involved in the day-to-day management of the campaign and the web analytics tool itself. Note that you need the category Enabled to even check the Display in Reports option.

Let me elaborate a bit on the campaign categorization that you have seen so far and provide an example of a five-level-deep classification. This is not to say that this is a best practice example, but merely an idea for you to see the flexibility:

Level 1, Channel Remember that this category is fixed. The options are Banner Campaigns, Email Campaigns, Affiliate Programs, Paid Search, or Other Campaigns.

Level 2, Vendor Any campaign management includes management of where and from whom you buy your impression, such as Yahoo!, Google, PriceRunner, or an industry-specific site.

Level 3, Subcategory Most major vendors will provide multiple campaign opportunities under a specified and unique channel, such as Banner Campaigns from Yahoo!, which is split into Display, Video, and so forth.

Level 4, Market Whether you are global or simply regional, you run optimized campaigns for different regions (such as New York, Boston, and San Francisco) and would like to track them.

Level 5, Campaign Manager This is where you designate your campaign manager by name.

Note that the campaign categories will be displayed in a tree structure in the Campaign Summary report (assuming you checked Display in Reports) in the order you created them, starting with Channel.

The campaign categories you created will be available every time you create a new campaign (see Figure 3.7), but much more about that in the section, "Setting Up New Campaigns."

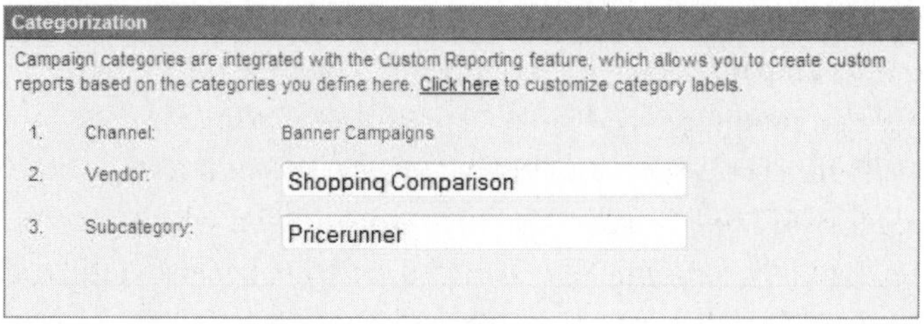

Categorization
Campaign categories are integrated with the Custom Reporting feature, which allows you to create custom reports based on the categories you define here. Click here to customize category labels.
1. Channel: Banner Campaigns
2. Vendor: Shopping Comparison
3. Subcategory: Pricerunner

Figure 3.7 Applying categories to new campaign

Once you deploy campaign tracking, a set of new dimensions, as presented in Table 3.2, becomes available throughout the system. Most important are the new campaign categories just discussed.

► **Table 3.2** Campaign Groups (Dimensions)

Group	Definition
Campaign	The name of the external campaign
Campaign Category (#1 through #10 if enabled)	The category the campaign has been located in
Internal Campaign	The name of the internal campaign
Paid Search Listings	Paid search campaign keyword
Paid Search Phrases	Search phrases used to initiate a paid search keyword

Let me ask some fairly simple marketing questions. Do my online campaign vendors provide leads of different product interest? If so, where do I have unique product marketing opportunities? To answer these, I set up a simple custom report, shown in Figure 3.8, with the campaign category Vendor as a top group, and then apply the merchandising group Product Name in the left column, and finally add two interest metrics, such as Visits and Amount (Revenue).

Product Name	Google		Shopping Comparison		Yahoo	
	Visits	Amount	Visits	Amount	Visits	Amount
Non-Categorized	24,183	$2,177.59	11,543	$2,175.59	13,828	$1,850.43
HITACHI 14.4V Drill Driver DS14DVF3 (14.4V)	8	$1,390.24	13	$2,259.14	2	$347.56
DeWalt 2kg SDS Plus Hammer Drill D25102K	9	$1,453.77	9	$1,453.77	2	$323.06
MAKITA Autofeed Screwdriver 6834	3	$1,394.93	2	$697.46	1	$348.73
Copper Cylinder	6	$1,380.09	1	$245.35	2	$472.58
Combi Kitchen Worktop Jig	1	$736.05	3	$736.05	2	$490.70
DeWalt 24V SDS Plus Rotary Hammer Drill DW005K2C	0	$0.00	0	$0.00	2	$1,545.84
Cordless Strip Nail Gun IM350 / 90 CTQ	0	$0.00	2	$1,468.14	0	$0.00
DeWalt 4kg SDS Plus Hammer Drill D25405K	0	$0.00	0	$0.00	2	$1,413.62
Corded Master 500EL Nail Gun & 1000 Nail Case & Nails	2	$461.24	2	$461.24	0	$0.00
Subtotal	**0**	**$8,993.91**	**0**	**$9,496.74**	**0**	**$6,792.52**
Total	**24,440**	**$26,491.46**	**11,733**	**$20,822.21**	**13,971**	**$20,451.53**

Figure 3.8 Custom campaign categories

Using our new campaign categorization, we immediately determine that we make about the same amount of revenue off Google, Yahoo!, and Shopping Comparison, but that some products—and that's just in the top ten—are completely missing from some vendors. Now you have instant insight and instant opportunity for action, as your first task after spotting this is asking the person in charge of the specific vendor why some products are left out, when you know they sell great with marketing efforts through other vendors.

Beyond categorizing the campaign, we need to know how to differentiate between web traffic generated by a campaign and traffic that is not generated by a campaign, and how to use our web analytics application to mark, or identify, campaigns from the arriving source.

Identifying Campaigns

Yahoo! Web Analytics does not catch campaign traffic automatically—no web analytics program does that—so it is your task to differentiate between what is campaign traffic and what is not. This is, and my apologies for applying strong wording here, where you will see who are the online marketing amateurs and who's got their act together! Remember my wording from the introduction to this chapter: This is one web analytics setup activity where good enough just isn't good enough. This section is where we get into the nitty-gritty of collecting data through campaign identification.

To identify visitors arriving to your site through an online marketing campaign, you must do one of two things: either define a pattern in the entry page URL of your website, or define a pattern in the referrer URL.

It is that simple, and it is not during the technology setup or understanding that people fail—it depends on having the right procedures in place to make this happen *every* time an online campaign is initiated.

There are certain cases where the referrer URL of a campaign cannot be detected and thus not specified, as visitors might not arrive from something as simple as a click on a link, but through multiple non-unique redirects or sources using multiple referrers. It is quite common in ad serving systems, and in particular in the paid search advertising systems, such as Google AdWords and Yahoo! Search Marketing. When this is the case, you are forced to create a unique entry page, also called a landing page, for each of your campaigns (e.g., `visualrevenue.com/example/dennis.html`). Therefore, to ensure that your paid search campaign visitors are correctly identified, you should always define a landing page URL for these campaigns.

To create a unique landing page for each of your campaigns, if you do not want to create unique files or URLs for all of them, you can use the URL parameter analysis method, which provides an exact match on a given URL parameter. To use this method, you append a tracking string to the end of the target URL of the campaign:

```
visualrevenue.com/example/dennis.html?campaign=1
```

This string is not used by your web server, unless you tell it to, as it is only for tracking purposes.

Landing Page

In online marketing, a landing page is the page that appears when a potential customer clicks on an online advertisement (this includes paid search engine result links). The page will usually display content that is a logical extension of the advertisement.

The reasoning for not using this method all the time is that it only works when you control the link sending the traffic to your web property, such as setting up paid search campaigns. If a high-traffic blog review of one of your products starts sending continuous good-quality traffic to your site, I suggest you set that up as a campaign. Instead of persuading a blogger to change the link to include a tracking string (which I discourage), you can catch the traffic on the referrer URL, which is likely to be a unique blog post.

How do you identify campaigns for which the tracking string is removed? In this not-so-unusual scenario, we have a campaign source where the referrer is not unique and your website setup and structure is so that the tracking string is removed. You are essentially left with nothing in the URL, either before or after, to work with.

The reason is that some websites use a redirect, which might remove the tracking string by not passing it on. This is not necessarily something you just fix server side, say, by deploying vanity URLs as part of a marketing campaign, which are then redirected to the permanent address on your site. This approach will not work if you do not own those vanity domains.

The good news is that Yahoo! Web Analytics has a way of working within this setup, using the variable `_S_CMPQUERY` to pass on the tracking string outside the URL.

Let's use our earlier example where we might use the following landing page URL to catch a campaign:

```
visualrevenue.com/example/dennis.html?campaign=1
```

And we envision that this is redirected to a permanent campaign URL as follows:

```
visualrevenue.com/example
```

You are in a situation where you might not be able to use the referrer URL, you cannot use the landing page URL, and there are no URL parameters to analyze. So you would use the `_S_CMPQUERY` variable, having it equal the original campaign tracking string. Thus, you apply the following variable to the tracking script:

Version 4

```
var _S_CMPQUERY='campaign=1';
```

Version 5

```
YWATracker.setCmpQuery("campaign=1");
```

This instrumentation will forward the campaign tracking information to Yahoo! Web Analytics without having the tracking string displayed in the URL.

Setting Up New Campaigns

Before I begin, let me repeat that you do not need to make any changes to the tracking script to activate campaign management in general. This is entirely something that is done in the Yahoo! Web Analytics settings and in collaboration with your ad serving partner, if you have one.

To set up a new campaign or edit an existing one, choose Settings > Manage Campaigns (see Figure 3.9).

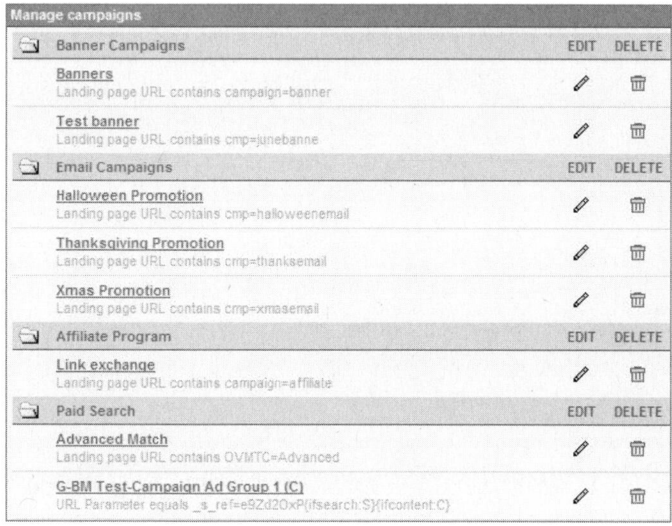

Figure 3.9 Manage Campaigns

You can edit any of the existing campaigns, or create an entirely new campaign by choosing one of the campaign channels and clicking Add New Campaign.

Setting up a new campaign is a three-step activity:

1. Apply the general campaign properties.
2. Apply the campaign categories.
3. Identify the campaign.

I'll expand on those three steps now.

The first step is to apply the general campaign properties (see Figure 3.10).

You are expected to name your campaign for future reference in reports and elsewhere in the campaign interface. If needed, you can apply a description to the campaign that details the campaign's objectives.

The most important choice you make here is the Cost Type, as introduced earlier in this chapter:

- Free Campaign / Other Cost Type
- One-time Cost
- CPC (Fixed Cost per Click)
- CPA (Fixed Cost per Action)
- PPC (Pay per Click)

CAMPAIGN PROPERTIES

Campaign type: Banner Campaigns

Campaign name: Free Y!WA Books

Description: Internal Y! Campaign giving away books with a new Y! Store Signup.

Cost Type:
Specify the cost model, and then define your costs, in order to calculate the profitability of this campaign in your reports.

- Free campaign / Other cost type
- One-time cost USD 5000
- CPC (Fixed Cost-per-Click)
- CPA (Cost per action)

NO OF IMPRESSION: 800000

Campaign start: 2009 June 01

Campaign end: 2009 August 04

Show campaign in reports: Show | Hide

Figure 3.10 Campaign properties

Your Cost Type choices depend on the specified channel, so you have to apply the right channel to make sure you have the ability to apply the right cost type.

You can choose Free Campaign / Other Cost Type if there is no direct cost attached to the campaign, such as a great review from a blogger, which you set up as a campaign. It can also be a general offline branding exercise that drives good traffic to a vanity URL that you want to track the impact of, but the cost center is placed elsewhere in the organization.

One-time Cost is a type you choose when you buy a campaign where the number of impressions, clicks, visits, or actions are related to the cost. This is typically display advertising, such as when you buy a one-week ad on the front page of your industry trade magazine's website.

CPC and CPA are two cost types that are used to automatically apply a summed up cost for the campaign. This is done in real time, and you will be able to see the running costs as they arrive. An example is a shopping comparison engine where you pay, for example, $1.20 per click in a given category.

PPC is almost self-explanatory; it represents the opportunity to apply the cost for every click you bid on and on the paid search engine, and then summarize the costs for the campaign.

The next step is to put the campaign categorization we talked about earlier to use (see Figure 3.11).

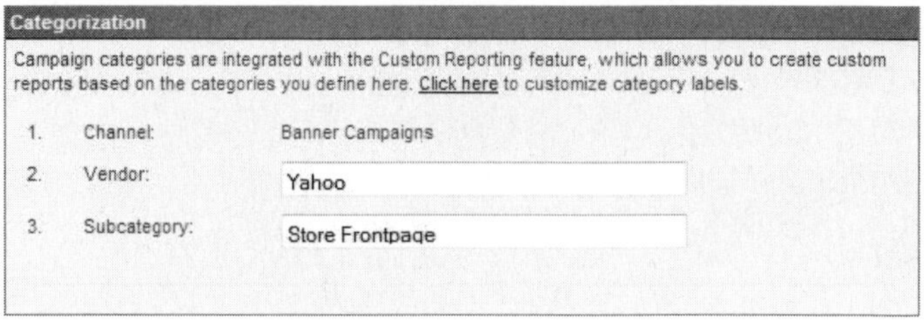

Categorization

Campaign categories are integrated with the Custom Reporting feature, which allows you to create custom reports based on the categories you define here. Click here to customize category labels.

1. Channel: Banner Campaigns

2. Vendor: Yahoo

3. Subcategory: Store Frontpage

Figure 3.11 Campaign categorization

You can apply any new value for one of the preset categories, or use the Ajax search to use an existing value. You are not forced to use Ajax search, but if you find yourself not using this, you probably created too many campaign categories.

However, note that if you do not enter a value for a particular category, then the campaign will appear as noncategorized for that category.

Finally, you need to apply your knowledge about how to identify the campaign (see Figure 3.12).

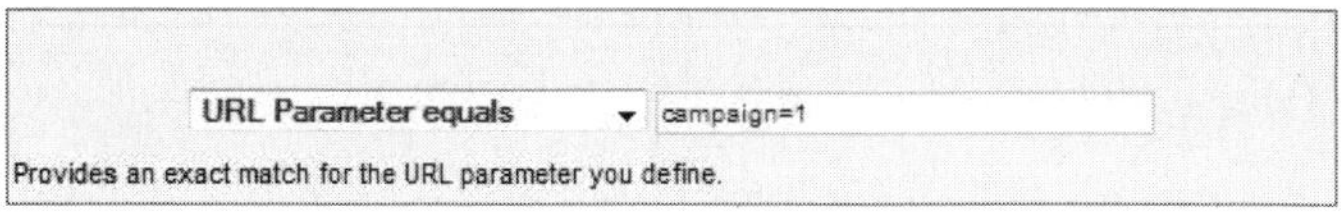

URL Parameter equals campaign=1

Provides an exact match for the URL parameter you define.

Figure 3.12 Identifying a campaign

Remember that since Yahoo! Web Analytics is a real-time system, you can do an instant test by accessing the landing page or the website serving your advertisement and see if your visit was properly recorded.

However, be aware of the fact that this does not mean that you can register campaigns retroactively. Your campaign is active from the time you create it, meaning that you should set up the campaign beforehand. You can, nevertheless, in panic and as a hack, create a segment based on entry page URL or referrer URL, but this is purely to report back on a missing campaign, and it will not be part of the campaign summary.

It is important to ensure that there are no campaign-tracking string conflicts, meaning two campaign identifiers that are overlapping. This is a typical error, and I have seen this overlooked numerous times, even by experienced technical support personnel. Envision the following campaign tracking strings:

- `campaign=Google`
- `campaign=GoogleEU`

Also, envision a campaign identifier as follows:

- `URL contains: "campaign=Google"`

Since both tracking strings are defined with URL contains and both strings contain the phrase `"campaign=Google"`, Yahoo! Web Analytics will report this as a conflict.

Having said that, I always recommend using `equal` as the indentifying option when possible, as this drastically decreases the opportunity for error.

It's worth noting, even if we are not there yet, that internal campaigns do not conflict with external campaigns.

Single Campaign Management

There is not much to say about single campaign management other than what you have seen so far in this section and in particular what Figure 3.9 tells us.

Under Manage Campaigns, you will see all of your campaigns listed, grouped by channel, and you'll have an edit icon on the right hand side of all campaign rows. This is how you view and manage the configuring of all your campaigns, which is fine as long as you do not have too many campaigns.

There is also a search function, which is not used unless you are working with hundreds and hundreds of campaigns.

I think the most advanced part of the single campaign management screen is the access to fallback campaign setup and to the bulk campaign management.

Bulk Campaign Management

In case you manage hundreds and hundreds of campaigns, you can choose to configure them in bulk by using the Yahoo! Web Analytics Bulk Campaign Management feature.

The interface, shown in Figure 3.13, bluntly notes:

The changes you make [with bulk campaign management] may have dramatic effects on your campaign tracking and report display. Please consult a technical support specialist for assistance in using this feature.

That is not to say that you cannot use this feature—just be aware that you might destroy the existing campaigns, not fully set up the new campaigns correctly, and generally end up in a situation where you are completely blind and have no valid online campaign data. Not good!

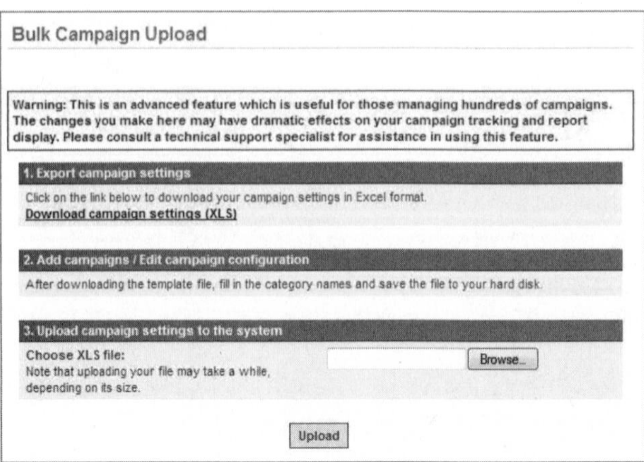

Figure 3.13 Bulk Campaign Upload

You will find the Bulk Campaign access at the end of the Manage Campaigns screen (see Figure 3.9). This will give you access to the Bulk Campaign Upload screen, which provides a straightforward set of tasks:

- Export Campaign Settings
- Add Campaigns / Edit Campaign Configuration
- Upload Campaign Settings to the System

This is not the difficult part; adding new campaigns is the risky part—small errors have huge impacts.

Yahoo! provides detailed explanations and warnings in the Microsoft Excel sheet. You can merge this Excel sheet with information from, for example, a Yahoo! Search Marketing account or a Google AdWords account, as shown in Figure 3.14.

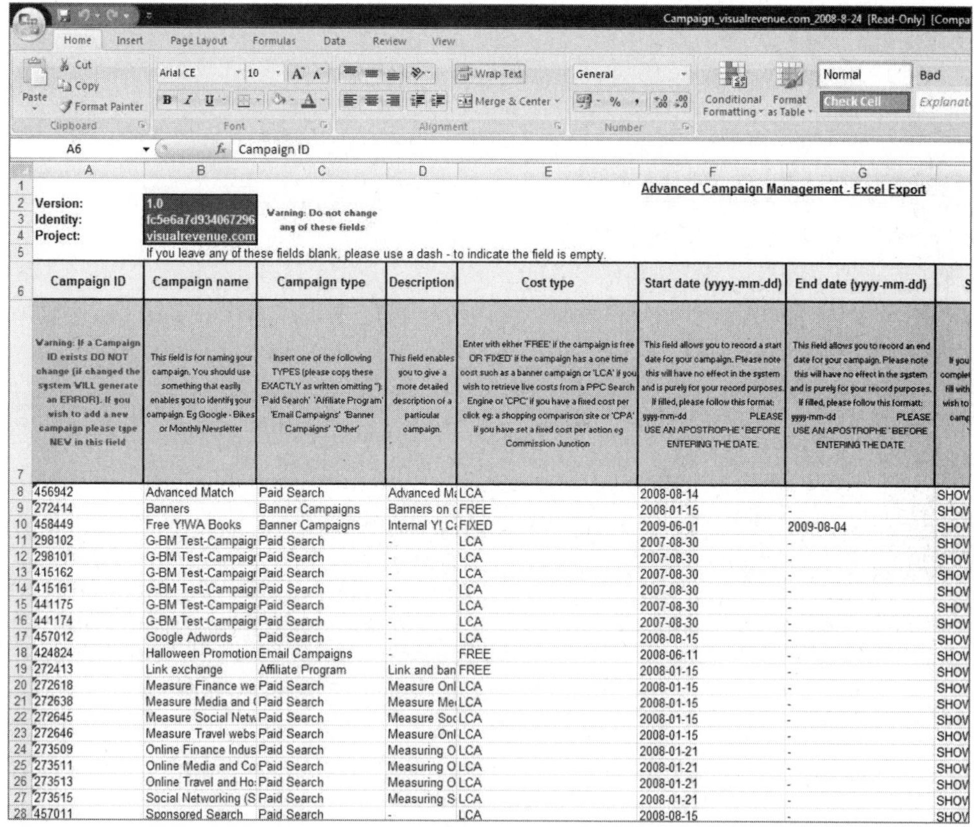

Advanced Campaign Management - Excel Export

Version: 1.0
Identity: fc5e6a7d934067296
Project: visualrevenue.com

Warning: Do not change any of these fields

If you leave any of these fields blank, please use a dash - to indicate the field is empty.

Campaign ID	Campaign name	Campaign type	Description	Cost type	Start date (yyyy-mm-dd)	End date (yyyy-mm-dd)	S
Warning: If a Campaign ID exists DO NOT change (if changed the system WILL generate an ERROR). If you wish to add a new campaign please type NEW in this field	This field is for naming your campaign. You should use something that easily enables you to identify your campaign. Eg Google - Bikes or Monthly Newsletter	Insert one of the following TYPES (please copy these EXACTLY as written omitting "): 'Paid Search' 'Affiliate Program' 'Email Campaigns' 'Banner Campaigns' 'Other'	This field enables you to give a more detailed description of a particular campaign.	Enter with either 'FREE' if the campaign is free OR 'FIXED' if the campaign has a one time cost such as a banner campaign or 'LCA' if you wish to retrieve live costs from a PPC Search Engine or 'CPC' if you have a fixed cost per click eg: a shopping comparison site or 'CPA' if you have set a fixed cost per action eg Commission Junction	This field allows you to record a start date for your campaign. Please note this will have no effect in the system and is purely for your record purposes. If filled, please follow this format: yyyy-mm-dd PLEASE USE AN APOSTROPHE ' BEFORE ENTERING THE DATE.	This field allows you to record an end date for your campaign. Please note this will have no effect in the system and is purely for your record purposes. If filled, please follow this formatt: yyyy-mm-dd PLEASE USE AN APOSTROPHE ' BEFORE ENTERING THE DATE.	If you complet fill with wish to camp
456942	Advanced Match	Paid Search	Advanced Ma	LCA	2008-08-14	-	SHOV
272414	Banners	Banner Campaigns	Banners on (	FREE	2008-01-15	-	SHOV
458449	Free Y!WA Books	Banner Campaigns	Internal Y! Ca	FIXED	2009-06-01	2009-08-04	SHOV
298102	G-BM Test-Campaigı	Paid Search	-	LCA	2007-08-30	-	SHOV
298101	G-BM Test-Campaigı	Paid Search	-	LCA	2007-08-30	-	SHOV
415162	G-BM Test-Campaigı	Paid Search	-	LCA	2007-08-30	-	SHOV
415161	G-BM Test-Campaigı	Paid Search	-	LCA	2007-08-30	-	SHOV
441175	G-BM Test-Campaigı	Paid Search	-	LCA	2007-08-30	-	SHOV
441174	G-BM Test-Campaigı	Paid Search	-	LCA	2007-08-30	-	SHOV
457012	Google Adwords	Paid Search	-	LCA	2008-08-15	-	SHOV
424824	Halloween Promotion	Email Campaigns	-	FREE	2008-06-11	-	SHOV
272413	Link exchange	Affiliate Program	Link and ban	FREE	2008-01-15	-	SHOV
272618	Measure Finance we	Paid Search	Measure Onl	LCA	2008-01-15	-	SHOV
272638	Measure Media and (	Paid Search	Measure Me	LCA	2008-01-15	-	SHOV
272645	Measure Social Netw	Paid Search	Measure Soc	LCA	2008-01-15	-	SHOV
272646	Measure Travel webs	Paid Search	Measure Onl	LCA	2008-01-15	-	SHOV
273509	Online Finance Indus	Paid Search	Measuring O	LCA	2008-01-21	-	SHOV
273511	Online Media and Co	Paid Search	Measuring O	LCA	2008-01-21	-	SHOV
273513	Online Travel and Ho	Paid Search	Measuring O	LCA	2008-01-21	-	SHOV
273515	Social Networking (S	Paid Search	Measuring S	LCA	2008-01-21	-	SHOV
457011	Sponsored Search	Paid Search	-	LCA	2008-08-15	-	SHOV

Figure 3.14 Advanced Campaign Management Excel Report

All of the fields in the Excel spreadsheet are the ones we explored earlier:

- Campaign Name
- Campaign Type
- Description

- Cost Type
- Start Date (yyyy-mm-dd)
- End Date (yyyy-mm-dd)
- Status
- URL/Referrer
- Equals/Contains
- Query String
- Currency
- Cost
- Action Name
- PPC Search Engine Name
- Quantity
- Keyword Identifier
- Search Engines

Once you have updated the information or added a bulk of campaigns, you upload the Excel sheet, and the campaigns are instantly available.

A good exercise is just to download the Excel spreadsheet, rename a few campaigns, or amend the description of them and then upload the spreadsheet. There is little risk, and you will get a feel for it while doing so.

Setting Up a Fallback Campaign

Fallback campaigns are by definition a funny thing, because, if everything is in order, why would you need a fallback campaign? However, I applaud Yahoo! for introducing the feature.

Fallback campaigns allow you to track campaigns that you might have overlooked when configuring them individually, but you still want them counted in your campaign reports. I use the term *you* loosely here, as I typically see this as an organizational fallback.

If you want to be sure every campaign is tracked as a campaign, the first thing you set up is a fallback campaign and then you provide your organization with the procedures for running campaigns, particularly the tracking string pattern needed, such as

```
?campaign="a unique name of the campaign"
```

You would expect all your campaigns to be of the following style, `campaign=1`, `campaign=2`, `campaign=dennis`, or `campaign=Google` (see Figure 3.15). Any forgotten campaign defined by the `campaign` variable will fall into the fallback campaign, and the traffic generated by the campaign you overlooked will still be counted as campaign traffic.

CAMPAIGN PROPERTIES

Campaign type: Fallback Campaign

Campaign name: General

Description:

CAMPAIGN SETTINGS

In order to identify visitors arriving to your site through this campaign you either have to define a pattern for the REFERRER or for the LANDING PAGE of your campaign.

In case of a PPC / CPC campaign, where the referrer cannot be defined, you must define the activity by LANDING PAGE URL. To do so, use one of the following methods:

1. Create a campaign-specific LANDING PAGE (*www.abc.com/ppccampaignoverture.html*)
2. Identify a LANDING PAGE on your web site by adding a "tracking string" to the destination URL
   - Regular URL: *www.abc.com/index.html*
   - Destination URL: *www.abc.com/index.html?campaign=overture*

Note that the "tracking string" is used for tracking purposes only. It does not affect your web server in any way and it reduces the number of pages that you need to maintain (campaign-specific Landing Pages).

Landing Page URL contains ▾ campaign=

Update Cancel

Figure 3.15 Fallback campaigns

Fallback campaigns are also helpful when you know certain sources, such as `shopping.com`, simply do not provide any free traffic and that anything from that domain should be defined as campaign traffic.

To be clear, the system first checks if traffic can be attributed to any of the campaigns you have defined. If Yahoo! Web Analytics cannot find any campaign match, it tries to attribute the traffic to a fallback campaign. Finally, if the traffic cannot be attributed to either defined campaigns or fallback campaigns it is considered noncampaign traffic.

Note that fallback campaigns can be defined only with the `Contains` operator. Also have in mind that a fallback campaign does not apply to historical data.

And as you might have expected as well, the fallback campaigns, of which you can have multiple, can be configured and managed through the bulk management system, just as you would ordinary campaigns.

Example Paid Search Deployment

I believe the deployment of regular external campaigns is a fairly straightforward process; however, deploying paid search campaigns is sadly not always a straightforward process because of Yahoo! Web Analytics' reliance on the paid search engine's APIs. It is also a tad trickier because you are eager to catch information beyond the campaign click and referrer only, such as the keyword.

Assuming that you have taken the appropriate steps described in the earlier section "Paid Search Setup," this leaves you with the task of setting up a new paid search campaign within Yahoo! Web Analytics (see Figure 3.16).

Figure 3.16 New paid search campaign

Here you will apply a PPC cost type under the campaign properties and instruct the application to grab the cost, as described in "Paid Search Setup." See Figure 3.17.

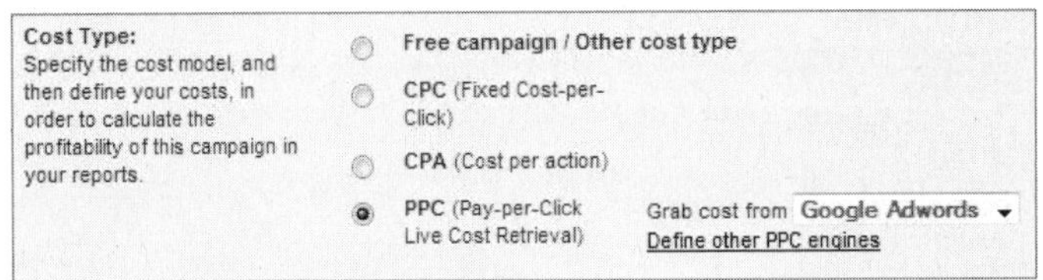

Figure 3.17 Paid search campaign cost type

This is all good and quite easy, isn't it? The challenge is that in most cases, you need to be aware of the setup and general settings in your paid search engine.

Finally, you are required to add a keyword identifier to match visitors arriving from this campaign. This identifier should be a variable in the campaign landing page URL, which you entered at the paid search engine. I suggest just going with the recommended keyword identifier kw.

Yahoo! Paid Search

As you might remember, Yahoo! acquired the paid search company Overture in 2003, and this legacy is apparent in some of its settings and variables.

Yahoo! Search Marketing (Overture) differs from the other major paid search engines partly in the following ways:

- The keyword identifier must be OVKEY.
- The Tracking URLs On option must be selected in the administration part of your account.

This means that you do not have to apply the keyword identifiers to your landing page URL since Yahoo! does that automatically. They extend the landing page URL with a number of valuable variables, but that is beyond the scope of this section. IndexTools (before its Yahoo! acquisition) used to have a full-blown Bid Management offering, but there is yet to be announced a combined strategy at the time of this writing.

Yahoo! did announce that the intelligent bidding would be discontinued. I suggest you follow my blog `visualrevenue.com/blog` and the official blog on `analytics.yahoo.com` for the latest up-to-date information.

So go ahead and use a landing page URL such as the following for your Yahoo! paid search campaigns:

```
http://visualrevenue.com/landingpage.html?campaign=yahoo
```

This looks standard compared to our external campaign setup discussion.

Google Paid Search

Google is a completely different animal, and you again have to take special precautions in order to track a paid search engine campaign from Google.

The keyword identifier can be anything you want it to be, so I suggest you just go with the suggested `kw`. I also suggest that you utilize the built-in Google AdWords keyword variable instead of writing a variable by hand. The variable is called `{keyword}`. So you would use the following landing page URL for your Google AdWords campaigns:

```
http://visualrevenue.com/landingpage.html?campaign=google&kw={keyword}
```

I know I'm repeating myself, but you have to set up the campaign in Yahoo! Web Analytics with the suggested `campaign=google` campaign identifier from earlier.

Do not confuse this task with activating analytics in Google AdWords. If you're interested, check out Avinash Kaushik's *Web Analytics: An Hour a Day* (Sybex, 2007), which offers great information on analytics as well.

As with Yahoo!, Google provides the opportunity to gain much more information beyond just the keyword. You can track three different match types: Broad, Exact, and Phrase—more on this in Chapter 4, "Merchandising Tracking and Reporting."

I believe your most tricky part will be that of actually connecting with and setting up the paid search engine with Google's multitiered MCC system. But if you are just running a blog, you will be in control with every element.

Microsoft Paid Search

Microsoft's paid search initiative is called Microsoft AdCenter, and it is not very different in setup than what you have seen in Google AdWords.

The keyword identifier can be anything you want it to be, so again I suggest you just go with the suggested `kw`. I also suggest that you utilize the built-in Microsoft AdCenter keyword variable, which is called `{keyword}`. So you would use the following landing page URL for your Microsoft AdCenter campaigns:

```
http://visualrevenue.com/landingpage.html?campaign=microsoft&kw={keyword}
```

Microsoft also provides extended opportunities for detailed paid search tracking.

Paid Search Verification Opportunities

In my role as the COO of IndexTools, now Yahoo! Web Analytics, I can attest to the fact that a large portion of our technical support hours and efforts was and partially still is spent on maintaining paid search cost tracking.

Paid search analytics is the lesser of two evils in a cutthroat paid search competitive world. It tends to fail or at least create challenges such as these:

- There are multiple search engines, with ever-changing setups and guidelines.
- There are multiple APIs that often change.
- There might be agency partners working the paid search element who are not in touch with the web analytics teams.
- There are typically thousands and thousands of keywords, and most of the time even thousands of landing page URLs.

Yahoo! Web Analytics has a feature under Settings that essentially eliminates support from paid search engines to create a more powerful self-service environment. This is called LCA Troubleshooting, but I think it likely you will see this renamed.

LCA stands for Live Cost Analysis. LCA Troubleshooting allows you to check the PPC results obtained by the system against the click and cost data provided by the paid search engines. LCA Troubleshooting provides a page that shows whether the system encountered any problems when retrieving data from paid search engines (see Figure 3.18).

LCA Troubleshooting — visualrevenue.com

Date	PPC Engine	Login Failed	No Matching Campaigns Found	Keyword Identifier Missing	Keyword Mismatch	Creative Identifier Missing	Creative Mismatch	Download Failed	Search Engine Unavailable	Keywords Retrieved Successfully
2008.02.05	Yahoo US (EWS API) [Yahoo EWS API]	0	0	0	0	0	0	0	0	38
2008.02.05	Google Adwords [Google Adwords]	0	0	0	0	0	0	0	0	18

Figure 3.18 LCA Troubleshooting results

Most paid search engines, for obvious reasons, are unable to provide same-day reporting, and therefore LCA Troubleshooting data is available only up until the previous day.

As you noticed in Figure 3.18, the system checks for the following types of potential errors:

Login Failed The credentials provided under Settings > Paid Search Setting are not valid or even more likely (if it is Google), the Google MCC information is missing or is inaccurate.

No Matching Campaigns Found One or more landing page target URLs used in the paid search engine cannot be mapped to any paid search campaigns set up on Yahoo! Web Analytics Campaigns.

Keyword Identifier Missing The keyword identifier, such as the suggested kw, is missing. This error appears when a landing page URL can be mapped to a campaign but there is no keyword identifier in the query string. If the search engine is Yahoo!, the keyword identifier is applied automatically as described earlier, but you need to have the feature turned on.

Keyword Mismatch The value in the keyword identifier does not match the keyword reported by the search engine. This is typically caused by a typo in the keyword identifier, which is why you should use the variables provided by the search engines and as displayed in our examples.

Download Failed The connection to the search engine was established, but data could not be successfully transferred. Time to contact support if this continues.

Search Engine Unavailable The search engine was temporarily unavailable. The system will try to access the search engine again later. It is unfortunately a fact that the API connection to the paid search engines is not always up.

Keywords Retrieved Successfully This field provides the number of keywords successfully retrieved and correctly consolidated on a given day, and is merely meant as a quick visual check to ensure that everything is in order.

Internal Campaigns

Internal campaigns give you the opportunity to relate cause and effect in marketing. Internal campaigns in Yahoo! Web Analytics are on-site activities designed to elicit a certain response from your visitors, not that far from any other external campaign. Remember that this does not have to be a direct banner looking like an advertisement; it might as well be a prominent navigational link. With internal campaigns, you get an easy way to test the effectiveness of these activities.

Any out-of-the-box tool that claims to do this should be viewed with suspicion, simply because most web analytics tools determine the cause based on the effect, such as a campaign banner click. Relating cause and effect is doable but quite a difficult task in external campaigns, and a very shaky proposition with internal campaigns.

This does not mean you cannot and should not use the feature—I highly recommend you do, as it is a good indicator as to what to look for—but just do not see it as the final truth. However, it is a whole lot better than just treating on-site inventory as free-of-charge inventory, because it is definitely not.

Causality

Causality indicates a necessary relationship between one event (cause) and another event (effect) that is the direct consequence (result) of the first.

You experience the same challenge when using internal search reports and you're trying to work out a cause-and-effect analysis—such as whether an internal search caused a sale, for example.

Imagine a scenario where you have a visitor arrive from a bookmark and he lands on your shoe store home page. From the home page, he clicks on a banner announcing sale prices on large shoe sizes; he then moves on and searches for large shoes in your internal search box; and finally uses the directory and navigates to the Gucci category and ends up buying a size 48 European Gucci shoe on discount.

Did he buy the shoe because of the banner click, because of the internal search, or just because of the general positive site usability? Determining cause and effect is difficult!

To set up internal campaigns, you work in an environment similar to that of external campaigns, but it's simplified. You find internal campaign options by choosing Settings > Manage Internal Campaigns (see Figure 3.19).

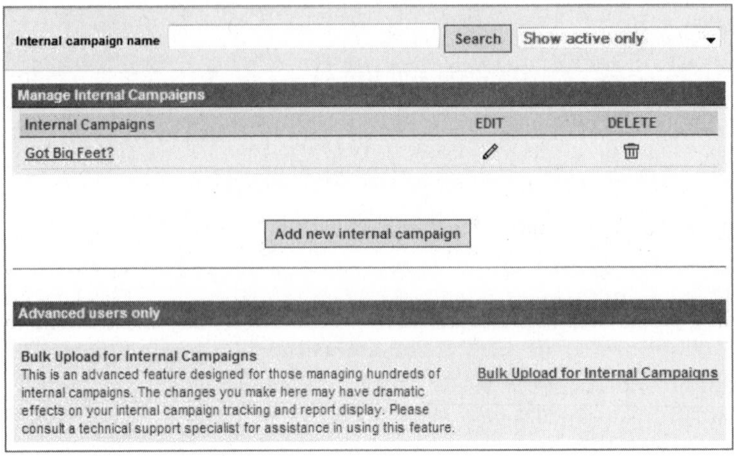

Internal campaign name | Search | Show active only

Manage Internal Campaigns

Internal Campaigns	EDIT	DELETE
Got Big Feet?		

Add new internal campaign

Advanced users only

Bulk Upload for Internal Campaigns
This is an advanced feature designed for those managing hundreds of internal campaigns. The changes you make here may have dramatic effects on your internal campaign tracking and report display. Please consult a technical support specialist for assistance in using this feature.

Bulk Upload for Internal Campaigns

Figure 3.19 Manage Internal Campaigns

The biggest difference between external campaigns and internal campaigns is the way you identify them. Identify internal campaigns with a unique URL string containing a variable called `_s_icmp`, which is used for internal campaigns only. So when you set the target (let's call it landing page) for your internal campaign, the link looks something like this:

```
http://visualrevenue.com/example/large-shoes-discount.html?_s_icmp=dennis1
```

Please note that the `_s_icmp` variable is case sensitive. And when you create a new internal campaign, Yahoo! Web Analytics will automatically provide you with a URL pattern such as `_s_icmp=b70w6X8V`, which you can edit if there is a conflict or if you just prefer to follow your own naming conventions (see Figure 3.20).

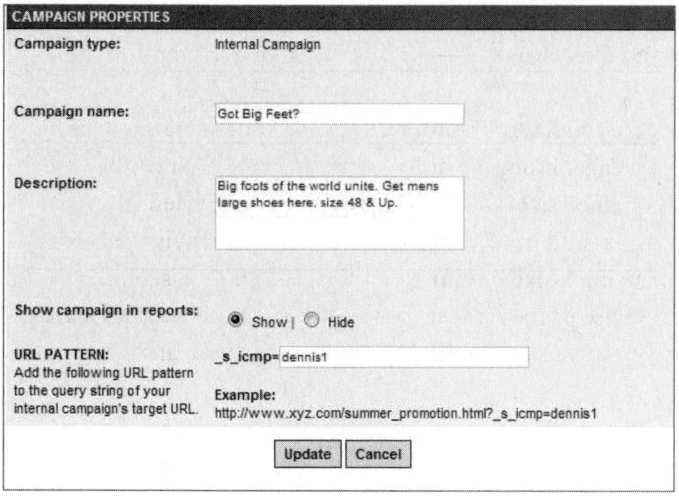

CAMPAIGN PROPERTIES
Campaign type: Internal Campaign
Campaign name: Got Big Feet?
Description: Big foots of the world unite. Get mens large shoes here, size 48 & Up.
Show campaign in reports: Show | Hide
URL PATTERN: Add the following URL pattern to the query string of your internal campaign's target URL. _s_icmp= dennis1
Example: http://www.xyz.com/summer_promotion.html?_s_icmp=dennis1
Update Cancel

Figure 3.20 Editing internal campaign properties

Once you decide what URL string to use, click the Add button, and your internal campaign will be saved. Make sure that you add the same URL string to your website in order to identify the campaign.

To track internal campaign clicks that point to both internal and external locations, call a standard function, which for Version 4 is called `submit_icmp()`. This function is similar to the standard Version 4 `submit()` function, except that it only triggers an internal campaign click and does not trigger a page view—much more about this in Chapter 5, "Advanced Instrumentation."

Finally, internal campaigns do not conflict with regular external campaigns, neither in the setup and recognition nor in the attribution of the actions taken. That said, I would like to remind you that categorization is indeed possible for internal campaigns but that it is separate from regular external campaigns.

You should by now be fully versed in campaign tracking and ready to move on to the exciting topic of merchandising tracking.

Merchandising Tracking and Reporting

Tracking and Reporting on Merchandising allows you to extend beyond the standard focus on content and pages. Unless you are in media and want to monetize your inventory, the pages on your site are little more than a means to more sales. Merchandising is not exclusive to physical products; it can include virtual products, such as downloads or bookings. Remember that reporting on merchandising is not just about the sale; it's also about the ability to use any interaction with your products and services as the backbone of your reporting. For example, you can see what product interest certain campaigns generate or if users arriving from highly qualified search phrases are served the right content and if that content is product focused.

4

Chapter Contents

Merchandising Basics
Setting Up Merchandising Tracking
Tracking Products Viewed
Tracking Products Added to the Cart
Tracking Pending Sales and Reconciling Orders
Tracking Products Purchased
Tracking Discount, Tax, and Shipping
Setting Up Merchandising Categories
Merchandising Setup Tips

Merchandising Basics

Yahoo! Web Analytics provides the opportunity for you to track the individual products or services that your visitors view, add to their basket, and purchase. When a visitor becomes a customer by purchasing one or more of your products and services, you track this information using the guidelines for conversion tracking, as explained in Chapter 2.

Merchandising tracking is much more than just collecting the name of the product sold. Yahoo! allows you to define your product categories and replicate them as merchandising categories. By doing this, you have the opportunity to create custom reports with product names and product categories as merchandising dimensions, which means you can analyze cost and revenue according to these dimensions.

The report in Figure 4.1 represents our most popular products sorted by the amount of revenue each generates.

Product Name Search Engines (Direct)	Revenue
⊞ Non-Categorized	$45,338.53
⊟ MAKITA Autofeed Screwdriver 6834	$17,087.89
Google	$8,369.64
Yahoo	$4,533.49
AOL Search	$4,184.76
⊟ HITACHI 14.4V Drill Driver DS14DVF3 (14.4V)	$12,685.94
Google	$4,344.50
AOL Search	$4,170.72
MSN Search	$2,085.36
Blueyonder	$2,085.36
⊟ DeWalt 24V SDS Plus Rotary Hammer Drill DW005K2C	$10,047.96
Yahoo	$10,047.96
⊞ Copper Cylinder	$8,355.84
⊞ Combi Kitchen Worktop Jig	$6,133.75
⊞ DeWalt Cordless Tools Radio Charger DC011	$6,085.20
⊞ MAKITA 2kg SDS Plus Hammer Drill HR2450T	$5,641.44
⊞ Belle 1600W Paddle Mixer PROM04	$5,023.98
⊞ DeWalt 9" Circular Saw D23700	$4,023.84
Subtotal	**$120,424.37**
Total	**$252,065.11**
« PREVIOUS 10	NEXT 10 »

Figure 4.1 Top products sorted by revenue

As a quick note, notice that the report is not a Most Popular Page report, but a report showing unique products sold, products that could be presented over multiple pages, on- and off-site and in multiple ways. We know they are unique products because they have been defined with a SKU code and later named by uploading your merchandising categories. The beautiful part of this is that we can apply something as simple as a search engine dimension, where we instantly see which search engines drive traffic and sales to our top products. Chapter 10, "Distinctive Reports and Usage," delves into detail on merchandising reports.

By applying the search engine dimension, you can spot an issue with our third most popular product, whose revenue appears to be derived only from Yahoo! visits. It is obviously an error and something to look into. Assuming Google is driving double the revenue as in our most sold product, this could be a USD $20,000 opportunity to work on. The task given to your web or marketing team would be, in part, to see if your web property is indexed correctly or if the specific page that drives traffic from Yahoo! is the one indexed by Google as well. In any case, you can take action on new insights such as this.

You can collect and maintain accurate information on your products and services, all the way down to updating your reports to reflect cancelled orders or changes to order amounts, by sending API requests to the system. You can also upload your individual product costs and calculate how each campaign contributes to your profits.

Activating this type of reporting involves customizing the tracking script. There are a number of different variables, but not to worry—they are easy to understand and implement. Setting up merchandise reporting requires you to perform three distinct activities:

- Set up merchandising tracking variables.
- Set up merchandising categories within the application.
- Upload your product information.

The merchandising variables are myriad, but you can start simple and build on them later. If you do not want to go all-out to begin with, you can even skip uploading the product information and just report on a SKU level. This is a common approach, and you can get Yahoo! Web Analytics technical support without uploading the product information as part of the interface.

Stock Keeping Unit (SKU)

A SKU is a unique identifier for each distinct product and service that can be ordered from a merchant. Use of the SKU system is rooted in data management, enabling a merchant to be in detailed control of inventory.

Tracking by SKU is fine because categorization and enhanced enabling of product information is a retrospective activity. You can track the SKU code for months and then at a later stage upload the product names and categorization, which will then affect your reporting back in time. Should a product change name or be recategorized, this can easily be done after the fact.

Setting Up Merchandising Tracking

Merchandising tracking is by nature closely related to the sales tracking described in Chapter 2, "Content and Advanced Conversion Tracking." Setting up merchandising tracking is similar to sales tracking: You simply add variables to your tracking code.

Yahoo! Web Analytics uses the following variables for merchandise tracking:

- ACTION
- ORDERID
- AMOUNT
- _S_DISCOUNT
- _S_TAX
- _S_SHIPPING
- _S_SKU
- _S_UNITS
- _S_AMOUNTS

The most important of these variables is the SKU code; it is the center around anything merchandising.

I strongly suggest that you build on the skills you learned in Chapter 2 on content tracking to understand merchandising. For example, you should be able to group sales using the DOCUMENTGROUP feature and be able to report on those as a collective process:

Version 4

```
var DOCUMENTGROUP='Checkout Pages';
```

Version 5

```
YWATracker.setDocumentGroup("Checkout Pages");
```

Tracking SKU Information

Let's get to the meat of the matter, the SKU code, which is not surprisingly tracked in the _S_SKU variable and is applied as follows:

Version 4

```
var _S_SKU='DM112899';
```

Version 5

```
YWATracker.setSKU("DM112899");
```

Be aware that the SKU code is always related to one of the following action values:

- PRODUCT_VIEW
- ADD_TO_CART
- PENDING_SALE
- 01
- CANCELLED_SALE

These products and actions typically register in the order presented here so that tracking a sale of a given product would look like this:

Version 4

```
var ACTION='01';
var _S_SKU='DM112899';
```

Version 5

```
YWATracker.setAction("01");
YWATracker.setSKU("DM112899");
```

The value of the variable corresponds to the specific product or products you wish to track, and the product SKU information is typically something you inflate at runtime. The reason for doing so is that it is unusual to see product pages managed manually, and they are generally created in runtime based on a product database. There is nothing wrong in hard-coding this in the `_S_SKU` variable if you have a limited number of products.

If you do not manage your own product pages—that is, if you use an outsourced e-commerce platform—you should expect, actually *demand*, that they provide you with a set of tracking variables that you can use.

Let me give you a simple example of a standard PHP-enabled e-commerce platform and what a runtime-inflated variable looks like:

Version 4

```
var ACTION='PRODUCT_VIEW';
var _S_SKU = "<?php echo $product_info['products_id']; ?>";
```

Version 5

```
YWATracker.setAction("PRODUCT_VIEW");
YWATracker.setSKU("<?php echo $product_info['products_id']; ?>");
```

If your company does not deploy SKU codes, you can just create your own proprietary numbering or naming system. It is absolutely essential to supply Yahoo! Web Analytics with a unique number for referencing each product, as grouping separate products into the same SKU would create more harm than good.

Tracking Units and Amounts

You should always track the individual units and individual amounts; otherwise you'll end up with flawed information, which is almost always worse than having no information at all.

So, using the previous sales example and applying the `_S_UNITS` and `_S_AMOUNTS` variables, we get:

Version 4

```
var ACTION='01';
var _S_SKU='DM112899';
var _S_UNITS='2';
var _S_AMOUNTS='100.00';
```

_S_UNITS tracks the number of each item sold, and S_AMOUNTS records the total price of a product (which is the individual price of an item multiplied by the total number of units of the respective item).

But no decent sale can be recorded without the total amount and a unique order ID, which we deploy by adding the ORDERID and AMOUNT variables. The following code results:

Version 4

```
var ACTION='01';
var _S_SKU='DM112899';
var _S_UNITS='2';
var _S_AMOUNTS='100.00';
var ORDERID='10099802';
var AMOUNT='USD100.00';
```

Version 5

```
YWATracker.setAction("01");
YWATracker.setSKU("DM112899");
YWATracker.setUnits("2");
YWATracker.setAmounts("100.00");
YWATracker.setOrderId("10099802");
YWATracker.setAmount("USD100.00");
```

There is a distinct difference between the _S_AMOUNTS and AMOUNT variables: The AMOUNT variable references the total sum of the sale, and the _S_AMOUNTS variable references the total amount of the individual product, in question. In the previous example, as we only reference one product, the two sums are the same, but as you will see later, this is not the case if a client purchases multiple products in the same basket.

I created a quick custom report, shown in Figure 4.2, that showcases the previous scenario. Products are grouped by individual customer, then by their unique order, and finally by the product items purchased within those orders.

You will notice that the orders with IDs equaling TB0000013021 and TB0000012895 very much fit our example in regard to identical values applied to the _S_AMOUNTS and AMOUNT variables, but it is also very visible that the order with the TB0000012894 ID is different, as a whole range of products are sold and we also see a very different number of units for every product. I will go into detail on how to track the latter shortly.

Member / Order ID / Product Name	Units	Revenue
██low_uk@btinternet.com	282	$168.53
TB0000012894	181	$128.75
End Feed - Tees	70	$42.11
End Feed - Straight Couplers	60	$8.99
End Feed - Elbows	20	$10.63
End Feed - 45? Elbows	10	$6.74
End Feed - Crossover Full	10	$39.66
End Feed - Reducing Couplers	10	$16.56
Radiator Valve with Lockshield	1	$4.06
TB0000013021	100	$22.49
End Feed - Elbows	100	$22.49
TB0000012895	1	$17.29
Double Open Pipe Clip	1	$17.29

Figure 4.2 A custom report showing individual items sold

Note that the same variable syntax from Chapter 2 applies here: The variable must not be longer than 75 characters, and you must not use non-ASCII characters. In addition, do not use any of the following characters in the variable:

```
' < > # & ; : ? - * ~ ` ´ ) ( = % ! "
```

Working with Multiple Currencies

You read the section in Chapter 2 about how to track revenue in multiple currencies, and working with multiple currencies in merchandising is similar. As you've probably noticed, we did not apply a currency code to the `_S_AMOUNTS` variable. That leaves you with one variable with a currency code applied and another one without any currency code.

Version 4

```
var ACTION='01';
var _S_SKU='DM112899';
var _S_UNITS='2';
var _S_AMOUNTS='100.00';
var ORDERID='10099802';
var AMOUNT='USD100.00';
```

Version 5

```
YWATracker.setAction("01");
YWATracker.setSKU("DM112899");
YWATracker.setUnits("2");
YWATracker.setAmounts("100.00");
YWATracker.setOrderId("10099802");
YWATracker.setAmount("USD100.00");
```

You have to enter the currency code in front of the AMOUNT variable, or it defaults to USD. But unlike the AMOUNT variable, the _S_AMOUNTS variable does not need to have the currency code entered, since the currency is inherited from the AMOUNT variable. In the previous example, a USD currency results for the two units sold of product numbered DM112899.

Tracking Products Viewed

I have been very focused on the nirvana of e-commerce actions, the sale, but I am sure you agree with me that there are many steps and many actions before getting to this point. You can track any number of steps and any number of activities with Yahoo! Web Analytics. The tool has a few hard-coded events, however, that come right out of the box—one of them is the unique action value called PRODUCT_VIEW.

The Product View variable provides you with the opportunity to expand your merchandising knowledge to activities, very close to the top of the sales funnel. In this way, you can see how often potential customers view your products, which products are the most popular, and whether a positive connection exists between product campaigns and product views.

Remember that selling only provides you with successful customer behavior, whereas events before the sale occurs can provide you with very powerful insights on unsuccessful customer outcomes. The product view can be used in a number of ways, and you will even see some use of it as a proxy for products added to cart or sales (if they do not have volume enough to perform significant campaign analysis on that parameter).

To enable this type of tracking, you apply the value PRODUCT_VIEW to the ACTION variable on all the pages where you display products:

Version 4

```
var ACTION='PRODUCT_VIEW';
var _S_SKU='DM112899';
```

Version 5

```
YWATracker.setAmount("PRODUCT_VIEW");
YWATracker.setSKU("DM112899");
```

The pages where this code is applied do not have to be unique and in fact rarely are. Products are displayed on product marketing pages, technical specification pages, in search results, in recommendation boxes—and I am sure you have even more suggestions. I recommend you enhance your document-naming and -grouping skills to create opportunities to split different product views over the site.

Which leads to our next topic: forwarding to pages where we display multiple products at the same time. A product search result is likely to do this, as shown in Figure 4.3.

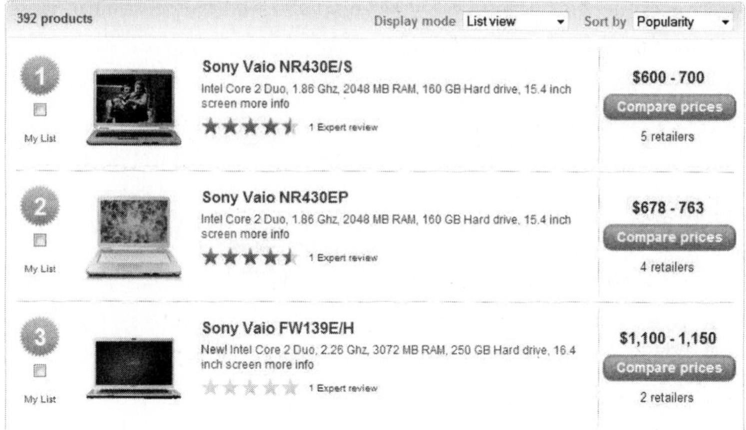

Figure 4.3 Standard product search result page

There are other scenarios where this is bound to happen. In order to track several product views at the same time, continue using the same syntax we've discussed in previous chapters, separating variable values by a semicolon. Tracking two product views at the same time looks like this:

Version 4

```
var ACTION='PRODUCT_VIEW';
var _S_SKU='DM112899;DM113834';
```

Version 5

```
YWATracker.setAction("PRODUCT_VIEW");
YWATracker.setSKU("DM112899;DM113834");
```

If you are not sure which product views to track together, the default merchandising report, shown in Figure 4.4, is a good starting point for you to play around with the various dimensions and metrics.

Product Category Product Type Brand or Supplier Name Product Name	Product Views	Add To Cart	Cart Complete	Units	Amount	Avg. Product Order Value
⊞ Plumbing	4,036	503	114	1,387	$3,638.54	$31.92
⊞ Electrical	1,382	229	35	314	$391.38	$11.18
⊞ Sealants & Adhesives	1,874	155	58	214	$557.82	$9.62
⊞ Building	3,215	374	4	129	$218.97	$54.74
⊞ Hand Tools	499	58	82	104	$2,068.86	$25.23
⊞ Safety	368	41	15	102	$369.99	$24.67
⊞ Bolts	76	108	18	71	$108.73	$6.04
⊞ Ironmongery	954	7	9	62	$97.55	$10.84
⊞ Abrasives	480	166	10	61	$92.83	$9.28
⊞ Screws	1,456	43	16	46	$237.65	$14.85
Subtotal	14,340	1,684	361	2,490	$7,782.32	$21.56
Total	19,014	2,219	522	2,740	$21,616.66	$41.41
« PREVIOUS 10						NEXT 10 »

Figure 4.4 Default merchandising summary report

Note that the report in Figure 4.4 and those from earlier include product naming and product categorization, which we are yet to talk about, and thus your reports will look different. However, you can view merchandising reporting and products on a SKU level, as shown in Figure 4.5. You only have this option, though, if you have not uploaded any merchandising information. If you proceed to the summary report, you will see the screen shown in Figure 4.5.

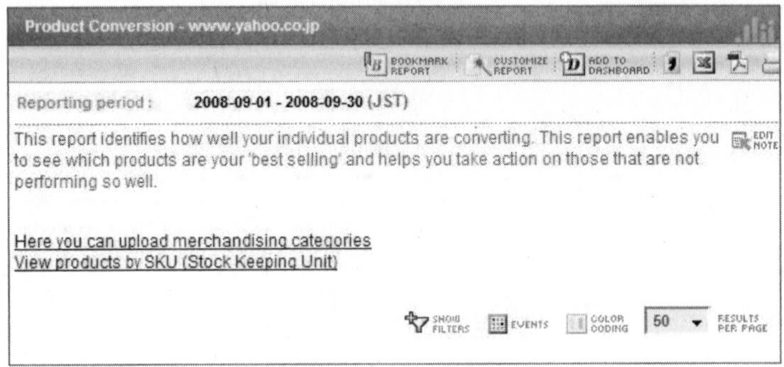

Figure 4.5 Viewing products by SKU

As I mentioned earlier, you can choose to view products by SKU to begin with and then associate product names and categorization later. Now, let's move on to tracking products added to your cart.

Tracking Products Added to the Cart

The next natural step after tracking product views is to track which products your visitors choose to add to their shopping carts on your website. Adding something to the shopping cart tells a lot beyond the action itself, and you can perform a lot of behavioral analysis later, armed with this event tracked.

It should not be possible to add anything to the cart without having tracked the product viewed first, making this a very natural extension to your general sales funnel analysis.

Yahoo! Web Analytics provides this feature out of the box as yet another hard-coded event very similar to `PRODUCT_VIEW`. The unique action value is called `ADD_TO_CART`.

This action is typically tracked as an on-click action on the Add to Cart button or on the cart page itself (see Figure 4.6). This all depends on your cart features and the overall e-commerce checkout-process technology.

Figure 4.6 On-click Add to Cart example

To activate Add to Cart tracking, add the ADD_TO_CART value to your ACTION variable, as shown here:

Version 4

```
var ACTION='ADD_TO_CART';
var _S_SKU='DM112899';
```

Version 5

```
YWATracker.setAction("ADD_TO_CART");
YWATracker.setSKU("DM112899");
```

While your products are viewed all over your web site, they are added to the cart through one system. However, we can imagine a scenario where your visitors have the opportunity to add more than one product to the cart at once, as shown in Figure 4.7.

Figure 4.7 Adding two or more products to the cart example

You continue using the same syntax mentioned in product views, separating variable values by a semicolon. Tracking two products added to the cart at the same time looks like this:

Version 4

```
var ACTION='ADD_TO_CART';
var _S_SKU='DM112899;DM113834';
```

Version 5

```
YWATracker.setAction("ADD_TO_CART");
YWATracker.setSKU("DM112899;DM113834");
```

The results appear in the Add to Cart column on the Merchandising Summary page, as shown in Figure 4.4. But this example just scratches the surface of what we can do with this metric added to your analysis arsenal.

Track Pending Sales and Reconciling Orders

Yahoo! Web Analytics provides a well-conceived concept of sales and merchandising. Although many web analytics users would think that the next natural step after tracking the Add to Cart activity would be the actual sale, there are many situations where this would not be ideal.

Let's look at a couple of examples where it is simply not possible to track the sale immediately and directly on the Thank You page.

Thank You Page

In online marketing, the term *Thank You page* typically refers to a page where it is made clear to customers that they successfully completed the transaction. A transaction could be anything from a sale to an RSS signup, but it's always a conversion point. A good rule of thumb is to make sure you always apply an ACTION variable to your Thank You page.

For example, suppose a visitor buys a new credit card that requires you to perform a credit check before final approval. If you track this as a sale on the "thank you for applying" page, you could end up with registered sales that did not materialize.

Imagine a scenario in which the final price is not necessarily determined upon sale, such as per-hour car rentals, where you would know that a sale occurred but have yet to determine the final sales value. If registered as a normal sale in the system, you would be reporting on erroneous sales data.

As you can see from these two examples, we must have an opportunity to "park" a sale until we know what the final status is. Parking a sale is a built-in functionality in Yahoo! Web Analytics known as Pending Sale. It allows you to reconcile your back office and your reporting interface, without having to worry about either aborted sales or incorrect sales amounts showing up in your reporting interface. Once the sale has been finally confirmed, you can update the status of the sale from Pending to Approved Sale.

To activate the Pending Sale tracking, you have to add the PENDING_SALE action value to your ACTION variable, as follows:

Version 4

```
var ACTION='PENDING_SALE';
```

Here's an example that explains the constraints as well as the freedom of the PENDING_SALE action value:

Version 4

```
var ACTION='PENDING_SALE';
var _S_SKU='DM112899; DM113834';
var _S_UNITS='2;1';
var _S_AMOUNTS='100.00;50.00';
var ORDERID='10099803';
var AMOUNT='USD150.00'
```

Version 5

```
YWATracker.setAction("PENDING_SALE");
YWATracker.setSKU("DM112899; DM113834");
```

```
YWATracker.setUnits("2;1");
YWATracker.setAmounts("100.00;50.00");
YWATracker.setOrderId("10099803");
YWATracker.setAmount("USD150.00");
```

You are not required to use the AMOUNT variable and can leave it blank if you don't yet know the final sales value. However, to reconcile the order, you can only change the Amount, Currency, and Status. This does not include any line items, such as the Units or the Unit Amounts, which when you think about it, might be a new order altogether. The suggested workaround, which you might make company policy, is to cancel the order and create a new one.

Updating the status of a sale from Pending to Approved, or deleting the sale altogether by setting it to Cancelled, is called *order reconciliation* and can be performed directly in the interface.

To approve or cancel a pending sale and to change the order amount and the currency for a specific sale, right-click on Order Line in the sale's Details report and select Modify Sale Action (see Figure 4.8). Be aware that, as of this writing, the order reconciliation feature can only be used for actions that are at least 24 hours old. Note that you must have the Order ID set up as shown in Figure 4.9.

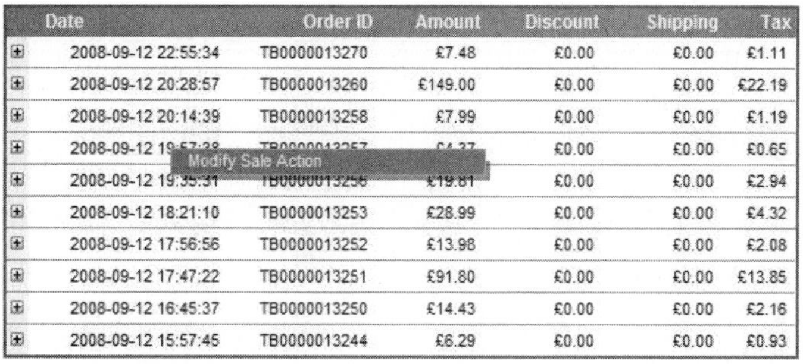

	Date	Order ID	Amount	Discount	Shipping	Tax
⊞	2008-09-12 22:55:34	TB0000013270	£7.48	£0.00	£0.00	£1.11
⊞	2008-09-12 20:28:57	TB0000013260	£149.00	£0.00	£0.00	£22.19
⊞	2008-09-12 20:14:39	TB0000013258	£7.99	£0.00	£0.00	£1.19
⊞	2008-09-12 19[illegible]	[illegible]	[illegible]	£0.00	£0.00	£0.65
⊞	2008-09-12 19:35:31	TB0000013256	£19.81	£0.00	£0.00	£2.94
⊞	2008-09-12 18:21:10	TB0000013253	£28.99	£0.00	£0.00	£4.32
⊞	2008-09-12 17:56:56	TB0000013252	£13.98	£0.00	£0.00	£2.08
⊞	2008-09-12 17:47:22	TB0000013251	£91.80	£0.00	£0.00	£13.85
⊞	2008-09-12 16:45:37	TB0000013250	£14.43	£0.00	£0.00	£2.16
⊞	2008-09-12 15:57:45	TB0000013244	£6.29	£0.00	£0.00	£0.93

Modify Sale Action

Figure 4.8 Modify Sale Action

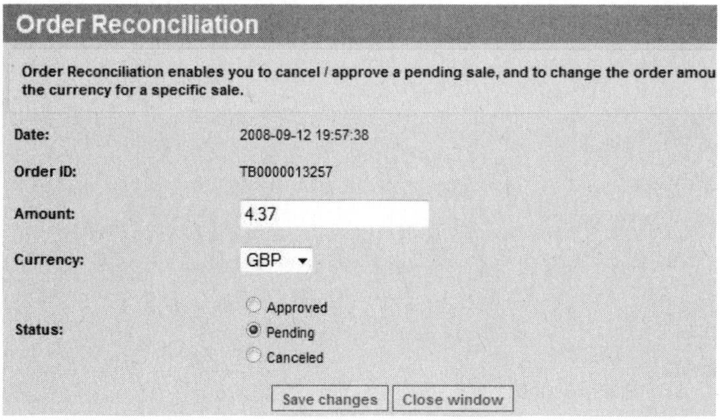

Order Reconciliation

Order Reconciliation enables you to cancel / approve a pending sale, and to change the order amou the currency for a specific sale.

Date: 2008-09-12 19:57:38

Order ID: TB0000013257

Amount: 4.37

Currency: GBP

Status: Approved / Pending / Canceled

Save changes | Close window

Figure 4.9 Order Reconciliation dialog

This approach is all good and fine if you are working with a manageable amount of orders on a daily basis, but it is completely unusable if you have thousands or even just hundreds of orders on a daily basis. For large numbers of sales, you can automate the order reconciliation process through the Yahoo! Web Analytics API.

Application Programming Interface (API)

An API is a set of functions that a service, such as Yahoo! Web Analytics, provides to support requests made by other applications.

I will go more in depth about the API in Appendix A.

Tracking Products Purchased

The final step in any funnel and the climax of our merchandising expectations is the ability to track products purchased. This is not to be confused with the ability to track a sale as whole, as that only records the fact that we had a sale and what the amount was, but beyond the fact that a conversion took place and that it had a value, we don't know much.

So after tracking Product Added to Cart and potentially a Pending Sale, we move on to tracking in detail which products your visitors purchased.

There are a plethora of positive reasons for wanting to do detailed merchandising tracking. And should you be completely out of ideas, let me suggest at least one value before moving into the nuts and bolts of how to use your tracking reports in Part II of this book.

Most online marketers understand that click-through rate (CTR) is not necessarily the best way to measure success. To some degree, when looking at your CTR metric, all you see is the match between, for example, search phrase and the search advertising creative, which is important but does not define success in the end. I am sure you can imagine us driving up the CTR by adding in a sentence saying "Click here to get a $500 discount," but if the offering does not match that, the CTR didn't do anything for you.

Click-Through Rate (CTR)

The CTR is a way of measuring the success of an online campaign. It is calculated by dividing the number of visitors who clicked on the campaign ad by the number of times the campaign ad was delivered (impressions). For example, if a banner ad was delivered 1,000 times (impressions delivered) and 15 visitors clicked on it, then the resulting CTR would be 1.5 percent.

Products purchased are an opportunity to gain a detailed understanding of the quality of your traffic acquisition programs. If you have two campaigns driving a similar amount of sales with a comparable campaign cost, you now have the power to drill into the actual products sold. The actual products sold will provide you with information on whether one campaign drove more high-profit products than the other, whether one campaign drove more strategically important sales, and all that good stuff you do when you normally analyze your merchandising (see Figure 4.10). You might even find that the price points are different from channel to channel and that you should have a different discount offering for a unique channel.

Search Engines (Direct)	DeWalt Revenue	MAKITA Revenue	HITACHI Revenue	Bosch Revenue	Albion Revenue	TREND Revenue
Google	$1,777.80	$1,402.65	$949.09	$567.09	$920.06	$163.54
AOL Search	$4.33	$444.56	$737.60	$480.05	$0.00	$490.70
Yahoo	$772.92	$697.46	$0.00	$360.13	$236.29	$490.70
Deal Time	$122.69	$66.63	$0.00	$89.65	$0.00	$0.00
MSN Search	$388.46	$0.00	$173.78	$143.28	$0.00	$0.00
Blueyonder	$0.00	$0.00	$347.56	$0.00	$0.00	$0.00
Altavista	$323.06	$0.00	$0.00	$0.00	$0.00	$0.00
Oingo	$253.40	$0.00	$0.00	$0.00	$0.00	$0.00
Tiscali	$0.00	$0.00	$0.00	$0.00	$0.00	$0.00
Gawwk	$0.00	$0.00	$0.00	$0.00	$0.00	$0.00
Total	**$3,642.66**	**$2,611.30**	**$2,208.03**	**$1,640.20**	**$1,156.35**	**$1,144.94**

Figure 4.10 Revenue from paid and organic search engines grouped by merchandising vendor category

To activate the Products Purchased tracking, you append the variables used on the Sale action tracking script. It could look like this:

Version 4

```
var ACTION='01';
var _S_SKU='DM112899';
var _S_UNITS='2';
var _S_AMOUNTS='100.00';
var ORDERID='10099803';
var AMOUNT='USD100.00'
```

Version 5

```
YWATracker.setAction("01");
YWATracker.setSKU("DM112899");
YWATracker.setUnits("2");
YWATracker.setAmounts("100.00");
YWATracker.setOrderId("10099803");
YWATracker.setAmount("USD100.00");
```

To enter the price of your purchased products, you need to use the `_S_AMOUNTS` variable.

While the variables in the following example are expressed as constants, I doubt that you will be able to implement it that way, as your shopping content depends on the visitor's choices. So expect to have values inflated from your e-commerce platform.

You can also track more products purchased at the same time. Here's an example:

Version 4

```
var ACTION='01';
var _S_SKU='DM112899; DM113834';
var _S_UNITS='2;1';
var _S_AMOUNTS='100.00;50.00';
var ORDERID='10099803';
var AMOUNT='USD150.00';
```

Version 5

```
YWATracker.setAction("01");
YWATracker.setSKU("DM112899; DM113834");
YWATracker.setUnits("2;1");
YWATracker.setAmounts("100.00;50.00");
YWATracker.setOrderId("10099803");
YWATracker.setAmount("USD150.00");
```


It is critical that you enter the sales prices in the proper order, as this is how it is associated in the Yahoo! system. In the previous example, that would be the sale of the following two products:

- 2 Units of Product DM112899 at a total of USD100.00
- 1 Unit of Product DM113834 at a total of USD50.00
- At a total sales price of USD150.00 recorded and saved under order ID number 10099803

Make sure you align the number of choices within the `_S_UNITS` and `_S_AMOUNTS` variables, as with the `_S_SKU` variable. That way, if you sell two products, the `_S_UNITS` variable will hold two different numbers of units sold, and the `_S_AMOUNTS` variable will list two different sales prices.

Once your purchased products are tracked as in the preceding example, you can check reports on products purchased in the reporting interface. At this stage, only the SKU information will be displayed.

Be aware that Yahoo! Web Analytics does not check whether the revenue registered under `S_AMOUNTS` adds up to the total sales value registered in the `AMOUNT` variable. So it is fine to write a tracking script like this:

Version 4

```
var ACTION='01';
var _S_SKU='DM112899; DM113834';
var _S_UNITS='2;1';
```

```
var _S_AMOUNTS='100.00;50.00'; //
var ORDERID='10099803';
var AMOUNT='USD150.00';
```

Make sure you have quality assurance (QA) in place, because once the tracking script is deployed, it is possible to collect incorrect data that is free of syntax errors.

Quality Assurance (QA)

QA refers to planned and systematic processes that provide confidence of a product's or service's effectiveness.

Note that not only is the Sale Action 01 used for merchandising reporting, but it is also positively applied to most conversion reports, scenario analysis, and so forth.

Tracking Discount, Tax, and Shipping

Yahoo! Web Analytics provides you with an opportunity to achieve detailed merchandising tracking. With the final set of variables I will present in this chapter, you will be able to track and report on:

- Discounts
- Taxes
- Shipping costs

Among other things, tracking these variables will provide you with the opportunity to do detailed promotional campaign analysis.

To activate any of the three variables, add one of the following individual variables and inflate it with the appropriate value:

- `_S_DISCOUNT`
- `_S_TAX`
- `_S_SHIPPING`

The variables are not dependent on each other, and you can add any one of them without the others. In my experience, though, once you reach this level of detail, all three are added at the same time as part of the same deployment project. Here's an example in which we have a price discount, a value-added tax, and a shipping cost:

Version 4

```
var ACTION='01';
var _S_SKU='DM112899';
var _S_UNITS='2';
var _S_AMOUNTS='100.00';
var _S_DISCOUNT ='5.00';
var _S_TAX ='8.00';
```

```
var _S_SHIPPING ='20.00';
var ORDERID='10099803';
var AMOUNT='USD123.00';
```

Version 5

```
YWATracker.setAction("01");
YWATracker.setSKU("DM112899");
YWATracker.setUnits("2");
YWATracker.setAmounts("100.00");
YWATracker.setDiscount("5.00");
YWATracker.setTax("8.00");
YWATracker.setShipping("20.00");
YWATracker.setOrderId("10099803");
YWATracker.setAmount("USD123.00");
```

Unlike with the previous set of variables, only one value can be associated with any of these three variables. Because they are all attached to the order ID, you cannot add a discount, tax, or shipping cost for each individual product. So in the case of multiple products purchased, the tracking script would look like this:

Version 4

```
var ACTION='01';
var _S_SKU='DM112899; DM113834';
var _S_UNITS='2;1';
var _S_AMOUNTS='100.00;50.00';
var _S_DISCOUNT ='5.00';
var _S_TAX ='8.00';
var _S_SHIPPING ='20.00';
var ORDERID='10099803';
var AMOUNT='USD173.00';
```

Version 5

```
YWATracker.setAction("01");
YWATracker.setSKU("DM112899; DM113834");
YWATracker.setUnits("2;1");
YWATracker.setAmounts("100.00;50.00");
YWATracker.setDiscount("5.00");
YWATracker.setTax("8.00");
YWATracker.setShipping("20.00");
YWATracker.setOrderId("10099803");
YWATracker.setAmount("USD173.00");
```

The AMOUNT variable should equal the final revenue amount, which then should be the sum of the following calculation:

```
AMOUNT = _S_AMOUNTS (DM112899) + _S_AMOUNTS (DM113834) + _S_TAX + _S_
SHIPPING - _S_DISCOUNT
```

The first place that you will see these new variable values is under the Default Sales Details report, shown in Figure 4.11.

Date	Order ID	Amount	Discount	Shipping	Tax
2008-08-31 23:48:43	TB0000013933	£2.98	£0.00	£0.00	£0.44
2008-08-31 23:04:07	TB0000013930	£269.95	£3.56	£5.00	£40.21
2008-08-31 21:52:58	TB0000013923	£55.15	£5.00	£0.00	£8.21
2008-08-31 20:48:46	TB0000013920	£57.76	£7.37	£0.00	£8.64
2008-08-31 20:46:50	TB0000013919	£70.99	£2.85	£0.00	£10.73
2008-08-31 20:21:57	TB0000013917	£22.22	£3.33	£0.00	£3.31
2008-08-31 20:09:14	TB0000013914	£33.58	£2.68	£0.00	£5.04
2008-08-31 19:49:46	TB0000013913	£28.00	£7.20	£0.00	£4.17
2008-08-31 19:27:10	TB0000013912	£44.92	£2.45	£0.00	£6.80
2008-08-31 19:27:06	TB0000013911	£20.90	£1.09	£0.00	£3.11
2008-08-31 19:14:09	TB0000013908	£7.99	£2.45	£0.00	£1.19
2008-08-31 18:20:01	TB0000013903	£8.99	£0.74	£0.00	£1.34
2008-08-31 18:03:55	TB0000013901	£36.48	£0.78	£0.00	£5.44

Figure 4.11 Default Sales Details report

As you know, Yahoo! Web Analytics does not check whether the revenue registered under S_AMOUNTS adds up to the total sales value registered in the AMOUNT variable. Also, keep in mind that the system will accept figures reported by your tracking code, regardless of whether all the elements of the price _S_DISCOUNT, _S_TAX, _S_SHIPPING, and _S_AMOUNTS add up to the total registered in the AMOUNT variable.

Setting Up Merchandising Categories

Completing a perfect merchandising setup is essentially a three-step activity:

1. Set up merchandise tracking.
2. Define product categories.
3. Upload the CSV file.

By far, the biggest part of the task is setting up merchandise tracking by altering the tracking scripts as shown in earlier sections.

If you want to receive reports broken down by the product categories in your product catalog, you need to add your merchandising categories to the Yahoo! Web Analytics interface and upload product information. Merchandising categories provide reports that are easier to use, as your reports will display your already familiar product categories. The categorization itself is not mandatory, and with a limited number of products, you might want to use this only for product naming—product naming in the sense that you would want to see real product names instead of SKUs in the interface.

While merchandise tracking involves changing the tracking code, you can add merchandising categories and upload product information from the reporting interface.

So to conclude, detailed product information is defined as applying:

- Product name
- Product categories

You can access the product categories definition settings (see Figure 4.12) by choosing Settings > Customize > Upload Merchandising Categories. You will see a number of predefined categories that you can activate or alter to fit your merchandising.

2. Define product categories

Tick the **Enabled** check box to include your merchandising categories in your Custom Report Wizard and Drill-down options.
Tick the **Display in reports** check box to have your merchandising categories displayed in your Products Conversion report.

ID	Category label	Enabled	Display in reports
Category #1	Product Name	☑	☑
Category #2	Product Category	☑	☑
Category #3	Product Type	☑	☑
Category #4	Brand or Supplier Name	☑	☑
Category #5	Product Category	☐	
Category #6	Product Category	☐	
Category #7	Product Category	☐	
Category #8	Product Category	☐	
Category #9	Product Category	☐	
Category #10	Product Category	☐	

Update Cancel

Figure 4.12 Defining product categories

Yahoo! Web Analytics provides the following predefined merchandising categories:

Category #1 – Product Name

Category #2 – Product Type

Category #3 – Product Subtype

Category #4 – Brand

The product name is fixed and cannot be changed; it is always presented as the last dimension in the reporting. The only thing you can specify here is whether you want to display the product category in reports. Any of the other categories, from #2 through #10, can be altered.

The merchandising categories are truly independent classifications, where you are limited only by your imagination. You have an opportunity to replicate your merchandising setup in your web analytics merchandising categories. I strongly recommend that your online and offline setups match.

As you probably noticed by now, this type of categorization is similar to the thinking behind campaign categorization. So if you chose to enable the product category, you make the category visible in the Custom Report Wizard, cross-reference filters, drill-down options, and so on. I find it difficult to imagine a situation where you would not want to do this, other than as a user rights management choice. So I recommend you check Display in Reports whenever you add a category.

If you chose to have the product category displayed in reports, you simply chose whether this category is displayed in the fixed merchandising summary report shown in Figure 4.4. Most of my clients end up having both options selected whenever they create a new product category, just as with campaign categories, unless only part of the merchandise is presented online. Note that you need to enable Category to make the Display in Reports option available.

A category name can have up to 100 characters, and the categories you enter are displayed in a hierarchical order. Once you have set up the categories, click the Update button and they are instantly visible in the system. You may not have any of the information there, but the grouping is in place for you to upload matching data.

Under Upload CSV File to the System (see Figure 4.13), you will be presented with the opportunity to finalize step 3 of our complete merchandising setup.

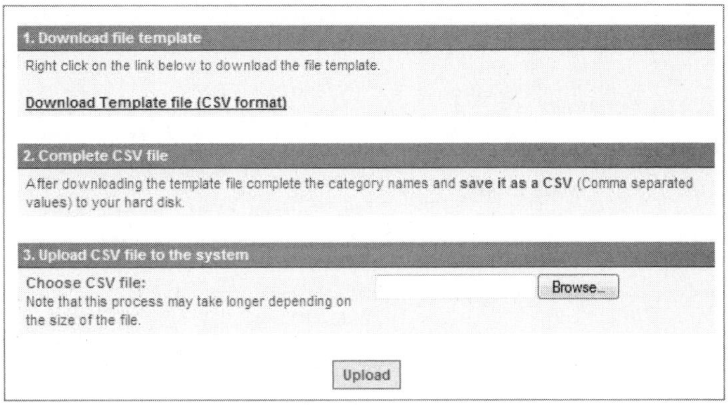

1. Download file template
Right click on the link below to download the file template.
Download Template file (CSV format)

2. Complete CSV file
After downloading the template file complete the category names and **save it as a CSV** (Comma separated values) to your hard disk.

3. Upload CSV file to the system
Choose CSV file:
Note that this process may take longer depending on the size of the file.
Browse...
Upload

Figure 4.13 Merchandising categories upload

Here your first task is to download the CSV template, which will help you do one of two things. Either you choose to fill in the products and their categorization by hand, which is a rare activity, or you perform an export from your products database.

Comma-Separated Value (CSV)

The CSV file is a simple data format that separates the values on one line by a comma.

The CSV file, with a product categorization choice as shown in Figure 4.12, would look like Figure 4.14. You will notice that the columns that appear in the CSV file are the merchandising categories you set up on the Custom Merchandising Categories page.

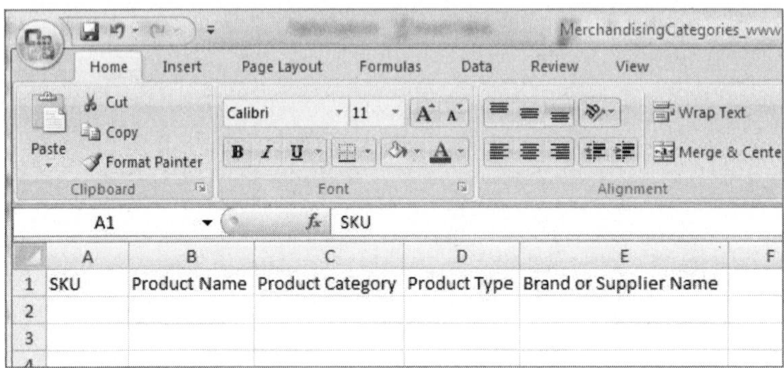

Figure 4.14 CSV template

Once the CSV is populated with data, you upload it to the system, and it will be immediately available for use (see Figure 4.15).

	A	B	C	D	E
1	SKU	Product Name	Product Category	Product Type	Brand or Supplier Na
2	V59179	Cat 5E Non Snag Boots	Electrical	Data Networking	Philex
3	V46698	Electro Brassed Picture Screw Eyes	Ironmongery	Picture Fixings	CENTURION
4	V59455	Plastic Expansion Plugs	Fixings	Cavity Fixings	SAFEGUARD
5	V59297	RJ45 Keystone Jack Punchdown Outlet	Electrical	Data Networking	Philex
6	V59124	RJ45 Keystone Jack Surface Mount Box	Electrical	Data Networking	Philex
7	V59137	RJ45 Keystone Jack Surface Mount Box	Electrical	Data Networking	Philex
8	V42520	Acrylic Sealant	Sealants & Adhesives	Building Sealants	DEN BRAVEN
9	H94799	Pink Grip	Sealants & Adhesives	Adhesives	Everbuild
10	V44059	Cable Tacks	Fixings	Staples, Tacks & Nails	RAPESCO
11	V44024	Ct45 ABS Cable Tacker	Hand Tools	Staplers & Riveters	RAPESCO
12	V58648	Programmable security light Switch	Electrical	RCD's and Timers	Foster
13	529026	Copper Push Fit - Elbows	Plumbing	Copper Push Fit	Yorkshire Fittings
14	529091	Copper Push Fit - Release Tools	Plumbing	Copper Push Fit	Yorkshire Fittings
15	529001	Copper Push Fit - Straight Couplers	Plumbing	Copper Push Fit	Yorkshire Fittings
16	306580	Danfoss RMT230 Room Thermostat	Plumbing	Heating Controls	Danfoss
17	338962	C17 Timeswitch	Plumbing	Heating Controls	Horstmann
18	N32386	DeWalt Cordless Tools Radio Charger DC01	Power Tools	Radio Charger	DeWalt
19	517718	Push Fit - Reducing couplers	Plumbing	Push Fit	J G Speedfit
20	V49228	All Purpose Filler	Sealants & Adhesives	Fillers	Kalon

Figure 4.15 Populated CSV template

As of this writing, the following restrictions apply to the CSV file:

- The CSV file can have a maximum of 60,000 rows, and its size should not be larger than 6MB.
- You can only use ASCII characters in the CSV file, and you should not use any ASCII Ctrl characters (e.g., Tab).
- You can have as many as 90 characters in each cell of the CSV file.

It is important to record the information about your products in their allotted columns. Do not change the category names, as this will result in an error.

As I've explained, you can always recategorize your products or change product information by simply uploading an updated CSV file.

If you add categories that do not match the existing uploaded CSV file, the reporting interface will not return an error but instead will give you the option to upload matching categories or view products by SKU (without any categories).

Merchandising Setup Tips

Once you have set up Yahoo! Web Analytics merchandise tracking, you can view the results in your reports. However, in order to troubleshoot these results, make sure that you only apply a reporting period where you did in fact collect the merchandising information you are trying to verify. If you examine a reporting period that includes sales recorded before you set up merchandise tracking, your results will be incorrect.

This section explores a few tips that might come in handy in your advanced setup or general troubleshooting.

Avoiding Duplicate Order IDs Captured in Different Visits

As I am sure you agree, using order IDs to track purchased products is mandatory when running an e-commerce property. When using the `ORDERID` variable, you ensure that order IDs are not duplicated since the system filters out duplicates within the same session.

However, imagine a scenario in which a visitor saves an order confirmation page (the Thank You page) and later that month reopens the page. Reopening the page will execute the tracking code, and the order ID would be tracked again. Yahoo! Web Analytics allows you to avoid order duplication in such an event.

You can apply a Unix time stamp in the `ACTION` variable, like this:

Version 4

```
var ACTION="ACTIONID:UNIXTIMESTAMP";
```

Version 5

```
YWATracker.setAction("ActionID:UNIXTIMESTAMP");
```

This is a syntax that still allows you to apply multiple actions in the same `ACTION` variable, such as:

Version 4

```
var ACTION="01:1221482942;02";
```

Version 5

```
YWATracker.setAction("01:1221482942;02");
```

Unix Time Stamp

Unix time is a system for describing points in time, defined as the number of seconds elapsed since midnight Coordinated Universal Time (UTC) of January 1, 1970, not counting leap seconds. It is widely used not only on Unix-like operating systems, but also in many other computing systems.

When using the Unix time stamp, the system will check the time of the request against the Unix time stamp in the `ACTION` variable and will disregard the action if the difference between the two dates is more than 30 minutes. This will avoid any order ID duplication that might be caused by reloading the order confirmation page from cache or from a local server.

A complete example enhanced with the Unix time stamp might look like this:

Version 4

```
var ACTION='01:1221482942';
var _S_SKU='DM112899; DM113834';
var _S_UNITS='2;1';
var _S_AMOUNTS='100.00;50.00';
var _S_DISCOUNT ='5.00';
var _S_TAX ='8.00';
var _S_SHIPPING ='20.00';
var ORDERID='10099803';
var AMOUNT='USD173.00';
```

Tracking Sales Across Secure and Nonsecure Domains

Envision a setup where you have a nonsecure marketing domain and a secure shopping cart domain, as in this example:

- Marketing domain: `http://www.dennis.com`
- Shopping cart domain: `https://secure.othercart.com`

Because we have an HTTPS request, recall the "Basic Installation" section in Chapter 1. The problem is that the visit session breaks when transferring between domains, and therefore the visit numbers are inflated and the referrer URL reports are not completely accurate. Exit links are registered, and the Exit Link report is adversely affected.

The following variable must be set in the customization code on all the pages that contain the links to the other domain, as in the following example, where the domains match the two websites mentioned earlier:

Version 4

```
var DOMAINS='*.dennis.com,*.othercart.com';
```

Version 5

```
YWATracker.setDomains("*.dennis.com,*.othercart.com");
```

Throughout the Checkout domain, the following variable must be inflated on the Checkout page:

Version 4

```
var _S_DOMAIN='othercart.com';
```

Version 5

```
YWATracker.setCookieDomain("othercart.com");
```

This will ensure that no Exit Link has been registered and that the visit session is not broken.

I am confident that what you've learned about tracking merchandising will have you well prepared for the last nerdy chapter on instrumentation, Chapter 5, "Advanced Instrumentation."

5 Advanced Instrumentation

With the emergence of Web 2.0, rich Internet applications are becoming more the standard than the exception. Together with new web approaches come new marketing methodologies and the need to track the initial usage and impact of those. The ability to collect the data, which Yahoo! Web Analytics provides, is only half the story—the other half is choosing what to collect. Just because you can collect every single event and action on a dynamic page does not mean you should.

Chapter Contents

Tracking Custom Fields
Tracking Internal Searches
Instrumentation for Flash-Based Objects
Instrumentation for Ajax-Based Objects
Setting Up External Data Sources
Validating Your Code

Tracking Custom Fields

Everything presented so far have been about fixed variables, which you could customize, name, and enhance to derive further value from them. You might, however, find yourself in a situation where you are asked to collect information that simply does not fit into any of the standard variables.

This could be as simple as a request from marketing to collect data from a business-specific dimension. Imagine that you are in the travel and hospitality industry and that your offering is in part based on a search interface like the one in Figure 5.1.

Figure 5.1 Search for flights user interface

From a search interface like the one in Figure 5.1, it would be extremely valuable to collect the following information:

- From airport
- To airport
- Number of travelers
- Cabin type

This search would create an opportunity to list the number of searches with New York City (NYC) as a starting point and the number of business trips. But this search would also create four new dimensions in the system that you could use in conjunction with campaign filtering, campaign segmentation, and conversion points.

For example, you could see if respectively a thousand visits from Google and a thousand visits from Yahoo! create the same number of searches for business class trips, which I would presume are much more valuable. This search is an instant opportunity to evaluate your traffic-acquisition strategies more closely. It is also an opportunity to see if your visitor-to-customer conversion is different from economy to business. And if that is the case, is it true on all destinations, or are you just not competitive on certain routes?

I am sure you see the bigger picture by now and just how powerful it can be to enhance your web analytics tool with business-specific metrics and dimensions.

Yahoo! Web Analytics provides an opportunity to collect custom information using custom fields. Custom fields enable you to add your specific reporting categories to the predefined reporting structures already available in the system and to obtain reports broken down by these categories. Using custom fields allows you to capture and report information that is not contained in standard reports but that is important and unique to your business.

Note that the availability of custom fields is different from Yahoo! offering to Yahoo! offering, and I suggest you connect with your account manager or support team to find out whether this feature is available to you.

To access your custom fields after they have been activated for your account, select Settings > Manage Custom Fields (see Figure 5.2).

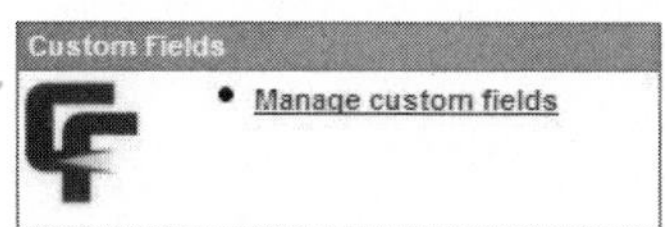

Figure 5.2 Manage Custom Fields

Management of custom fields is both a categorization of existing variables and an opportunity to append those categories by adding your own new custom fields, as you can see under the content hierarchy in Figure 5.3.

Content Hierarchy

These custom fields capture visitor information in relation to your web site's structure / content.

Tracking code ID	Custom Field Name	Custom Param	Carry-over Option	Status	Scope
DOCUMENTNAME	Page Title		No carry-over	Valid	Page view (String)
DOCUMENTGROUP	Document Group		No carry-over	Valid	Page view (String)

Contact your Account Manager to add new custom fields to this category.

Figure 5.3 Content Hierarchy

Here you could choose to append the content hierarchy with another level called `DocumentSubGroup` (if you believe the two levels provided are not sufficient to cover your needs).

Or if we are to use our previous example from the travel and hospitality industry, specifically the search function, you could choose to add a custom field such as From Airport, as shown in Figure 5.4.

Non categorized

These custom fields do not belong to a specific category.

Tracking code ID	Custom Field Name	Custom Param	Carry-over Option	Status	Scope
_s_cf01	From Airport		No carry-over	Valid	Action (String)

Contact your Account Manager to add new custom fields to this category.

Figure 5.4 Noncategorized custom fields

As you have noticed, the custom fields belong to a group. The custom field grouping has no influence on your tracking or reporting and is merely created for you to be in control of all the data fields. Thus there is no error to be made by placing the fields in the wrong group. More importantly, a custom field has the following public properties available:

- Tracking code ID
- Custom field name
- Custom parameter
- Carry-over option
- Status scope

The tracking code ID is the most important in regard to the actual tracking, as this is what you deploy in your tracking script. Continuing with the first examples of creating a custom field to capture a document subgroup, the tracking script variables would look like this:

Version 4

```
var ACTION='07';
var DOCUMENTNAME='Wedding gift list promotions';
var DOCUMENTGROUP='Gift lists';
var _s_cf01='Wedding';
```

Version 5

```
YWATracker.setAction("07");
YWATracker.setDocumentName("Wedding gift list promotions");
YWATracker.setDocumentGroup("Gift lists");
YWATracker.setCF(1, "Wedding");
```

The custom field name is the friendly name that will be shown in the interface when you want to create reports using this new dimension. This name can be changed at any time, and it will affect data already collected as it is simply a lookup.

The custom parameter, carry-over option, and status scope describe the type of data that we want to collect and how to treat it in the system.

Let me explain the scope with an example. Imagine that as part of a sign-in process you ask people to supply their gender and that you collect that information in a custom field. As this information is the same throughout the whole visit (I am assuming most people do not change their gender during a web visit), you would choose a session scope. However, on the other hand, you might have a search function as described earlier, where you collect the From Airport data. This data could have multiple values during a single session, and you could choose to set the scope to No Carry-Over, as you do not want to attribute all searches to one value. The carry-over options include:

- No Carry-Over
- Carry-Over Until Visit Ends

- Carry-Over Until Any Next Action Occurs
- Carry-Over Until Next Defined Action Occurs

The process becomes a bit hairy when we think about the option to carry-over until the next defined action occurs. The system will hold the value for the custom field, such as the From Airport field, until another defined action, such as a flight search, occurs. The reason for doing so involves attribution; you can define and attribute success to certain actions. In this example it would be of great value if you could attribute actual bookings to searches for flights. And for that to happen, you would have to use Carry-Over Until Next Defined Action Occurs.

Adding a new custom field is shown in Figure 5.5. Notice the option for attributes such as Carry-Over or No Carry-Over.

Figure 5.5 Adding a custom field

Here are the variables needed for our Search for Flights form shown in Figure 5.1:

Version 4

```
var DOCUMENTGROUP='Search'; //(All Search related pages)
var DOCUMENTNAME='Flight Search Result Page'; //(The specific flight SERP)
var ACTION='07'; // (action number for flight search)
var MEMBERID='dennis.mortensen@evcrp.com'; //(represent member ID)
var _s_cf01='NYC'; //(represent From Airport)
var _s_cf02='SFO'; //(represent To Airport)
var _s_cf03='1'; //(represent The number of Travelers)
var _s_cf04='Business'; //(represent Cabin type)
```

Version 5

```
YWATracker.setDocumentGroup("Search"); //(All Search related pages)
YWATracker.setDocumentName("Flight SERP"); //(The specific flight SERP)
YWATracker.setAction("07"); //(action number for flight search)
YWATracker.setMemberId("dennis.mortensen@evcrp.com"); //(represent member ID)
YWATracker.setCF(1, "NYC"); //(represent From Airport)
YWATracker.setCF(2, "SFO"); //(represent To Airport)
YWATracker.setCF(3, "1"); //(represent The number of Travelers)
YWATracker.setCF(4, "Business"); //(represent Cabin type)
```

Note that the variables _s_cf01, _s_cf02, and so on are always lowercase in the Version 4 code example.

Also note that no reports are attached to the custom fields and that any interaction with this new data collected is something that happens within the Custom Report Wizard. The Custom Report Wizard (see Figure 5.6) works in real time, and as soon as you have collected the visit data, including these new dimensions, you can start to add them to your reports.

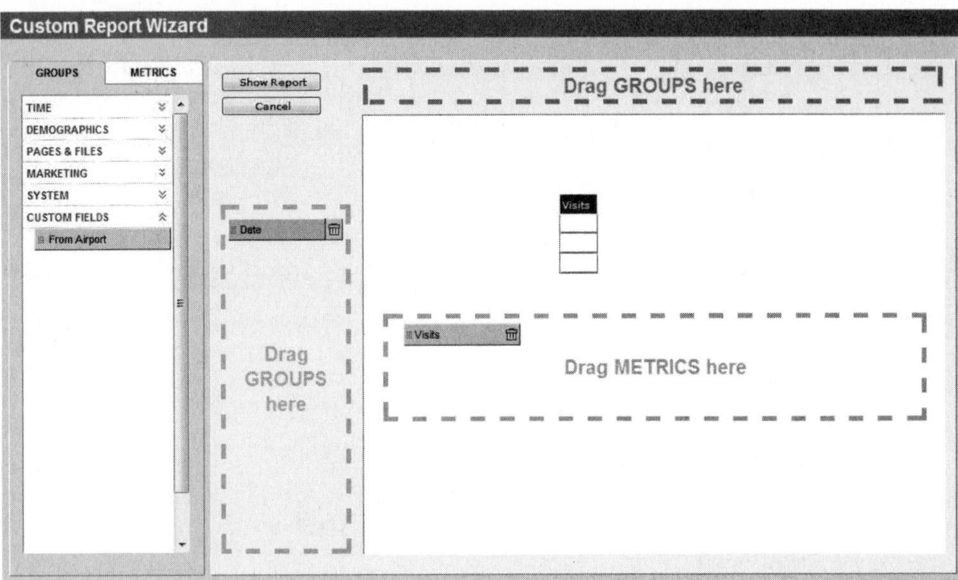

Figure 5.6 Custom Report Wizard: custom fields

Tracking Internal Searches

Tracking internal search is a wonderful feature for obtaining deep and honest insight into the intent of your customers. By tracking pages and products, even with full merchandising setup, all you see is the interaction with content and products people can find. You will not see any interaction with pages they cannot find, with products you do not have, or with products you have but customers can't find.

With Internal Search you walk in the shoes of your customers for a second, and it is the closest you get to qualitative data without conducting any surveys. Do not be fooled by the fact that this section is short and that collecting the information is fairly simple, because this is, if you ask me, one of the juiciest low-hanging fruits in web analytics. There is so much insight to get from this information that it is almost unfair. See Chapter 10, "Distinctive Reports and Usage," for more details on what you can gain from tracking Internal Search.

You can track Internal Search using a set of variables, which have to be inflated on the internal search results page, also called the Search Engine Results page (SERP).

Search Engine Results Page (SERP)

The SERP is the listing of web pages returned by a search engine in response to a keyword query. The results normally include a list of web pages with titles, a link to the page, and a short description showing where the keywords have matched content within the page.

To track that an internal search has occurred and to be in control of the number of internal search actions in general, use the INTERNAL_SEARCH standard action:

Version 4

```
var ACTION='INTERNAL_SEARCH';
```

Version 5

```
YWATracker.setAction("INTERNAL_SEARCH");
```

The most important part of Internal Search is the ability to track the search query itself and if and how many results were included in your SERP. You do this using the variables _S_ISK and _S_ISR:

Version 4

```
var _S_ISK='manhattan airport'; // represent the search phrase
var _S_ISR='0'; // represent the number of search results
```

Version 5

```
YWATracker.setISK("manhattan airport"); // represent the search phrase
YWATracker.setISR("0"); // represent the number of search results
```

What follows is a full example. I strongly suggest you add in at least two additional variables when you deploy internal search tracking.

Version 4

```
var DOCUMENTGROUP='Search';
var DOCUMENTNAME='Blog SERP';
var ACTION='INTERNAL_SEARCH';
var _S_ISK='KPI';
var _S_ISR='10';
```

Version 5

```
YWATracker.setDocumentGroup("Search");
YWATracker.setDocumentName("Blog SERP");
YWATracker.setAction("INTERNAL_SEARCH");
YWATracker.setISK("KPI");
YWATracker.setISR("10");
```

It becomes obvious that both the search phrase and the search result number are elements that need to be inflated at runtime. A number of reports are provided out of the box, such as the Top Internal Searches report.

Yahoo! also provides a number of other internal search reports beyond what is shown in Figure 5.7; you'll learn more in Chapter 10.

Internal Search Phrase	Unique Internal Searches	Internal Searches
kpi	3	4
dennis	2	2
emetrics	1	1
mortensen	1	1
metrics	1	1
jim	1	1
candidates	1	1
ggg	1	1
ggglkjf	1	1
more	1	1
mobile analytics	1	1
mobile	1	1
mobile web	1	1
most used	1	2
community management	1	1
fat	1	1
Unknown	**1**	**1**
Total	**20**	**22**
« PREVIOUS 25		NEXT 25 »

Figure 5.7 Default Top Internal Searches report

Instrumentation for Flash-Based Objects

There is no argument for not tracking activity and events within your Flash applications. Yahoo! Web Analytics unfortunately does not support native Flash tracking at this point, but I am confident that this is a feature that is on Yahoo!'s roadmap.

This lack of support does not mean that you cannot track any Flash activity; it just means that you have to apply a somewhat known and acceptable hack: a hack accomplished simply by calling a JavaScript from within your code, which is not a specific Yahoo! Web Analytics functionality as such but more of a general opportunity to expand the code.

I am not going to delve too much into this topic as I am sure you will see more native tracking coming from Yahoo!, and I believe that most of the web analytics vendors will end up supporting true and native Flash tracking at some point in time.

That said, the standard plain-vanilla HTTP tracking script from Yahoo! Web Analytics is suitable for tracking a Flash application. You simply add a number of code lines to your SWF file.

Shockwave Flash (SWF)

SWF is a partially open file format for multimedia and especially vector graphics developed by Adobe.

Add the following line of code to the SWF file that you want to extend with tracking:

Version 4

```
getURL("javascript:__IT.page(\"\",\"\",\"\",\"\",\"\")");
```

Version 5

```
getURL("javascript:YWA.getTracker('your project id'
).page(\"\",\"\",\"\",\"\",\"\")");
```

Adding this code will allow you to track any of the five following parameters:

- DOCUMENTNAME
- DOCUMENTGROUP
- MEMBERID
- ACTION
- AMOUNT

These parameters are set in the line of code shown earlier, and each \"\" contains one of the parameters, where the order is:

```
\"documentname\",\"documentgroup\",\"member id\",\"action\",\"amount\"
```

This order cannot be changed, and the parameter must be entered in its correct place. If you do not use a parameter, leave its placeholder as is. In case of a fixed variable, you have to enter the name you want for the parameter; for example:

Version 4

```
getURL("javascript:__IT.page(\"Sales Confirmation\",\" Checkout Pages
\",\"dennis.mortensen@evcrp.com\",\"01\",\"USD100.00\")");
```

Version 5

```
getURL("javascript:YWA.getTracker('your project id'
).page(\"Sales Confirmation\",\" Checkout Pages \",\"dennis.mortensen@evcrp.
com\",\"01\",\"USD100.00\")");
```

In case of a dynamic variable, you have to enter it within plus signs, as shown here:

Version 4

```
getURL("javascript:__
IT.page(\""+vardocumentname+"\",\""+vardocumentgroup+"\",\""+varmemberid+"\"
,\""+varaction+"\",\""+varamount+"\")");
```

Here, any of the suggested Flash variables, such as vardocumentname, can be any name you need it to be.

You must install this line of code into the action script wherever the new section of Flash is loaded, usually in the SectionLoader. The line should be placed at the bottom of this script. If the variable has multiple cases, you will still be able to track it using a condition statement. For example:

Version 4

```
if(sectionToLoad=="download")
  vardocumentname = "file1";
else
  vardocumentname = "file2";
getURL("javascript:__
IT.page(\""+vardocumentname+"\",\""+vardocumentgroup+"\",\""+varmemberid+"\"
,\""+varaction+"\",\""+varamount+"\")");
```

I'm sure you can make up 10 other programming examples where the use of this one JavaScript call would work.

There is an opportunity to test the code as well. However, most of the users I know use the fact that the system is real time and test directly by collecting the data on the fly and confirm that the code is correct implemented and set up. If needed, you can test the code by adding the following line to the very end of the script after the getURL command:

Version 4

```
trace("getURL("javascript:__
IT.page(\""+vardocumentname+"\",\""+vardocumentgroup+"\",\""+varmemberid+"\"
,\""+varaction+"\",\""+varamount+"\")");
");
```

You need to match any parameters entered in the getURL command with the test line. Use the Test Movie function in Flash to run the test. A box will appear showing the parameters that were successfully set up. An error box will appear if there are any problems with the code.

We introduced something we called a wrapper function in Chapter 2 ("Content and Advanced Conversion Tracking") in the section on conversion actions, and it looked like this:

Version 4

```
<script language="Javascript">
function recordsale(orderid, amount) {
       var tracking_object = createITT();
       tracking_object.ACTION = "01";
       tracking_object.ORDERID = orderid;
       tracking_object.AMOUNT = amount;
       tracking_object.submit_action();
}
</script>
```

Version 5

```
<script language="Javascript">
function recordsale(orderid, amount) {
var YWATracker = YWA.getTracker("1000123xxxx");
        YWATracker.setAction("01");
        YWATracker.setOrderId(orderid);
        YWATracker.setAmount(amount);
        YWATracker.submit_action();
}
</script>
```

The wrapper function idea is also possible when using Flash, and is typically something you would use if you need to inflate dynamic variables on the fly. It is possible to refer to the relevant function on the preceding HTML page and pass variables to this function, in the same way that we reference the version 4 `javascript:__IT.page`. A typical example is when we only want to record an action.

In such a case we can add a `getURL` like the following to our Flash FLA file, which calls a wrapper function named `newwrap`:

```
getURL("javascript:newwrap.newpage(\"07\")");
```

This line of code passes the number 7 to the function on the referrer HTML page, located after the JavaScript file, which then sets the action only and does not register a full-page view:

FLA

FLA files contain source material for the Flash application. Flash authoring software can edit FLA files and compile them into SWF files.

Version 4

```
<script type="text/javascript">

 var _s_itt=createITT();
 _s_itt.ol();
 _s_itt._submit();

 var __newwrap=_s_itt;
 ITT.prototype.newpage=function(action)
  {
  this.ACTION=action;
  this.submit_action();
  }

</script>
```

Note that this method should not be used when multiple projects are being tracked from the same website.

Also note that you have to relax the security rules to allow JavaScript access across domains. Therefore, `AllowScriptAccess` should be set to `always` (any domain:

```
<object width="250" height="250">
 <param name="movie" value="configurator.swf">
 <param name="allowScriptAccess" value="always">
 <embed src="configurator.swf" width="250" height="250"
AllowScriptAccess="always"></embed>
</object>
```

Tracking an action without a page view is probably more typical in Flash than the general HTML content that you serve. Most Flash elements tend to be in-site elements that people interact with and not entirely new pages (see Figure 5.8).

Figure 5.8 Typical Flash video

Any interaction with a typical embedded Flash element should be considered an action only, and the interaction should not be considered new page views. Looking at Figure 5.8, you can see that possible actions you might want to track include:

- Play/Pause
- Full Screen
- Mute

These three online video actions are unique from site to site, and should you deploy online video, yours will be specific as well. If you want a complete rundown of the essential online video key performance indicators (KPIs), I suggest you go have a look at the following post:

`http://visualrevenue.com/blog/2008/02/online-video-analytics-kpis.html`

Before we get too specific, I would like to focus on one of the KPIs mentioned in this post: Online Video Played, Seconds. Tracking this KPI takes a bit more than the usual effort and involves adding another hack.

We can set a timer within the Flash file using ActionScript, and then report the time spent watching the video each time the file is paused. In ActionScript 2, add the following to the existing ActionScript `onClipEvent` functions:

```
on (playing) {
 getURL("javascript:timestart.timepage(\"07\")");
 var timer1:Number = setInterval(getTime, 1000); // 1 second
 timeViewed = 0;
 function getTime():Void {timeViewed = timeViewed + getTimer();}
}

on (paused) {
getURL("javascript:Pausedtime.newpage(\""+timeViewed+"\",\"12\")");
        }
```

The second function passes the action, and then passes a value containing the time spent watching the file to an action-based custom field.

In ActionScript 3, the timer is initialized differently:

```
function getTime(event:TimerEvent) {
 timeViewed = timeViewed + getTimer();
}

var timer1:Timer = new Timer(1000);
timeViewed = 0;
timer1.addEventListener(TimerEvent.TIMER,getTime);
timer1.start();
```

The function `getTime()` can then be called when the video is paused. I am surprised that the Flash framework, as the prominent web client video platform of choice today, does not provide easier access to metrics like this, but I am sure this fact will change over time.

Instrumentation for Ajax-Based Objects

The Internet changed from consisting mostly of static pages through the period known as Web 1.0 to become the interactive environment known today as Web 2.0. Whether we recognize that the Web has entered a new phase in its development does not matter too much, as I am sure we can all agree that users expect a much richer experience using websites today. Websites are so interactive in nature that we might as well call them applications, just as we would call Microsoft Word an application.

A fundamental part of this revolution is the ability to develop applications that can behave in a manner similar to what we know from our day-to-day operating system. The technology to do so has been around for a long time but has taken off over the last five years, mostly under the name Ajax. A typical Ajax object is shown in Figure 5.9.

Ajax

Asynchronous JavaScript and XML, more commonly known as Ajax, is a group of interrelated web development techniques used for creating interactive web or rich Internet applications. With Ajax, web applications can retrieve data from the server asynchronously in the background without interfering with the display and behavior of the existing page. Data is retrieved using the `XMLHttpRequest` object or through the use of Remote Scripting in browsers that do not support it. Despite the name, the use of JavaScript, XML, or its asynchronous use is not required.

We won't debate whether or not you should track Ajax-enabled sites—the answer is obviously yes. I still believe, though, that the most difficult part is not so much collecting the events but choosing which events to collect and then finally making sense of it all. Our first task, which has been the theme of this first part of the book, is to understand how to collect the data.

Figure 5.9 Typical Ajax object

Ajax-based websites require different tracking, as these sites do not always refresh the page to perform various actions such as adding an item to the shopping cart, subscribing to a newsletter, or as in Figure 5.9, flicking through the pictures.

Technically, upon loading the page, the Yahoo! Web Analytics include file is loaded and will track the initial page view. As you work the page, every subsequent event or change on the page can be tracked as a new page view or as an action only. Keep in mind that tracking Ajax objects does not change any of the previously mentioned elements from Chapter 1 through 4—all it changes is the methodology to do so.

To enable Ajax tracking, you have to create a JavaScript tracking object:

Version 4

```
var tracking_object = createITT();
```

You can then apply values to defined properties of this object and submit it. When submitting it, you have two possibilities:

Version 4

```
tracking_object.submit();
tracking_object.submit_action();
```

Depending on your Ajax application, you may decide whether you want to track a page view before you track an action, or you may want to track the action only. You can only submit once, so you would never have both submits in the same function.

Imagine a scenario where you would have an on-screen Ajax pop-up that shows the shipping costs, ensuring people do not navigate away from your basket. I recommend that you track such a pop-up as a page view:

Version 4

```
var tracking_object = createITT();
tracking_object.DOCUMENTGROUP='Shipping Costs';
tracking_object.DOCUMENTNAME='Shipping Costs ZIP 10010';
tracking_object.submit();
```

The values in this example are inflated at runtime, depending on the actual ZIP code. For complex Ajax websites, I suggest that you create wrapper functions to perform the JavaScript calls and that you make the functions somewhat generic, like this:

Version 4

```
<script language="Javascript">
function ypageview(vardocumentgroup, vardocumentname)
 {
 var tracking_object = createITT();
 tracking_object.DOCUMENTGROUP=vardocumentgroup;
 tracking_object.DOCUMENTNAME=vardocumentname;
 tracking_object.submit();
 }
</script>
```

We would call the new `ypageview` function with the following values:

```
ypageview('Shipping Costs','Shipping Costs ZIP 10010')
```

Using the on-click knowledge from Chapter 2, we could write an HTML link like this:

```
<a href='#' onclick='showshippingcosts(10010); ypageview('Shipping
Costs','Shipping Costs, ZIP 10010')'>CLICK HERE FOR SHIPPING COSTS</a>
```

The JavaScript object offers the opportunity to track the full suite of variables we've discussed so far. To illustrate, let's replicate the standard merchandising example from Chapter 4 in a dynamic environment. The code would look like this:

Version 4

```
var tracking_object = createITT();
tracking_object.ACTION='01';
tracking_object.DOCUMENTNAME='Confirmation';
tracking_object.DOCUMENTGROUP='Shopping cart';
tracking_object._S_SKU='DM112899;DM113834';
tracking_object._S_UNITS='2;1';
tracking_object._S_AMOUNTS='100.00;50.00';
tracking_object._S_DISCOUNT ='5.00';
tracking_object._S_TAX ='8.00';
tracking_object._S_SHIPPING ='20.00';
tracking_object.ORDERID='10099803';
tracking_object.AMOUNT='USD173.00'; ;
tracking_object.submit();
```


All of our Version 4 examples are not completely obsolete in Version 5, but Version 5 includes this Ajax functionality as a standard, and no specific code is needed for you to track Ajax elements and the like. The Version 4 Ajax tracking is similar to the Version 5 standard tracking. Here we've replicated the Version 4 code:

Version 5

```
var YWATracker = YWA.getTracker("1000123xxxx");
YWATracker.setDocumentName("Confirmation");
YWATracker.setDocumentGroup("Shopping cart");
YWATracker.setAction("01");
YWATracker.setSKU("DM112899; DM113834");
YWATracker.setUnits("2;1");
YWATracker.setAmounts("100.00;50.00");
YWATracker.setDiscount("5.00");
YWATracker.setTax("8.00");
YWATracker.setShipping("20.00");
YWATracker.setOrderId("10099803");
YWATracker.setAmount("USD173.00"); ;
YWATracker.submit();
```

If you only wish to trigger an action without tracking a page view, you should use the Version 4 `submit_action()` or the Version 5 `YWATracker.submit_action();` function instead. Again, the technical part is almost obvious; the harder part is figuring out when to choose one type of data instead of another type—such as choosing when to register a full page view.

Tracking Page Views vs. Actions Alone

As a director of the Web Analytics Association (WAA), I am a huge advocate of the standards we create. Having a look at the latest published definitions is a good starting point.

Page View: WAA definition

Content, such as XML feeds (RSS or Atom) and emails, that can be delivered to both web browsers and nonbrowser clients are not typically counted as page views because the request or receipt of the content does not always correspond to the content being displayed. As an alternative, image-based page tags can be placed inside such content to track the views of all or portions of the content. Web server responses returning status codes indicating the requested content was missing (400 to 499) or there was a server error (500 to 599) should not be counted as a page view unless the web server has been configured to return a real page in the same response with the status code. Returning a page such as a site map, search page, or support request form instead of the default missing or error messages is configurable in the most widely used web serving applications (Apache and IIS). Web server responses returning status codes indicating redirection to another page (300 to 399) are also not typically counted as page views but can be used to track events such as click-throughs with systems specifically designed to use the redirect as a counting mechanism. Most redirect counting is done with a status code of 302. Within the status codes that indicate a successful response (200 to 299) there are few status codes that also may or may not be counted as a page view. The 202 status code (Accepted) is returned in cases where the request has been accepted by the server and the server might or might not return content to the request at a later time. It is not possible from this response to determine if the content was ever sent, so it would typically be excluded from page view counts. The 204 status code (No Response) tells the web browser there is no content to return but that no error has occurred, so the browser should stay on the page prior to the request. It is essentially a nonevent. The 206 status code (Partial Download) usually occurs with the delivery of larger file downloads, such as PDFs. This code indicates that only a part of the file was delivered, so it typically should not be counted as a page view. Filtering by status codes to remove requests that should not be counted is generally needed only when processing raw web server log files and is not usually needed in page tag–based implementations.

If you would like to know the specifics about how Yahoo! as a vendor adheres to the WAA standards, check out the complete compliance list on all the definitions:

`http://visualrevenue.com/blog/2008/03/web-analytics-definitions-waa.html`

This is not the only issue we have when implementing Ajax tracking, but it is a good example of something that seems simple in concept but might not be as simple in deployment.

Let's look at an example where an action related to an Ajax object adheres to the WAA definition of a page view and where the value of tracking such an action is obvious. Imagine a scenario where you have a list of products and the user can zoom in on the product pictures, as shown in Figure 5.10.

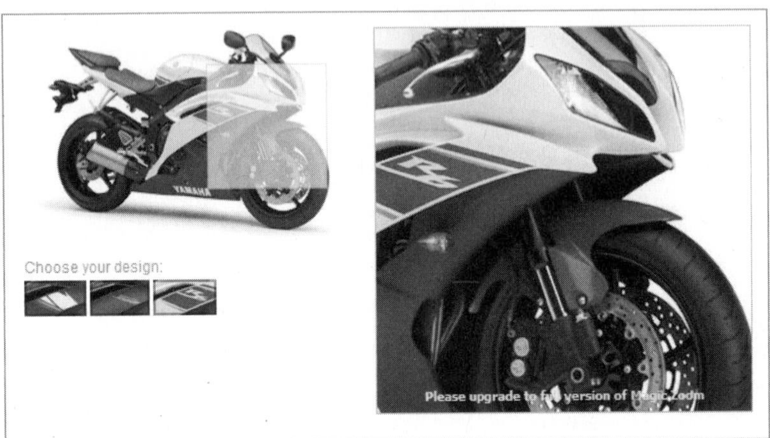

Figure 5.10 Typical Ajax product zoom

You want to track how many users use the product zoom functionality and how that is related to sales conversions. However, you do not want to see your page views inflated with fake page views and with those fake page views also a somewhat destroyed visitor path. So you could deploy a tracking code like this:

Version 4

```
var tracking_object = createITT();
tracking_object.ACTION = '09';
tracking_object.submit_action();
```

Version 5

```
var YWATracker = YWA.getTracker("1000123xxxx");
YWATracker.setAction("09");
YWATracker.submit_action();
```

Or perhaps, if this new view extends to the level of a full product view, you could choose to incorporate that as part of your merchandising tracking, including a SKU and using the `PRODUCT_VIEW` value:

Version 4

```
var tracking_object = createITT();
tracking_object.ACTION = 'PRODUCT_VIEW';
tracking_object._S_SKU = 'DM113834';
tracking_object.submit_action();
```

Artificially Triggering Campaigns

Campaigns are an important part of Yahoo! Web Analytics. The goal is to identify the visitor with existing paid search advertising and to assess the success of existing online marketing strategies. To artificially trigger a campaign during a visit session, you can use the _S_CMPQUERY command.

Version 4

```
function camp(camppattern)
{
var tracking_object = createITT();
tracking_object._S_CMPQUERY = camppattern;
tracking_object.submit();
}
```

Version 5

```
function camp(camppattern)
{
var YWATracker = YWA.getTracker("1000123xxxx");
YWATracker.setCmpQuery("camppattern");
YWATracker.submit();
}
```

This code will also generate a page view. It's not likely that you will use this function extensively, as campaigns are normally triggered on the entry page of a site. However, some websites use a server-side redirect to automatically remove the tracking strings and all the variables from the target URL of the campaign for branding and other purposes. In this scenario, Yahoo! Web Analytics will not be able to pick up a campaign source, and you are forced to use the CmpQuery function to pass the tracking information to Yahoo!

Yahoo! Web Analytics also has the capacity to track internal campaigns as distinct from the normal campaigns that relate to external traffic sources. These internal campaigns are more relevant to Ajax-based tracking and can be monitored using the following syntax:

Version 4

```
function internalcamp()
{
var tracking_object = createITT(intcamppattern);
tracking_object._S_CMPQUERY = "_s_icmp="+intcamppattern
tracking_object.submit_icmp();
}
```

In this example, pattern needs to be populated with the internal campaign pattern as described in Chapter 3, "Enterprise Campaign Tracking."

Finally, if for campaign purposes you need to record a different URL in reports than the one displayed in the address bar, you can use the _S_URL variable:

Version 4

```
var _S_URL="http://www.mysite.com?campaign=pattern";
```

Version 5

```
YWATracker.setUrl("http://www.mysite.com?campaign=pattern");
```

This code overwrites the URL as recorded by Yahoo! and therefore changes the reports.

Setting Up External Data Sources

I think it is appropriate to end this part of the book with the final frontier, external data. Yahoo! Web Analytics provides an External Data Sources framework, which enables you to integrate data from external sources with your existing analytics data.

The ability to collect external data is not accessible by everyone. If you don't have it now but later gain access to this feature, it might look different from how I describe it here. But this discussion should help you understand how to use the External Data Sources feature.

To begin, select Settings > External Data Sources (EDS) > Manage External Data Sources to open the screen shown in Figure 5.11.

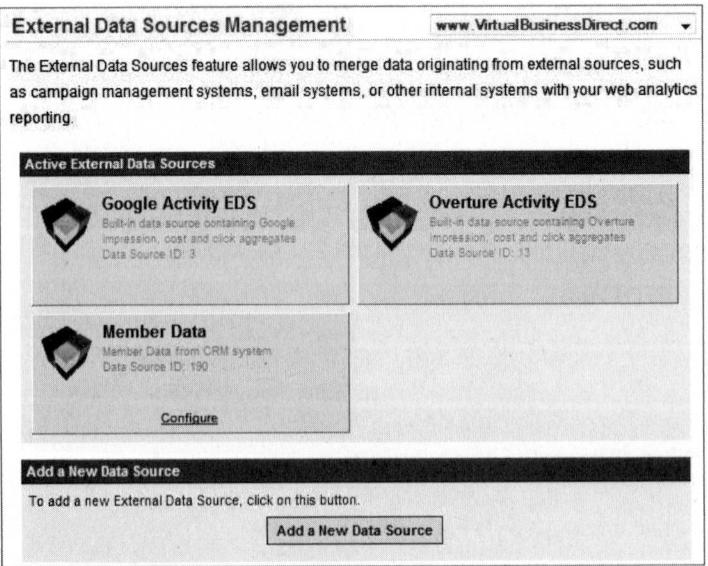

Figure 5.11 External Data Sources Management

This window displays the data sources that have already been configured and lets you either add a new one or edit an existing one. You can essentially upload two types of data:

- Lookup table data
- Aggregate data

You'll recall the use of lookup data from our discussion on merchandising, where we collect the SKU through the tracking script and then enhance it with a number of fields such as the product name and other category information. This process is in fact based on the same technology as external data sources.

Suppose that you collect unique member identification in the `MEMBERID` variable. You are then later able to enhance that member-specific information with fields that you collect offline or as part of a process that is not tied to your web analytics data collection. Or imagine that you collect the number of support calls generated by every customer, a number you can then later attach to the `MEMBERID` variable and thus be able to run analysis on that.

On the other hand, there is an opportunity to upload data in aggregate. By *aggregate*, I mean data that is not necessarily connected as such to a specific key in the system, as is the case with lookup data. One of my favorite examples is uploading the absolute temperature on a daily basis for your favorite market, and thus creating an opportunity to see how the weather has an effect on your online endeavors. And trust me—the weather has a surprisingly high correlation to other metrics in the system.

To create a new external data source, your first task is to select the type. Currently, the following types of external data sources are available:

- Banner Campaign Activity
- Email Campaign Activity
- Customer Relationship Management (CRM)

Depending on the type of data source, different predefined fields are built into the data source template. After naming the data source and providing the correct encoding, you can specify the fields to be included in the data source file. You can choose from two types:

- Key fields
- Data source fields

Key fields, which I described as lookup data, are those fields that establish the connection between the Yahoo! Web Analytics database and the external data source you are creating, thus making possible the integration of the visitor data collected by Yahoo! with the data you collect from other sources.

Depending on the type of data source you selected, the key fields will be different. For example, the Banner Campaign Activity data source contains the following key fields: Start Time, Duration, and Campaign ID. A CRM data source contains only the Member ID as a key field.

The data source fields contain the external source data that you are uploading to the Yahoo! Web Analytics database. You can select from two types of fields:

- In-built fields
- User-defined fields

In-build fields are already defined in your database and can be used in an external data source when you are collecting this information from different external sources, such as an open rate for an email campaign activity data source.

User-defined fields are new fields that you add to your database. They contain the specific information that you would like to have integrated with Web Analytics.

Once you have configured the external data source, the fields contained in the data source will be available in the Custom Report Wizard.

By completing the sequence of steps outlined in this section, you have configured the data source. To check how the data source file needs to be organized, download the sample data template by clicking the Download Data Template button. The template that you download contains all the external data source fields that you have configured and an example for each field (see Figure 5.12). Format the data source file according to the same format used in the downloaded template.

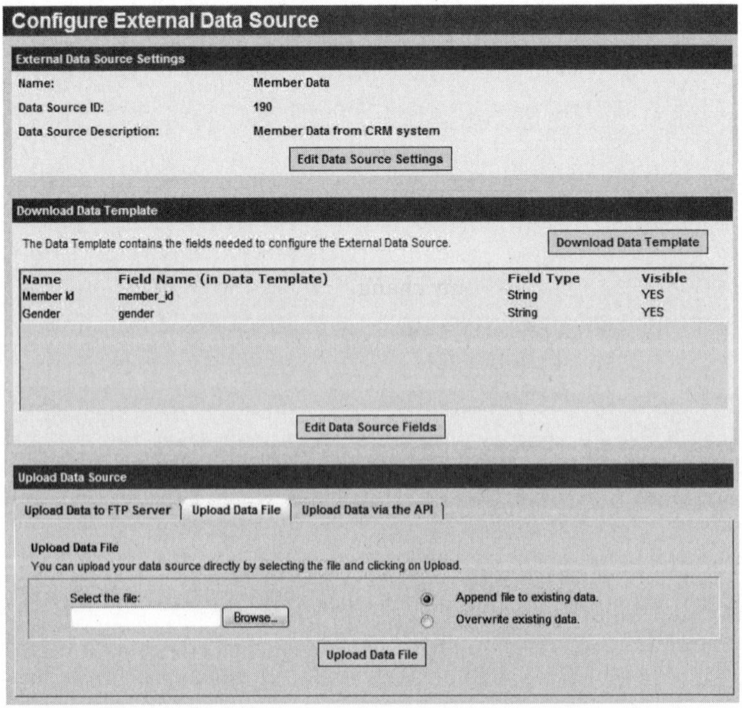

Configure External Data Source

External Data Source Settings

Name: Member Data

Data Source ID: 190

Data Source Description: Member Data from CRM system

Edit Data Source Settings

Download Data Template

The Data Template contains the fields needed to configure the External Data Source. Download Data Template

Name	Field Name (in Data Template)	Field Type	Visible
Member Id	member_id	String	YES
Gender	gender	String	YES

Edit Data Source Fields

Upload Data Source

Upload Data to FTP Server | Upload Data File | Upload Data via the API

Upload Data File

You can upload your data source directly by selecting the file and clicking on Upload.

Select the file: Browse...

Append file to existing data.

Overwrite existing data.

Upload Data File

Figure 5.12 Configure External Data Sources

Once you finish formatting your data, you must specify the method through which your data will be uploaded to your system. You have the following options:

- Web Analytics Interface
- FTP Server
- API

Your choice of upload method all depends on the type of data and the urgency of getting it into the system.

Validating Your Code

There might be reasons for you to validate the Yahoo! Web Analytics tracking script against an XHTML validator for compliance, such as company standards for XHTML validity, thus assuring consistency in document code across the organization. If that is the case, you have to make slight changes to some elements of the tracking script, such as the script type and the `img` tag.

Find the elements that you need to change and their changed versions here:

Version 4

```
<script language="Javascript" type="text/javascript">


<img alt=""src="http://yourwebsite.com/p.pl?a=1000xxxxxxxxxx&amp;js=no"
width="1" height="1"/></noscript><!-//->
```

This code shows a few small edits to the tracking script. Once this is done, you should be able to have your code XHTML validated.

- Add a script type: `type="text/javascript"`
- Add an `ALT` tag: `alt=""`
- Add a reference to the entity `&`

The Version 5 code validates without any changes to the tracking script.

Utilizing an Enterprise Web Analytics Platform

II

The task throughout Part I of this book was collecting data—the right data. Remember that reports are never better than the data you collect. Having said that, you need an exceedingly good understanding of how to work with your data, as random report surfing is unlikely to create a situation where you can truly compete on analytics. In Part II, you will learn reporting tools and features that will help you gain an understanding of how you can work with your collected data through the reporting interface.

Chapter 6 **Working with Report Results**

Chapter 7 **Customizing Report Results**

Chapter 8 **Using Basic Reports as Templates for Customization**

Chapter 9 **Using Dashboards**

Chapter 10 **Distinctive Reports and Usage**

Working with Report Results

A web analytics report is typically a visual display of a subset of your data. It consists of a set of dimensions and metrics, a sorting choice, applied filters or segments—all for a specific time period. With dozens of choices in each individual category, some requiring your free text or number input, we end up with an infinite number of ways to report results.

Your vendor's out-of-the-box reports are starting points that turn into true web analytics reports only after applying your inquiries and actions to them.

This chapter will help you translate questions about how your web business is doing in specific reporting strategies.

Chapter Contents

What to Expect from a Report
A Traditional Reporting Interface
Using Calendars for Time Period Reporting
Using Cross-Reference Filters
Using Drill-downs and Drill-throughs
Sorting Report Results
Color-Coding Data
Applying Report Notes and Reasoning
Exporting Data

What to Expect from a Report

First, let's agree on just what you should expect from out-of-the-box reports versus reports that answer specific business questions you have formulated.

Vendors such as Yahoo! Web Analytics can create a few reporting starting points; having too many starting points is a usability disaster and does nothing but confuse and detract value from the better starting points. Those starting points can begin to take shape only when you have defined the business questions you want your reports to answer for you.

Out of the Box

Items, functionalities, or features provided out of the box are those that do not require any additional installations, plug-ins, expansion packs, or products. In the case of implementation, out of the box also has the connotation of using a system without customization, such that it is usable with a plain-vanilla installation.

Therefore, I suggest that you ask yourself three business-related questions that you would like answered *before* you open up your web analytics tool. Then try to answer those three questions through your tool using anything from standard reports, custom reports, filters, segments, and other tools.

An example of a marketing- and business-related question is "Are my recent SEO initiatives paying off?"

This is a fair question from a marketing manager who just finished a search engine optimization program to improve on the company's organic efforts. But it also becomes clear that, even before opening up the web analytics tool, you would have to debate or at least think about how to answer this. Breaking down the big question, smaller related questions that come to mind include:

- What is the time period in question?
- What is the baseline index?
- How do we define "paying off"?
- How do we measure success?
- What are the success and failure thresholds?
- If any specific search phrases stand out, should they be reported on?
- What was the cost of the initiative and where is this data coming from?
- Did the initiative end, or are we reporting on the progress?
- What does the manager expect: a simple yes/no or a detailed report from which to draw conclusions?
- Should you provide suggestions for actions on how to improve?

I hope the question and "subquestions" outlined here confirm that you should never expect to be so lucky as to find the magic report provided out of the box. By now it should be obvious that a skill set is needed to work with your reports to the extent that you can use them to answer marketing questions.

Note: For more information about report surfing versus developing reports in response to business questions, see this blog post:

`http://visualrevenue.com/blog/2007/09/web-analytics-report-surfing-and-how-to.html`

A Traditional Reporting Interface

When you enter Yahoo! Web Analytics, you are immediately presented with the Control Center, which holds all the projects you have set up. This is presented as a simple list of projects, as shown in Figure 6.1, accompanied by a small chart icon that will give you access to the reporting for the individual projects.

View reports

VIEW REPORTS	BASE URL	EDITION NAME
	http://www.fourseasons.com	Enterprise Edition
	http://test.fourseasons.com	Enterprise Edition
	http://dev1.fourseasons.com	Enterprise Edition

You can manage more than one web site under your account. Please note that a distinct tracking code will be generated for each site. Add new web site (project)

Figure 6.1 List of projects

Once you enter Reports, you will either see a traffic summary or a default dashboard. Dashboards are described in Chapter 9, "Using Dashboards."

Choose a random report, and you are left in an interface, as shown in Figure 6.2.

Throughout this chapter I will deconstruct the primary reporting interface, as it will be the basis for most of our information on report use.

The project header, shown in Figure 6.3, is the first element I would like to point out, as it does not actually belong to the report itself. You use the project header to access other projects and to navigate between the reporting interface and the settings for the project in question.

Pay no mind to the small Operator link to the right in Figure 6.3, which is exclusive to people inside the Yahoo! firewall. Wink!

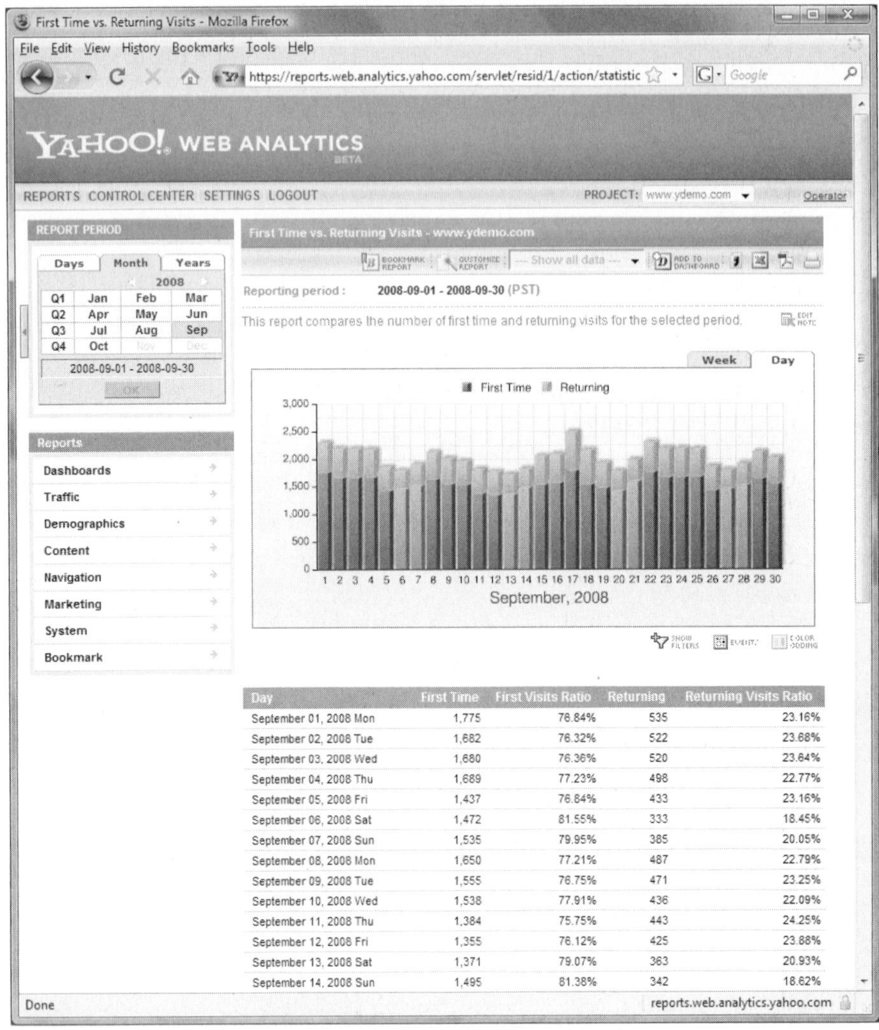

Day	First Time	First Visits Ratio	Returning	Returning Visits Ratio
September 01, 2008 Mon	1,775	76.84%	535	23.16%
September 02, 2008 Tue	1,682	76.32%	522	23.68%
September 03, 2008 Wed	1,680	76.36%	520	23.64%
September 04, 2008 Thu	1,689	77.23%	498	22.77%
September 05, 2008 Fri	1,437	76.84%	433	23.16%
September 06, 2008 Sat	1,472	81.55%	333	18.45%
September 07, 2008 Sun	1,535	79.95%	385	20.05%
September 08, 2008 Mon	1,650	77.21%	487	22.79%
September 09, 2008 Tue	1,555	76.75%	471	23.25%
September 10, 2008 Wed	1,538	77.91%	436	22.09%
September 11, 2008 Thu	1,384	75.75%	443	24.25%
September 12, 2008 Fri	1,355	76.12%	425	23.88%
September 13, 2008 Sat	1,371	79.07%	363	20.93%
September 14, 2008 Sun	1,495	81.38%	342	18.62%

Figure 6.2 Primary reporting interface

REPORTS CONTROL CENTER SETTINGS LOGOUT PROJECT: www.ydemo.com

Figure 6.3 Project header

On a more serious matter, in the upper-left corner, shown in Figure 6.4, is a calendar that displays the reporting time period and also acts as the user interface for choosing new reporting time periods and comparative periods.

The calendar is removed when you view your dashboards, simply due to the fact that anything on a dashboard should be rolling periods, such as Today, This Week, This Quarter, or Last 30 Days.

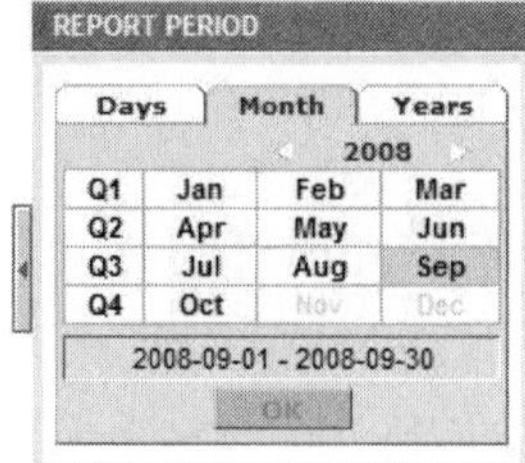

Figure 6.4 Report time period

Moving on to the actual report header, we find the name of the report in question as well as shortcuts to the most powerful features of Yahoo! Web Analytics. These features include:

- Bookmark Report
- Customize Report
- Segment Report
- Add Report to Dashboard
- Export Report Data
- Print Report

All of these features are discussed separately throughout this section, but I will note that Customize Report is the nirvana of Web Analytics play!

Finally—and this should not be neglected just because it is a simple implementation task—there is an opportunity to add notes directly to the report (see Figure 6.5). You would typically add notes when you change a report; for example, by adding a filter or a specific set of metrics or dimensions. Notes can explain why the report was changed and how other users are expected to interpret the data.

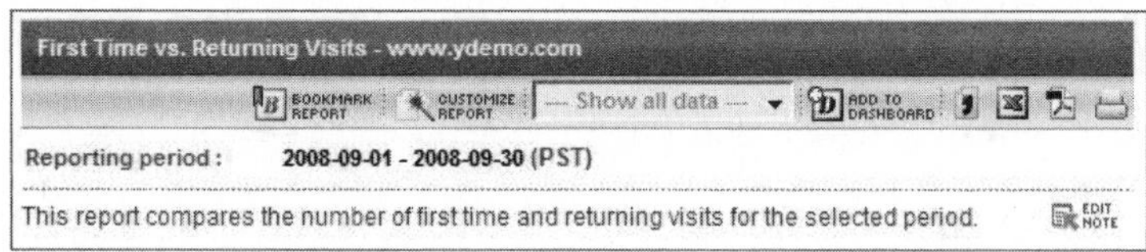

Figure 6.5 Report header

Most reports are accompanied by a chart that visualizes the quantitative information that was requested through the report choice, filter choice, sorting choice, and so on.

It is with great regret that I have to say that the visualizations are essentially fixed and decided upon beforehand. The freedom that you have in data selection and data setup is not replicated in data visualization. The chart allows you to quickly spot trends and abnormalities, but not at a level you deserve!

You can choose data grouping, such as whether you want to see the chart on a daily, weekly, or monthly basis. As you can see in Figure 6.6, this provides some power to visualize a trend more accurately.

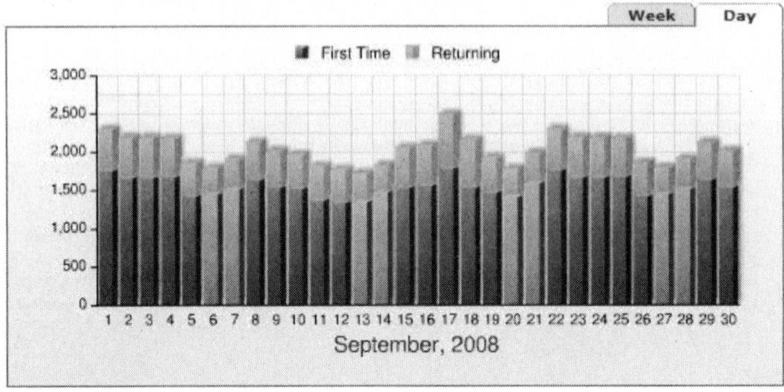

Figure 6.6 Report chart

Depending on the type of report, the report data contains the reporting entries and the metrics pertaining to them in a tabular form. This is true for most reports; even when you don't have the table, as in a path analysis report, you are still looking at the report data modifiers. The report data modifiers, as shown in Figure 6.7, include:

- Filters
- Sorting
- Events
- Alerts
- Color-Coding
- Drill-Downs
- Ask IT Tutor

These modifiers are accessible by clicking the three icons you see at the top right; by clicking the sorting arrow on top of the metric columns; by clicking the magnifying glass on the left column; or by right-clicking any of the metrics or dimensions. The report data modifiers are tremendously valuable, and this is where you can drill into and work with your data.

SHOW FILTERS EVENTS COLOR CODING

Day	First Time	First Visits Ratio	Returning	Returning Visits Ratio
September 01, 2008 Mon	1,775	76.84%	535	23.16%
September 02, 2008 Tue	1,682	76.32%	522	23.68%
September 03, 2008 Wed	1,680	76.36%	520	23.64%
September 04, 2008 Thu	1,689	77.23%	498	22.77%
September 05, 2008 Fri	1,437	76.84%	433	23.16%
September 06, 2008 Sat	1,472	81.55%	333	18.45%
September 07, 2008 Sun	1,535	79.95%	385	20.05%

Figure 6.7 Report data and report data modifiers

The menu, or Report Chooser as I like to call it, allows you to access different types of standard and customized reports. It is shown in Figure 6.8.

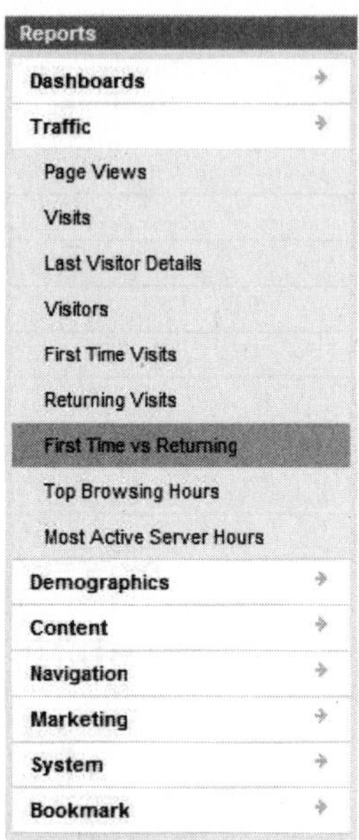

Figure 6.8 Report Chooser (menu)

I believe the best way to use the Report Chooser is not to blindly look for the perfect report—that report is unlikely to exist—but to become familiar with the template reports to the extent that you can get to a reasonably qualified starting point.

Keep in mind that Yahoo! Web Analytics has metrics such as Revenue Participation and Action Participation, which can only be found as page drill-downs, not as template reports. The only way you can access metrics such as these is by creating a custom report.

Your task is to find a decent reporting starting point and go from there. You don't need somebody to create a report for you from scratch; you should be able to quickly build it yourself.

Using Calendars for Time Period Reporting

Using the calendar date selection box may seem obvious, but please indulge me as there are a few important notes to take away from the choices you make here.

You can select the following periods directly from the calendar date selection box:

- Day
- Week
- Month
- Quarter
- Year
- Custom Period

Note that the first day of the week can be set on a project basis, as shown in Figure 6.9. For example, you can set the first day of the week to be the day when you edit your website profile, providing you with an opportunity to align the calendar view and shortcuts to match your region.

Figure 6.9 Project setting for first day of the week

You will probably end up using the custom period functionality most of the time. The reason is that if you want to report on a given campaign, the start and end date is unlikely to be supported by the time period shortcuts, and you would simply select that custom period, as shown in Figure 6.10.

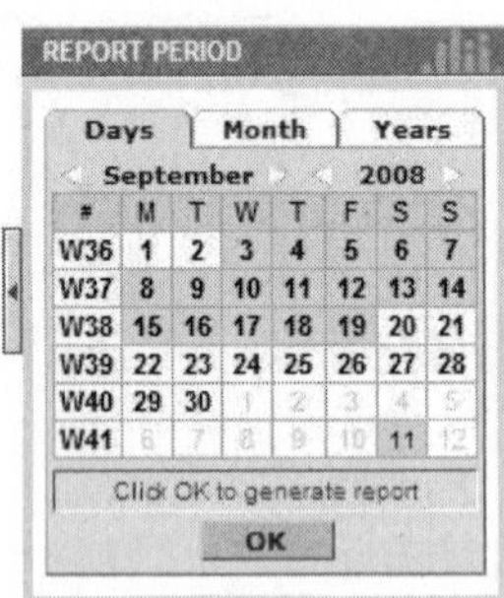

Figure 6.10 Custom data period

Reporting on Unique Visitors over Specific Time Periods

Be aware that the way the number of unique visitors is calculated changes depending on the time period.

Depending on whether you have been upgraded to the newest visitor calculation methodology, you will have one of the following two aggregation opportunities. The latter is the newest and most correct and flexible way of doing things:

- Daily Unique Visitors
- Weekly Unique Visitors
- Monthly Unique Visitors

or

- Visitors (Custom Period Unique Visitor)

You cannot add up unique visitors in reports yourself; you have to use the date selection box to do that for you. See Figure 6.11 for a visual display showing the number of unique visitors on a given day.

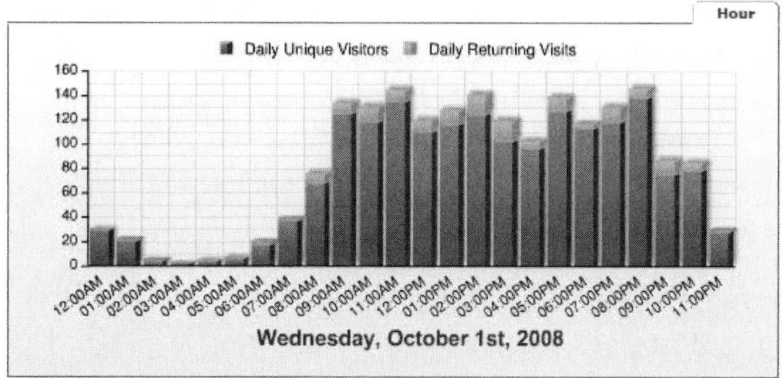

Figure 6.11 Daily unique visitors on October 1, 2008

This report shows you that there were 1,814 unique visitors on October 1, 2008. If you then viewed reports for daily unique visitors on October 2, you would find that there were 1,680; for October 3, there were 1,642 daily unique visitors.

From there we conclude that we had 5,136 unique visitors for the three-day period October 1 to October 3 (1,814 + 1,680 + 1,642 = 5,136). However, this is not true, and we cannot add up unique visitors in that way. The reason is that some of those who were unique on the first day might turn up the next day and thus be a repeat visitor when looking over the three-day period. So expect the unique visitor count to decrease.

Figure 6.12 shows an example report of weekly unique visitors over the three-day period.

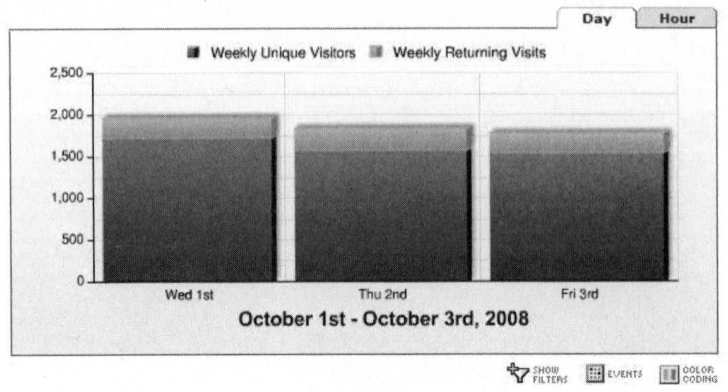

Day	Weekly Unique Visitors	%	Weekly Returning Visits	%
October 01, 2008 Wed	1,730	35.58%	240	32.52%
October 02, 2008 Thu	1,583	32.56%	261	35.37%
October 03, 2008 Fri	1,549	31.86%	237	32.11%
Total	**4,862**	**100.00%**	**738**	**100.00%**

Figure 6.12 Weekly unique visitors, October 1 to October 3, 2008

Figure 6.12 illustrates my point: We did not have 5,136 but more like 4,862 unique visitors—a conclusion I came to by using the data selection box.

This is not perfect; doing a count of unique visitors for the three-day period would have been better, but I am sure you get my point.

The beautiful part of Yahoo! Web Analytics is that it is in real time and you can essentially play with your data by changing the dates and see the impact. This approach is a great way to spot seasonality and gain insights that you did not know about.

Unique Visitor

A unique visitor is a statistic describing a unit of traffic to a website, counting each visitor only once in the time frame of the report. This statistic is relevant to site publishers and advertisers as a measure of a site's true audience size, equivalent to the term *reach* used in other media.

Time Comparative Reporting

You can always save a report, export data, take a note, or otherwise save the information from one period and then compare it to another. However, Yahoo! Web Analytics allows you to do comparative reporting in the interface.

What I like the most is that once you compare two periods, say Q1 2009 to Q2 2009, you stay in what I call *comparative mode*. Comparative mode means that if you move from one report to another, the new report shows differences between old and new data for each metric you have chosen to display. Comparative mode is useful if you are on a quest to solve an anomaly between Q1 and Q2, but would be less helpful should you just want to compare a one-off question.

You cannot compare reports grouped by date, as this would not make sense, with you choosing a new date in the date selection box. And if you want to compare a specific data point, such as visits, over more than one date, I suggest you just choose a longer period and use the default trended view to compare.

Let's take a simple report of visits grouped by search engine referrals, as shown in Figure 6.13, as an example.

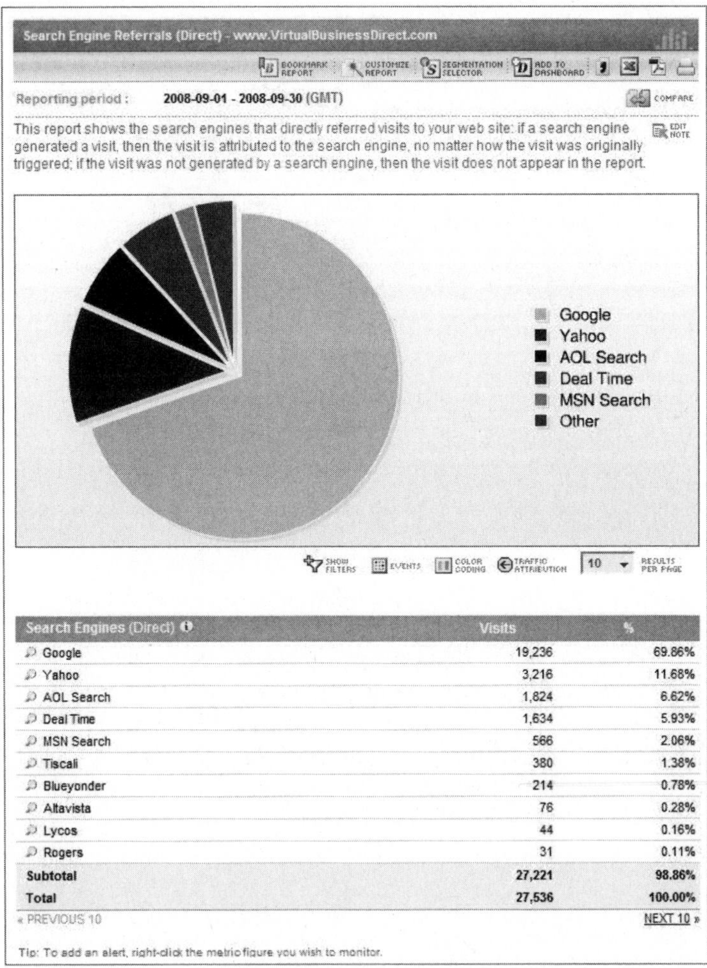

Search Engines (Direct)	Visits	%
Google	19,236	69.86%
Yahoo	3,216	11.68%
AOL Search	1,824	6.62%
Deal Time	1,634	5.93%
MSN Search	566	2.06%
Tiscali	380	1.38%
Blueyonder	214	0.78%
Altavista	76	0.28%
Lycos	44	0.16%
Rogers	31	0.11%
Subtotal	**27,221**	**98.86%**
Total	**27,536**	**100.00%**

Figure 6.13 Search engine referrals report

The report shows us that about 70 percent of our direct search engine referrals are coming from Google. A natural marketing question is how this result compares with the previous month's results, and thus provides an opportunity to use the comparative reporting feature.

You access the comparative reporting by clicking the Compare button in the upper-right corner. Doing so will expand the calendar date selection box beyond the existing period, which in our example was September (see Figure 6.14).

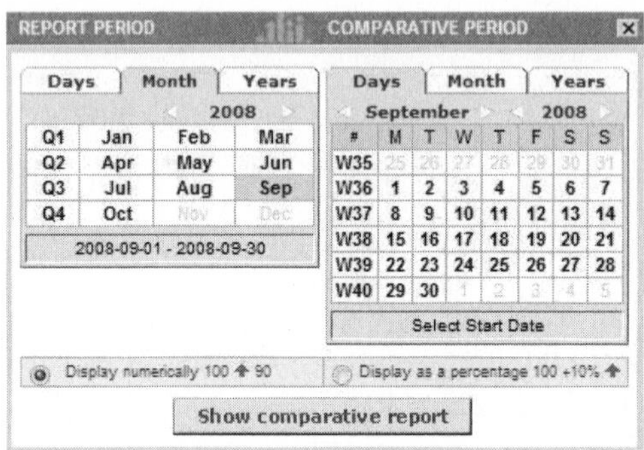

Figure 6.14 Expanded calendar date selection box

The expanded date selection box lets you choose the comparative period that you want to use. Note that Yahoo! Web Analytics enables you to choose any arbitrary period you want. This includes periods before, after, and, most surprisingly, overlapping periods, but also periods that do not necessarily match in length.

There can be multiple reasons for choosing the not-so-obvious overlapping periods and uneven periods. For example, suppose you do not want to compare the dates themselves, but instead investigate two different SEO initiatives, where one took 17 days and another took 24 days.

Also notice that you can choose to have the comparative result presented to you in two ways: numerically or as a percentage. See Figure 6.15 for an example of a comparative report with a numeric column and a percentage column.

Search Engines (Direct)	Visits		%	
	01 Sep 08 - 30 Sep 08	01 Aug 08 - 31 Aug 08	01 Sep 08 - 30 Sep 08	01 Aug 08 - 31 Aug 08
Google	19,236 ↓	19,692	69.86% ↓	70.00%
Yahoo	3,216 ↑	3,192	11.68% ↑	11.35%
AOL Search	1,824 ↓	1,939	6.62% ↓	6.89%
Deal Time	1,634 ↑	1,592	5.93% ↑	5.66%
MSN Search	566 ↑	552	2.06% ↑	1.96%
Tiscali	380 ↓	418	1.38% ↓	1.49%
Blueyonder	214 ↓	219	0.78% ↓	0.78%
Altavista	76 ↓	77	0.28% ↑	0.27%
Lycos	44 –	44	0.16% ↑	0.16%
Rogers	31 ↓	42	0.11% ↓	0.15%
Subtotal	**27,221 ↓**	**27,767**	**98.86% ↑**	**98.70%**
Total	**27,536 ↓**	**28,132**	**100.00% –**	**100.00%**
« PREVIOUS 10				NEXT 10 »

Figure 6.15 Numerically displayed comparative search engine referrals report

Keep in mind that it is not just the standard reports where you can use comparative reporting; it is a valid function on any of the more exotic reports as well, such as the scenario analysis reports, as shown in Figure 6.16.

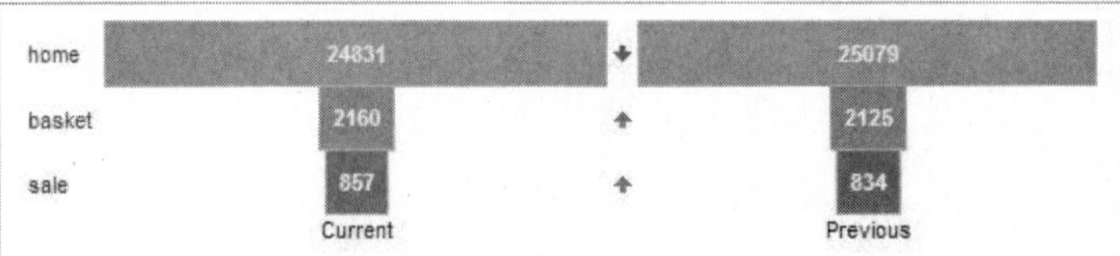

Figure 6.16 Comparative scenario analysis report

Note that, in reports showing a row-based set of data below the chart, every single metric gets compared. Consequently, if you choose to use the results to communicate a point, I suggest you delete some metrics that are not absolutely necessary, as the report can otherwise become quite confusing to look at.

Using Cross-Reference Filters

I think it is important that we agree on what a filter is and how to interpret a filter with Yahoo! Web Analytics before we discuss how to use it and where you should use it.

Filters are not data collection filters that chop off some of your data. Filters are not bucket definitions, where you put a certain part of your data into a bucket. Filters are not necessarily just simple drill-downs, even though they can be used in the same way.

Drill-down

Drill-down (also data drilling) refers to any of various operations and transformations on tabular, relational, and multidimensional data and is very often implemented as a simple way to execute a cross-reference lookup in web analytics applications (essentially a subset of the data you view).

Filters are a simple way of doing real-time segmentation, on the fly, in a report. Filters create a subset of the data you are looking at based on the criteria you set. However simple this may sound, filters are probably one of the best and most powerful features you have in your toolbox.

Let's have a look at a simple visits report in Figure 6.17, as we all have a good understanding of that particular metric.

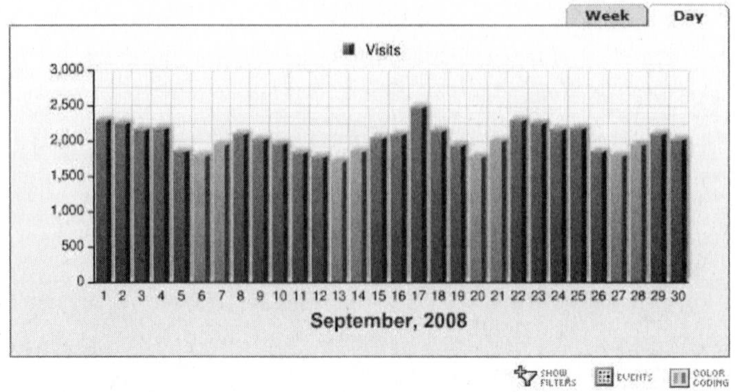

Figure 6.17 Visits report

Again, you activate the filter options by clicking the Show Filters icon in the lower-right corner. You will then see the filter selection box shown in Figure 6.18.

CROSS-REFERENCE FILTERS

-- Select Filter --

- -- Select Filter --
  - Visit Frequency
- Metric filters
  - Visits
- Demographics filters
  - City
  - Member
  - Visiting Countries
  - Visiting Organizations
- Campaign filters
  - Campaign (Direct)
  - Campaign (Intelligent)
  - Campaign (Original)
  - Channel (Direct)
  - Channel (Intelligent)
  - Paid Search Listings (Direct)
  - Paid Search Listings (Intelligent)
  - Search Engines (Direct)
  - Search Engines (Intelligent)
- Entry filters

Day	Visits	%
Sept	2,302	3.77%
Sept	2,259	3.70%
Sept	2,172	3.56%
Sept	2,186	3.58%
Sept	1,857	3.04%
Sept	1,802	2.95%
Sept	1,954	3.20%
Sept	2,105	3.45%
Sept	2,031	3.33%
Sept	1,970	3.23%
Sept	1,844	3.02%
Sept	1,786	2.93%
September 13, 2008 Sat	1,718	2.81%

Figure 6.18 Cross-Reference Filters selection box

You choose between two distinct groups of filters:

- Most available dimensions set up
- All metrics displayed in the report

Welcome to Analytics Nirvana. Let's apply a simple filter to get an understanding of how quick and easy it is.

Choosing a demographic filter and dimension called City, we can look at the subset of visitors who originated from London only, as in Figure 6.19. Imagine that we have an offline marketing campaign and event going on there and want to see how many visits that counts for.

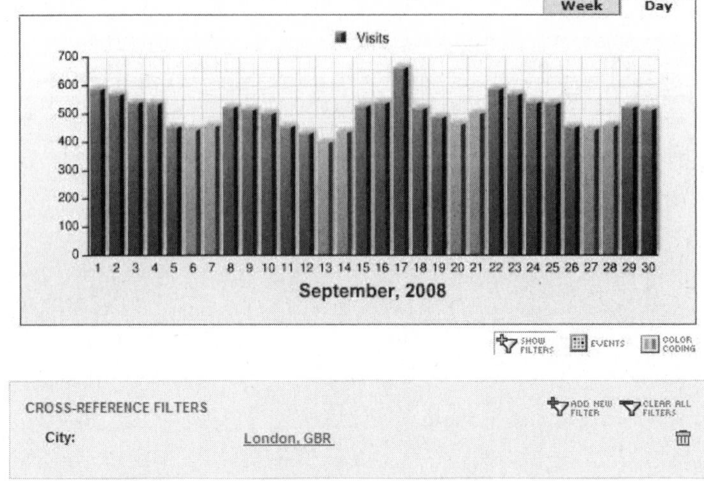

Figure 6.19 Visits report with a demographic cross-reference filter applied

You might argue that this particular filter could have been achieved by a simple drill-down, and you are absolutely right—but the power is that some filters can be measured and that you can apply multiple filters.

So expanding our example, we can assume that we do another campaign and event in Manchester at the same time, which showcases that we can use an OR function in our filter as well. Furthermore, we want to see only those who have not visited us before, so we can get a better idea of our campaign and event ROI. See Figure 6.20.

Return on Investment (ROI)

Return on investment, or sometimes just return, is the ratio of money gained or lost (realized or unrealized) on an investment relative to the amount of money invested.

CROSS-REFERENCE FILTERS

ADD NEW FILTER   CLEAR ALL FILTERS

Visit Frequency: First time

City: London, GBR

OR Mancheste   Add

Manchester Center, VT, USA
Manchester, CT, USA
Manchester, GA, USA
Manchester, GBR
Manchester, IA, USA
Manchester, KY, USA
Manchester, MA, USA
Manchester, MD, USA
Manchester, ME, USA
Manchester, MI, USA
15 results

Week	%
Week 36, 2008	23.87%
Week 37, 2008	21.56%
Week 38, 2008	23.78%
Week 39, 2008	23.87%
Week 40, 2008	6.91%
Total	100.00%

Figure 6.20 Cross-reference filter with multiple metrics and OR function added

Note that when you provide input and a unique value is expected, the system is prepopulated, and you simply type until you have the preferred result presented. So in the previous example, I typed **Lon** and ended up choosing London, GBR and not the one in Canada, for example.

When defining a cross-reference filter that does not contain a drop-down list with prepopulated options, the following operators are available:

- Equals
- Does Not Equal
- Begins With
- Does Not Begin With
- Ends With
- Does Not End With
- Contains
- Does Not Contain
- Is Empty
- Is Not Empty

Note that if the cross-reference filter is not properly defined, or if two of your selected filters are incompatible, the system will not generate any report results.

There are no limitations to the number of filters you can add; the important thing is to make sure your filters match the business question you are trying to answer. Applying too many filters may result in a report that answers a business question you didn't mean to ask!

Imagine that the campaign and event in London was something to do with our unique hardware drills, and that we wanted to see the direct product sales in relation to the campaign. And by that setup, we decide to look at all those who enter the site on a page that had something to do with drills—product category pages, product-specific pages, product guides, or other content about drills. In addition, we want to see the immediate output, such as in sales revenue related to those visits. To answer this question, we could create a custom report and apply two filters, as shown in Figure 6.21.

One thing that you will notice throughout this process is that when you start working with custom reports, the charting disappears. Yahoo! Web Analytics does not yet provide custom charting options.

Note: You can also use a wildcard (*) to define cross-reference filters, for example, Entry Page Title equals "dri*".

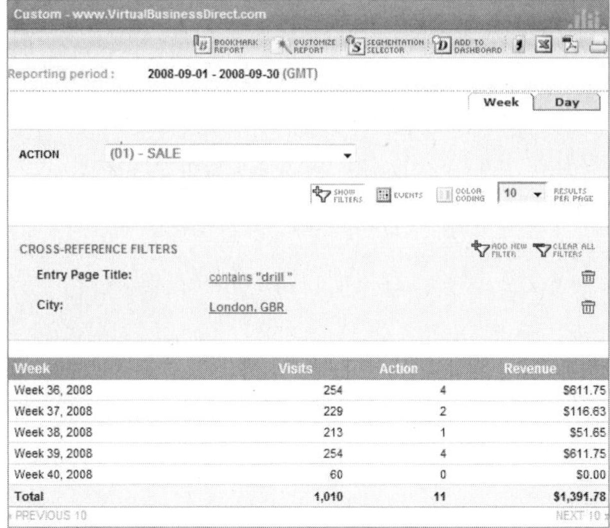

Figure 6.21 Custom report with two filters

For string cross-reference filters (such as Document Group, Page URL, Page Title), you can use the Is Empty or Is Not Empty operator. This operator is especially useful for filtering custom fields; you can filter on whether values were recorded for specific custom fields.

As with time comparative reporting, you can use filters throughout the system and not just on the standard reports, such as the scenario report shown earlier. And to make it really exciting, you can apply comparative reporting on a filtered scenario like the one in Figure 6.22. Endless opportunities for insight!

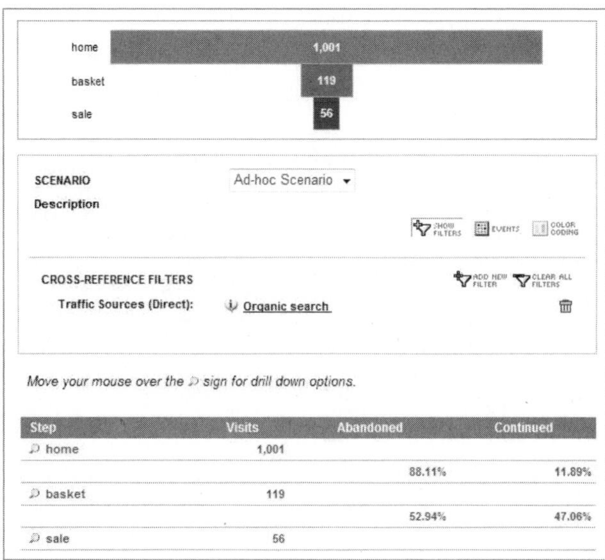

Figure 6.22 Filter scenario analysis report

Choosing Scope of Filter

When you create filters that are attributed to your content, such as:

- Document Group
- Internal Search Phrase
- Page Title
- Page URL

you have the option of selecting whether the cross-reference filter will be based on:

- Visits (Session Scope)
- Page Views (Page View Scope)
- Action (Action Scope)

The Session Scope filter includes all the page views of the visitor sessions that also included pages for which the filter matched. The Session Scope filter will help you answer questions concerning the visitors who viewed the pages defined by the filter. See Figure 6.23.

Figure 6.23 Session Scope filter

The Page View Scope filter includes only the page views for which the filter matched. The Page View Scope filter will help you answer questions concerning only the specific page views identified by the filter.

This subject is something we will touch on in a bit more detail when we discuss segmentation in Chapter 7, "Customizing Report Results." In the meantime, let's look at one example so you can better understand when to choose one filter over the other.

Imagine that you would like to figure out if people who read about your company are more or less likely to convert into customers, with the hypothesis that knowing who you are creates more trust. If you created a scenario where you filtered by `Page Title = About Us` with a page view scope, you would not receive any results—all you would be looking at would be the About Us pages themselves. Extending this to a session scope, as shown in Figure 6.24, you get all the pages within the sessions (visits) where somebody viewed the About Us pages at one point.

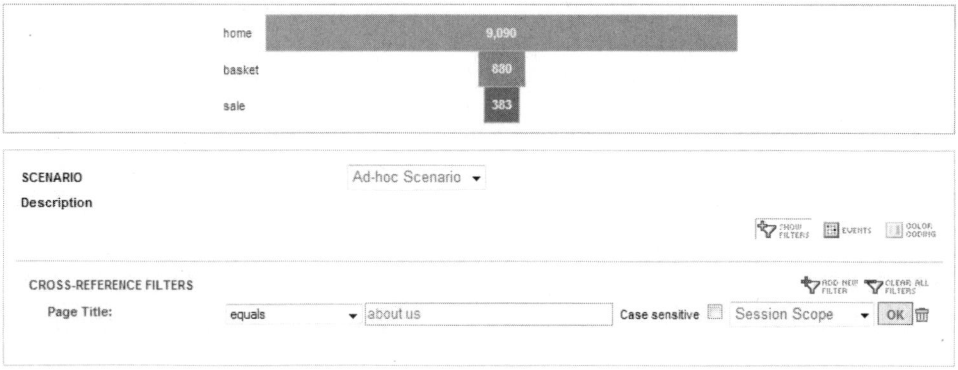

Figure 6.24 Search Engine Filter

Using the Right Traffic Attribution Filters

As you've probably noticed by now, Yahoo! Web Analytics provides three distinct traffic attribution filters:

- Direct
- Intelligent
- Original

These are not unique filters by themselves, but a way of attributing credit to a given completion. The following example is provided by my good friend Tami Dalley:

> *Imagine a game of football… The quarterback throws the ball to the receiver in a perfect pass. The receiver runs like the wind all the way to the 5-yard line before running into the defense. Before he is tackled he gives the ball to another player who dodges the defense and takes it into the end zone to score a touchdown. The crowd goes wild!*
>
> *The quarterback's mother thinks, "My son is a star! Without his excellent pass, there would be no touchdown at all!" The receiver's mother is there also and says to her friends, "Without that brilliant 80-yard run from my son, there would have been no touchdown." Then the girlfriend of the scorer says, "Wait a minute, it was my boyfriend who scored the touchdown—the full credit belongs to him!"*
>
> *So who does deserve the credit?*

And this is what traffic attribution is all about, and for a lot of people, it goes way beyond the simple attribution models provided in Yahoo! Web Analytics.

Although the available attribution models are simple, Yahoo! should indeed receive some praise for providing more than one model. Many tools available on the Internet use only one attribution model, the last-click model (Direct).

The Direct attribution model attributes everything to the last click of the source in question. The Original attribution model attributes everything to the first original click of the source in question. See Figures 6.25 and 6.26 for examples of reports with these filters applied.

Feel free to explore the Intelligent model that Yahoo! provides, which essentially translates to the Original (first) paid-for (campaign) click, on your own. This is a huge subject and unfortunately beyond the scope of this book.

CROSS-REFERENCE FILTERS — ADD NEW FILTER — CLEAR ALL FILTERS

Search Engines (Direct): Google

Week	Visits	%
Week 36, 2008	4,122	21.44%
Week 37, 2008	3,997	20.79%
Week 38, 2008	4,586	23.85%
Week 39, 2008	4,772	24.82%
Week 40, 2008	1,753	9.12%
Total	**19,230**	**100.00%**

Figure 6.25 Visits filtered by search engine referrals with the Direct attribution model applied

CROSS-REFERENCE FILTERS — ADD NEW FILTER — CLEAR ALL FILTERS

Search Engines (Original): Google

Week	Visits	%
Week 36, 2008	4,271	21.60%
Week 37, 2008	4,025	20.35%
Week 38, 2008	4,826	24.40%
Week 39, 2008	4,942	24.99%
Week 40, 2008	1,713	8.66%
Total	**19,777**	**100.00%**

Figure 6.26 Visits filtered by search engine referrals with the Original attribution model applied

Notice how the impact of a simple visits report increases by filtering it with two different attribution models? Traffic attribution might be a minor issue in this particular report, but it becomes a huge issue when you are trying to allocate money spent on campaigns to sales generated. Which campaign should rightfully continue, and which campaign can be optimized?

Applying Regular Expression Filters

As mentioned earlier, cross-reference filters require you to enter a string such as Document Group, Page URL, or Page Title, but you can also have a Regular Expression filter type enabled, which Yahoo! Web Analytics calls RegExp.

> **RegExp**
>
> Regular expressions provide a concise and flexible means for identifying strings of text of interest, such as particular characters, words, or patterns of characters. Regular expressions are written in a formal language that can be interpreted by a regular expression processor that serves as a parser and examines text and identifies parts that match the provided specification.

If you are familiar with regular expressions, you know the power and freedom provided by this functionality. That said, a regular expression is still just a filter, though more advanced, so as long as you can fulfill your need with the existing filter types, you are not missing out on anything. For example, if you want to include two different page groups, you can do so by using OR. I suggest that you take a mental note that regular expression filters exist and are particularly useful when you are stuck in a string-based filter.

This is also a feature that, at the time of this writing, was not enabled on all accounts, so you may have to request it to be enabled.

Note: For more information about regular expressions, I recommend the following sources:
`http://regexlib.com/`
`http://www.regular-expressions.info/`

Adding and Using Metric Filters

Most users of Web Analytics tools will not directly differ between filters on Dimension and filters on Metrics, simply because the ability to use metric filters is less of a feature by itself and more of a natural extension of what you would have expected already. As you have noticed, the filters are based on dimensions. In addition to the dimensions that you can use for filtering are the metrics used in the actual report.

So, in a search engine visit report, you have the entire dimension set available, including the search engine dimension, but you also have the metric Visit available for filtering.

When filtering on metrics, you filter a bit differently and have the following operators available:

- Equals
- Does Not Equal
- Is Greater Than
- Is Greater Than or Equal To
- Is Less Than
- Is Less Than or Equal To
- Between

As an example, suppose you are about to initiate an SEO initiative and you want to know which keyword to focus on. A standard search phrase report might not be what you are looking for as this is about yesterday's facts, and the reasoning for the initiative is that you are not happy to begin with. You might even apply Revenue, or any other metric that indicates value, as a metric to the report and sort by that, but this again talks to yesterday's news.

You could apply Average Order Value per Search Phrase, but that alone will provide you with a long list of Search Phrases. You could also apply a metric filter, filtering only orders above $150, and then you could sort the report by visits and discover your high-value keywords (see Figure 6.27).

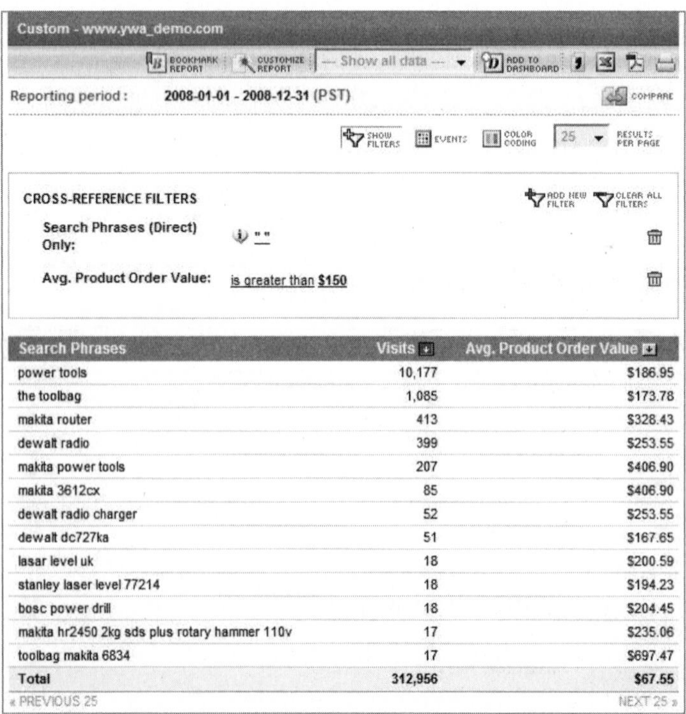

Search Phrases	Visits	Avg. Product Order Value
power tools	10,177	$186.95
the toolbag	1,085	$173.78
makita router	413	$328.43
dewalt radio	399	$253.55
makita power tools	207	$406.90
makita 3612cx	85	$406.90
dewalt radio charger	52	$253.55
dewalt dc727ka	51	$167.65
lasar level uk	18	$200.59
stanley laser level 77214	18	$194.23
bosc power drill	18	$204.45
makita hr2450 2kg sds plus rotary hammer 110v	17	$235.06
toolbag makita 6834	17	$697.47
Total	**312,956**	**$67.55**

Figure 6.27 This custom report on search phrases generates average order value above $150.

Note that we used the Direct attribution here. You would have to decide which traffic attribution model fits your audience.

Using Drill-downs and Drill-throughs

The reason for putting the less sophisticated feature of using drill-downs and drill-throughs below our pages-long chat about filters is that it is a shortcut for you to apply a set of filters and metrics. I work less with drill-downs and drill-throughs, which are essentially the same, and more with filters and custom reports directly.

Most of the standard reports in the system provide a drill-down opportunity, which is indicated by a magnifying glass to the left of the row of data, as shown in Figure 6.28.

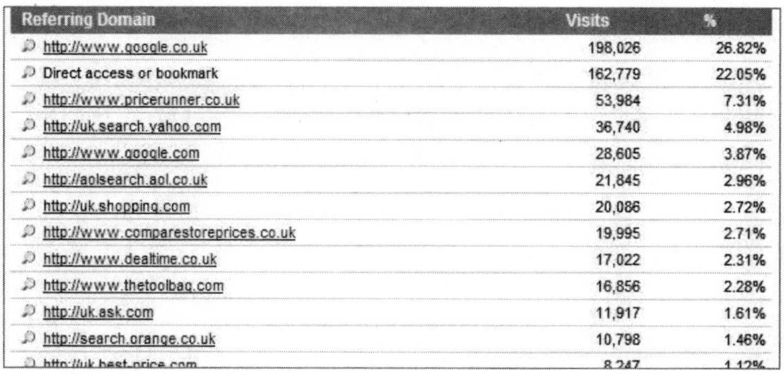

Referring Domain	Visits	%
http://www.google.co.uk	198,026	26.82%
Direct access or bookmark	162,779	22.05%
http://www.pricerunner.co.uk	53,984	7.31%
http://uk.search.yahoo.com	36,740	4.98%
http://www.google.com	28,605	3.87%
http://aolsearch.aol.co.uk	21,845	2.96%
http://uk.shopping.com	20,086	2.72%
http://www.comparestoreprices.co.uk	19,995	2.71%
http://www.dealtime.co.uk	17,022	2.31%
http://www.thetoolbag.com	16,856	2.28%
http://uk.ask.com	11,917	1.61%
http://search.orange.co.uk	10,798	1.46%
http://uk.best-price.com	8,247	1.12%

Figure 6.28 Click the magnifying glass to drill down on a row of data.

Using Figure 6.28 as an example, if you want to drill down into the number of visits that are coming from PriceRunner, a natural question would be, "How much money am I making from the traffic PriceRunner sends me?"

You activate a drill-down by clicking the magnifying glass to the left of a row. You can then drill down into the data or drill through to another report (see Figure 6.29).

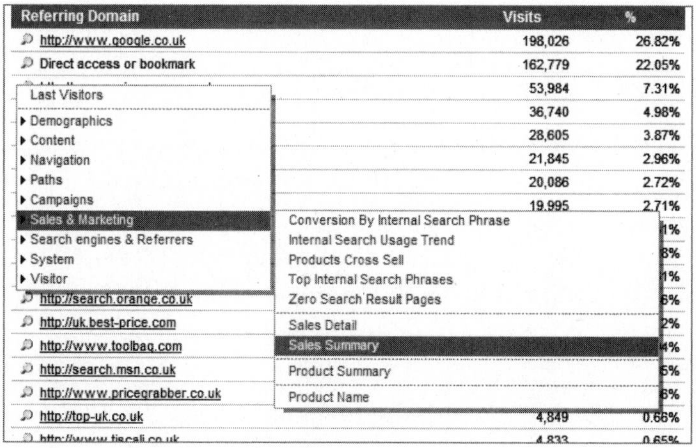

Referring Domain	Visits	%
http://www.google.co.uk	198,026	26.82%
Direct access or bookmark	162,779	22.05%
	53,984	7.31%
	36,740	4.98%
	28,605	3.87%
	21,845	2.96%
	20,086	2.72%
	19,995	2.71%
		1%
		8%
		1%
http://search.orange.co.uk		6%
http://uk.best-price.com		2%
http://www.toolbag.com		4%
http://search.msn.co.uk		5%
http://www.pricegrabber.co.uk		6%
http://top-uk.co.uk	4,849	0.66%
http://www.tiscali.co.uk	4,833	0.65%

Last Visitors
- Demographics
- Content
- Navigation
- Paths
- Campaigns
- Sales & Marketing
- Search engines & Referrers
- System
- Visitor

Conversion By Internal Search Phrase
Internal Search Usage Trend
Products Cross Sell
Top Internal Search Phrases
Zero Search Result Pages
Sales Detail
Sales Summary
Product Summary
Product Name

Figure 6.29 Drilling down into the Referring Domain report

The first thing you will notice about the results, as shown in Figure 6.30, is that your screen looks like a standard sales summary, with a cross-reference filter applied. And that is indeed what it is.

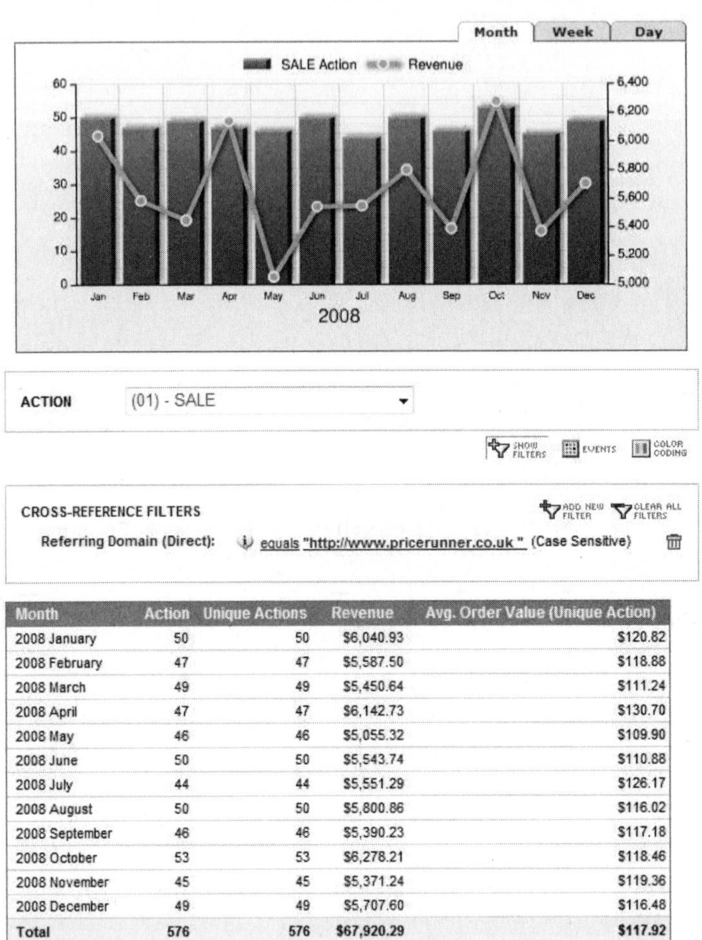

Month	Action	Unique Actions	Revenue	Avg. Order Value (Unique Action)
2008 January	50	50	$6,040.93	$120.82
2008 February	47	47	$5,587.50	$118.88
2008 March	49	49	$5,450.64	$111.24
2008 April	47	47	$6,142.73	$130.70
2008 May	46	46	$5,055.32	$109.90
2008 June	50	50	$5,543.74	$110.88
2008 July	44	44	$5,551.29	$126.17
2008 August	50	50	$5,800.86	$116.02
2008 September	46	46	$5,390.23	$117.18
2008 October	53	53	$6,278.21	$118.46
2008 November	45	45	$5,371.24	$119.36
2008 December	49	49	$5,707.60	$116.48
Total	**576**	**576**	**$67,920.29**	**$117.92**

Figure 6.30 Drill-down results

One case in which the drill-down feature provides additional functionality, beyond ease of use, is when the report result is not just segmented but presented in an entirely different manner. An example is when you are drilling down on a scenario analysis on Abandonment Path by Title, which results in the path analysis report. I will talk more about path analysis in Chapter 10, "Distinctive Reports and Usage."

Sorting Report Results

The ability to sort reports is much more valuable than you might think. Not only can you sort what appears on your screen, but you can also determine whether what appears on your screen includes the right metrics for you to sort on. For example, take the Most Requested Pages by Page Title report, partially shown in Figure 6.31.

Page Title	Page Views	%	Avg. Time On Page
home	210,791	10.11%	0m 3s
Products	180,500	8.65%	0m 5s
all - Toolbag	96,764	4.64%	0m 18s
Toolbag - Tools, Fixings & Consumables at Trade Prices!	69,029	3.31%	0m 50s
search	56,551	2.71%	0m 48s
Power Tools	42,572	2.04%	0m 5s
largetoolbag	41,882	2.01%	0m 26s
Power Tools - Toolbag, Next Day Delivery at Trade Prices!	41,612	1.99%	0m 32s
Plumbing - Toolbag, Next Day Delivery at Trade Prices!	23,876	1.14%	0m 27s
Plumbing	22,021	1.06%	0m 5s
Subtotal	**785,598**	**37.66%**	**0m 16s**
Total	**2,085,988**	**100.00%**	**0m 19s**
« PREVIOUS 10			NEXT 10 »

Figure 6.31 Most Requested Pages by Page Title report

Is a report on the most popular pages, sorted by number of page views, really what you are looking for? A content review initiative would focus on pages that did indeed actively participate in revenue generation, suggesting that you add a Revenue Participation metric to the report and sort by that, as shown in Figure 6.32, instead of merely impression.

Page Title	Page Views	%	Avg. Time On Page	Revenue Participation
Confirmation	2,734	0.13%	0m 1s	$281,691.15
Payment and Verification	3,220	0.15%	1m 33s	$281,382.03
Billing & Delivery Addresses	7,642	0.37%	0m 26s	$281,074.59
Delivery Options	6,318	0.30%	0m 20s	$280,589.21
home	210,791	10.11%	0m 3s	$274,421.97
baskettoolbag	16,986	0.81%	0m 27s	$274,297.97
confirmationtoolbag	5,222	0.25%	0m 49s	$274,213.09
Order Confirmed	2,766	0.13%	0m 14s	$272,383.70
add to basket	20,375	0.98%	0m 3s	$269,788.83
PRODUCTS	20,585	0.99%	0m 38s	$269,253.16
Products	180,500	8.65%	0m 5s	$249,921.37
Header	8,989	0.43%	0m 48s	$225,700.58
my_accounttoolbag	6,497	0.31%	0m 48s	$217,142.55
user registered	2,841	0.14%	3m 44s	$204,977.85
Toolbag - Tools, Fixings & Consumables at Trade Prices!	69,029	3.31%	0m 50s	$176,906.82
search	56,551	2.71%	0m 48s	$138,628.07

Figure 6.32 Most Requested Pages by Page Title sorted by the Revenue Participation metric

Adding metric sorting columns can create instant insight. In this example, we learn that Delivery Options, which is not a mandatory page, still participates in almost all of our revenue. This is the value of report sorting!

You perform sorting by simply clicking the small gray arrow on top of all the columns that you can sort.

Color-Coding Data

Yahoo! Web Analytics allows you to color-code the row-based data output. You can add a mark to the end of each row of data, using the following colors:

- Red (interpreted as negative)
- Green (interpreted as positive)
- Yellow (interpreted as neutral)

The vertical marks shown in Figure 6.33—green on line 6 and red on line 10—are applied at runtime and dependent on the results, so if the data rows displayed change when different filters are applied, so will the coloring.

Number Of Visits	Action	Revenue	Visits	Avg. Order Value (Unique Action)
1 visit(s)	440	$43,547.73	47,106	$99.88
2 visit(s)	236	$25,359.05	7,648	$109.31
3 visit(s)	82	$9,255.78	2,064	$112.88
4 visit(s)	49	$4,937.31	909	$100.76
5 visit(s)	30	$3,677.76	515	$126.82
6 visit(s)	20	$3,363.69	397	$168.18
7 visit(s)	7	$872.79	244	$124.68
8 visit(s)	10	$731.01	182	$73.10
9 visit(s)	6	$297.95	137	$49.66
10 visit(s)	4	$94.90	128	$23.72
Subtotal	**884**	**$92,137.97**	**59,330**	**$105.30**
Total	**907**	**$93,559.14**	**61,038**	**$104.42**

Figure 6.33 Report showing the color-coded number of visits until conversion

The coloring is done on a metric level, as shown in Figure 6.33 (on Avg. Order Value).

You activate the color-coding feature by clicking the color-coding icon just below the chart, which brings up another set of icons just above the columns, indicating which ones that you can apply color coding to. Clicking the Edit icon takes you to the Edit Color Coding screen, shown in Figure 6.34.

The Edit Color Coding screen lets you apply the threshold for Red, Green, and Yellow, but more importantly, offers a choice for *what* to display and *when* to display it. You are given these options:

- Which of the three colors to display
- What reports to apply it to
- What projects to apply it to

Remember, though, that if you use color coding too aggressively, you are merely adding "chart junk" to your account—not insights!

Chart Junk

Chart junk refers to all visual elements in charts and graphs that are not necessary to comprehend the information represented on the graph, or that distract the viewer from this information.

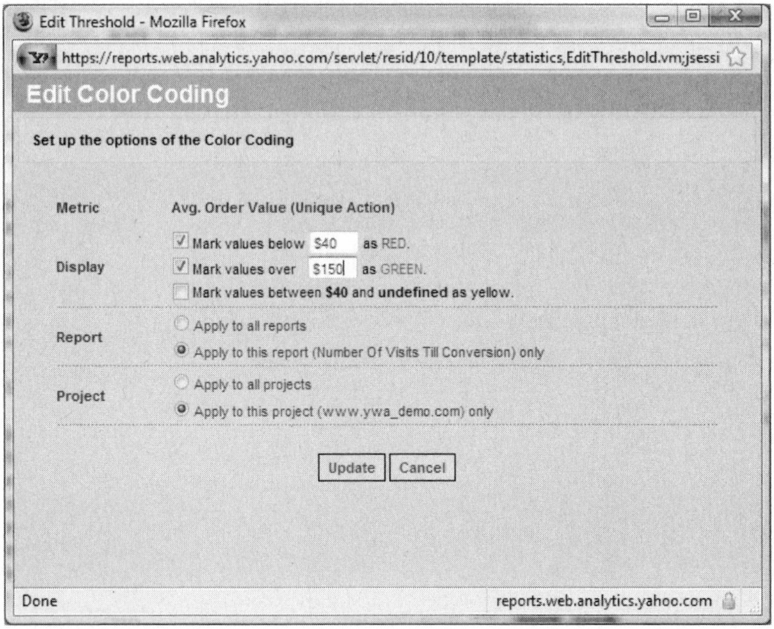

Edit Threshold - Mozilla Firefox

https://reports.web.analytics.yahoo.com/servlet/resid/10/template/statistics,EditThreshold.vm;jsessi

Edit Color Coding

Set up the options of the Color Coding

Metric: Avg. Order Value (Unique Action)

Display:
- Mark values below $40 as RED.
- Mark values over $150 as GREEN.
- Mark values between **$40** and **undefined** as yellow.

Report:
- Apply to all reports
- Apply to this report (Number Of Visits Till Conversion) only

Project:
- Apply to all projects
- Apply to this project (www.ywa_demo.com) only

Update | Cancel

Done | reports.web.analytics.yahoo.com

Figure 6.34 Edit Color Coding

I suggest that you avoid using yellow (neutral) unless you have a good reason to do so. The color coding is a visual alert that indicates additional action is needed. If you apply yellow to indicate the data is neutral, you just drew attention to data that does not need attention. At the same time, use green sparingly, unless you have verified processes and actions aligned to positives.

Red is the color I tend to use the most. But even when using only red, you should be conservative. If half the rows in every report are color-coded red, the color loses its meaning, and you might as well not use the functionality. Reserve the color red to indicate a warning.

Imagine that your goal is a visit-to-sale conversion rate of 1 percent, and on all reports—out of the box or custom built—anything below that level should be marked red. You could wind up coloring a lot of reports red throughout. Or suppose you have traffic sources that drive interest and not sales. If they are to be color-coded by a default value, you could end up with chart junk again. So be careful.

The same warning goes for applying color to all projects. You can only do so if all projects are aligned or if a given metric means the same, no matter what you do. I have never applied color coding to all projects.

Applying Report Notes and Reasoning

The Report Notes feature allows you to add notes to reports and share them with your colleagues. Your notes will be displayed above the graph for each report, as shown in Figure 6.35.

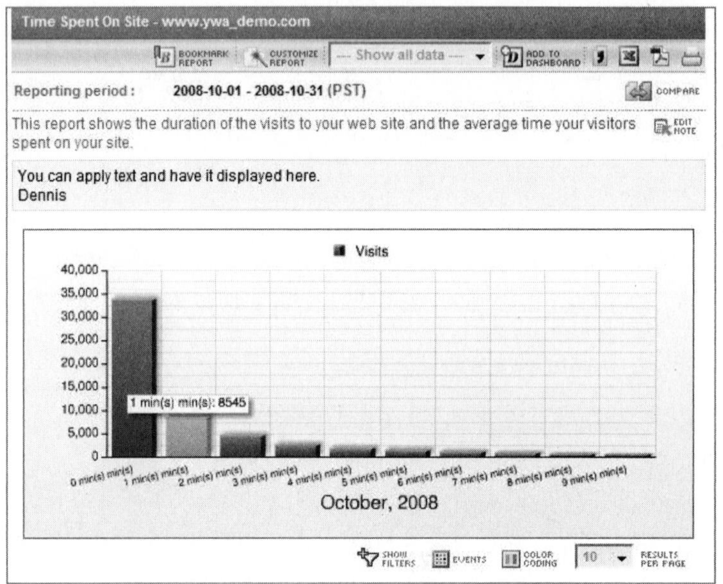

Figure 6.35 Your notes are displayed above the graph for each report.

If you have nothing to say, do not add any notes, but you will likely want to add report notes on the most used reports. The notes should hold information such as:

- How to interpret the data, including your reasoning for color-coding thresholds
- What actions to take if the data reads a certain way
- Why a custom report has been assembled

Returning to the report shown in Figure 6.33, a valid report note could be:

Please note that about half our revenue is generated on the first visit. It is therefore of the utmost importance that we keep people beyond the first minute. It should be noted that the average time spent for a buyer, excluding the process of checking out, is 4 min.

You activate this feature by clicking the Edit Note icon in the upper-right corner, just above the chart. Enter your notes, and click the Save Note button, which will immediately display and save your notes without refreshing the page. You can edit report notes by using basic HTML syntax.

Exporting Data

Whether you export data to do separate analysis and modeling, to connect it to your data warehouse, or just to share it with a partner, having access to large raw exports offers a plethora of opportunities.

This section focuses less on how you can utilize the raw data output and more on how you gain access to it.

The reporting interface allows you to export report results in the following formats:

- HTML
- Microsoft Excel (XLS)
- Comma-separated values (CSV)
- PDF

Three of these output formats are directly accessible through the icons presented on the right side of the report header, as shown in Figure 6.36. We clicked the HTML icon and the Export Reports dialog opened with the HTML radio button selected (see Figure 6.37).

Figure 6.36 Access the output formats by clicking the icons in the report header.

Export Reports

This allows you to export reports in different formats and have them delivered instantly, by email or via an FTP connection.

Export options

No. of rows 1,000

Email note

Select format

HTML

Microsoft Excel

Comma-separated values (CSV)

PDF

Compressed file (.zip)

Instant Export | Email Export | Upload Export to FTP Server

Enter an email address and the exported report will be sent to you by email.

E-mail dennis.mortensen@evcrp.com

E-mail BCC all@yahoo-inc.com

Notify these recipients when the report export is completed.

Export Report | Cancel

Figure 6.37 The resulting Export Reports dialog

You can select from the following delivery methods:

Instant Export The export is immediately generated and is ready to be saved.

Email Export You enter your email address, and the exported report will be delivered to your inbox.

Upload Export to FTP Server You provide the FTP connection where the exported report will be uploaded and enter an email address to be notified in case of an FTP upload error.

You can also have the report exported as a compressed file by clicking the Compressed File (.zip) radio button.

The instant export is, well, instant, and the file will pop up as a download.

To use the Email Export feature, select the number of rows you want to export, apply an optional note, select the format of the exported report, and enter the email address of the report recipient.

Note that if the report you selected for Email Export contains more than 100,000 rows, the report will not be sent by email but will be saved under the Volume Export Download Center. You will be notified by email that your selected report is available under the Volume Export Download Center when the export is ready.

To use the Upload Export to FTP Server feature, select the number of rows you want to export, apply an optional note, select the format of the exported report, and select a preconfigured FTP connection you want to use for this export.

Before exporting, consider just printing a report result and handing it over to the person. Most reports can be printed as a default, and they actually don't look that bad.

Yahoo! Web Analytics lets you download volumes of data, such as the true long tail. If you want to do some keyword research, what better place to start than with the 150,000 organic search phrases that you have collected throughout the past year?

This chapter provided a foundation for using Yahoo! Web Analytics reports, which means our next step is learning how to customize report results. Chapter 7 shows how to go beyond the data presented, using features such as the Custom Report Wizard and the Segmentation Wizard.

Customizing Report Results

By now I am sure you appreciate the fact that most reports provided out of the box will not help you answer your unique business questions, at least not without some level of customization. In addition to customizing the reports, it is also important that you move beyond the general dataset and group of averages, as they are unlikely to give you true insight. For true insight you are almost forced to segment your data. Think of segments as a subgroup of people sharing the same characteristics. As my good friend Avinash would say, it is a sin against humanity to look at unsegmented data.

7

Chapter Contents

Using Metric Alerts
Event Management
Using Scheduled Reports
Building Custom Reports
Bookmarking Reports
Using Segments in Reporting
User Rights and Role Administration

Using Metric Alerts

Although we've talked about various ways to query your data and even combine queries for reports that help create insight, there is still value in reporting on your KPIs and generally important metrics. Rather than randomly surfing reports, you can delve in to your analytics tool to get critical business information on single metrics, once you have defined those that are important to report back to your team or management.

In many situations, the absolute value of a metric is not important as such, but it becomes critical if that number goes beyond or below a set of predefined thresholds. As you'll recall from our discussion on color-coding your data in Chapter 6, "Working with Report Results," when you read the results of a report, you should be able to easily discern whether a metric is performing poorly.

The ability to color-code the data is still extremely valuable for communicating about abnormal metric behavior. But keep in mind that color-coding your data is not the same as monitoring the data. Monitoring the data is a manual task. The effort you expend on monitoring data should be comparable to the level of business risk you assume if the target metric does not meet its performance goals.

You can set up scheduled emails and receive 50 reports daily. This might be something to consider when you're monitoring important metrics. However, receiving anything beyond a small handful of web analytics emails a day is not likely to allow you to consume all the numbers and at the same time monitor them for abnormalities. In addition, you would damage the reporting structure by poisoning valuable data communication with irrelevant "noise"—in other words, emails with little or no action attached to them.

Yahoo! Web Analytics provides a function called Alerts that monitors the data and alerts you if anything out of the ordinary happens. You can stay on top of your website's performance by setting up customized email metric alerts. The Alerts function allows you to schedule email alerts for you and your colleagues, depending on the performance of your website. You can define email alerts by identifying high/low values for your key metrics or significant percentage changes based on past performance.

Alerts can save you time by letting you automatically scout dozens of reports at the same time and essentially thousands of metrics, and receive an email only if something unusual happens.

What to Monitor with an Alert

The option to set up alerts is not apparent in the interface, so it's easy to forget if you do not know how to access it. As you can see in Figure 7.1, the Add Alert option pops up when you right-click any acceptable metric in a report.

In our example we've clicked the Visits metric from AOL Search. This opens the Edit Alert dialog shown in Figure 7.2.

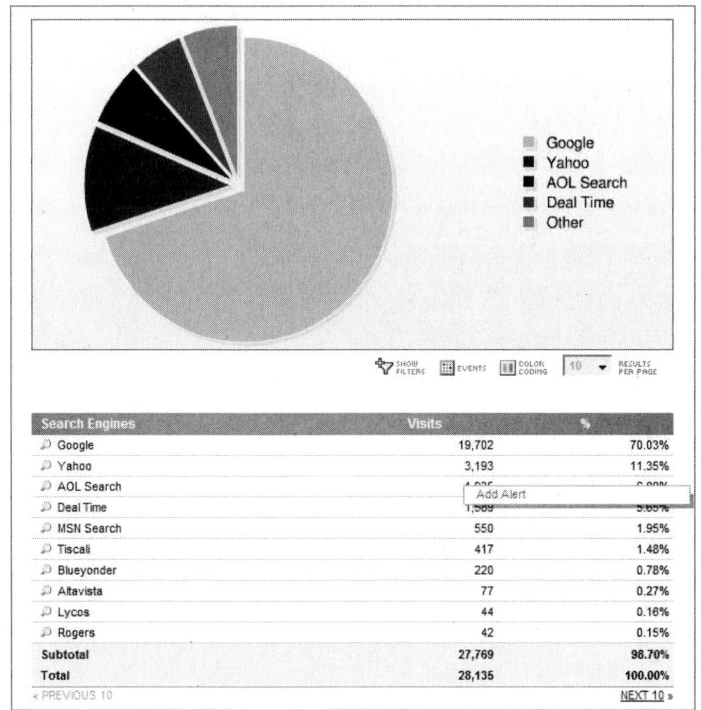

Search Engines	Visits	%
Google	19,702	70.03%
Yahoo	3,193	11.35%
AOL Search	[illegible]	[illegible]
Deal Time	[illegible]	[illegible]
MSN Search	550	1.95%
Tiscali	417	1.48%
Blueyonder	220	0.78%
Altavista	77	0.27%
Lycos	44	0.16%
Rogers	42	0.15%
Subtotal	**27,769**	**98.70%**
Total	**28,135**	**100.00%**

« PREVIOUS 10 NEXT 10 »

Figure 7.1 Adding an alert

Edit Alert

Set an automated alert based on key metrics.

Name Monitor visits from AOL

Monitor
- AVERAGE
- EACH ITEM INDIVIDUALLY
- ONE UNIQUE ITEM

Monitor the **Visits** of this one specific item:
Search Engines (Direct) **AOL Search**
Search Engines (Direct) Only
You will monitor this specific item against your chosen triggers.

Timing
Perform check each month on the 1 st After 1 AM according to your project's time zone.
Check last full 30 days compared to last full 30 days before

Trigger alert if
- [x] Visits is above 2500.0
- [ ] Visits is below 0.0
- [ ] Visits has increased by 0.0
- [ ] Visits has decreased by 0.0
- [ ] Visits has increased by 0.0 %
- [ ] Visits has decreased by 0.0 %

Email dennis.mortensen@evcrp.com

Comment
```
Visits from AOL Search has increased and
is now at 2500 per month.
```

Enable [x]

Update | Test this alert | Cancel

Figure 7.2 Edit Alert dialog

In the Edit Alert dialog, you'll specify a name, comments, and a destination email, as well as the three most important parts of most alert systems: what to monitor, when to perform the checks, and what should trigger the monitoring process. Let's look at each of these choices.

Your first is how to monitor the metric that you initially chose. Yahoo! Web Analytics, quite elegantly, provides you with three choices that are all quite different:

Average You can monitor the average of the metric for the specified column. Suppose you allow marketing to do any campaign they want, as long as the overall visit-to-sale conversion from campaigns is above a certain level. Setting up an alert that monitors the average will look at a total for all your campaigns, and you will not be alerted if a single campaign performs badly, as long as the overall conversion rate is where it is supposed to be.

Each Item Individually Choose this option if you want to ensure that every metric in that column is measured against the triggers. Suppose you want to monitor the visit-to-sale conversion rate on all referring visits from several campaigns. You might have hundreds of marketing campaigns running at any given point in time, and they are always changing. Setting up an alert is a way to ensure that you are instantly warned about campaigns going below a given negative threshold, even as marketing is setting up new campaigns and deleting old ones.

One Unique Item This is the most specific of all the alerts: It lets you monitor the metrics that you clicked against the triggers on that one item only. Suppose you engage in a narrow SEO activity, which is intended to drive up your visits from AOL Search. If the promised output and closure of the project is expected to occur at a visit number above 2,500, you can create the alert shown in Figure 7.2 and wait for an email to arrive.

Your situation will determine which option you choose. In general, I have observed that the Average alerts tend to go to managers, who might not even log into the tool but rely solely on scheduled emails and alerts. Each Item Individually is somewhat the same as setting up 20 alerts on each unique item, and thus those two options tend to go together and are mostly used on an operational level—for example, if you are a Search Engine Marketing (SEM) or SEO manager or if you are in charge of specific website optimization tasks.

Alert Timing and Triggers

Having decided which metrics you want to monitor, it is time to choose what the timing should be. You might assume that you should just monitor as often as technically possible, but that does not necessarily make sense. If you are serving business customers and monitor a metric such as visits on a daily basis, you are likely to receive an alert every Saturday and Sunday when traffic is bound to decline. In that scenario, you might want to monitor traffic on a weekly basis to average things out so expected fluctuations are not noted.

Dashboard Examples

In this set of examples I am not showcasing the best dashboards you can create with Yahoo! Web Analytics; rather, I'm providing you with a source for discovery and inspiration. Even though some of the dashboards apply elements that go against my recommendations in Chapter 9, I think they will get you started on your own journey toward the perfect dashboard for you and your organization. The most important element is that you gain the confidence to get started and create your own unique dashboard without feeling that you have to apply a default dashboard or copy any of the following 15 directly.

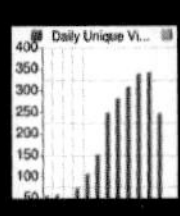

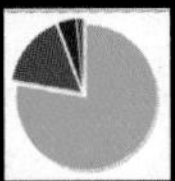

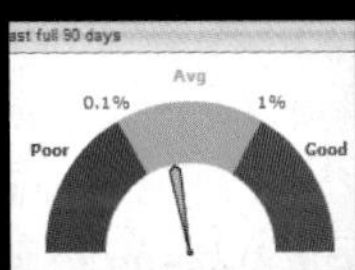

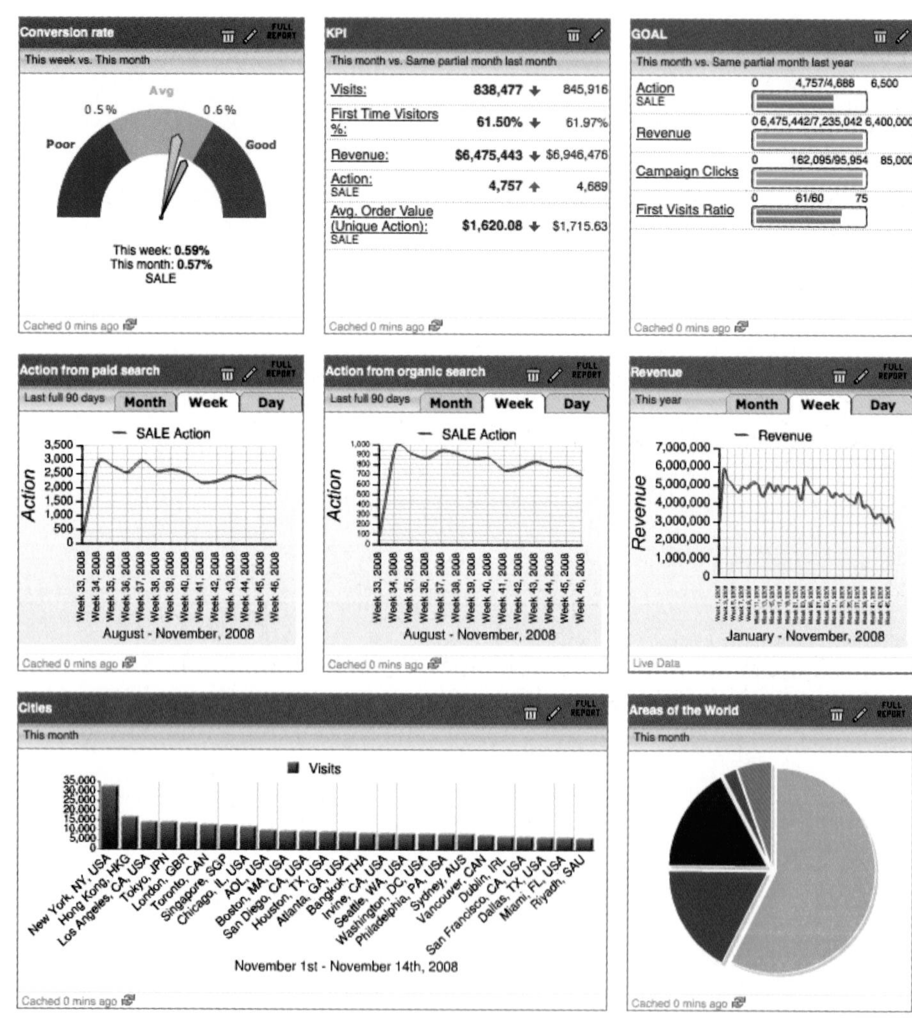

Hospitality SEM Dashboard Tami Dalley, Acronym Media Inc., using Yahoo! Web Analytics

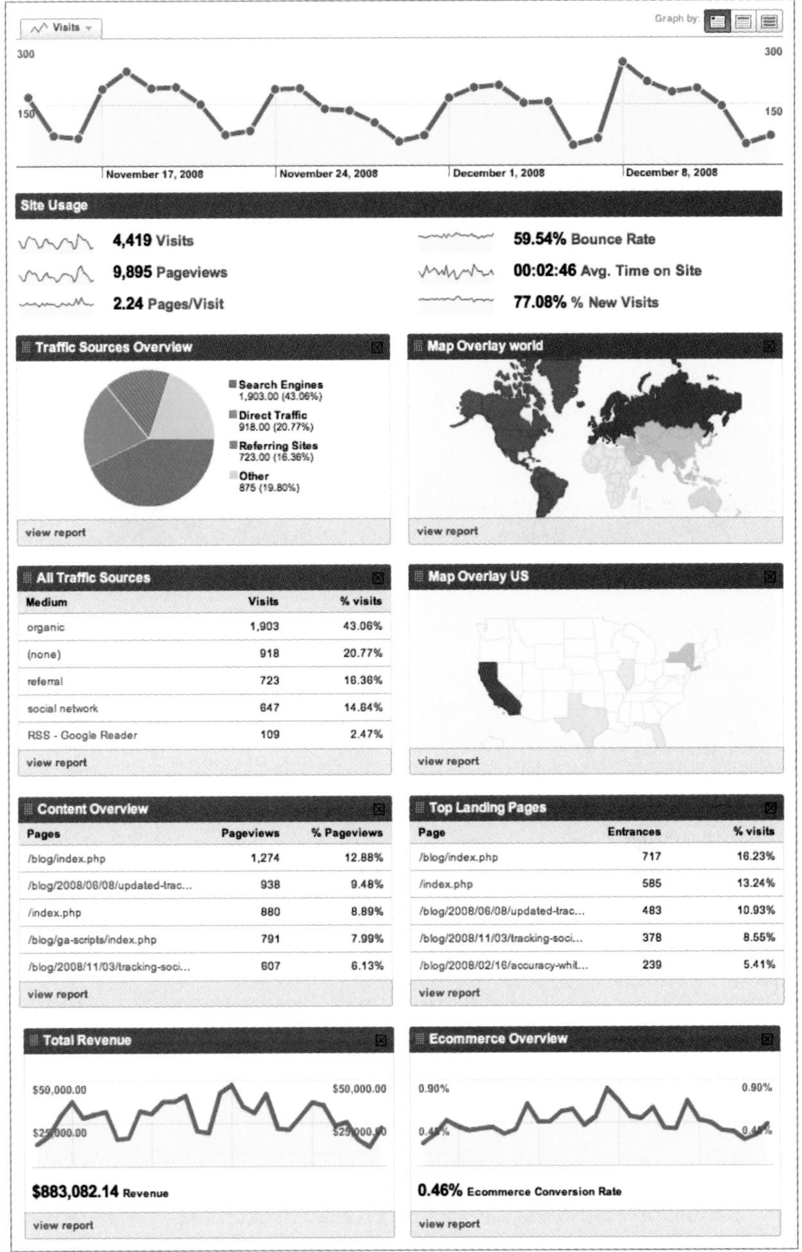

E-commerce Dashboard This dashboard is for a retail website with a global target audience, though there is specific interest in U.S. visitors. The initial chart and site usage report are fixed. However, you can customize the remaining eight summary reports to contain any report content from Google Analytics. The dashboard can contain up to 12 such reports.

Brian Clifton, author of *Advanced Web Metrics* (Sybex, 2008), using Google Analytics

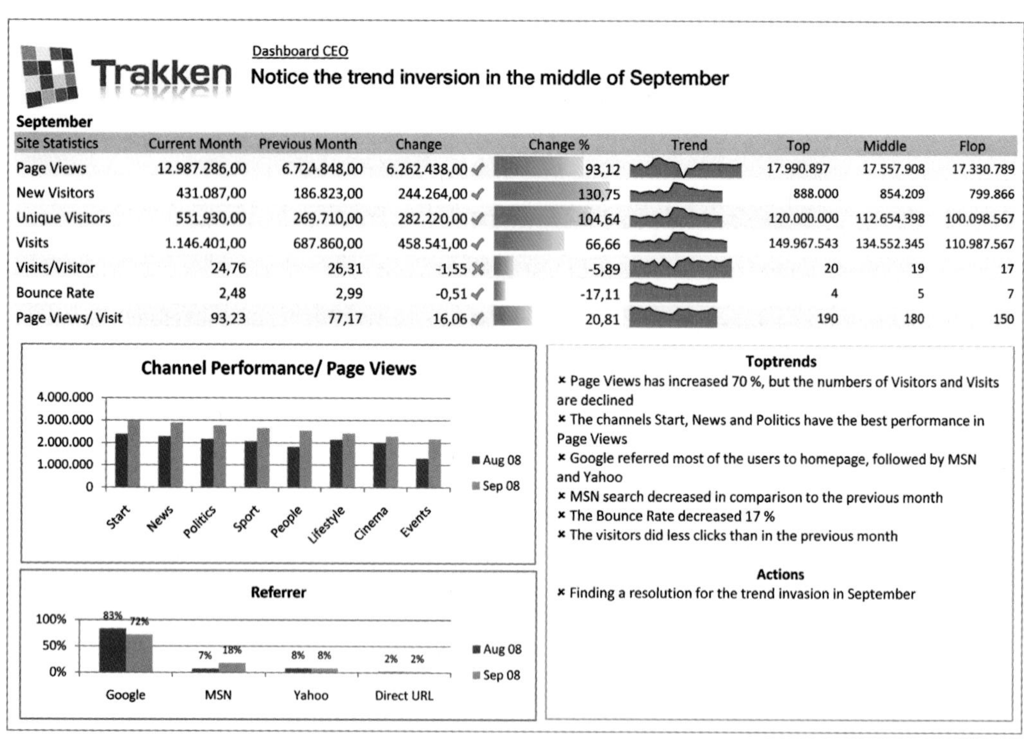
Trakken
Dashboard CEO
Notice the trend inversion in the middle of September
September

Site Statistics	Current Month	Previous Month	Change	Change %	Trend	Top	Middle	Flop
Page Views	12.987.286,00	6.724.848,00	6.262.438,00 ✓	93,12		17.990.897	17.557.908	17.330.789
New Visitors	431.087,00	186.823,00	244.264,00 ✓	130,75		888.000	854.209	799.866
Unique Visitors	551.930,00	269.710,00	282.220,00 ✓	104,64		120.000.000	112.654.398	100.098.567
Visits	1.146.401,00	687.860,00	458.541,00 ✓	66,66		149.967.543	134.552.345	110.987.567
Visits/Visitor	24,76	26,31	-1,55 ✗	-5,89		20	19	17
Bounce Rate	2,48	2,99	-0,51 ✓	-17,11		4	5	7
Page Views/ Visit	93,23	77,17	16,06 ✓	20,81		190	180	150

Channel Performance/ Page Views
4.000.000
3.000.000
2.000.000
1.000.000
0
Start
News
Politics
Sport
People
Lifestyle
Cinema
Events
Aug 08
Sep 08
Referrer
100%
50%
0%
83%
72%
7%
18%
8%
8%
2%
2%
Google
MSN
Yahoo
Direct URL
Aug 08
Sep 08
Toptrends
× Page Views has increased 70 %, but the numbers of Visitors and Visits are declined
× The channels Start, News and Politics have the best performance in Page Views
× Google referred most of the users to homepage, followed by MSN and Yahoo
× MSN search decreased in comparison to the previous month
× The Bounce Rate decreased 17 %
× The visitors did less clicks than in the previous month
Actions
× Finding a resolution for the trend invasion in September

Content Site Dashboard This is an example of a top-level dashboard for content sites.

Timo Aden, Trakken GmbH, using Google Analytics and Microsoft Excel

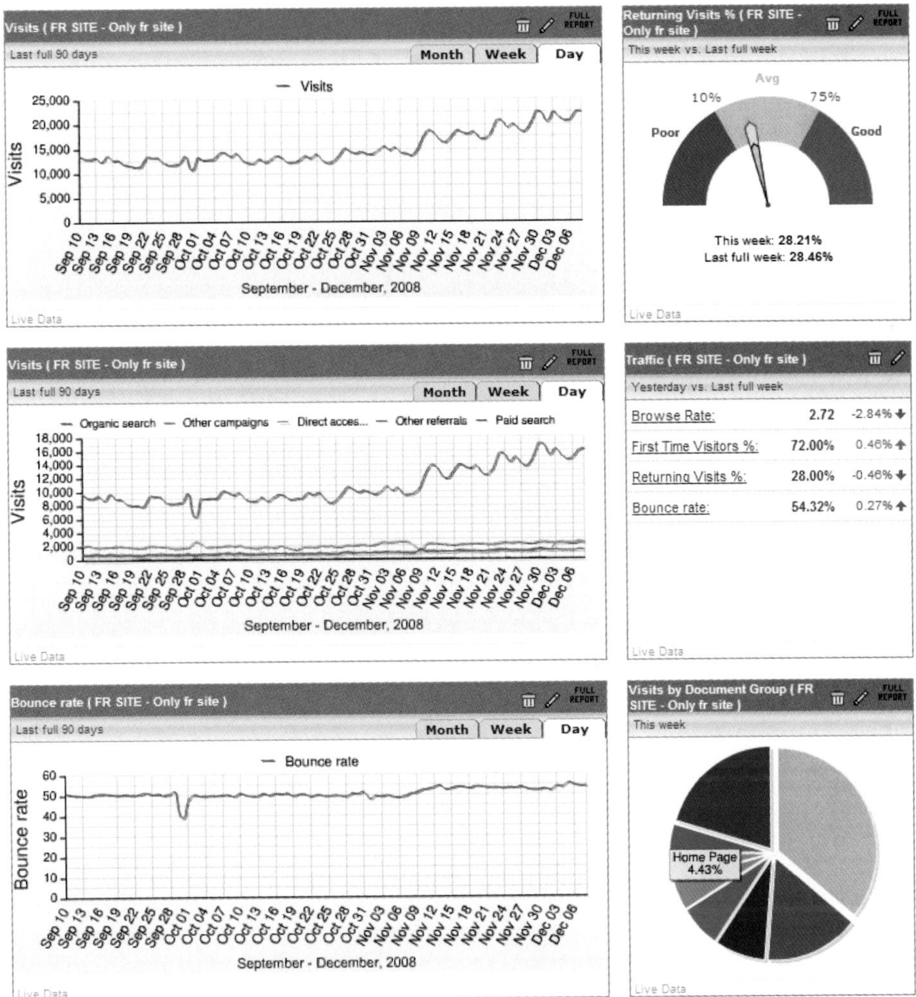

Regional Traffic Dashboard This dashboard looks at visits, traffic type, and bounce rate over a longer period; tracks returning visitors on a weekly basis; and gives an overview of visits by page type.

Per Hedén, using Yahoo! Web Analytics

% tracked Conversions attributed to Social Media	0.34%						
Total Conversions by Orig Source	4974	6263	375	3182	46140	7368	1974
Social Media Conversions by OrigSource	7	11	0	8	192	10	9
Percentage of Social Media Conversion by Source	0.14%	0.18%	0.00%	0.25%	0.42%	0.14%	0.46%
Traffic from Social Media	Action 1	Action 2	Action 3	Action 4	Action 5	Action 6	Action 7
Social Media Returns by Orig Source	June '07	June '07	June '07	June '07	June '07	June '07	June '07
babycenter.com	4	2		4	44	1	8
babyzone.com					4		
friendster.com							
supermama.lt					1		
celebrity-babies.com					9		
blogdelbebe.com					8		
babychic101.blogspot.com							
blog.gracobaby.com							
forum.bg-mamma.com							
boards.babycenter.com							
windsorpeak.com		1					
forums.slickdeals.net							
car-seat.org	1				6		
breastfeeding.com							
bebechouchou.qc.ca					3		
fixya.com							
community.thenestbaby.com							
perekool.ee							
jeeptrip.com							
mumsnet.com							

Social Media Dashboard This dashboard shows the number of conversions from Social Media Referral traffic to the site in question.

Marshall Sponder, WebMetricsGuru.com, using Omniture SiteCatalyst and Microsoft Excel

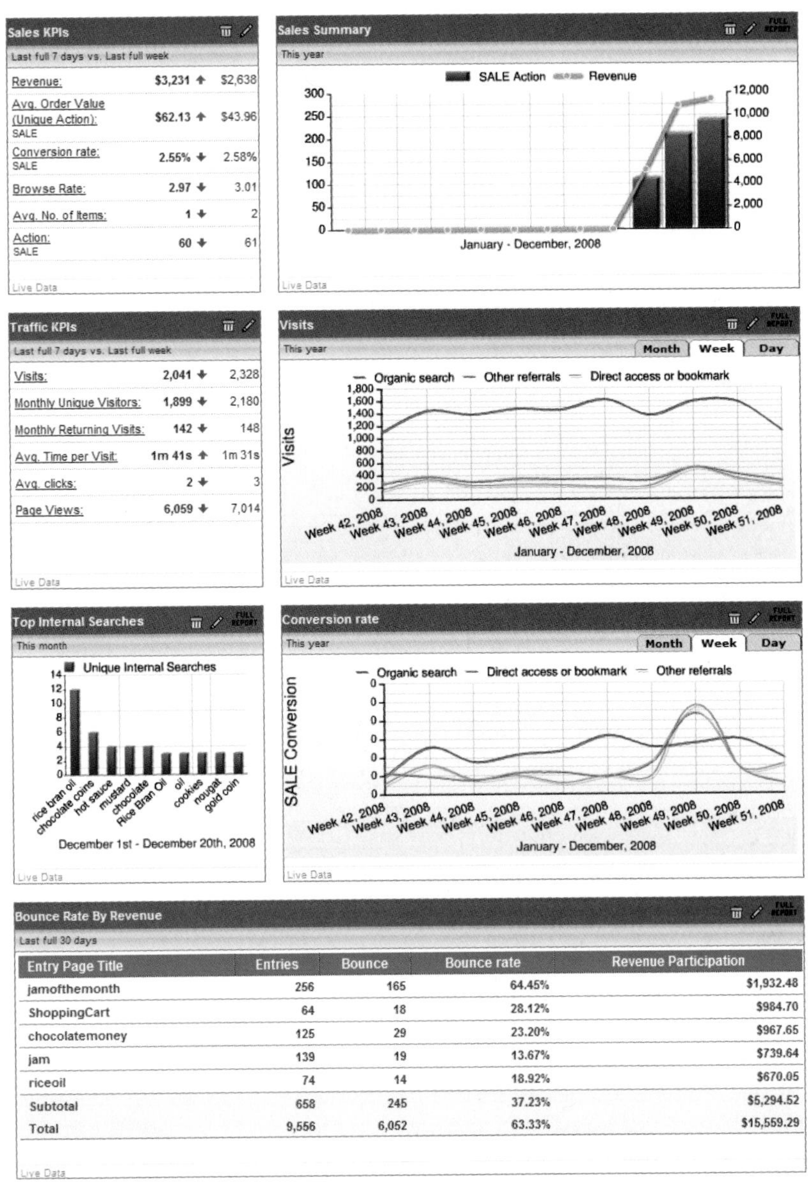

Entry Page Title	Entries	Bounce	Bounce rate	Revenue Participation
jamofthemonth	256	165	64.45%	$1,932.48
ShoppingCart	64	18	28.12%	$984.70
chocolatemoney	125	29	23.20%	$967.65
jam	139	19	13.67%	$739.64
riceoil	74	14	18.92%	$670.05
Subtotal	658	245	37.23%	$5,294.52
Total	9,556	6,052	63.33%	$15,559.29

Yahoo! Store E-commerce Dashboard The Yahoo! Store dashboard is meant to serve as not only a traditional analytics dashboard for KPIs (visitors, page views, revenue, average order value, etc.), but also as a starting point into the top reports on which merchants just starting with analytics should focus (bounce rate, conversion rate by search phrase, top internal search phrases). Visitor and conversion rate charts are broken out by traffic sources for immediate visualization of performance by traffic source. Weekly KPIs are placed side by side with year-to-date trend reports to put current performance into a longer historical context.

Paul Boisvert, Yahoo! Small Business, using Yahoo! Web Analytics

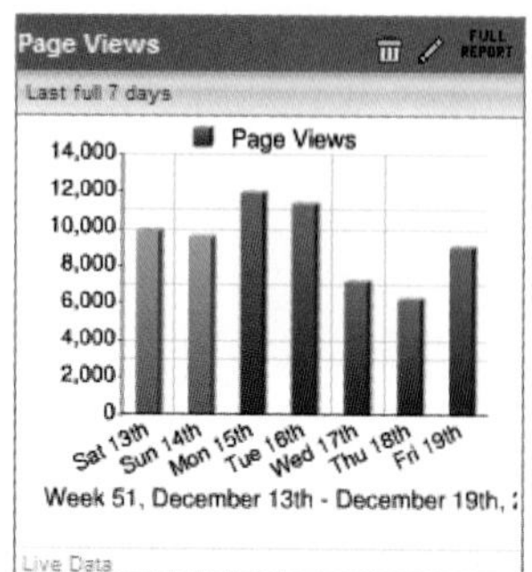

Module Interactions

Last full 7 days

Day | Hour

Day	flickrcontent Action	qa Action	SALE Action	domore Action	bestblogs Action	groups Action	arti Ac
December 13, 2008 Sat	1,589	146	25	125	83	52	
December 14, 2008 Sun	1,933	228	40	87	36	64	
December 15, 2008 Mon	1,650	251	36	79	92	81	
December 16, 2008 Tue	1,505	202	28	65	70	61	
December 17, 2008 Wed	297	49	9	18	21	20	
December 18, 2008 Thu	165	64	8	2	9	18	
December 19, 2008 Fri	1,629	236	21	100	78	96	

Live Data

Browser Type

Last full 7 days

Live Data

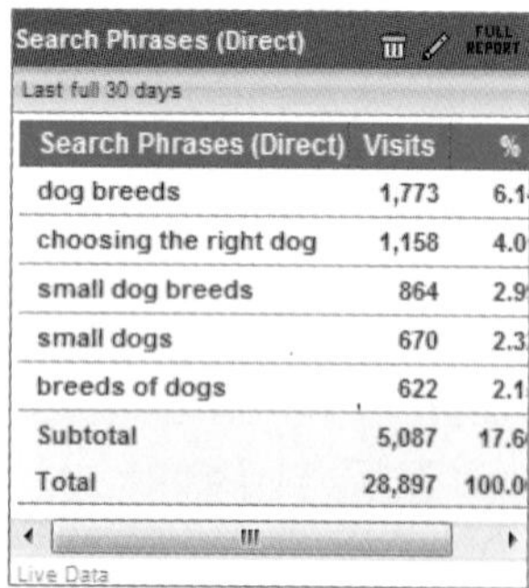

Search Phrases (Direct)

Last full 30 days

Search Phrases (Direct)	Visits	%
dog breeds	1,773	6.1
choosing the right dog	1,158	4.0
small dog breeds	864	2.9
small dogs	670	2.3
breeds of dogs	622	2.1
Subtotal	5,087	17.6
Total	28,897	100.0

Live Data

Referring Domains (Direct)

Last full 30 days

Referring Domain (Direct)	Visits
Direct access or bookmark	31,110
http://search.yahoo.com	20,384
http://shopping.yahoo.com	5,792
http://www.local.com	4,160
http://www.blurtit.com	4,012
Subtotal	65,458
Total	112,014

Live Data

Exit Links (grouped by domain)

Last full 30 days

Domain	Clic
http://www.goldenwestsf.com	3,9
http://www.valrhona.com	2,8
http://www.gwsfoods.com	1,7
http://www.amazon.com	1,4
http://www.honestfoods.com	1,2
Subtotal	11,1
Total	16,5

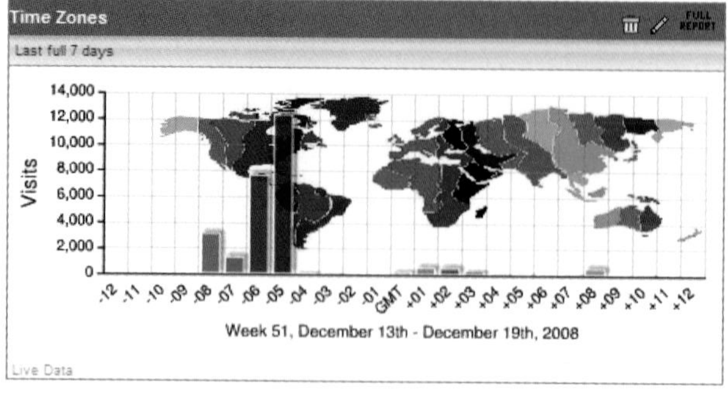

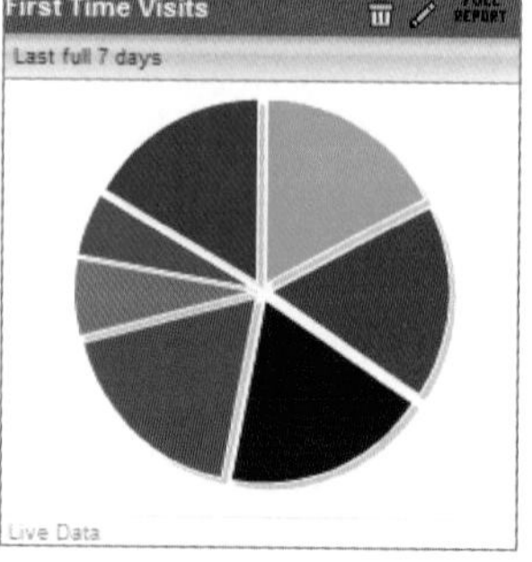

Large Campaign Landing Page Dashboard Julie Schmitt, Yahoo! Buzz Marketing, using Yahoo! Web Analytics

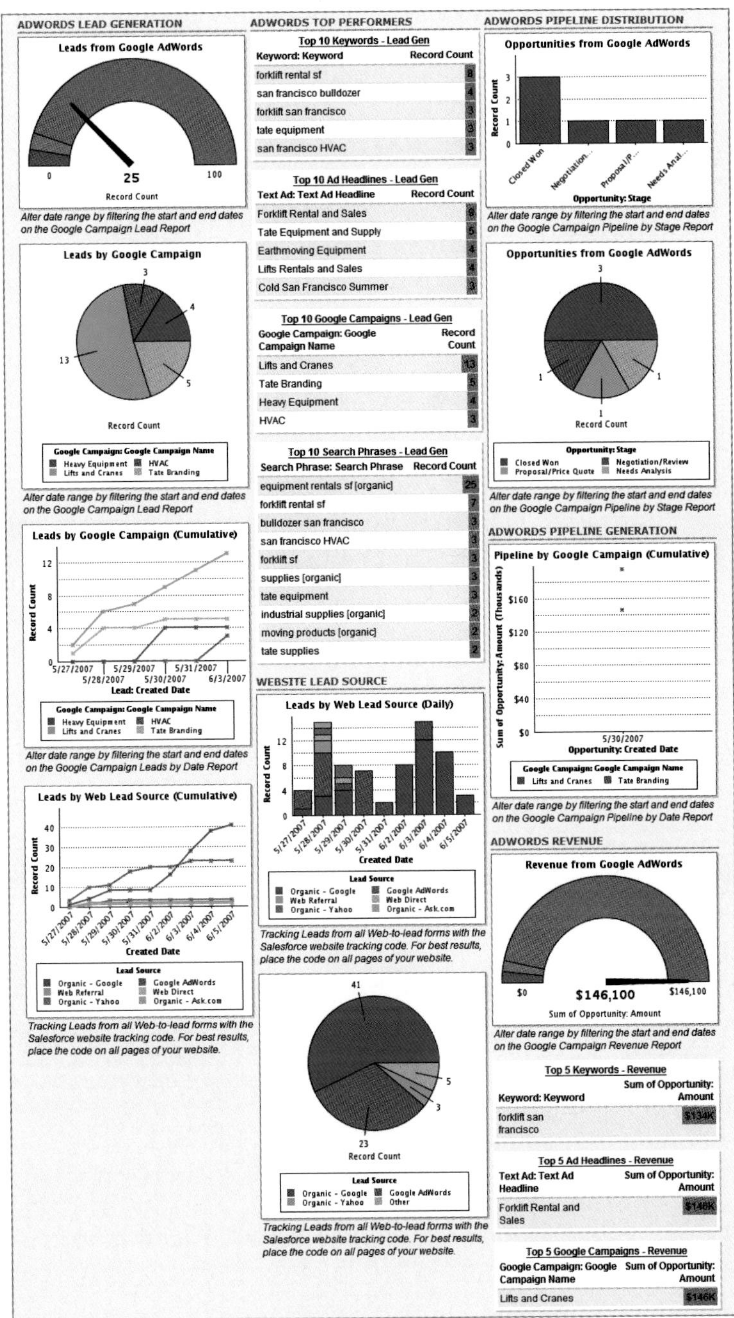

Google AdWords Dashboard The Google AdWords Dashboard allows you to analyze Google advertising programs. You can use it to understand how Google AdWords helps to deliver leads, opportunities (pipeline), and revenue. Drill into any of the components to find detailed reports.

SalesForce.com, Inc., using SalesForce, AppExchange Google AdWords

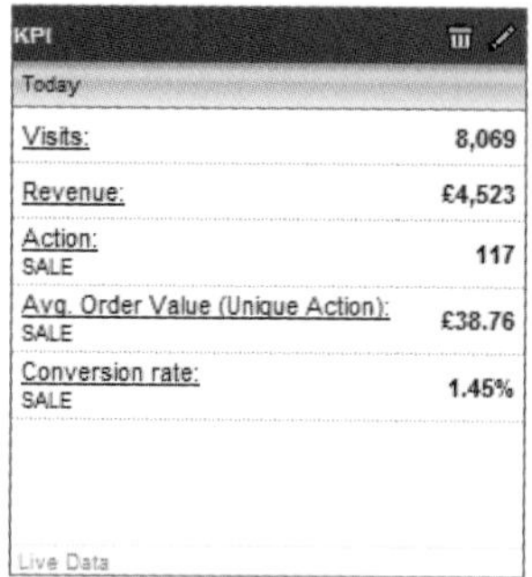

KPI

Today	
Visits:	8,069
Revenue:	£4,523
Action: SALE	117
Avg. Order Value (Unique Action): SALE	£38.76
Conversion rate: SALE	1.45%

Live Data

Sales Summary
Today
SALE Action Revenue
Sunday, December 21st, 2008
Live Data

KPI 2

Yesterday vs. Same full day last year		
Visits:	9,879	16.86% ↑
Revenue:	£8,659	34.75% ↑
Action: SALE	249	54.65% ↑
Avg. Order Value (Unique Action): SALE	£34.90	-13.91% ↓
Conversion rate: SALE	2.52%	0.62% ↑

Live Data

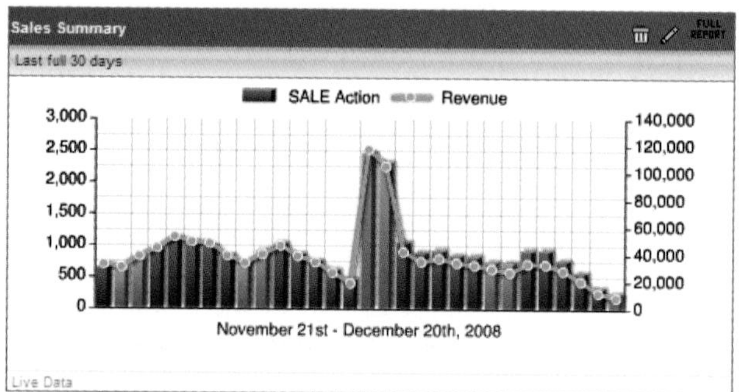

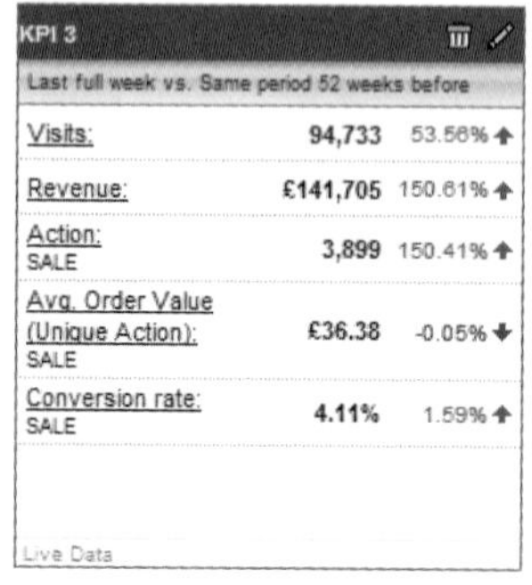

KPI 3

Last full week vs. Same period 52 weeks before		
Visits:	94,733	53.56% ↑
Revenue:	£141,705	150.61% ↑
Action: SALE	3,899	150.41% ↑
Avg. Order Value (Unique Action): SALE	£36.38	-0.05% ↓
Conversion rate: SALE	4.11%	1.59% ↑

Live Data

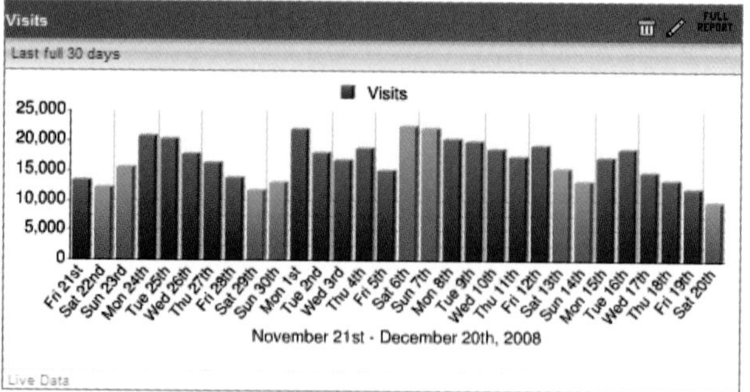

Sales Visit Standard Dashboard Snow Valley Ltd., using Yahoo! Web Analytics

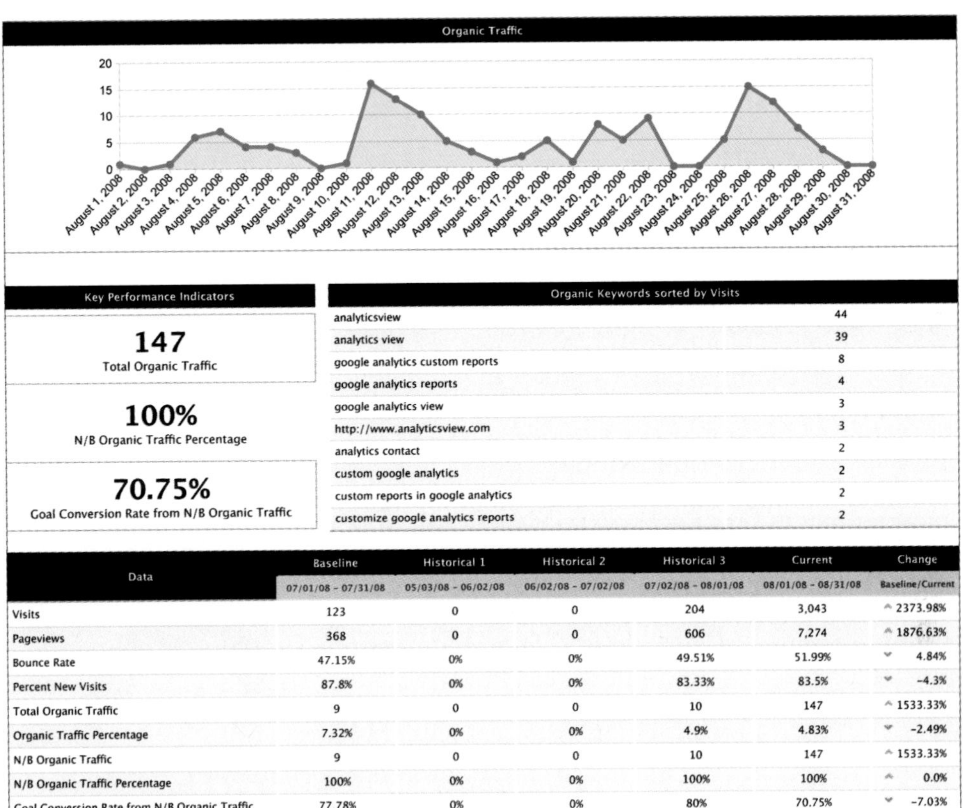

Organic Keywords sorted by Visits	
analyticsview	44
analytics view	39
google analytics custom reports	8
google analytics reports	4
google analytics view	3
http://www.analyticsview.com	3
analytics contact	2
custom google analytics	2
custom reports in google analytics	2
customize google analytics reports	2

Data	Baseline	Historical 1	Historical 2	Historical 3	Current	Change
	07/01/08 - 07/31/08	05/03/08 - 06/02/08	06/02/08 - 07/02/08	07/02/08 - 08/01/08	08/01/08 - 08/31/08	Baseline/Current
Visits	123	0	0	204	3,043	2373.98%
Pageviews	368	0	0	606	7,274	1876.63%
Bounce Rate	47.15%	0%	0%	49.51%	51.99%	4.84%
Percent New Visits	87.8%	0%	0%	83.33%	83.5%	-4.3%
Total Organic Traffic	9	0	0	10	147	1533.33%
Organic Traffic Percentage	7.32%	0%	0%	4.9%	4.83%	-2.49%
N/B Organic Traffic	9	0	0	10	147	1533.33%
N/B Organic Traffic Percentage	100%	0%	0%	100%	100%	0.0%
Goal Conversion Rate from N/B Organic Traffic	77.78%	0%	0%	80%	70.75%	-7.03%

SEO Dashboard The SEO report gives you insight on what keywords are driving the most qualified visitors to your site. You are able to remove branded keywords from your organic visits so that you can accurately track the most important keywords driving traffic to your site. The SEO report contains 68 KPIs pulled from 25 different Google Analytics reports.

EpikOne, Inc., using Google Analytics and Microsoft Excel

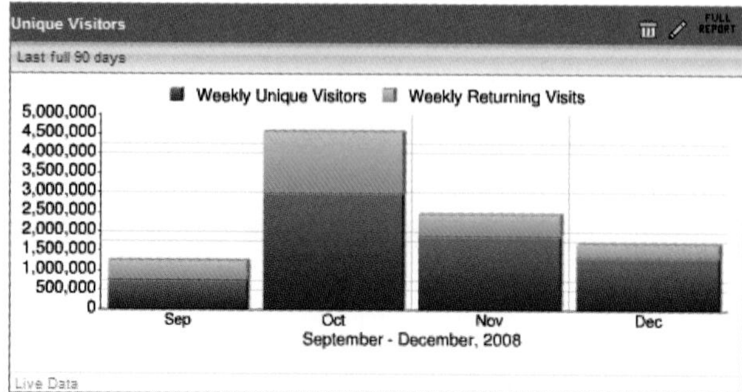

Total Inquiries

This month vs. Same partial month last month

Action: Any inquiry	16,610 ↓	19,833
Conversion rate: Any inquiry	0.95% ↓	1.03%
Action: Create Profile Confirmation	8,113 ↓	10,252
Conversion rate: 06 Create Profile Confirmation	0.46% ↓	0.53%
Action: Contact Us Confirmation	5,396 ↓	6,205
Conversion rate: Contact Us Confirmation	0.31% ↓	0.32%

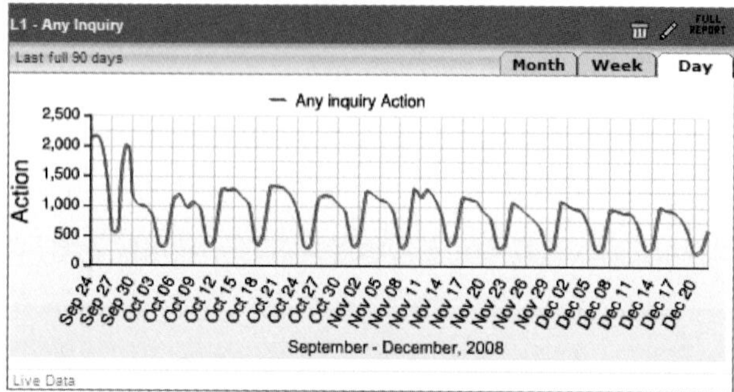

GOAL

This month

Action Any inquiry	0	16,610	7,000
Action Create Profile Confirmation	0	8,113	8,000
Action Contact Us Confirmation	0	5,396	8,000

Live Data

Inquiry by Traffic Source

This month

Traffic Sources (Intelligent)	Visits	Action	Conversion
Direct access or bookmark	774,046	7,352	0.95%
Organic search	524,220	5,258	1.00%
Other referrals	364,732	3,371	0.92%
Paid search	56,709	454	0.80%
Other campaigns	29,260	175	0.60%
Total	1,748,967	16,610	0.95%

Live Data

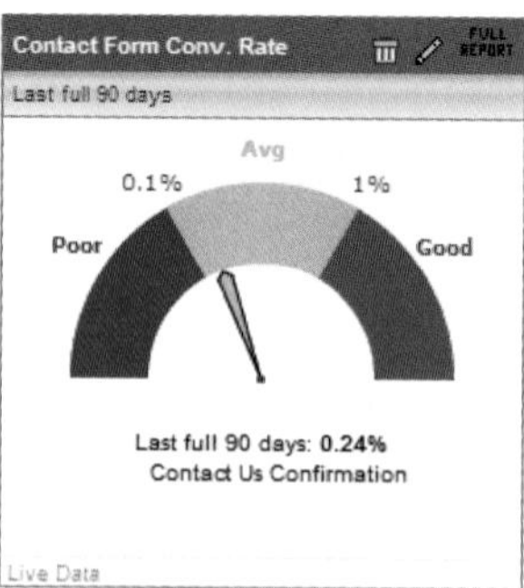

Conversion Dashboard Yahoo! Web Analytics

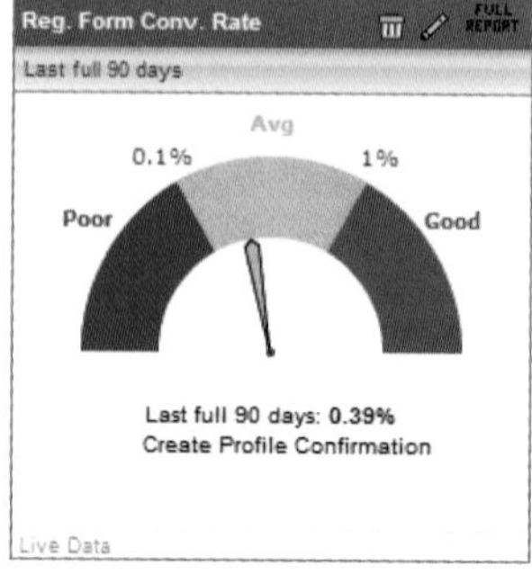

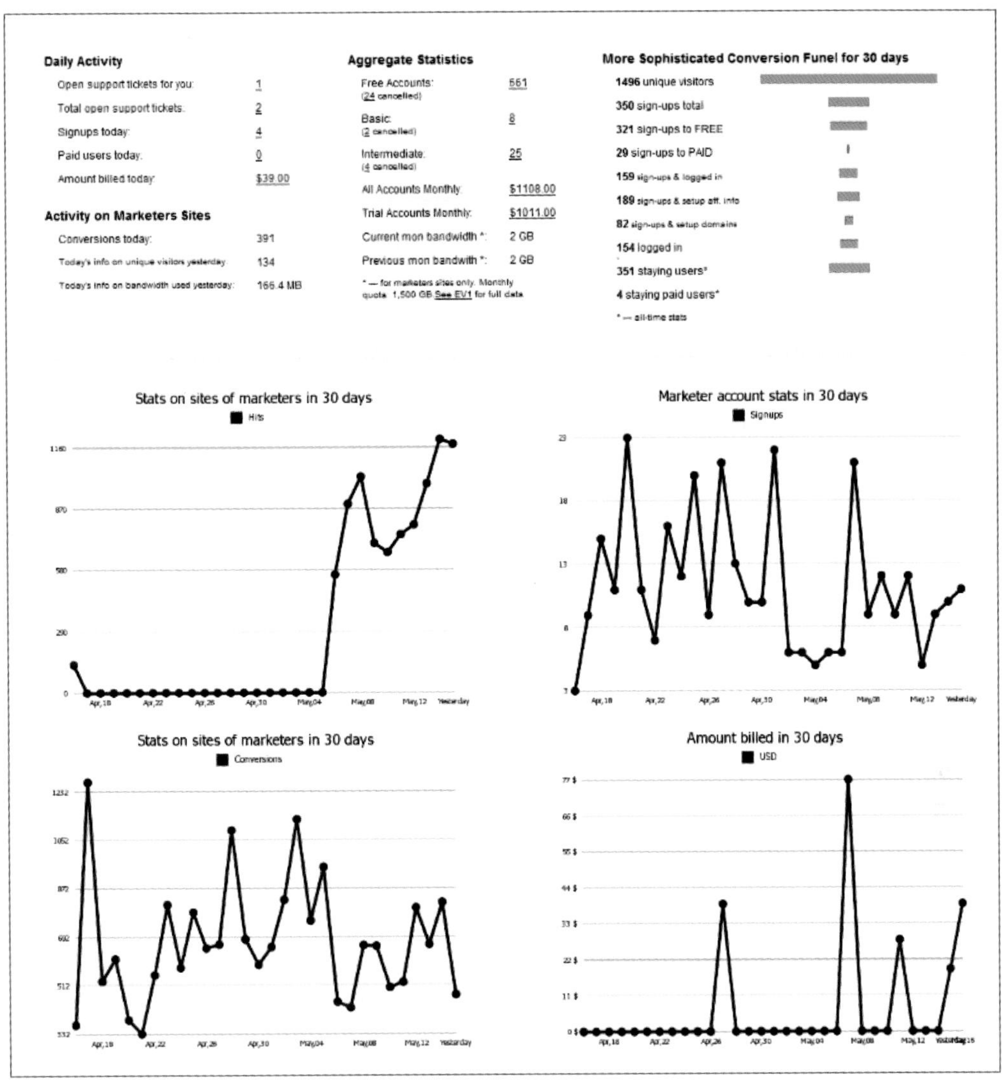

Affiliate Performance Dashboard This dashboard provides at-a-glance data into the daily affiliate performance. It tracks the visits and conversions on affiliate sites over trailing 30 days. It also tracks the number of new signups and the amount billed each day. A conversion funnel tracks the user's journey from Visits to Signups for Free and Paid Accounts, Paying User, and finally to Staying User. It shows the active support tickets for any administrator.

Chris Schultz, Voodoo Ventures, LLC

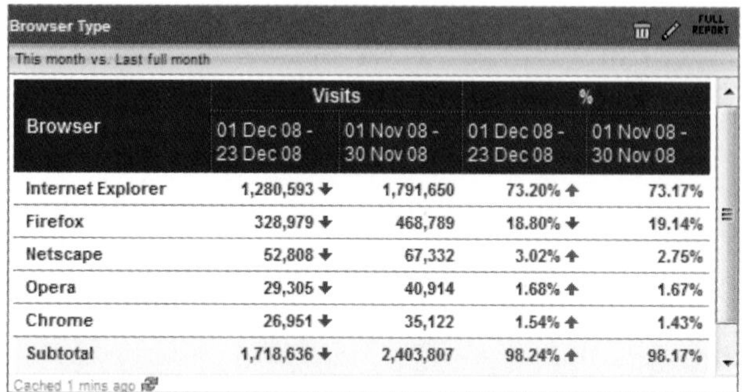

Browser Type
This month vs. Last full month

Browser	Visits 01 Dec 08 - 23 Dec 08	Visits 01 Nov 08 - 30 Nov 08	% 01 Dec 08 - 23 Dec 08	% 01 Nov 08 - 30 Nov 08
Internet Explorer	1,280,593 ↓	1,791,650	73.20% ↑	73.17%
Firefox	328,979 ↓	468,789	18.80% ↓	19.14%
Netscape	52,808 ↓	67,332	3.02% ↑	2.75%
Opera	29,305 ↓	40,914	1.68% ↑	1.67%
Chrome	26,951 ↓	35,122	1.54% ↑	1.43%
Subtotal	1,718,636 ↓	2,403,807	98.24% ↑	98.17%

Cached 1 mins ago

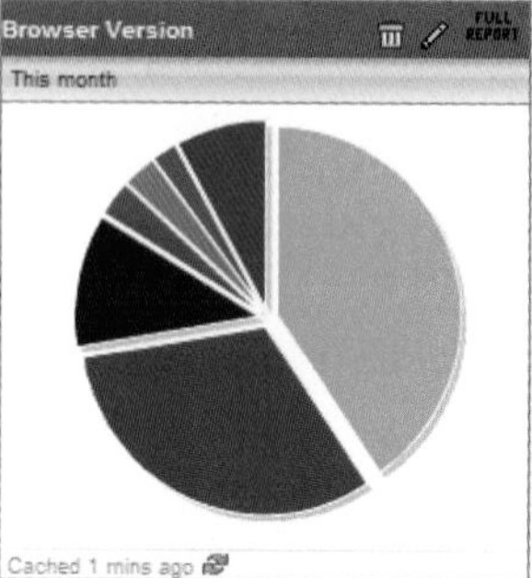

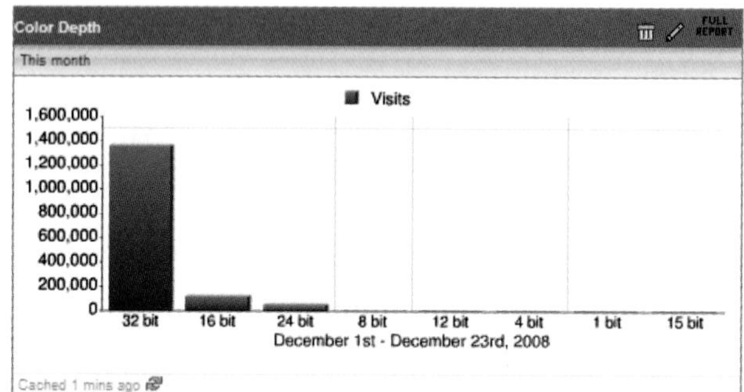

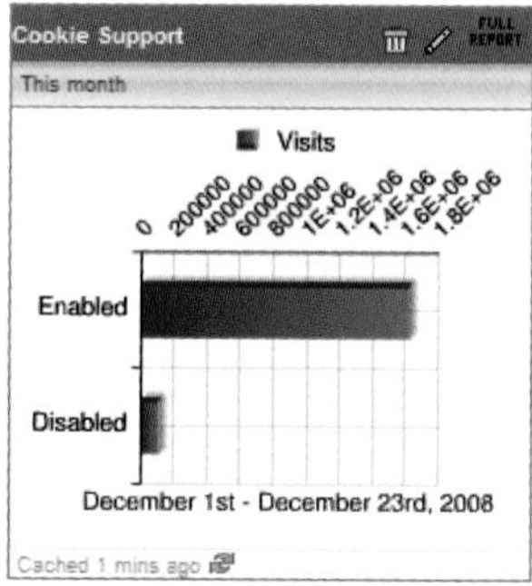

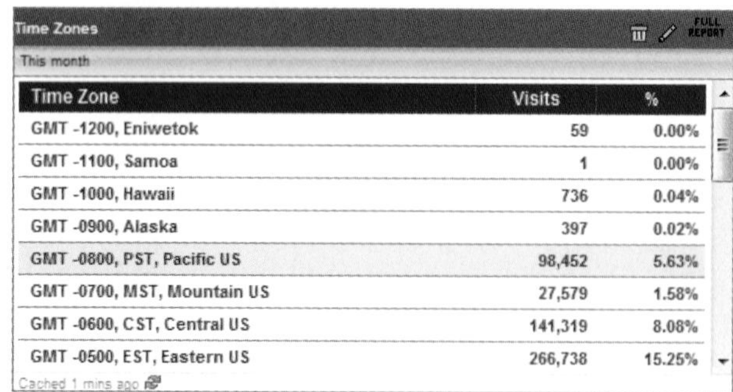

Time Zones
This month

Time Zone	Visits	%
GMT -1200, Eniwetok	59	0.00%
GMT -1100, Samoa	1	0.00%
GMT -1000, Hawaii	736	0.04%
GMT -0900, Alaska	397	0.02%
GMT -0800, PST, Pacific US	98,452	5.63%
GMT -0700, MST, Mountain US	27,579	1.58%
GMT -0600, CST, Central US	141,319	8.08%
GMT -0500, EST, Eastern US	266,738	15.25%

Cached 1 mins ago

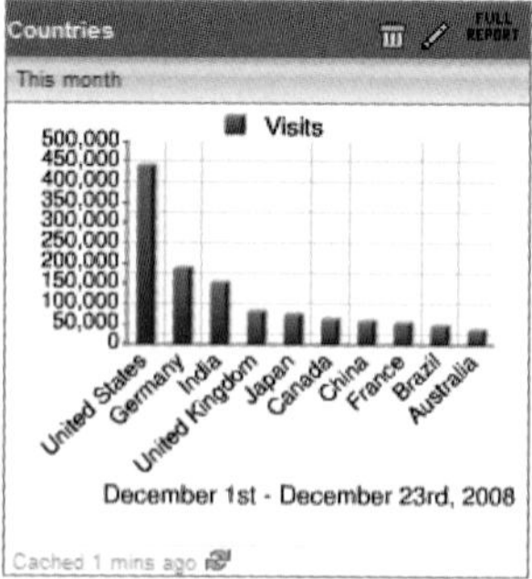

Demographic Dashboard Yahoo! Web Analytics

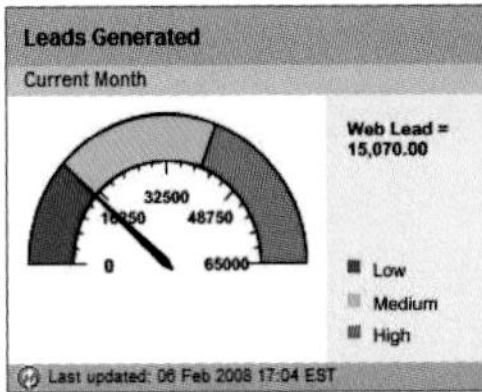

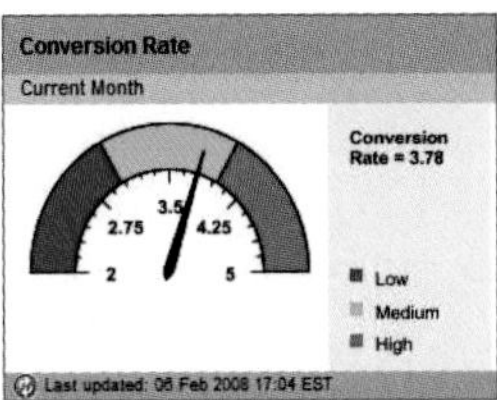

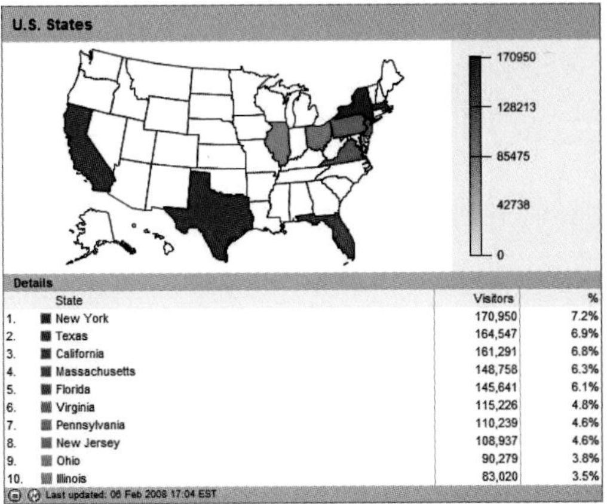

Details

	State	Visitors	%
1.	New York	170,950	7.2%
2.	Texas	164,547	6.9%
3.	California	161,291	6.8%
4.	Massachusetts	148,758	6.3%
5.	Florida	145,641	6.1%
6.	Virginia	115,226	4.8%
7.	Pennsylvania	110,239	4.6%
8.	New Jersey	108,937	4.6%
9.	Ohio	90,279	3.8%
10.	Illinois	83,020	3.5%

Last updated: 06 Feb 2008 17:04 EST

Conversion Rate

Last 12 months

Details

	Date	Selected Period
1.	Feb 2007	4.14%
2.	Mar 2007	4.34%
3.	Apr 2007	4.37%
4.	May 2007	4.38%
5.	Jun 2007	4.36%
6.	Jul 2007	4.55%
7.	Aug 2007	4.41%
8.	Sep 2007	4.43%
9.	Oct 2007	4.34%
10.	Nov 2007	4.12%
11.	Dec 2007	3.97%
12.	Jan 2008	3.99%
	Total	n/a

Last updated: 06 Feb 2008 17:04 EST

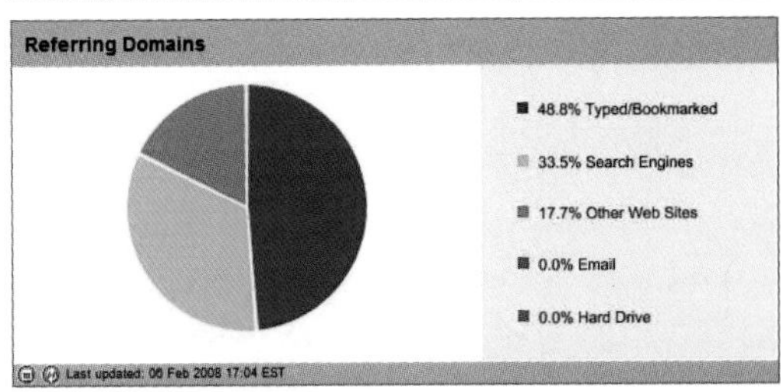

Monthly Unique Visitors

Details

	Date	Selected Period
1.	Feb 2007	1,413,665
2.	Mar 2007	1,499,226
3.	Apr 2007	1,418,191
4.	May 2007	1,517,651
5.	Jun 2007	1,453,907
6.	Jul 2007	1,533,546
7.	Aug 2007	1,561,974
8.	Sep 2007	1,473,793
9.	Oct 2007	1,538,978
10.	Nov 2007	1,477,683
11.	Dec 2007	1,449,392
12.	Jan 2008	1,700,677
	Total	18,038,683

Last updated: 06 Feb 2008 17:04 EST

Natural Search Engines

	Natural Search Engine	February 2... Searches		February 2... Searches		Change	
1.	Google	384,996	68.9%	114,873	70.2%	-270,123	-70.2%
2.	Yahoo!	84,746	15.2%	24,309	14.9%	-60,437	-71.3%
3.	MSN	52,287	9.4%	7,395	4.5%	-44,892	-85.9%
4.	AOL.com Search	13,357	2.4%	3,589	2.2%	-9,768	-73.1%
5.	Live.com	6,954	1.2%	4,071	2.5%	-2,883	-41.5%
6.	Ask Jeeves	4,717	0.8%	1,687	1.0%	-3,030	-64.2%
7.	Google - Canada	3,153	0.6%	4,736	2.9%	1,583	50.2%
8.	MyWay.com	2,614	0.5%	372	0.2%	-2,242	-85.8%
9.	Netscape Search	2,068	0.4%	521	0.3%	-1,547	-74.8%
10.	Google - United Kingdom	813	0.1%	234	0.1%	-579	-71.2%
	Total	559,067		163,553			

Last updated: 06 Feb 2008 17:04 EST

Web Leads

Details

	Date	Selected Period
1.	Feb 2007	75,112
2.	Mar 2007	83,870
3.	Apr 2007	79,997
4.	May 2007	86,238
5.	Jun 2007	82,331
6.	Jul 2007	91,884
7.	Aug 2007	91,081
8.	Sep 2007	85,505
9.	Oct 2007	88,029
10.	Nov 2007	79,458
11.	Dec 2007	74,784
12.	Jan 2008	89,202
	Total	1,007,491

Last updated: 06 Feb 2008 17:04 EST

Top Keywords

	Paid Search Keyword	Searches ▼	%
1.	used cars	10,280	1.6%
2.	used cars for sale	4,697	0.7%
3.	dodge charger	4,321	0.7%
4.	honda civic	3,725	0.6%
5.	tucson dodge	3,505	0.5%
6.	willey honda	2,621	0.4%
7.	dodge trucks	2,600	0.4%
8.	rick case acura	2,513	0.4%
9.	honda accord	2,506	0.4%
10.	metro honda	2,443	0.4%
	Total	658,548	

Last updated: 06 Feb 2008 17:04 EST

Lead Generation Dashboard Omniture SiteCatalyst

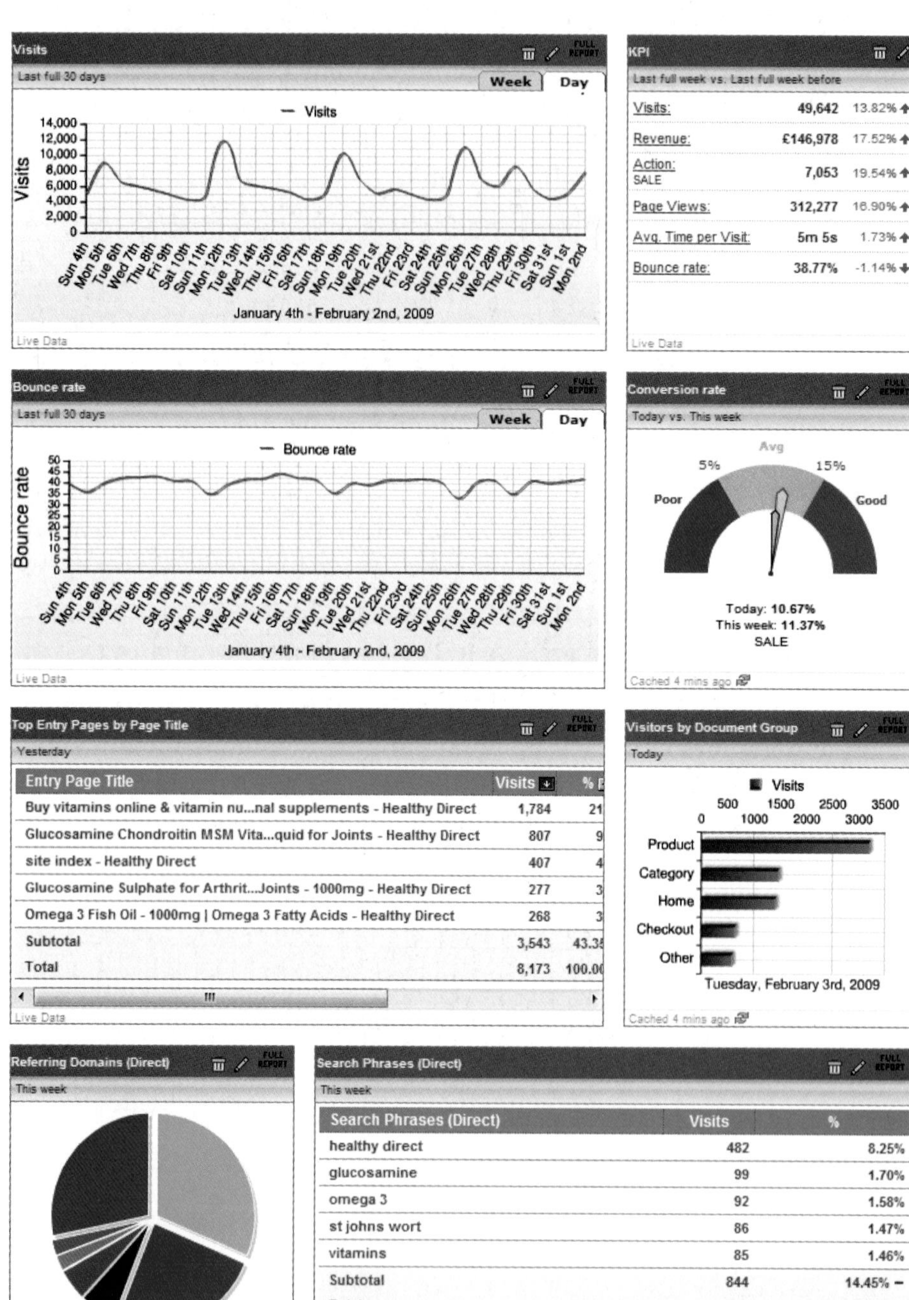

Global Traffic Dashboard Carl Rowlands, Yahoo! Service Engineer, using Yahoo! Web Analytics

Handling Alerts

As I recommended with color coding, only set up alerts that you plan to take action on. Before you set your alerts, have a clear set of processes in place for handling an alert. These processes might include:

- Closing a campaign down
- Flagging a campaign for optimization
- Asking the web optimization team to explain why the average time spent on site declined more than 20 percent last month

The alert triggers only deal with positives and negatives. You can use an absolute number—such as the number of visits above 2,500, as you saw in Figure 7.2—or an increase, defined as an absolute number or percentage. You can define an increase as more than 500 visits or more than 10 percent, for example.

Just as with color coding, remember that this is an alert service, so if you receive 10 alerts a day but do not act on them, you might as well not receive any alerts at all. So think hard about where to set the triggers, and you should not be afraid to adjust them later.

You can practice by first applying a number so low that the alert is triggered immediately, as shown in Figure 7.3. That way, you receive an email and confirm that the trigger is working properly before applying the final number.

Once your triggers are saved—and I am sure you can envision a scenario where you have dozens and dozens of alerts running around the system checking metrics—you will need a way to see what alerts you have running. Begin by choosing Settings > Scheduled Email Reports > Setup Alerts, as shown in Figure 7.4.

Trigger alert if
☑ Visits is above 200.0
Alert triggered!
☐ Visits is below 0.0
☐ Visits has increased by 0.0
☐ Visits has decreased by 0.0
☐ Visits has increased by 0.0 %
☐ Visits has decreased by 0.0 %

Figure 7.3 Testing this alert

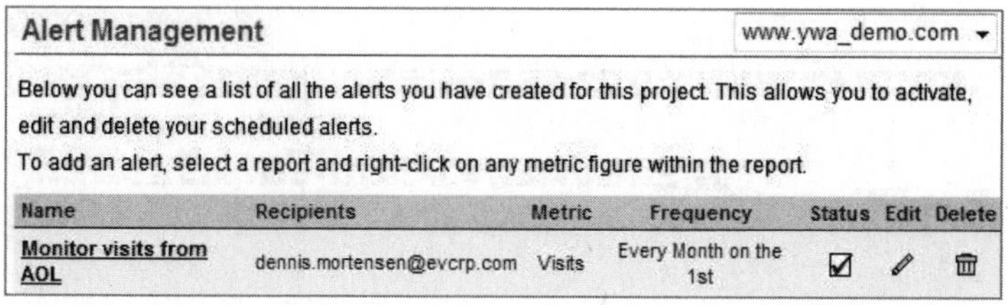

Alert Management www.ywa_demo.com

Below you can see a list of all the alerts you have created for this project. This allows you to activate, edit and delete your scheduled alerts.
To add an alert, select a report and right-click on any metric figure within the report.

Name	Recipients	Metric	Frequency	Status	Edit	Delete
Monitor visits from AOL	dennis.mortensen@evcrp.com	Visits	Every Month on the 1st	☑		

Figure 7.4 Alert management

All this alert chatter and setup leaves you with one task, which is for you to go fetch a diet soda, sit back, and relax and wait for an alert email. Until that happens, everything is supposedly cool.

The alert email is simple and does the job, even though it is not nicely designed (see Figure 7.5).

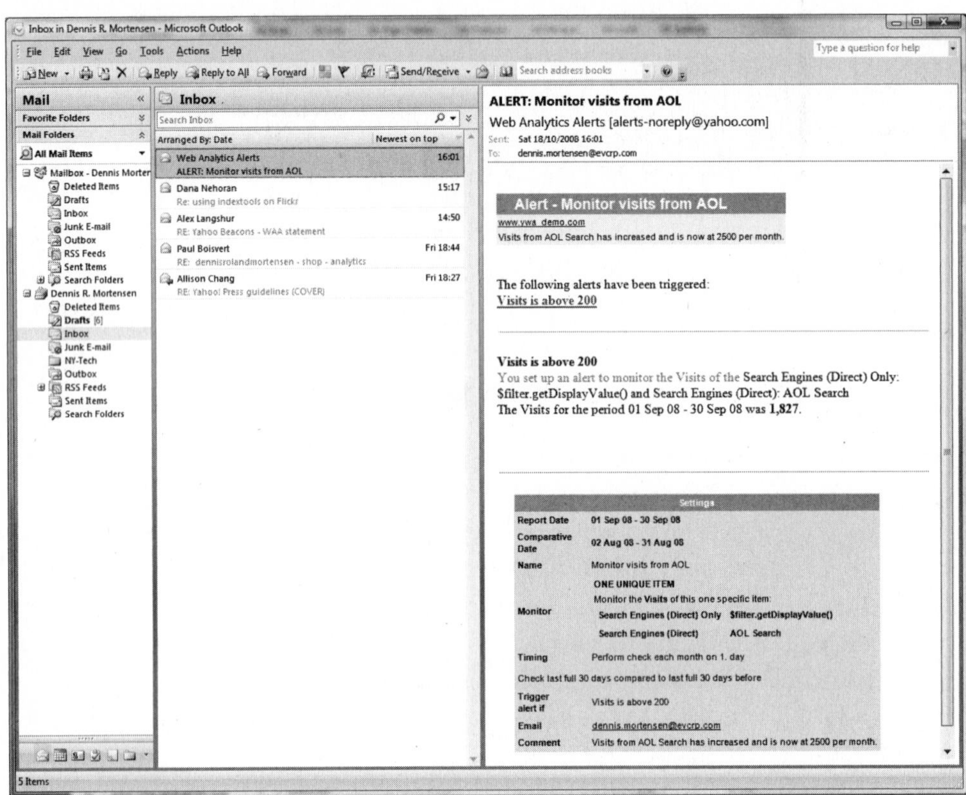

Figure 7.5 Alert email

Event Management

Event management is administered the same way as alerts, but it is a completely different animal. The Event Management feature allows you to keep track of events that might impact your website's metrics, such as website changes, public holidays, marketing campaigns, or system outages. This feature enables you to schedule these events and examine their effects on your website. For example, you can schedule a website change and then compare the metrics before and after the change took place.

Unlike alerts, you do not right-click metrics but instead right-click a dimension, such as a date or a page title, as shown in Figure 7.6.

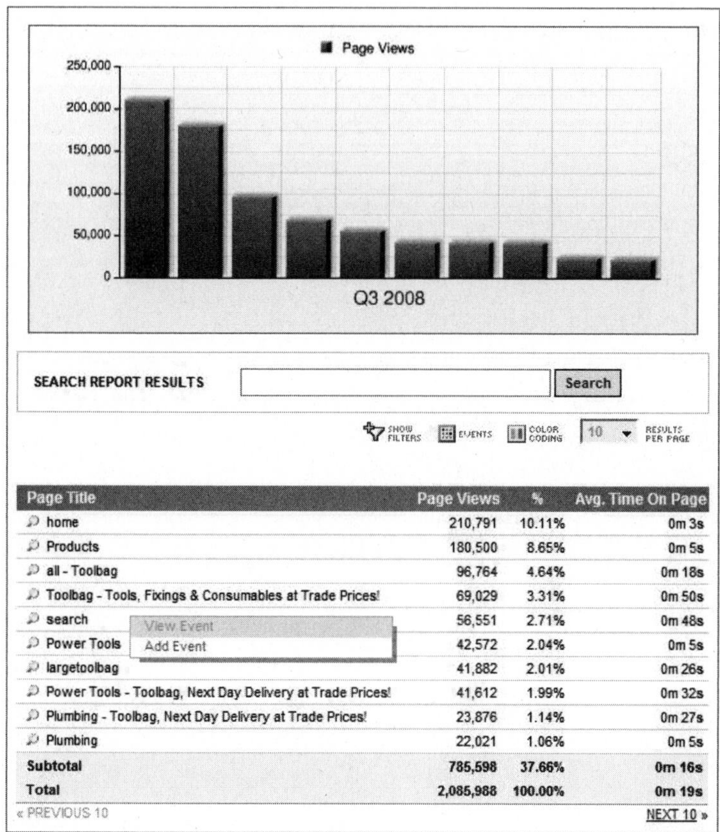

Page Title	Page Views	%	Avg. Time On Page
home	210,791	10.11%	0m 3s
Products	180,500	8.65%	0m 5s
all - Toolbag	96,764	4.64%	0m 18s
Toolbag - Tools, Fixings & Consumables at Trade Prices!	69,029	3.31%	0m 50s
search	56,551	2.71%	0m 48s
Power Tools	42,572	2.04%	0m 5s
largetoolbag	41,882	2.01%	0m 26s
Power Tools - Toolbag, Next Day Delivery at Trade Prices!	41,612	1.99%	0m 32s
Plumbing - Toolbag, Next Day Delivery at Trade Prices!	23,876	1.14%	0m 27s
Plumbing	22,021	1.06%	0m 5s
Subtotal	**785,598**	**37.66%**	**0m 16s**
Total	**2,085,988**	**100.00%**	**0m 19s**

Figure 7.6 View Existing Event or Add New Event

Events are more about adding informational value to your data points and less about driving your attention to a specific report or metric. A word of caution: As in any other informational system, too much information results in no information at all.

You can easily add 40 public holidays for your main markets and at the same time add 40 website-wide changes without poisoning the system. Remember that you have time working on your behalf, because events like holidays have a definite start and end time. You can set any event to begin and expire on particular dates, as shown in Figure 7.7.

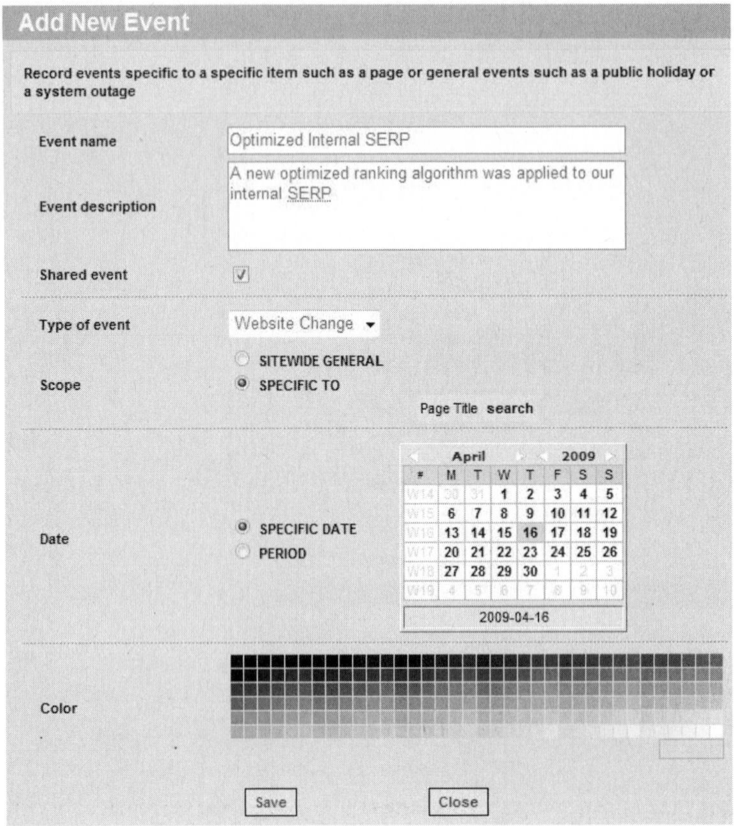

Add New Event

Record events specific to a specific item such as a page or general events such as a public holiday or a system outage

Event name: Optimized Internal SERP

Event description: A new optimized ranking algorithm was applied to our internal SERP

Shared event

Type of event: Website Change

Scope: SITEWIDE GENERAL / SPECIFIC TO — Page Title search

Date: SPECIFIC DATE / PERIOD — April 2009 — 2009-04-16

Color

Save Close

Figure 7.7 Edit or Add New Event dialog

When you edit or add new events, be sure to include an accurate event name and detailed description, but most of all, think about how you will define the type of event, scope, and date:

Type of Event The two choices of Holiday or Website Change are a bit limited, but I expect Yahoo! to expand on this. Type of Event is mostly for classification only and has no impact on the event or data comparison done on the event.

Scope You can create both sitewide and site-specific events for the Most Requested Pages and the Entry Pages reports and so on, whereas for other reports where you are not looking at specific pages, you can only create sitewide events.

Date Apply the date or date range when this event is active so that you and other system users are able to see events that are within the reporting period.

Activate a new event by clicking the Events icon just below the chart area, which will expand an area showing the active event for the period in question (see Figure 7.8).

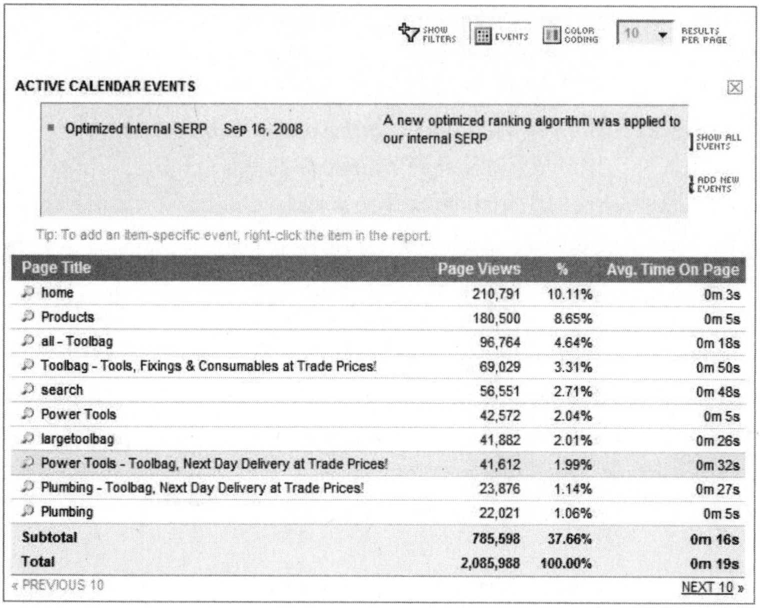

SHOW FILTERS | EVENTS | COLOR CODING | 10 | RESULTS PER PAGE

ACTIVE CALENDAR EVENTS

- Optimized Internal SERP Sep 16, 2008 A new optimized ranking algorithm was applied to our internal SERP

SHOW ALL EVENTS

ADD NEW EVENTS

Tip: To add an item-specific event, right-click the item in the report.

Page Title	Page Views	%	Avg. Time On Page
home	210,791	10.11%	0m 3s
Products	180,500	8.65%	0m 5s
all - Toolbag	96,764	4.64%	0m 18s
Toolbag - Tools, Fixings & Consumables at Trade Prices!	69,029	3.31%	0m 50s
search	56,551	2.71%	0m 48s
Power Tools	42,572	2.04%	0m 5s
largetoolbag	41,882	2.01%	0m 26s
Power Tools - Toolbag, Next Day Delivery at Trade Prices!	41,612	1.99%	0m 32s
Plumbing - Toolbag, Next Day Delivery at Trade Prices!	23,876	1.14%	0m 27s
Plumbing	22,021	1.06%	0m 5s
Subtotal	**785,598**	**37.66%**	**0m 16s**
Total	**2,085,988**	**100.00%**	**0m 19s**

« PREVIOUS 10 NEXT 10 »

Figure 7.8 Active Calendar Events screen

It's easy to understand when and why you would use the specific date option, such as for a holiday, but it might be a bit more confusing when an event spans multiple dates. You might have a three-week product launch, which includes a period of launch activities that all contributes to increased site traffic. Suppose you want to mark all three weeks as out of the ordinary and you would like to analyze the effect based not on the starting date of this period but on the end date.

You probably noticed that you can choose whether the event is shared, which means all users can see it, or not shared, which means only you can see it. This is an opportunity, and a great one, for you to ensure that you do not clutter the system with information that holds no value for people other than you.

As with alerts, I am sure you can envision a scenario where you have dozens and dozens of events in the system. You will need a way to see what events you have. Choose Settings > Set Calendar Events to open the screen shown in Figure 7.9.

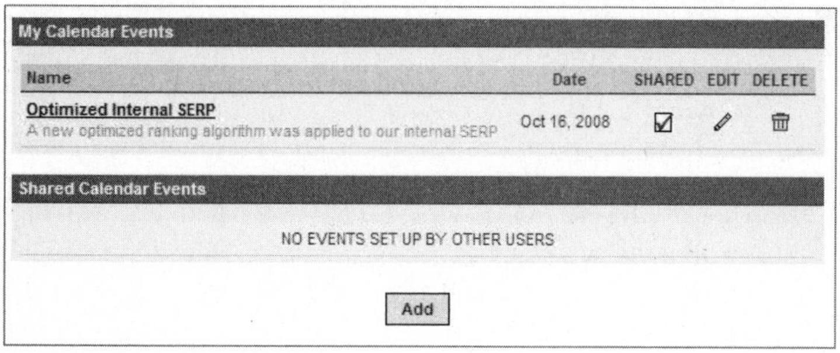

My Calendar Events

Name	Date	SHARED	EDIT	DELETE
Optimized Internal SERP A new optimized ranking algorithm was applied to our internal SERP	Oct 16, 2008	☑		

Shared Calendar Events

NO EVENTS SET UP BY OTHER USERS

Add

Figure 7.9 Managing event settings

Beyond the obvious value of having good event information in your system for yourself and others to use as a backbone for some of your data insights and general interpretations, you can use events as a shortcut. You can click any active event and quickly do an analysis of the effects before and after the dates in question, as shown in Figure 7.10.

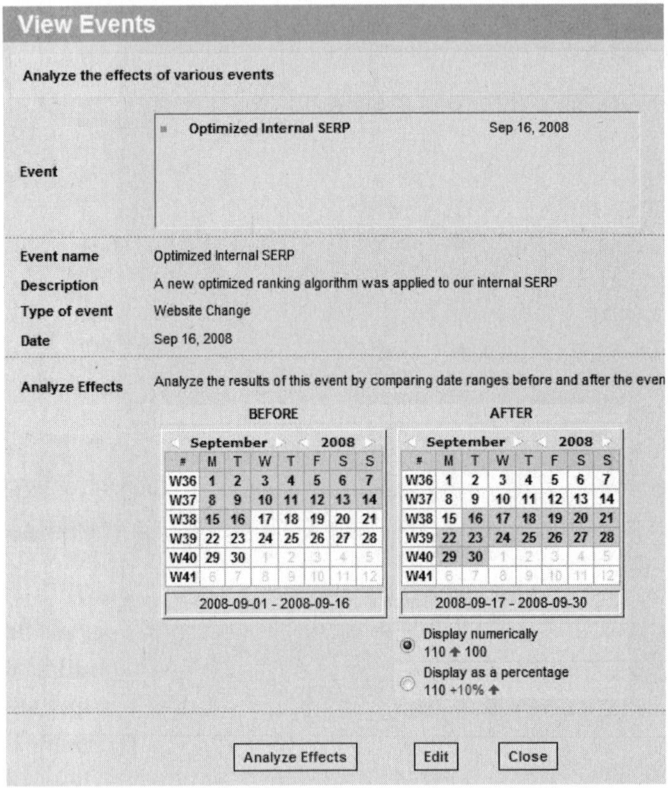

Figure 7.10 Viewing and analyzing the effect of an event

As you might have spotted, this is essentially a way to do a comparison directly from within the event report system. Remember from Chapter 6 that you could have done the comparison simply by using the Compare feature. Figure 7.11 shows the result of a comparison from within an event pop-up.

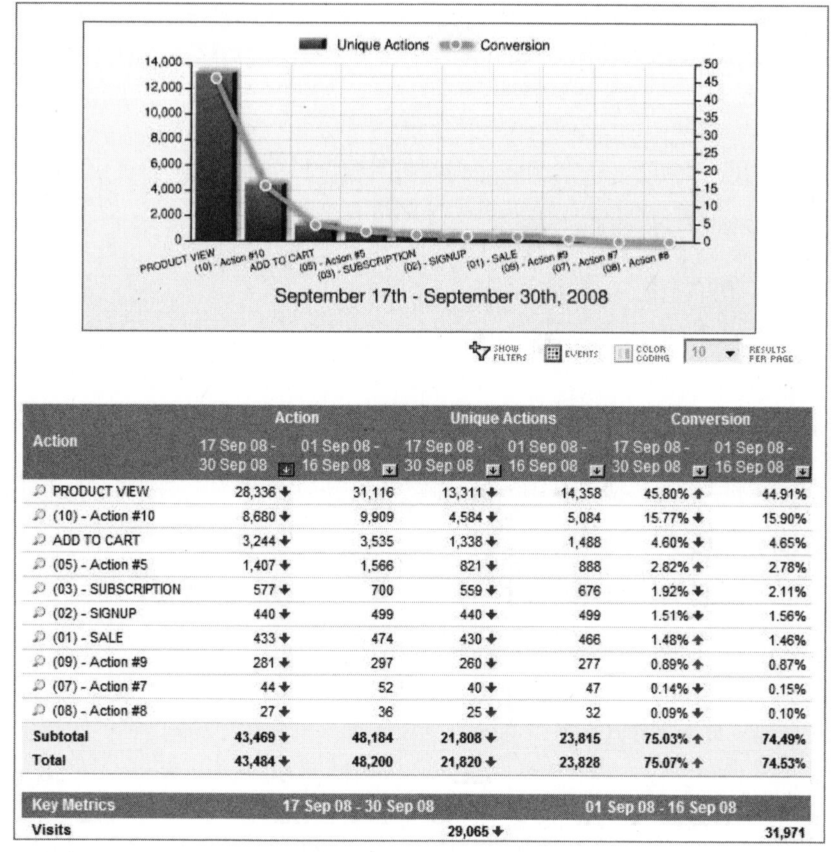

Action	Action		Unique Actions		Conversion	
	17 Sep 08 - 30 Sep 08	01 Sep 08 - 16 Sep 08	17 Sep 08 - 30 Sep 08	01 Sep 08 - 16 Sep 08	17 Sep 08 - 30 Sep 08	01 Sep 08 - 16 Sep 08
PRODUCT VIEW	28,336 ↓	31,116	13,311 ↓	14,358	45.80% ↑	44.91%
(10) - Action #10	8,680 ↓	9,909	4,584 ↓	5,084	15.77% ↓	15.90%
ADD TO CART	3,244 ↓	3,535	1,338 ↓	1,488	4.60% ↓	4.65%
(05) - Action #5	1,407 ↓	1,566	821 ↓	888	2.82% ↑	2.78%
(03) - SUBSCRIPTION	577 ↓	700	559 ↓	676	1.92% ↓	2.11%
(02) - SIGNUP	440 ↓	499	440 ↓	499	1.51% ↓	1.56%
(01) - SALE	433 ↓	474	430 ↓	466	1.48% ↑	1.46%
(09) - Action #9	281 ↓	297	260 ↓	277	0.89% ↑	0.87%
(07) - Action #7	44 ↓	52	40 ↓	47	0.14% ↓	0.15%
(08) - Action #8	27 ↓	36	25 ↓	32	0.09% ↓	0.10%
Subtotal	**43,469 ↓**	**48,184**	**21,808 ↓**	**23,815**	**75.03% ↑**	**74.49%**
Total	**43,484 ↓**	**48,200**	**21,820 ↓**	**23,828**	**75.07% ↑**	**74.53%**

Key Metrics	17 Sep 08 - 30 Sep 08	01 Sep 08 - 16 Sep 08
Visits	**29,065 ↓**	**31,971**

Figure 7.11 The result of a comparison from within an event pop-up

Using Scheduled Reports

Communicating the results of your reporting can be done in multiples ways:

- Provide a login and password and thus provide direct access to the Yahoo! Web Analytics application for your users.
- Color-code the information for better interpretation.
- Have metric alert services running so that when certain thresholds are exceeded you are warned.
- Set up report notes on how to interpret the report.
- Create and display events within the reports.
- Set up specific reports to be emailed to users on a recurring schedule.

Depending on the situation, sending out custom-designed, scheduled email reports may be one of the strongest ways of communicating information on a recurring basis. Another is using user rights management and giving access to a preset dashboard only. Managing user rights is described in general terms at the end of this chapter; its application to dashboards is covered in Chapter 9, "Using Dashboards."

Note: As with alerts, it is so simple to set up scheduled email reports that you may be tempted to overcommunicate or communicate without enough interpretation. Recipients can unsubscribe to the emails. If this happens, that is a strong sign that you are sending the wrong information or that you are sending too many emails.

You access the Scheduled Reports screen, shown in Figure 7.12, by choosing Settings > Scheduled Email Reports > Customize and Schedule Reports for Email Delivery. This screen lets you add and manage your scheduled emails, each with multiple reports and recipients.

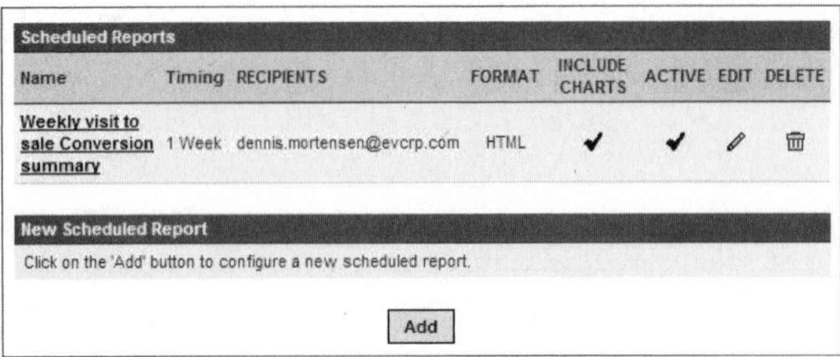

Figure 7.12 Scheduled Reports screen

The settings include simple properties such as the name and description and who is supposed to receive the report. The most important options are:

Timing Most email marketers have done research on timing scheduled reports. Reviewing that research is beyond the scope of this book, but as an example, imagine that the agenda for the weekly Wednesday marketing meeting goes out a day before the meeting. The data that serves as backup for the decisions to be made at the meeting could be emailed at the same time as the agenda. Make sure that the recipients are only those who attend the meeting and that the report title identifies the report as support material for the agenda.

Reporting Period Continuing our example, you can set the reporting period to the same time period as the one discussed in the meeting, such as last week's results, or what Yahoo! Web Analytics would call Last Full Week.

Format The reporting format is again almost as important as the timing. First, choose whether you want to communicate results (in HTML or PDF) or data (as an Excel or CSV file). I am a bigger fan of sending HTML, simply due to the fact that people can cut copy and paste it into other media as part of their meeting preparations.

Figure 7.13 shows the Scheduled Report Settings screen.

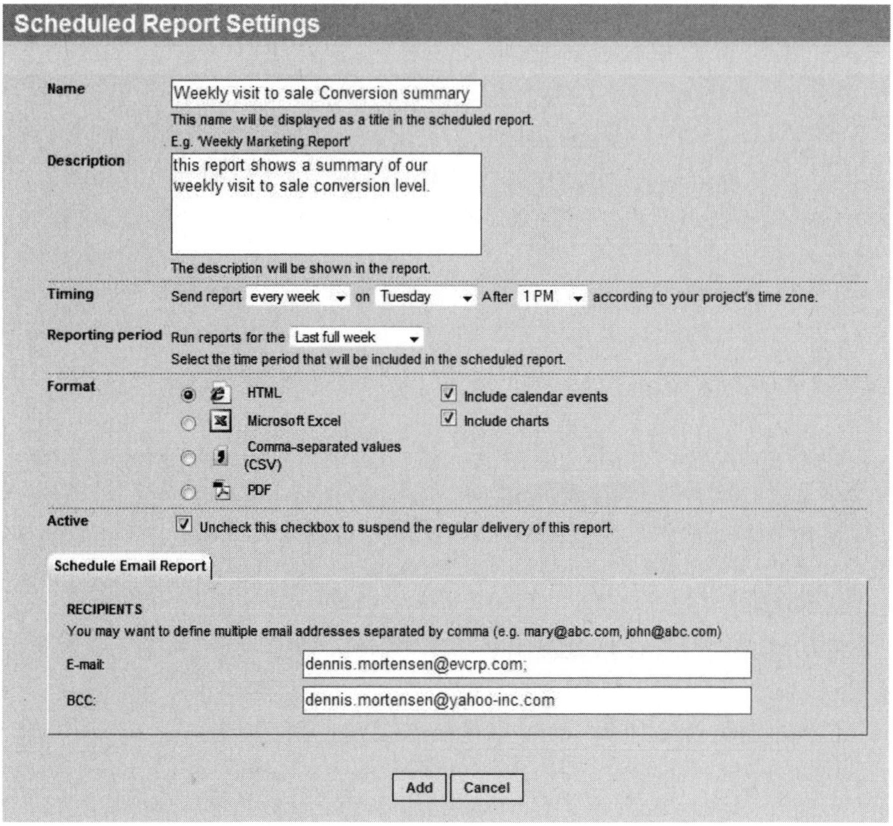

Figure 7.13 Scheduled Report Settings

You can add a number of reports to the scheduled email (see Figure 7.14). All the standard reports are available, but the most important fact is that you can choose custom-built reports, which is definitely the road to take.

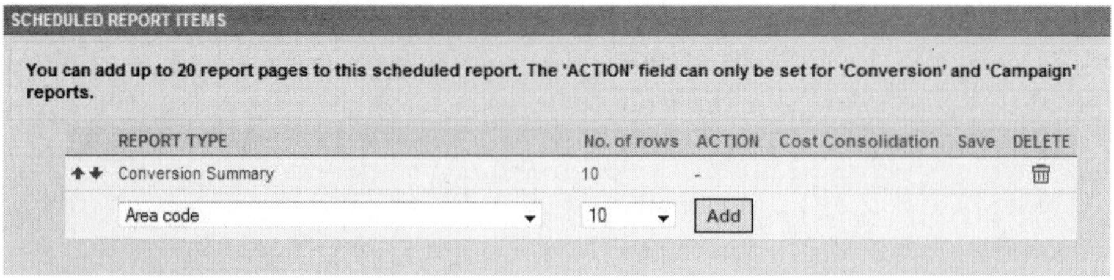

Figure 7.14 Scheduled Report Items screen

As with alerts, you can check to see how the emails look. Figure 7.15 shows how to choose a calendar date to create a test email.

Figure 7.16 is an example of a scheduled email report.

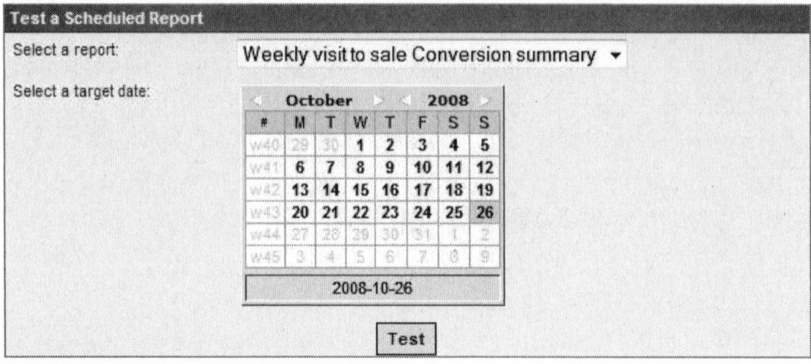

Figure 7.15 Test a Scheduled Report screen

Scheduled Report - www.ywa demo.com - Weekly visit to sale Conversion summary

noreply@yahoo.com

Sent: Sun 26/10/2008 13:01

To: dennis.mortensen@evcrp.com

Weekly visit to sale Conversion summary
www.ywa demo.com

Description	this report shows a summary of our weekly visit to sale conversion level.
EMAIL	dennis.mortensen@evcrp.com
Timing	Oct 12, 2008 - Oct 18, 2008

CONVERSION SUMMARY - www.ywa_demo.com

This report lists all action occurrences and corresponding conversion rates for the selected period. Use this report to understand how well your visitors respond to various calls-to-action on your web site and what you can do to increase their propensity to convert.

Action	Action	Unique Actions	Conversion
PRODUCT VIEW	14,234	6,755	46.34%
(10) - Action #10	4,219	2,304	15.80%
ADD TO CART	1,557	664	4.55%
(05) - Action #5	709	396	2.72%
(03) - SUBSCRIPTION	235	231	1.58%
(02) - SIGNUP	219	219	1.50%
(01) - SALE	213	212	1.45%
(09) - Action #9	119	110	0.75%
(07) - Action #7	22	18	0.12%
(06) - Action #6	12	9	0.06%
Subtotal	21,539	10,918	74.89%
Total	21,545	10,923	74.93%

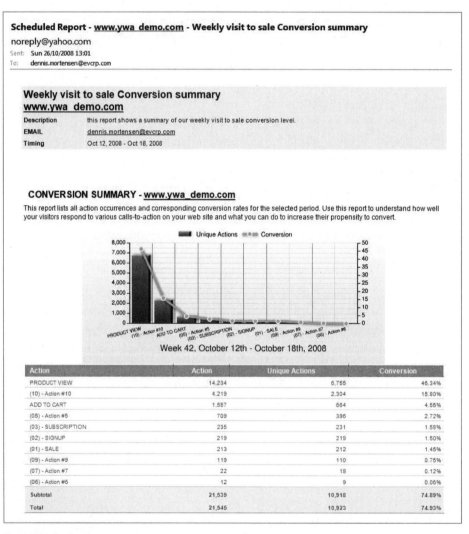

Figure 7.16 Email report

Finally, you can apply your company corporate identity to the email as a top-centered GIF or JPG file. Adding a logo can sometimes increase the perceived validity of the information and the number of people reading it. Figure 7.17 shows the screen where you can upload your logo.

Figure 7.17 Adding a company logo

As an alternative to emails, you can choose to have the reports uploaded to an FTP server on a scheduled basis. This is a data export functionality more than a scheduled email. For this to work, you have to have set up an FTP connection and use this select destination for your scheduled data transfers. Enter an email address that will be used in case of FTP upload error.

Building Custom Reports

Building custom reports and segmenting your data (discussed in the next section) are the two skills you need to reach the highest level of data analysis and professional polish in Yahoo! Web Analytics.

Most of the reports available in the system today can be customized, or you can build a completely new report from scratch. I tend to find the report that is closest to what I need and then mold that into the new report needed to answer my question. And if I am creating a report that is an answer to a recurring question, I will save it and then access the bookmarked report next time that question crops up.

You can access the Customize Report feature in two ways. Either click the Customize Report icon on the report header, or select Settings > Build Custom Reports. Either way you end up in the Custom Report Wizard. The only visible action is that, if you have multiple projects and are creating a brand-new report, you have to choose which project you want to build it for. This is preselected if you are already in a project report and start to customize it.

Looking at a simple report like the one shown in Figure 7.18, we might notice a trend or something out of the ordinary.

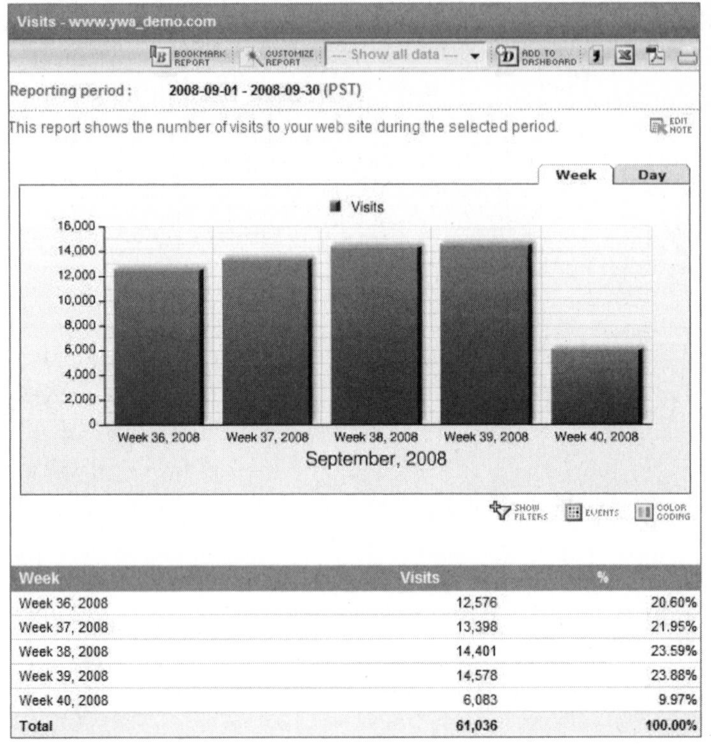

Week	Visits	%
Week 36, 2008	12,576	20.60%
Week 37, 2008	13,398	21.95%
Week 38, 2008	14,401	23.59%
Week 39, 2008	14,578	23.88%
Week 40, 2008	6,083	9.97%
Total	**61,036**	**100.00%**

Figure 7.18 Visits report

Suppose we want to know if increased traffic over the last weeks increased our revenue. To answer this question and to initiate an investigation, we should customize this report instead of hunting for a unique revenue visits report.

Clicking the Customize Report button at the top of the wizard screen opens the screen shown in Figure 7.19, which resembles a traditional pivot table and visually shows how the report was built so that you can continue from there. The table headers Visits and Visits % in the background resemble how the final report will look. The data under each of these headers is dynamically updated as you change the report.

Pivot Table

A pivot table is a data summarization feature found in data management and visualization applications, such as a spreadsheet like Microsoft Excel. Among other functions, this feature lets you automatically sort, count, and total the data stored in one table or spreadsheet and create a second table displaying the summarized data. Pivot tables are useful for quickly creating cross tabs. The user sets up and changes the summary's structure by dragging and dropping fields graphically. This "rotation," or pivoting of the summary table, gives the concept its name.

> **Cross Tabs**
>
> A cross tabulation displays the joint distribution of two or more variables. Variables are usually presented as a contingency table in a matrix format, as you will find it inside a spreadsheet. Whereas a frequency distribution provides the distribution of one variable, a contingency table describes the distribution of two or more variables simultaneously. Each cell shows the number of respondents who gave a specific combination of responses—that is, each cell contains a single cross tabulation.

Before we go into the magic of the Custom Report Wizard—which I am quite confident you can see already from Figure 7.19—let's outline its functioning. That way, you'll be aware of the basic limitations before the creation of magic begins.

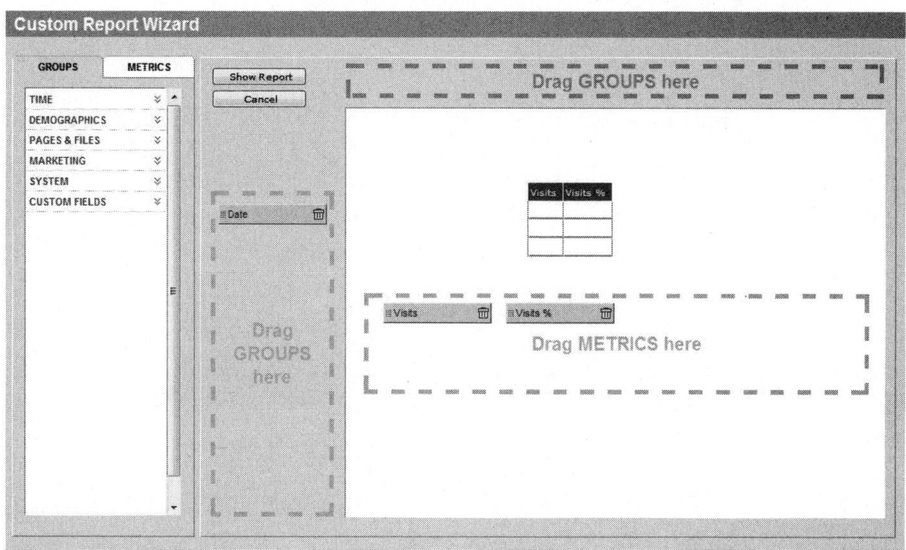

Figure 7.19 Custom Report Wizard

The Custom Report Wizard is based on pivot table technology, which allows you to drag and drop dimensions (groups) and metrics into a table for instant rendering. To use it, follow these steps:

1. To develop your custom report, drag groups and metrics into their respective dashed boxes. When dragging items across, you will notice that a black horizontal bar appears when you add a new item to the custom report. This bar illustrates the item's position after you drop it. In Figure 7.20, we've applied a Revenue metric to the visit report.
2. As soon as you drop a dimension (group) item or a metric, an example grid appears in the background, essentially creating an instant and real-time preview of how the report will look when you render it.

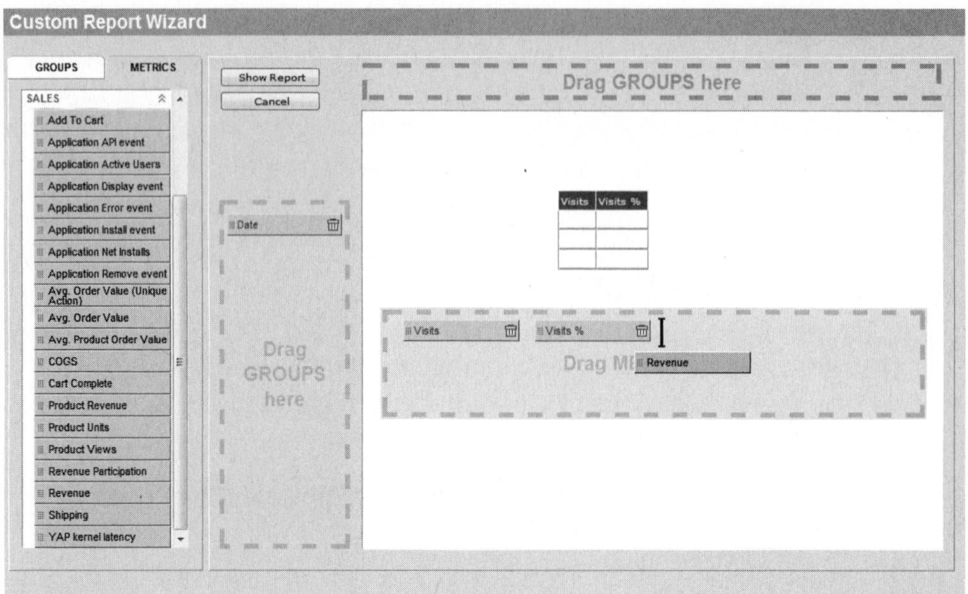

Figure 7.20 Custom Report Wizard: dragging in a new metric

3. Once you have added the dimensions, you can switch to metrics by clicking on the Metrics heading in the menu tree. Do the same as you did for dimensions, expanding the metrics menu tree and dragging and dropping the desired metrics into the metrics dashed box.
4. When you have added all the dimensions and metrics you are interested in, click the Show Report button.

Note that you cannot drag a dimension (group) menu item into a metric box, or vice versa. If an item is grayed out, you cannot use it in the report you are generating.

The Custom Report Wizard also allows you to change the order of the report group items or metrics just by moving them around. You can also delete a dimension or a metric by clicking the trashcan.

Clicking the Show Report button displays your custom report. And this is where it becomes sexy, as the report generation is done on the fly and not saved for later. You can easily play around with your data—true data porn!—and I would be surprised if you initially have the right report and instantly find the insight you are looking for. You should not be disappointed if you do 15 different custom report iterations to find your next piece of golden insight.

The custom reports can be bent in all the ways a normal report can. So you can apply any time period you want, apply comparative periods, apply segments and filters, export the data, or use it on a dashboard.

To save your custom report for future use, simply bookmark it, which you also need to do if you want to send it out as a scheduled email or use it on the dashboard.

Once you bookmark a custom report, it is saved in the Reports menu under Bookmarks. Bookmarking a custom report is useful because you do not have to generate the same custom report every time you need it, and you can access it the same way as you would select a standard report.

The results of the action in Figure 7.20 are shown in Figure 7.21.

Week	Visits	%	Revenue
Week 36, 2008	12,576	20.60%	$18,183.24
Week 37, 2008	13,398	21.95%	$22,777.36
Week 38, 2008	14,401	23.59%	$20,278.29
Week 39, 2008	14,578	23.88%	$20,706.84
Week 40, 2008	6,083	9.97%	$11,613.41
Total	**61,036**	**100.00%**	**$93,559.14**

« PREVIOUS 10 NEXT 10 »

Figure 7.21 Custom Report Wizard: report results

The report results reveal that the steady increase in traffic does not directly translate into a steady increase in revenue (note that week 40 was not a full week in Figure 7.18 and figure 7.21).

Beyond the dimensions shown on the left-hand side of the Custom Report Wizard, you have yet another opportunity: using grouping (shown at the top of the Custom Report Wizard). Let me illustrate the use of this with a set of example figures. I am sure you noticed by now that I use the words *groups* and *dimensions* interchangeably. The reason is that other tools and the industry in general would use the word *dimensions*, but Yahoo! chose to call them *groups*.

Figure 7.22 represents a standard out-of-the-box Visits per Search Engine report.

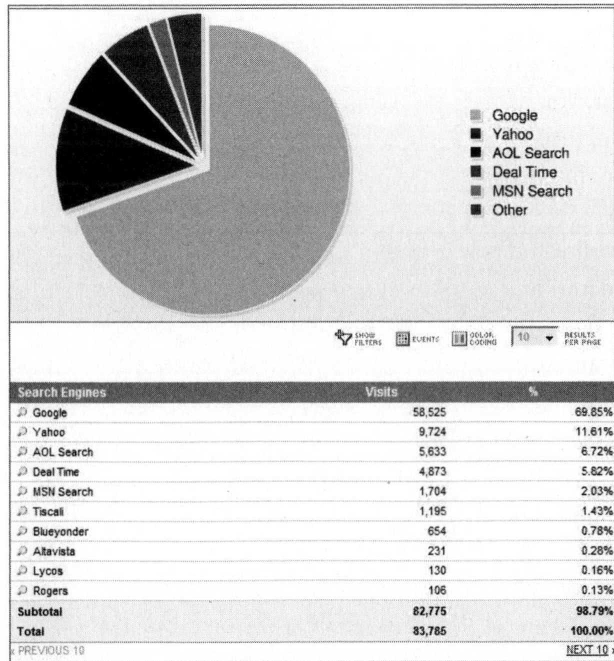

Search Engines	Visits	%
Google	58,525	69.85%
Yahoo	9,724	11.61%
AOL Search	5,633	6.72%
Deal Time	4,873	5.82%
MSN Search	1,704	2.03%
Tiscali	1,195	1.43%
Blueyonder	654	0.78%
Altavista	231	0.28%
Lycos	130	0.16%
Rogers	106	0.13%
Subtotal	**82,775**	**98.79%**
Total	**83,785**	**100.00%**

« PREVIOUS 10 NEXT 10 »

Figure 7.22 Search engine referrals

If we add yet another dimension, Search Phrase, to the Visits Per Search Engine report, as shown in the custom report in Figure 7.23, we'd see the custom report results in Figure 7.24.

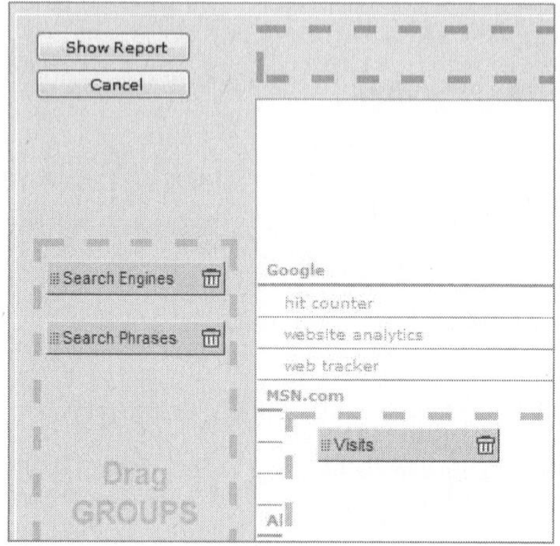

Figure 7.23 Custom Report Wizard on search engines and search phrases

Search Engines / Search Phrases	Visits
⊞ Google	58,525
⊟ Yahoo	9,724
power tools	634
toolbag	503
bathroom taps	259
jigsaws	197
bath taps	138

Figure 7.24 Custom report results on search engine referrals with added search phrases as a left group

A slightly different question, which I'll illustrate in Figures 7.25 and 7.26, is whether the distribution of search phrases differs from search engine to search engine. If so, which phrases occupy the top places in the distribution? Knowing the answer to this question would help you identify potential optimization opportunities. This report is a great example of how you can utilize the top groups.

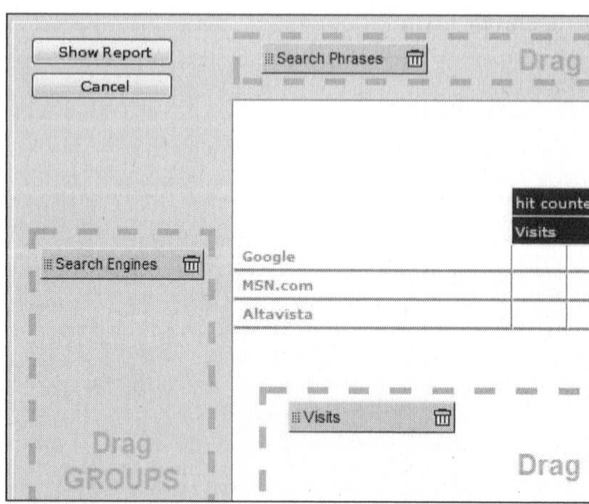

Figure 7.25 Custom Report Wizard on search engines and search phrases as a top group

Search Engines	toolbag Visits	power tools Visits	plumbing supplies Visits	tool bag Visits	bosch power tools Visits	tool bags Visits	thetoolbag.com Visits	toolbag Visi
Google	3,154	1,609	1,606	794	568	482	354	
Yahoo	503	634	25	61	0	31	98	
AOL Search	519	270	151	122	46	58	40	
Deal Time	0	5	0	0	0	0	0	
MSN Search	220	8	0	22	0	8	66	
Tiscali	70	46	33	9	23	9	25	
Blueyonder	28	30	8	14	13	9	16	
Altavista	24	4	0	0	0	5	0	
Lycos	8	9	0	0	0	0	0	
Rogers	0	0	0	0	0	0	0	
Subtotal	**4,526**	**2,615**	**1,823**	**1,022**	**650**	**602**	**599**	
Total	**4,539**	**2,619**	**1,832**	**1,022**	**654**	**607**	**603**	
« PREVIOUS 10								

Figure 7.26 Custom report results on search engine referrals with added search phrases as a top group

The results presented in Figure 7.26 let you immediately spot abnormalities. To begin with, any search phrases that return zero visits on one search engine while performing as top phrases on another engine should be a note in your to-do list for tomorrow.

If you look at the result set in Figure 7.26, you will notice that the search phrase "bosch power tools" is among the most popular search phrases on Google but creates zero visits on Yahoo!. Why is that? This should have been one of the most popular search phrases on Yahoo! as well, and if not, you need to figure out why that is.

As a final note, keep in mind that using top groups does not provide you with any additional data that you could not get by just applying the same dimension to the left-hand side. However, using top groups does allow you to quickly compare multiple dimensions at the same time.

Bookmarking Reports

I have repeatedly pitched the fact that the reports provided out of the box are merely templates and you should use them as starting points for something more insightful. With that sales pitch in mind, you need to be able to save your findings. Saving a custom report or any customization to a report is a functionality that Yahoo! calls *bookmarks*.

A custom report does not have to be advanced; it could just be an out-of-the-box report that you chose to sort differently. Or maybe you added a meaningful title for your organization. I am a big fan of being aggressive to the point where all you use are the reports in your bookmark folder.

Imagine that you create an insightful search engine report and generally a better view of search engine traffic than provided out of the box, as shown in Figure 7.27.

Search Engines	Visits	Revenue	Conversion	Avg. Order Value
Google	58,525	$43,324.28	0.80%	$91.98
AOL Search	5,633	$23,630.15	2.01%	$209.12
Yahoo	9,724	$18,328.88	1.48%	$127.28
Deal Time	4,873	$4,625.00	2.11%	$44.90
MSN Search	1,704	$2,297.34	1.82%	$74.11
Blueyonder	654	$1,073.00	0.61%	$268.25
Altavista	231	$678.56	3.46%	$84.82
Gawwk	49	$629.75	10.20%	$125.95
Tiscali	1,195	$516.27	1.09%	$39.71
Oingo	46	$506.84	8.70%	$126.71
Subtotal	**82,634**	**$95,610.07**	**1.08%**	**$106.71**
Total	**83,785**	**$95,610.07**	**1.07%**	**$106.71**

« PREVIOUS 10 NEXT 10 »

Figure 7.27 Search engine revenue insight and referrals report

There is an icon in the report header called Bookmark Report. Once you have created the report the way you want it, click this icon. For a reminder of what the icon looks like, refer back to Figure 6.5, which shows a report header.

You'll use the Bookmark Report screen (see Figure 7.28) to name and describe the report, and more importantly, apply the report properties Timing, Segment, and Sorting, as well as certain user rights:

Bookmark Report

NAME: ngine Revenue Insight and Referrals Report

Description: The Search Engine Revenue Insight and Referrals Report provides a visit and revenue centered report on our search engine referral traffic. Sorted by revenue.

Read Rights: All users / Me only

Edit Rights: All users / Me only

Timing: 2008-07-01 - 2008-09-30 / Display data based on current calendar settings

Save segment selection
Check this box to save the currently selected segment with this bookmark

Save sorting
Check this box to save the currently selected sorting with this bookmark

Folder: Search Engines

Create Bookmark

Figure 7.28 Bookmark Report

Timing I usually recommend that you don't save timing with the report. You may find it annoying to have to change the period back to where you started.

The only justification for using fixed timing is if you bookmark reports specifically to a period and folder, such as Q3 2009 results. Fixed timing can also be justified if you report on a marketing campaign that spanned a specific period, such as a summer campaign. The bigger question here is whether you should use the Yahoo! Web Analytics User Interface to communicate such information. I rarely recommend you use the user interface to communicate elements such as these directly, as they typically lack a clear communicative conclusion by themselves.

Save Segment Selection Whether you choose this option depends on your report. For example, looking back at Figure 7.27, I would hesitate to save the segment as this is a view on the dimension search engine itself and not a demographic or similar dimension.

Save Sorting I recommend that you save your method of sorting, since it is a big part of presenting a report and influencing people's way of interpreting it. Sorting is simply an instant way to say a certain metric is the most important one.

Read Rights and Edit Rights The user rights are very straightforward and provide you with an opportunity to lock in the report itself so that it stays the same and nobody changes it. Or you can choose to keep the report private so that you will be the only one able to see it. In this scenario, where the report is private, it makes more sense to save the report with fixed time periods and fixed segments, and they might just be draft reports for assignments you are working on.

The Bookmark menu, shown in Figure 7.29, is displayed only when at least one bookmark has been created and is the last of the folders in the main menu.

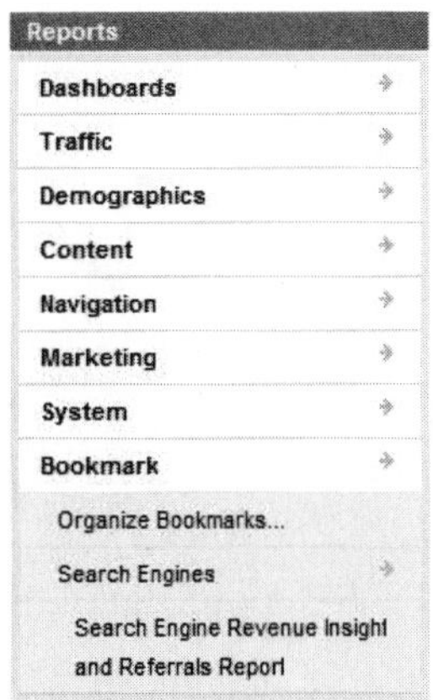

Figure 7.29 Bookmark menu

You can manage and organize your reports pretty much as you would manage your browser bookmarks. The first item under the Bookmark menu is called Organize Bookmarks. Clicking it takes you to a management screen (shown in Figure 7.30), where you copy, edit, and delete bookmarks.

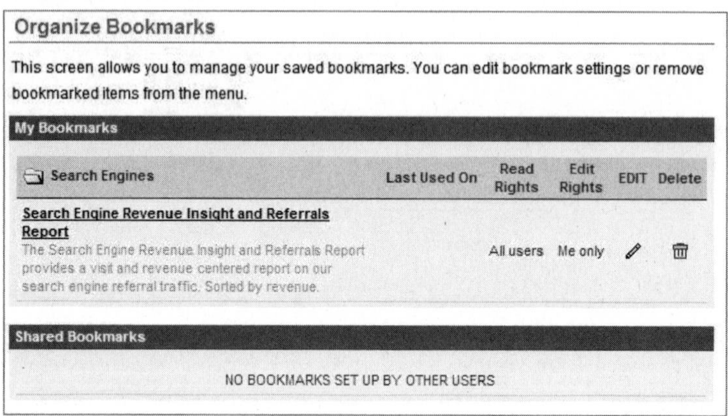

Figure 7.30 Organize Bookmarks

To change a bookmarked report—which is typically a custom report—you simply go the report and change it. The interface will ask you if you want to overwrite the existing report.

Using Segments in Reporting

Yahoo! Web Analytics provides a powerful, real-time segmentation module. It will let you analyze, for example, how different groups of visitors respond to a specific campaign, a specific group of content, and more. The segments you create also apply to historical data.

But before I describe how to use the segmentation module, let me provide at least some conceptual introduction to segmentation. This is by no means expected to be the final word, and I suggest you go beyond this book if marketing segmentation is all new to you. It does not mean you cannot play around with segments before getting your segmentation masters degree; in fact, there are plenty of simple, yet extremely powerful segments you can create.

Marketing and general market segmentation is something that existed long before web analytics came around. It is a methodology for dividing a population into specific groups, also called segments, that share one or more attributes. A population is defined by a set of visits or, even better, visitors from your web analytics tool. The reason you would use segmentation is that most optimization and most results reporting do not make much sense if just reported on the complete population.

Remember the old saying: Half of your advertising is wasted—the trouble is you do not know which half it is. The idea behind segmentation, especially online, is that you might be able to figure out which half that is.

Any report you look at, whether out of the box or a custom report you created and bookmarked, is likely to tell you completely different stories about your visitors when looking at it from a segmented view. This segmented view can be as simple as the day of week, the country of origin, or first-time or returning visits. Generally an opportunity to split or combine visitors into groups is based on attributes like the following:

- Behavior
- Demographics
- Psychographics
- Geography
- Money

Segmentation Pointers

In case you are yet to pass your segmentation exam, here are a few pointers on how to get started. Again, this is by no means everything there is to say about segmentation:

- Use your existing objectives and goals as thresholds for how to approach segmentation. Say that you have an overall site goal of a 1 percent visit-to-sale conversion rate and that your site average for the given period is indeed a positive 1 percent. By the definition of the word average, we know with certainty that some groups of visitors are converting above this ratio and some are converting below this ratio. It is your task to isolate the better-performing segments to learn from their attributes. It is also your task to find less optimal segments, so you can eliminate the campaigns that drive these visitors or try to optimize the way you serve them.
- Define and create segments based partly on your intuition and understanding of the business and partly by looking through sorted reports to spot winning sources, campaigns, and other attributes.
- Measure segmented behavior to the extent where you can conclude that you have a unique segment that, for example, converts within a certain percentage range. This sounds easy, but you should be very careful in how you do this—don't jump to conclusions based on too little data or polluted data.
- Create an optimization hypothesis on the poorer-performing segments, or just aggressively cut support for campaigns and general activities that support this traffic influx.
- Take action and execute the suggested optimization, and measure if the results live up to the hypothesis using your newly defined segments.

When you start using segmentation for the first time, you will be surprised to see how badly some of your initiatives are doing. Or to put it differently, I cannot remember when I was not completely horrified when segmenting on just campaign activity and results. But then again, money flushed down the toilet is an unsettling picture.

Creating and Configuring Segments

This section describes how to create different sets of segments using the Yahoo! Web Analytics drag-and-drop wizard. First, select Settings > Create Visitor Segments to open the Segmentation Wizard, which is a simple drag-and-drop feature that will allow you to create the segments you want. The Segmentation Wizard is shown in Figure 7.31.

The process of creating a segment is quite easy, and this is what makes it so powerful. You don't have to change your tracking scripts to grab new data types.

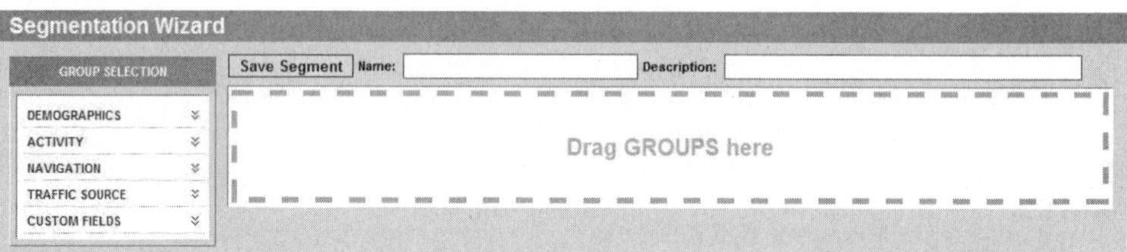

Figure 7.31 Segmentation Wizard

The Segmentation Wizard very much looks like the Custom Report Wizard. You simply add in dimensions you want to use for your segment definition. All you do when creating a segment is create a definition of it, which you then later apply as a view on a specific report and dataset; you never alter the data itself. So you are not segmenting any data by creating it but are merely setting it up for later use.

The wizard lets you create a name and description of your segment. I'd like to add a personal note on the importance of the naming and description. In any other place, the name and description do not mean more than just the ability to find the element you named. In segmentation, the naming typically defines the use and the perceived insight and understanding of the segment. So if you create a segment called "Loyal Customers," you have to think hard about how you include and exclude data that describes loyal customers and how others will perceive this segment name, before just winging the name and description.

Segmenting Loyal Customer Data

Before we move on, let's look at an example. Figure 7.32 defines loyal customers using dimensions such as the following:

- Action
- Number of Visits
- Traffic Source

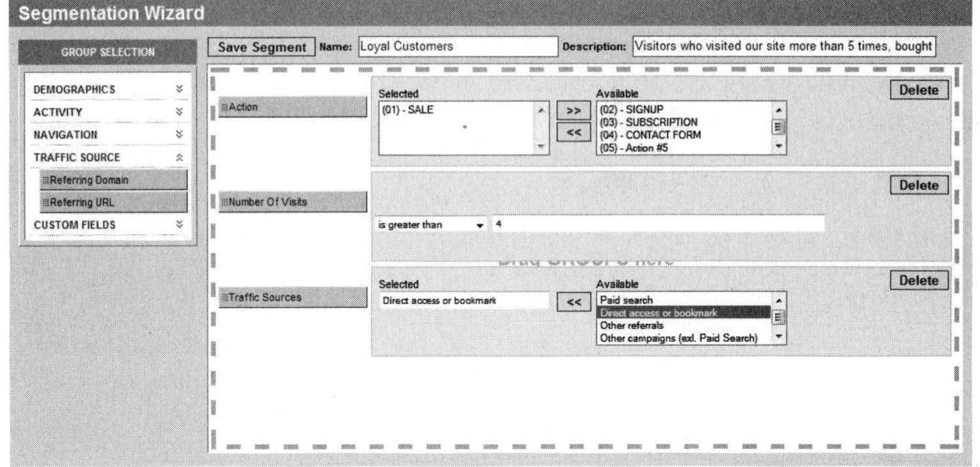

Figure 7.32 Segmentation Wizard, with the Loyal Customers Segment setup

Once created, the segment can be saved and used on any of the reports in the system. Report headers for both out-of-the-box reports and custom-designed reports provide an opportunity for you to apply any of the segments that you have created. You simply choose the segment by name and apply it to the report, which will give you an extra column in your report for all your metrics in question, so you can compare the segmented result to the overall population.

I created a simple visit revenue custom report and applied our newly created segment on top of it and got the result shown in Figure 7.33.

Week	Visits		Revenue	
	ALL	Loyal Customers	ALL	Loyal Customers
Week 27, 2008	10,266	12	$15,027.78	$843.81
Week 28, 2008	13,398	19	$22,777.36	$3,665.56
Week 29, 2008	14,401	29	$20,278.29	$2,694.32
Week 30, 2008	14,578	21	$20,706.84	$2,085.92
Week 31, 2008	13,398	19	$22,777.36	$3,665.56
Week 32, 2008	14,401	29	$20,278.29	$2,694.32
Week 33, 2008	14,578	21	$20,706.84	$2,085.92
Week 34, 2008	13,398	19	$22,777.36	$3,665.56
Week 35, 2008	14,401	29	$20,278.29	$2,694.32
Week 36, 2008	14,578	21	$20,706.84	$2,085.92
Week 37, 2008	13,398	19	$22,777.36	$3,665.56
Week 38, 2008	14,401	29	$20,278.29	$2,694.32
Week 39, 2008	14,578	21	$20,706.84	$2,085.92
Week 40, 2008	6,083	10	$11,613.41	$743.60
Total	**185,857**	**298**	**$281,691.15**	**$35,370.61**

« PREVIOUS 10 NEXT 10 »

Figure 7.33 Visit revenue report segmented by loyal customers

While not necessarily revealing the word of God, this report might produce an "aha" moment for this retailer. You see, only about 20 visitors per week make up

12 percent of all their revenue. This is a completely different picture than you would get if these visits stay buried in averages, as they represent only 0.1 percent of the overall traffic and click-stream data that is analyzed.

I would carefully research every single one of those 20 customers to learn more about why so few people make up so much of our revenue. I would furthermore have an alert on this segment. If I start losing my loyal customer base, there could be a negative spiral starting to form, which I would want to catch immediately.

Additional Tips on Setting Up Data Segments

Returning to the task of setting up a segment and the various dimension items, here's how you can work with the items:

Radio button segmentation items Use the radio buttons to select the value you are interested in by clicking the icon to add your selected items to the list.

Multiple values list segmentation item You can add multiple values by clicking the icon to add your selected items to the list.

Numerical segmentation item Here you can use the following set of operators: Equals, Does Not Equal, Is Greater Than, Is Greater Than or Equal To, Is Less Than, Is Less Than or Equal To.

Alphanumerical segmentation items Here you can use the following set of operators: Equals, Does Not Equal, Begins With, Does Not Begin With, Ends With, Does Not End With, Contains, Does Not Contain. For certain alphanumerical segmentation items, such as Document Group, Domain, Page Title, and Directory, you have the option of selecting whether the segment will be based on visitor sessions (session scope) or on page views (page view scope):

> The session scope segment includes all the page views of the visitor sessions that also included pages for which the segmentation item is true. The session scope segment will help you answer questions concerning the visitors who viewed the pages defined by the segment.
>
> The page view scope segment includes only the page views for which the segmentation is true. The page view scope segment will help you answer questions concerning only the specific page views identified by the segment.

A segment is available for use in the reporting interface immediately after it is created. Segments are applied to reports in real time. You should review the segments you construct, as there is no built-in mechanism that prevents the creation of stupid segments such as Country is Denmark and State is New York. But of course, a zero result will help you notice this.

When you enter the segmentation setup screen, you can edit or delete existing segments, as shown in Figure 7.34. To edit an existing segment, simply click the icon next to it. This opens the Segmentation Wizard with the criteria you have previously selected. Make your changes, click the Save Segment button, and your new settings will be saved.

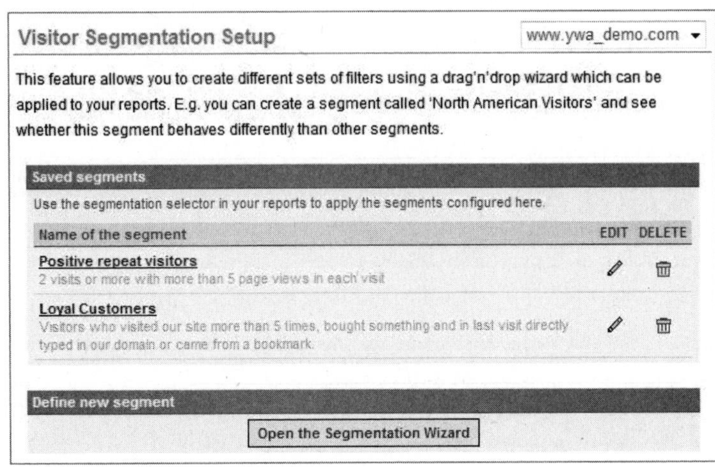

Figure 7.34 Managing visitor segmentations

User Rights and Role Administration

When defining user rights in Yahoo! Web Analytics, you can define how users view reports based on time zone and currency.

Profile is one of the first items under the general settings. You access the administration by clicking Edit Your User Profile.

Let's dig into the User-Level Display Settings dialog, shown in Figure 7.35.

USER-LEVEL DISPLAY SETTINGS

User Specific Time Zone — Use project default

You can define a user specific time zone, which might be different from the project default time zone (e.g., a user lives in London-GMT and monitors a project based on GMT-8). If this setting is enabled, all reports and dashboards will be displayed in the user's time zone.

User Specific Reporting Currency — USD

You can define a user specific reporting currency, which might be different from the project default reporting currency. If this setting is enabled, all campaign costs and sales figures except the ones in the Sales Details report will be converted to this currency, which will override the project default reporting currency.

User Specific Report Cache Timing — 1 minute

The Report Cache stores the most recently accessed reports and KPIs and serves them from cache to all account users, resulting in considerably faster loading times. Select a user-defined time period for which reports / KPIs are stored in the cache, which will override the project default Report Cache setting.

Locale Settings — Default

Select one of the stored profiles defining local time and date settings for reports and charts.

Figure 7.35 User-Level Display Settings

The user-specific time zone allows you to select your own time zone, which might be different from the time zone of your project. Say you live in New York, like me, and you have to monitor a British retailer's operations in the United States. They might have set up global reporting (default project settings) to London, (GMT time zone) as that is where they are headquartered, but you would set up your user profile to an EST time zone. When doing this, all your reports and dashboards will be adjusted to your own time zone.

The user-specific time zone affects only the reporting interface. It will not affect user-independent features such as alerts or scheduled email reports.

The user-specific reporting currency allows you to select the currency you want displayed in your reports, which might be different from the default currency of your project. Using the previous example, the project settings might be set to GBP, but you would want to report on everything in USD. You can select from the currencies presented in Chapter 2. If you enable this setting, all your reports except the Sales Details report will be displayed with your selected currency.

As a final note, Yahoo! uses monthly average exchange rates to convert the campaign costs and sales figures into the project default reporting currency. So your annual revenue displayed in your project default reporting currency is calculated by multiplying the monthly figures obtained in the tracking currency by the monthly average exchange rates.

In this chapter you were introduced to a number of concepts. Knowing how to customize reports and set up segments is fundamental to the most advanced analysis that you are likely to perform. The sooner you start using these tools, the better.

The next chapter goes into more depth on report customization. I will go through most of the standard out-of-the-box reports and show you how much additional value you can get out of them with just a few small, yet powerful, changes.

Using Basic Reports as Templates for Customization

This chapter builds on the customization features and techniques from the previous chapter and will showcase a large number of out-of-the-box reports and a pool of creative ideas on how you can get started on customizing them for more insights. This is not a chapter-long advertisement for Yahoo!'s standard reports, but without knowing where to start, you might not find out where to end. This is by no means a catalog of all possible iterations of custom reports but a handpicked few reports and a handpicked number of customization suggestions. Let's get started.

Chapter Contents

Visit Reports
Demographics Reports
Content Reports
Navigation Reports
Search Engines and Referrers Reports
Conversion Reports
System Reports

Visit Reports

We are all suckers for a standard visit report. Do not deny it, as I will proudly proclaim that I look at this particular standard report once every other day as well.

We were taught from the beginning of Internet time (for me that started in 1996) that it was all about eyeballs, and that quickly translated into the embarrassing term and key performance indicator *hits*, which later translated into the slightly better indicator *visits*.

> **Hits**
>
> In the early 1990s, web analytics consisted primarily of counting the number of client requests, also known as *hits*, made to the web server. This was a reasonable method initially, since each website often consisted of a single HTML file. However, with the introduction of images in HTML, and websites that spanned multiple HTML files, this count became less useful, and hits is now widely known as "how idiots track success"—which should be enough reason not to use it.

The fair reasoning and justification behind a look at the visit report is not so much because it tells us much by itself. Think about it: What does the visit report tell you about your business, blog, or other web property? It is valuable because we can usually do 10 crosstabs in our head on what 2,000 visits a day means to our business. We can quickly evaluate visits against the other factors involved in the Key Performance Indicators (KPIs) that drive revenue, profit, and so forth for the website. Look at Figure 8.1. What conclusions can we draw from it?

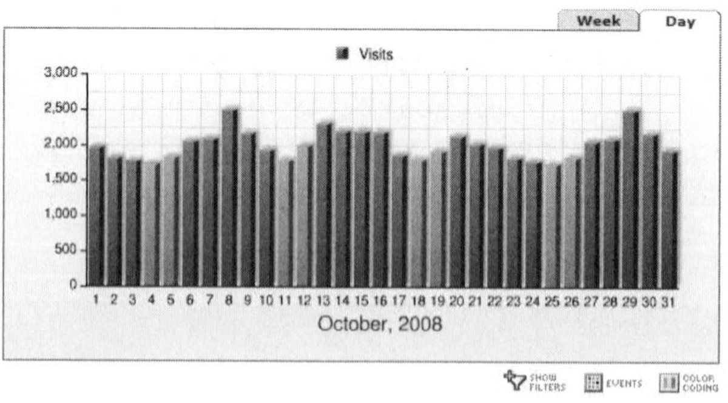

Figure 8.1 What conclusions can you draw from this visit report?

All that is shown in Figure 8.1 is a visit trend that does nothing but prompt us to ask further questions—which, by the way, is super valuable. A question could be whether the increase from October 7 to October 8 had an impact on revenue. The increase in visitors was as follows:

October 7: 2,099 visits

October 8: 2,502 visits

This is a noticeable 19 percent increase from one day to another. We should customize the report and add a success metric, such as Revenue, to investigate further. Figure 8.2 shows a visit report with a Revenue column added.

October 07, 2008 Tue	2,099	$3,139.46
October 08, 2008 Wed	2,502	$2,060.26
October 09, 2008 Thu	2,173	$3,036.51

Figure 8.2 Customized visit report; we added the Revenue metric.

Customizing the report quickly turns the initial "woohoo" moment into a "boohoo" moment. You can see that the days before and after the traffic increase are averaging about $3,000 in revenue, but on the day of the 19 percent visit increase, we are only at $2,000.

October 7: 2,099 visits, $3,139.46 revenue

October 8: 2,502 visits, $2,060.26 revenue

This indicates not just a 35 percent revenue decrease; it is a 35 percent revenue decrease coupled with a 19 percent increase in traffic. To get a better understanding of what the heck happened, I suggest drilling into the money part first, adding in the Average Order Value and the Visit to Sale Conversion Rate, as shown in Figure 8.3.

October 07, 2008 Tue	2,099	$3,139.46	$120.75	1.24%
October 08, 2008 Wed	2,501	$2,060.26	$62.43	1.32%

Figure 8.3 Adding in multiple revenue-related metrics

Doing so quickly shows us that we do indeed convert visits to sales at much the same rate, but for some reason the average order value tanked to about half of what it used to be. Your next step is to investigate the traffic sources, zeroing in on a potential bad source. You again use the Custom Report Wizard, but this change is about adding *not* another metric but another dimension—traffic sources. You then expand the tree on the result report, as shown in Figure 8.4.

October 06, 2008 Mon	2,061	$3,762.79	$110.67	1.65%
⊟ October 07, 2008 Tue	2,099	$3,139.46	$120.75	1.24%
Other campaigns	1,676	$2,560.20	$142.23	1.07%
Direct access or bookmark	214	$442.77	$88.55	2.34%
Organic search	106	$136.49	$45.50	2.83%
Other referrals	103	$0.00	$0.00	0.00%
⊟ October 08, 2008 Wed	2,501	$2,060.26	$62.43	1.32%
Other campaigns	2,072	$1,616.22	$80.81	0.97%
Direct access or bookmark	227	$378.29	$31.52	5.29%
Other referrals	107	$0.00	$0.00	0.00%
Organic search	95	$65.75	$65.75	1.05%
⊞ October 09, 2008 Thu	2,175	$3,036.51	$82.07	1.70%

Figure 8.4 Adding multiple revenue-related metrics and a traffic source dimension

Now it is quite visible that the negative impact on the average order value was caused by campaign activity, also called Other Campaigns. Aha! That's where the money was wasted. Now you should move on to your campaign reporting for October 8 or perhaps even just add in a third campaign dimension to this report to get more details.

This approach works on other primary dimensions such as Visitors, First or Returning Visitors, and so on. The success metric does not have to be Revenue—it could be any other metric you defined as one of your KPIs.

Moving on, but still within the visit sphere, I would like to showcase two other reports that help you gain insight with very little work on your part. The first one is the first-time versus returning visitors report, shown in Figure 8.5.

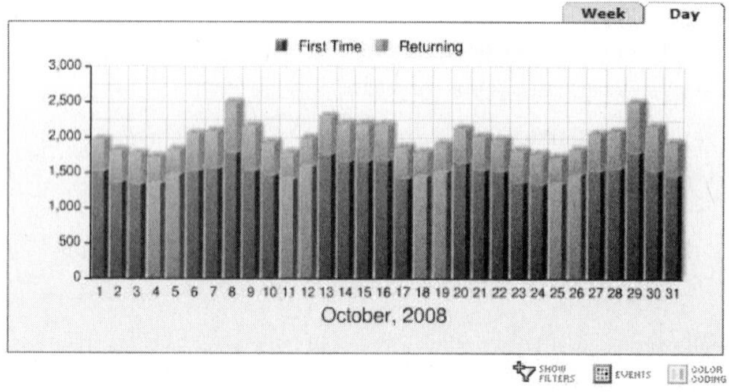

Figure 8.5 First-time versus returning visitors report

This report shows you, to some extent, how loyal your users are and, indirectly, how valuable your traffic sources are. I am sure we agree that you are keen to have people make return visits to your web property (unless you are running the technical support part of your website, where I assume you would rather people never had to visit in the first place).

Think up a number of segments, or just simply use the filters on the report itself and apply them to learn something about the quality of different visitor segments. An example is to look into the quality of different keywords, such as "bosch power tools" versus "power tools."

Comparing Figures 8.6 and 8.7, you can see that there is little difference in the returning visitor rate among a branded product-specific search phrase and a generic product-specific search phrase.

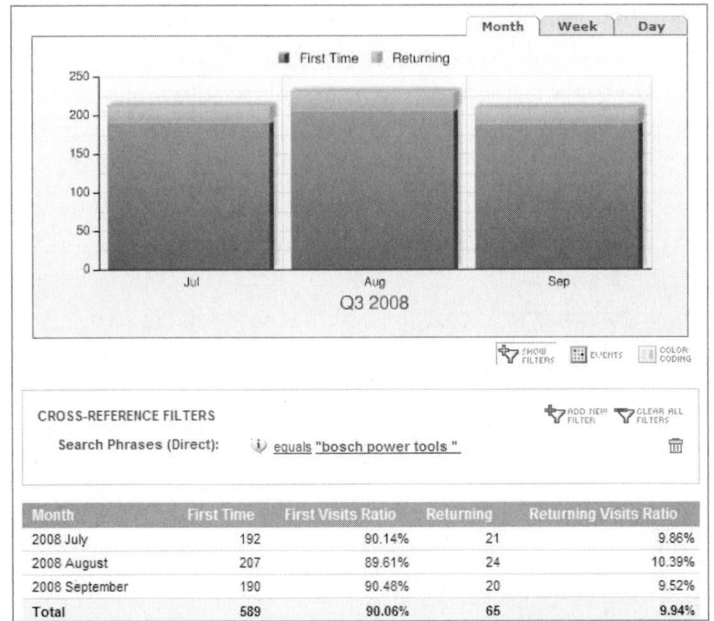

Month	First Time	First Visits Ratio	Returning	Returning Visits Ratio
2008 July	192	90.14%	21	9.86%
2008 August	207	89.61%	24	10.39%
2008 September	190	90.48%	20	9.52%
Total	**589**	**90.06%**	**65**	**9.94%**

Figure 8.6 First-time versus returning visitors report segmented by branded product search phrase

Month	First Time	First Visits Ratio	Returning	Returning Visits Ratio
2008 July	756	85.91%	124	14.09%
2008 August	726	86.12%	117	13.88%
2008 September	769	85.83%	127	14.17%
Total	**2,251**	**85.95%**	**368**	**14.05%**

Figure 8.7 First-time versus returning visitors report segmented by generic product search phrase

Probably an even more valuable experiment is to do the same exercise on a company name and see if people, once they find your company, are likely to return. See Figure 8.8, which shows the brand name Toolbag as the unique search phrase.

Month	First Time	First Visits Ratio	Returning	Returning Visits Ratio
2008 July	947	60.90%	608	39.10%
2008 August	924	61.64%	575	38.36%
2008 September	885	59.60%	600	40.40%
Total	2,756	60.72%	1,783	39.28%

Figure 8.8 First-time versus returning visitors report segmented by company name search phrase

This strategy provides valuable information—you could even consider increasing spending on your company brand-name terms, as people are returning at a rate of 40 percent. Some might say you should decrease spending, but that does not change the data gathered.

You can make up dozens of other hypotheses. Because the system is in real time, this kind of segmentation is doable over an afternoon.

Let's look at another visit report: last visitor details. This report offers you a great opportunity to get up close and personal with your visitors—that is, your customers or prospective customers. A last visitor details report is shown in Figure 8.9.

This report shows in real time what is happening on your site, right now, this instant. And it shows you the following information in the report on every visitor:

- Date
- IP/Host
- Country
- No. of visits
- Entry page
- Visit path
- Referrer
- Search phrase

	Visit path:	VIEW VISIT PATH - 3 page views	Resolution:	1680x1050
	Referrer:	http://www.google.co.uk/search...	Cookies:	Enabled
	Search phrase:	single lever tap		
22.	Date:	2008-09-30 22:59:18	System:	Windows XP
	Member ID:	woodlanddell@tiscali.co.uk	Browser:	MSIE 6.0
	IP/Host:	88.111.15.11 (as9105.com)	Language:	English (United Kingdom)
	Country:	United Kingdom	Javascript:	Enabled [1.5]
	No. of visits:	New visitor	Monitor color:	32 bit
	Entry page:	Toolbag - Tools...t Trade Prices!	Resolution:	1152x864
	Visit path:	VIEW VISIT PATH - 150 page views - 1h 31m 0s 89.19 USD	Cookies:	Enabled
	Referrer:	Direct access or bookmark		
	Search phrase:	n / a		
23.	Date:	2008-09-30 22:59:10	System:	Unknown
	IP/Host:	86.134.228.108 (btcentralplus.com)	Browser:	Netscape 7.0
	Country:	United Kingdom	Language:	English (United Kingdom)
	No. of visits:	New visitor	Javascript:	Enabled [1.5]
	Entry page:	Products	Monitor color:	16 bit
	Visit path:	VIEW VISIT PATH - 1 page view	Resolution:	800x600
	Referrer:	http://www.pricerunner.co.uk/d...	Cookies:	Enabled
	Search phrase:	n / a		
24.	Date:	2008-09-30 22:56:59	System:	Windows XP
	IP/Host:	82.46.66.190 (blueyonder.co.uk)	Browser:	MSIE 6.0
	Country:	United Kingdom	Language:	English (United Kingdom)
	No. of visits:	New visitor	Javascript:	Enabled [1.5]
	Entry page:	Toolbag - Tools...t Trade Prices!	Monitor color:	32 bit
	Visit path:	VIEW VISIT PATH - 4 page views - 0m 9s	Resolution:	1024x768
	Referrer:	http://www.blueyonder.co.uk/bl...	Cookies:	Enabled
	Search phrase:	compact tool case		
25.	Date:	2008-09-30 22:37:13	System:	Windows XP
	IP/Host:	212.32.114.61	Browser:	MSIE 6.0
	Country:	United Kingdom	Language:	English (United Kingdom)
	No. of visits:	New visitor	Javascript:	Enabled [1.5]
	Entry page:	Toolbag - Tools...t Trade Prices!	Monitor color:	32 bit
	Visit path:	VIEW VISIT PATH - 21 page views - 4m 6s	Resolution:	1400x1050
	Referrer:	Direct access or bookmark	Cookies:	Enabled
	Search phrase:	n / a		
26.	Date:	2008-09-30 22:34:08	System:	Windows 2000
	IP/Host:	199.164.160.4 (sharp.com)	Browser:	MSIE 6.0
	Country:	United States , CA, California	Language:	English (United States)

Figure 8.9 Last visitor details report

It also shows a number of system-related metrics, which are of less value in this particular setting. It is not the metrics themselves that are the most important information. These are merely a few handpicked metric indicators that you can use to choose which visitors to drill into.

You would be looking into either random visitors or handpicked visitors, because of abnormalities in their immediate behaviors. Looking into random visitors is not necessarily as useless as it sounds. Look at it this way: Imagine that you are the store manager of a Wal-Mart. You can sit in the backroom and perform endless analyses on the numbers and never get a feel for what your customers are doing. Or you can choose to walk the floor and get a sense of how things are working around the store. I think this latter approach is immensely valuable. What you will find on a visitor-by-visitor level is not statistically significant, but it will give you a much better idea of what people are doing on your web property.

Alternatively, you might choose to handpick visitors based on indicators such as the following:

- Lots of page views, but no action
- Very large sale amounts (remember it does not have to be about negative scenarios all the time)

- Lengthy visit time
- Lots of visits
- Peculiar search phrases

Figure 8.9 earlier showed a new visitor who spent a considerable amount of time on the site and looked at a lot of pages. Click the View Visit Path link, which will take you to a detailed view of every single page and action that visitor took. See Figure 8.10.

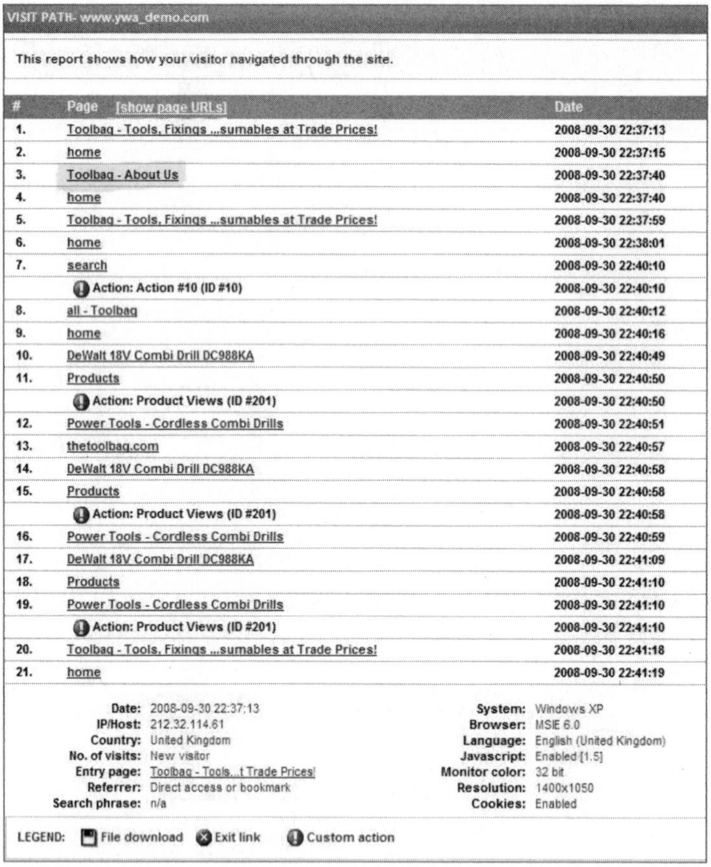

VISIT PATH- www.ywa_demo.com

This report shows how your visitor navigated through the site.

#	Page [show page URLs]	Date
1.	Toolbag - Tools, Fixings ...sumables at Trade Prices!	2008-09-30 22:37:13
2.	home	2008-09-30 22:37:15
3.	Toolbag - About Us	2008-09-30 22:37:40
4.	home	2008-09-30 22:37:40
5.	Toolbag - Tools, Fixings ...sumables at Trade Prices!	2008-09-30 22:37:59
6.	home	2008-09-30 22:38:01
7.	search	2008-09-30 22:40:10
	Action: Action #10 (ID #10)	2008-09-30 22:40:10
8.	all - Toolbag	2008-09-30 22:40:12
9.	home	2008-09-30 22:40:16
10.	DeWalt 18V Combi Drill DC988KA	2008-09-30 22:40:49
11.	Products	2008-09-30 22:40:50
	Action: Product Views (ID #201)	2008-09-30 22:40:50
12.	Power Tools - Cordless Combi Drills	2008-09-30 22:40:51
13.	thetoolbag.com	2008-09-30 22:40:57
14.	DeWalt 18V Combi Drill DC988KA	2008-09-30 22:40:58
15.	Products	2008-09-30 22:40:58
	Action: Product Views (ID #201)	2008-09-30 22:40:58
16.	Power Tools - Cordless Combi Drills	2008-09-30 22:40:59
17.	DeWalt 18V Combi Drill DC988KA	2008-09-30 22:41:09
18.	Products	2008-09-30 22:41:10
19.	Power Tools - Cordless Combi Drills	2008-09-30 22:41:10
	Action: Product Views (ID #201)	2008-09-30 22:41:10
20.	Toolbag - Tools, Fixings ...sumables at Trade Prices!	2008-09-30 22:41:18
21.	home	2008-09-30 22:41:19

Date:	2008-09-30 22:37:13	System:	Windows XP
IP/Host:	212.32.114.61	Browser:	MSIE 6.0
Country:	United Kingdom	Language:	English (United Kingdom)
No. of visits:	New visitor	Javascript:	Enabled [1.5]
Entry page:	Toolbag - Tools...t Trade Prices!	Monitor color:	32 bit
Referrer:	Direct access or bookmark	Resolution:	1400x1050
Search phrase:	n/a	Cookies:	Enabled

LEGEND: File download Exit link Custom action

Figure 8.10 Last visitor details visit path

This detail report shows at least one piece of priceless insight: the importance of your About Us page. The first thing the visitor did after landing at a category front page was to click back to Home and then click About Us, before even considering looking into your merchandise. You can investigate how much revenue the About Us page participates in and, in general, how up to date that page is.

Demographics Reports

Demographic reporting in Yahoo! Web Analytics consists of the following standalone reports:

- Languages
- Organizations
- Countries
- Areas of the World
- Time Zones
- Region/State code
- City
- Zip code (US & Canada)
- Area code (US & Canada)

Depending on where you are located and whether they have been enabled for your account, you may also have these reports:

- NAICS (North American Industry Classification System)
- DMA/MSA (Designated Market Area) codes

Using these default reports can give you a nugget or two of helpful information. Without customization, however, much of it is known information from somewhere else in your organization. Taking a report like Time Zones at face value is stating the obvious fact for a British retailer, that all their visits come from a UK time zone, as showcased in Figure 8.11.

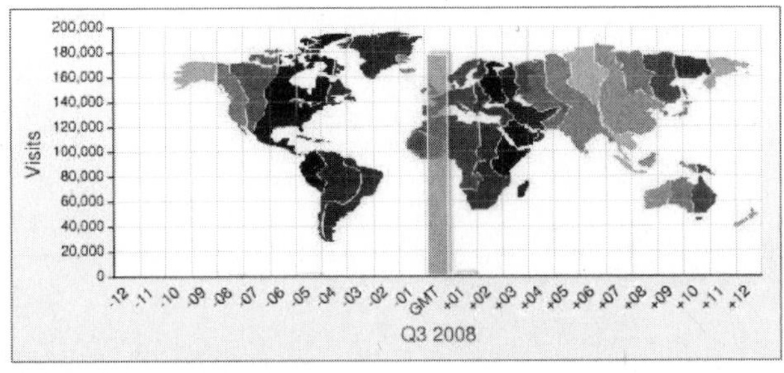

Figure 8.11 Time Zones report

Applying a simple filter can add some nuance to the report. Figure 8.12 shows a time zone report with a filter applied.

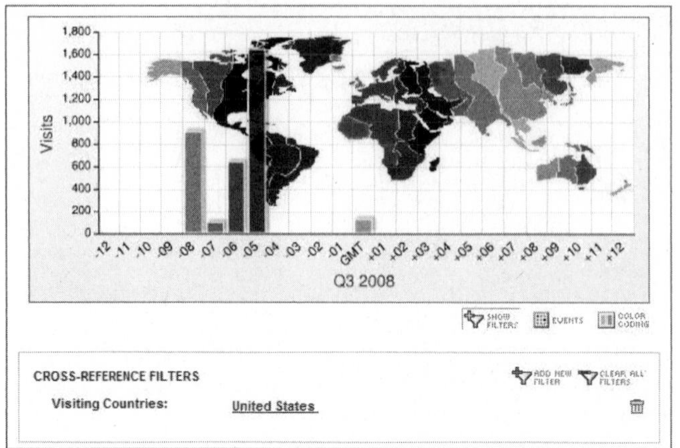

Figure 8.12 Time Zones report filtered by United States visitors

But this is not where the power of demographics lies; the power is in using these dimensions as part of other reports. These dimensions are particularly valuable when used together with marketing reports. Using demographic dimensions is exceptionally valuable when you try to optimize your marketing expense through paid search engines and their geographic targeting options, or any other advertising platform that lets you target specific demographics.

Our next example shows how you can combine demographics reports with other metrics. First, let's create a simple campaign summary report focused on one unique channel—Banners—and a number of typical campaign metrics. See Figure 8.13.

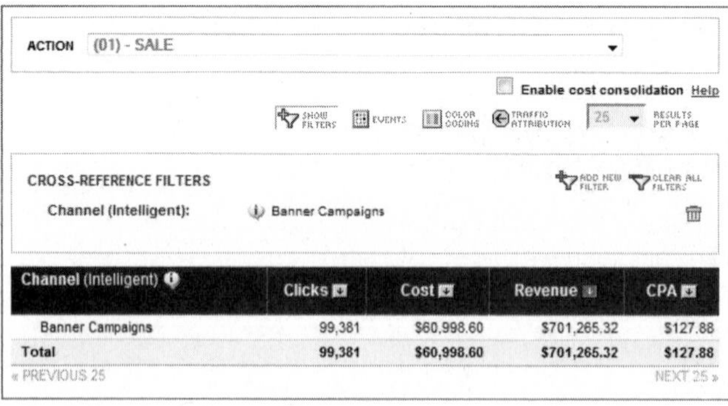

Channel (Intelligent)	Clicks	Cost	Revenue	CPA
Banner Campaigns	99,381	$60,998.60	$701,265.32	$127.88
Total	99,381	$60,998.60	$701,265.32	$127.88

Figure 8.13 Custom campaign summary report

This report shows us that for the online marketing channel Banners, we spent $60,998.60 and generated $701,265.32 in revenue, with an average cost per actual sale (CPA) of $127.88.

However, there is additional value to be derived from this report by adding in demographic dimensions. In Figure 8.14 you can see how I expanded on the custom report by adding in the demographic dimension City. You must determine which demographic dimension holds the most value for you.

Channel (Intelligent) City	Clicks	Cost	Revenue	CPA
⊟ Banner Campaigns	99,381	$60,998.60	$701,265.32	$127.88
London, GBR	2,785	$1,524.15	$24,336.44	$108.87
New York, NY, USA	2,531	$1,325.45	$45,239.78	$45.71
Madrid, ESP	2,489	$1,334.90	$9,583.40	$222.48
AOL, USA	1,347	$699.75	$15,557.15	$58.31
Los Angeles, CA, USA	1,297	$709.75	$20,657.00	$59.15
Toronto, CAN	1,260	$627.95	$2,665.75	$209.32
Milan, ITA	1,203	$669.70	$676.94	$669.70
Rome, ITA	1,176	$834.30	$2,790.00	$417.15
Milton Keynes, GBR	1,150	$712.10	$2,750.00	$712.10
Paris, FRA	1,063	$919.40	$7,029.30	$183.88
Irvine, CA, USA	1,048	$547.10	$16,886.03	$42.08
Manchester, GBR	1,048	$584.30	$0.00	$0.00
Bucharest, ROM	946	$598.50	$2,175.00	$598.50
Chicago, IL, USA	930	$439.40	$6,773.63	$62.77
Birmingham, GBR	920	$479.45	$3,523.78	$159.82
Zurich, CHE	911	$492.75	$7,738.42	$246.38
Dublin, IRL	880	$519.20	$9,414.68	$74.17
Montreal, CAN	850	$524.80	$1,820.93	$524.80
Buenos Aires, ARG	812	$542.35	$0.00	$0.00
Atlanta, GA, USA	743	$344.80	$9,011.84	$57.47
"Other"	73,992	$46,568.50	$512,635.25	$132.30
Total	**99,381**	**$60,998.60**	**$701,265.32**	**$127.88**

« PREVIOUS 25 NEXT 25 »

Figure 8.14 Adding a demographic dimension and sorting by campaign clicks

One conclusion you can draw from this report is that the number of campaign clicks has no direct relation to the success of the campaign in that particular city. Furthermore, there is another red flag: the fact that we are not making any revenue at all from visitors coming from Manchester and Buenos Aires. You could break down that question and many others by studying the report in Figure 8.14.

Using different metrics for sorting can change your view of the data almost as much as a completely new report. In Figure 8.15 I sorted the report in Figure 8.14 by campaign cost instead, even though Figure 8.14 showed us a close correlation between clicks and costs.

Channel (Intelligent) City	Clicks	Cost	Revenue	CPA
⊟ Banner Campaigns	99,381	$60,998.60	$701,265.32	$127.88
Bellevue, WA, USA	154	$3,574.70	$1,340.00	$3,574.70
London, GBR	2,785	$1,524.15	$24,336.44	$108.87
Madrid, ESP	2,489	$1,334.90	$9,583.40	$222.48
New York, NY, USA	2,531	$1,325.45	$45,239.78	$45.71
Kiev, UKR	46	$1,109.80	$0.00	$0.00
Paris, FRA	1,063	$919.40	$7,029.30	$183.88
Rome, ITA	1,176	$834.30	$2,790.00	$417.15
Milton Keynes, GBR	1,150	$712.10	$2,750.00	$712.10
Los Angeles, CA, USA	1,297	$709.75	$20,657.00	$59.15
AOL, USA	1,347	$699.75	$15,557.15	$58.31
Milan, ITA	1,203	$669.70	$676.94	$669.70
Toronto, CAN	1,260	$627.95	$2,665.75	$209.32
Halton, GBR	620	$604.60	$5,525.96	$151.15
Bucharest, ROM	946	$598.50	$2,175.00	$598.50
Manchester, GBR	1,048	$584.30	$0.00	$0.00
Irvine, CA, USA	1,048	$547.10	$16,886.03	$42.08
Buenos Aires, ARG	812	$542.35	$0.00	$0.00
Montreal, CAN	850	$524.80	$1,820.93	$524.80
Dublin, IRL	880	$519.20	$9,414.68	$74.17
Edinburgh, GBR	723	$516.80	$5,357.90	$258.40
"Other"	75,953	$42,519.00	$527,459.06	$117.13
Total	**99,381**	**$60,998.60**	**$701,265.32**	**$127.88**

« PREVIOUS 25 NEXT 25 »

Figure 8.15 Adding a demographic dimension and sorting by campaign cost

Yet again, we are provided with instant insight, such as another outlier not making any revenue (in this example, Kiev). Even more important is the fact that the most costly city, from a campaign point of view, drives very little revenue.

I finally chose to sort the report by revenue to get yet another view of this particular channel (see Figure 8.16). As with the previous reports, I sorted with my CPA in mind.

Channel (Intelligent) City	Clicks	Cost	Revenue	CPA
⊟ Banner Campaigns	99,381	$60,998.60	$701,265.32	$127.88
New York, NY, USA	2,531	$1,325.45	$45,239.78	$45.71
London, GBR	2,785	$1,524.15	$24,336.44	$108.87
Los Angeles, CA, USA	1,297	$709.75	$20,657.00	$59.15
Irvine, CA, USA	1,048	$547.10	$16,886.03	$42.08
Houston, TX, USA	716	$381.70	$16,102.99	$47.71
AOL, USA	1,347	$699.75	$15,557.15	$58.31
Almaty, KAZ	25	$11.25	$14,400.00	$5.62
Miami, FL, USA	455	$254.25	$13,950.00	$28.25
Philadelphia, PA, USA	543	$286.50	$13,313.47	$40.93
San Diego, CA, USA	610	$294.10	$13,235.77	$36.76
Seattle, WA, USA	411	$239.70	$13,190.00	$59.92
Brough, GBR	591	$275.70	$11,813.35	$55.14
Galway, IRL	56	$24.75	$11,778.38	$6.19
Perth, AUS	245	$198.90	$10,270.26	$66.30
Dallas, TX, USA	505	$325.95	$9,955.00	$36.22
Vancouver, CAN	506	$284.15	$9,888.88	$71.04
Raleigh, NC, USA	180	$83.35	$9,660.00	$27.78
Madrid, ESP	2,489	$1,334.90	$9,583.40	$222.48
Dublin, IRL	880	$519.20	$9,414.68	$74.17
Atlanta, GA, USA	743	$344.80	$9,011.84	$57.47
"Other"	81,418	$51,333.20	$403,020.90	$164.53
Total	**99,381**	**$60,998.60**	**$701,265.32**	**$127.88**
« PREVIOUS 25				NEXT 25 »

Figure 8.16 Adding a demographic dimension and sorting by revenue

With this report you bring Irvine into the picture again—it was lost at the bottom of the previous reports—but more importantly, Houston is brought in near the top and appeared out of nowhere. There might be a great optimization opportunity to pursue here.

All of the reports heavily depend on the attribution model chosen, but that just makes it ever more valuable to play with. You can see from the figures that intelligent attribution was applied.

If this isn't just absolutely beautiful, then I do not know what is. And this is just one dimension (a unique campaign channel) and one demographic dimension (City) that is paired. There are literally hundreds of other reports that you can pair, and then again, reports where you can go beyond just two dimensions.

Yahoo! derives its demographic information through IP lookup, which is not 100 percent accurate. In some narrow dimensions, IP lookup is close to 80–85 percent accurate. This does not mean you cannot trust the data—it just means that you should ensure you are looking at enough data. It also means that you will see discrepancies (for example, AOL is a city in the United Kingdom as well as America Online).

Content Reports

Yahoo! Web Analytics provides four types of content analysis reporting out of the box:

- Pages
- Document Groups
- Directories
- Downloads

From this list we can discard Directories as it is nothing but a lazy person's Document Groups. That leaves us with Downloads, which is not that bad a success metric, and Pages (Documents), grouped or not. Let's use the report called Most Requested Pages by Page Title as a customization example—this is yet another example of a report that we all look at without getting the full benefits.

The Most Requested Pages by Page Title report, shown in Figure 8.17, is similar to the visit report. We can use it to mentally gauge how we are doing in several other categories. However, this report is not the way to prove a point and run a data-driven organization.

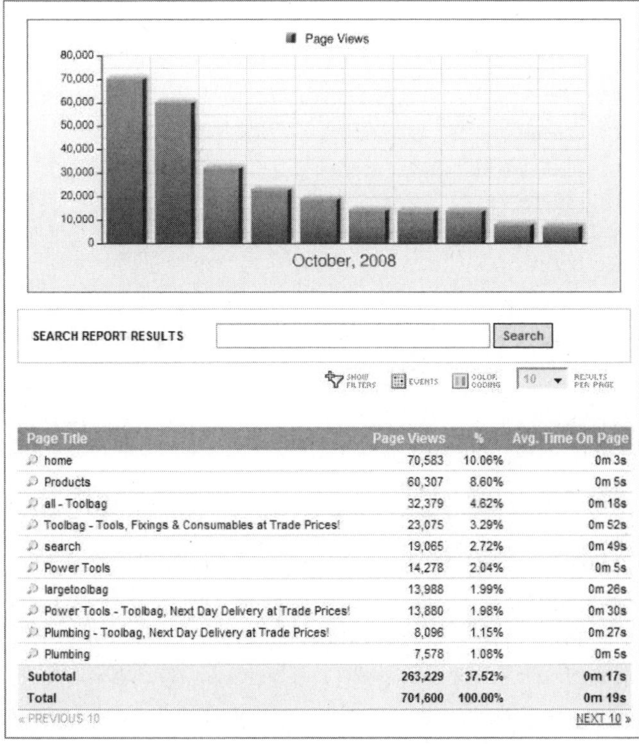

Page Title	Page Views	%	Avg. Time On Page
home	70,583	10.06%	0m 3s
Products	60,307	8.60%	0m 5s
all - Toolbag	32,379	4.62%	0m 18s
Toolbag - Tools, Fixings & Consumables at Trade Prices!	23,075	3.29%	0m 52s
search	19,065	2.72%	0m 49s
Power Tools	14,278	2.04%	0m 5s
largetoolbag	13,988	1.99%	0m 26s
Power Tools - Toolbag, Next Day Delivery at Trade Prices!	13,880	1.98%	0m 30s
Plumbing - Toolbag, Next Day Delivery at Trade Prices!	8,096	1.15%	0m 27s
Plumbing	7,578	1.08%	0m 5s
Subtotal	**263,229**	**37.52%**	**0m 17s**
Total	**701,600**	**100.00%**	**0m 19s**

« PREVIOUS 10 NEXT 10 »

Figure 8.17 The Most Requested Pages by Page Title report

This report provides you with a top list of the most viewed pages but does not tell you much information about the importance of those pages. Yahoo! provides two participation metrics on this subject:

- Revenue Participation
- Action Participation

Revenue Participation is interpreted as how much revenue was generated from people who also viewed this page and not how much revenue the page generated. Action Participation is how many actions in total were generated from people who also viewed this page.

You apply these two metrics only from the Custom Report Wizard, shown in Figure 8.18.

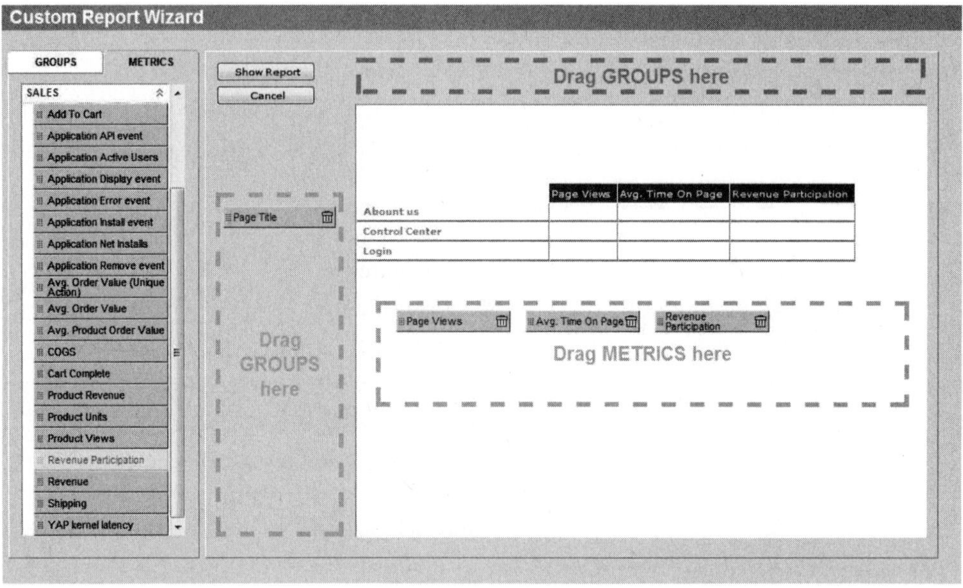

Figure 8.18 Custom Report Wizard for a Most Requested Pages report with a Revenue Participation metric added

The results, when sorted on Revenue Participation, are a lot different than when the report is sorted on pages viewed. You will always get a bunch of pages that are a forced part of the revenue generation, such as checkout pages—which is okay, but you would have them removed if you show the report to colleagues.

The first direct insight that we get from the new report, shown in Figure 8.19, is that it is less about us talking up Search as a successful site element, but more about us knowing the value of internal site search. Before, all I knew was that it was used 19,065 times in October 2008.

Page Title	Page Views	Avg. Time On Page	Revenue Participation
Confirmation	897	0m 1s	$92,393.38
Payment and Verification	1,050	1m 32s	$92,305.90
Delivery Options	2,083	0m 21s	$92,170.13
Billing & Delivery Addresses	2,474	0m 26s	$92,112.53
Order Confirmed	907	0m 15s	$89,603.33
home	70,583	0m 3s	$89,190.09
baskettoolbag	5,575	0m 25s	$89,165.29
confirmationtoolbag	1,724	0m 46s	$89,097.00
add to basket	6,798	0m 3s	$87,801.75
PRODUCTS	6,871	0m 38s	$87,716.34
Products	60,307	0m 5s	$80,901.10
Header	2,982	0m 47s	$71,850.47
my_accounttoolbag	2,148	0m 48s	$68,351.46
user registered	934	3m 37s	$66,098.98
Toolbag - Tools, Fixings & Consumables at Trade Prices!	23,075	0m 52s	$56,820.30
search	19,065	0m 49s	$46,051.90
all - Toolbag	32,379	0m 18s	$44,492.53
logintoolbag	1,219	0m 53s	$33,418.20
largetoolbag	13,988	0m 26s	$29,320.77
My Account	646	0m 29s	$26,264.03
Power Tools	14,278	0m 5s	$24,677.28
Power Tools - Toolbag, Next Day Delivery at Trade Prices!	13,880	0m 30s	$23,848.17
Toolbag - Special Offers	4,026	0m 42s	$17,447.92
Hand Tools - Toolbag, Next Day Delivery at Trade Prices!	7,191	0m 36s	$15,113.90
Plumbing - Toolbag, Next Day Delivery at Trade Prices!	8,096	0m 27s	$14,160.18
Subtotal	**303,176**	**0m 20s**	**$1,520,372.93**
Total	**701,600**	**0m 19s**	**$2,717,657.01**
« PREVIOUS 25			NEXT 25 »

Figure 8.19 Customized Most Requested Pages report sorted by Revenue Participation

Now I know that internal site search participates in $46,051.96 of revenue generated. This indicates that half my revenue is generated from people who use internal site search, which is indeed a strategic piece of information and especially valuable if you find out that you have high usage but little revenue generated from those visitors. It also tells you not to fiddle around with the Search element as if it did not matter—we know now that half the company's online revenue might be attached to it.

Now let's look at a third view of your pages. Beyond pure page views and revenue, you can apply an Action Participation metric, such as the Subscription action that I applied and sorted on in Figure 8.20.

Here we can see that the internal site search, as expected, does not drive more than one fifth of the subscriptions.

However, it becomes quite evident that the internal Subscribe advertisement that we have on product and category pages, such as Power Tools, Plumbing, and Electrical, are the drivers for people subscribing. This tells you that people are likely to subscribe because of your products. It might also indicate that there should be some product focus in the newsletters.

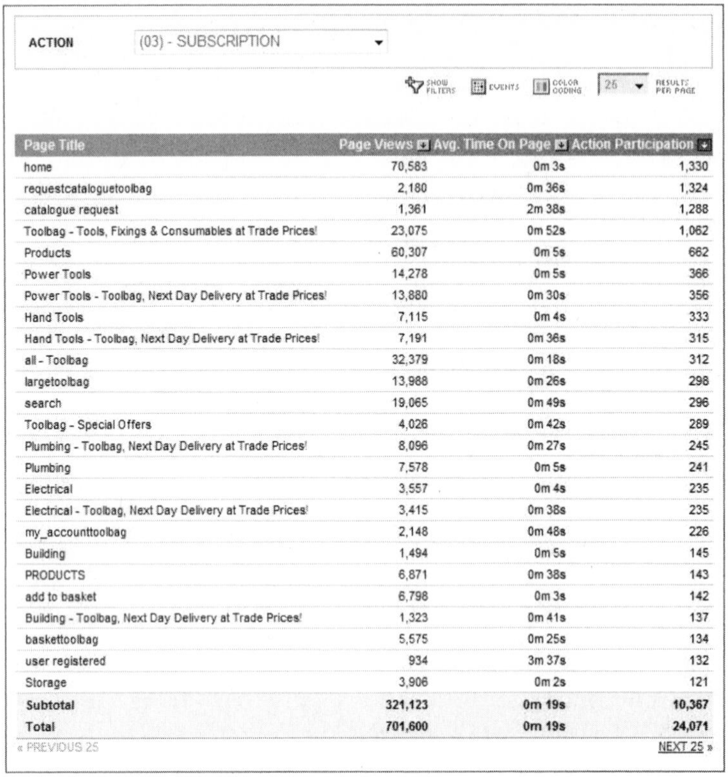

ACTION (03) - SUBSCRIPTION

SHOW FILTERS EVENTS COLOR CODING 25 RESULTS PER PAGE

Page Title	Page Views	Avg. Time On Page	Action Participation
home	70,583	0m 3s	1,330
requestcataloguetoolbag	2,180	0m 36s	1,324
catalogue request	1,361	2m 38s	1,288
Toolbag - Tools, Fixings & Consumables at Trade Prices!	23,075	0m 52s	1,062
Products	60,307	0m 5s	662
Power Tools	14,278	0m 5s	366
Power Tools - Toolbag, Next Day Delivery at Trade Prices!	13,880	0m 30s	356
Hand Tools	7,115	0m 4s	333
Hand Tools - Toolbag, Next Day Delivery at Trade Prices!	7,191	0m 36s	315
all - Toolbag	32,379	0m 18s	312
largetoolbag	13,988	0m 26s	298
search	19,065	0m 49s	296
Toolbag - Special Offers	4,026	0m 42s	289
Plumbing - Toolbag, Next Day Delivery at Trade Prices!	8,096	0m 27s	245
Plumbing	7,578	0m 5s	241
Electrical	3,557	0m 4s	235
Electrical - Toolbag, Next Day Delivery at Trade Prices!	3,415	0m 38s	235
my_accounttoolbag	2,148	0m 48s	226
Building	1,494	0m 5s	145
PRODUCTS	6,871	0m 38s	143
add to basket	6,798	0m 3s	142
Building - Toolbag, Next Day Delivery at Trade Prices!	1,323	0m 41s	137
baskettoolbag	5,575	0m 25s	134
user registered	934	3m 37s	132
Storage	3,906	0m 2s	121
Subtotal	**321,123**	**0m 19s**	**10,367**
Total	**701,600**	**0m 19s**	**24,071**

« PREVIOUS 25 NEXT 25 »

Figure 8.20 Customized Most Requested Pages report sorted by Action Participation

Note that the Subtotal and Total rows in these tables do not represent anything but the summing of the numbers. Some columns are not worth summing up, as the sum by itself makes little sense, and you should not use that as part of any decision.

Moving beyond the participation metrics, let's look at content reporting in general. Yahoo! Web Analytics allows you to check reports by URL and by title (`DOCUMENTNAME`) because, in certain cases, running reports by URL and by title for the same project might output different results based on how your web pages are named. For example, if you have a number of welcome pages in different languages, all of them named "Welcome," you will see the aggregate page views figure in the "by title" report while figures for each welcome page will be displayed in the "by URL" report. This is a great way of grouping pages together, as we discussed when talking about the `DOCUMENTNAME` variable.

When you're tracking downloads, this information is collected automatically. Because of the restraints of page tagging, the number presented is likely to be only an indication of the actual number of downloads.

Navigation Reports

Yahoo! clustered a number of great reports together under the header Navigation, and I picked two of them for later discussion in Chapter 10, "Distinctive Reports and Usage." The two reports are:

- Scenario Analysis
- Path Analysis

This leaves us with the following seemingly simple, but yet very powerful, reports:

- Entries
- Bounce Rate
- Exits
- Page Depth
- Time Spent on Site
- Page Views per Visit

These reports become even more powerful when you start customizing them. The general theme is how your visitors navigate your site. Let's look at a customization example using the Bounce Rate reports.

The *bounce rate* is the percentage of people exiting the site immediately after entering. Yahoo! Web Analytics records a *bounce* for each single page access event.

Bounce Rate

The bounce rate is defined by the Web Analytics Association as follows: "If bounce rate is being calculated for a specific page, then it is the number of times that page was a single page view visit divided by the number of times that page was an entry. If bounce rate is calculated for a group of pages, then it is the number of times pages in that group was a single page view visit divided by the number of times pages in that group were entry pages. A site-wide bounce rate represents the percentage of total visits that were single page view visits." I encourage you to read the Yahoo! compliance table to see how their method of calculation squares with this definition: `http://visualrevenue.com/blog/2008/03/web-analytics-definitions-waa.html`.

The tool provides some segmentation out of the box by letting you select Bounce Rate reports for:

- All Visits
- First Time Visits
- Returning Visits

This is neat, but somewhat redundant, as we can do this segmentation and filtering ourselves using the Segmentation Wizard or the filtering on the reports themselves. What is more important is the reports themselves, which are:

- Bounce Rate by Entry Page URL
- Bounce Rate by Entry Page Title
- Bounce Rate over Time

Assuming that you have a decent title (DOCUMENTNAME) grouping, you could use this as your standard for reporting grouping, especially if you need to communicate beyond your own analytics team.

The beautiful thing about bounce rate is that it is simple to understand and you do not have to juggle it much to get great value out of it. Even the standard report out of the box provides direct value (see Figure 8.21).

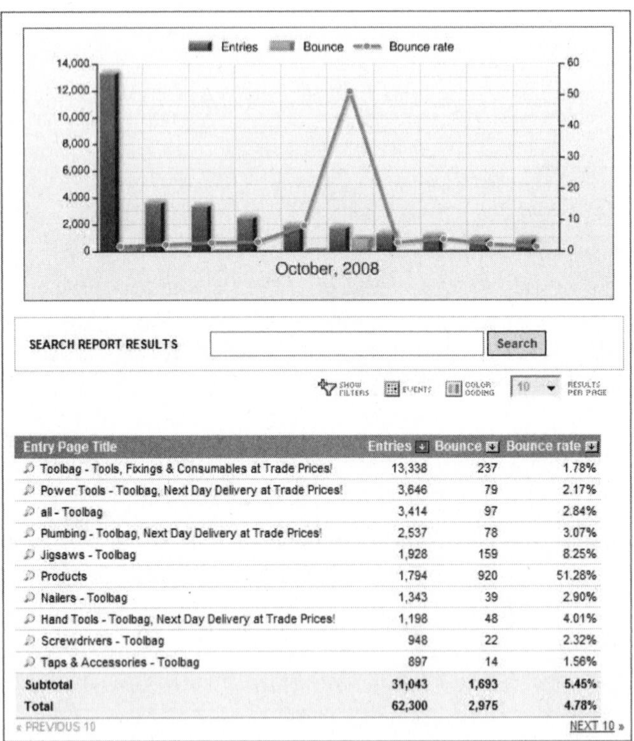

Entry Page Title	Entries	Bounce	Bounce rate
Toolbag - Tools, Fixings & Consumables at Trade Prices!	13,338	237	1.78%
Power Tools - Toolbag, Next Day Delivery at Trade Prices!	3,646	79	2.17%
all - Toolbag	3,414	97	2.84%
Plumbing - Toolbag, Next Day Delivery at Trade Prices!	2,537	78	3.07%
Jigsaws - Toolbag	1,928	159	8.25%
Products	1,794	920	51.28%
Nailers - Toolbag	1,343	39	2.90%
Hand Tools - Toolbag, Next Day Delivery at Trade Prices!	1,198	48	4.01%
Screwdrivers - Toolbag	948	22	2.32%
Taps & Accessories - Toolbag	897	14	1.56%
Subtotal	**31,043**	**1,693**	**5.45%**
Total	**62,300**	**2,975**	**4.78%**

« PREVIOUS 10 NEXT 10 »

Figure 8.21 All Visits Bounce Rate by Title report

You can instantly spot poor-performing pages just by looking at the report as is. Figure 8.21 shows a successful site with a bounce rate of only 5 percent on average, but it also shows that there is something wrong with the landing page called Products. There may also be a problem with a product-specific page about Jigsaws, which has about an 8 percent bounce rate.

This information is helpful by itself, but might not represent enough clarity. You might even pay dearly for this traffic, in which case half the money is directly down the drain.

But to ensure we have the best picture of poor-performing pages—those with the biggest bounce rate—you can sort on bounce rate. You may see a list of pages with a 100 percent bounce rate, simply because you might have pages with one entry and one bounce. To get a better picture—a list of pages with limited visits does not provide great optimization opportunities—you should apply a filter on the number of entries. Set the filter to the number of entries that represents a significant number to your business. See Figure 8.22.

CROSS-REFERENCE FILTERS

ADD NEW FILTER | CLEAR ALL FILTERS

Entries: is greater than 500

Entry Page Title	Entries	Bounce	Bounce rate
Products	1,794	920	51.28%
search	559	154	27.55%
Jigsaws - Toolbag	1,928	159	8.25%
Measuring - Toolbag	588	40	6.80%
all Power Tools - Toolbag	516	26	5.04%
Hand Tools - Toolbag, Next Day Delivery at Trade Prices!	1,198	48	4.01%
Plumbing - Toolbag, Next Day Delivery at Trade Prices!	2,537	78	3.07%
Nailers - Toolbag	1,343	39	2.90%
SDS Plus Hammer Drills - Toolbag	840	24	2.86%
all - Toolbag	3,414	97	2.84%
Wrenches - Toolbag	571	15	2.63%
Lasers & Levels - Toolbag	804	19	2.36%
Screwdrivers - Toolbag	948	22	2.32%
Routers - Toolbag	531	12	2.26%
Skil 9.6V Cordless Drill Driver 2201 (9.6V)	532	12	2.26%
Power Tools - Toolbag, Next Day Delivery at Trade Prices!	3,646	79	2.17%
Radiator Valves - Toolbag	658	13	1.98%
toolbag	790	15	1.90%
Circular Saws - Toolbag	819	15	1.83%
Toolbag - Tools, Fixings & Consumables at Trade Prices!	13,338	237	1.78%
Taps & Accessories - Toolbag	897	14	1.56%
Sanders - Toolbag	588	7	1.19%
Storage - Toolbag, Next Day Delivery at Trade Prices!	622	7	1.13%
Total	**62,300**	**2,975**	**4.78%**

« PREVIOUS 25 | NEXT 25 »

Figure 8.22 Sorted and filtered All Visits Bounce Rate by Title report

Customizing the Bounce Rate report with a simple filter and sort takes it from being valuable to being a truly great report. You can bookmark such a sorted and filtered version as your new standard Bounce Rate report.

In Figure 8.22, we see a new entry, Search, with a 28 percent bounce rate. As we saw earlier, internal search made a lot of money, so learning that this high bounce rate is attached to it, we know there is real money to be made if we improve the internal search tool.

Now let's delve into details of using the bounce rate. First look at the traffic sources and their potential cost to you. The bounce rate is a great indicator of the quality of the traffic you receive.

Using the previous example, let's add another dimension that reflects the traffic we want to investigate, as shown in Figure 8.23.

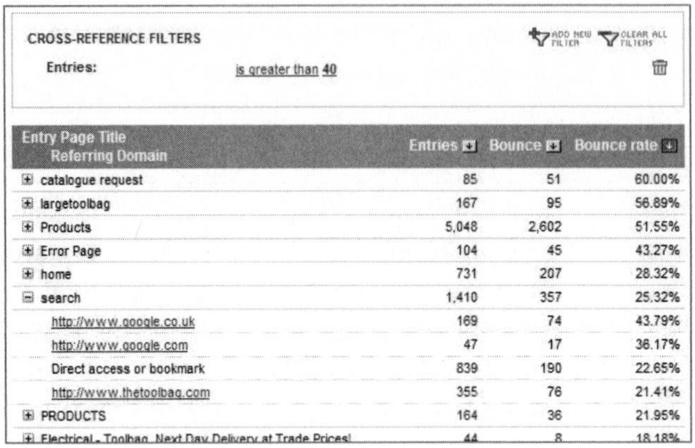

CROSS-REFERENCE FILTERS

ADD NEW FILTER | CLEAR ALL FILTERS

Entries: is greater than 40

Entry Page Title / Referring Domain	Entries	Bounce	Bounce rate
catalogue request	85	51	60.00%
largetoolbag	167	95	56.89%
Products	5,048	2,602	51.55%
Error Page	104	45	43.27%
home	731	207	28.32%
search	1,410	357	25.32%
http://www.google.co.uk	169	74	43.79%
http://www.google.com	47	17	36.17%
Direct access or bookmark	839	190	22.65%
http://www.thetoolbag.com	355	76	21.41%
PRODUCTS	164	36	21.95%
Electrical - Toolbag, Next Day Delivery at Trade Prices!	44	8	18.18%

Figure 8.23 Custom Bounce Rate report with added traffic dimension

As you can see, I lowered the entry page filter, as we are drilling into greater detail. I also expanded the period to get a bit more data. Figure 8.23 undoubtedly tells us a story about internal search engine results pages (SERPs) indexed in Google and that they are obviously not working as landing pages.

SERP

A search engine results page, internal or external, is the listing of web pages returned by the search engine in response to a keyword query. The results normally include a list of web pages with titles, a link to the page, and a short description showing where the keywords have matched content within the page. A SERP may refer to a single page of links returned, or to the set of all links returned for a search query.

You could mark those pages in your `robots.txt` file and make sure they are not indexed. You could then focus on getting more valuable pages indexed on the same keywords instead.

`robots.txt`

The robot exclusion standard, also known as the Robots Exclusion Protocol or `robots.txt` protocol, is a convention to prevent cooperating web spiders and other web robots from accessing all or part of a website that is otherwise publicly viewable. Robots are often used by search engines to categorize and archive websites.

Remember there is no home page anymore; the home page is where people enter your site, and the bounce rate tells us how good those landing pages are. For some content sites, such as a blog, reading one page might not be as negative as the bounce rate suggests.

Consider setting up an alert on the bounce rate metric so that when a given page with enough entries reaches a specified level, you are appropriately warned.

Search Engines and Referrers Reports

There is not much difference between a search engine and a traditional referrer beyond the fact that search engines are likely to be the most popular referrer you have. You are provided with feedback on the search phrase when talking about organic search and campaign information when talking about paid search. Yahoo! provides access to this in the form of six standard reports, which are concise and also great starting points:

- Search Engines
- Search Phrases
- Organic Search Engines
- Organic Search Phrases
- Referring Domains
- Referring URLs

A given visitor will be reported in as many different sources as appropriate.

The standard search engine report, shown in Figure 8.24, may not help you much beyond listing the traffic drivers.

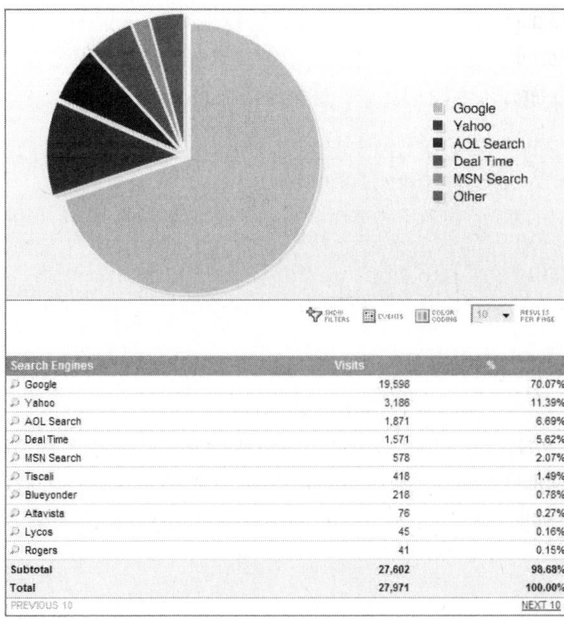

Search Engines	Visits	%
Google	19,598	70.07%
Yahoo	3,186	11.39%
AOL Search	1,871	6.69%
Deal Time	1,571	5.62%
MSN Search	578	2.07%
Tiscali	418	1.49%
Blueyonder	218	0.78%
Altavista	76	0.27%
Lycos	45	0.16%
Rogers	41	0.15%
Subtotal	**27,602**	**98.68%**
Total	**27,971**	**100.00%**

PREVIOUS 10 NEXT 10 »

Figure 8.24 Search engine report

Looking at the report, you see that Google provides you with the most visits, then Yahoo!, and on to the smaller search engines. But this doesn't tell you much, does it? I suggest that you append the metrics with something that describes the value of the visit and sort on that metric.

I deleted the Visit percentage, applied a Revenue metric, changed to a different sorting, and ended up with the result report shown in Figure 8.25.

Search Engines	Visits	Revenue
Google	19,598	$14,684.16
Yahoo	3,186	$7,075.16
AOL Search	1,871	$5,158.86
Deal Time	1,571	$1,114.23
MSN Search	578	$842.10
Blueyonder	218	$536.50
Altavista	76	$339.28
Oingo	20	$253.42
Gawwk	16	$125.95
Tiscali	418	$121.41
Subtotal	**27,552**	**$30,251.07**
Total	**27,971**	**$30,251.07**
« PREVIOUS 10		NEXT 10 »

Figure 8.25 Customized search engine referrals report

When looking at figure 8.25, you might have concluded to primarily focus on Google if visit was your only metric. This conclusion is obviously wrong, which is visible when you apply a revenue metric.

The revised report shows that Google only generates half the revenue (based on the applied direct attribution) and that sources like Yahoo! Search (with one sixth of the traffic) generate *half* the revenue of Google Search. Even more significant is that AOL Search, which is powered by Google, is generating $5,158.86, with one tenth of the traffic of Google ($14,684.16).

You can append the custom report with the Avg. Order Value and Visit to Sale Conversion Rate metrics and change the sorting to Avg. Order Value. This strategy is bound to reveal obscure engines in the top 10 that randomly gave you a few visits. Apply a filter on minimum visits as well so that you get the true cream of the crop. The report result, shown in Figure 8.26, paints a different picture than what we started with. Not only that, we have a good understanding of why our revenue generated from organic search engines is distributed as it is.

Imagine if you could get your Google visits to convert at the same rate as your AOL visits; that would be another $15,000 for this retailer every month.

You probably noticed that I use Revenue as a success metric in a lot of my examples. You can change that for other actions, such as signups, leads, subscriptions, and catalog requests. The Revenue success metric is just a great way to illustrate a point, using dollars as a metric.

CROSS-REFERENCE FILTERS

ADD NEW FILTER | CLEAR ALL FILTERS

Search Engines (Direct) Only:

Visits: is greater than 500

Search Engines	Visits	Conversion	Avg. Order Value	Revenue
AOL Search	1,871	1.50%	$184.24	$5,158.86
Yahoo	3,186	1.44%	$153.81	$7,075.16
Google	19,598	0.74%	$101.27	$14,684.16
MSN Search	578	1.90%	$76.55	$842.10
Deal Time	1,571	1.78%	$39.79	$1,114.23
Total	**27,971**	**0.97%**	**$112.04**	**$30,251.07**

« PREVIOUS 10 NEXT 10 »

Figure 8.26 Detailed customized search engine referrals report

Yahoo! identifies search engines by matching the referrer URL to a database of search engine URLs, which can be either domain names or IP addresses. This identification includes both organic traffic and traffic from paid search engine campaigns.

Note: Yahoo! differentiates between paid and organic traffic by allowing you to mark the paid traffic; the rest are expected to be organic. Not marking your paid traffic will skew things drastically!

Conversion Reports

The Conversion section under the Marketing menu is nothing more than a collection of segmented reports that allow you to quickly view the conversion according to another dimension. Yahoo! provides conversion reports according to:

- SEO & SEM
- Referrers
- Demographics
- Landing Pages

Yahoo! also provides two distinct reports, the Conversion Summary shown in Figure 8.27 and the Number of Visits Till Conversion report.

I see conversion metrics as something you should either utilize together with another report or as KPIs and goals on your dashboard. If you take a month's worth of data, you could have a view like Figure 8.28.

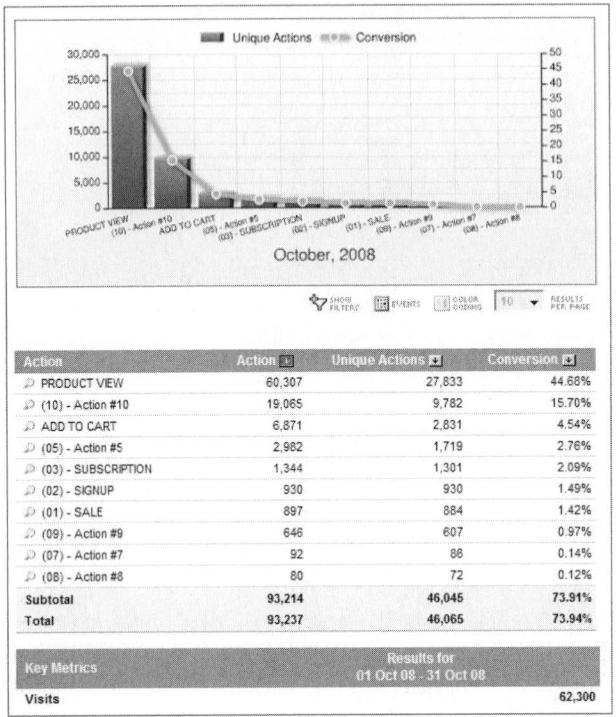

Action	Action	Unique Actions	Conversion
PRODUCT VIEW	60,307	27,833	44.68%
(10) - Action #10	19,065	9,782	15.70%
ADD TO CART	6,871	2,831	4.54%
(05) - Action #5	2,982	1,719	2.76%
(03) - SUBSCRIPTION	1,344	1,301	2.09%
(02) - SIGNUP	930	930	1.49%
(01) - SALE	897	884	1.42%
(09) - Action #9	646	607	0.97%
(07) - Action #7	92	86	0.14%
(08) - Action #8	80	72	0.12%
Subtotal	**93,214**	**46,045**	**73.91%**
Total	**93,237**	**46,065**	**73.94%**

Key Metrics	Results for 01 Oct 08 - 31 Oct 08
Visits	**62,300**

Figure 8.27 Conversion Summary report

Month of Year	Visits	Revenue
October	62,300	$92,393.38
Total	**62,300**	**$92,393.38**
« PREVIOUS 10		NEXT 10 »

Figure 8.28 Simple customized Visit Revenue report

We can now apply a complete new dimension, either by looking at the out-of-the-box report or just by applying the Number of Visits dimension to the report in Figure 8.28, which will provide us with the expanded result tree shown in Figure 8.29.

This report provides good information and shows us how important that first and second visit is for the month in question. Now let's try to segment. For the report shown in Figure 8.30, I extended the time period to get more data and expanded the organic search tree.

We now see a distribution that does not hold the typical characteristics of the long tail. This is all head. I will go into greater detail in Chapter 13 about what the long tail is and what optimization opportunities we might get from it. The results show that we should make no more than three tries to convert an organic search visitor into a buyer; after that, they are either persuaded or gone forever. The results show that we should seriously consider optimizing our landing page.

Month of Year Number Of Visits	Visits	Revenue
⊟ October	62,300	$92,393.38
1 visit(s)	47,742	$41,153.86
2 visit(s)	7,877	$24,832.40
3 visit(s)	2,079	$8,930.67
4 visit(s)	999	$3,502.10
5 visit(s)	575	$6,466.40
6 visit(s)	432	$3,469.13
7 visit(s)	262	$1,225.62
8 visit(s)	205	$398.31
9 visit(s)	169	$421.53
10 visit(s)	158	$189.80
11 visit(s)	137	$23.65
12 visit(s)	121	$377.34
13 visit(s)	106	$813.80
14 visit(s)	84	$14.70
17 visit(s)	69	$0.00
16 visit(s)	60	$86.04
15 visit(s)	59	$0.00
19 visit(s)	50	$49.85
20 visit(s)	47	$11.49
18 visit(s)	41	$0.00
Other	1,028	$426.69
Total	**62,300**	**$92,393.38**
« PREVIOUS 10		NEXT 10 »

Figure 8.29 Customized Visit Revenue report with additional dimensions

Traffic Sources Number Of Visits	Visits	Conversion	Revenue
⊞ Other campaigns	628,052	1.22%	$838,963.86
⊞ Direct access or bookmark	60,177	3.49%	$169,559.26
⊞ Other referrals	25,463	1.85%	$51,983.64
⊟ Organic search	24,577	2.18%	$49,664.87
1 visit(s)	21,942	1.97%	$43,581.29
2 visit(s)	1,799	1.89%	$1,917.94
3 visit(s)	420	16.67%	$4,165.64
4 visit(s)	105	0.00%	$0.00
5 visit(s)	85	0.00%	$0.00
17 visit(s)	53	0.00%	$0.00
8 visit(s)	52	0.00%	$0.00
7 visit(s)	34	0.00%	$0.00
6 visit(s)	18	0.00%	$0.00
10 visit(s)	18	0.00%	$0.00
15 visit(s)	17	0.00%	$0.00
19 visit(s)	17	0.00%	$0.00
20 visit(s)	17	0.00%	$0.00
Total	**738,269**	**1.46%**	**$1,110,171.63**
« PREVIOUS 10			NEXT 10 »

Figure 8.30 Customized Number of Visits Till Conversion report

Conversions are entirely based on our action tracking. Therefore, every time the page on which we configured an action is viewed, an action is recorded. So make 100 percent sure the page is unique to that action.

System Reports

System reports are generally used for engineering and tend to drive decisions related to technology and usability studies. System reports are useful for marketing because they tell you the technical specifications of your visitors so that your web development efforts reflect the settings and capabilities of your audience.

The system reports Yahoo! provides out of the box include:

- Browsers
- Browser Versions
- JavaScript Support
- JavaScript Version
- Operating Systems
- Operating System Versions
- Screen Resolutions
- Color Palettes
- Connection Type
- Cookie Support
- Java Support
- Flash Support
- Flash Version

Conversions are not optimal reports by themselves, but better used along with other reports. For example, looking at a standard system report, such as the Browser Versions, provides technical information on your audience in general (see Figure 8.31).

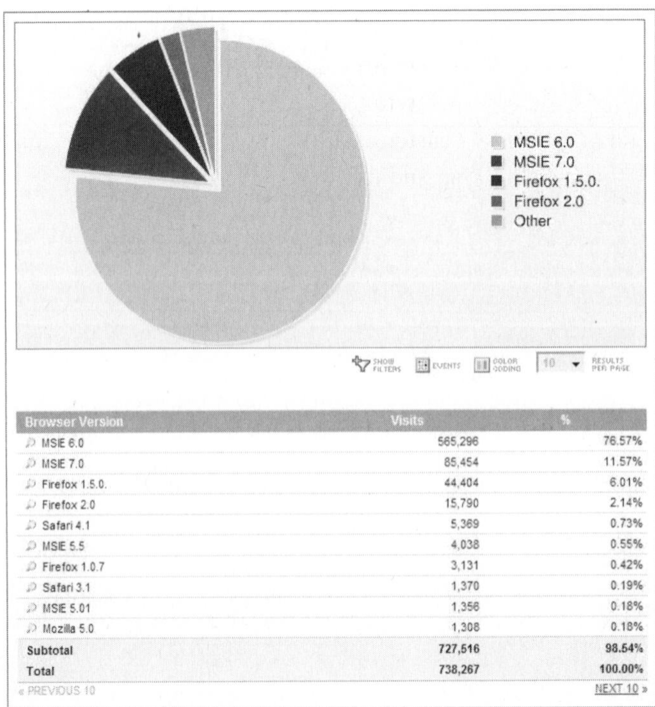

Browser Version	Visits	%
MSIE 6.0	565,296	76.57%
MSIE 7.0	85,454	11.57%
Firefox 1.5.0.	44,404	6.01%
Firefox 2.0	15,790	2.14%
Safari 4.1	5,369	0.73%
MSIE 5.5	4,038	0.55%
Firefox 1.0.7	3,131	0.42%
Safari 3.1	1,370	0.19%
MSIE 5.01	1,356	0.18%
Mozilla 5.0	1,308	0.18%
Subtotal	**727,516**	**98.54%**
Total	**738,267**	**100.00%**

« PREVIOUS 10 NEXT 10 »

Figure 8.31 Browser Versions report

Always segment between first-time and returning visitors when looking at system reports. If your site is incompatible with a browser version, you are not likely to see people coming back many times. If you don't differentiate between first-time and returning visitors, the results will be skewed, and you'll assume this is a smaller problem than it really is.

With that in mind, I applied a visit-to-sale conversion metric and an Avg. Order Value metric to the Browser Versions report, as shown in Figure 8.32.

Browser Version	Visits	Conversion	Avg. Order Value
MSIE 6.0	565,298	1.32%	$106.03
MSIE 7.0	85,454	1.82%	$102.82
Firefox 1.5.0.	44,404	2.24%	$108.77
Firefox 2.0	15,790	2.21%	$53.57
Safari 4.1	5,369	3.28%	$127.97
MSIE 5.5	4,038	0.89%	$142.37
Firefox 1.0.7	3,131	0.00%	$0.00
Safari 3.1	1,370	2.48%	$23.50
MSIE 5.01	1,356	1.25%	$122.68
Mozilla 5.0	1,308	6.65%	$12.25
Subtotal	**727,518**	**1.47%**	**$103.59**
Total	**738,269**	**1.46%**	**$102.98**
« PREVIOUS 10			NEXT 10 »

Figure 8.32 Customized Browser Versions report

This instantly shows us that there is an issue with Firefox 1.0.7; it generates visits like the others but for some reason does not generate any conversions. This is likely because of some sort of incompatibility—incompatibility that is costing the retailer just below $10,000 in the current time period. That is just the immediate revenue, not the lifetime revenue, and does not reflect the negative branding cost of being unable to serve 3,000 people. At the very least, we need to redirect these potential customers to a page that tells visitors where they can obtain a Firefox upgrade.

This brings us to the end of our report customization adventure. Now let's move on to another type of customization: setting up and using dashboards.

Using Dashboards

Effectively visualizing large sets of quantitative information has become a vital task in most organizations today. It has also become an extremely time-consuming task. This is solved by the introduction of the information dashboard. An information dashboard, simply put, allows its audience to monitor the status of their business in an instant. This chapter focuses on applying visualization techniques using the dashboard items provided by Yahoo! Web Analytics. This is not a best practice guide on choosing the best possible KPIs for your business, division, or unit, but a guide on what to do once you have them.

Chapter Contents

Defining a Dashboard
Adding a New Dashboard
Adding New Dashboard Items
Understanding Dashboard Items

Defining a Dashboard

Before we move forward, let's agree on exactly what a dashboard is. I like Stephen Few's definition as provided in his book, *Information Dashboard Design: The Effective Visual Communication of Data* (O'Reilly Media, Inc., 2006).

Dashboard

A dashboard is a visual display of the most important information needed to achieve one or more objectives, consolidated and arranged on a single screen so you can monitor the information at a glance.

By this definition, Yahoo! Web Analytics dashboards are not entirely where they are supposed to be.

In my blog I went through the dashboard features and functionality of the three free web analytics vendors: Yahoo!, Google, and Microsoft. Check the following post if you want to look into alternatives:

`http://visualrevenue.com/blog/2008/09/google-microsoft-yahoo-web-analytics-dashboards.html`

In the post I conclude that Google, Microsoft, and Yahoo! Web Analytics dashboards are, at worst, just a report collage, and, at best, an aspiring opportunity for end users to have an easy ascent toward true dashboards. Yahoo! provides the best flexibility as to what data to show and how to visualize it, but Google provides, through their solution, the best understanding of how to visually communicate quantitative data. The Microsoft dashboard lacks both data flexibility and good understanding of data visualization. This leaves us with the question of whether these web analytics tools should even consider themselves dashboard tools at this point or if they should acknowledge that they are meant for report collages.

What distinguishes a dashboard from a report collage? Dashboards focus on the KPIs that drive your business and nothing else. Figure 9.1 shows an example of a Yahoo! Web Analytics dashboard. Notice how much information it includes. Do you think it is a good at-a-glance tool?

My critique of the Yahoo! Web Analytics dashboard as a report collage is not meant to discourage you from using it; my purpose is for you to demand more and take great pride in the dashboard that you build and for you to truly bend the technology as much as you can. Most important, make sure that you do not fall into the easy trap of just creating a report collage and convincing yourself it is a dashboard.

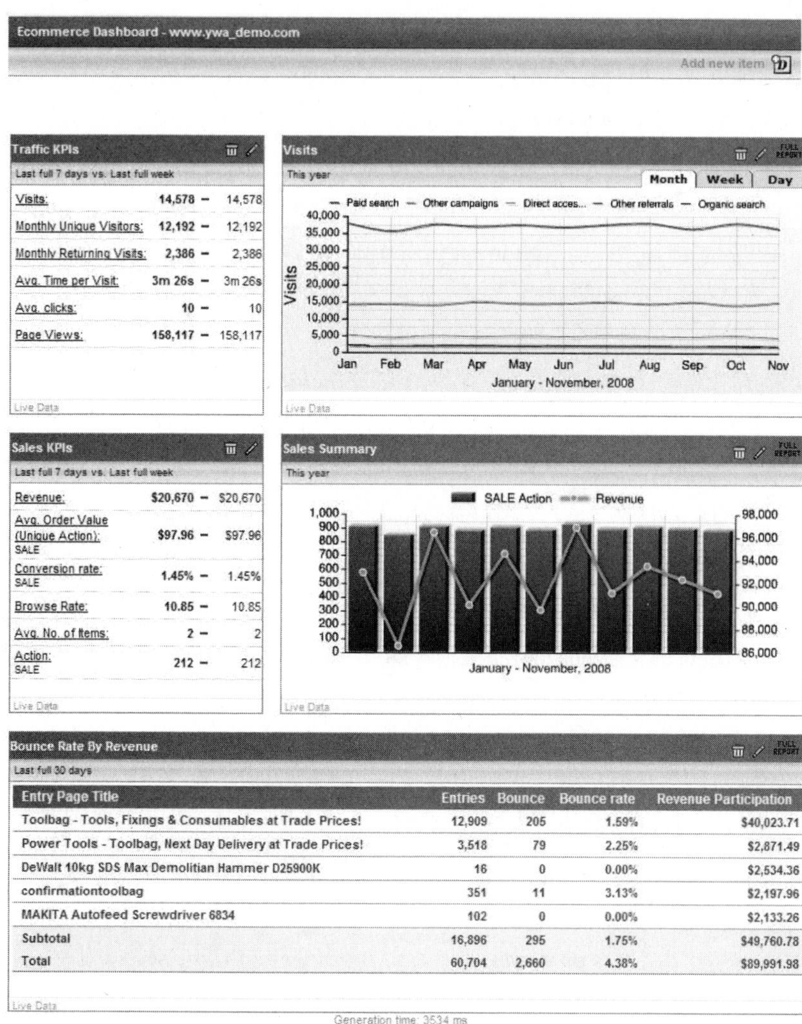

Figure 9.1 Yahoo! Web Analytics dashboard

Yahoo! Web Analytics dashboards provide a number of features that I find extremely interesting—features such as the opportunity to freely choose visualization and the ability to use any of the collected metrics and dimensions. Yahoo! also provides the ability to segment the dashboard items and to do all this with real-time data.

The reporting interface offers you (depending on where you created your Yahoo! Web Analytics Account) a series of preconfigured dashboards, which you'll find under Reports > Dashboards.

You can edit the default Executive Dashboards or create new ones. You can also drag and drop your dashboard items to customize the layout of your dashboard pages. You can achieve this without refreshing the page, and it is instantly saved. You can have as many as 10 different Executive Dashboards per user account.

For comparison, Figures 9.2 and 9.3 show examples of the dashboards provided by Google and Microsoft.

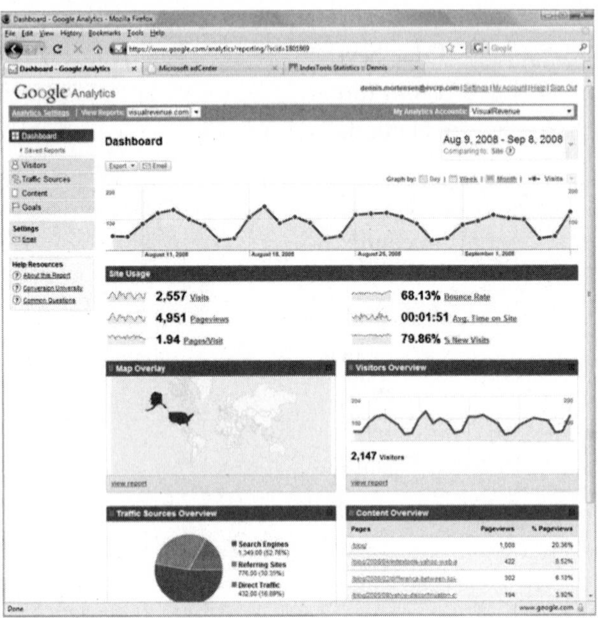

Figure 9.2 Google Analytics dashboard

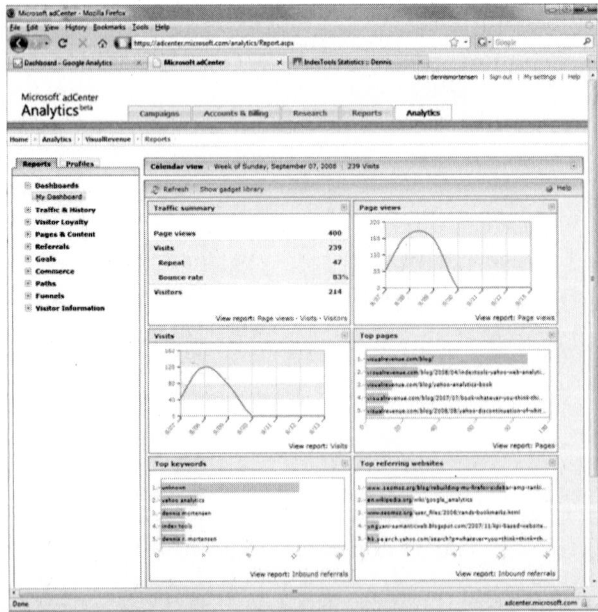

Figure 9.3 Microsoft adCenter Analytics dashboard

Adding a New Dashboard

A dashboard is unique from company to company and from function to function, and it is acceptable to have different dashboards for different objectives. Given that, providing fixed, preset dashboards is rarely of much value beyond making the tool look good. (Glitter!) The dashboard should be delivered blank, forcing you to set it up from the ground up. As with out-of-the-box reports, the blank dashboards are great starting points for something bigger.

You have to make your dashboard actionable (otherwise, it is *not* a dashboard). If you cannot compare data or generally put it in context, there is little reason for presenting the data to begin with.

Yahoo! allows you to compare data columns and define what is to be perceived as success and what is perceived as failure. Success or failure can be gauged by visualizing a conversion rate for a given segment where you determine that a visit-to-sale conversion below 4 percent should be marked.

To add a new dashboard, select Reports > Dashboards > Manage Dashboards, as shown in Figure 9.4.

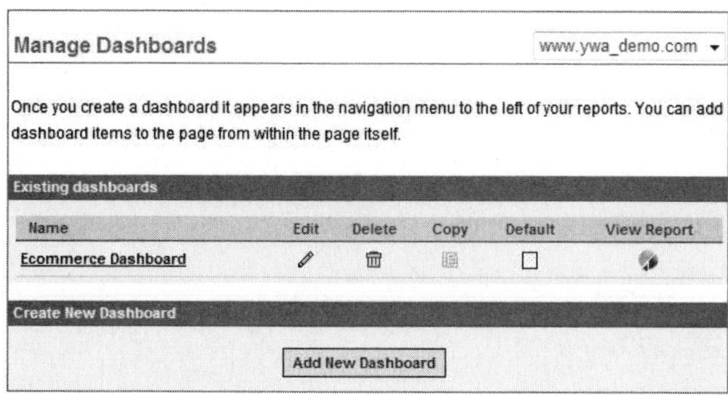

Figure 9.4 Manage Dashboards

The Manage Dashboards screen shows a list of your existing dashboards, but you are also allowed to perform the following functions from this screen:

- Add a Dashboard
- Edit an Existing Dashboard
- Copy a Dashboard
- Make a Dashboard the Default Report

The Add a Dashboard function is perhaps not as grand as you would expect; all it does is create an empty shell with a name and description, as Figure 9.5 shows.

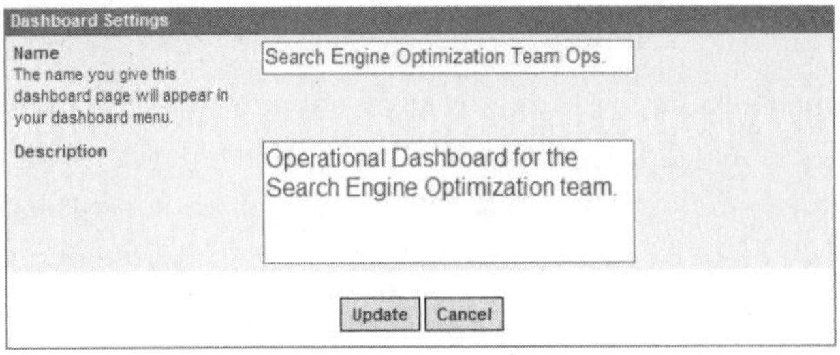

Figure 9.5 Adding a dashboard

Once a new dashboard is added, you are taken back to the Manage Dashboard screen, which shows you your latest addition (see Figure 9.6).

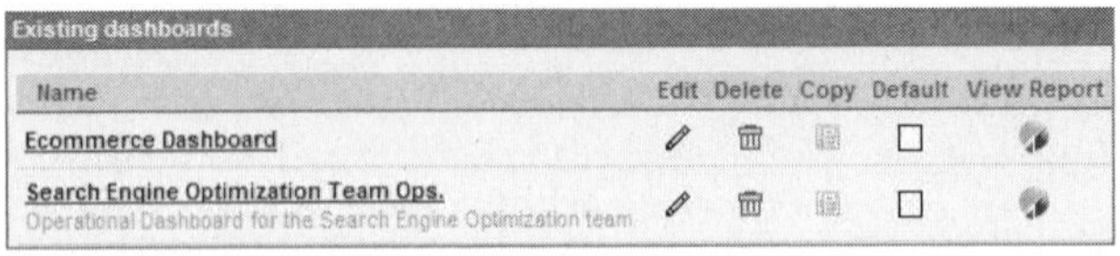

Figure 9.6 Updated Manage Dashboards screen

You have a number of options and actions for each dashboard:

Edit This title might be a bit confusing as it is not a link to set up dashboard items; it is merely a link to change the title and the description, as shown in Figure 9.5. Simply make your changes, click the Update button, and your new settings will be saved.

Delete To delete a dashboard, simply click the trashcan icon next to it, but beware, there are *no* warnings.

Copy The Copy function, which is available by clicking the Copy icon, allows you to copy a dashboard across multiple projects, enabling you to quickly share your dashboard setups and settings with other projects. Choose the project you wish to copy the dashboard to from the dropdown menu, or choose to copy to all projects. Click the Copy button, which copies the dashboard to your selected projects. You cannot replicate a dashboard within the same project but can use it as a starting point for the next one. This is shown in Figure 9.7.

Default When you enter Yahoo! Web Analytics, you are taken to the Control Center. Your next move is typically to the reports themselves, where the default report is the traffic overview. You can change the first default report and use one of your dashboards. Select the Dashboard checkbox to make this particular dashboard appear by default upon login.

View Report Yahoo! includes a shortcut so that you can go directly to the dashboard by clicking View Reports. This is no different than choosing the dashboard from the menu.

Copy Dashboard
This function allows you to copy dashboards across projects.
Copy the Ecommerce Dashboard to www.ywa_demo.com
Copy Cancel

Figure 9.7 Copying dashboards across projects

Depending on your account type, you can create up to 10 different dashboards. The difficult parts are choosing the right KPIs, choosing the right time periods, choosing the right visualization, and creating a unique departmental dashboard. The next section focuses on adding new dashboard items.

Adding New Dashboard Items

Now that you know how to set up and manage a blank dashboard, let's move on to the juicy part: adding dashboard items. You have two important tasks:

- Choosing *which* data to visualize (including context)
- Deciding *how* it should be visualized

Data should be any of the metrics or dimensions you already collected.

An example of viewing the data is comparing revenue from paid search to revenue from email advertising for the last 30 days running, displayed as a trend graph.

Yahoo! Web Analytics is the best of the three free tools when it comes to dashboard management. Yahoo! does limit the metrics and dimensions you can add depending on the chosen visualization. This might seem like a limitation, but you can view it as a polite education on which metrics and dimensions go best with which visualizations. I agree with most of the choices they have made.

When you start adding dashboard items, you might quickly come to the point where you simply aren't able to display all the information on a single screen. This is a problem with Yahoo!'s approach: Yahoo! uses only about 50 percent of screen real estate for data presentation, which means that it wastes half the potential data visualization space on items such as the logo, the top menu, the left menu, and other navigational fluff.

On a positive note, Yahoo! does allow users to remove the left menu by clicking the Hide button. That does not change the data/ink ratio, as dashboard items are not resized to use the extra space, though.

Data-Ink Ratio

The data/ink ratio is the proportion of ink (or pixels, when displaying information on a screen) used to present actual data, without redundancy, compared to the total amount of ink (or pixels) used in the entire display, such as in a table or graph. The goal is to design a display that has the highest possible data-ink ratio.

Coming back to the dashboard, you will find that you can add dashboard items in one of the following ways:

- Add new dashboard items from the dashboard itself.
- Add new dashboard items from reports.

To add new dashboard items from the dashboard, you go into the dashboard that you would like to amend and click the Add New Item button in the header of the dashboard. Clicking this button displays the Add Dashboard Item window, as shown in Figure 9.8, where you can select what types of items to add to the dashboard. Each dashboard item and its functionality is discussed in detail in the following section.

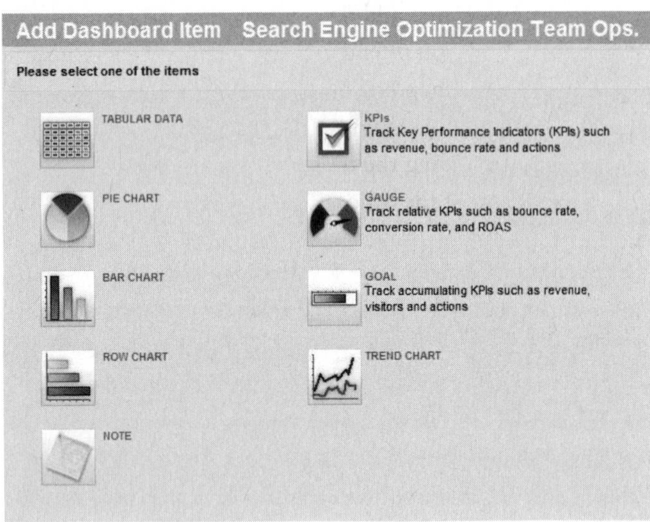

Figure 9.8 Add Dashboard Item screen

You can add new dashboard items from reports, but when you think about it, this approach is not optimal, unless it is part of some strict planning. You can quickly end up with the previous discussed report collage. You can select the report you want added to the dashboard from the Reports menu by clicking the Add to Dashboard button in the Report toolbar.

Not all reports, such as a Path Analysis report, can be added to a dashboard. If the Add to Dashboard button is grayed out, then that report is not currently available for the dashboard.

Clicking the Add to Dashboard button displays a pop-up window, where you choose which dashboard you want to add a new report to. Dashboards are presented in a dropdown list, as shown in Figure 9.9.

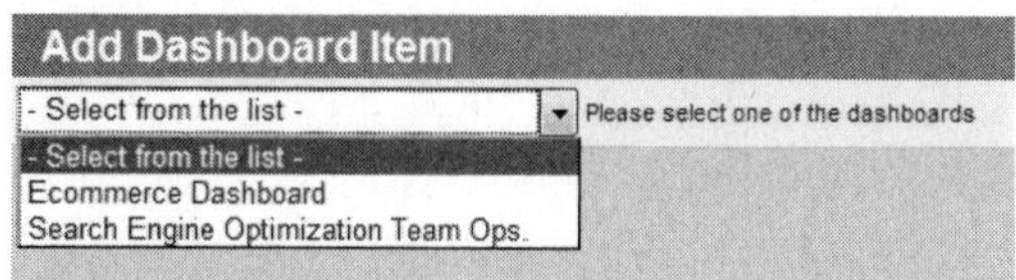
Add Dashboard Item
- Select from the list -
Please select one of the dashboards
- Select from the list -
Ecommerce Dashboard
Search Engine Optimization Team Ops.

Figure 9.9 Adding a dashboard item

Select the dashboard you want to add a new report item to. This will take you to the Add Dashboard Item window shown in Figure 9.8.

No matter how you ended up at the Add Dashboard Item window, your first task is to choose the visualization form. Think about your choice carefully. You cannot change it later, and a random visualization form could destroy an otherwise great KPI, simply because it will not have the effect that you intended if it is not visualized in the correct way. (More details on this later in the chapter.)

You choose the visualization by clicking the appropriate icon, which takes you into the second and most important step of adding the dashboard item. This second step, shown in Figure 9.10, allows you to select the following:

- Reporting Metric
- Dashboard Item Name
- Reporting Period
- Action
- Placement
- Comparative period
- Optional Top Group
- Visitor Segment

These properties are specific to the item, which means that you will never see all of them at the same time.

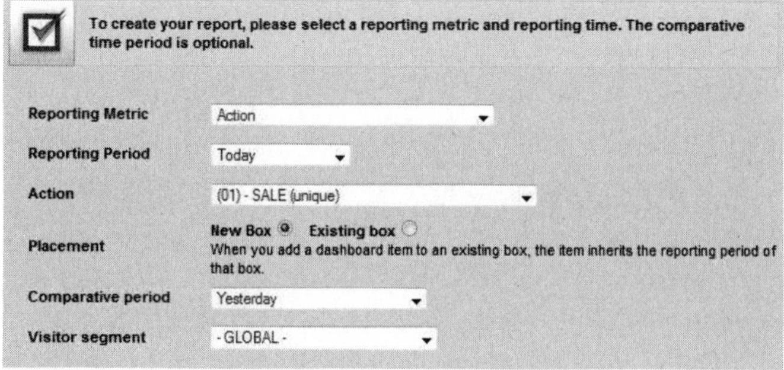
To create your report, please select a reporting metric and reporting time. The comparative time period is optional.

Reporting Metric	Action
Reporting Period	Today
Action	(01) - SALE (unique)
Placement	New Box ◉ Existing box ○ When you add a dashboard item to an existing box, the item inherits the reporting period of that box.
Comparative period	Yesterday
Visitor segment	- GLOBAL -

Figure 9.10 On this screen, you select properties specific to the item.

I advise that you change the default name, which is set to the name of the primary metric. You change the name by clicking the Modify Default Name link to the right of the metric.

Choosing a reporting period for a dashboard item is mandatory, while choosing a comparative period is optional. Avoid adding too many different time periods on your dashboard. I tend to use one time period and one comparative period. The comparative period does not need to match the main reporting period of the item from a technical point of view, whereas from a logical point of view you need a good reason and the right metric to use two different period sizes, such as comparing this week to the last 30 days. It would make sense to compare, for example, a conversion rate for a longer historical period, getting a fair average number, to the latest weekly conversion rate average.

Understanding Dashboard Items

The topic of choosing the correct KPI for your business could consume an entire book by itself. Therefore, it is more important that you invest time in KPI investigation than actual dashboard setup. While I'll go into detail for every visualization opportunity you have in the Yahoo! Web Analytics dashboard, I'll allow myself to apply one or two suggestions for a potentially good KPI and important metric. If you wonder what the difference is between a KPI and a metric, here is a list of seven things that distinguish KPIs from the rest of your metrics:

- A KPI echoes organizational goals.
- A KPI is decided by management.
- A KPI provides context.
- A KPI creates meaning on all organizational levels.
- A KPI is based on legitimate data.
- A KPI is easy to understand.
- A KPI leads to action!

That's serious, eh? But there is no escaping it when creating KPIs and especially when using those KPIs for your dashboard.

Note: For more information about choosing KPIs, including a Microsoft PowerPoint presentation, see my blog: `http://visualrevenue.com/blog/2008/02/difference-between-kpi-and-metric.html`

Now, on to the actual items you can use. I am going to use the previously setup dashboard, Search Engine Optimization Team Ops, as a canvas for all the examples in this section. Keep in mind that the items we will add are not SEO related, though.

Tabular Data

Tabular data is similar to the tabular data presented in most reports. Use tabular data for displaying data when not only the split between points is important, but also the value.

To add this item, you are presented with the options shown in Figure 9.11.

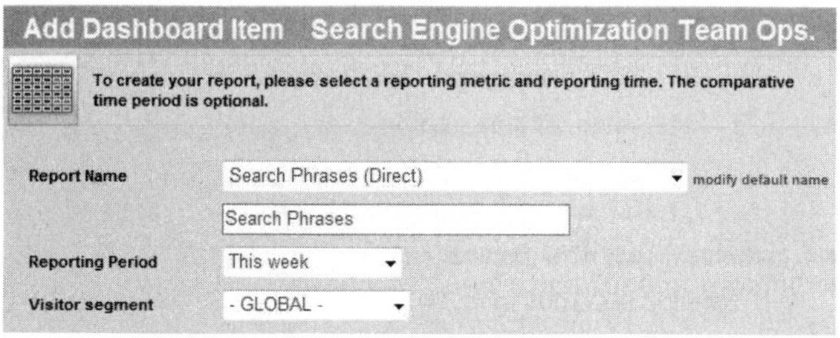

Add Dashboard Item Search Engine Optimization Team Ops.

To create your report, please select a reporting metric and reporting time. The comparative time period is optional.

Report Name	Search Phrases (Direct) ▾ modify default name
	Search Phrases
Reporting Period	This week ▾
Visitor segment	- GLOBAL - ▾

Figure 9.11 Adding the Tabular Data dashboard item

The fantastic thing about this item is that you can choose any report from the system, even a custom report created a minute ago. This, along with the reporting period, is mandatory input.

The result of the input in Figure 9.11 is shown in Figure 9.12.

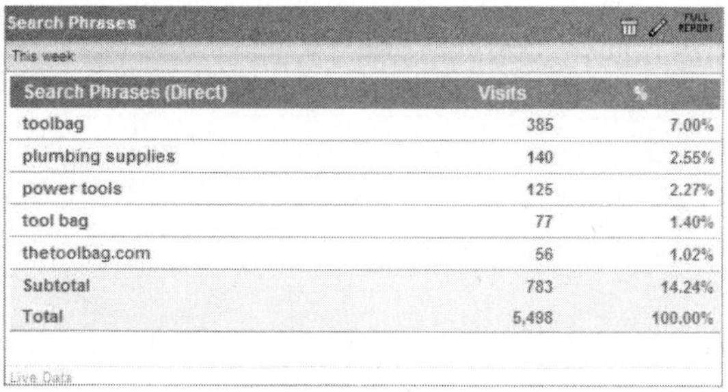

Search Phrases

This week

Search Phrases (Direct)	Visits	%
toolbag	385	7.00%
plumbing supplies	140	2.55%
power tools	125	2.27%
tool bag	77	1.40%
thetoolbag.com	56	1.02%
Subtotal	783	14.24%
Total	5,498	100.00%

Live Data

Figure 9.12 Search Phrases presented in a Tabular Data dashboard item

A newly added item appears at the end of the dashboard. You can then move the item to its final destination. It might take a bit of juggling to do this as Yahoo! automatically positions an item if you move another in its place.

Attached to the Dashboard Item box header is a number of functions, which are represented by icons:

- Delete Dashboard Item
- Edit Dashboard Item
- Go to Full Report
- Move Dashboard Item

The Delete function will warn you before the item is deleted, and once the item is deleted, you are forced to create a new item; there is no undo for this function. This is all about visualization, so no data is deleted. The Edit function will take you back to the Add Dashboard Item screen shown in Figure 9.11, but with a few added attributes (see Figure 9.13).

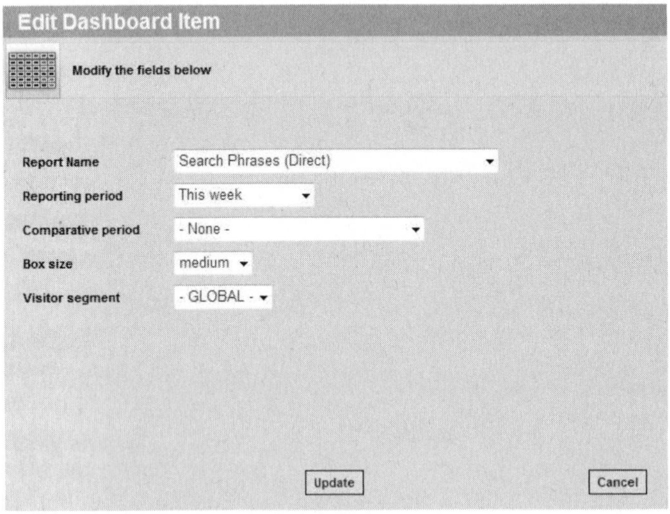

Figure 9.13 We've added a few attributes to this screen.

The Full Report function will take you to a report showing an in-depth view of the data and will allow you to work with it in greater detail—which is exactly why you should use a dashboard: Whenever you spot something out of the ordinary, you must drill into the data and figure out why that is. The full report for the item in Figure 9.12 looks like Figure 9.14.

Notice that the rolling period from the dashboard, This Week, is replaced with the actual date range in the full report.

You can move the whole item to another position on the dashboard simply by clicking the header, dragging the item to another position, and then releasing the mouse button.

These general functions are applied to all dashboard items. I will not repeat these descriptions as we move along to other kinds of visualizations.

I tend to use Tabular Data only when it comes from custom reports, but when utilized correctly, Tabular Data can be quite powerful. An example is the custom report we created earlier, the Search Engine Revenue Insight and Referrals report.

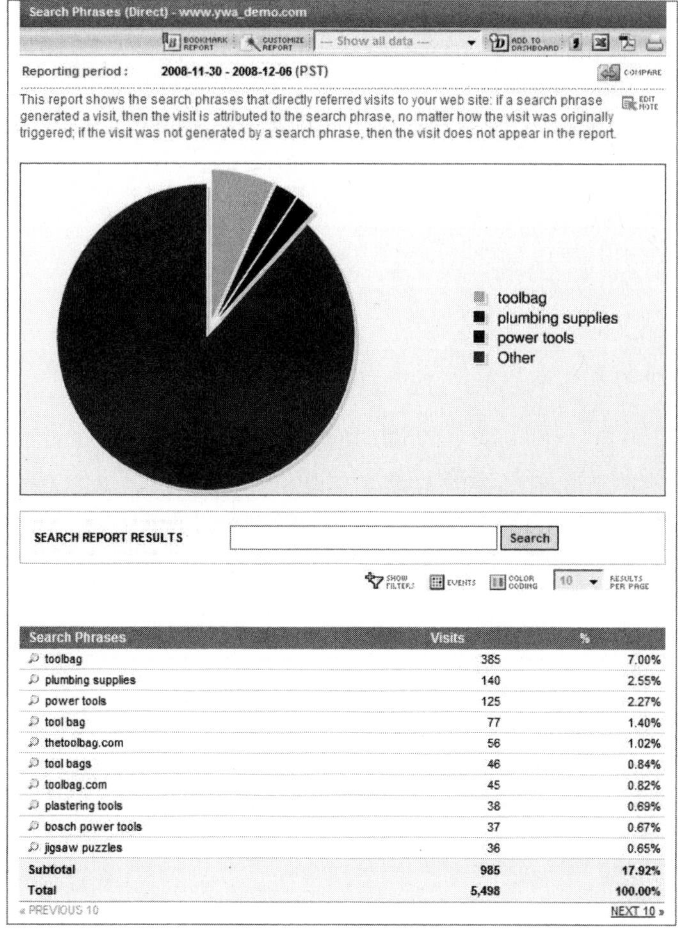

Search Phrases	Visits	%
toolbag	385	7.00%
plumbing supplies	140	2.55%
power tools	125	2.27%
tool bag	77	1.40%
thetoolbag.com	56	1.02%
tool bags	46	0.84%
toolbag.com	45	0.82%
plastering tools	38	0.69%
bosch power tools	37	0.67%
jigsaw puzzles	36	0.65%
Subtotal	**985**	**17.92%**
Total	**5,498**	**100.00%**

« PREVIOUS 10 NEXT 10 »

Figure 9.14 Search Phrases report

Pie Charts

Pie charts display percentages and are used to show and compare different parts of the same whole. Use pie charts for representing how something is divided among various groups. First, let's look at how to add them and which attributes to use. Figure 9.15 shows the screen we'll use to add the pie chart.

Add Dashboard Item Search Engine Optimization Team Ops.

To create your report, please select a reporting metric and reporting time.

Report Name	Visiting Countries	modify default name
Reporting Period	Last full 30 days	
Visitor segment	- GLOBAL -	

Figure 9.15 Adding a pie chart dashboard item

Here you are forced to apply the report (metric) and the reporting period. The results of the values in Figure 9.15 appear in Figure 9.16.

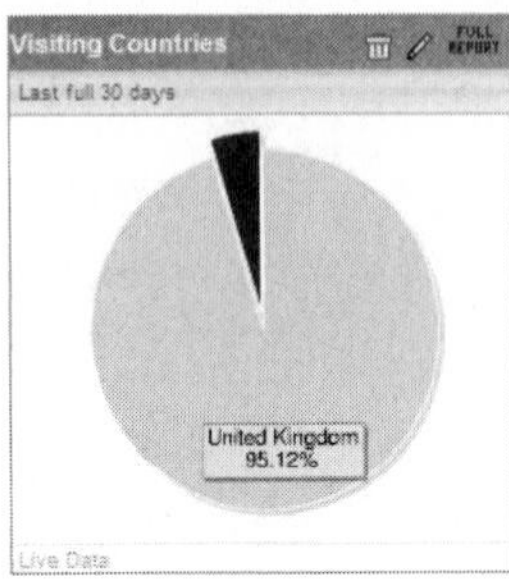

Figure 9.16 The pie chart of the values in Figure 9.15

You should use the pie chart visualization technique sparingly. Pie charts make it easy to judge the magnitude of a slice only when it is close to 0, 25, 50, 75, or 100 percent. Any percentages other than these and the angles, if there are many, are difficult to discern.

Looking at the pie chart presented in Figure 9.16, we could assume that this UK retailer wants information on how much traffic is coming from outside their delivery region. You could answer this with a simple KPI percentage—you don't need a full pie chart to show that. In a case like this, why color your numbers at all when they are better presented as is?

Percentages and other parts of the whole can be much more accurately shown in a bar chart, simply due to the fact that there is a numbered scale. So let's move on to one of the most useful visualization techniques you can use on the Yahoo! dashboards: the bar chart.

Bar and Row Charts

A bar chart, or bar graph as some call it, is a chart with rectangular bars with lengths proportional to the values that they represent. Bar charts are used for comparing two or more values. The bars can be horizontally (what Yahoo! calls row charts) or vertically oriented.

I am very fond of bar charts, whether shown vertically or horizontally. And I think, even beyond the Yahoo! Web Analytics dashboard solution, that this is one of the simplest and yet most powerful visualization techniques for quantitative data. Bar charts are great for displaying measures that are associated with some sort of categorization, which is what we see as dimensions within Yahoo! Web Analytics.

I would even be so bold as to conclude that using the bar chart with the KPI box is all you need in a dashboard.

Bar and row charts are similar to traditional line graphs, called trend charts in Yahoo!. However, rather than using a point on a plane to define a value, bar and row charts use a horizontal or vertical rectangular bar that levels off at the appropriate level.

Adding a bar chart is straightforward, and you can see an example in Figure 9.17.

Add Dashboard Item   Search Engine Optimization Team Ops.

To create your report, please select a reporting metric and reporting time.

Report Name	Returning Visits	modify default name
Reporting Period	Last full 30 days	
Visitor segment	- GLOBAL -	

Figure 9.17 Adding a bar chart dashboard item

The only mandatory fields are the Report Name (metric or dimension) and the Reporting Period. The result of the values in Figure 9.17 appears in Figure 9.18.

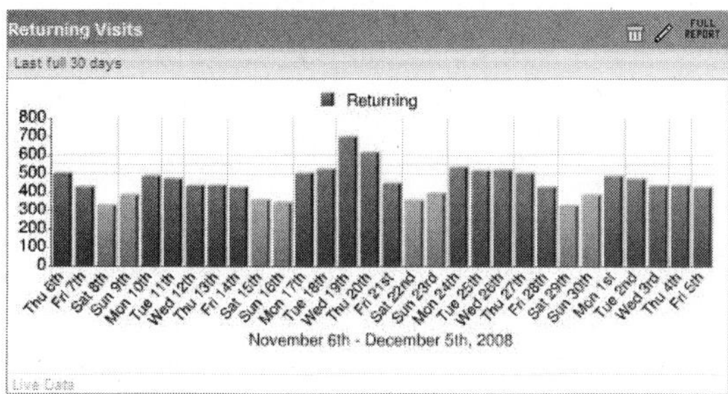

Figure 9.18 The bar chart of the values in Figure 9.17

You can monitor the chart shown in Figure 9.18 and be alerted when you are moving into a downward negative spiral. You might have an increase in traffic due to aggressive campaign strategies or a poor review on a site. If you see a decline in returning visitors, it is time to figure out what's wrong with your business—no company can survive on first-time visitors only.

You add the row chart in a similar way, as you can see in Figure 9.19.

Add Dashboard Item   Search Engine Optimization Team Ops.

To create your report, please select a reporting metric and reporting time.

Report Name	Referring Domains (Direct)	modify default name
Reporting Period	Last full 30 days	
Visitor segment	- GLOBAL -	

Figure 9.19 Adding a row chart dashboard item

The only mandatory fields are the Report Name (metric or dimension) and the Reporting Period. The result of the values in Figure 9.19 appears in Figure 9.20.

When looking at similar data, choose a bar graph, as it makes comparison easy across dashboard items. Think about how you size and stack these items on the actual dashboard.

You cannot choose stacked bar charts; however, if you choose reports like First Time Visits vs. Returning Visits, this metric comparison is provided automatically and without you applying anything.

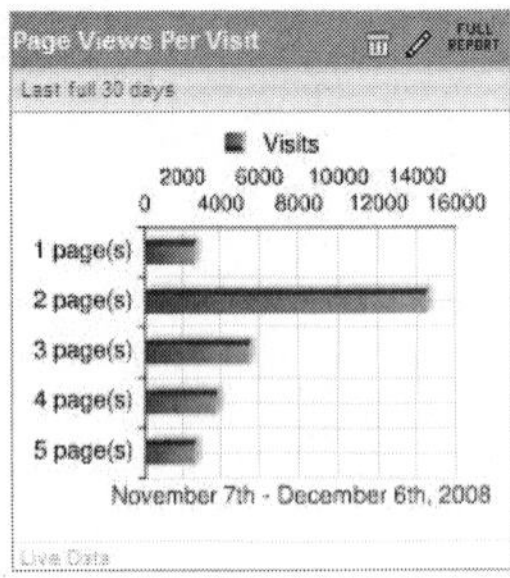

Figure 9.20 The row chart of the values in Figure 9.19

Key Performance Indicators (KPIs)

The Yahoo! Web Analytics KPI dashboard item displays key performance indicators (KPIs) such as revenue, return on advertising spending (ROAS), and unique actions. Choosing the right KPIs to display and how to display them is challenging; KPIs are one of the most important dashboard items that you have in your arsenal. As I stated earlier, you will be able to get by with bar graphs and KPIs alone.

I believe, however naive it might sound, that one of the best visualization methods is just showing the number. I don't need any magic applied to a metric such as Revenue So Far This Month. Just show me the number!

Almost any of the tracked metrics can be promoted, from a logical point of view, to KPIs and presented in a KPI dashboard item box.

When adding your first KPI (see Figure 9.21), you are presented with a number of options, which change a bit depending on the metric you choose. Most of the other dashboard visualization types provide a presorted and selected list of metrics, whereas the KPI list is essentially making all of the metrics in the system available.

When you select Action as a reporting metric, you get another mandatory field: which action you want to display.

Figure 9.22 shows the result of adding a sale Action KPI in a KPI item box for this week compared to the same partial period four weeks ago.

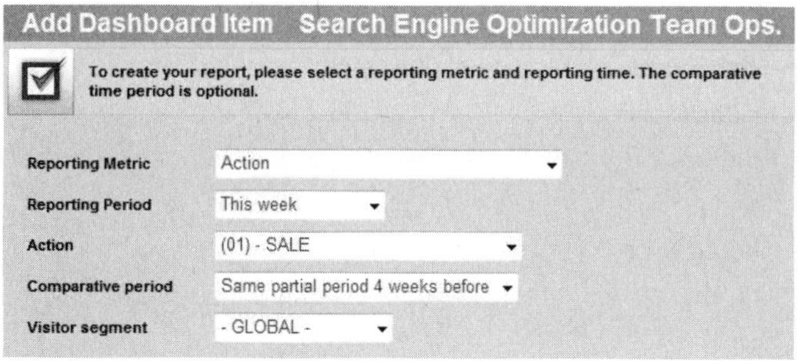

Figure 9.21 Adding a KPI dashboard item

Figure 9.22 The result of adding a sale Action KPI

You will likely have more than one KPI item box on your dashboard, and the categorization should either be done on the metric or the period. The reason for categorizing on the period is that this is fixed for the entire box.

When you add a second KPI to the dashboard, as shown in Figure 9.23, you are asked whether you want to create a new box or add to an existing box. If you choose the latter option, you are provided with a dropdown listing the existing KPI's boxes that you have.

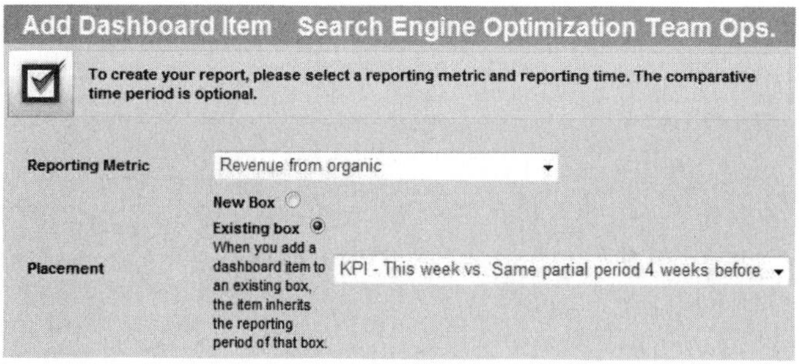

Figure 9.23 Adding a metric to the existing KPI box

In Figure 9.24 multiple metrics are presented in one KPI box.

The KPI box typically appears in the upper-left corner and is thus the most visible box you have. So to make it more appealing, sort the order of the individual KPIs in the box (see Figure 9.25).

While not the perfect sorting mechanism, it will do what you need.

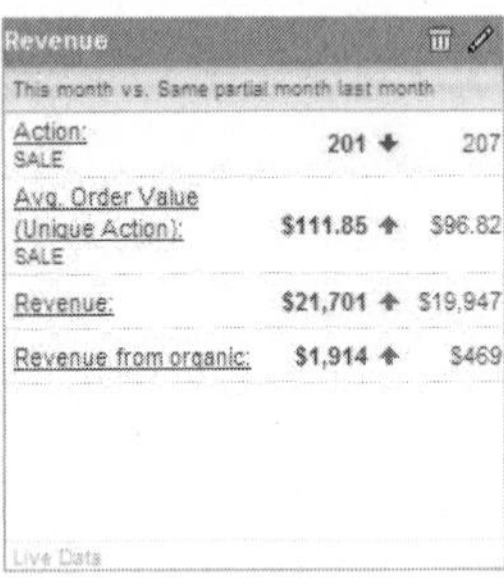

Figure 9.24 Multiple metrics in one KPI box

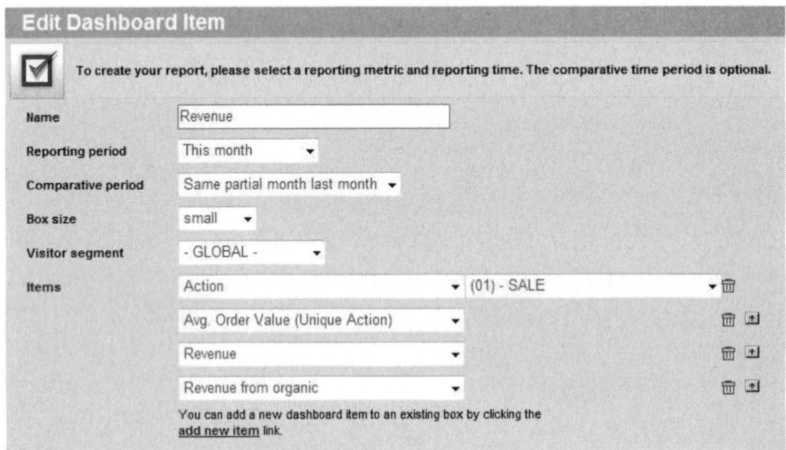

Figure 9.25 Sorting and managing KPI box items

Gauge

I am not too fond of gauges as central dashboard items in general, but let me begin with the facts about gauges in Yahoo! Web Analytics.

A gauge displays fluctuating data such as the bounce rate or conversion rate. At the same time, it allows you to display the performance of the KPI. The performance is displayed as green, yellow, and red and is based on your own set targets.

The most important thing to remember about gauges is that they do not function very well, if at all, on accumulating data values, such as visits, page views, or revenue. The reason that gauges are not working for such metrics is that the metric value will be small, and thus represented as highly negative in the beginning of the period, and by the end of the period, the metric could be visualized as overly positive. Furthermore, in between the start of a reporting period and the end of a reporting period, the gauge provides very little insight. For this type of data, you would be better off using a goal chart (discussed in the next section).

When you add a gauge dashboard item, as shown in Figure 9.26, you must provide a lower and a higher limit, which may be the best thing about gauges—they force you to think about success and failure.

The result of the numbers input for the metric conversion rate and the lower and higher limits appears in Figure 9.27.

Add Dashboard Item Search Engine Optimization Team Ops.

To create a gauge you need to define your success criteria, eg the lower and upper limits of performance. A gauge can track relative KPIs such as your bounce rate, conversion rate and ROAS.

Reporting Metric	Conversion rate ▾ modify default name
Reporting Period	This month ▾
Action	(01) - SALE ▾
Comparative period	Same partial month last month ▾
Lower Limit	1.0
Higher Limit	1.8
Visitor segment	- GLOBAL - ▾

Figure 9.26 Adding a gauge dashboard item

Figure 9.27 Displaying the gauge dashboard item

The Good portion of the display is always colored in green. Looking at a conversion rate metric (as shown in Figure 9.27), the higher the value, the better and thus the green part appears to the right.

The reverse is also possible, where a metric such as Cost per Action (CPA) is more successful the lower it is. Therefore, the gauge shows the green part to the left, as you can see in Figure 9.28.

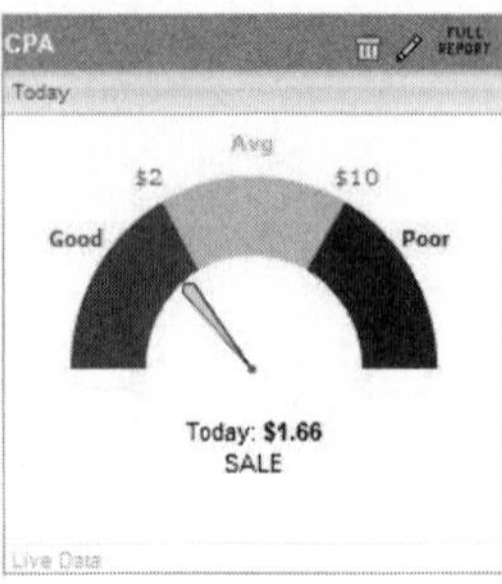

Figure 9.28 The gauge dashboard Item with reverse success visualization

It's time for me to provide you with my personal warning about gauges: I find them less than optimal, to put it mildly. Don't get me wrong; they look great and add a lot of authenticity and color to the dashboard, but when you think about it, are they really the best way to present a conversion rate?

Most of the time, a conversion rate is much better displayed as a single KPI number instead of wasting a whole dashboard item on one KPI. Furthermore, if you have three conversion rates you would like to compare, comparing values across gauges becomes very difficult. So I suggest you avoid gauges unless somebody who pays your salary demands them.

Goal Charts

A goal chart displays KPIs with accumulating data such as visits, page views, actions, and revenue. Use goal displays when you have a clear goal for your KPI and you want to track progress toward your target. You should not use a goal chart for a conversion rate, a bounce rate, or anything else that does not progress and accumulate toward a goal.

The goal chart holds the same characteristics as the KPI box since you can apply multiple items to the same box.

When setting up a new goal, as you can see in Figure 9.29, you have to choose whether to create a complete new goal dashboard item box or apply your new goal to an existing box. Then you have to enter the metric, period, and most important, a target for your goal, which Yahoo! calls the limit.

The results of the choices in Figure 9.29 are presented in Figure 9.30.

Notice that the numbers presented on top of the goal are not the usual sorted set. They represent the following values:

- The start value, which is always 0
- KPI, which is the current value of the KPI
- The goal (limit), which is the number you specified when you created the item

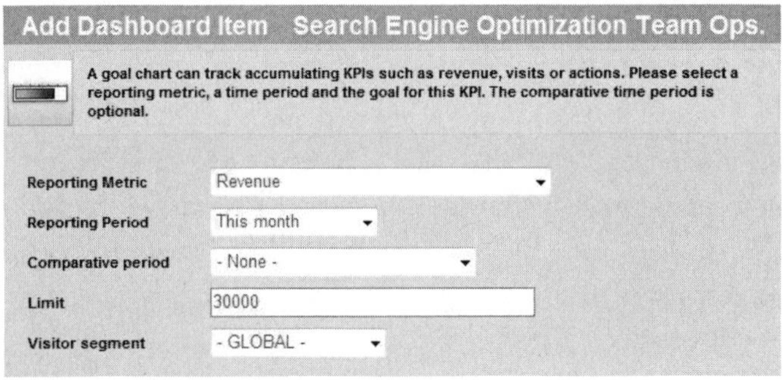

Figure 9.29 Adding a goal dashboard item

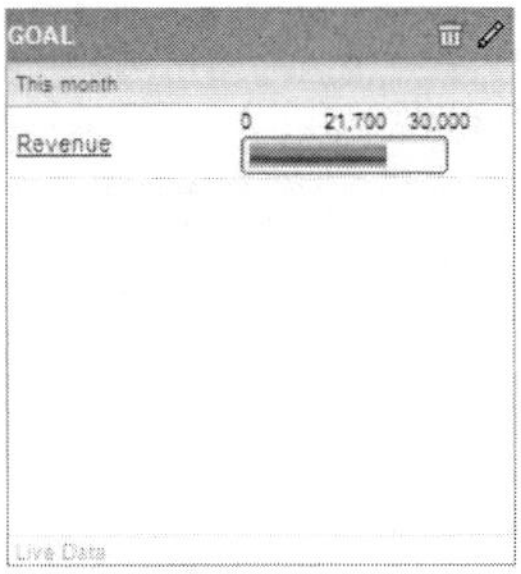

Figure 9.30 The results of the choices in Figure 9.29

In order for the bar to turn green, the middle KPI value must become greater than the set goal (limit).

You can add a comparative period, which appears as a horizontal split on the bar. For examples, see some of the dashboard examples in appendix 2.

Trend Charts

Line graphs, or trend charts as they are called by Yahoo!, do an excellent job of displaying the shape (trend) of data and how it moves up or down. We can compare two variables by plotting them along a vertical axis and a horizontal axis, and can show specific values of data, determine data trends, and make predictions.

The trend chart is almost as valuable as the bar chart. If you have to expand beyond the KPI box and the bar chart, this is the visualization item to use. Trend charts are the best possible way to illustrate a time series–based dataset. The focus is less on the actual values—for that you would use a bar chart—and more on the overview and comparison.

With this in mind, I suggest adding a top group, as that provides a great third dimension to the chart. You'll learn more about this in a moment.

It is important to understand when to use a trend chart rather than a bar chart. If in doubt, you should go with the bar chart and leave the trend chart for later.

The three types of scales that appear in graphs based on dimensions as we know them in Yahoo! Web Analytics are as follows:

Nominal Scales Nominal scales are lists of items that belong to one shared dimension but do not relate to each other in any way other than that. Therefore, the order of this list has no meaning. This could for example be dimensions such as Country, City, and Browser Type.

Ordinal Scales Ordinal scales are lists of items that belong to the same dimension. And opposite from what we know from nominal scales, ordinal scales do have a unique order. This could, for example, be dimensions such as Weeks, Day of Week, and Page Views per Visits.

Interval Scales Interval scales are lists of items that, like ordinal scales, belong to the same dimension and have a unique order, but they represent a value as well. An interval scale is a quantitative scale, such as the sum of visits in a month, which is then divided into a set of smaller ranges, perhaps a day, thus showing the sum of visits per every day in that month.

For nominal and ordinal scales, I recommend that you go with the bar chart and only use trend charts for interval scales. There is little lost and no major harm done in using bar charts on all three scales, but from a visualization point of view, it is wrong to use trend charts on nominal and ordinal scales.

Adding a trend chart involves filling in the usual suspects, but with the notable difference of a top group (see Figure 9.31).

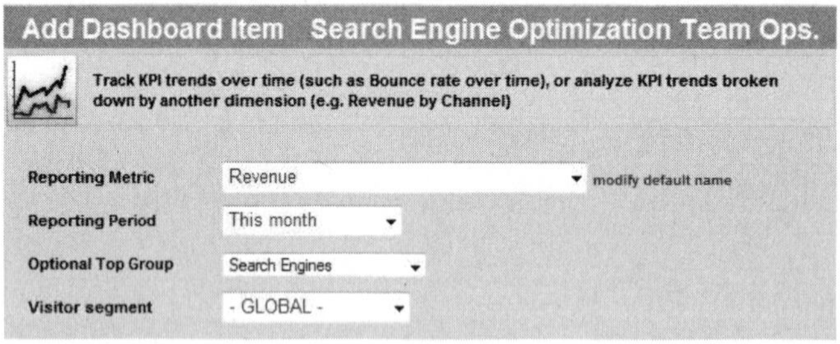

Add Dashboard Item Search Engine Optimization Team Ops.

Track KPI trends over time (such as Bounce rate over time), or analyze KPI trends broken down by another dimension (e.g. Revenue by Channel)

Reporting Metric: Revenue — modify default name
Reporting Period: This month
Optional Top Group: Search Engines
Visitor segment: - GLOBAL -

Figure 9.31 Adding a trend chart dashboard item

We wanted to generate a trended revenue line graph in Figure 9.31, and added in a top group based on the dimension Search Engines. Remember that you can easily have multiple visualizations based on the same data on the dashboard. For example, you could have Revenue This Month as part of a KPI box and then still have a trended revenue line graph to the right of it.

The result of the values added in Figure 9.31 appears in Figure 9.32.

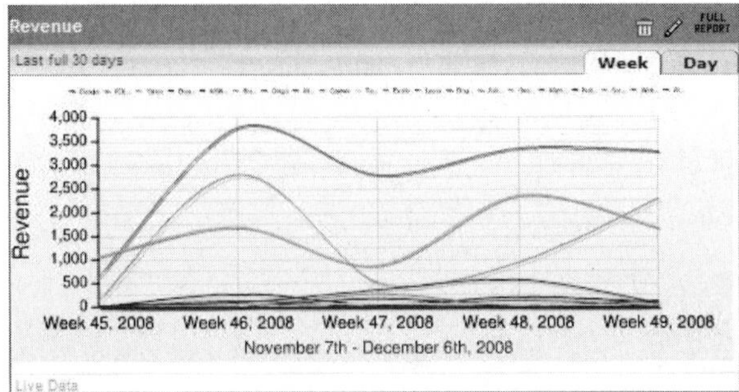

Figure 9.32 The result of the values added in Figure 9.31

The trend chart dashboard item contains a Resolution tab, which allows you to select the time unit on the dashboard element. You can select Hour, Day, Week, or Month depending on the reporting period you initially selected. If the reporting period for a trend dashboard element is set to Year, then the Resolution tab will not contain the Hour option.

The time unit you select is saved and the page is refreshed. Your selected time unit will be maintained until you make a new selection. This feature helps you avoid unsatisfactory displays in which accumulating data is trending downward if the selected period extends into the first few days of a given month.

I created, for inspiration purposes, a second trend chart example, shown in Figure 9.33, the trended visit-to-sale conversion rate segmented on campaign sources.

One thing that annoys me a bit is that Yahoo! displays too many items in the top group you apply. If you look at Figure 9.32, we would have been better off with a top 5 or an option to choose how many items in that category we would like to display.

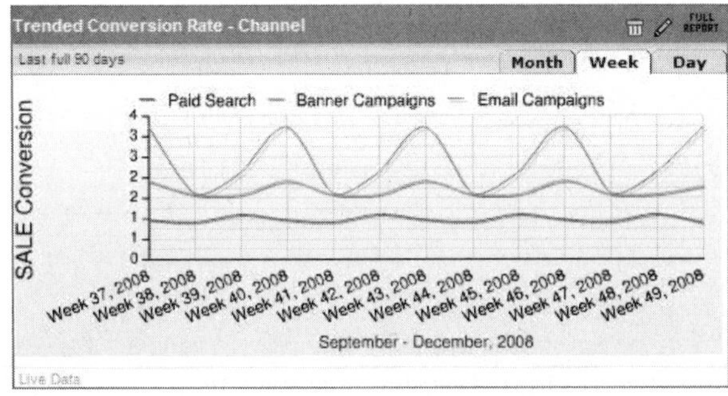

Figure 9.33 Trended conversion rate dashboard item with channel top group

Notes

The Notes dashboard item from Yahoo! lets you add notes and subsequently edit them. I am ambivalent when it comes to notes. If we think about the perfect dashboard and the definition of dashboards as a whole, there should be no need for notes on the dashboard. I do, however, like the functionality and try to see this feature as a sticky note added to a printout.

The notes support standard HTML syntax. As you can see in Figure 9.34, you must first enter the note's title.

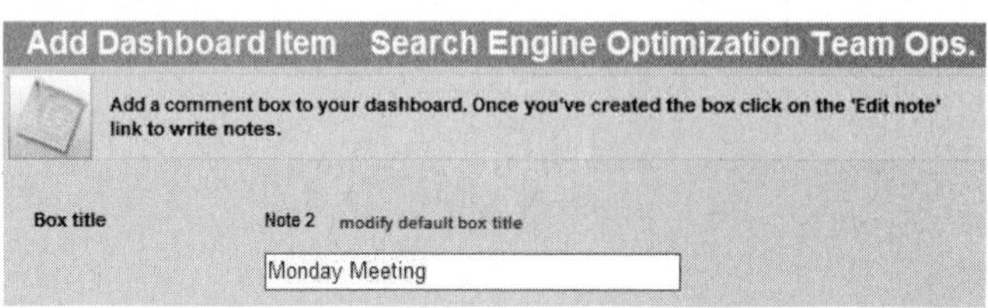

Figure 9.34 Adding a note dashboard item

Once you enter the title, you are taken back to the dashboard, where an empty note has been added. Click the edit button to apply the text. For our example, I added the following text:

```
<H2>SEO Dashboard</H2>
This Dashboard is created for the Search Engines Optimization Operational
Team. The Dashboard is also used as a reference point in Monday morning
meetings. Send change suggestions to
<a href="mailto:dennis.mortensen@evcrp.com">Dennis</a>.
```

The text results in a formatted dashboard note item that looks like the one in Figure 9.35.

Figure 9.35 Our formatted note

In Figure 9.36 we have all the items we created on one dashboard. Does this mean this is a great dashboard? No! It is just a representation of all the items for your reference, and it should by no means be seen as the perfect dashboard or as a unique SEO team dashboard.

I will provide a number of real dashboard examples in the insert, so you can get some inspiration from those.

Search Engine Optimization Team Ops. - www.ywa_demo.com

Add new item

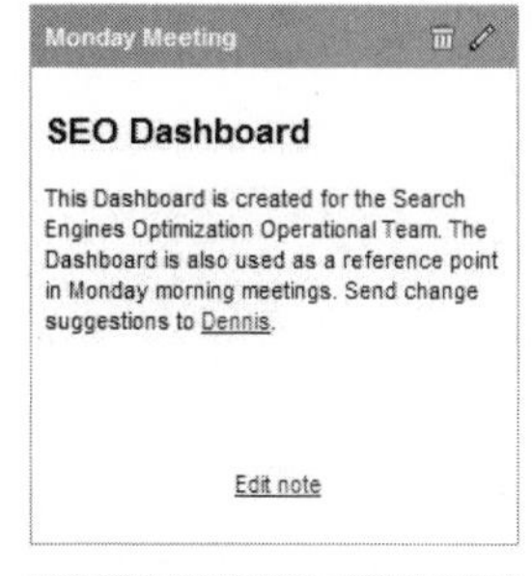

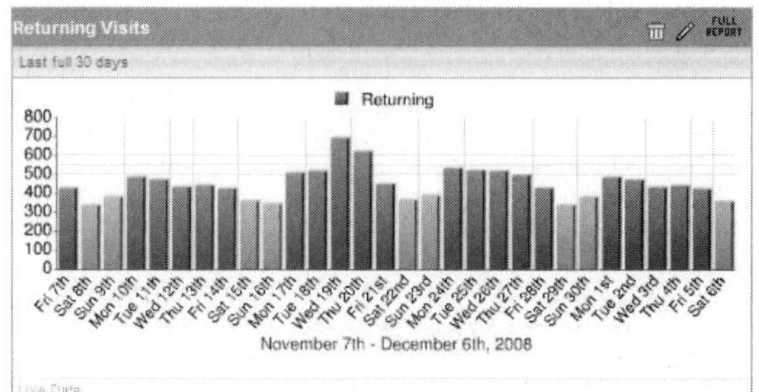

Revenue

This month vs. Same partial month last month

	This month		Last month
Action: SALE	201	↓	207
Avg. Order Value (Unique Action): SALE	$111.85	↑	$96.82
Revenue:	$21,701	↑	$19,947
Revenue from organic:	$1,914	↑	$469

Live Data

Search Engine Revenue Insight and Referrals Report

This month

Search Engines (Direct)	Visits	Revenue	Conversion	Avg. Order Value
Google	4,021	$3,801.38	0.80%	$118.79
Yahoo	716	$2,809.06	1.82%	$216.08
AOL Search	405	$1,700.46	1.48%	$283.41
MSN Search	142	$275.52	2.11%	$91.84
Oingo	7	$126.71	14.29%	$126.71
Subtotal	5,291	$8,713.13	1.04%	$158.42
Total	5,898	$8,810.05	1.07%	$139.84

Live Data

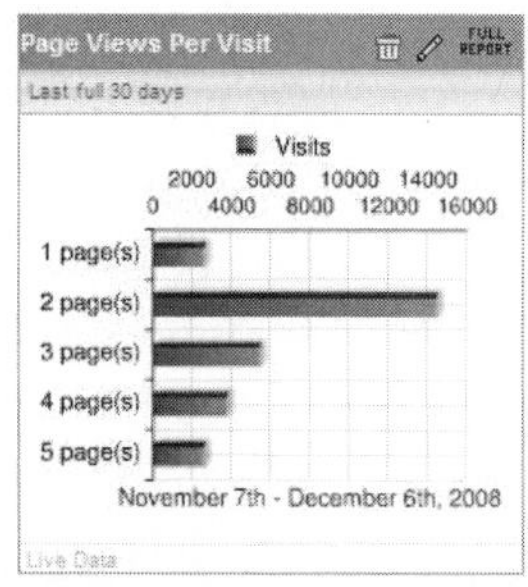

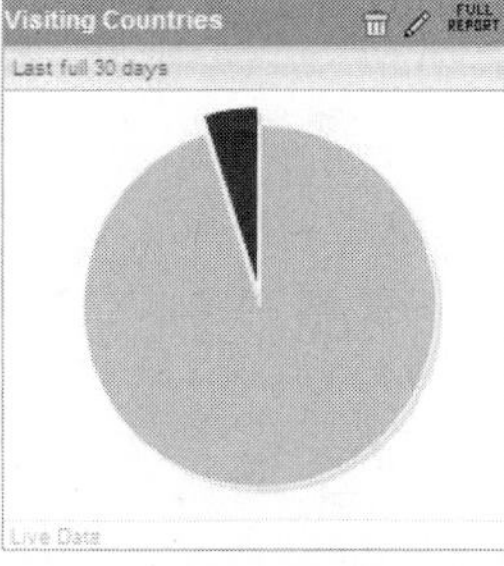

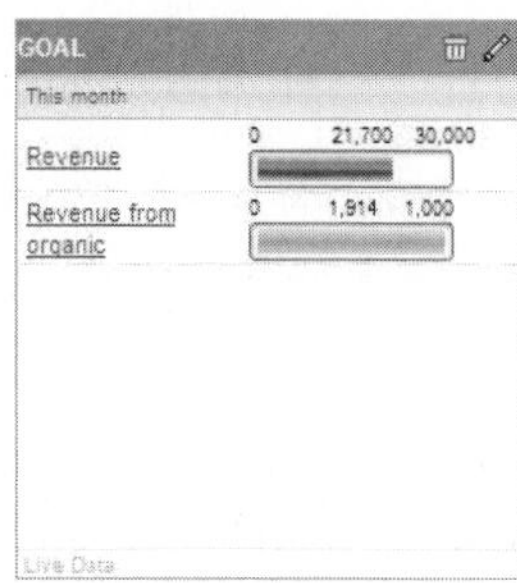

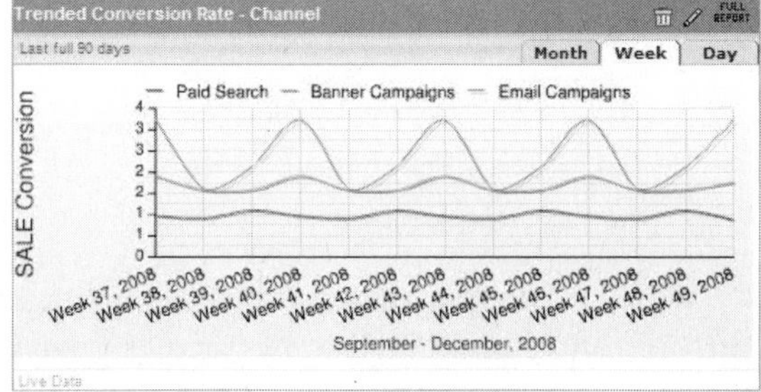

Figure 9.36 Sample dashboard with all items available

Distinctive Reports and Usage

10

Some reports are unique in that they cannot be re-created by the Custom Report Wizard. Examples of such reports include those that allow you to analyze paths, funnels, and merchandising cross-sells. This chapter delves into specific out-of-the-box reports that Yahoo! has to offer. You will learn how to use them as well as bend them.

Chapter Contents

Understanding Path Analysis
Using Scenarios for Funnel Analysis
Merchandising Reports
Using Campaign Reports
Using Internal Search Reports

Understanding Path Analysis

Path analysis allows you to identify the most popular paths your visitors pursue through your website, mapped out in a hierarchical tree structure. You can expand the branches of this tree to follow your visitors through as many levels of navigation as you wish. I left out Yahoo! Web Analytics' path analysis features in our discussion of navigational reporting in Chapter 8, "Using Basic Reports as Templates for Customization," because they deserve a section of their own.

Yahoo! provides the following path analysis reports out of the box:

- Path Analysis by URL
- Path Analysis by Title
- Path Analysis by Document Group
- Path Analysis During Visit 1–4
- Paths for Conversion
- Paths for Conversion by Title
- Paths for Conversion by Document Group

In addition to these standalone reports, you can use path analysis as a drill-down feature on other reports—in fact, it makes a lot more sense to use the feature that way.

Standalone Path Analysis Reports

Figure 10.1 shows a sample Path Analysis by Title report. The report you see here has been shrunk to fit the page, so you cannot read the text, but you can see the general tree structure. Next to each "branch" of the tree is an arrow. To navigate further into the visitor path, click on the arrow next to the display.

I know it is almost evident how the feature works, but indulge me for a second, so we can agree on the basics before we discuss how to use it, customize it, filter it, and finally criticize it.

The standard Path Analysis by Title report shown in Figure 10.1 is a tree from All Entries, which means that your home page is not the only starting point taken into account. I do not recommend using All Entries as a starting point to analyze visitor navigational behavior because it gives you too much data from which to make generalizations.

You can choose to have your path analysis reporting displayed based on two distinct criteria:

- Show Site Entries Only (visit paths for the visits that started on this page)
- Show All Transit Traffic (visit paths for the visits that included this page)

Neither option is better than the other; it just depends on what data you want to see and what you plan to do with the data.

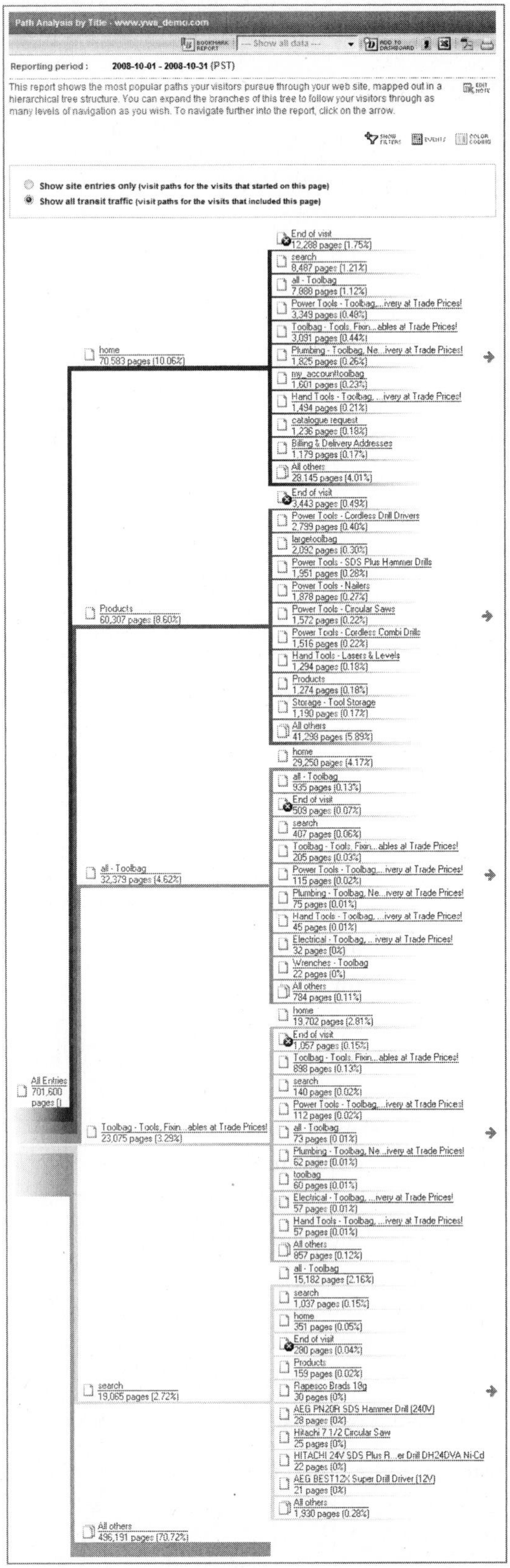

Path Analysis by Title - www.yws_demo.com

BOOKMARK REPORT | --- Show all data --- | ADD TO DASHBOARD

Reporting period : 2008-10-01 - 2008-10-31 (PST)

This report shows the most popular paths your visitors pursue through your web site, mapped out in a hierarchical tree structure. You can expand the branches of this tree to follow your visitors through as many levels of navigation as you wish. To navigate further into the report, click on the arrow.

EDIT NOTE

SHOW FILTERS | EVENTS | COLOR CODING

Show site entries only (visit paths for the visits that started on this page)
Show all transit traffic (visit paths for the visits that included this page)

All Entries
701,600 pages

home
70,583 pages (10.06%)

End of visit
12,288 pages (1.75%)
search
8,487 pages (1.21%)
all - Toolbag
7,888 pages (1.12%)
Power Tools - Toolbag,...ivery at Trade Prices!
3,349 pages (0.48%)
Toolbag - Tools, Fixin...ables at Trade Prices!
3,091 pages (0.44%)
Plumbing - Toolbag, Ne...ivery at Trade Prices!
1,825 pages (0.26%)
my_accounttoolbag
1,601 pages (0.23%)
Hand Tools - Toolbag, ...ivery at Trade Prices!
1,494 pages (0.21%)
catalogue request
1,236 pages (0.18%)
Billing & Delivery Addresses
1,179 pages (0.17%)
All others
28,145 pages (4.01%)

Products
60,307 pages (8.60%)

End of visit
3,443 pages (0.49%)
Power Tools - Cordless Drill Drivers
2,799 pages (0.40%)
largetoolbag
2,092 pages (0.30%)
Power Tools - SDS Plus Hammer Drills
1,951 pages (0.28%)
Power Tools - Nailers
1,878 pages (0.27%)
Power Tools - Circular Saws
1,572 pages (0.22%)
Power Tools - Cordless Combi Drills
1,516 pages (0.22%)
Hand Tools - Lasers & Levels
1,294 pages (0.18%)
Products
1,274 pages (0.18%)
Storage - Tool Storage
1,190 pages (0.17%)
All others
41,298 pages (5.89%)

all - Toolbag
32,379 pages (4.62%)

home
29,250 pages (4.17%)
all - Toolbag
935 pages (0.13%)
End of visit
509 pages (0.07%)
search
407 pages (0.06%)
Toolbag - Tools, Fixin...ables at Trade Prices!
205 pages (0.03%)
Power Tools - Toolbag... ivery at Trade Prices!
115 pages (0.02%)
Plumbing - Toolbag, Ne...ivery at Trade Prices!
75 pages (0.01%)
Hand Tools - Toolbag, ...ivery at Trade Prices!
45 pages (0.01%)
Electrical - Toolbag, ... ivery at Trade Prices!
32 pages (0%)
Wrenches - Toolbag
22 pages (0%)
All others
784 pages (0.11%)

Toolbag - Tools, Fixin...ables at Trade Prices!
23,075 pages (3.29%)

home
19,702 pages (2.81%)
End of visit
1,057 pages (0.15%)
Toolbag - Tools, Fixin...ables at Trade Prices!
898 pages (0.13%)
search
140 pages (0.02%)
Power Tools - Toolbag,...ivery at Trade Prices!
112 pages (0.02%)
all - Toolbag
73 pages (0.01%)
Plumbing - Toolbag, Ne ..ivery at Trade Prices!
62 pages (0.01%)
toolbag
60 pages (0.01%)
Electrical - Toolbag, ...ivery at Trade Prices!
57 pages (0.01%)
Hand Tools - Toolbag, ...ivery at Trade Prices!
57 pages (0.01%)
All others
857 pages (0.12%)

search
19,065 pages (2.72%)

all - Toolbag
15,182 pages (2.16%)
search
1,037 pages (0.15%)
home
351 pages (0.05%)
End of visit
280 pages (0.04%)
Products
159 pages (0.02%)
Rapesco Brads 18g
30 pages (0%)
AEG PN20R SDS Hammer Drill (240V)
28 pages (0%)
Hitachi 7 1/2 Circular Saw
25 pages (0%)
HITACHI 24V SDS Plus R...er Drill DH24DVA Ni-Cd
22 pages (0%)
AEG BEST12X Super Drill Driver (12V)
21 pages (0%)
All others
1,930 pages (0.28%)

All others
496,191 pages (70.72%)

Figure 10.1 Path Analysis by Title report

The distinction is important enough that I would like to show a couple of unrelated reports, to make sure we are on the same page. When you look at the out-of-the-box Path Analysis by Title report (and thus All Entries as shown in Figure 10.1) and choose the option Show All Transit Traffic, you are looking at every single page view on the site for the time period in question.

Compare the Path Analysis by Title report to the much simpler, standard Most Requested Pages by Page URL report shown in Figure 10.2.

This report shows us all page views to the site within the reporting period (701,600 views), just as our Path Analysis report does, but in a more concise format. So my first suggestion is that if you want to use a Path Analysis report starting from All Entries, you should choose to show site entries only, as shown in the partial Path Analysis report in Figure 10.3.

Figure 10.3 shows us 62,300 entries. We should be able to validate this by looking at the Top Entry Pages by Page URL report, as shown in Figure 10.4.

Page URL	Page Views	%	Avg. Time On Page
http://www.thetoolbag.com/	17,871	2.55%	0m 35s
https://www.thetoolbag.com/basket/	14,122	2.01%	0m 20s
http://www.thetoolbag.com/Power-Tools/	13,858	1.98%	0m 21s
http://www.thetoolbag.com/Hand-Tools/	9,361	1.33%	0m 22s
http://www.thetoolbag.com/Plumbing/	6,929	0.99%	0m 19s
http://www.thetoolbag.com/offers/index.php	6,860	0.98%	0m 23s
http://www.thetoolbag.com/?campaign=awppc	6,551	0.93%	0m 17s
http://www.thetoolbag.com/Electrical/	6,237	0.89%	0m 21s
http://www.thetoolbag.com/index.php	5,900	0.84%	0m 23s
http://www.thetoolbag.com/Po.../?campaign=ysmppc&ovkey=power+tool&x	5,769	0.82%	0m 16s
Subtotal	**93,458**	**13.32%**	**0m 23s**
Total	**701,600**	**100.00%**	**0m 19s**
« PREVIOUS 10			NEXT 10 »

Figure 10.2 Most Requested Pages by Page URL report

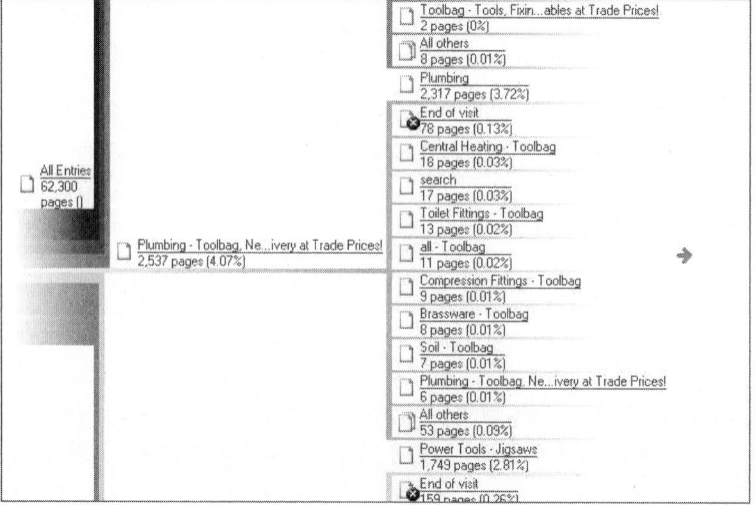

Figure 10.3 Path Analysis by Title report showing site entries only

Entry Page URL	Visits	%	Page Views	Browse Rate
http://www.thetoolbag.com/	5,593	8.98%	121,785	21.77
http://www.thetoolbag.com/?campaign=awppc	2,310	3.71%	36,885	15.97
http://www.thetoolbag.com/Po.../?campaign=ysmppc&ovkey=power+tool&x	1,850	2.97%	21,516	11.63
http://www.thetoolbag.com/?campaign=awppc&kw=Toolbag&x	1,654	2.65%	41,336	24.99
http://www.thetoolbag.com/?campaign=ysmppc	1,272	2.04%	29,671	23.33
http://www.thetoolbag.com/?campaign=buyat	1,263	2.03%	17,455	13.82
http://www.thetoolbag.com/Power-.../?campaign=awppc&kw=power+tool&x	1,007	1.62%	10,690	10.62
http://www.thetoolbag.com/Scre.../?campaign=awppc&kw=screwdrivers&x	927	1.49%	7,372	7.95
http://www.thetoolbag.com/Jigsaws/?campaign=awppc&kw=jigsaw&x	824	1.32%	2,000	2.43
http://www.thetoolbag.co.../?campaign=awppc&kw=plumbing+equipment&x	818	1.31%	9,715	11.88
Subtotal	**17,518**	**28.12%**	**298,425**	**17.04**
Total	**62,301**	**100.00%**	**701,600**	**11.26**
« PREVIOUS 10				NEXT 10 »

Figure 10.4 Top Entry Pages by Page URL report

By now, you might be asking why it is that Yahoo! only chose to illustrate two level deep paths and not illustrate horizontally three levels, four levels, or all the way to the end of the path. You can move further into the path, which you do by clicking the arrow next to the last branch of the three. It will remove the first level and essentially just shift everything one step left.

But before you get carried away doing this, know that there are an unlimited number of paths a visitor can take and the longer that path is, the more likely it is to be unique. The more unique paths you have, the fewer conclusions you can draw. Imagine 50,000 unique paths out of 62,300 visits. So the shorter the distance your Yahoo! report looks ahead, the more likely you are to be able to group paths together and form a conclusion. Note, however, that some industry experts question full-path analysis as a valid methodology for gaining insight.

Now that you know the difference between site entries and all transit traffic path analysis reporting, I want to show you another element of path analysis reporting that I call forward-looking versus backward-looking path analysis reporting.

Don't worry; we are coming to the insights shortly. What you have seen so far is the forward-looking path analysis, which has a fixed starting point and can branch out in an unlimited number of ways. The backward-looking path analysis views paths with a fixed ending point and explores how certain path visitors used the most to get to this point.

This also turns around the criteria on which you want your path analysis to be displayed:

- Show Site Exits Only (visit paths for the visits that ended on this page)
- Show All Transit Traffic (visit paths for the visits that included this page)

Site entry is exchanged for site exit. Unlike with site entry path analyses, with site exit analyses it is a good idea to look at all transit traffic. We probably don't care too much if people exit after this point (a confirmation page, for example)—we just want to figure out how they got here.

Looking at Figure 10.5, you see how people ended up at the Order Confirmed page, which surprisingly to a lot of people, even those managing their sites, is not as linear as they mentally persuaded themselves.

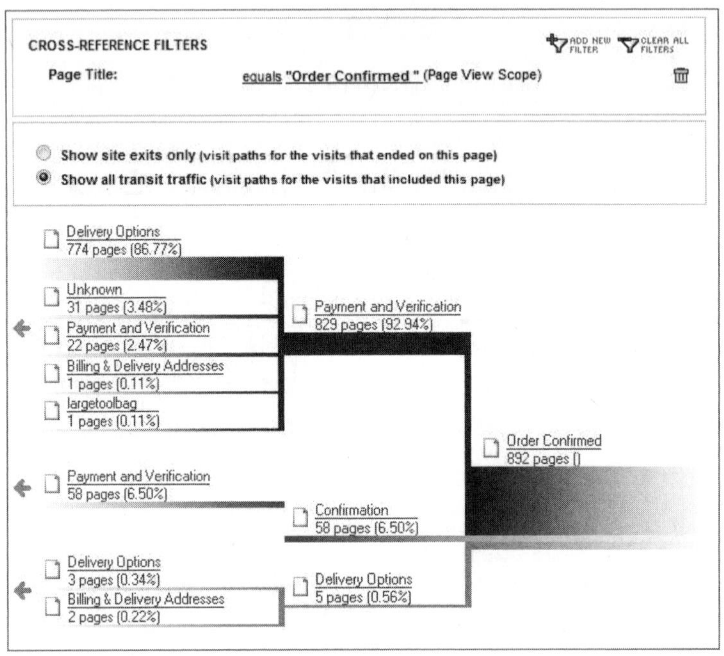

Figure 10.5 Backward-looking Path Analysis report

For path analysis reports to be of any value on their own, I suggest that you always use segmentation when looking at paths. Each of your segments is likely to behave differently, and an understanding of how different they are can be valuable. I provided a set of examples on the same path segmented by two unique traffic sources in the Path Analysis Drill-Down Examples section.

Path Analysis Drill-Down Examples

In this section I will show you how to use path analysis as a drill-down feature on other reports.

Looking at our Most Popular Pages report and searching for *basket*, we get an output like that shown in Figure 10.6.

When you click the magnifying glass to the left of the row result, you can run a Show Path from Here by Title path analysis report. This is an easier way to do a cross-reference rather than using the path analysis report.

On the returning path analysis screen, you append your filters with a Traffic Source filter and apply two distinct filters, one after the other, on Other Referrals (see Figure 10.7) and Organic Search (see Figure 10.8).

SEARCH REPORT RESULTS	basket	Search	
SHOW FILTERS	EVENTS	COLOR CODING	10 RESULTS PER PAGE

Page Title	Page Views	%	Avg. Time On Page
add to basket	20,375	54.54%	0m 3s
baskettoolbag	16,986	45.46%	0m 27s
Total	**37,361**	**100.00%**	**0m 13s**
« PREVIOUS 10			NEXT 10 »

Figure 10.6 The result of a search on our Most Popular Pages report

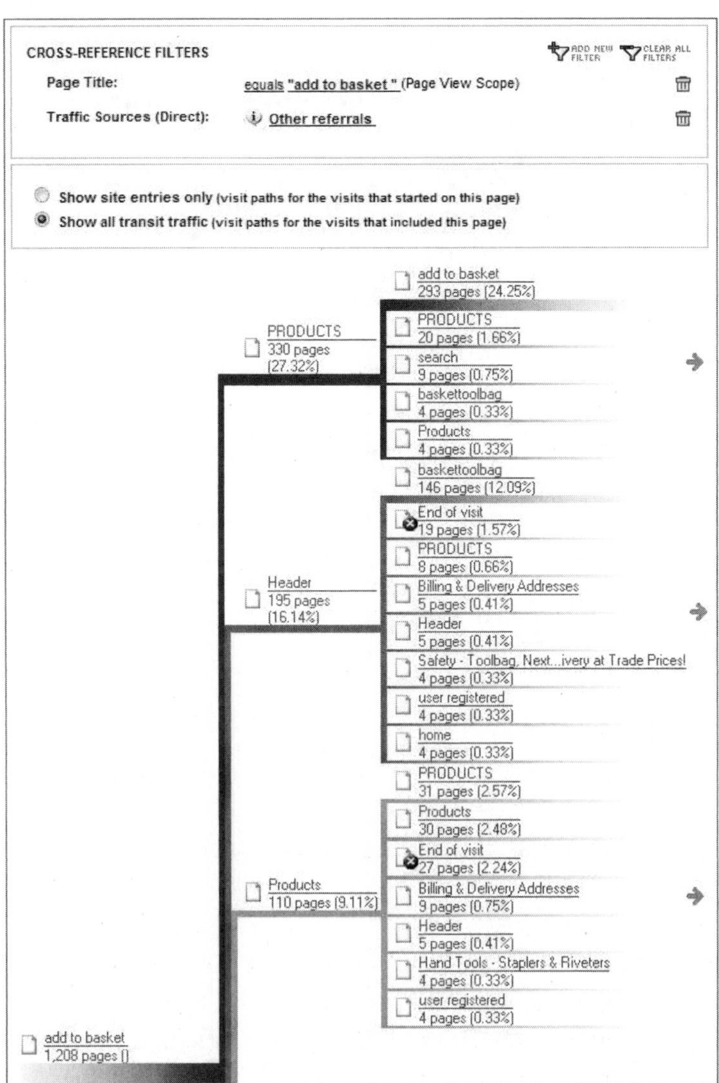

Figure 10.7 A unique page drill-down, filtered by direct traffic from Other Referrals

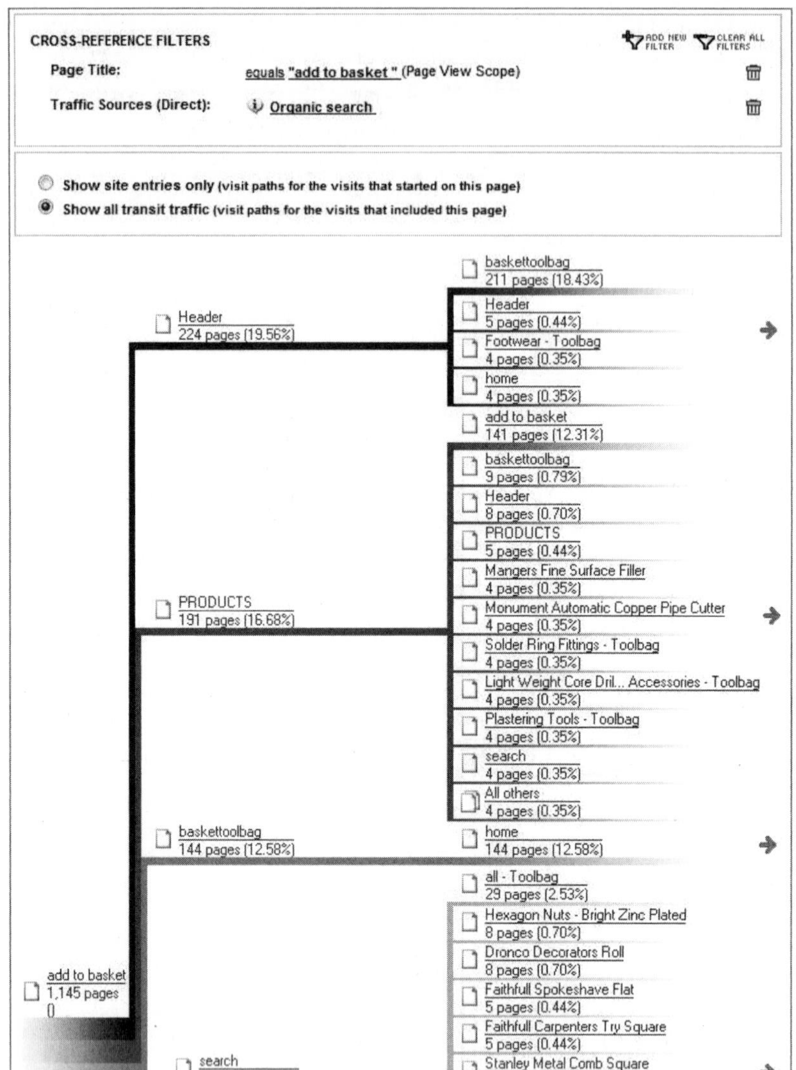

Figure 10.8 A unique page drill-down, filtered by direct traffic from Organic Search

Comparing these two reports, we are provided with valuable insights, such as the fact that visitors coming from Organic Search are somewhat more qualified and determined. We can hypothesize this because when these visitors are at the basket, they tend to move forward. Visitors coming from other referrals, such as blogs, links, and other reference points, abandon the basket funnel at a disturbing rate of 10 percent.

It is also interesting to see that visitors arriving from Organic Search seem more comfortable doing internal site search than visitors from other referrals. As you can see, something as simple as segmenting on the direct traffic source shows two very different behaviors. From here you could choose to provide some basic behavioral targeting.

As a final note, I would once again like to caution you on site-wide entry point path analysis reporting, as it is unlikely to tell you much about anything. So always do specific path analysis on unique entry points or destination points, and preferably on parts of a well-understood funnel within your organization, or finally as a simple yet powerful next-page analysis feature.

Using Scenarios for Funnel Analysis

Scenarios are the term Yahoo! uses for what is generally known as *funnels*. (A funnel typically describes a process and a set of steps toward a goal. For a sales process, this is typically visualized as a number of prospects at the top of the funnel and a number of follow-up steps where prospects drop out of the funnel; and from the large number of initially interested people, the funnel narrows toward the end where a sale might complete it, keeping only interested people on each step as you move forward.) There are two types:

- Predefined scenarios
- Ad hoc scenarios

When you think about it, funnels are not that much different from paths. Funnels are multipurpose and better utilized than paths. But there are multiple ways to look at a funnel:

Linear fixed funnel toward conversion In this type of funnel, you set the number of pages that have to be visited in a specific order without jumping out of the funnel in between them. An example of this is a funnel starting at the last steps of an e-commerce cart, where you provide payment and delivery details. In this example you cannot provide half the payment and delivery details and come back later. Thus, it is fixed, and you optimize with that in mind.

Linear nonfixed funnel toward conversion In this type of funnel, you set a number of pages that have to be visited in a specific order, but you could jump out of the funnel and come back in later. An example of this is a funnel starting from the SERP (an internal search engine result page), then moving on to the Added to Cart page. Here you can do multiple searches and click back and forth between the SERP and the chosen product page before you move forward and later add a product to the cart.

Nonlinear path toward conversion This type of path is an unplanned path by the visitor who can visit *n* number of undefined pages before ending up on a successful conversion page. An example is a high-value lead generation form where the visitor typically has questions that need to be resolved before a conversion can take place.

Note: For more on conversion funnels, visit the following blog post:

`http://visualrevenue.com/blog/2007/02/use-conversion-funnel-analysis-to.html`

There is no difference in the output of the two types of scenarios. Think of a predefined scenario as a bookmarked report so you do not have to do it over and over again.

If you supply Yahoo! Web Analytics with information on funnels that you know are fixed and do not change very often, it can sum some parts and create the report a lot faster. Report creation is faster only if you are in the tens or hundreds of millions of page views per month—if not, it does not really matter from a speed point of view. Note that if you track revenue, the predefined scenario output will include a revenue number at the end of the funnel, if the end of your funnel is a sale action. Keep in mind that predefined scenarios cannot be applied to historical data.

Now let's jump directly into a Yahoo! Web Analytics predefined scenario.

Setting Up a Predefined Scenario

To set up a predefined scenario, begin by choosing Scenario Analysis > Define > Settings. In the resulting screen, you'll outline a series of steps toward a sale or other defined action. Your first task is to name and apply a description for your scenario.

The most important part of setting up a funnel is setting up the criteria for each step of the funnel, as shown in Figure 10.9.

You can set up scenarios based on five criteria:

- Page Name Equals
- Page Name Contains
- URL Equals
- URL Contains
- Action Equals

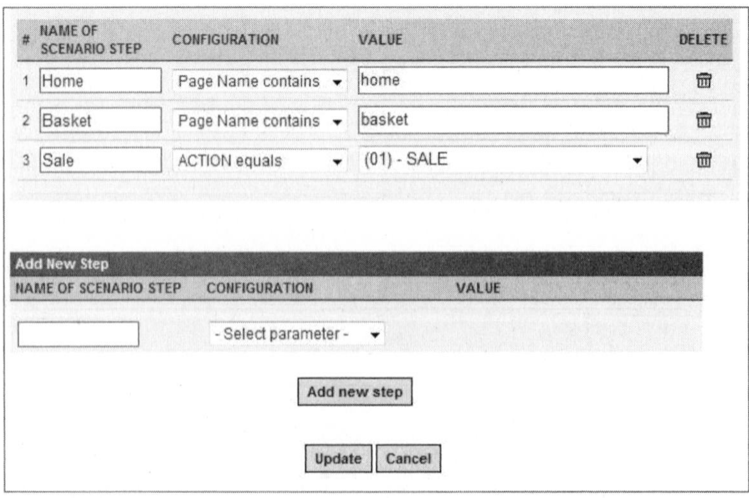

Figure 10.9 Creating a new scenario

The only difference between predefined and ad hoc scenarios is that you can use the OR operator for the values you assign to the step configuration—for example, the OR operator is available for all the configuration options just listed except the Action Equals option.

For an ad hoc scenario you can add up to eight steps, and for a predefined scenario you can add up to 15. However, analyzing 15 steps might not be any more helpful than multiple funnels with fewer steps.

The beautiful thing about an ad hoc scenario is that it allows you to try various combinations of steps before deciding on the final sequence. You can use ad hoc scenarios to research past visitor behavior, or to test possible scenario steps in preparation for setting up a standard scenario.

Once you have created a predefined scenario, it is available under Settings and is listed together with the other predefined scenarios you have. Figure 10.10 shows the predefined scenario I just created and saved, the Entry to Sale funnel analysis.

Now let's move on to the fun part: the resulting funnel reports. The result of the predefined scenario setup in Figure 10.9 is a funnel like the one shown in Figure 10.11.

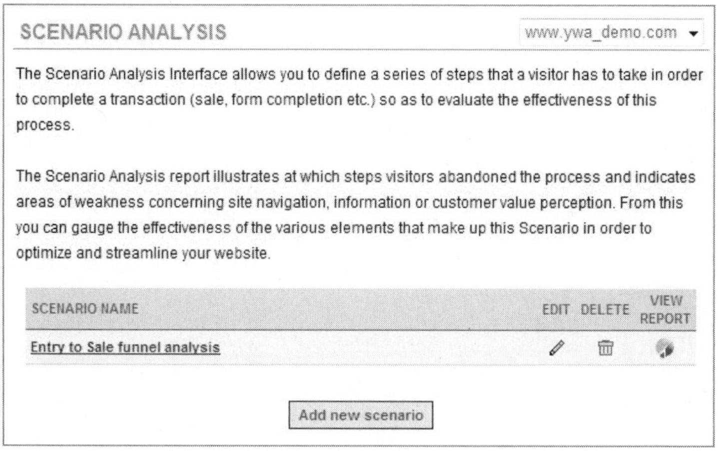

Figure 10.10 Manage your pre-configured scenarios

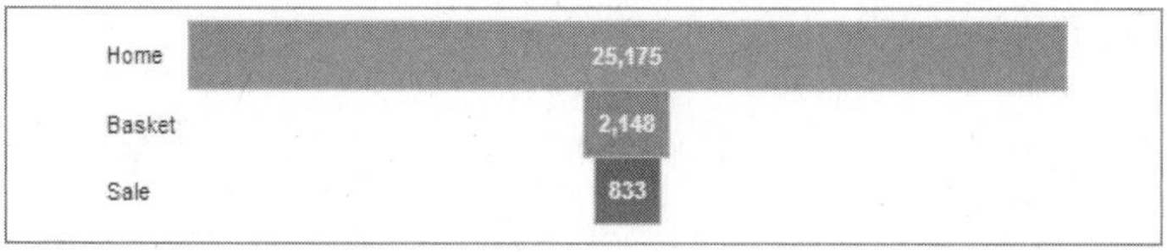

Figure 10.11 Predefined scenario result

Setting Up an Ad Hoc Scenario

Figure 10.12 shows a four-step ad hoc scenario. The first thing you notice is that you can edit steps directly from the report, which gives you the opportunity to try out numerous iterations of the same funnel. The Edit Steps icon is located in the upper-right corner, just above the chart.

In Figure 10.12, you can see that the abandonment rate from the basket to the delivery page is 29.43 percent and from the delivery page to the actual sale is 43.26 percent.

First we need to figure out where the people go and whether they are lost to the extent that they just leave the site, or whether they are confused and move somewhere else.

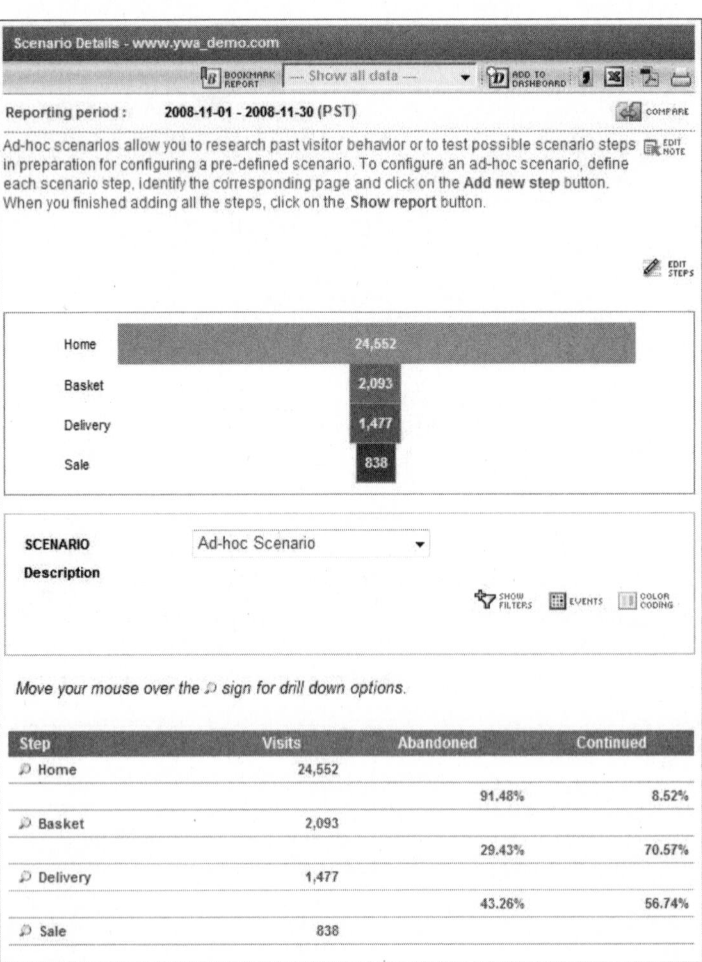

Figure 10.12 An ad hoc scenario

You can drill into the funnel abandonment using the Path Analysis function. That way, you can figure out, for example, where those 639 visitors who did not go from delivery to sale actually went (the 43.26 percent). Click the magnifying glass on the Delivery step and choose Show Abandonment Path by Title, which will immediately take you to a path analysis report, as partially shown in Figure 10.13.

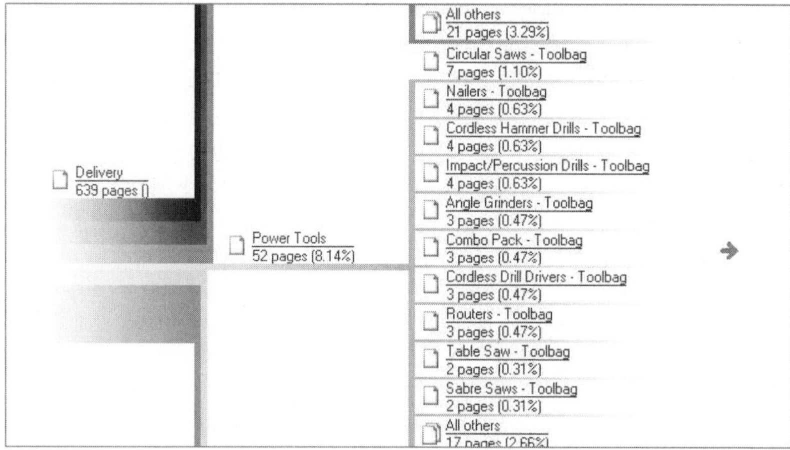

Figure 10.13 Partial Path Analysis report

This is an exciting feature to play with, because suddenly it is not just about abandonment alone—it is about real visibility into where people go, as they obviously aren't moving through your funnel as you want them to. This could be due to overly aggressive cross promotions or unclear information on delivery costs. It sometimes becomes clear where you've failed by looking at that subset of visitors who move away from the planned path.

Now let's look at the various visit segments of your funnel. I expanded the time period to get a bit more data and applied two very simple filters: looking at how visitors arriving from Google funnel through (Figure 10.14), versus visitors arriving from Yahoo! (Figure 10.15).

Here we immediately see a difference in behavior and abandonment rates, which should not necessarily be viewed as a competition between the search engines. This might be an optimization opportunity where you look at the SERP snippets in Google and in Yahoo! and then come to the conclusion that you are not indexed as well in Google as in Yahoo!, and that the Yahoo! snippets are a lot better at prequalifying your visitors. And based on the result, we obviously have a task of working toward having better snippets in Google search results.

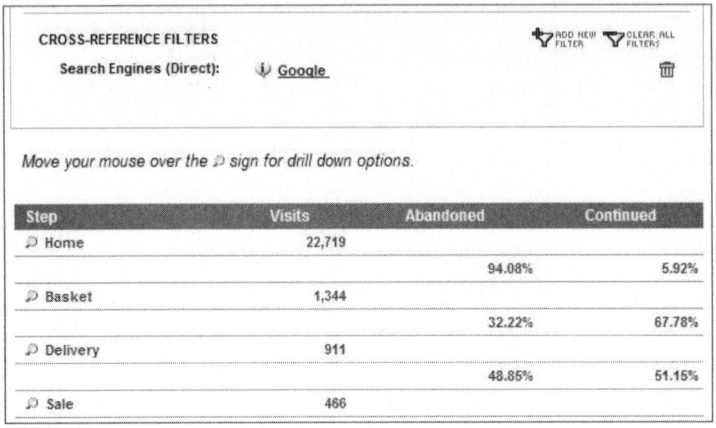

CROSS-REFERENCE FILTERS

ADD NEW FILTER CLEAR ALL FILTERS

Search Engines (Direct): Google

Move your mouse over the sign for drill down options.

Step	Visits	Abandoned	Continued
Home	22,719		
		94.08%	5.92%
Basket	1,344		
		32.22%	67.78%
Delivery	911		
		48.85%	51.15%
Sale	466		

Figure 10.14 Ad hoc scenario result filtered by direct search engine Google

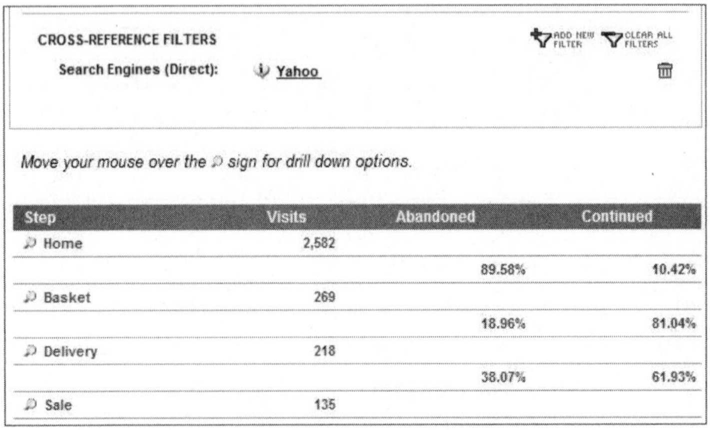

CROSS-REFERENCE FILTERS

ADD NEW FILTER CLEAR ALL FILTERS

Search Engines (Direct): Yahoo

Move your mouse over the sign for drill down options.

Step	Visits	Abandoned	Continued
Home	2,582		
		89.58%	10.42%
Basket	269		
		18.96%	81.04%
Delivery	218		
		38.07%	61.93%
Sale	135		

Figure 10.15 Ad hoc scenario result filtered by direct search engine Yahoo!

Make sure you input URLs and fractional URLs correctly, as any small error will result in no data. Test your scenarios by completing them yourself to ensure they work correctly. Whenever you create a new predefined scenario, you have to allow the system roughly an hour to collect data for your scenario. This is why I rarely use predefined scenarios myself, as I like to play around with my historical data, which is easy with ad hoc scenarios.

For dynamically generated pages (such as a shopping cart), select URL Contains and enter an identifying string (for example, `'/ship.aspx'`) if the string is unique, or select Page Name Equals if the page name is unique.

Scenarios are not exclusive. Two or more scenarios may share pages, entry points, or exit points, which means that some visitor transactions may be recorded in more than one scenario. And they should be!

Merchandising Reports

You should be on a constant quest to move your reporting from a focus on URLs to a focus on documents and then to a focus on products or services. This is what Yahoo! Web Analytics Merchandising allows you to do. You access this functionality and its standard reports by choosing Marketing > Merchandising. Only two standard reports are provided out of the box:

- Merchandising Summary
- Cross-Sell Analysis

Merchandise reporting, as you learned in Chapter 4, "Merchandising Tracking and Reporting," allows you to track specific information about your products, such as how many times individual products are viewed, added to a shopping cart, and purchased. This includes the SKU information, number of units sold, and revenue per product. You can also associate any applicable discount and tax with each purchase, and receive reports including this information.

This section focuses on how you can use the collected information beyond the two standard reports, but first, let's review what you get from those two reports.

Merchandising Summary Report

The Merchandising Summary report identifies how well your individual products are converting and how much revenue you are making on a category basis, all the way down to an individual product basis. The report is displayed and broken down by the custom categories you created and the product information you uploaded (as described in Chapter 4).

All reports show 10 rows by default (unless you've changed the global settings to show more). I strongly recommend that you always show all available categories on one screen. If you don't, then the report loses considerable value. If your categories cannot be shown on one screen, you can use suboptimal product categorization. Figure 10.16 shows an example of all top-level categories on one page.

To view product-specific information, you simply drill down into your merchandising categories and expand the tree as needed, as shown in Figure 10.17.

Product Category / Product Type / Brand or Supplier Name / Product Name	Product Views	Add To Cart	Cart Complete	Units	Amount	Avg. Product Order Value
Plumbing	0	0	1,432	12,476	$38,282.45	$26.73
Electrical	0	0	507	2,607	$6,311.93	$12.45
Sealants & Adhesives	0	0	675	2,220	$6,574.46	$9.74
Hand Tools	0	0	1,162	1,348	$30,135.05	$25.93
Ironmongery	0	0	182	781	$4,290.04	$23.57
Drill Bits	0	0	348	775	$6,532.19	$18.77
Abrasives	0	0	133	768	$1,872.34	$14.08
Building	0	0	25	662	$1,026.15	$41.05
Safety	0	0	174	639	$4,959.54	$28.50
Power Tools	0	0	526	534	$104,282.07	$198.26
Screws	0	0	252	515	$2,618.93	$10.39
Lighting	0	0	122	429	$2,472.25	$20.26
Blades	0	0	215	394	$12,785.47	$59.47
Bolts	0	0	118	370	$706.03	$5.98
Fixings	0	0	200	336	$3,383.34	$16.92
Site Equipment	0	0	179	319	$15,418.97	$86.14
Storage	0	0	230	249	$6,098.28	$26.51
Driver Bits	0	0	108	154	$2,132.75	$19.75
Nails	0	0	63	128	$461.32	$7.32
Ventilation	0	0	62	127	$1,345.61	$21.70
Non-Categorized	0	0	76	76	$28,632.41	$376.74
Packs	0	0	59	73	$1,244.02	$21.09
Total	0	0	6,848	25,980	$281,565.60	$41.12

« PREVIOUS 25 NEXT 25 »

Figure 10.16 Merchandising Summary report of all top-level categories

Product Category / Product Type / Brand or Supplier Name / Product Name	Product Views	Add To Cart	Cart Complete	Units	Amount	Avg.
Plumbing	0	0	1,432	12,476	$38,282.45	
Electrical	0	0	507	2,607	$6,311.93	
Sealants & Adhesives	0	0	675	2,220	$6,574.46	
Hand Tools	0	0	1,162	1,348	$30,135.05	
Ironmongery	0	0	182	781	$4,290.04	
Drill Bits	0	0	348	775	$6,532.19	
Abrasives	0	0	133	768	$1,872.34	
Building	0	0	25	662	$1,026.15	
Safety	0	0	174	639	$4,959.54	
Power Tools	0	0	526	534	$104,282.07	
Cordless Drill Drivers	0	0	129	133	$20,815.24	
SDS Plus Hammer Drills	0	0	100	100	$20,806.62	
DeWalt	0	0	69	69	$13,871.97	
DeWalt 2kg SDS Plus Hammer Drill D25102K	0	0	64	64	$10,337.92	
DeWalt 4kg SDS Plus Hammer Drill D25405K	0	0	5	5	$3,534.05	
MAKITA	0	0	17	17	$3,996.02	
HITACHI	0	0	14	14	$2,938.63	
Nailers	0	0	43	43	$12,250.08	
Circular Saws	0	0	40	40	$8,683.12	

Figure 10.17 Expanded Merchandising Summary report tree

Cross-Sell Analysis Report

The second out-of-the-box merchandising report is the Cross-Sell Analysis report.

Cross-sell analysis might be too grand a term for what Yahoo! provides. This report shows products sold together within a shopping cart or even within different shopping carts during the same visit. Analyzing your customers' acquisition patterns allows you to fine-tune your cross-selling efforts by offering products that are known to sell together. This is all good but might be too simple a way to look at cross-sell strategies.

Combining cross-sell analysis and campaign segmentation can provide you with real insight. You cannot create the Cross-Sell Analysis report using the Custom Report Wizard, so having a look at this particular report once in a while is not a bad idea. Figure 10.18 shows a sample Cross-Sell Analysis report.

Product sold in conjunction with	Cross Sell %	Amount	Units	Cart Complete
⊟ HITACHI 14.4V Drill Driver DS14DVF3 (14.4V)		$45,704.14	263	263
HITACHI 2kg SDS Plus Hammer Drill DH24PB3	5.70%	$2,784.90	15	15
HITACHI 550W Impact Drill FDV16VB2	5.70%	$1,532.85	15	15
Pre Worn In Plaster Trowel	6.08%	$1,144.64	16	16
25mm Standard	6.08%	$461.28	16	16
7 Piece Bi-torsion Contractors Set	5.70%	$398.70	15	15
Plasteres Quick Mix	6.08%	$366.72	16	16
Flat Wood Set	6.08%	$153.28	16	16
SDS Plus Extreme	6.08%	$90.24	16	16
SDS Plus Extreme	6.08%	$77.12	16	16
High Speed Twist Drill Bits - Metric	6.08%	$72.48	16	16
{Others}	12.17%	$41.12	32	32
⊞ DeWalt 2kg SDS Plus Hammer Drill D25102K		$34,728.95	215	215
⊞ Non-Categorized		$30,657.16	47	47
⊞ Combi Kitchen Worktop Jig		$30,178.05	123	93
⊞ Non-Categorized		$24,820.90	61	61
⊞ Cordless Strip Nail Gun IM350 / 90 CTQ		$22,756.17	31	31
⊞ MAKITA Autofeed Screwdriver 6834		$21,272.68	61	46
⊞ Non-Categorized		$19,015.35	15	15
⊞ Tar Boiler Kit		$17,482.50	30	30
⊞ DeWalt 18V 4 Piece Combo Pack DC4KITA (18V)		$15,947.85	15	15
{Others}	2,632,000.00%	$723,433.70	91,532	26,367

Figure 10.18 A sample Cross-Sell Analysis report

Figure 10.18 lists our most popular products, sorted by revenue. We can expand the tree and see the top 10 products sold in conjunction with each product.

The Cross-Sell Analysis report is also a good example of how you can choose to use the Yahoo! Web Analytics IT Tutor (see Figure 10.19).

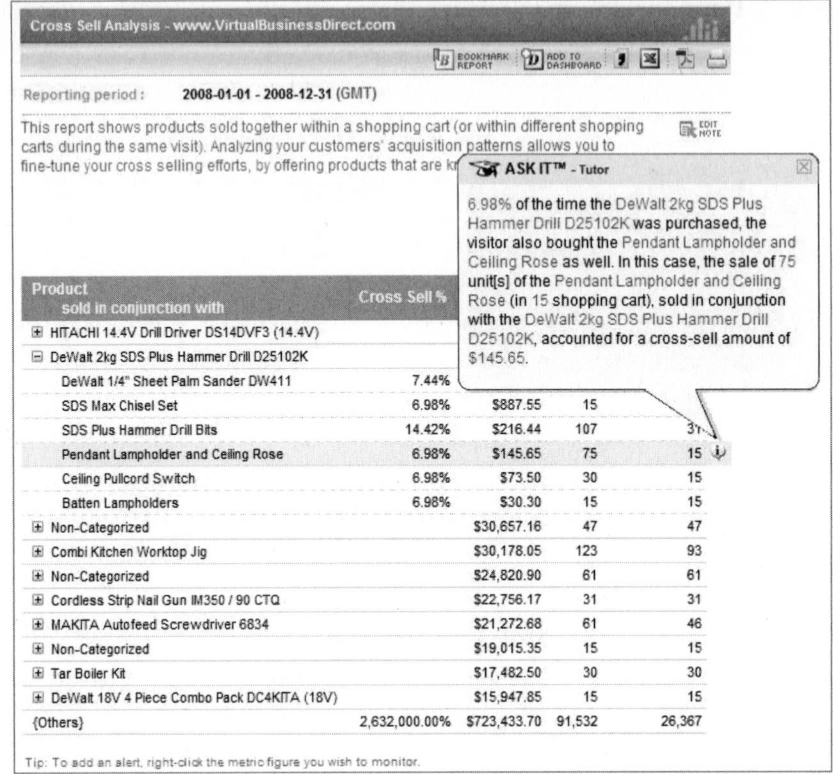

Figure 10.19 ASK IT Tutor

The screen might be confusing at first, but the ASK IT Tutor provides facts in plain English about the row in question. Here's an example:

> *6.98% of the time the DeWalt 2kg SDS Plus Hammer Drill D25102K was purchased, the visitor also bought the Pendant Lampholder and Ceiling Rose as well. In this case, the sale of 75 unit[s] of the Pendant Lampholder and Ceiling Rose (in 15 shopping cart), sold in conjunction with the DeWalt 2kg SDS Plus Hammer Drill D25102K, accounted for a cross-sell amount of $145.65.*

A Sample Custom Merchandising Report

You can create a new custom report, as shown in Figure 10.20, or use the Merchandising Summary report as a starting point.

Notice that we've associated intent (the search phrase) with action (actual products being sold). The result of the report created in Figure 10.20 is presented in Figure 10.21.

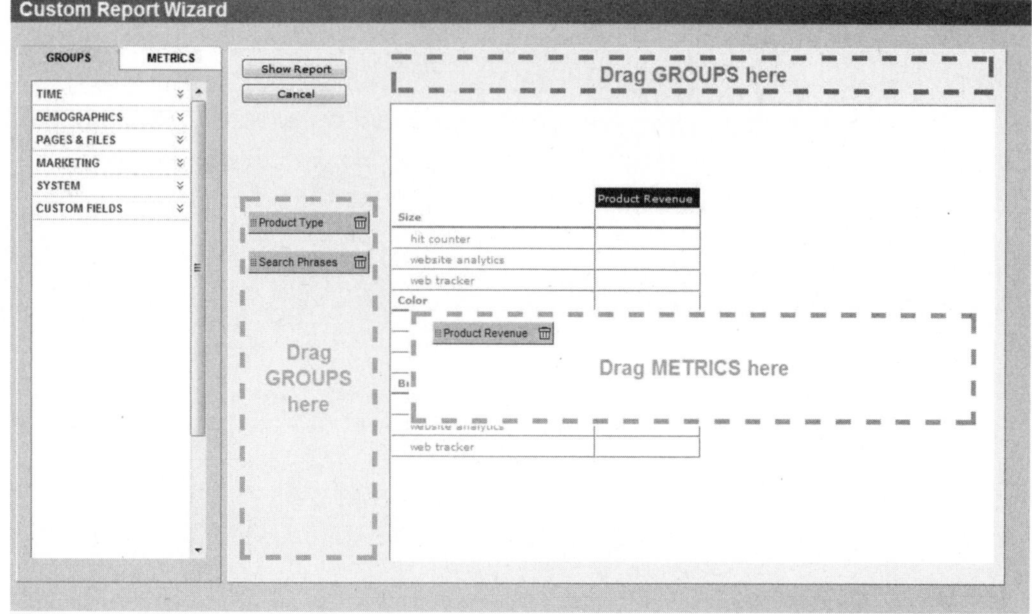

Figure 10.20 Setting up a Product Type by Search Phrases custom report

Product Type / Search Phrases (Direct)	Amount
⊞ Non-Categorized	$100,803.56
⊟ Cordless Drill Drivers	$73,167.16
toolbag	$3,502.50
bosc power drill	$3,271.20
the toolbag	$2,780.48
power tools	$2,780.48
hitachi cordless drill drivers.	$2,780.48
toolbag.com	$2,606.70
tool bag	$2,606.70
dewalt dc727ka	$2,514.75
skil 2302	$1,308.32
skil power tools	$955.52
"Other"	$48,060.03
⊞ SDS Plus Hammer Drills	$69,614.19
⊞ Nailers	$38,128.79
⊞ Jigs	$36,535.49
⊞ Various	$32,686.99
⊞ Circular Saws	$29,661.50
⊞ Central Heating	$27,915.19
⊞ Lasers & Levels	$25,455.20
⊞ Heating Controls	$19,794.80
Subtotal	**$453,762.87**
Total	**$989,525.93**
« PREVIOUS 10	NEXT 10 »

Figure 10.21 The result of the report created in Figure 10.20

This is an almost perfect example of the power of having merchandising available as another dimension in your analytics reporting. I'm not a fan of most traditional SEO practices, which involve keyword research. With Yahoo! Web Analytics, you can pinpoint the specific and factual keywords (search phrases) used that led to sales.

Now you are able to answer marketing questions on how to drive increased sales—not just traffic—to your Cordless Drill Drivers department by supplying gold keywords such as the following:

- bosc power drill
- power tools
- hitachi cordless drill drivers
- dewalt dc727ka
- skil 2302
- skil power tools

This process is likely quite different from any keyword research you've done. I'm not saying this is the only way to look at keywords, but it is a great way to conclude which keywords help sell specific product groups.

Now imagine the report reversed and that you have search phrases on top. Instead of seeing which keywords were used to sell a product, you could see what people buy after they type in a generic phrase like "power tools." Very exciting, isn't it?

Using Campaign Reports

Most people choose to use a campaign summary when performing online campaign analytics. Assembling a campaign summary is of utmost importance as this report is one of the most valuable out-of-the-box reporting elements available. Figure 10.22 shows a sample Campaign Summary report.

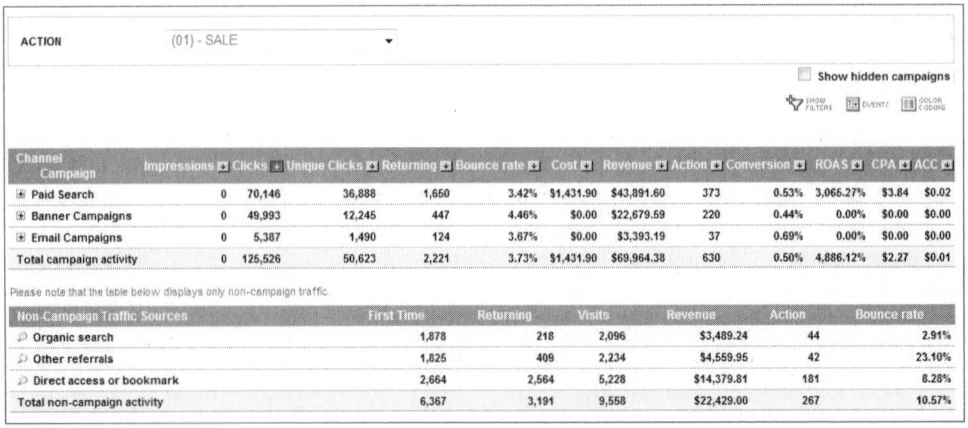

ACTION (01) - SALE

Show hidden campaigns

SHOW FILTERS EVENTS COLOR CODING

Channel Campaign	Impressions	Clicks	Unique Clicks	Returning	Bounce rate	Cost	Revenue	Action	Conversion	ROAS	CPA	ACC
Paid Search	0	70,146	36,888	1,650	3.42%	$1,431.90	$43,891.60	373	0.53%	3,065.27%	$3.84	$0.02
Banner Campaigns	0	49,993	12,245	447	4.46%	$0.00	$22,679.59	220	0.44%	0.00%	$0.00	$0.00
Email Campaigns	0	5,387	1,490	124	3.67%	$0.00	$3,393.19	37	0.69%	0.00%	$0.00	$0.00
Total campaign activity	0	125,526	50,623	2,221	3.73%	$1,431.90	$69,964.38	630	0.50%	4,886.12%	$2.27	$0.01

Please note that the table below displays only non-campaign traffic.

Non-Campaign Traffic Sources	First Time	Returning	Visits	Revenue	Action	Bounce rate
Organic search	1,878	218	2,096	$3,489.24	44	2.91%
Other referrals	1,825	409	2,234	$4,559.95	42	23.10%
Direct access or bookmark	2,664	2,564	5,228	$14,379.81	181	8.28%
Total non-campaign activity	6,367	3,191	9,558	$22,429.00	267	10.57%

Figure 10.22 Top-level default Campaign Summary report

The default Campaign Summary report shows the activity that originated as a result of a campaign such as Paid Search, Banner Campaign, and so on, as discussed in Chapter 3, "Enterprise Campaign Tracking." The report also lists the Non-Campaign Traffic Sources for comparison purposes, bringing all incoming traffic, and its immediate impact, onto one screen.

You must have enabled cost retrieval to use some metrics, such as Paid Search Cost Data. This feature combines the live data on your bid costs with the revenue generated by your website sales to measure the profitability of each pay-per-click (PPC) keyword. Figure 10.23 shows Email Campaigns expanded.

Channel Campaign	Impressions	Clicks	Unique Clicks	Returning	Bounce rate	Cost	Revenue	Action
⊞ Paid Search	0	70,146	36,888	1,650	3.42%	$1,431.90	$43,891.60	373
⊞ Banner Campaigns	0	49,993	12,245	447	4.46%	$0.00	$22,679.59	220
⊟ Email Campaigns	0	5,387	1,490	124	3.67%	$0.00	$3,393.19	37
December Prospect Email 1	0	2,181	540	35	4.83%	$0.00	$1,276.15	18
December Christmas Email	0	1,689	390	13	3.18%	$0.00	$771.96	4
October Prospect Email 1	0	694	212	22	2.95%	$0.00	$576.66	7
Sept FF customer last chance email	0	380	143	1	5.13%	$0.00	$173.78	1
November Prospect Email 2	0	163	125	1	2.88%	$0.00	$388.46	2
October Prospect Email 2	0	121	35	10	0.00%	$0.00	$103.30	2
October Customer Email 2	0	72	24	7	0.00%	$0.00	$85.46	2
October Customer Email 1	0	40	8	3	0.00%	$0.00	$0.00	0
July_Email_01	0	23	9	21	0.00%	$0.00	$17.42	1
January Cold List	0	12	2	5	0.00%	$0.00	$0.00	0

Figure 10.23 Expanded Campaign Summary report

It should be noted that the default report, beyond what is shown in figure 10.23, provides the following metrics as well: Conversion, ROAS, CPA, and ACC.

Having a look at the campaign summary from a categorized point of view definitely makes sense when you have a lot of campaigns running. But if you have fewer than 50 active campaigns running at any point in time, you can build a simple campaign summary that will give you an instant view of the status of all your campaigns; see Figure 10.24.

This is a great campaign communication report, assuming you have validated which campaign specific metrics are important to your organization.

The campaign dimensions are useful beyond the campaign summary. Figure 10.25 shows a customized visit and bounce rate report with Campaign as a top group. The report is filtered on the two most successful campaigns: Yahoo! PCC and a display campaign named CP. We also applied a demographic left group. This report could show you whether it is time to start using demographic segmentation within your ad serving systems; there is obviously a huge difference from demographic area to area and, very likely, from advertising platform to advertising platform.

CROSS-REFERENCE FILTERS

Campaign (Intelligent): Show all active campaign

ADD NEW FILTER CLEAR ALL FILTERS

Campaign	Clicks	Unique Clicks	Returning	Bounce rate	Cost	Revenue	Action	Conversion	CPA
Yahoo PPC	39,671	13,091	628	2.58%	$0.00	$22,160.24	160	0.40%	$0.00
CP	28,638	23,441	1,008	3.85%	$1,431.90	$21,588.28	211	0.74%	$6.79
Croatia	23,153	5,201	258	4.77%	$0.00	$9,914.45	108	0.47%	$0.00
FF email confirmation banner	18,378	4,330	149	5.00%	$0.00	$9,751.69	81	0.44%	$0.00
Pricerunner DIY	3,808	1,175	20	4.14%	$0.00	$1,599.88	19	0.50%	$0.00
Pricerunner Power Tools	3,985	1,295	17	0.96%	$0.00	$1,413.57	12	0.30%	$0.00
December Prospect Email 1	2,181	540	35	4.83%	$0.00	$1,276.15	18	0.83%	$0.00
December Christmas Email	1,689	390	13	3.18%	$0.00	$771.96	4	0.24%	$0.00
October Prospect Email 1	694	212	22	2.95%	$0.00	$576.66	7	1.01%	$0.00
November Prospect Email 2	163	125	1	2.88%	$0.00	$388.46	2	1.23%	$0.00
Sept FF customer last chance email	380	143	1	5.13%	$0.00	$173.78	1	0.26%	$0.00
Pricegrabber	1,479	270	4	2.81%	$0.00	$143.08	2	0.14%	$0.00
October Prospect Email 2	121	35	10	0.00%	$0.00	$103.30	2	1.65%	$0.00
October Customer Email 2	72	24	7	0.00%	$0.00	$85.46	2	2.78%	$0.00
July_Email_01	23	9	21	0.00%	$0.00	$17.42	1	4.35%	$0.00
December Customer Email 1	0	0	2	0.00%	$0.00	$0.00	0	0.00%	$0.00
FROOGLE	16	3	5	0.00%	$0.00	$0.00	0	0.00%	$0.00
HRB broadcast	0	0	4	0.00%	$0.00	$0.00	0	0.00%	$0.00
January Cold List	12	2	5	0.00%	$0.00	$0.00	0	0.00%	$0.00
KELKOO	0	0	4	0.00%	$0.00	$0.00	0	0.00%	$0.00
MIbanners	20	2	0	0.00%	$0.00	$0.00	0	0.00%	$0.00
October Customer Email 1	40	8	3	0.00%	$0.00	$0.00	0	0.00%	$0.00
Pricerunner Skyscraper	350	127	1	5.84%	$0.00	$0.00	0	0.00%	$0.00
Pricerunner.co.uk	193	75	1	11.11%	$0.00	$0.00	0	0.00%	$0.00
Sept customer	12	2	0	0.00%	$0.00	$0.00	0	0.00%	$0.00
Shopping	149	8	0	0.00%	$0.00	$0.00	0	0.00%	$0.00
WNIlbanners	299	115	2	6.15%	$0.00	$0.00	0	0.00%	$0.00
Total	**125,526**	**50,623**	**2,221**	**3.73%**	**$1,431.90**	**$69,964.38**	**630**	**0.50%**	**$2.27**

« PREVIOUS 50 NEXT 50 »

Figure 10.24 This simple customized Campaign Summary report gives you an instant view of the status of all your campaigns.

Consolidating Costs from Paid Searches and Tracked Campaigns

In a Campaign Summary report like the one in Figure 10.24, you can check the Enable Cost Consolidation box in the upper-right corner of the report (not shown in the figure). If you do this, your PPC/CPC report results will be consolidated. That means the PPC results obtained by your tracking system will be automatically consolidated with click and cost data provided by the paid search engines. If you leave the Enable Cost Consolidation box unchecked, the PPC/CPC report results will be based only on your tracking system.

The current day's data will always come from your tracking system, as most search engines are unable to provide same-day reporting. Once every 24 hours, you can automatically consolidate the data collected by your tracking system with the cost and click data reported by the paid search engines. Search engines may occasionally take up to 18 hours to provide cost and click data.

When you enable Consolidated PPC/CPC Reporting, your report results will be based on your tracking data consolidated with the impressions, clicks, and costs that the search engines reported. Metrics such as CPA, ROAS, and Conversion Rate will be calculated based on consolidated data.

CROSS-REFERENCE FILTERS

ADD NEW FILTER CLEAR ALL FILTERS

Campaign (Direct): Yahoo PPC

OR CP

City	CP		Yahoo PPC		Total	
	Visits	Bounce rate	Visits	Bounce rate	Visits	Bounce rate
London, GBR	66,889	2.76%	46,790	1.90%	112,726	2.43%
AOL, GBR	30,617	5.93%	12,978	4.01%	43,317	5.40%
Cambridge, GBR	15,626	1.91%	12,411	1.43%	27,726	1.71%
Milton Keynes, GBR	14,460	1.47%	7,043	1.75%	21,311	1.58%
Manchester, GBR	12,594	2.06%	7,744	1.81%	20,059	1.99%
Birmingham, GBR	10,596	1.99%	7,599	2.76%	18,109	2.32%
Sheffield, GBR	8,420	1.83%	4,027	2.16%	12,207	1.97%
Watford, GBR	5,461	3.50%	5,242	3.64%	10,615	3.60%
Leeds, GBR	3,488	2.47%	2,173	4.00%	5,608	3.08%
Ipswich, GBR	2,655	1.28%	1,788	2.01%	4,390	1.59%
Nottingham, GBR	2,606	5.45%	1,228	2.85%	3,783	4.68%
Stevenage, GBR	2,499	2.12%	1,206	0.00%	3,670	1.44%
St Albans, GBR	2,600	7.27%	815	6.38%	3,381	7.13%
Exeter, GBR	2,223	4.72%	855	1.99%	3,025	4.03%
Reading, GBR	1,952	0.92%	864	1.97%	2,782	1.26%
Edinburgh, GBR	1,869	6.63%	910	0.00%	2,779	4.46%
Brighton, GBR	2,020	7.03%	663	0.00%	2,629	5.40%
Rochdale, GBR	1,953	3.53%	626	0.00%	2,562	2.69%
Bristol, GBR	1,562	5.57%	771	2.20%	2,333	4.46%
Gloucester, GBR	1,366	2.56%	842	2.14%	2,190	2.42%
Hull, GBR	1,343	5.29%	820	2.07%	2,145	4.10%
Welwyn Garden City, GBR	1,600	2.12%	545	3.30%	2,109	2.47%
Aylesbury, GBR	1,448	4.83%	580	0.00%	2,028	3.45%
Belfast, GBR	1,270	0.00%	733	2.46%	1,969	0.91%
Northampton, GBR	1,380	5.22%	542	3.32%	1,922	4.68%
Subtotal	**0**	**0.00%**	**0**	**0.00%**	**0**	**0.00%**
Total	**276,946**	**3.35%**	**159,200**	**2.46%**	**432,428**	**3.05%**

« PREVIOUS 25 NEXT 25 »

Figure 10.25 Custom demographic campaign and bounce rate report

Methods of Counting Visitors

You may find that campaign traffic measured by Yahoo! Web Analytics is less than campaign traffic reported by other traffic sources (e.g., a PPC/CPC engine or a directory link). This discrepancy is due to differences in how your traffic source measures a visitor and how Yahoo! Web Analytics measures a visitor. The traffic source counts a click on a link to your website as a visitor. However, Yahoo! only counts a visitor if the web page is loaded in a browser and the tracking script is executed. Whether or not the tracking script executes depends on a number of things, such as the position of the code on the page, whether the page is fully loaded, and whether JavaScript is turned off in the visitor's browser.

Typically, you will see that the Yahoo! Web Analytics visitor numbers will be up to 10–15 percent lower than advertising serving systems traffic numbers.

Figure 10.25 shows that we are successful: as the bounce rate is below 10 percent all over. However, there is always room for optimization, such as the outlier city St Albans, GBR, which does not perform according to standard in any of our biggest campaign traffic contributors.

Using Internal Search Reports

Internal site search is represented as a query box on your site, which clearly lets people believe that all content on the site in question can be searched. It is also represented as a site-specific SERP page. Yahoo! Web Analytics offers four usage and insight reports:

- Top Internal Searches
- Zero Results Internal Searches
- Internal Search Conversion
- Internal Search Usage

Remember that this is data that you can get only if you specifically set up your tracking code to do so. First, let's explore the standard reports.

The Top Internal Searches report (see Figure 10.26) shows the search phrases that you used when performing an internal search on your website. The report is sorted on Unique Internal Searches by default.

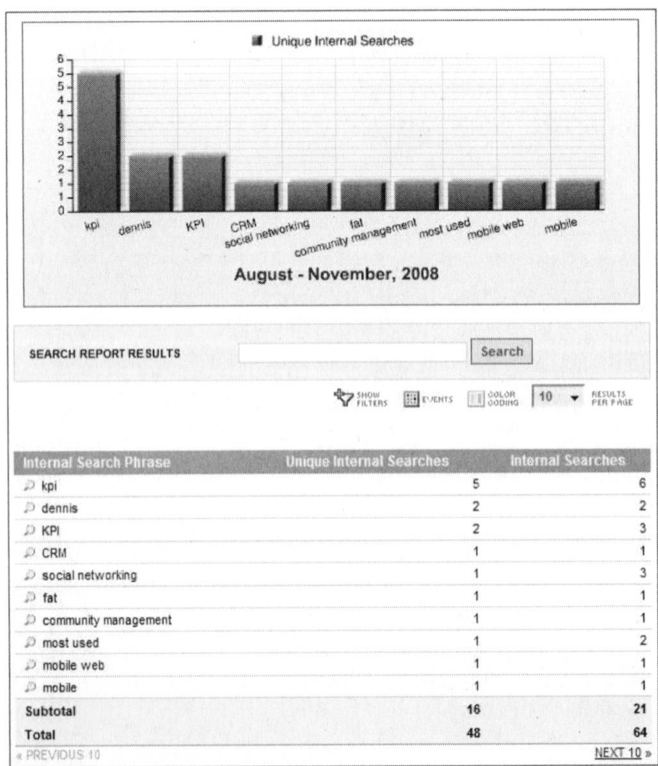

Internal Search Phrase	Unique Internal Searches	Internal Searches
kpi	5	6
dennis	2	2
KPI	2	3
CRM	1	1
social networking	1	3
fat	1	1
community management	1	1
most used	1	2
mobile web	1	1
mobile	1	1
Subtotal	16	21
Total	48	64

« PREVIOUS 10 NEXT 10 »

Figure 10.26 Top Internal Searches report

An internal site search phrase shows visitor interest by showing their true intent. Therefore, in this out-of-the-box report, it makes sense to sort on unique visitor phrases and show the most popular visitor interest areas. The intent does not change no matter how many times the person searches for a specific widget.

From a value point of view, this list cannot be compared to other top lists such as Most Popular Pages. This report is as close as you can get to doing qualitative studies, such as site surveys, without actually conducting them. Visitors who search for unique content on your sites are telling so many stories that just following the keywords on this list is like having a daily conversation with your prospects on their needs and wants. Who does not want that?

If you look at Figure 10.26, you see that there is a request for "mobile" as a subject (forget about the limited volume for the moment). With that request in mind, let's move on to the Zero Results Internal Searches report shown in Figure 10.27 for the same time period.

This report is similar to the Top Internal Searches report. The major difference is that the report is filtered to include only those internal search phrases that did not display any results on the SERP.

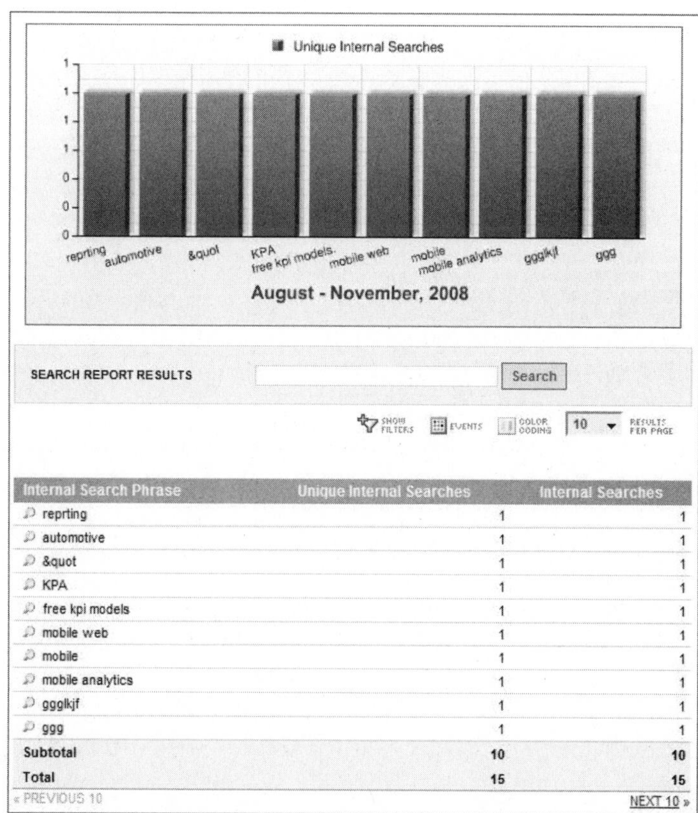

Internal Search Phrase	Unique Internal Searches	Internal Searches
reprting	1	1
automotive	1	1
"	1	1
KPA	1	1
free kpi models	1	1
mobile web	1	1
mobile	1	1
mobile analytics	1	1
ggglkjf	1	1
ggg	1	1
Subtotal	**10**	**10**
Total	**15**	**15**

Figure 10.27 Zero Results Internal Searches report

We immediately notice that there is interest for a unique item and there is no content to support it. As you'll recall, we saw interest for "mobile" content, but none is provided. You should check every item and confirm that you do not provide content that matches this search term. Watch this list to make sure your internal site search engine is always tuned the way it should be.

Suppose you do not offer Widget A but you have many requests for it; should you start offering it? This is a great debate to take on, and depending on your volume, the discussion might help you decide what to research (though it doesn't replace market research).

The Internal Search Conversion report shows the number of actions performed during a visit that contained an internal search as well as the corresponding internal search conversion rates. Use this report to determine how well your visitors respond to various calls to action on your website in conjunction with their use of internal search. The Internal Search Conversion metric is calculated by dividing the number of actions by the number of unique internal searches and shows the conversion rate for visitors who performed an internal search.

I am hesitant in using internal campaign management and internal conversions, including internal site search, as it is extremely difficult to measure true cause and effect. Therefore, I have not included an example of that report in this book.

Yahoo! also provides an Internal Search Usage report, which shows the occurrence of internal searches on a daily, weekly, or monthly basis. The Internal Search Usage metric is calculated by dividing the number of unique internal searches by the total number of visits. The metric reveals the proportion of visits that included internal searches out of the total number of visits. Figure 10.28 is an example of an Internal Search Usage report.

The Internal Search Usage report, as shown in Figure 10.28 without any filters or segments applied, is not too useful as is. I recommend that this is not the typical trend chart that you focus on driving up and to the right.

You would, however, like to watch the trends for unique segments over time. Imagine that you changed your layout or your Merchandising categorization; you would want to watch a specific document group or a specific product subcategory and the use of internal site searches.

I believe it is important for you to understand why people search, beyond the traditional debate on whether they are search- or navigational-dominant visitors.

The most obvious way to figure out why visitors search and what brought them to this point is to determine from which pages they search and how they got there. Imagine the scenario where your visitors keep searching for Widget A in a different product category than you initially put it in? The answer is a great eye-opener beyond the search phrases themselves.

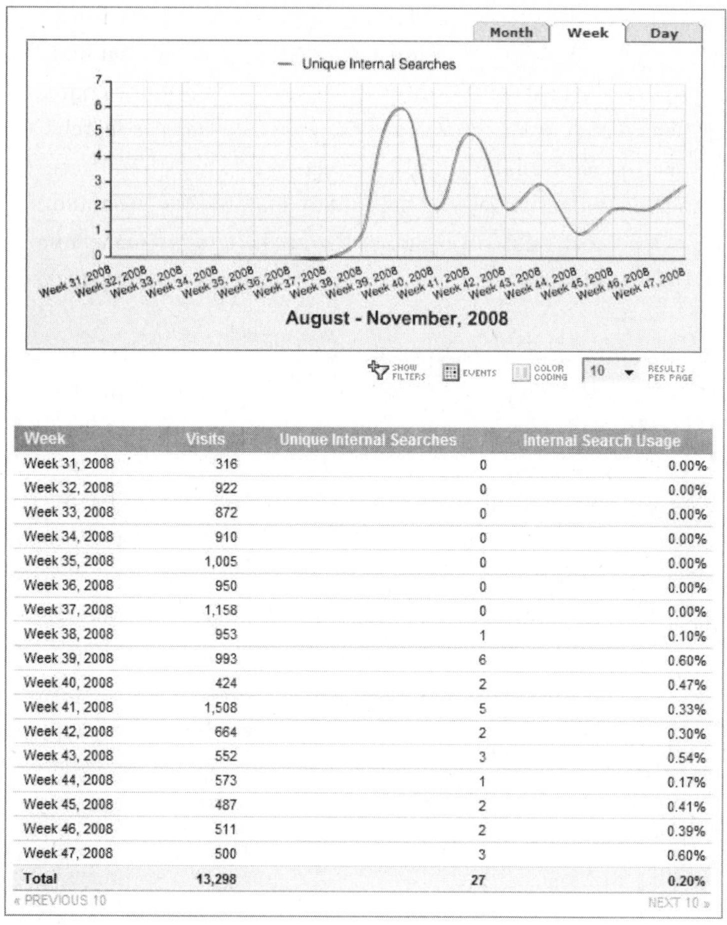

Week	Visits	Unique Internal Searches	Internal Search Usage
Week 31, 2008	316	0	0.00%
Week 32, 2008	922	0	0.00%
Week 33, 2008	872	0	0.00%
Week 34, 2008	910	0	0.00%
Week 35, 2008	1,005	0	0.00%
Week 36, 2008	950	0	0.00%
Week 37, 2008	1,158	0	0.00%
Week 38, 2008	953	1	0.10%
Week 39, 2008	993	6	0.60%
Week 40, 2008	424	2	0.47%
Week 41, 2008	1,508	5	0.33%
Week 42, 2008	664	2	0.30%
Week 43, 2008	552	3	0.54%
Week 44, 2008	573	1	0.17%
Week 45, 2008	487	2	0.41%
Week 46, 2008	511	2	0.39%
Week 47, 2008	500	3	0.60%
Total	**13,298**	**27**	**0.20%**

« PREVIOUS 10 NEXT 10 »

Figure 10.28 Internal Search Usage report

Search-Dominant Visitors

Search is one of the most important user interface elements in any large website. As a rule of thumb, sites with more than about 200 pages should offer search. Usability studies show that more than half of all users are search dominant, about a fifth of the users are link dominant, and the rest exhibit mixed behavior. The search-dominant users will usually go straight for the search button when they enter a website. They are not interested in looking around the site; they are task focused and want to find specific information as fast as possible. More on the difference between the two types of visitors and how to use web analytics to segment them can be found on my blog:

`http://visualrevenue.com/blog/2007/10/search-dominant-visitors-vs-navigation.html`

When customizing an internal search report, differentiate between home page and category pages as they serve as potential starting points. Some see the home page as an invitation to search and prefer to start there. For others, pages that hold original content may be the desired entry page if visitors landed there from a search engine.

Figure 10.29 shows us that about half of our visitors are search dominant and search directly from the home page. It also tells us that about 5 percent of our visitors who come from, say, the Power Tools page, do a search. We might want to expand this report to document groups so we get a better understanding of these figures.

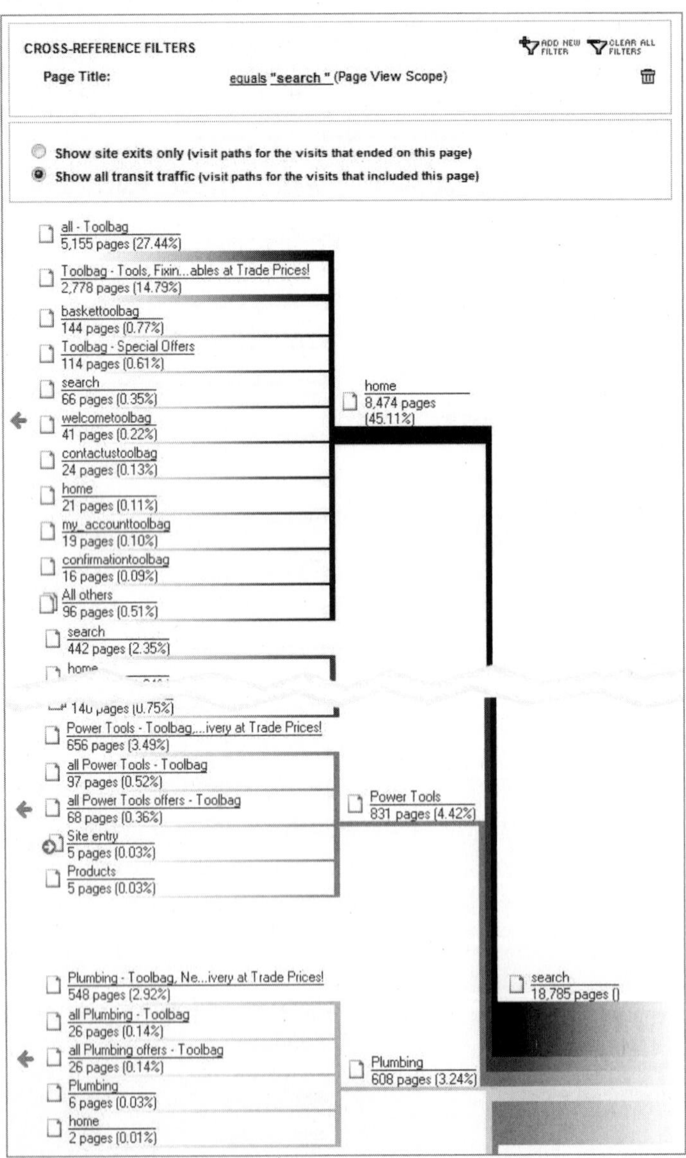

Figure 10.29 Custom backward-looking path analysis for internal SERP

You can filter this report by the unique internal search phrase and figure out on exactly which pages people search for a unique term.

Note: I wrote a blog post about how you can use web analytics to determine the width of your internal search query box. Almost nerdy, but quite powerful:
`http://visualrevenue.com/blog/2007/05/use-web-analytics-to-determine-width-of.html`

This concludes Part II of this book, and you now know how to utilize an enterprise-level web analytics platform with these reports. Part III focuses on actionable insights and contains a number of examples you can pursue in your business.

Actionable Insights

The task in Part I of this book involved collecting the right data. Part II provided you with detailed information on how you can work with this marvelous data. We should never forget why we undertake the tremendous effort of collecting and reporting on our data: to gain insight, start an optimization process, and move our business forward! Part III introduces you to optimization using a set of actionable insights. This is merely an appetizer; the three avenues for optimization I present are not, by any means, the only ones to pursue. The concepts behind them can carry you down other optimization avenues.

III

Chapter 11 **Paid Search Analysis and Optimization**

Chapter 12 **Form Analysis and Optimization**

Chapter 13 **Content Optimization and Competitive Analysis**

11 Paid Search Analysis and Optimization

This chapter is not about how to work with the Yahoo! Search Marketing or Google AdWords interface; instead, we'll focus on evaluating and optimizing your paid search initiatives. I'll start by discussing the basic objectives of running a paid search campaign and how you perform detailed reporting on it. Then we'll jump into optimization for both e-commerce and content sites, and explore the implications of organic search.

Chapter Contents

Defining Paid Search Objectives
Getting Started with Paid Search Analysis
Detailed Paid Search Reporting
Optimizing Paid Search for an E-commerce Site
Optimizing Paid Search for a Content Site
Balancing Paid Search with Organic Search

Defining Paid Search Objectives

Let's establish paid search objectives before we talk about the optimization itself. Paid search can be used for many reasons, such as increasing sales, customers, orders, leads, traffic, or to help decrease costs and be more cost efficient overall. Paid search can also help you build the brand.

With all these possible uses for paid search, I want to emphasize the importance of putting together a detailed plan for how and what you want to measure. You need a set of crystal-clear objectives before you begin thinking about optimization.

This plan must clarify what web analysis should accomplish according to your paid search objectives. Make sure you have a framework that cuts through the clutter and lets you focus on the right problems and the methods suggested for solving those problems.

Tips for Clarifying Your Objectives

When defining these objectives—a process that includes management or other key stakeholders—you are bound to end up with a set of tasks that goes beyond optimization alone. That's absolutely acceptable. For example, you may be advertising your limited participation in a specific industry conference while continuously advertising a major product or service. These are two different animals when it comes to the results you want paid search to help you achieve.

For you to create clear-cut optimization objectives, it helps to be able to look at a *part* of something—whether that is the landing page, the keywords, or the call to action—and, based on the analysis, recommend a change to that part.

I suggest you choose to see search and paid search as channels by themselves. This decision depends on the size of your budget allocation. When you run traditional mass media campaigns, you will see that they have a strong impact on your web traffic. Effective mass media will impact your direct, organic search, and paid search traffic.

Note: Search has become omnipresent as a finding method and typically the glue between channels. I have general comments on this topic in my post on search-dominant visitors versus navigation-dominant visitors:

`http://visualrevenue.com/blog/2007/10/search-dominant-visitors-vs-navigation.html`

Even if your organization focuses on mass media and you are aware of the traffic effects, you might miss the opportunity to measure the impact and value of other channels based on your superior measurability in paid search.

Paid Search as a Cross-Channel Optimization Tool

With the amount of money spent on traditional mass media campaigns, your online endeavors might be more useful as a cross-channel optimization tool than as a revenue-generating channel in its own right. You can achieve this by setting up a control group, but a simpler approach is to establish a separate segment. You could use any type of segment, such as a geographic segment. This setup is supported in most channels, including paid search.

Imagine that you have two full-page ad creatives for a specific product. You can choose to run both of them in two segments (for example, two different geographic regions). But before you do this, you must set up strict baselines on incoming traffic and its quality. Once you have a baseline—which could be as simple as the number of visitors and the average visit-to-sale conversion rate—you have created a powerful method for measuring the differential effectiveness of the full-page advertisements. Simply track the baseline periods for the control groups compared to the target media markets. You can measure traffic impact, qualification impact, and impact by visitor type.

While this type of web analytics tracking may not replace your traditional mass media analysis, it does provide a number of benefits. This is an easy, and cost-effective process.

To summarize, know your business and know your advertising mission all the way down to having clear objectives for your paid search campaigns.

Getting Started with Paid Search Analysis

Before we get started, take action on the Campaign Tracking items recommended in Chapter 3. Without data, no analysis can be done. Likewise, without a good understanding of report customization (see Chapters 7 and 10), you will find it hard to do good paid search optimization.

Despite the amount of money spent on paid search marketing initiatives today, it would not be fair to assume that someone within your organization is handling this. Just because paid search initiatives might be run by the Marketing department, you cannot expect them to have a complete view of paid search's impact across all online channels. Web analysts need to take charge and evaluate the behavior of online customers acquired from paid search. Paid search is so expensive that providing insight may mean the difference between a well-run program and a half-baked one. Paid search visitors cannot be optimized on a separate channel; they must be optimized as a part of a whole. These visitors have their own distinct behavioral patterns, and they enter the site in unique and controlled places (landing pages) with well-defined keywords and interests in mind.

I am not suggesting that your web analytics program replace your bid management program. I do believe that web analytics are vital for helping your company allocate funds among paid search, SEO, and other online and offline marketing initiatives, while ensuring that proper optimization plans and initiatives are in place.

Bid Management

The term "bid management" encapsulates tools and processes that help manage bids on PPC search engines such as Google and Yahoo! in an automated manner.

Once you can truly measure the value of a visitor, and in particular a search visitor, you can begin thinking about optimization. Start your optimization efforts around the following:

- Campaigns
- Ad groups
- Search listings (keywords)
- Search phrases

In paid search, the higher the position of the listing, the more incoming traffic you are likely to get, but the higher the listing, the higher the costs are. A set of variables are involved, some set by the search engine, but more importantly, we must understand that search listings are not equal.

Many of the paid search programs I've worked with are amazingly large and have embraced the concept of a *long tail*. I am not surprised when I see ten thousand keywords or even one hundred thousand keywords. The reason I mention this is that when using web analytics, you may never see any of those single clicks, as they are by themselves so limited in volume.

Long Tail

A data distribution pattern, which when applied to an e-commerce business, shows a small number of top-selling products and a large number of products sold in small quantities that together make up a large percentage of revenue.

The long tail becomes a challenge for a number of reasons. First, you might not have full access to the tail as it is sometimes cropped by your web analytics solution. Yahoo! Web Analytics does not crop any of its data, but bulk exports are currently maxed at 200,000 rows, which if not filtered, might not be enough for you. Remember, you can always add a geographic filter and split the export into two or three and then combine everything in Microsoft Excel later.

Second, if you have a search listing that generates less than one hundred clicks within the reporting period, you will have statistically limited conversion actions (or proxies) recorded and little action to take, simply because you do not know whether the impact is significant and valid. In Figure 11.1 you can see that we have lots of keywords generating limited clicks and no revenue.

Search Listings	Clicks	Bounce rate	Cost	Revenue	Action	Conversion	CPA
central controller heating&x	485	4.02%	$24.05	$255.45	5	1.03%	$4.81
bosch router&x	483	2.62%	$24.15	$374.35	5	1.04%	$4.83
nail gun&x	455	5.93%	$22.75	$0.00	0	0.00%	$0.00
plumbing shop&x	450	7.11%	$22.10	$234.80	5	1.11%	$4.42
stanley knife&x	436	2.92%	$21.80	$66.78	9	2.06%	$2.42
discount plumbing&x	409	3.94%	$20.25	$171.95	5	1.22%	$4.05
thermostatic radiator valve&x	407	2.04%	$20.35	$0.00	0	0.00%	$0.00
makita reciprocating saw&x	380	0.00%	$19.00	$0.00	0	0.00%	$0.00
laser level&x	373	2.12%	$17.75	$940.40	8	2.14%	$2.22
hammer&x	369	7.07%	$18.05	$0.00	0	0.00%	$0.00
garden fork&x	349	2.24%	$17.45	$392.24	8	2.29%	$2.18
makita router&x	349	2.72%	$17.20	$1,627.60	4	1.15%	$4.30
power saw&x	343	2.33%	$17.15	$0.00	0	0.00%	$0.00
skil saw&x	343	1.44%	$17.15	$358.20	5	1.46%	$3.43
merchant plumbing&x	340	1.18%	$17.00	$0.00	0	0.00%	$0.00
dewalt cordless&x	337	3.52%	$16.65	$0.00	0	0.00%	$0.00
trend router&x	330	2.42%	$16.25	$0.00	0	0.00%	$0.00
paslode nail gun&x	325	2.73%	$16.25	$0.00	0	0.00%	$0.00
makita jigsaw&x	324	1.20%	$15.80	$0.00	0	0.00%	$0.00
diy plumbing&x	318	4.40%	$15.90	$0.00	0	0.00%	$0.00
bosch circular saw&x	312	1.60%	$15.60	$0.00	0	0.00%	$0.00
dewalt jigsaw&x	302	1.66%	$14.90	$0.00	0	0.00%	$0.00
dewalt radio&x	301	1.61%	$14.65	$1,014.20	4	1.33%	$3.66
cheap power tool&x	299	1.30%	$14.95	$0.00	0	0.00%	$0.00
estwing hammers&x	276	3.56%	$13.80	$285.10	5	1.81%	$2.76
Subtotal	**9,095**	**0.00%**	**$450.95**	**$5,721.07**	**63**	**0.69%**	**$7.16**
Total	**383,029**	**3.59%**	**$4,193.40**	**$211,975.00**	**1,954**	**0.51%**	**$2.15**
« PREVIOUS 25							NEXT 25 »

Figure 11.1 Custom search listings cost and revenue report

Does this mean that we should immediately remove those keywords? No! It simply means that we have too limited a dataset to make any solid conclusions. So it becomes your task to group some of these words to create meaningful analysis and suggestions for actions. Remember that your customers already group search phrases, so there is no sin in doing this. A simple way of grouping keywords is to look at a unique organic landing page, such as a product page, and the search phrases used to reach it.

By reviewing search listings for "nailers," Figure 11.2 shows us that only one of our keywords is successful.

However, it's likely that some of our other keywords are "upstream" keywords used to get to this one. To learn more, let's add a dimension, as shown in Figure 11.3.

CROSS-REFERENCE FILTERS

Search Listings (Direct): contains "nailers "

ADD NEW FILTER · CLEAR ALL FILTERS

Search Listings	Clicks	Bounce rate	Cost	Revenue	Action	Conversion	CPA
nailers&x	515	6.02%	$25.75	$0.00	0	0.00%	$0.00
floor nailers&x	202	3.96%	$10.10	$0.00	0	0.00%	$0.00
air nailers&x	97	4.12%	$4.85	$0.00	0	0.00%	$0.00
paslode nailers&x	48	8.33%	$2.40	$0.00	0	0.00%	$0.00
framing nailers&x	47	0.00%	$2.35	$0.00	0	0.00%	$0.00
electric nailers&x	32	0.00%	$1.60	$0.00	0	0.00%	$0.00
brad nailers&x	23	0.00%	$1.15	$402.80	5	21.74%	$0.23
nailers stapler&x	20	0.00%	$1.00	$0.00	0	0.00%	$0.00
nail gun&x	4	0.00%	$0.20	$0.00	0	0.00%	$0.00
paslode impulse framing nailers&x	4	0.00%	$0.20	$0.00	0	0.00%	$0.00
pneumatic nailers&x	4	100.00%	$0.20	$0.00	0	0.00%	$0.00
Subtotal	**996**	**0.00%**	**$49.80**	**$402.80**	**5**	**0.50%**	**$9.96**
Unknown	**138**	**0.00%**	**$0.00**	**$0.00**	**0**	**0.00%**	**$0.00**
Total	**1,134**	**5.14%**	**$49.80**	**$402.80**	**5**	**0.44%**	**$9.96**

« PREVIOUS 25 · NEXT 25 »

Figure 11.2 Filtered custom search listings report

Channel / Search Listings	Clicks	Bounce rate	Cost	Revenue	Action	Conversion	CPA
⊟ Paid Search	1,037	5.14%	$49.80	$402.80	5	0.48%	$9.96
nailers&x	515	6.02%	$25.75	$0.00	0	0.00%	$0.00
floor nailers&x	202	3.96%	$10.10	$0.00	0	0.00%	$0.00
air nailers&x	97	4.12%	$4.85	$0.00	0	0.00%	$0.00
paslode nailers&x	48	8.33%	$2.40	$0.00	0	0.00%	$0.00
framing nailers&x	47	0.00%	$2.35	$0.00	0	0.00%	$0.00
electric nailers&x	32	0.00%	$1.60	$0.00	0	0.00%	$0.00
brad nailers&x	23	0.00%	$1.15	$402.80	5	21.74%	$0.23
nailers stapler&x	20	0.00%	$1.00	$0.00	0	0.00%	$0.00

Figure 11.3 Grouped and filtered custom search listings report

Figure 11.3 shows a group of "nailers" converting at 0.48 percent rather than just one single keyword converting at almost 22 percent. We can only hope that your internal search marketing team has already done this by grouping keywords in logical ad groups. But even if they have, you could wind up wanting to do analysis on keywords across ad groups.

Organizing Ad Groups

This brings us to our next area of optimization: ad groups. You should ask the paid search team to group intelligently in ad groups for the long tail, make single bids from the groups, and have single landing pages for each group. You can still use multiple creatives as long as this is done as an ad group activity.

In Chapter 4, where we talked about tracking and collecting information on paid search, we focused on the search listing itself and not the ad group. You are forced to do the hard work yourself in grouping these search listings into the proper categories;

this is not done automatically by Yahoo! Web Analytics. Yahoo! is working on that so that not only the ad group, but also the campaign, creative, and so forth are passed on down to the Yahoo! Web Analytics application.

When organizing your ad groups, your first priority must be to replicate the reporting from all your paid search channels and—if necessary because of a potentially flawed reporting setup—group long-tail search listings. You can accomplish all this with your measurable objective in mind.

I call this ad group *cleansing*. Your first action for optimization could be offering feedback to your search marketing team about whether keywords in ad groups center on a single concept. If they don't, you can achieve the same thing on your end through filters or segments.

Matching Options

Classifying your keywords into meaningful groups might not be enough. The reason is that each search listing will have a search phrase matching option applied to it. Matching options include the following:

- Broad Match
- Phrase Match
- Exact Match
- Negative Match

This means that a search phrase (search) for "Viggo Mortensen" will match a search listing for "Mortensen" with Broad Match. Why does this matter? Because any way you put it, there is a huge difference between the search intent for searches on "Dennis Mortensen" and searches for "Viggo Mortensen." So you need to know how matching options are set before you start analyzing either keywords or ad groups. Remember, it is all about grouping visitor intent and optimizing that.

If you are disconnected from your search marketing team or if it's an outsourced activity, I recommend that you refer to actual search phrases and make your recommendations using them. It then becomes the search team's responsibility to match these phrases the best way possible.

Search Engine Content Networks

In this section, we'll explore another flavor of search: search engine content networks, such as Google AdSense.

Introducing content networks to your paid search web analysis is a much bigger undertaking than just checking the box to participate on the engine side. So devote some thought as to how you want to track the traffic. If you decide to participate in content networks, be sure to isolate this traffic and do not combine it with either your traditional paid search campaigns or your organic results.

Search Engine Content Networks

Search engine content networks help publishers monetize their inventory by matching a site's content with a keyword and thus an audience, as if they have searched. The content network automatically crawls the content of the publisher's pages and delivers text and image ads that are relevant to the publisher's audience and site content. You see these ads on websites such as CNN.com, where they are delivered by Google and identified as "Ads by Google."

Comparing Search Engine Data to Your Website Data

The traditional paid search consists of the following metrics on the search engine side:

- Search Listing (Keyword)
- Matching Options
- Max CPC (Bid)
- Ad Impressions
- Clicks
- Search Listing Total Cost
- Search Listing Avg. Cost per Click
- Average Position

These paid search engine metrics are all metrics you have to compare with your website-side behavioral data. But as farfetched as it may sound, some marketers do paid search engine optimization using only these metrics. It is your task to make sure that this does not happen, however sophisticated the search engine's setup might be.

For you to truly optimize, you must know what happened after the paid search click. It is *after* the click when you make your money.

So what's the conclusion to all this? Well, it is important that you agree that we just have to live with two systems and two sets of data: the search engine data and your web analytics data. With two sets of data, collected and presented from two different systems, we cannot expect everything to match up 100 percent. But you must try to connect the two to achieve paid search optimization.

Detailed Paid Search Reporting

Not only is the campaign summary the most obvious place to start your detailed paid search reporting, it is also the *best* place to start.

Any decent campaign summary will provide you with information on the high-level facts, such as the following:

- Paid Search
- Organic Search
- Other Campaigns
- Other Referrals
- Direct Traffic

These rows appear in the sample campaign summary shown in Figure 11.4.

Channel Campaign	Impressions	Clicks	Unique Clicks	Returning	Bounce rate	Cost	Revenue	Action	Conversion	ROAS	CPA	ACC
Paid Search	0	70,219	36,820	1,649	3.40%	$1,420.85	$43,506.21	378	0.54%	3,061.98%	$3.76	$0.02
Banner Campaigns	0	49,269	12,066	460	4.54%	$0.00	$21,628.31	215	0.44%	0.00%	$0.00	$0.00
Email Campaigns	0	5,641	1,564	126	3.41%	$0.00	$4,022.62	44	0.78%	0.00%	$0.00	$0.00
Total campaign activity	0	125,129	50,450	2,235	3.71%	$1,420.85	$69,157.14	637	0.51%	4,867.31%	$2.23	$0.01

Please note that the table below displays only non-campaign traffic.

Non-Campaign Traffic Sources	First Time	Returning	Visits	Revenue	Action	Bounce rate
Organic search	1,885	226	2,111	$5,054.92	45	2.98%
Other referrals	1,818	404	2,222	$5,106.81	41	22.86%
Direct access or bookmark	2,811	2,607	5,418	$15,039.81	189	8.16%
Total non-campaign activity	6,514	3,237	9,751	$25,201.54	275	10.39%

Figure 11.4 Default top-level campaign summary

This is not where you will get the bulk of your insights, but it does put in perspective some interesting facts. Using Figure 11.4 as an example, we see that paid search is driving about 50 percent of our traffic generation and approximately 45 percent of our online revenue. That only confirms the importance of paid search within this organization. But it also illustrates another fact: With this amount of traffic attributed to paid search, the optimization task ahead is less likely to be about volume and a whole lot more about effectiveness of such elements as visit-to-sales conversion. Acknowledging this moves you toward making a decision on whether future optimization projects should focus on growth or effectiveness.

In our campaign summary, we should be concerned about the limited contribution organic search has to our search marketing program.

So don't underestimate the value of using high-level numbers to determine your strategy for growing the organic channel and optimizing the effectiveness of the paid channel. These are important decisions, and just because getting the numbers is easy, that does not mean it is any less valuable.

Our next step (concentrating on just one channel, paid search) is to add a search engine dimension to our report, as shown in Figure 11.5. Remember, you can make a setup like this the default in your campaign summary.

Now, repeat the custom report exercise from earlier, but this time think about whether the individual engine is a growth or an effectiveness opportunity. I suggest you look at Visits as the primary traffic share metric, with an eye to Revenue or other successful conversion metrics.

Channel / Search Engines	Impressions	Clicks	Unique Clicks	Returning	Bounce rate	Cost	Revenue	Action	Conversion	ROAS	CPA	ACC
Paid Search	0	70,219	36,820	1,649	3.40%	$1,420.85	$43,506.21	378	0.54%	3,061.98%	$3.76	$0.02
Google	0	22,921	17,009	90	3.38%	$924.80	$12,087.19	109	0.48%	1,307.01%	$8.48	$0.04
Yahoo	0	8,906	2,826	41	1.53%	$0.90	$6,378.11	36	0.40%	708,679.00%	$0.02	$0.00
AOL Search	0	2,322	1,696	17	5.94%	$97.30	$3,136.71	22	0.95%	3,223.75%	$4.42	$0.04
Blueyonder	0	237	191	0	1.04%	$10.25	$536.50	2	0.84%	5,234.15%	$5.12	$0.04
Altavista	0	283	74	0	8.11%	$0.10	$339.28	4	1.41%	339,280.00%	$0.02	$0.00
Oingo	0	50	19	0	0.00%	$2.50	$253.42	2	4.00%	10,136.80%	$1.25	$0.05
Gawwk	0	30	15	0	0.00%	$0.50	$125.95	1	3.33%	25,190.00%	$0.50	$0.02
Deal Time	0	273	161	0	1.59%	$8.75	$88.35	1	0.37%	1,009.71%	$8.75	$0.03
Tiscali	0	465	350	0	1.42%	$19.60	$74.59	1	0.22%	380.56%	$19.60	$0.04
Excite	0	57	31	0	12.90%	$0.60	$0.00	0	0.00%	0.00%	$0.00	$0.01
Lycos	0	118	46	0	4.35%	$0.25	$0.00	0	0.00%	0.00%	$0.00	$0.00
MSN Search	0	4	1	39	0.00%	$0.00	$0.00	0	0.00%	0.00%	$0.00	$0.00
Dogpile	0	29	13	0	0.00%	$0.60	$0.00	0	0.00%	0.00%	$0.00	$0.02
Ask Jeeves	0	6	6	0	0.00%	$0.30	$0.00	0	0.00%	0.00%	$0.00	$0.05

Figure 11.5 Custom campaign summary with the search engine dimension added

My next suggestion is to look at the split between engines. I suggest you create a table like the one shown here, comparing site share and market share:

Search Engine	Site Share	Market Share
Google	67% (22,921)	64%
Yahoo!	26% (8,906)	21%
AOL	7% (2,322)	4%

This table (which takes the numbers from Figure 11.4, using the three most popular search engines) concludes that their search programs are very much aligned with the overall market distribution.

As we have done with the traffic channels and search engines, comparing the sourcing rates by engine can help us identify growth opportunities. Most sites should expect their numbers by engine to track reasonably to the overall market share by that engine. If the site numbers deviate from this, there's a potential for either growth or improved effectiveness. For example, if Google provides you with only 30 percent of your paid search traffic, you have a traffic growth opportunity.

These types of numbers form the background for the deeper analysis that will help you achieve most of your detailed optimization tasks. These tasks involve grouping this information on such dimensions as campaigns, ad groups, landing pages, creatives, and so on (see Figure 11.6). And, with access to custom fields, you can attach additional campaign attributes to a specific campaign, which will give you an even greater opportunity to do detailed analysis.

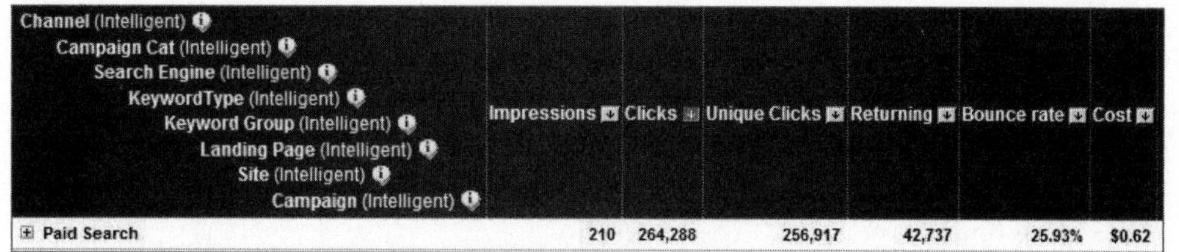

Figure 11.6 Detailed campaign summary with additional dimensions

Figure 11.6 shows extensive detail in the number of dimensions and thus drill-down opportunities. But more importantly, you don't just get the drill-down opportunities; you get analysis opportunities on every single level and across levels.

At the lowest level, Yahoo! Web Analytics provides you with reporting about the actual search phrases entered and search listings used. This data will typically be associated with each of the higher levels already described. So you can look at all search traffic by keyword or search engine traffic by keyword, as shown in Figure 11.7.

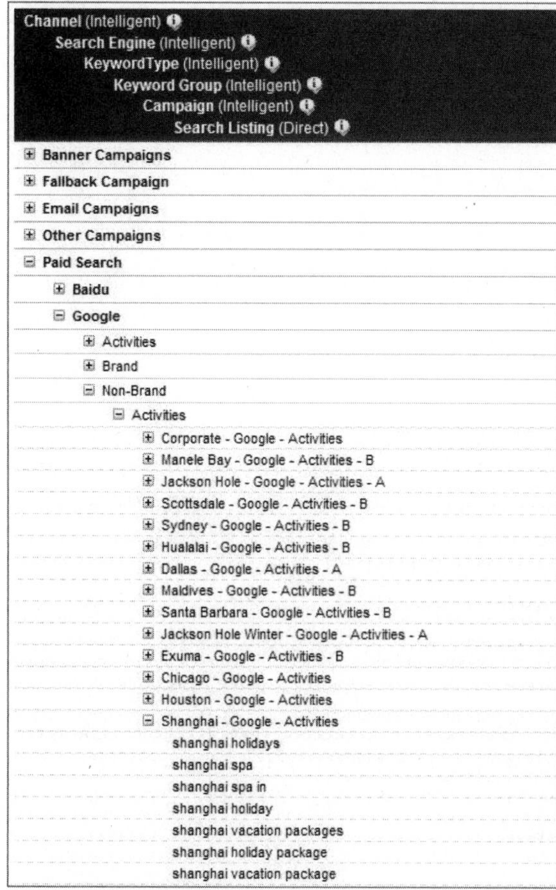

Figure 11.7 Custom campaign summary tree

Where you see the detail, you can drill into the tree shown in Figure 11.7. This is not all the detailed reporting you can do with paid search, but merely an indication of what you can do to make your reporting more useful.

Optimizing Paid Search for an E-commerce Site

As you have noticed throughout this book, I have often used e-commerce as an example foundation, simply because it is very quick and easy to understand. E-commerce has clear conversion points, and most of the time, these are sales conversion points. In addition, a conversion point is assigned a value, the actual revenue, and perhaps even a true profit.

Therefore, most of this book provides input for paid search optimization for an e-commerce site. You might also be able to achieve a large part of your e-commerce optimization with your bid management software, simply because the optimization process is so well defined. If that's not entirely the case, you can use your web analytics package as your primary optimization tool. For the most part, this strategy does not seem particularly challenging—and it's more of a reporting issue than an analysis issue.

On the surface, this strategy may look fairly easy, but it is not a trivial task. You have to choose optimizing goals, and this is probably the most important task in any campaign optimization process. If you are not optimizing toward the right goal, you probably won't be successful. Even worse, you may end up "de-optimizing" your campaigns.

Note: Remember, you are likely to worsen your campaigns if you optimize toward the wrong goal!

Here are some possible optimization goals for an e-commerce site:

- CTR
- Visit-to-Sales Conversion
- Visitor-to-Sales Conversion
- Revenue per Visit
- Revenue per Visitor
- Profit per Visitor
- Lifetime Value of the Visitor

Looking at this list, you should immediately ask yourself which of these optimization goals you are using. You cannot use more than one optimization metric for one campaign.

Just identifying which optimization metric to use is enough to justify the time spent reading this book. Any optimization done on the CTR alone is prone to instant "mis-optimization." The reason is, if clicks are truly what you are going for, an ad saying something along the lines of "$1,000 to click here" will create a high CTR, but unless you actually give away money, it will create an even higher bounce rate and essentially create no value. So to begin with, see CTR only as a component and direct your energy toward another optimization goal. With this rule of thumb in mind, how would you evaluate the ad shown in Figure 11.8?

Disclaimer: I don't know anything about the actual results of the campaign running the ad shown in Figure 11.8. But it illustrates my concern about being overly aggressive in your message to the extent that this becomes the goal itself. Remember, there is no value in a visit by itself—there is only a cost associated with it. The keywords that produce valuable visits and visitors are driven out of the paid search program in exchange for cheap clicks. Once you can think through this chain of results, the better you will be at optimizing the results for your business.

Moving on to a more serious optimization metric, the Visit-to-Sales Conversion metric, we get something that might start to make a difference. See Figure 11.9.

Name Brand Bikes
Discounted up to 60%
Road, Mountain, Track & Tri Bikes - save hundreds. New with Warranty.
www.bikesdirect.com

Figure 11.8 Paid search ad, with an aggressive CTR focus

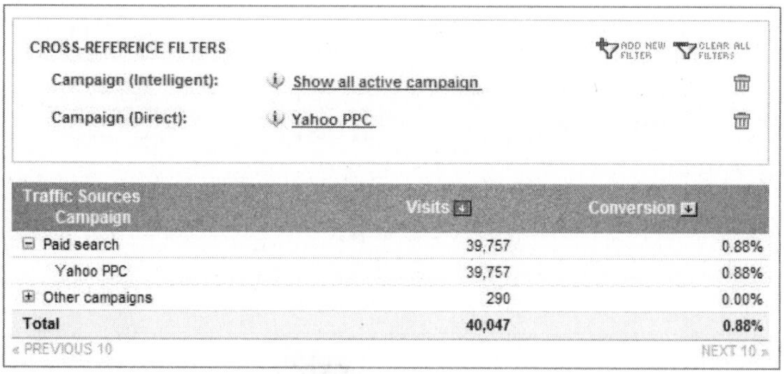

CROSS-REFERENCE FILTERS
Campaign (Intelligent): Show all active campaign
Campaign (Direct): Yahoo PPC

Traffic Sources Campaign	Visits	Conversion
⊟ Paid search	39,757	0.88%
Yahoo PPC	39,757	0.88%
⊞ Other campaigns	290	0.00%
Total	**40,047**	**0.88%**

« PREVIOUS 10 NEXT 10 »

Figure 11.9 Custom paid search report on the visit-to-sales conversion rate

As Figure 11.9 shows, we will be optimizing on our current 0.88 percent visit-to-sale conversion. We should have the ability to drill into this report on a campaign, ad group, or keyword listing level.

Visit-to-Sales Conversion is a reasonable metric to use, and it might even work for you, but only if you have all your sales within that first visit, and only if you don't expect to sell any other products to this person over time. There are a number of other constraints as well.

In the report shown in Figure 11.10, you can see that only a few keywords provide us with a visit-to-sale conversion.

Traffic Sources Campaign Search Listing	Visits	Conversion
Paid search	**39,757**	**0.88%**
Yahoo PPC	39,757	0.88%
circular saw blade&x	79	0.00%
power tool&x	36	0.00%
screwdrivers&x	36	0.00%
skil&x	33	0.00%
circular saw&x	29	0.00%
cordless drill&x	24	0.00%
bosch jigsaw&x	23	0.00%
bosch cordless drill&x	22	0.00%
hand tool&x	22	0.00%
nail gun&x	21	0.00%
Toolbag&x	20	0.00%
bosch circular saw&x	20	0.00%
nailers&x	18	0.00%
dewalt sander&x	18	27.78%
cordless makita&x	17	0.00%
power saw&x	17	0.00%
makita jigsaw&x	13	0.00%
bosch hammer drill&x	10	0.00%
hitachi power tool&x	10	50.00%
dewalt cordless&x	9	0.00%
"Other"		
Other campaigns	**290**	**0.00%**
Total	**40,047**	**0.88%**
« PREVIOUS 10		NEXT 10 »

Figure 11.10 Visit-to-sales conversion rate on a search listings level

Does this mean that all the other keywords are worthless and we should put all our money on those few, very high visit-to-sales conversion keywords? I think that is unlikely. What we are seeing here is that companion keywords are used as part of the visitors' (not visits) navigation and search for what they are going to buy. Again, if we removed all the nonconverting keywords without any further analysis and just focused on this visit-to-sales conversion, we would again end up "mis-optimizing" our campaign.

However, if we move on to the Visitor-to-Sales Conversion metric, we might be able to fix some of the flaws. If we optimize the overall campaign toward a better visitor-to-sales conversion rate, we might be doing some good. The challenge with using this metric is that we have to accept that Yahoo! Web Analytics is not a true visitor-based system. I know Yahoo! is moving into this, but that's not the case as of this writing. This means you have to do a bit of hacking to use this metric.

Another problem is campaign attribution. When can we peg Yahoo! PCC as the owner of a conversion? Furthermore, by using this metric we do not necessarily take care of the optimization problem, and we might be driving low-value shopping carts, where value is defined as anything from revenue to profits.

If you look at Figure 11.11, you will notice that we define and optimize toward success on sales varying from approximately $4 to $143.

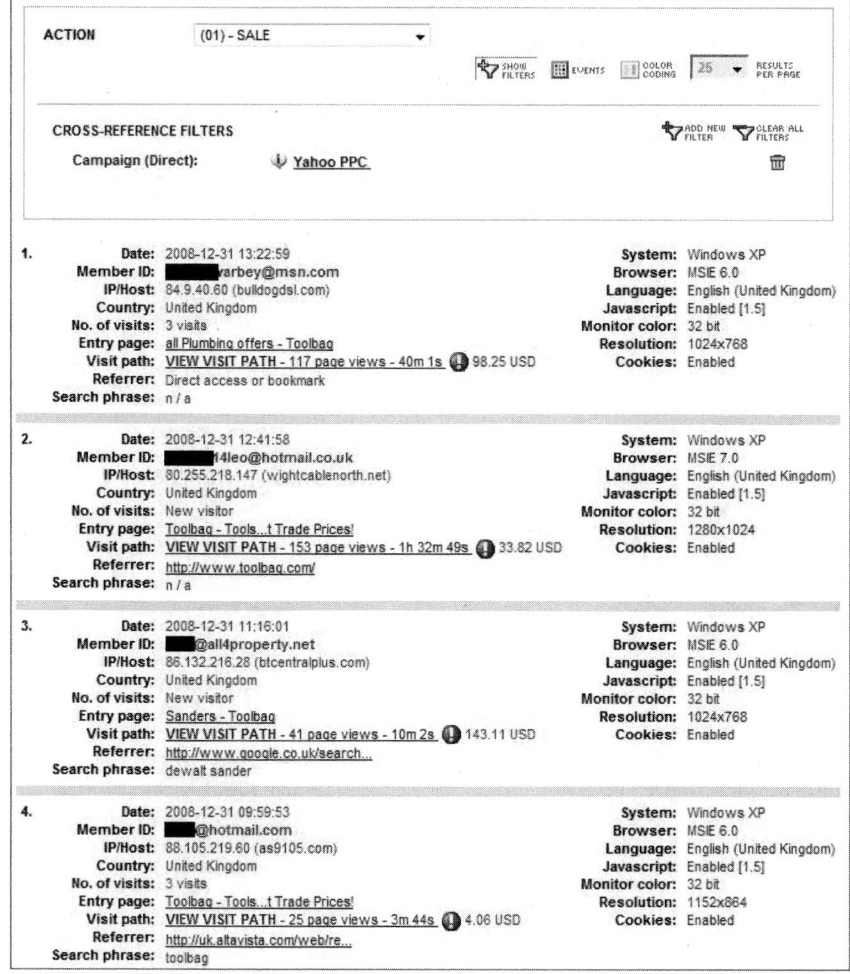

Figure 11.11 Last visitor details filtered by paid search and sales conversion

Is it fair to optimize toward a goal that equals a sale on $4 and $143 in the optimization process? Perhaps it is, but most of the time I would think it is not.

Let's move on to another optimization metric, one that takes the previous potential flaw into consideration: Revenue per Visit. See Figure 11.12.

Channel	Visits	Avg. Order Value
Paid Search	114,425	$116.91
Banner Campaigns	39,521	$101.47
Email Campaigns	5,334	$92.66
Total	**157,458**	**$110.02**

« PREVIOUS 10 NEXT 10 »

Figure 11.12 Average paid search revenue per visit report

As you can see, this report moves us beyond the CTR, as it does not impact this metric; it also goes beyond the conversion metric since the value of the actual sale is taken into consideration. In this case, we will optimize toward getting a better average value of each visit sale action. Our task is to move the needle on $116.91.

Using the Revenue per Visit metric, we have fixed a great deal of these potential issues simply by taking into account the revenue of products sold. However, if you have a great deal of sales that take place not in a single visit but over multiple visits, then you will unfortunately still be prone to mis-optimizing.

This brings us to the next potential paid search optimization metric: Revenue per Visitor. This one promises to be almost everything we want. In situations where you expect ongoing sales to existing visitors, you may considerably undervalue the campaign, ad group, or search listing. Because it is obvious that optimization takes place within a defined period of time, optimizing toward revenue per visitor can have negative effects, such as failing to take into consideration the value generated over the next coming sales.

The last optimization metric, Lifetime Value of the Visitor, is definitely the hardest to implement and, quite frankly, something that you need to work hard to do in Yahoo! Web Analytics. Expect to do exports and use Microsoft Excel. See the following post for more:

`http://visualrevenue.com/blog/2007/10/customer-lifetime-value-kpi.html`

I would like you to leave this section with a couple of takeaways. First, think hard about what optimization strategy you choose, and think hard about the potential built-in limitations of that metric. Second, expect that you might have to choose a metric because of limitations in your technology, and use that as sort of a proxy for what you are really trying to do.

That said, if you are a traditional e-commerce property, why couldn't you just use the Lifetime Value of the Visitor metric all the time? The reason is that your site might not have the volume to generate enough data for meaningful analysis and optimization on that metric. You should then fall back and use something else as a proxy.

Optimizing Paid Search for a Content Site

You've seen that e-commerce is not really as straightforward to optimize as you might have expected. If we then add to the equation the idea that we can analyze sites that have no direct conversions (as in sales), things get trickier. Welcome to paid search optimization for non-e-commerce sites: content sites.

I won't discuss all imaginable content site scenarios, so expect my advice to serve as general pointers.

For me, optimizing paid search for content sites is all about proxies. By that, I mean conversion proxies. This is almost as important as choosing the right optimization metric when talking about e-commerce sites.

You might be coming from an e-commerce situation where you might not have enough traffic and conversion to do any decent analysis. The low traffic does not have to be due to a small budget; you might just sell very expensive items. For the conversion proxy, you choose something that in a best-case scenario should happen before the actual sale. This can be an Add to Cart action, which must take place before a sale. No one can have a 100 percent Add to Cart–to-sales conversion rate. So you will have a lot more volume and data at the Add to Cart level than the actual sales level. This means you will be able to use Add to Cart as a proxy for sales and as an optimization point.

You're looking for those highly correlated points as proxies for conversion when optimizing. You're seeking events before the actual conversion. With a conversion proxy like Add to Cart, you can be less concerned about other behaviors, such as how people navigate and behave in general.

Figures 11.13, 11.14, and 11.15 show the ad hoc scenario I built for the three paid search filtered steps: Basket (Add to Cart), Checkout, and Sale, in Weeks 1, 2, and 3, respectively. You will notice that the limited volume in actual sales is closely related to the checkout step in the process. We might even be able to use this checkout step as a decent proxy for our analysis.

When using a proxy, your goal is not to predict future behavior. We cannot conclude that those visitors in checkout are more likely to convert. They might, but it doesn't matter.

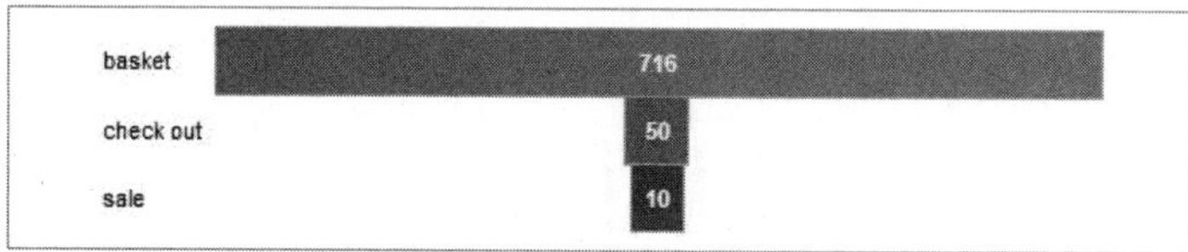

Figure 11.13 Paid search filtered ad hoc checkout scenario: Week 1

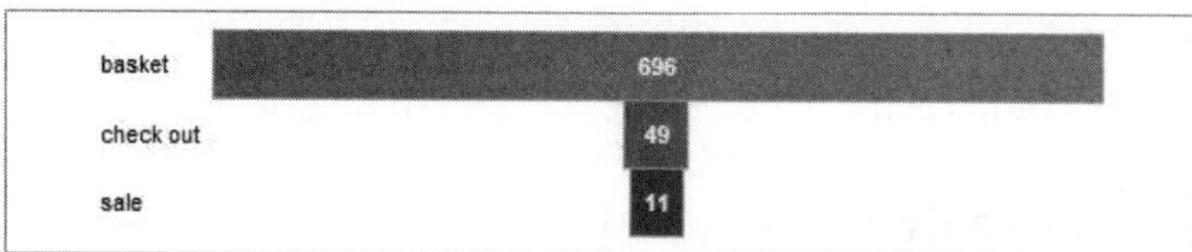

Figure 11.14 Paid search filtered ad hoc checkout scenario: Week 2

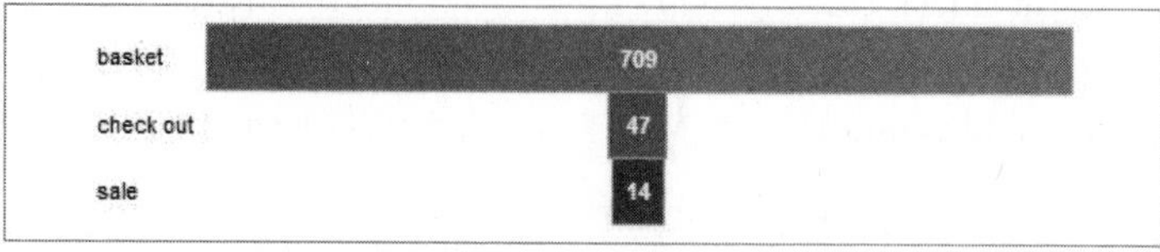

Figure 11.15 Paid search filtered ad hoc checkout scenario: Week 3

When you have few direct or indirect conversions to measure the impact of your paid search program, you should use conversion proxies. You can correlate various actions on the site, such as checkout page view, page views, document group views, downloads, numbered actions, or time on site.

Choosing the conversion proxy is not something you should look upon lightly. Your first task is to make sure that the proxy is not connected to your paid search program—connected in such a way that you could move the proxy based on paid search attributes alone.

Imagine your content site is funded through sponsorships. You choose to use whitepaper downloads as a proxy for success, because you only have three or four sponsorship sales a month. However, if one of your paid search campaigns is directly related to whitepaper downloads, this particular campaign will look overly successful, and your budget will steer toward this one, when that is probably not the best thing to do.

When the first data comes in, it's your task to judge whether the proxy is influenced so that it favors certain campaigns. If that's the case, you can still use it; you might just have to exclude it as a proxy for those particular campaigns.

Let's move on to another type, the lead-generation site. You might judge this to be a pure sale, but you should take a couple of points into consideration.

In our discussion of e-commerce, we explored the problem of assigning all sales the same value. The same goes with leads: You cannot apply the same value to all leads. When you sign up for webinars or other marketing subjects online, some sites ask questions about budget, time to buy, country, or other information. These are all qualifying elements that can be used to value the lead and determine the way you conduct your paid search campaigns. If you do not qualify your leads and just value them all the same, you are likely to replace well-qualified traffic with less-qualified traffic. This is an evitable result, because your competitors will figure out which keywords generate high-value leads that are likely to convert and at a much higher end value. You are left with the leftovers from your competitors. I am sure you do not want that.

Adding to this complexity is the fact that most sites provide the customer with an opportunity to connect over the phone; perhaps the phone might even be a primary lead-generation channel. This is easy if you value your phone leads the same as the online leads, as you can then use online leads as a proxy for phone leads. If you do not value these leads the same, you have a separate set of tasks you should look into. One of them is the potential of using unique 800 numbers, but this is a separate matter I suggest you investigate on your own if you are in this situation.

Moving along to another scenario, suppose you run a site where your primary revenue source is advertising. You could optimize toward goals like:

- Page Views per Visit
- Advertising Revenue per Visit (multiply your current CPM value with your number of page views)

- Page View after First Paid Search Visit
- Advertising Revenue Generated after First Paid Search Visit

One caution on using advertising revenue as a simple multiplication of page views with an overall site CPM: Most sites charge very different rates for different placements. The Yahoo! front page CPM and the Yahoo! Mail CPM, for example, are far, far apart!

Finally, I suggest you think about optimization as either considerably delayed or in real time.

If you choose a delayed method, you can use Yahoo! Web Analytics to do most of what you want to do. For instance, you can analyze a paid search campaign run in January 2009 through March 2009, giving you an opportunity to see the return rate and engagement of those users.

However, if you need real-time optimization, you are forced to generate a proxy for the return rate and engagement. The validity of an engagement metric is wildly debated in the industry, and I will let you decide whether that is the route for you to take. I suggest you start by looking at this whitepaper by Eric Peterson and Joseph Carrabis (see Figure 11.16):

`http://www.webanalyticsdemystified.com/sample/Web_Analytics_Demystified_and_NextStage_Global_-_Measuring_the_Immeasurable_-_Visitor_Engagement.pdf`

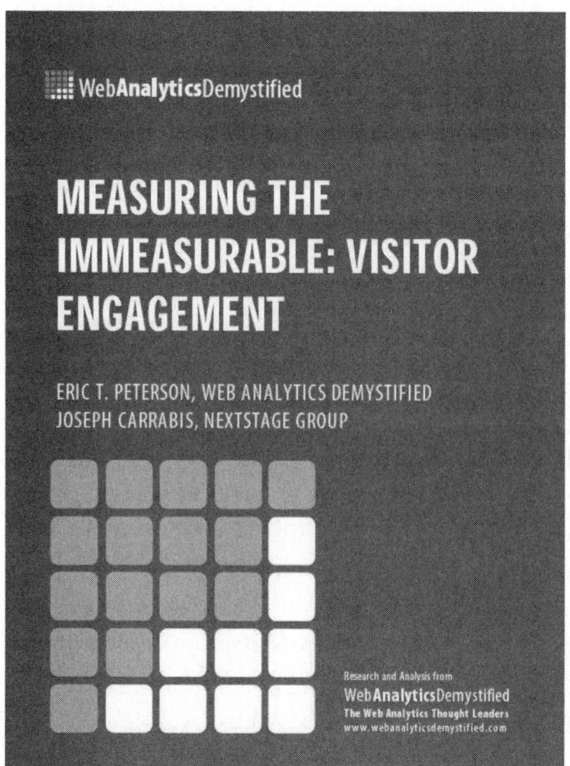

Figure 11.16 Visit this site for a whitepaper on Visitor Engagement.

The prevalent mistake in paid search optimization is to optimize toward more traffic. We keep coming back to the obvious conclusion that less costly traffic is likely to be less valuable.

So what to do? I am sorry to revert to the engagement metric, but this time, let me try to simplify it by suggesting that you use the following elements:

- Time spent on site > 2 min.
- Page views per visits > 3
- Visits per visitor > 2

These might seem simple and almost naive, but they could be great engagement proxies for your site. If you are optimizing your paid search campaigns on visits only today, any of these optimization metrics, or a simple combination, is sure to yield a remarkable increase in performance.

A question comes to mind: When do you know you have picked the right engagement metric? This is probably not something we can measure within our web analytics application, but it is something that can be solved by using surveys and other panel measures.

Tips for Choosing Your Optimization Metric

Choosing your optimization metric is one of the most important things you'll ever do in paid search. Keep the following in mind:

- Does the chosen optimization metric truly reflect your site's success?
- Can the optimization metric be captured by your web analytics tool? Can it be captured and used in real time?
- Is the optimization metric destined to be biased?

These two posts discuss using KPIs for media and social networking sites, respectively:

`http://visualrevenue.com/blog/2007/07/what-and-how-to-measure-media-and.html`

`http://visualrevenue.com/blog/2007/07/what-to-measure-on-social-networking.html`

Balancing Paid Search with Organic Search

This is a chapter about paid search, so why am I writing about organic search? Because there is a strong correlation between what happens in organic and what happens in paid search, and vice versa.

I believe this can be summed up in one word: cannibalization. The more aggressive you are on paid search, the more traffic you are destined to take away from organic search. This is one of the low-hanging fruits of any nonoptimized paid search campaign: making sure a natural balance exists between paid and organic search.

The simple way to test this is (if you dare) to turn off all of your paid search for a week and measure the impact on the expected organic lift. Most organizations are not willing to do something as drastic as this. In that case, I suggest you choose specific campaigns, ad groups, or just a set of keywords that you turn off and then measure the organic search equal to those.

I am not saying that the effect is always negative; it may prove that organic supports your paid search, and again vice versa. My point is that you need to have an understanding of how they are related so that you don't end up optimizing your paid search in the wrong direction because of an impact on organic rankings.

I am fully aware that this book has turned from direct and easy-to-use suggestions in Parts I and II to a more theoretical discussion in Part III with concepts that are less easy to directly apply to your business. This shift is intentional, and I hope that it gets you thinking and that it opens your eyes so you aren't fooled by overly simple paid search optimization schemes. Now let's move on to form analysis and optimization, or more directly, how you can get more leads.

12 Form Analysis and Optimization

Forms might seem too insignificant a topic to which to devote an entire chapter. The objective for most websites is tied to a conversion of some kind, and most conversions include an HTML form element, typically at the most crucial part of a transaction. Therefore, any optimization on this part of your website has the potential for a huge impact on performance.

Chapter Contents

Form Analysis and Form Actions
Form Abandonment
Form Page Optimization
Form Submit Optimization

Form Analysis and Form Actions

Like any other task you perform as the person responsible for web analytics in your organization, the form optimization task has to be part of a greater project plan where the optimization project is justified and measured against other potential projects that drive your business forward.

Form creation, analysis, and improvement are just part of the bigger picture in this process; factors like the following must be taken into consideration as well:

- Website design
- Funnel flow
- Text copy
- Usability studies
- Voice-of-customer studies
- Testing (such as multivariate testing)
- Behavioral analysis (web analytics)

Each point is crucial in achieving the perfect conversion form experience: the highest possible conversion rate.

When you start a form-based analysis and optimization project, you should begin with the business requirements. Using the previous list, make sure that the form fits well into the overall website design and that there is a natural flow. Also ensure that you have performed some basic usability studies.

Traditional form analysis, as will be illustrated later, is imperfect by itself without further investigation. You shouldn't see form analysis as all you need to do when running a form optimization process.

HTML Form

An HTML form is a form on a web page that allows a user to enter data that is typically sent to a server for processing. The form often replicates a traditional paper form.

Usability Studies

Usability studies can be as simple as observing three or four people from another department going through the form-based pages and taking notes on their difficulties. I am a big fan of limited usability studies. For further input on that matter, see my post on the positive impact of limited users in qualitative studies:

`http://visualrevenue.com/blog/2007/05/in-qualitative-analysis-5-8-users-are.html`

It is difficult to do analysis and come back with significant optimization suggestions if the process is broken and poorly conceived to begin with.

Now getting to the actual form page, let's start with a traditional form-based page. Look at Figure 12.1 and evaluate it based on the following questions. These are great starters when you are first setting up your forms.

- Are the form fields and form flow set up logically?
- Do you capture the right amount of information, making sure you do not capture too much or too little information?
- Can the fields be navigated easily using a keyboard?
- Has the setup and placement of each form field compared to the others been carefully considered?
- Are your form field validations too strong or too weak?
- Are instructions on how to fill out the form fields appropriate and accurate?
- How is the performance of the form? Are elements such as JavaScript instant validation or Help seen as a help or an annoyance?

This package includes:
Phone
Apple iPhone 3G - 8 GB - Black
Included in package
Feature
Please note: Data plan for iPhone is required for the life of your iPhone service and cannot be removed in the future.
Data Plan for iPhone
$30.00/month
Your choice of individual plan
Choose the plan that works best for you.
Nation Unlimited
$99.99/month
Nation 1350 w/Rollover® Minutes
$79.99/month
Nation 900 w/Rollover® Minutes
$59.99/month
Nation 450 w/Rollover® Minutes
$39.99/month
Recommended Features
Add a text messaging feature to get the most out of your iPhone.
Your choice of preferred feature
iPhone Text Messaging Unlimited
$20.00/month
iPhone Text Messaging 1500
$15.00/month
iPhone Text Messaging 200
$5.00/month
None - $0.20 per message
Safety/Insurance
AT&T Roadside Assistance
$2.99/month
Voice Services
VoiceDial
$4.99/month
Parental Controls
Smart Limits for Wireless Parental Controls
$4.99/month
Optional Features and Accessories
Interested in adding more items? See below for other features and accessories that are compatible with your selected package.

Figure 12.1 A typical web-based conversion form

The form presented in Figure 12.1 is not, well, optimal. That was very polite, wasn't it?

So let's assume that you've finished basic usability testing. Then you might ask, "What do I need web analytics for?" Because the data you retrieve from your web analytics application, such as Yahoo! Web Analytics, truly represents your customers, whereas usability studies give you only a model of what customers might do, and the problems they might run into, on your site. Web analytics data is valuable because you have the opportunity to work with data on a granular level, both up- and downstream from the form itself.

Web analytics allow you to answer questions such as these:

- Did people get all their questions answered before they completed the form?
- Did the form arrive at an expected point in the process for the customer?
- What information is missing from the form?
- How do different visitor segments behave, such as first-time visitors versus returning visitors or paid-for and non-paid-for visitors?
- Is the number of fields on the form itself appropriate?

Analyzing the form, while helpful, doesn't tell you how to take on the bigger issue of funnel abandonment, which is typically your first optimization angle. We'll turn to that next.

Using Funnels in Form Optimization

Along with paid search optimization projects, landing page optimization projects, and organic search optimization projects, more often than not most organizations include some sort of funnel optimization. Funnel optimization can be anything from the last steps in an e-commerce funnel, as shown in Figure 12.2, to usability studies on how many steps are needed all in all. Funnel optimization projects are used on many governmental form-based sites or lead-generating sites, such as in finance and insurance.

Why am I talking about funnel optimization? Because most funnel steps consist of an information retrieval form, and for us to be able to decide which form to optimize and why, we must understand our funnel.

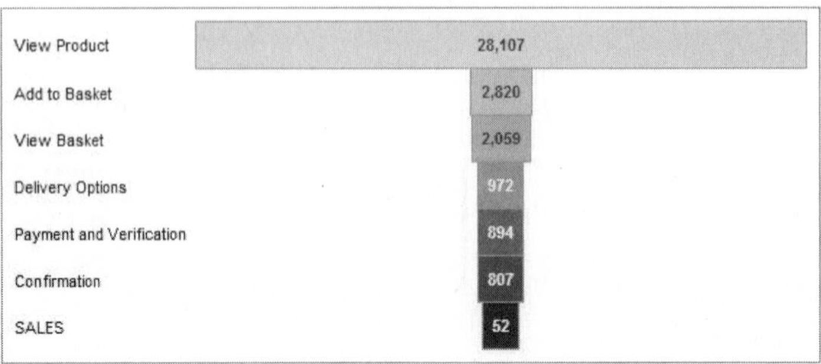

Figure 12.2 A traditional e-commerce sales funnel

The most common methodology is an examination of the abandonment rate of one or more steps. For example, look at the abandonment rates from Figure 12.2, which are shown in Figure 12.3.

It is quick and easy, at least from a user interface point of view, for you to drill into the abandonment between Delivery Options and Payment and Verification, as Figure 12.4 shows.

Step	Visits	Abandoned	Continued
View Product	28,107		
		89.97%	10.03%
Add to Basket	2,820		
		26.99%	73.01%
View Basket	2,059		
		52.79%	47.21%
Delivery Options	972		
		8.02%	91.98%
Payment and Verification	894		
		9.73%	90.27%
Confirmation	807		
		93.56%	6.44%
SALES	52		

Figure 12.3 Funnel abandonment

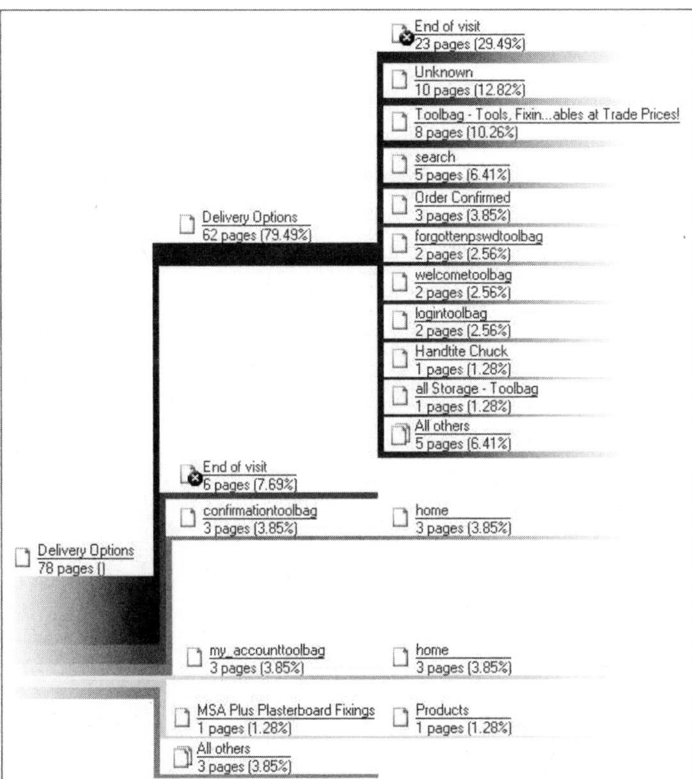

Figure 12.4 Funnel abandonment visualized in a path analysis report

The sales persuasion process starts and sometimes ends before the funnel shown in Figure 12.2. This is typically part of your overall site persuasion architecture, of which the form is only one part.

Prequalifying Traffic Sent to the Funnel

Let's focus on your site setup so we can examine some of the elements that persuade visitors to enter the sales funnel. The following is not the only possible setup, but it is a great way of classifying your content:

- Creating an outline
- Defining the problem
- Explaining the solution
- Providing a call to action
- Presenting the conversion form

Your call to action is likely different from page to page; it may be subtle on the front page and a whole lot more aggressive on the product page. That alone makes a difference in how visitors enter the funnel and how they perform on your form—in other words, their conversion rate.

Therefore, you can't just optimize on the form itself; nor can you just decide to overexpose your call to action everywhere on your site.

Certain factors within the form optimization process exist that you simply cannot optimize much on. Say you are in the business of selling mortgages. Although I am not a mortgage expert, I am quite sure you cannot change the sales cycle much.

So in the case of selling mortgages, you might look at your funnel and decide to be less aggressive on those final steps, in case this is not the right time to drive people into taking out mortgages. Essentially, you would hold back on your call to action early on in the sales cycle. You shouldn't always assume that the increase in form-fills offsets the expected decline in conversion.

Think about the type of traffic you throw to the funnel and to the form itself. High-value paid search traffic is likely to perform differently than low-value paid search traffic. Therefore, you must be able to tell whether people are qualified to make a purchase or other conversion, and if they are not qualified, you must discover why.

Now, how do you do determine if people are qualified to enter the form? Begin by looking at the following metrics, keeping in mind that this list is dependent on your industry and the type of clients you are working with:

- The number of previous visits to the website
- The number of pages viewed in the current session
- The type of pages read in the last session, according to our classification from earlier
- The average time spent on the site

This is not a complete list. You might want to take a more scientific approach to this, such as applying a customized engagement metric. But whatever you do, first have a look at one or more of these prequalification metrics and see if there are any behavioral differences. This is exactly what I did in Figure 12.5 and Figure 12.6, using the metrics First Time Visitors and Returning Visitors.

Looking at not just the actual conversion rate, but also the details on every one of the steps, you can see that the previous two figures show a reasonable level of similar behaviors. The biggest dissimilarity is the difference in abandonment from viewing the basket to choosing and agreeing to the delivery options. First-time visitors abandon this at approximately 60 percent and returning visitors at approximately 40 percent.

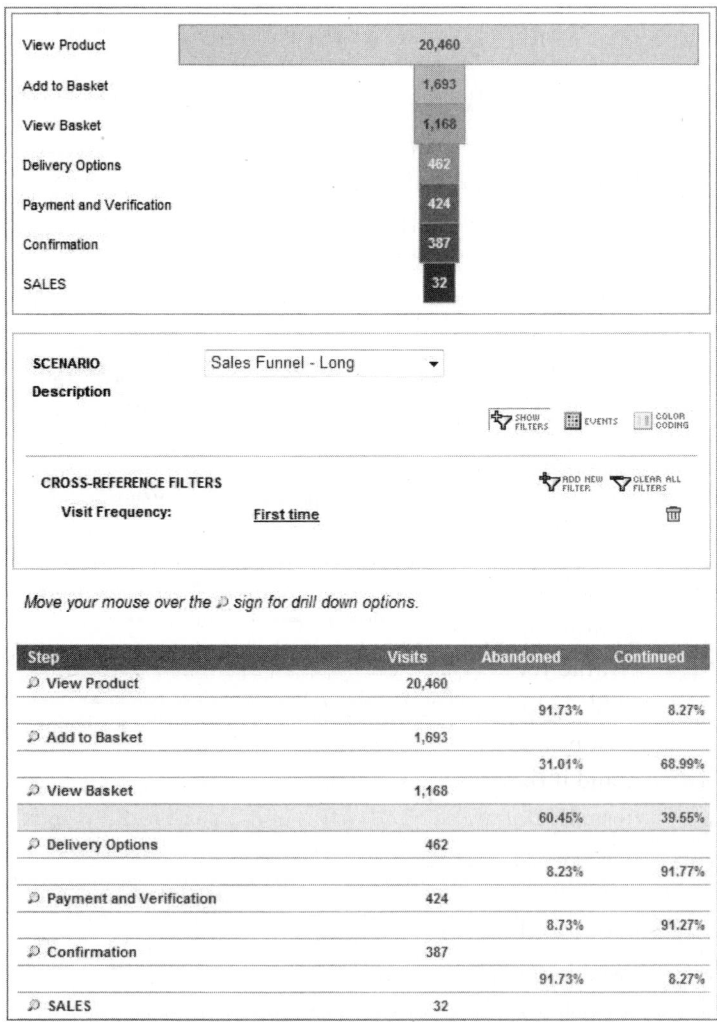

Figure 12.5 A funnel filtered on the prequalification metric First Time Visitors

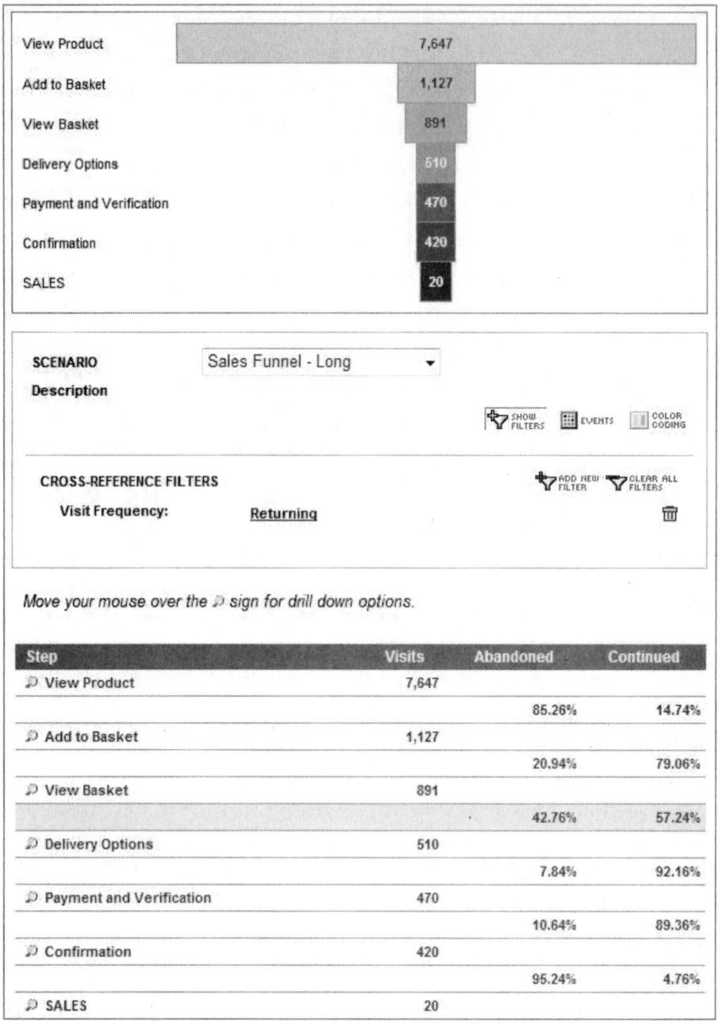

View Product 7,647
Add to Basket 1,127
View Basket 891
Delivery Options 510
Payment and Verification 470
Confirmation 420
SALES 20

SCENARIO Sales Funnel - Long
Description

SHOW FILTERS EVENTS COLOR CODING

CROSS-REFERENCE FILTERS ADD NEW FILTER CLEAR ALL FILTERS
Visit Frequency: Returning

Move your mouse over the sign for drill down options.

Step	Visits	Abandoned	Continued
View Product	7,647		
		85.26%	14.74%
Add to Basket	1,127		
		20.94%	79.06%
View Basket	891		
		42.76%	57.24%
Delivery Options	510		
		7.84%	92.16%
Payment and Verification	470		
		10.64%	89.36%
Confirmation	420		
		95.24%	4.76%
SALES	20		

Figure 12.6 A funnel filtered on the prequalification metric Returning Visitors

This fact has nothing to do with the delivery options form itself, but it has everything to do with the prequalification of the visitor ending up at this page.

I am not saying that you shouldn't send your first-time visitors down the path of conversion, but that there might be an optimization opportunity to investigate; for example, being more up front with information on delivery costs before they end up at this screen and abandon it. This is something that needs to be measured carefully so you don't end up making the outcome worse than where you started from.

The rule of thumb is that the better educated the visitor is before you throw her into the conversion funnel, the better the outcome. This is why I recommend the call-to-action principle, but I suggest you be cautious in just how aggressive you are.

I also suggest that you take traffic sources into consideration, simply because the actual visitors could have done all their prequalification at a different site, such as a search engine or a price comparison engine or a set of unique industry blogs. For traffic arriving from these sources, you might want to be super aggressive on your call to action. The reason is that it skews your prequalification metrics, as you are likely not to register the 15 pages they read before ending up on your site. Thus it might look like their behavior—such as fewer pages viewed or less time spent—is successful.

In your quest for figuring out and classifying the content that moves you toward optimizing your form conversion rate, you can use the Action Participation metric provided by Yahoo!.

I created a custom report from the old IndexTools website, as shown in Figure 12.7, on the most popular pages. I applied and sorted on the Action Participation metric, with the Action set to Unique Partner Applications.

Page Title	Page Views	Action Participation
Partnership Application Form	1,063	49
Partners Home	7,006	44
IndexTools: Numbers that mean business	216,981	40
Partners Overview	1,664	21
IndexTools: Test drive IndexTools 8 E-Business	21,634	18
Partner Application - Thanks	19	17
IndexTools: Your essential online business tool	20,432	16
Key Alliance Partner	599	16
Authorised Partner	735	15
White Label Partnership	641	13
Strategic Alliance Partner	872	12
About Home	7,219	9
Agency Interface	406	9
web analytics	20,227	8
The Co-Branded Alliance	1,419	8
IndexTools: Which edition is right for you?	7,602	7
IndexTools: IndexTools delivers real-time results	7,876	7
IndexTools: Try an IndexTools demo	6,188	5
Analysis	645	4
IndexTools: Contact Us	4,734	4

Figure 12.7 Most popular pages sorted by Action Participation

It is not surprising that the Partnership Application form is the most popular content in regard to this action. What is really exciting is the fact that pages such as the Agency Interface are viewed modestly compared to other pages but are active in persuading people to complete the form. The same goes for the About Home page.

You must do a bit more investigation than this, but your task is to figure out not only the right amount of content, but also which content is needed before you start to hit visitors with the call to action. You should sometimes opt for not having a call to action on a page and rather educate people a bit more. This approach will increase the opportunity for them to buy or otherwise convert.

This approach is also likely to change the shape of your funnel, which may not be a bad idea.

Form Abandonment

I indicated earlier that the standard funnel analysis of looking at the abandonment rate at each step involves more than just finding the step with the highest abandonment rate. The funnel shape and typical optimization view resembles Figure 12.8.

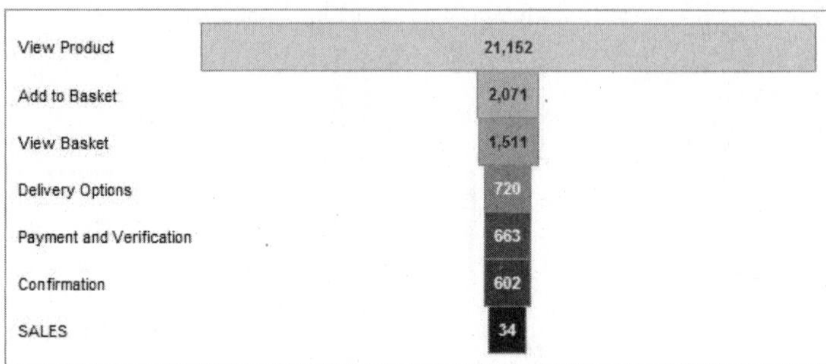

Figure 12.8 Traditional funnel abandonment rate

A typical funnel is defined as one where you will see a first step with an ultra-high abandonment rate, followed by a set of somewhat similar steps with less of an abandonment rate, and a final step of ultra-high abandonment rate.

You can change this funnel by simply changing the user interface and navigation path for your visitors. However, that's not the point; the point is that most people tend to focus on the steps with the highest abandonment rates with the belief that this area represents the best funnel and form optimization opportunities. This would only be true if every single step had the same probability of being abandoned, which is not true at all. There is a huge mental step from viewing a product on a website to adding it to your basket. Compare the following two lines:

View Product to Add to Basket abandonment rate: 90.21%

Add to Basket to View Basket abandonment rate: 27.04%

It is not immediately possible to conclude which of the two steps is the one with the highest potential output in an optimization project. And even more important, as soon as we have accepted this obvious fact, we must also accept that perhaps there are no immediate problems to fix in some of the steps and the abandonment rate could be seen as normal.

This brings me to my point that any improvement must be viewed in a larger context. The following makes the same conclusion in the usual 140 characters:

> *Positive siloed optimization is likely to cannibalize and create new negative siloed effects in other parts of your business.*

TAKEN FROM `http://twitter.com/DennisMortensen/status/1075552712`

Figure 12.9 illustrates what can happen when you look at any optimization impact out of context.

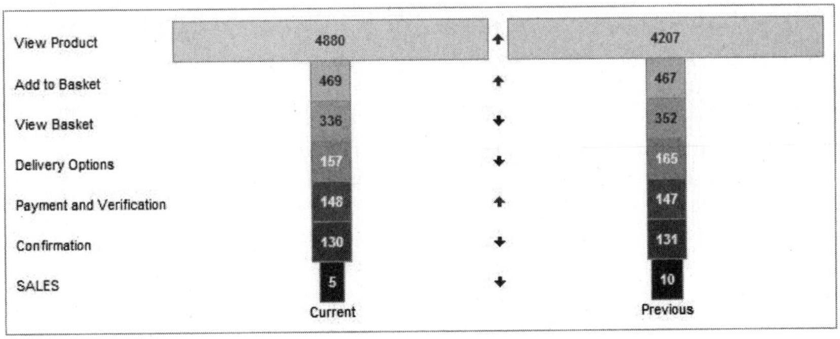

	Current		Previous
View Product	4880	↑	4207
Add to Basket	469	↑	467
View Basket	336	↓	352
Delivery Options	157	↓	165
Payment and Verification	148	↑	147
Confirmation	130	↓	131
SALES	5	↓	10

Figure 12.9 Funnel comparison, current week to previous week

Information Silo

An *information silo* is a system incapable of reciprocal operation with other related systems. Your online sales, for example, are considered a silo if they cannot exchange information (analytics) with your offline sales systems.

No changes were made to the Confirmation form between the two weeks compared, but we still have twice the amount of sales. So we know the form itself has not magically improved. We thus need to take other variables into consideration, such as new display campaigns, paid search optimization, or content optimization… which brings me back to my point that you do not have to look at the form page to optimize its performance.

So armed with this information, let's make a few conclusions on a conversion process where a form is involved:

- Each step in a funnel is not equal and should not be measured as being equal to other steps.
- Each form on each step is not equal and should not be measured as being equal to others.
- There is built-in resistance to any form you create, no matter how optimized. The more fields you use, the higher the resistance is likely to be. People don't like to fill in forms!
- Some form fields, in particular those with some sort of PII (Personally identifiable information) or commitment, embrace a higher resistance that others. Obvious fields such as a credit card number as well as fields like your phone number have a very high built-in resistance.

Given these facts, it's important to understand that some visitors never intend to finish your funnel and thus your forms—they simply use them to get to an answer that they would otherwise find difficult to get. This could be information such as a total sum for four items, the total cost including shipping, or whether you ship to Europe.

Resistance increases as you decrease the prequalification of your visitors. Let's look at a form (see Figure 12.10) and see how the principles I've listed apply to real life.

Step 1: Apply for a Citi® Diamond Preferred® Card

• Ver aplicación en Español

Before You Apply

Please note that:
- You must be 18 years of age or older
- You must have a valid Social Security Number

Already a Citi® cardmember?
Take a Shortcut.

Need Help?

Read our Credit Card Application FAQs.

Contact Information

*Required Field

Email:

If you provide your email address, we may use it to contact you about your account and tell you about useful products and services.
Email Policy

* First Name:
MI:
* Last Name:
Suffix: None
(No P.O. Boxes)
* Street Address:
Apt./Suite:
* City:
* State: Select one
* ZIP Code:
* Phone Number:
Last Name on Home Phone Bill:
* Social Security Number:
* Date of Birth: MM DD YYYY
* Security Word Hint: Other

Need help choosing? Read our Security Word Guidelines. (Must be 10 characters or less with letters or numbers)

* Security Word:
* Re-enter Security Word:

Employment Information

Company/Employer Phone Number:
Occupation: Select one

Figure 12.10 Partial application form for Citi credit card

Looking at Figure 12.10, it's safe to conclude that we should accept some abandonment rate simply because of the built-in resistance. We should accept that form fields like Employer Phone Number have a higher built-in resistance than other fields.

This does not make step 1 any less significant than step 2. The removal of any field, no matter the resistance level, will have a positive effect. This is the simplest and most powerful optimization tip in any form: Remove fields that are not 100 percent necessary, because in these types of funnels, there is simply no room for nice-to-have fields.

The abandonment is likely to be highly influenced by the traffic you are sending to it, so you should not immediately assume that a high abandonment rate, such as the almost 92 percent in Figure 12.5, is a complete fiasco. It might just be part of the process.

You may be wondering whether you should focus on optimization fields with a high built-in resistance. The answer is not necessarily, as the built-in resistance is completely impossible to optimize from your perspective of working on the form. Or, for some fields the resistance might be more closely related to trust in the brand than to anything within the funnel or on the actual page. Fields that ask you to hand over your email, phone, or credit card number are typically ones that hold less resistance with highly trusted brands than with unknown brands. Life is unfair.

Being able to identify the field that the visitor was in when he abandoned the form is rarely of much importance. If you have done your basic usability testing, that should catch the obvious mistakes of visitors unable to decipher just how you want your phone number input.

The one thing I hope you've learned by now is that a high form abandonment rate is not necessarily your top optimization priority. In the next section, you'll learn how you can use web analytics in place of, or to complement, some of the other methodologies we've discussed.

Form Page Optimization

So far you've learned that there is much more to a form than the abandonment rate. I expect that you will be catching data such as form error messages thrown, form help messages thrown, and form mandatory field messages thrown. And you will be doing your usability studies, but will you really be able to know just how well your form is helping you increase revenue?

This might be controversial (especially in light of my earlier statement that any field removal decreases the resistance and thus decreases the funnel abandonment rate), but sometimes it might not be that bad an idea to sell on the form itself. Continue with caution, as this might work in the opposite direction as well.

The reason for selling on the form is that, while you have resistance on a per-form field level, you are also building up prospect friction. Some people who aren't truly committed to completing the sale need support. The reason that this is difficult to test using a usability study is that unless you, as a test person, are spending your own real money and not make-believe money in a lab, you cannot re-create that emotional level of friction.

We can set up three form exits:

- Site Exit
- Site Stay, Form Exit, but no real engagement with the site
- Site Stay, Form Exit, but positive engagement with the site

We can use these form exits to decide whether our form helps us sell more stuff. The third group—people who stay on the site and move on to engage with other products—is especially significant. From the first group, those who exited the site altogether, we have no data and no opportunity to look into their state of mind when they exited. From the second group, those who stayed on the site after exiting the form but did not engage further, we find little value in their data. But from the third group, those who stayed on the site and continued to engage (looking at more products, searching, delving into terms and conditions), we can learn a lot. This is not always the biggest segment of the three, but that should not discourage us.

The third group is not an easy segment to create in Yahoo! Web Analytics, but you can still create some good methods, using the scenarios and the path analysis features, of viewing the pages your visitors went to after the form exit.

Look for pages that attracted positive engagement on the site. You should also try to classify the pages in groups of navigation pages, information pages, product pages, and aggressive call-to-action pages.

The beautiful thing about Yahoo! Web Analytics is that you can collapse steps when working with the ad hoc scenario and look at multiple steps at the same time.

Let's look at a simple ad hoc scenario. Figure 12.11 illustrates a four-step funnel of nonmembers arriving at the login page and shows how many people successfully sign up and then sign in.

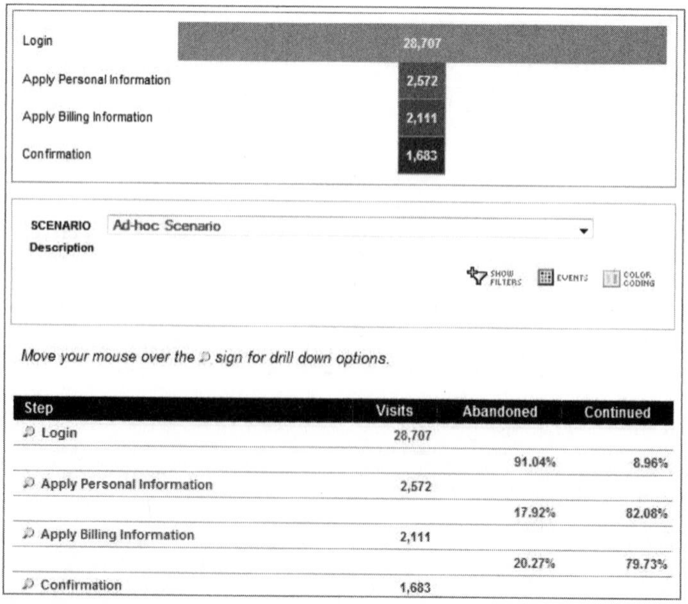

Login 28,707
Apply Personal Information 2,572
Apply Billing Information 2,111
Confirmation 1,683

SCENARIO Ad-hoc Scenario
Description
SHOW FILTERS EVENTS COLOR CODING

Move your mouse over the sign for drill down options.

Step	Visits	Abandoned	Continued
Login	28,707		
		91.04%	8.96%
Apply Personal Information	2,572		
		17.92%	82.08%
Apply Billing Information	2,111		
		20.27%	79.73%
Confirmation	1,683		

Figure 12.11 Login ad hoc scenario

The first thing you notice, even in this shortened funnel, is that it is quite similar to the ones from earlier: We have a first step with a huge abandonment rate. But knowing that this is not the biggest optimization opportunity, we will drill into the step between Apply Billing Information and the confirmation, where we have an abandonment rate of approximately 20 percent (see Figure 12.12).

Looking at the path shown in Figure 12.12, your task will be to find a pattern that could suggest this step might not be performing at its best.

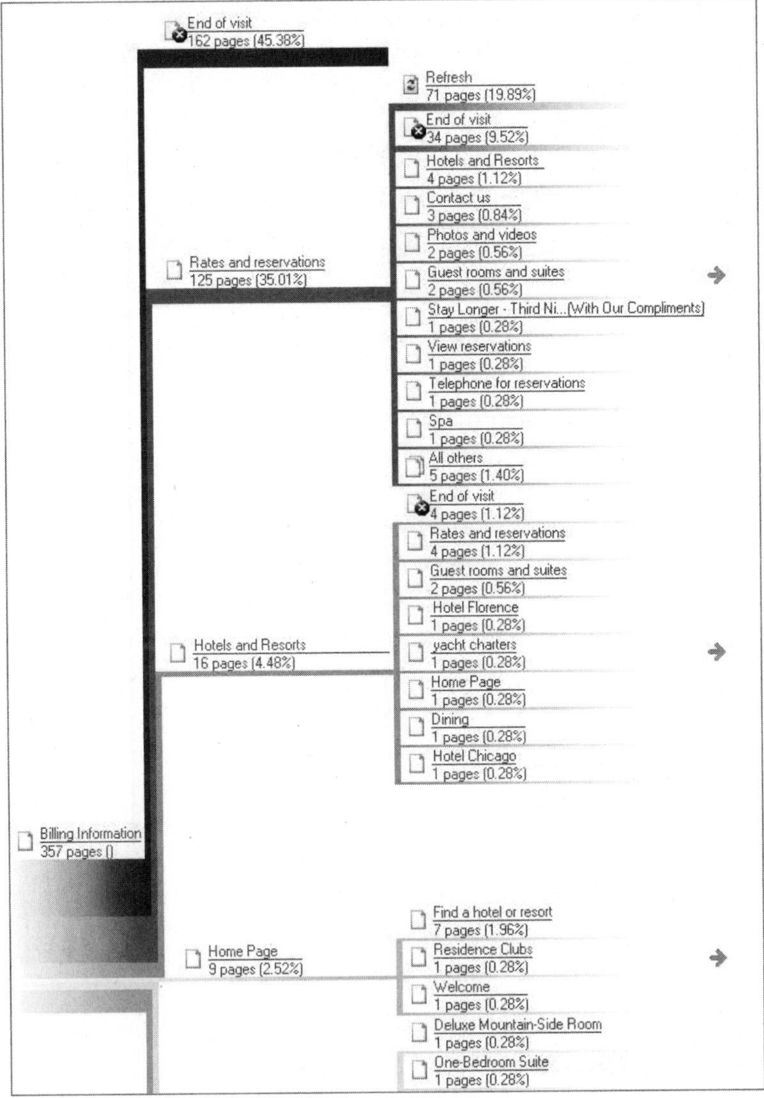

Figure 12.12 Login page path analysis

We start with the almost 400 page views at the beginning of our funnel. We are fully aware of what happens to the rest (the go to confirmation). It is interesting to see the following:

- 45% – Site Exit
- 13% – Site Stay, Form Exit, but no real engagement with the site
- 42% – Site Stay, Form Exit, but positive engagement with the site

With this high level of direct exit, we might conclude that we're too aggressive on our call to action. Therefore, a form with typical high resistance, such as billing information, shouldn't be presented here just yet, as it seems we are losing the opportunity to register visitors.

If visitors do not exit the site altogether or wander around doing nothing, most end up engaging with the site again. This engagement might include rechecking the price (the rates and reservations page). And this segment is the one that we would like to look more closely into.

Taking one more step into the path, we get a very interesting view, as illustrated in Figure 12.13.

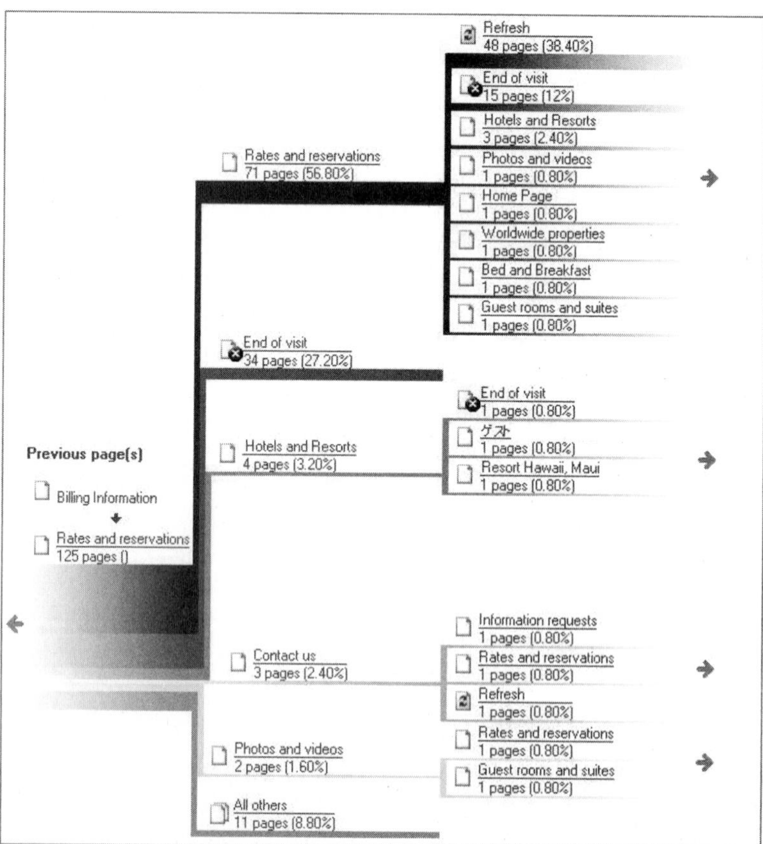

Figure 12.13 Login page path analysis, next step

Figure 12.13 reveals that people who were just about to log in and register with their billing information didn't feel completely convinced and then (after we lost about half the visitors to a site exit) went on to check rates and reservations. Then on that page we have almost 57 percent who go on to check the rates and reservations again. Finally, if you look at the step after this, nearly 39 percent refresh this page.

From this, we conclude that any important optimization to the "registering people with billing information" page is done on the rates and reservations page. If we expand the time period, we reveal a potential opportunity in the Contact Us page as well.

I strongly suggest that you compare this step-by-step analysis with the original visitor intent, which could be represented by the referring search phrase or the internal search phrase.

Be cautious in your interpretation of search phrases as they are created within a particular session. Some form-abandonment visitors might have seen different pages in different sessions, and this is where it becomes complicated in Yahoo! Web Analytics.

Coming back to the funnel, selling within the form might not have been such a bad idea after all. It's not all that different from any sales situation—nothing is sure until the actual conversion takes place.

Form Submit Optimization

There is an end to every funnel, and this is probably the last place you would think about optimization. The conversion just occurred, so why waste the time? However, the thank-you page is not an unimportant page, and unless you have the utmost trust in the brand you just did business with, you are consuming this page quite seriously. Figure 12.14 shows the traditional thank-you page as we all know it.

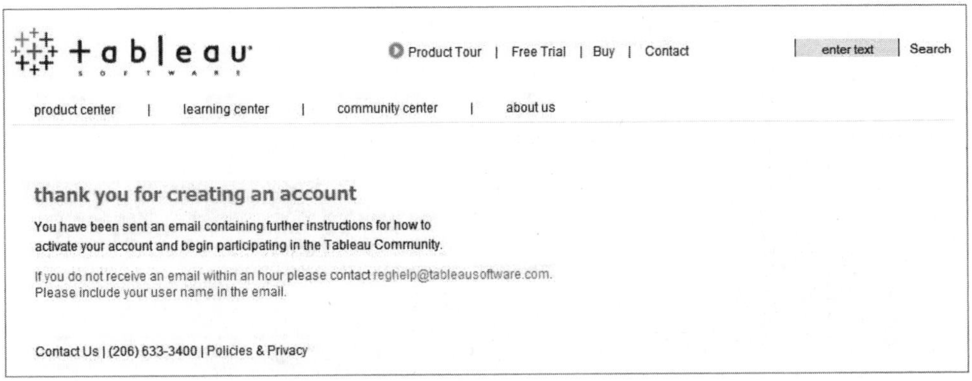

Figure 12.14 Traditional thank-you page

Think of the thank-you page as an opportunity to re-engage with a highly engaged visitor. This page is a great place to provide cross-sells and cross-promotions.

You can be aggressive in tempting visitors back into your store, or employ less aggressive tactics such as having them sign up for a next-buy coupon, asking them to tell a friend, or requesting that they participate in a survey.

The thank-you page is also a great place to inform the visitor about anything important in regard to their current situation. This includes such information as basic company contacts, upcoming sales promotions, user groups, and forums for your products.

Finally, reassure the visitor that everything is in order, you did indeed receive their information, you understood it, and you are crystal clear about the next steps, including what they should expect from you. This includes such information as expected delivery date and links to tracking services or help pages. Make sure you ease any post-transaction nervousness. For the visitor, this is not just a conversion!

With Amazon.com, as shown in Figure 12.15, it becomes obvious that they definitely incorporate the same thinking on their thank-you page. Amazon.com is taking the postconversion process and optimization opportunity seriously.

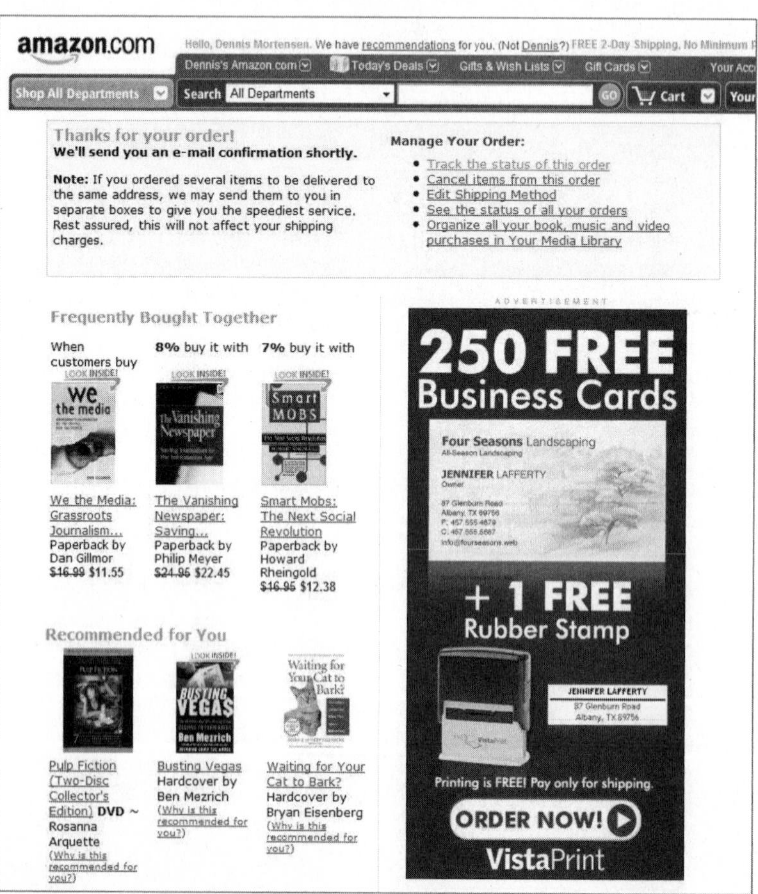

Figure 12.15 Amazon.com thank-you page

I understand why you might assume that the visitor leaves after the thank-you page simply because that's what most of your data is telling you. What excites me the most about this optimization opportunity is that, for the most part, the thank-you page is almost an empty canvas. You can use some of my suggestions or come up with an even better idea for this page. I think this is a rare opportunity, and I am hard put to find other pages that, in terms of optimization, are this open and have as little risk and friction applied to them.

How do we measure this page? This is a pretty straightforward split between those who do indeed exit and those who do not.

Let's create a simple funnel; it doesn't matter how it looks as long as we include the conversion we want to examine. I created a two-step funnel in Figure 12.16 that goes from the visitor adding the billing information and then moving to buy the product.

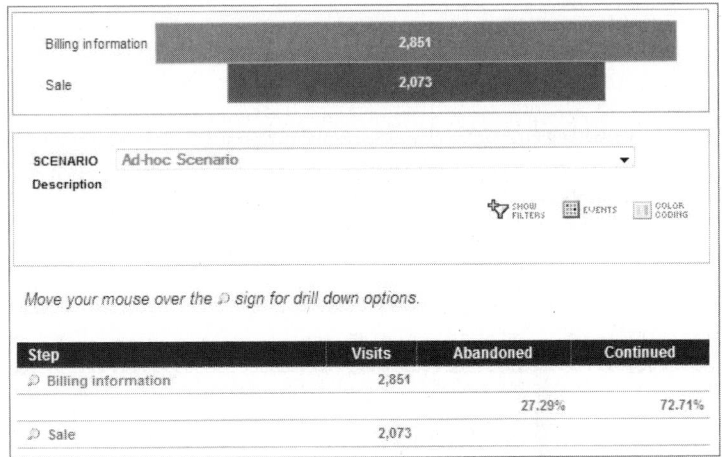

Figure 12.16 Simple ad hoc funnel to show a sales conversion

The optimization opportunity might be highest on those that exit altogether, but that is not how I suggest you sell it. I believe there is value in learning how many stay on the site. So let's examine, as shown in Figure 12.17, those 2,073 visits that converted to sales in the given period.

Figure 12.17 shows us the expected high site exit rate of approximately 57 percent, but what about those 43 percent who did not exit? What are they doing, and how can we serve them?

Your task is twofold when optimizing this page:

- Decrease the total site exit abandonment rate
- Move staying visitors across a planned path

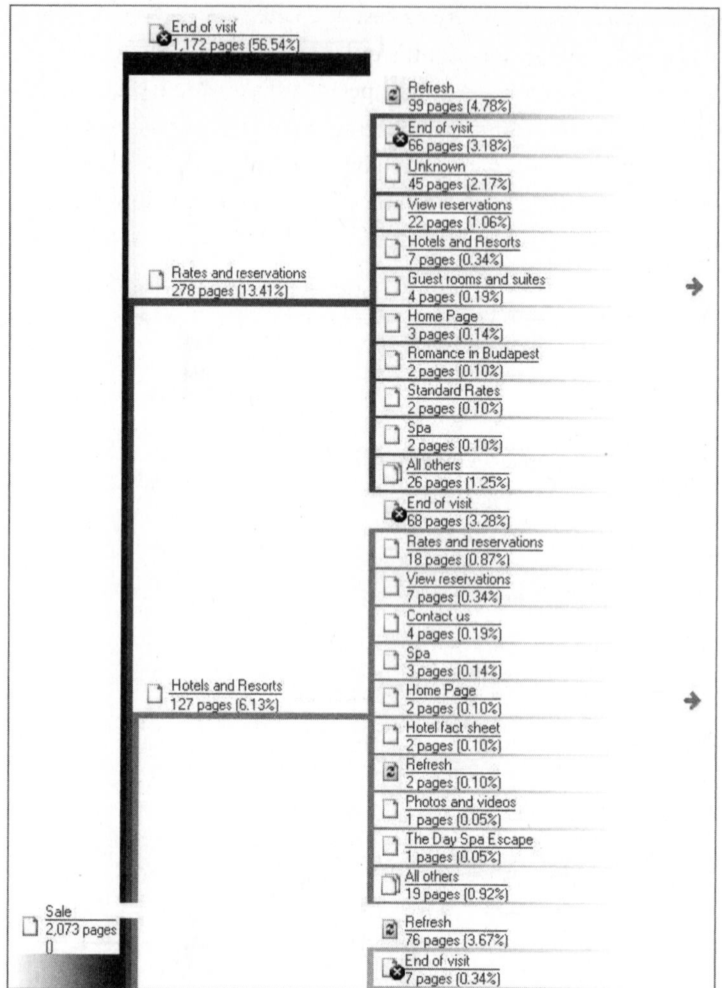

Figure 12.17 Path analysis after a positive sales conversion

Remember that the planned path may not be the current session; you might want to optimize this page for more return visitors. I commented on this subject in the following post:

`http://visualrevenue.com/blog/2009/01/optimizing-the-thank-you-page-using-web-analytics.html`

Let's talk about the impact of segments in form conversions and why you should use them in most of the optimization scenarios we've discussed. I'll introduce some of the obvious segments; you are tasked with setting up business-specific segments for your own site and industry.

Probably the best-known segment and the easiest to create is First-Time Visitor Resistance, but do not be fooled by its simplicity. It's quite handy because you can make sure that you look at a given metric in the right perspective. Assume that you look at the billing step in your sales funnel and the average amount of time spent on that page as part of an optimization process. We have two very different results when viewing this from two different segments, as you can see in Figure 12.18 and Figure 12.19 using Yahoo! Web Analytics filters.

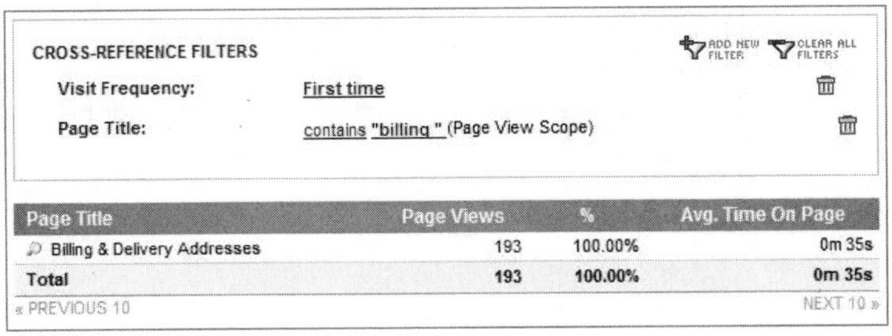

CROSS-REFERENCE FILTERS — ADD NEW FILTER — CLEAR ALL FILTERS

Visit Frequency: First time

Page Title: contains "billing " (Page View Scope)

Page Title	Page Views	%	Avg. Time On Page
Billing & Delivery Addresses	193	100.00%	0m 35s
Total	193	100.00%	0m 35s

« PREVIOUS 10 — NEXT 10 »

Figure 12.18 First-time visitor segmented report on average time spent on billing step

CROSS-REFERENCE FILTERS — ADD NEW FILTER — CLEAR ALL FILTERS

Visit Frequency: Returning

Page Title: contains "billing " (Page View Scope)

Page Title	Page Views	%	Avg. Time On Page
Billing & Delivery Addresses	221	100.00%	0m 25s
Total	221	100.00%	0m 25s

« PREVIOUS 10 — NEXT 10 »

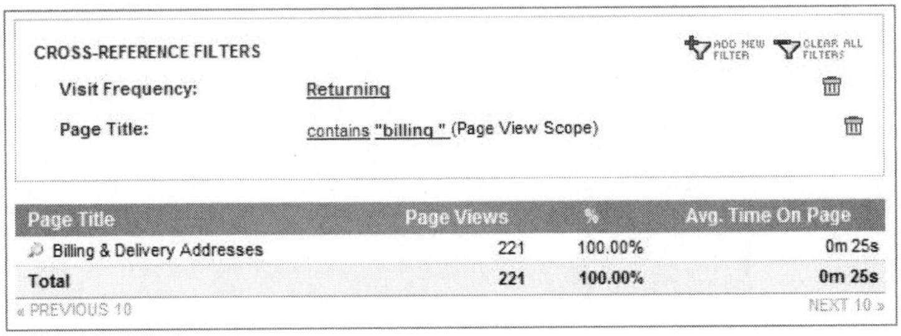

Figure 12.19 Returning visitor segmented report on average time spent on billing step

This is just one metric, where common sense concludes that first-time visitors are slower than returning visitors in filling out a form. In this case we see a 40 percent difference between the two segments. Any of the other metrics that you would use for optimization are likely to fluctuate just as much when looking at different segments.

Another segment worth mentioning is the one where you try to compare the form resistance impact (deleting fields) to the addition of sales information to the form. Create a segment of visitors who come directly to the site and have more than five visits, and use this as a control group. This segment is likely to be committed to your brand and will need little sales reinforcement. Use the opposite group for optimization impact analysis, so that it becomes clear if you do need more sales information on your form and if you are applying the right information.

I am most sure you have heard this a thousand times, but the importance of applying visit or visitor segments is critical. These segments work great in form analysis as well. They work so well that you might end up doing "mis-optimization" (as you learned in Chapter 11) if you do not apply this attitude.

If process conversion rates have improved because of a change in the mix of visitor types entering the form, it is absolutely essential that you identify the cause—not simply the existence—of that change!

Now on to the last chapter of the book, which will be less theoretical than the last two optimization chapters and a whole lot more hands-on. Let's get to it.

13

Content Optimization and Competitive Analysis

In this chapter, we will focus on a set of techniques that will help you optimize your content and develop a certain attitude and pattern of thinking about optimization. You will learn how to take your data out of the analytics tool and even enhance it with third-party data.

Chapter Contents

Using the Long Tail for Keyword Optimization
Using the Long Tail for Content Optimization
Determining the Width of Your Internal Search Query Box
Optimizing Content for Search- and Navigation-Dominant Visitors
Using Competitive Intelligence

Using the Long Tail for Keyword Optimization

The term "long tail" was originally coined by *Wired*'s Chris Anderson. The long tail is derived from traditional power laws and refers to the distribution of data in general. But in Chris's terminology, as I read it, the long tail describes a business strategy.

Power Law

A power law is a mathematical relationship between two quantities. If one quantity is the frequency of an event, the relationship is a power law distribution, and the frequencies decrease very slowly as the size of the event increases, thus generating a distribution with a clear head and, more importantly, the long tail.

The long tail describes the niche strategy of businesses such as Amazon or Apple iTunes that sell a large number of unique items, each in relatively small quantities. It is easier to adopt on the Internet than any other channel. Figure 13.1 shows the general shape of the long tail graph.

The long tail can also refer to the demographic group that purchases a large number of what we could call "non-hit" items. Given a large enough availability of choice, a large population of customers, and negligible stocking and distribution costs, the selection and buying pattern of the population results in a power law distribution curve. This suggests that a market with a high freedom of choice will create a certain degree of inequality by favoring the upper part of the items, hits, over the other items, the long tail.

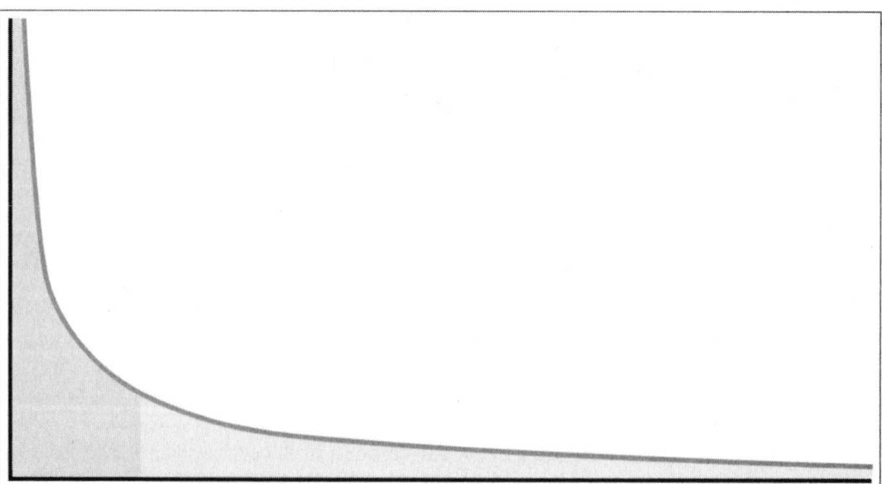

Figure 13.1 Traditional long tail graph

Now that you are familiar with the long tail, you should be able to use it to your advantage in any number of ways. Although there are plenty of metrics to play with, I like to showcase two interesting ideas for optimizing your keywords using long tail data from within Yahoo! Web Analytics.

Let's look at a traditional Search Phrases report, as shown in Figure 13.2.

Search Phrases	Visits	%
toolbag	1,612	6.15%
power tools	756	2.89%
plumbing supplies	622	2.37%
tool bag	335	1.28%
thetoolbag.com	247	0.94%
bosch power tools	211	0.81%
tool bags	200	0.76%
toolbag.com	178	0.68%
jigsaw puzzles	168	0.64%
plastering tools	163	0.62%
Subtotal	**4,492**	**17.14%**
Total	**26,200**	**100.00%**
« PREVIOUS 10		NEXT 10 »

Figure 13.2 Search Phrases report

This is a great report by itself, and you can do some exciting stuff with this dimension. However, take a closer look, and you'll notice that the data you see on screen is very limited and only represents a small section of not only the organic traffic influx, but the total number of unique search phrases.

Listed on the screen are 10 unique search phrases, accounting for 4,492 visits (just below 20 percent of all traffic). If we believe in the traditional long tail and that this dimension follows it, we should expect this to be the head of our distribution. Thus there should be a long tail of unique search phrases generating very little traffic, but altogether generating over 80 percent of the total traffic influx.

An easy way to test this is by showing 100 rows per screen and scrolling into the subsequent pages. I suggest that in such cases you use Yahoo! Web Analytics' export functionality and export all the search phrases. When you export, just go with the maximum number when asked; why settle for anything less? For our example, I chose to export 200,000 rows in a Microsoft Excel format. The Excel file for the data in Figure 13.2 is shown in Figure 13.3.

Scroll to the bottom to get a sense of the true volume of unique search phrases. In this scenario, we have 8,834 unique search phrases.

Our first optimization opportunity involves correlating this complete list of 8,834 phrases with our entire catalog of paid search listing keywords. This will create a list of phrases that we are not bidding on, and we need to determine why that is.

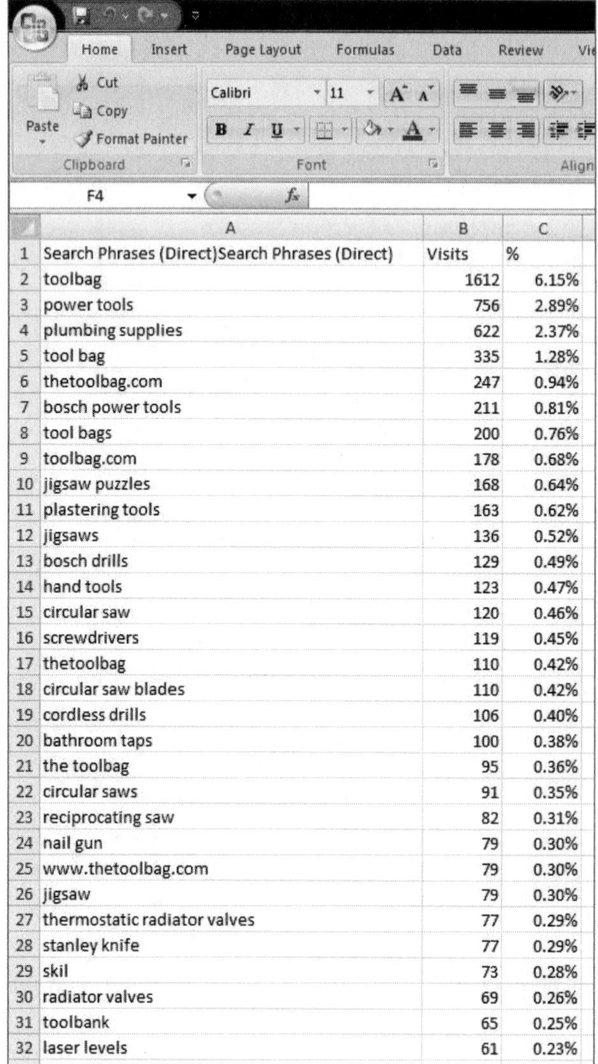

	A	B	C
1	Search Phrases (Direct)Search Phrases (Direct)	Visits	%
2	toolbag	1612	6.15%
3	power tools	756	2.89%
4	plumbing supplies	622	2.37%
5	tool bag	335	1.28%
6	thetoolbag.com	247	0.94%
7	bosch power tools	211	0.81%
8	tool bags	200	0.76%
9	toolbag.com	178	0.68%
10	jigsaw puzzles	168	0.64%
11	plastering tools	163	0.62%
12	jigsaws	136	0.52%
13	bosch drills	129	0.49%
14	hand tools	123	0.47%
15	circular saw	120	0.46%
16	screwdrivers	119	0.45%
17	thetoolbag	110	0.42%
18	circular saw blades	110	0.42%
19	cordless drills	106	0.40%
20	bathroom taps	100	0.38%
21	the toolbag	95	0.36%
22	circular saws	91	0.35%
23	reciprocating saw	82	0.31%
24	nail gun	79	0.30%
25	www.thetoolbag.com	79	0.30%
26	jigsaw	79	0.30%
27	thermostatic radiator valves	77	0.29%
28	stanley knife	77	0.29%
29	skil	73	0.28%
30	radiator valves	69	0.26%
31	toolbank	65	0.25%
32	laser levels	61	0.23%

Figure 13.3 Exported Search Phrases opened in Excel

Second, just by scrolling through the list freely, you are likely to gain valuable insights on how your customers use search phrases to find your products. Using some of the 8,834 phrases from our examples, you might note the following characteristics:

- Very unique phrases
  - black & decker laserplus laser level with detector
  - where can i buy a skil wormdrive saw in the uk
  - boschhammer gbh 24 vre sds plus cordless hammer drill
- Common misspellings that you might not be aware of
  - bosch powr tools

- Negative keywords that have nothing to do with your business
  - jigsaw puzzles of guardsmen at buckingham palace
  - skil logo
- New geographic targeting opportunities
  - plastering tool stores in Liverpool
  - offers makita power tools Nottingham
  - makita balta planer wood abbey uk

This list is by no means complete but just serves to tell you that something as simple and nontechnical as skimming a list will create value for you.

Next, let's create a scatter plot of our data to get a visual presentation of the data distribution, essentially confirming that it does indeed follow the long tail. Follow these steps:

1. Mark your Search Phrase and Visits columns (in our example, that means all 8,834 rows). Do not include the header or the total at the bottom, but only the raw data itself.
2. Insert a scatter chart in Excel (or another spreadsheet), based on the data selected, which should result in a long tail graph (see Figure 13.4).

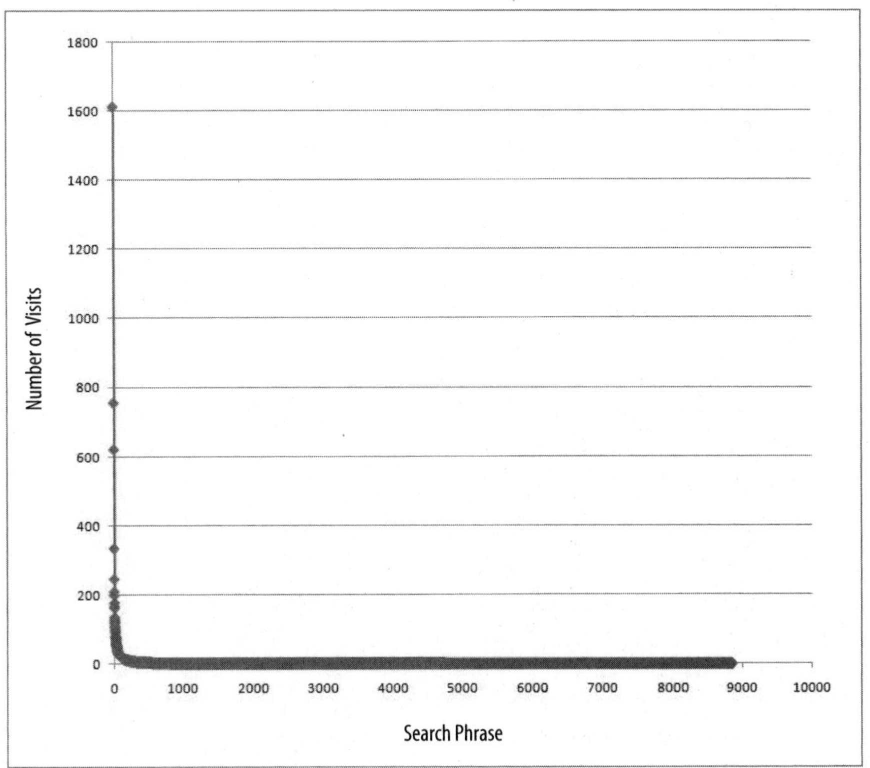

Figure 13.4 Search phrases scatter plot

In Figure 13.4, the first keyword, as represented by the leftmost plot on the x-axis, has a value a bit above 1,600, as represented by the y-axis. This seems to fit just fine with our most popular keyword, which drove 1,612 visits to the site. Also notice that we have nearly 9,000 plots, which again seems to fit very well with our 8,834 unique search phrases.

Looking at Figure 13.4, you confirm that your search phrases do indeed follow the long tail and that you can apply long tail thinking to your data set.

Note: The following post by Avinash Kaushik gives several suggestions for how to strategize around the long tail:

`http://www.kaushik.net/avinash/2007/03/excellent-analytics-tip-10-how-thick-is-your-head-and-how-long-is-your-tail.html`

If your data does not follow the traditional long tail distribution, you should follow the data with curiosity and try to figure out why. There might be simple answers to this, having the above data in mind, such as not having your site fully indexed in search engines.

Now, let's move on to a direct optimization example for content owners: the task of spotting a drooping tail.

Using the Long Tail for Content Optimization

Let's take what you've learned so far about the long tail one step further and explore a direct content optimization opportunity.

If you are a content owner with revenue derived from page view–based advertising, you can calculate how much revenue you are potentially leaving on the table by spotting what is generally called a "drooping tail."

Drooping Tail

A drooping tail is a long tail graph that does not follow the expected power law distribution, and thus creates a different-shaped tail when plotted on a double logarithmic chart.

To find whether your data has a drooping tail, first look up your Most Popular Pages report, for a 3 month period or more, and export all the data to Excel as described earlier. Then create a linear graph based on your data, as illustrated in Figure 13.5.

You will notice that the most popular page got about 16,000 visits, which seems correct. The website's home page got 16,241 visits in the same period and was the most popular page.

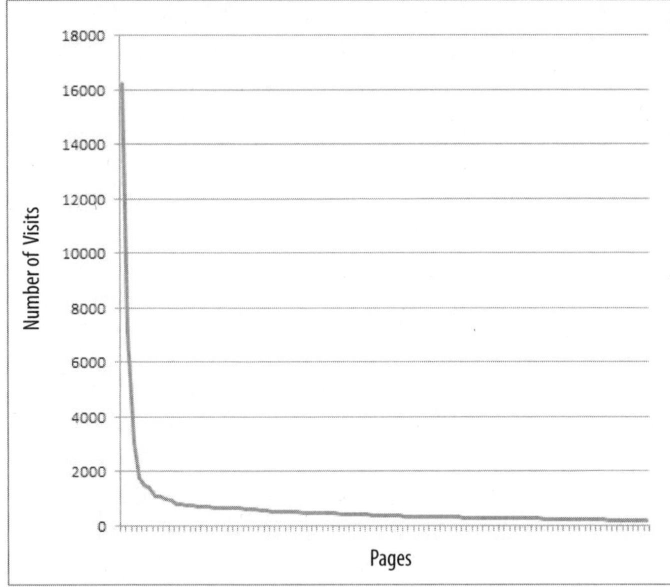

Figure 13.5 The number of visits per page, example 1

This is the traditional long tail, telling us that a few pages generated a lot of traffic but the same amount of traffic is generated by a large pool of lesser-visited pages. Without going into greater detail, it is fair to assume (just by looking at it) that a standard long tail distribution like this is inversely proportional and thus follows the power law.

Then, we should be able to plot the same information on a double-logarithmic chart. If a straight line appears, it confirms that we are talking about the traditional long tail.

So we need to add two more steps to our list:

3. Mark your y-axis, click Format Axis, choose Logarithmic as the Scale, and then click Apply to Chart.

4. Mark your x-axis, click Format Axis, choose Logarithmic as the Scale, and then click Apply to Chart.

Using the same dataset as Figure 13.5, we get a changed chart, as shown in Figure 13.6.

I applied a straight line through the graph. We can thus conclude that we have a perfect long tail distribution.

Now let's try to look at a less optimal dataset that does not necessarily create a straight line. I did a similar export and linear graph and ended up with the chart shown in Figure 13.7.

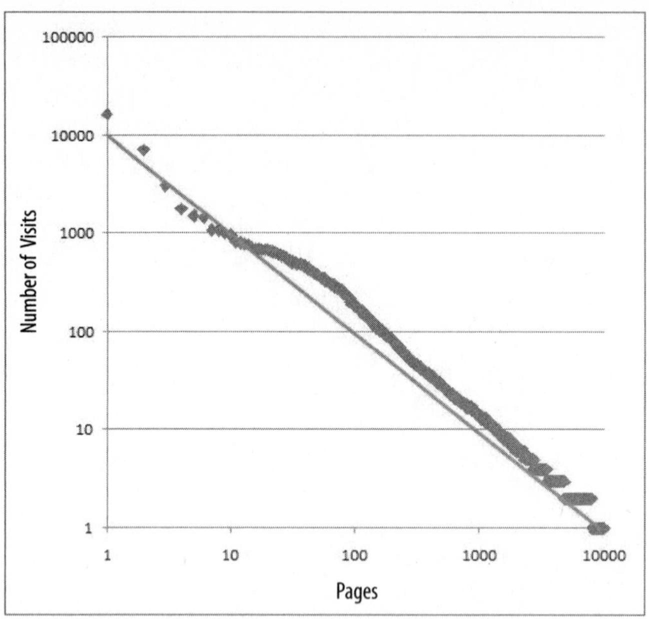

Figure 13.6 The number of visits per page in a double-logarithmic chart, example 1

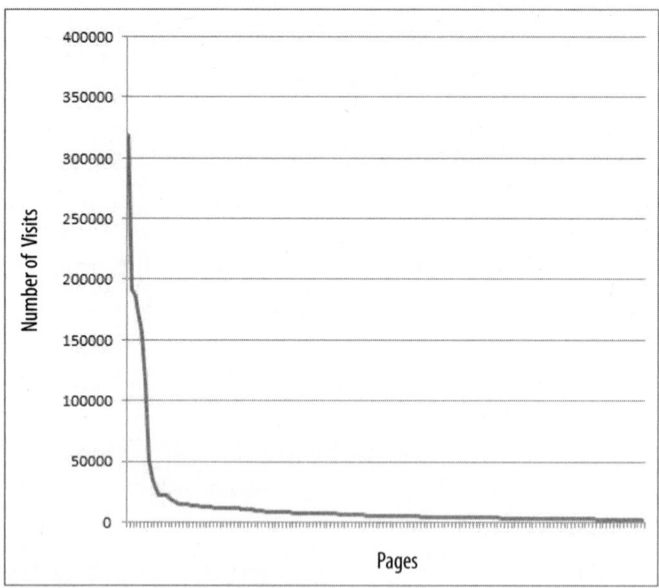

Figure 13.7 The number of visits per page, example 2

At first sight, Figure 13.7 looks just like any other long tail distribution. Most users might be fooled into believing everything is cool, unless they apply a different scale. Using a double-logarithmic chart (see Figure 13.8), we can see that there is no straight line and a drooping tail appears.

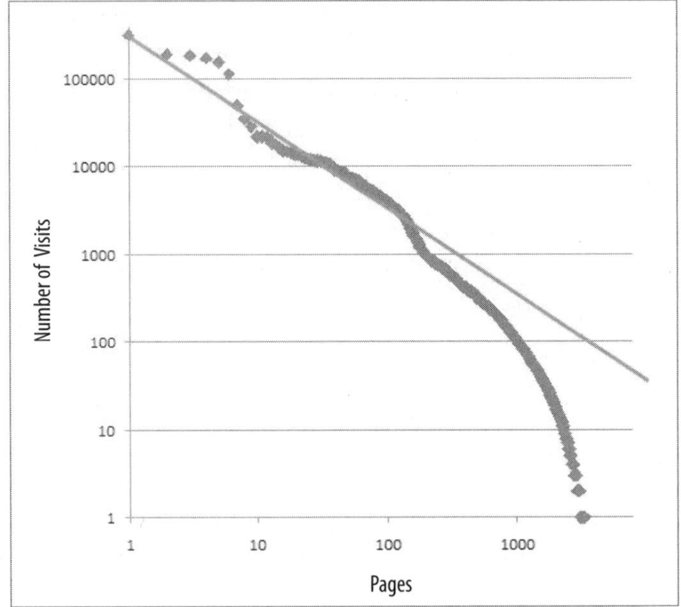

Figure 13.8 The number of visits per page in a double-logarithmic chart, example 2

Figure 13.8 tells a different story; there might be an opportunity to optimize for more traffic if we assume that the long tail should be inversely proportional and follows a power law. If that is the case, it becomes obvious that we are missing content to fill up the tail. The client, with the dataset shown, simply does not have enough content to support the long tail.

As you know, revenue is derived from content; thus, any additional visits and by that additional page views could realistically increase revenue. With our example dataset, the perfect distribution would roughly add an additional 1.7 million visits per week. It would also mean that they had to move from some 3,600 content pages to more than 300,000 content pages.

Making this even more concrete, let's assume that the cost per thousand impressions (CPM) is $2 and that each visit resulted in five page views. Under this assumption, we'd generate an additional $17,000 per week in revenue.

Now comes the billion-dollar question: Would this increase in revenue offset the cost of creating 300,000-plus pages? Does the content owner have a realistic opportunity to create this many more pages? A handy way to create content quickly and fill out the long tail might be to unleash one of your internal databases and make it publicly available.

I discuss this subject in the following post:

`http://visualrevenue.com/blog/2007/03/long-tail-and-how-to-calculate-missing.html`

But before you pop open the champagne, ask yourself whether this theory has a fair predictive power. I believe that in most cases it does. Any signs of bottlenecks should be seen as the actual opportunity and not a limitation. A bottleneck is what stands between supply and demand; a bottleneck is destined to be removed, if not by you, then by somebody else, and perhaps using a different channel at the same time.

Chris Anderson shares his input on the predictive power debate and how to deal with bottlenecks between supply and demand in this post on his long tail blog:

`http://www.longtail.com/the_long_tail/2006/08/a_billion_dolla.html`

Before we move on, I want to draw your attention to a distribution that provides a "fat head," as shown in Figure 13.9.

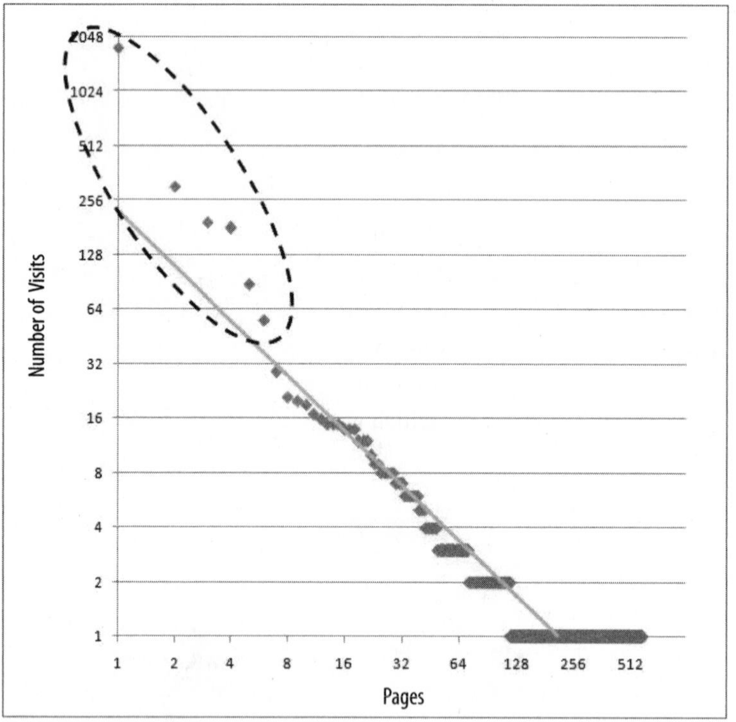

Figure 13.9 The number of visits per page in a double-logarithmic chart, fat head example

This creates a number of fantastic questions on why this is, if it is, a positive phenomena and what actions to take from it. The answers depend heavily on the metric you look at and on the organization and industry.

Such questions might lead you to conclude that there is an unjustified demand for certain keywords, such as the four or five outliers in the dataset with the fat head tendency, shown in Figure 13.9. This could be due to specific circumstances, such as overly aggressive SEO optimization, on those keywords in particular.

Determining the Width of Your Internal Search Query Box

As you noticed from the previous two sections, there are plenty of opportunities to access your data from Yahoo! Web Analytics. You must have access to your raw, non-aggregated data, because you can learn a lot by exporting and manipulating it. When discussing raw, non-aggregated data, we must take into account the complete dataset, not just the top 1,000 or top 10,000.

I included the following example (however narrow it might seem) for three reasons. First, it is yet another great example of accessing your data; second, it's a great follow-up to our chapter-long discussion on form optimization; and third, I believe this is a great little optimization nugget by itself.

I talked a lot about including usability studies when we discussed form optimization. I believe conducting such studies is worth your time and money here as well, simply because it does not take more than five friends, a couple of pizzas, and few soft drinks. Check out my blog post on the ideal number of users for usability studies:

```
http://visualrevenue.com/blog/2007/05/in-qualitative-analysis-5-8-
users-are.html
```

Why should a search query box be part of your usability study? For most websites, the search query box is one of the most important utilities, so you want to make sure it contributes to the optimal user experience and optimal site success.

If you doubt that the search utility is among the most important tools, run a basic Revenue Participation report, a metric we've mentioned a couple of times. In Figure 13.10 I created a custom content report, which shows revenue participation on a page level.

Page Title	Page Views	Revenue Participation
Confirmation	2,488	£120,529.88
Billing & Delivery Addresses	8,999	£120,134.98
Payment and Verification	3,616	£119,729.70
Delivery Options	5,825	£119,451.23
baskettoolbag	16,404	£116,836.70
confirmationtoolbag	5,088	£116,736.41
home	201,102	£116,728.31
Order Confirmed	2,514	£115,807.51
add to basket	17,781	£114,495.03
PRODUCTS	17,952	£114,416.67
Products	175,321	£103,182.23
Header	7,969	£95,776.08
my_accounttoolbag	6,549	£91,936.37
user registered	2,746	£88,979.63
Toolbag - Tools, Fixings & Consumables at Trade Prices!	62,457	£69,267.04
search	54,626	£51,416.62
all - Toolbag	92,344	£50,830.12
largetoolbag	39,056	£39,401.98
logintoolbag	3,411	£36,317.67
Power Tools - Toolbag, Next Day Delivery at Trade Prices!	45,574	£30,030.56

Figure 13.10 Custom Search Revenue Participation report

Going through the results, you will notice that the search utility participates in £51,416.62 of the overall £120,529.88 revenue for the given period. This means that 43 percent of all revenue-generating visits touched site search. My rule of thumb is that half your revenue is in some way, shape, or form mingled in with your site-search functionality.

This being the case, our first conclusion is that everything related to site search is important and should be optimized to the best of your ability. This includes everything from the SERP to the actual design of the search box, such as its width.

I've found that even when width testing is done, which to begin with is rare, it rarely takes into consideration the actual search phrase. Usability studies from Jacob Nielsen has shown that users use longer queries when the search box is wider.

Going back to our dataset, let's dig into the site search data and look at the number of searches per unique search query, as shown in Figure 13.11.

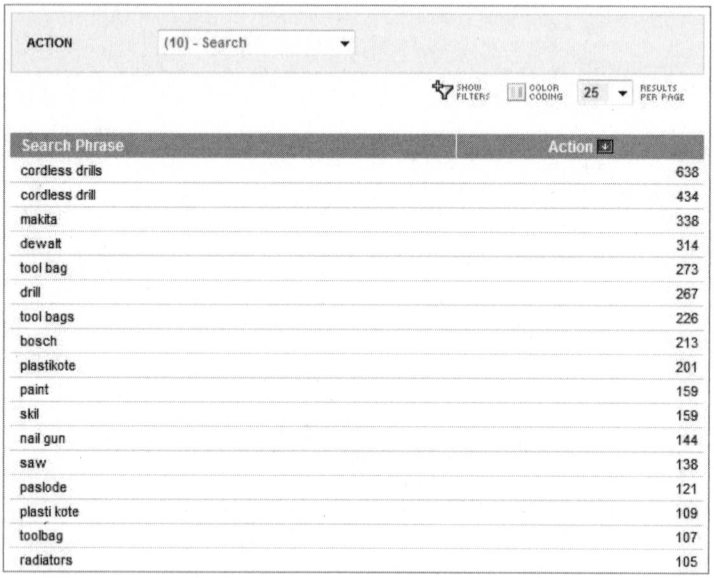

ACTION (10) - Search

SHOW FILTERS | COLOR CODING | 25 RESULTS PER PAGE

Search Phrase	Action
cordless drills	638
cordless drill	434
makita	338
dewalt	314
tool bag	273
drill	267
tool bags	226
bosch	213
plastikote	201
paint	159
skil	159
nail gun	144
saw	138
paslode	121
plasti kote	109
toolbag	107
radiators	105

Figure 13.11 Custom Searches per Search Phrase report

The report output is interesting on many levels, and when you look at the distribution of this dataset, it very much looks like a standard long tail. But for now we have a different interest in the data.

What we need to do now is determine how many characters (width) are needed to accommodate a certain percentage of all search queries in full. To do so, follow these steps:

1. Do a volume export of the data shown in Figure 13.11, which consists of a long list of unique search phrases with the number of searches for each phrase.

2. Import this dataset into Microsoft Excel or your favorite spreadsheet. This is likely to be a very long list since you should use a time period of at least 6 months. For this example, choose 24,000 unique site search phrases for the given period.

3. Add a third column and name it **Length**. This column will hold the number of characters in each search phrase. You will make this a calculated cell in your spreadsheet; in Excel the command is LEN(). The result appears in Figure 13.12.

	A	B	C
1	**Search Phrase**	**# Actions**	**Length**
2	cordless drills	638	15
3	cordless drill	434	14
4	makita	338	6
5	dewalt	314	6
6	tool bag	273	8
7	drill	267	5
8	tool bags	226	9
9	bosch	213	5
10	plastikote	201	10
11	paint	159	5
12	skil	159	4
13	nail gun	144	8
14	saw	138	3
15	paslode	121	7
16	plasti kote	109	11

Figure 13.12 Our search phrases, count, and length spreadsheet

This exercise is not about the uniqueness of the actual search phrase, but about the uniqueness in the number of characters in that search phrase. Therefore, let's do one more grouping based on our new calculated length number.

4. Group all the search phrases (rows) with similar length to get a total sum of searches per search length. In Excel, you can do so by creating a PivotTable; use whatever grouping mechanism your spreadsheet software provides. Figure 13.13 shows the new grouping, which should hold the same number of searches: 24,000.

   Now we have all the data we need. We can determine how many characters we need for our search box just by looking at this report. But let's take this process just one step further to get an even clearer picture by adding in a simple percentage column.

5. Add a column that calculates the percentage of all search queries. This column will show us a total percentage of how many queries we can accommodate in a search box of a specific length.

In Figure 13.14 you can see that I added the column. By just looking at the row-based data, we can conclude that with as few as 16 characters, we will be able to accommodate full usability on 71 percent of our internal search queries. Isn't that an exciting conclusion?

	A	B
1	Length	Count of # Actions
2	1	13
3	2	45
4	3	251
5	4	528
6	5	866
7	6	3471
8	7	1032
9	8	1152
10	9	1249
11	10	1272
12	11	1323
13	12	1448
14	13	1401
15	14	1199
16	15	1053
17	16	994
18	17	925
19	18	743
20	19	696
21	20	606
22	21	545

Figure 13.13 Our grouped search phrase length and actions spreadsheet

	A	B	C
1	Length	Count of # Actions	Percent of all Queries
2	1	13	0.1%
3	2	45	0.2%
4	3	251	1.3%
5	4	528	3.5%
6	5	866	7.0%
7	6	3471	21.4%
8	7	1032	25.6%
9	8	1152	30.4%
10	9	1249	35.5%
11	10	1272	40.8%
12	11	1323	46.3%
13	12	1448	52.2%
14	13	1401	58.0%
15	14	1199	63.0%
16	15	1053	67.3%
17	16	994	71.4%
18	17	925	75.3%
19	18	743	78.3%
20	19	696	81.2%

Figure 13.14 Grouped search phrase length percentage distribution spreadsheet

Finally, as part of your persuasion tactics when presenting this to the web development team, I suggest you visualize this in a scatter chart, as shown in Figure 13.15.

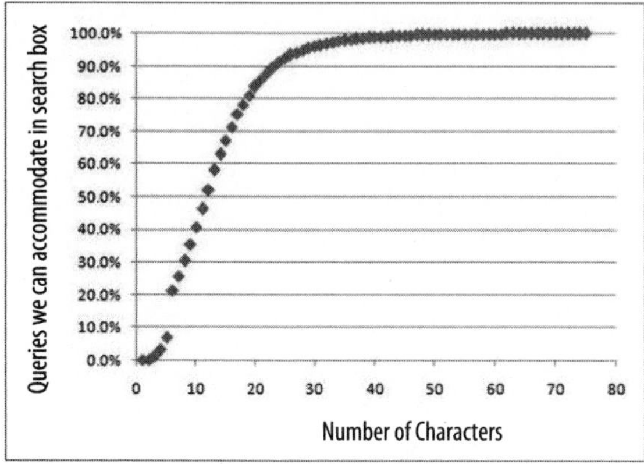

Figure 13.15 Search phrase length scatter chart

So armed with this data, we are left with only one question to answer: How many search queries should we support in full?

I assume we agree that we cannot accommodate 100 percent, simply because of outliers that have little meaning to the site's overall success. I suggest that you focus on accommodating about 90 percent of your internal search queries and make sure they fit in your search box. For our example, our internal search query box width should be 23 characters.

The site currently has an internal search box width of 35 characters, as shown in Figure 13.16. Following these guidelines, the site could "save" 12 characters and thus free up space and achieve optimal usability as a reward.

Figure 13.16 The search box today, which can benefit from our guidelines

Note: You can follow the debate on the width of search query boxes and add a comment here: `http://visualrevenue.com/blog/2007/05/use-web-analytics-to-determine-width-of.html`

Search query box width is only part of the story when exploring visitor behavior. Let's move on to the topic of search- and navigation-dominant visitors.

Optimizing Content for Search- and Navigation-Dominant Visitors

Search is one of the most important user interface elements in any large website today. As a rule of thumb, sites with more than 100 pages should offer site search. Keep the following in mind:

- Place a search query box on every page.
- Global search is better than scoped search.
- And, Or, Boolean, and other advanced queries should be moved to an advanced search page.

You can choose to split your visitors into two categories: search-dominant visitors and navigation-dominant visitors. Create a set of segments so that you can actively work with these visitor groups and achieve more precise content optimization based on how they navigate your site. The segments should include:

- Search-dominant visits
- Navigation-dominant visits
- Bounces (which consist of one page view only, by a visitor who used neither traditional navigation nor internal search)

Before showing you how to set up the segments in Yahoo! Web Analytics, I want to tell you why I think this is a significant discovery. I strongly believe that making a visitor suffer through poor direction-finding elements (in other words, traditional navigation or internal search) is bad for business. And "poor" means your visitors are not able to find the content they are looking for.

When you set up the segments, I suggest using the following filters:

- Search-dominant visit segment
  - Exclude all bounces
  - Include all visitors who searched on the first page of their visit path
- Navigation-dominant visit segment
  - Exclude all bounces
  - Exclude all visitors who searched on the first page of their visit path
- Bounce segment
  - Include all bounces

For some websites, it will be obvious how people navigate; for other sites this behavior will be less obvious, and as indicated earlier, might differ from section to section or from referring source to referring source. For instance, people may search to get closer to the section on a specific product, but browse and navigate through your 14 offerings.

My blog includes basic navigation and an internal site search. I set up three segments as described earlier and applied them to a basic visit report, as shown in Figure 13.17.

Month	Visits		
	ALL	Search-dominant visits	Navigation-dominant visits
2007 July	2,433	16	704
2007 August	2,654	20	719
2007 September	2,607	15	638
Total	**7,694**	**51**	**2,061**

Figure 13.17 Segmented Visit report

This report concludes that the visitors aren't focused on search and that most people navigate through the site. With this knowledge alone, we can make content decisions, such as applying a content widget like "Related Pages" rather than investing further in search at this point in time.

You might want to include first-time visitors and returning visitors as well, ensuring that you create a fair representation.

So to conclude, if you have mainly search-dominant visitors, you should engage in serious usability analysis focused on incorporating internal search into your overall site navigation. You might include such goals as determining the width of your internal search box or listing the five most-searched-for terms.

On the other hand, if you have mainly navigation-dominant users, you will be wasting valuable screen real estate on unused search elements. Not only that, you will be sending your users down a path they are not comfortable with. So perform the analysis to figure out which path (search or navigation) you should focus on.

And keep in mind that this behavior is most likely different from section to section of your web property.

Using Competitive Intelligence

Forming conclusions about overall market trends based on your own site-specific behavioral data may be dangerous. The surrounding market has, at most, a direct impact on your data; at the least, it can help you put your site-based conclusions in perspective. For example, I would hesitate to conclude that Yahoo! News was super successful during the Beijing Olympics without comparing the competitive news sites. If all major news sites covering the event had an increase in articles read or a metric like page views of 12 percent while Yahoo! News only had 7 percent, we should probably keep the champagne in the cooler for another day.

Competitive Intelligence Tools

There are a great deal of resources out there, both free-of-charge and expensive solutions that will provide you with all sorts of competitor information. So you can make sure that when you optimize your website you are optimizing with the whole universe in which you belong in mind. The following is a short list of vendors and applications that provide competitive intelligence (in order of cost):

- Alexa
- Compete
- Quantcast
- Hitwise
- comScore

Figure 13.18 shows a simple unique visitor comparison between the websites of luxury brands Prada and Gucci. (I can see now that I need a new dress shirt.)

You can also obtain competitive information from channels such as the following (in particular on search):

- Google AdWords
- Yahoo! Search Marketing
- Microsoft adCenter
- Google Ad Planner

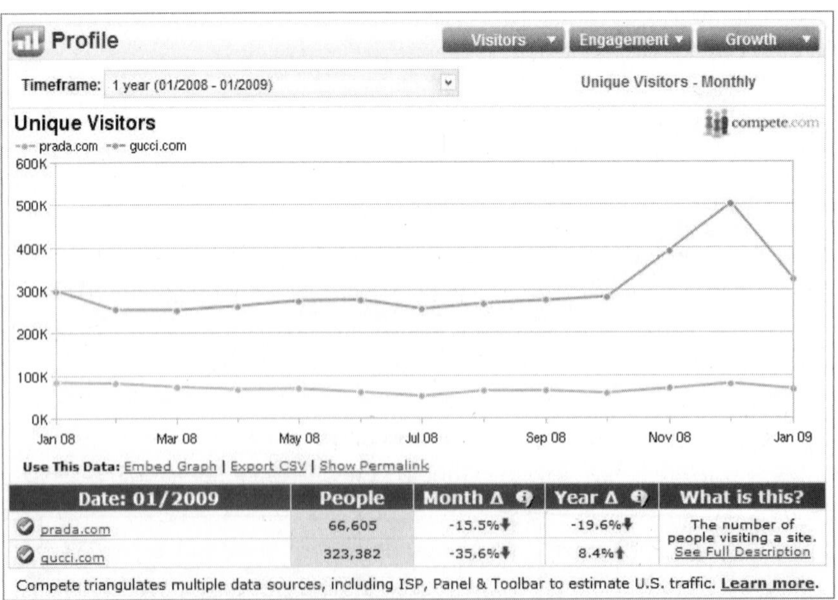

Figure 13.18 Unique visitor comparison using Compete

You shouldn't discount these channels just because the data comes from the search engines; the general marketplace insights they provide are generally valuable.

Let's use the same data shown in Figure 13.18 in the free (and for some people, infamous) Alexa. This is a great way to see if the sample data of either service is valid simply by looking at the trended data and confirming similar trends (see Figure 13.19).

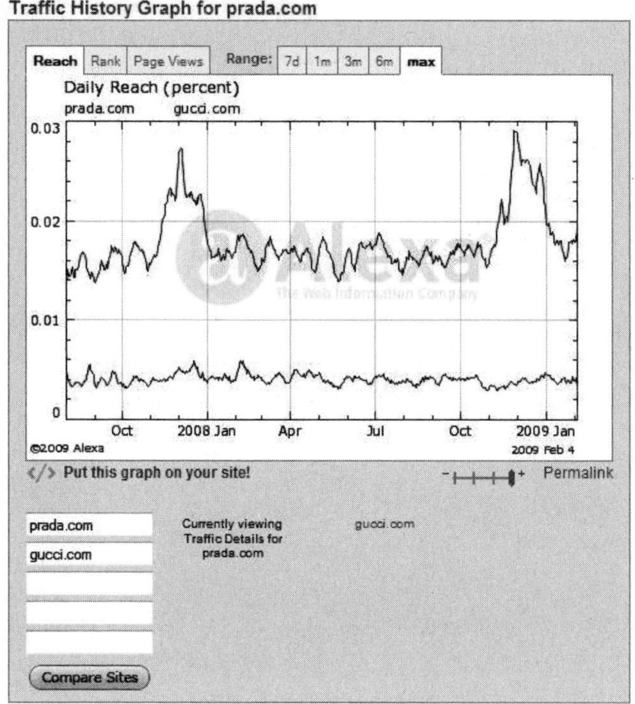

Figure 13.19 Daily reach (unique visitor) comparison using Alexa

As we have similar trends, I can then comfortably continue to use the Related Sites functionality in Alexa, which is essentially an up- and downstream analysis of what sites people visit in conjunction with visits to prada.com, as shown in Figure 13.20.

The upstream/downstream data coming from a service like Hitwise is a whole lot more meaningful, but this will do for now. I suggest you outgrow free tools before you move on to paid tools.

In our example, I know now that my primary competitor from a consumer traffic point of view is Paul Smith. Let's use the Google Keyword Suggestion tool to figure out specific content and product focus in regard to the Paul Smith website.

In Figure 13.21 we see primarily two things: first, a list of related keywords that hold information about content and products in general, and just as fascinating, the interest volume represented as the volume of search.

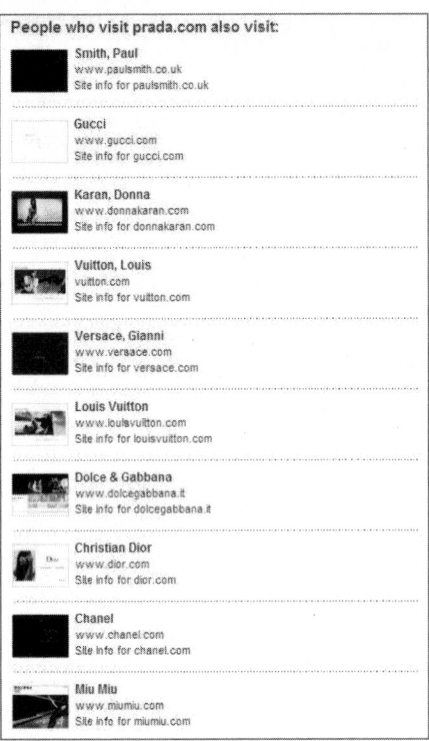

People who visit prada.com also visit:
Smith, Paul
www.paulsmith.co.uk
Site info for paulsmith.co.uk
Gucci
www.gucci.com
Site info for gucci.com
Karan, Donna
www.donnakaran.com
Site info for donnakaran.com
Vuitton, Louis
vuitton.com
Site info for vuitton.com
Versace, Gianni
www.versace.com
Site info for versace.com
Louis Vuitton
www.louisvuitton.com
Site info for louisvuitton.com
Dolce & Gabbana
www.dolcegabbana.it
Site info for dolcegabbana.it
Christian Dior
www.dior.com
Site info for dior.com
Chanel
www.chanel.com
Site info for chanel.com
Miu Miu
www.miumiu.com
Site info for miumiu.com

Figure 13.20 Related Sites competitive intelligence using Alexa

Choose columns to display: Show/hide columns

Keywords	Advertiser Competition	Approx Search Volume: January	Approx Avg Search Volume	Match Type: Broad
Keywords related to term(s) entered - sorted by relevance				
paul smith		8,100	8,100	Add
paul smith wallet		46	58	Add
paul smith shoes		260	320	Add
paul smith cufflinks		36	36	Add
paul smith perfume		16	12	Add
paul smith clothing		Not enough data	12	Add
paul smith clothes		Not enough data	12	Add
paul smith shirts		16	22	Add
paul smith wallets		Not enough data	Not enough data	Add
paul smith sunglasses		12	16	Add
paul smith extreme		46	58	Add
paul smith women		22	28	Add
paul smith sale		58	73	Add
paul smith uk		73	73	Add
paul smith floral		22	28	Add
paul smith men		36	36	Add
paul smith sneakers		46	110	Add
paul smith socks		12	36	Add
paul smith shop		91	73	Add
paul smith shoe		73	46	Add
paul smith trainers		28	16	Add
paul smith belt		Not enough data	36	Add
paul smith jeans		73	28	Add

Figure 13.21 Related Sites Paul Smith keywords

> **Note:** The biggest issue when playing around with competitor data (and when we dig into some of the other metrics) is that everything is sampled data that is extrapolated to some extent. So the less traffic your and your competitor's websites have, the more likely the data is inaccurate. That does not mean you can't use it; just use it with caution.

Comparing Metrics Appropriately

Keep in mind that some metrics do not compare, or it makes little sense to compare them. For example, let's consider the conversion rate, which might seem simple, but there are so many variables coming into play here, that it is probably not worth comparing. To begin with, you don't know what they are trying to drive toward, which could be fewer total conversions but higher value conversions or something completely different.

So make sure that the metrics you use in competitive intelligence can be compared. Some, such as keywords, might not need to be compared but just used as inspiration for optimizing or refreshing your own campaigns.

A good example of using a competitive intelligence tool to compare metrics is the market share report. It is simple to create but quite interesting (see Figure 13.22).

	Rank	Website	Domain	Market Share	01/10
	1.	Yahoo! News	news.yahoo.com	7.05%	1
	2.	The Weather Channel - US	www.weather.com	3.77%	2
	3.	CNN.com	www.cnn.com	3.30%	3
	4.	MSNBC	www.msnbc.msn.com	3.00%	4
	5.	Google News	news.google.com	2.35%	5
	6.	Drudge Report	www.drudgereport.com	2.02%	6
△	7.	Yahoo! Weather	weather.yahoo.com	1.88%	10
	8.	Fox News	www.foxnews.com	1.75%	8
▽	9.	People Magazine	www.people.com	1.75%	7
▽	10.	The New York Times	www.nytimes.com	1.62%	9

Figure 13.22 News & Media Market Share report by Hitwise

The market share report will show who the players are in your industry. If you are not in the top 10, you will get a good understanding of the size of the market and how much there is to share. From a report like this, you can strategize about whom to attack in unique campaign messages, if not directly then at least indirectly.

For most competitive intelligence tools, you are allowed to create a custom segment—that is, a pool of sites you might believe you compete with more directly than the larger segment set up by the tool vendor.

Finding Your Competitors in Upstream and Downstream Visits

I recommend that you look at upstream visitors (visits to other websites prior to yours) and downstream visitors (visits to other websites subsequent to yours).

Remember that exit tracking is not the same as downstream traffic. Exit links are links on your website that, by design, send people somewhere else. Downstream traffic is simply where people go after visiting your site by typing in a new URL in the address bar.

In regard to upstream traffic, you again have some of this information in your referring URL report, when it is a link sending you the traffic. But I am sure that Prada.com does not link to Gucci.com, and you will never be able to get a look into the visitor's intentions without using competitive intelligence.

There is all sorts of great information, such as Yahoo! Web Analytics showing that your SERP is an exit page, but your competitive tool showing that the downstream site is Google Search, providing you with a different story about the visitor not being able to find what he is looking for on your site.

Comparing Traffic from Search Engines

You can compare other information, such as the influx of traffic from search engines, against your direct competitors. There are again a number of stories you can learn from this, information such as brand loyalty. Remember, it is not a competition about getting the most traffic from search engines; it is about getting the most traffic coming to your site directly. The search engine should always be seen as an intermediary element.

If you engage in SEO, the information you get from Yahoo! Web Analytics and other website analytics tools is an absolute set of numbers (and metrics) about the actual incoming traffic. It is difficult to say if your SEO agency and in-house efforts are successful when a 5 percent increase is measured. What if the market grew 8 percent over the measured period, or what if your main competitor grew 15 percent?

The report in Figure 13.23 shows the market share of a given term, such as "Dubai," so you can measure yourself against the competition.

A report like this also provides you with information on where the most traffic volume related to this term goes. You would want to compete on some of the terms, whereas others you have no interest in competing on at all. The terms you typically would not want to compete on are those related to items outside your industry.

Websites that received traffic from 'dubai'
Displaying 1 to 10 of 62 websites. **4 weeks ending March 4, 2006**

	Website	Volume
1.	www.dubaitourism.ae	19.44%
2.	www.dubaicityguide.com	11.34%
3.	www.wikipedia.org	9.77%
4.	www.dubaitourism.co.ae	5.26%
5.	www.godubai.com	5.26%
6.	www.burjdubai.com	4.91%
7.	www.dubai.com	4.10%
8.	www.dubaiairport.com	3.24%
9.	travel.yahoo.com	2.83%
10.	news.google.com	2.02%

Most Popular search terms containing 'dubai'
Displaying 1 to 10 of 999 search terms

	Search Term	Volume
1.	dubai	15.03%
2.	dubai ports world	4.21%
3.	dubai jobs	1.67%
4.	where is dubai	1.27%
5.	dubai ports	1.21%
6.	jobs in dubai	0.86%
7.	dubai map	0.81%
8.	dubai desert classic	0.81%
9.	dubai open	0.81%
10.	cnn weather dubai	0.75%

Figure 13.23 Search term market share intelligence by Hitwise

Who Owns Which Part of the Funnel?

Using competitive intelligence is also a great way to figure out who owns what part of the funnel. For some items, there is a decision process that can be spontaneous or that can last for months. This process is pretty well defined for most industries. People don't sign up for a new mortgage at the supermarket on their way home, and people don't spend four months researching the best options to buy the new U2 CD.

There is also a well-researched keyword trail in most industries, which starts with industry/category keywords at the beginning of the funnel and ends with brand terms. Using competitive intelligence, you can learn who owns what part of the funnel and if you should reallocate some of your money to keywords earlier in the funnel. Or you might find affiliates (who, per definition, do not compete at the end of the funnel) who own huge parts at the top of the funnel, people with whom you can engage.

I find that most companies I work with define their competitors as those participating at the end of the funnel. In my world you compete on every single step in the funnel, and if somebody outside your usual competitors owns the initial persuasion dialogue on, for example, why you should buy this product, not from whom, you are indeed competing!

Note: By the beginning of Q2 2009, you will have the opportunity to do extended demographics and psychographic analysis in Yahoo! Web Analytics. This activity has been a feature of competitive intelligence tools or similar market segment information applications only.

Begin by using some of the free tools as well as the free functionality from the paid tools and move on from there. And always go for trends when using competitive intelligence; if using absolute numbers, be very cautious about the conclusion you derive from them. It is, after all, sample data!

I sincerely hope that after reading this book you know how to determine what data you need to collect and how to retrieve it; how to report on the collected data; and how to customize your reports, filters, and segments to make them more meaningful to you. And in this process, I hope you will gain the insight to take on optimization projects.

I will continue blogging about web analytics and online marketing on my blog, Twittering about the industry on my Twitter account, and speaking on these subjects at conferences around the world. So I am sure we will meet again, and you are always welcome to email me directly at `dennis.mortensen@evcrp.com`.

Appendix: Yahoo! Web Analytics Web Services API

The Yahoo! Web Analytics Web Services API enables you to create software programs and applications beyond and in conjunction with Yahoo! Web Analytics. You can read and execute most reports from within the system. The exported data can be used in any number of ways, such as building your own custom dashboards, adding to information on your intranet, and performing analysis using the Yahoo! Analytics platform. It is not just a pull (read) API, but also a push (write) API, which lets you put data back into the Yahoo! system. Such data might include merchandising categories, as described in Chapters 4 and 10. Use this appendix as a reference and inspiration for what is possible. You can supplement this appendix with the official Yahoo! API guides and manuals.

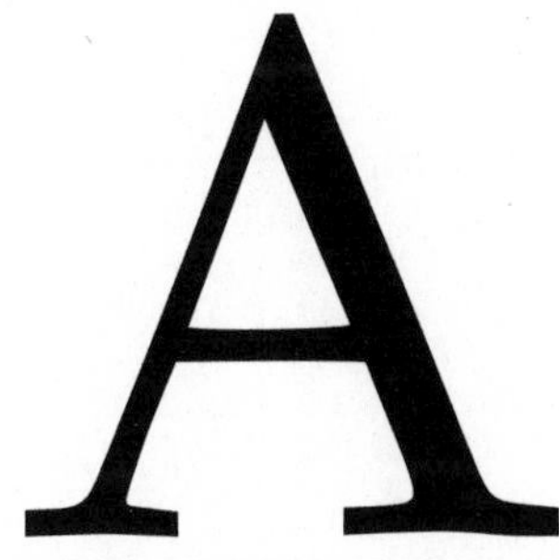

API Framework

As of the time of this writing, only a select number of users have access to the API. I anticipate that we will see this policy changed to include all accounts or at least a broad selection of them. It is simply too great a thing to hide!

The Yahoo! Web Analytics Web Services API provides programmatic means of interacting with the Yahoo! Web Analytics platform and serves as a way for you to read and write data for the main entities on the platform. Yahoo! provides API call opportunities all the way up to creating new accounts, new projects, and new users. This all depends on your API user rights.

The API provides access to the objects listed in Table A.1 and selectively supports the operations listed in Table A.2.

► **Table A.1** API Objects

Object	Description
`account`	`account` is the primary object and the parent of all other objects.
`user`	A `user` belongs to an `account`. One `account` may have multiple `users` with different user rights. When creating a new `account`, a `user` is created automatically with the same username as the `account` name and with full administrative rights.
`project`	A `project` belongs to an `account`. One `account` may have multiple `projects` with separate tracking scripts and thus separate data buckets. When creating a new `account`, a `project` object is created automatically.
`campaign`	A `campaign` belongs to a `project`. One `project` may have multiple `campaigns`.
`scenario`	A `scenario` belongs to a `project`. A `project` may have multiple `scenarios`.
`action`	An `action` belongs to a `project`. A `project` may have multiple actions.
`Edition`	The project's edition is an object property you will probably never have to set, as I see Yahoo! move towards a one-size-fits-all solution.

► **Table A.2** API Object Operations

Operation	Description
`login`	Starts a session.
`logout`	Finishes a session.
`createAccount`	Creates an account.
`createProject`	Creates an additional project within an account.
`createCampaign`	Creates a campaign within a project.
`getActions`	Retrieves the available actions of a project.
`getBookmarks`	Retrieves the bookmarks of a project.
`getCampaigns`	Retrieves the campaigns of a project.
`getEditions`	Retrieves editions.
`getProjects`	Retrieves the projects of an account.

► **Table A.2** API Object Operations *(Continued)*

Operation	Description
`getReport`	Retrieves a report.
`getReportFromBookmark`	Retrieves a bookmarked report.
`getReportFromBookmarkV2`	Retrieves a bookmarked report. New parameters include Offset and Limit.
`getReports`	Retrieves the available reports of a user/account.
`getTrackingCode`	Retrieves the tracking script for a project.
`getScenarios`	Retrieves scenarios for a project.
`approveOrder`	Changes the status of a previously recorded pending sale action to an approved sale.
`changeOrder`	Changes the order's (sale action) amount or currency.
`cancelOrder`	Deletes an order that was previously recorded in the system.
`ScheduleReportJobStandard`	Returns statistical data for a project.
`ScheduleReportJobBookmark`	Returns statistical data for a project.

The API works like any other API: Each call is initiated by a request from you (the client) and obtains a response from the server (Yahoo!). API calls are never initiated from the server to the client. Each API call has a method name, which is one of the operations described in Table A.2.

The API only supports the Simple Object Access Protocol (SOAP), so you encode your calls using SOAP.

Simple Object Access Protocol (SOAP)

SOAP is a protocol specification for exchanging structured information in the implementation of web services. It relies on XML as its message format and usually relies on other Application layer protocols, most notably remote procedure calls (RPC) and HTTP for message negotiation and transmission.

You can find the Yahoo! Web Analytics Web Services API WSDL here:

`http://www.indextools.com/download/IndexToolsApiV3.wsdl`

Yahoo! will release a new URL once it updates the address from the IndexTools location. Note that Yahoo! uses a number of custom types for its SOAP implementation, which are described in the WSDL schema.

Web Services Description Language (WSDL)

The WSDL is an XML-based language that provides a model for describing web services.

In the next section, we'll explore object operations. I am not going to list all of the constants or fault codes, but you can look those up in the reference manual.

API Calls

You initialize and create an API session using the login call. The URL (which includes a session ID returned by the login call) should be reused during subsequent calls until the session expires. The session should always be closed using the logout call.

login

The SOAP login call must be made to the following URL:

```
https://ondemand.indextools.com/IndexTools/services/IndexToolsApiV3
```

Succeeding calls are made to the URL returned by the login call. Keep in mind that this URL will change once the API is fully out in the open.

The login call takes an API partner ID and password as well as an optional user ID and password, and then validates them. Note that the API partner ID and password are different from the Yahoo! Web Analytics Consultant partner ID and password in the user interface.

There are two types of login privileges. If only the partner ID and password are supplied, a partner session will be created and only the `createAccount` operation will be allowed. If both the partner and user login information are supplied, a user session will be created with almost nonrestricted privileges.

Table A.3 lists the fields included in a login request. Fields marked by an asterisk (*) in the description are mandatory (this applies to all object tables in this appendix). Table A.4 lists the returned output fields after a login request has been made.

Table A.3 Fields for Login Calls

Name	Format	Description
`partner_id`	String	API partner identifier supplied by Yahoo! (*)
`partner_password`	Maximum of 32 characters	API partner password supplied by Yahoo! (*)
`user_id`	Maximum of 32 characters	Account's administrative user ID. If the `user_id` and `user_password` parameters are not supplied, the session will have limited privileges and only the `createAccount` operation will be allowed.
`user_password`	Maximum of 32 characters	If the `user_id` and `user_password` parameters are not supplied, the session will have limited privileges and only the `createAccount` operation will be allowed.
`secure`	Boolean	Specifies whether the login response should return a secure URL in the `server_url` parameter. This is an obsolete parameter, as all responses will be sent to secure URLs. This parameter must be set to `true` at all times. (*)

► **Table A.4** Return Fields for Login Calls

Name	Format	Description
`session_id`	Maximum of 64 characters	API partner identifier supplied by Yahoo!
`server_url`	Maximum of 128 characters	API partner password supplied by Yahoo!

As mentioned earlier, you should use the retrieved server URL for subsequent calls.

What follows is a code example of the login request and response so you can get a better idea of what the fields represent.

Login request:

```
<?xml version="1.0" encoding="utf-8"?>

<soapenv:Envelope xmlns:soapenv="http://schemas.xmlsoap.org/soap/envelope/"
xmlns:xsd="http://www.w3.org/2001/XMLSchema"
        xmlns:xsi="http://www.w3.org/2001/XMLSchema-instance">

 <soapenv:Body>
  <Login xmlns="http://v3.soap.api.indextools.com">
  <PartnerId>PARTNERID</PartnerId>
  <PartnerPassword>PARTNERPASSWORD</PartnerPassword>
  <UserId>USERID</UserId>
  <UserPassword>USERPASSWORD</UserPassword>
  <secure>true</secure>
  </Login>
 </soapenv:Body>

</soapenv:Envelope>
```

Login response:

```
<?xml version="1.0" encoding="utf-8"?>

<soapenv:Envelope xmlns:soapenv="http://schemas.xmlsoap.org/soap/envelope/"
xmlns:xsd="http://www.w3.org/2001/XMLSchema"
xmlns:xsi="http://www.w3.org/2001/XMLSchema-instance">

 <soapenv:Body>
  <LoginResponse xmlns="http://v3.soap.api.indextools.com">
  <ServerUrl> https://ondemand.indextools.com/IndexTools/services/IndexTools
ApiV3;jsessionid=FA60577E4AA2E30447D7502956C0D681
  </ServerUrl>
  <SessionId>FA60577E4AA2E30447D7502956C0D681</SessionId>
  </LoginResponse>
 </soapenv:Body>

</soapenv:Envelope>
```

This particular login call goes hand in hand with the logout call, which must be executed at the end of the API session.

ScheduleReportJobStandard

`ScheduleReportJobStandard` may be one of the most exciting pull (read) calls that you can do. A set of reporting calls is available that provides operations for getting reports out of your Yahoo! Web Analytics Account. The report is returned in an XML format, as you will see later in this section.

To retrieve reports, initialize your API session and send a `ScheduleReportJobStandard` or `ScheduleReportJobBookmark` request. The response is a `reportJobId` for the scheduled report job. Get the status of the report job by sending the `getReportJob` request. The status is Completed, Pending, or Failed. When the status is Completed, the response also includes the download URL for the report. The returned URL is valid for 5 minutes. If you need to obtain another URL, simply send another `getReportJob` request. Make sure you keep the returned URL confidential since it allows access to the report without the need to log in.

Download the report by sending an HTTP GET request to the download URL using any HTTP client library.

If you select a user-specific time zone in the user interface that is different from the project default, the reports you access via the API will be adjusted to the time zone you specify.

The `ScheduleReportJobStandard` call returns the aggregated data for a project and requires the fields listed in Table A.5.

Table A.5 Fields for `ScheduleReportJobStandard` Calls

Name	Format	Description
`project_id`	Digits	Numeric identifier of the project. (*)
`start_date`	Date, iso8601	Beginning of the reporting period, such as 2006-04-01. Note that dates must be entered in the year-month-day format. (*)
`end_date`	Date, iso8601	End of the reporting period, such as 2006-05-01. Note that dates must be entered in the year-month-day format.
`report_id`	`ReportId`	Use the `getReports()` call to get the available report IDs of the selected project.
`Offset`	Digits	Number of rows omitted from the beginning of the report. The default value is 0, and the report starts with the first row. If you are interested in looking at rows 20–30, the offset should be 19.
`Limit`	Digits	Number of rows to be displayed in the report.
`action_id`	Digits	Numeric action identifier. This parameter is only needed for conversion reports.
`campaign_id`	Digits	Numeric campaign identifier. This parameter is only needed for generating campaign details and campaign conversion reports.

► **Table A.5** Fields for `ScheduleReportJobStandard` Calls *(Continued)*

Name	Format	Description
`scenario_id`	Digits	Use the `getScenarios()` call to get the available scenario IDs of the selected project.
`session_id`	Maximum of 10 characters	Session identifier. This parameter is only needed for the session path report.
`sort`	Digits	Specifies the sort value of the columns: 0 means the first column, 1 the second column, and so on. Note that the sorting order always starts with the sort values of the left-hand labels.
`sort_direction`	Maximum of 4 characters	Sorts the column specified in the sort field. Possible values are `asc` (for ascending) and `desc` (for descending).
`show_help`	Boolean	Indicates whether report help should be included in the response.
`show_description`	Boolean	Indicates whether report description should be included in the response.
`Filters`	Structure	For details, see Table A.7.

Table A.6 lists the returned output fields after a `ScheduleReportJobStandard` request has been made.

► **Table A.6** Return Fields for `ScheduleReportJobStandard` Calls

Name	Format	Description
`ReportJobId`	Long	The ID of the report job to be used in subsequent `getReportJob` calls.

When using filters, you perform filtering much as you would in the interface. The `ScheduleReportJobStandard` call returns the exceptions based on the filter fault codes. The filter structure is described in Table A.7.

► **Table A.7** Fields for Filters Structure

Name	Format	Description
`Type`	String	Indicates the ID type of the filter.
`Operator`	String	Indicates the operator to be used for a filter. It can be a String or a Number operator. String operators include Equals, NotEquals, BeginsWith, NotBeginsWith, EndsWith, NotEndsWith, Contains, NotContains, Empty, NotEmpty, and Regexp. Number operators include Equals, NotEquals, Greater, GreaterOrEquals, Less, and LessOrEquals.
`Value`	String	Indicates the value of the filter (e.g., when filtering by the Browser report, the value can be Firefox).
`CaseSensitive`	Boolean	Indicates whether the value is case-sensitive.
`Scope`	String	Indicates the scope of the filter. Possible values are `Session`, `Action`, and `Page View`.

The `ScheduleReportJobStandard` request looks like this:

```
<?xml version="1.0" encoding="utf-8"?>

<soapenv:Envelope xmlns:soapenv="http://schemas.xmlsoap.org/soap/envelope/"
xmlns:xsd="http://www.w3.org/2001/XMLSchema"
xmlns:xsi="http://www.w3.org/2001/XMLSchema-instance">

 <soapenv:Body>
  <ScheduleReportJobStandard xmlns="http://v3.soap.api.indextools.com">
   <ProjectId>1234</ProjectId>
   <ReportId>182</ReportId>
   <StartDate>2009-01-01</StartDate>
   <EndDate>2009-01-10</EndDate>
   <Limit>2</Limit>
   <Sort>1</Sort>
   <SortDirection>Ascending</SortDirection>
   <IsShowDescription>true</IsShowDescription>
  </ScheduleReportJobStandard>
 </soapenv:Body>

</soapenv:Envelope>
```


Notice the report ID, which in the previous example is set to 182. You can look this ID up in Table A.8 and see that it equals a Campaign Summary.

► **Table A.8** API Report ID Constants

Operation	Description
104	Areas of the World
98	Bounce Rate (by Page Title)
97	Bounce Rate (by Page URL)
172	Bounce Rate of First-Time Visitors (by Page Title)
171	Bounce Rate of First-Time Visitors (by Page URL)
175	Bounce Rate of Returning Visitors (by Page Title)
174	Bounce Rate of Returning Visitors (by Page URL)
31	Browser Type
32	Browser Version
101	Campaign Conversion
102	Campaign Conversion Details
100	Campaign Details
99	Campaign Summary (Old version)
182	Campaign Summary
26	Clicks to Pages (listed by Page Title)

► **Table A.8** API Report ID Constants *(Continued)*

Operation	Description
25	Clicks to Pages (Listed by Page URL)
36	Color Depth
92	Content Groups Hosting Exit Links
106	Conversion Ratio by Countries
62	Conversion Ratio by Languages
55	Conversion Ratio by Referring Domains
56	Conversion Ratio by Referring URLs
58	Conversion Ratio by Search Engine Referrals
135	Conversion Ratio by Search Engine Referrals
59	Conversion Ratio by Search Phrases
136	Conversion Ratio by Search Phrases
66	Conversion Ratio by Top Entry Pages (by Page Title)
65	Conversion Ratio by Top Entry Pages (by URL)
63	Conversion Ratio by Visiting Organizations
67	Conversion Ratio Summary
39	Cookie Support
103	Countries
107	CPC Search Engine Campaigns
112	CPC Search Listings
111	CPC Search Phrases
8	Daily Unique Visitors
109	Demographics Regions
86	Download Pages by Content Groups
85	Download Pages by Title
84	Download Pages by URL
83	Downloaded Files (by File Name)
81	Downloaded Files (by Full URL)
82	Exit Links (by Full URL)
89	Exit Links (Grouped by Domain)
9	First-Time Visitors
11	First-Time vs. Returning Visits
227	Flash Version
40	Java Support
37	JavaScript Support
38	JavaScript Version
46	Languages
13	Last Visitors
148	Monthly Unique Visitors

Continues

▶ **Table A.8** API Report ID Constants *(Continued)*

Operation	Description
50	Most Active Server Hours
15	Most Requested Pages by Page Title
14	Most Requested Pages by Page URL
33	Operating System
34	Operating System Versions
133	Organic Search Engine Referrals
134	Organic Search Phrases
12	Page Views
27	Page Views by Document Group
2	Page Views Per Session
91	Pages Hosting Exit Links (by Title)
90	Pages Hosting Exit Links (by URL)
41	Referring Domains
42	Referring URLs
10	Returning Visitors
146	Sales Detail
165	Sales Summary
127	Scenario Summary
35	Screen Resolution
44	Search Engine Referrals
45	Search Phrases
110	Time Spent on Site
4	Time Zones
49	Top Browsing Hours
52	Top Directories
143	Top Domains
18	Top Entry Pages by Page Title
16	Top Entry Pages by Page URL
19	Top Exit Pages by Page Title
17	Top Exit Pages by Page URL
29	Traffic Summary
154	Visit Path
47	Visiting Organizations
28	Visitors by Document Group
7	Visits

Flipping through this list, it becomes obvious that this resembles almost every out-of-the-box report in the Yahoo! Web Analytics system.

You are able to apply, on the fly, API filtering inputs. You can also create a custom report using the conventional user interface, save it as a bookmarked report, and request that unique report to be called.

As mentioned earlier, when the report is returned, it will be in XML. A campaign summary result from the `ScheduleReportJobStandard` will look something like this:


```
<GetReportResponse>

<Title>Campaign Summary</Title>

<Description>This report summarizes the activity that originated as a result
of a specific campaign. For more information on specific campaigns use the
drill down call.</Description>

<HasMoreRows>false</HasMoreRows>

<TopHeadRows>
<Row>
<Item>
<Name>Impressions</Name>
<Span>1</Span>
</Item>
<Item>
<Name>Clicks</Name>
<Span>1</Span>
</Item>
<Item>
<Name>Uniques</Name>
<Span>1</Span>
</Item>
<Item>
<Name>Returning</Name>
<Span>1</Span>
</Item>
<Item>
<Name>Bounce rate</Name>
<Span>1</Span>
</Item>
<Item>
<Name>Cost</Name>
<Span>1</Span>
</Item>
<Item>
```

```
<Name>Revenue</Name>
<Span>1</Span>
</Item>
<Item>
<Name>Action</Name>
<Span>1</Span>
</Item>
<Item>
<Name>Conversion</Name>
<Span>1</Span>
</Item>
<Item>
<Name>ROAS</Name>
<Span>1</Span>
</Item>
<Item>
<Name>CPA</Name>
<Span>1</Span>
</Item>
<Item>
<Name>ACC</Name>
<Span>1</Span>
</Item>
</Row>
</TopHeadRows>

<LeftHeadLabels>
<Name>Channel</Name>
<Name>Market</Name>
<Name>Vendor</Name>
<Name>Category 44</Name>
<Name>Campaign</Name>
</LeftHeadLabels>
<LeftHeadItems>
<Item>
<Name>Paid Search</Name>
<Indent>0</Indent>
</Item>
<Item>
<Name>US</Name>
<Indent>1</Indent>
```

```
</Item>
<Item>
<Name>Paid Search</Name>
<Indent>2</Indent>
</Item>
<Item>
<Name>Google</Name>
<Indent>3</Indent>
</Item>
<Item>
<Name>Google</Name>
<Indent>4</Indent>
</Item>
<Item>
<Name>Google test</Name>
<Indent>4</Indent>
</Item>
<Item>
<Name>Overture</Name>
<Indent>3</Indent>
</Item>
</LeftHeadItems>

<DataRows>
<Row>
<Cell>
<Value>0</Value>
<FormattedValue>0</FormattedValue>
<Type>Int</Type>
</Cell>
<Cell>
<Value>268</Value>
<FormattedValue>268</FormattedValue>
<Type>Int</Type>
</Cell>
<Cell>
<Value>266</Value>
<FormattedValue>266</FormattedValue>
<Type>Int</Type>
</Cell>
<Cell>
```

```
<Value>894</Value>
<FormattedValue>894</FormattedValue>
<Type>Int</Type>
</Cell>
<Cell>
<Value>26.09%</Value>
<FormattedValue>26.09%</FormattedValue>
<Type>Percent</Type>
</Cell>
<Cell>
<Value>22.82</Value>
<FormattedValue>$22.82</FormattedValue>
<Type>Currency</Type>
</Cell>
<Cell>
<Value>0.00</Value>
<FormattedValue>$0.00</FormattedValue>
<Type>Currency</Type>
</Cell>
<Cell>
<Value>0</Value>
<FormattedValue>0</FormattedValue>
<Type>Int</Type>
</Cell>
<Cell>
<Value>0.00%</Value>
<FormattedValue>0.00%</FormattedValue>
<Type>Percent</Type>
</Cell>
<Cell>
<Value>0.00%</Value>
<FormattedValue>0.00%</FormattedValue>
<Type>Percent</Type>
</Cell>
<Cell>
<Value>0.00</Value>
<FormattedValue>$0.00</FormattedValue>
<Type>Currency</Type>
</Cell>
<Cell>
```

```
<Value>0.08</Value>
<FormattedValue>$0.08</FormattedValue>
<Type>Currency</Type>
</Cell>
</Row>
<Row>
<Cell>
<Value>0</Value>
<FormattedValue>0</FormattedValue>
<Type>Int</Type>
</Cell>
<Cell>
<Value>268</Value>
<FormattedValue>268</FormattedValue>
<Type>Int</Type>
</Cell>
<Cell>
<Value>266</Value>
<FormattedValue>266</FormattedValue>
<Type>Int</Type>
</Cell>
<Cell>
<Value>894</Value>
<FormattedValue>894</FormattedValue>
<Type>Int</Type>
</Cell>
</Row>
</DataRows>

<TotalCells>
<Cell>
<Value/>
<FormattedValue/>
<Type>Text</Type>
</Cell>
<Cell>
<Value>0</Value>
<FormattedValue>0</FormattedValue>
<Type>Int</Type>
</Cell>
<Cell>
```

```
<Value>342</Value>
<FormattedValue>342</FormattedValue>
<Type>Int</Type>
</Cell>
<Cell>
<Value>330</Value>
<FormattedValue>330</FormattedValue>
<Type>Int</Type>
</Cell>
<Cell>
<Value>1694</Value>
<FormattedValue>1,694</FormattedValue>
<Type>Int</Type>
</Cell>
<Cell>
<Value>33.23%</Value>
<FormattedValue>33.23%</FormattedValue>
<Type>Percent</Type>
</Cell>
<Cell>
<Value>22.82</Value>
<FormattedValue>$22.82</FormattedValue>
<Type>Currency</Type>
</Cell>
<Cell>
<Value>5108.52</Value>
<FormattedValue>$5,108.52</FormattedValue>
<Type>Currency</Type>
</Cell>
<Cell>
<Value>84</Value>
<FormattedValue>84</FormattedValue>
<Type>Int</Type>
</Cell>
<Cell>
<Value>24.56%</Value>
<FormattedValue>24.56%</FormattedValue>
<Type>Percent</Type>
</Cell>
<Cell>
```

```
<Value>22386.15%</Value>
<FormattedValue>22,386.15%</FormattedValue>
<Type>Percent</Type>
</Cell>
<Cell>
<Value>0.27</Value>
<FormattedValue>$0.27</FormattedValue>
<Type>Currency</Type>
</Cell>
<Cell>
<Value>0.06</Value>
<FormattedValue>$0.06</FormattedValue>
<Type>Currency</Type>
</Cell>
</TotalCells>

<SubtotalCells/>
<UnknownCells/>

</GetReportResponse>
```

You might feel exhausted when you finish reading the code, but most applications that you choose to use this data in will find the code easy to read!

cancelOrder

Let's move on to a simpler and less-text-heavy example, the `cancelOrder` call, which deletes an order that was previously recorded in the system.

The `cancelOrder` request requires the fields listed in Table A.9.

Table A.9 Fields for `cancelOrder` Calls

Name	Format	Description
`project_id`	Digits	Numeric identifier of the project. (*)
`OrderId`	String	Order identifier. (*)
`Date`	Date	Order's creation date. The date must be older than 24 hours.

If the method execution is not successful, an exception will be thrown.

This is typically a call you would make from your back-office systems, and it's a great example of the value of the push (write) API. If you only have a few orders a day, it doesn't make much sense—you would just do this from the user interface itself—but if you have hundreds or thousands of orders, the story is different.

Your web analytics solution is a business-critical application, and cleaning the data is of the utmost importance. Cleaning data involves making sure that orders you registered that were later cancelled are cancelled in your web analytics data as well; that way, the cancellations are reflected in future web analytics reporting.

If you do not take this strong stance against poor data, you might not catch those campaigns in which people buy but later cancel their orders. Missing such a transaction is much more expensive than the customer not buying at all.

The API is a great way of extending your use of Yahoo! Web Analytics. You don't have to create manual processes for changing orders or for moving orders from pending to completed, and you don't have to ask an assistant to move data from Yahoo! to the intranet.

Now find out if the API is enabled for your account and, if not, how you can get it enabled.

Index

Note to the Reader: Throughout this index **boldfaced** page numbers indicate primary discussions of a topic. *Italicized* page numbers indicate illustrations.

A

abandonment rates
  vs. behavior rates, 261
  form, **312–315**, *312–314*
  funnel optimization, 307, *307*
About Us pages, 152, 202
ACC metric, 60
account object, 350
accounts
  opening, **6–8**, *7–8*
  paid search, 62–63
Action Equals criteria, 258
Action filter, 152
`action_id` field, 354
Action Name field, 74
action object, 350
Action option for dashboards, 231
Action Participation metric
  accessing, 141
  content analysis reports, 208–210, *210*
  sales funnel, 311, *311*
ACTION variable
  description, 23
  on-click actions, 43
  pending sales, 94
  products added to cart, 93
  products viewed, 90
  revenue tracking, 48
  Thank You pages, 94
  time stamps, 105–106
actionable dashboards, 227
actions, conversion, **34–38**, *35–37*
  fixed-system, 34–35, *35*
  multiple actions on same web page, **38–42**
  multiple sales during same visit, 38
  on-click actions, **42–44**, *43*
  visitor conversion count methodology, **44–45**, *45*
Active Calendar Events screen, 173, *173*
ad groups, **286–287**
ad hoc funnel analysis scenarios, **260–263**, *260–262*
Ad Impressions metric, 288
Ad Planner, 342
AdCenter
  competitive information, 342
  paid search, 77
Add a Dashboard function, 227
Add Alert option, 166
Add Campaigns/Edit Campaign Configuration task, 73
Add Dashboard Item screen, 230–231, *230*, 234
Add Event option, 171
Add New Campaign option, 69
Add New Event dialog, 171–172, *172*
Add Report to Dashboard feature, 139
ADD_TO_CART action, 34
  paid search, 297
  SKU codes, 86
  working with, 92–93
Add to Dashboard option, 230
Advanced Encryption Standard (AES), 51–53
advanced queries, 340
Advanced Web Metrics with Google Analytics (Clifton), 5
AdWords
  accounts, 61–62
  API, 63
  campaigns, 77
  competitive information, 342
AES (Advanced Encryption Standard), 51–53
affiliate campaigns, 58
aggregate data
  content reports, 210
  leftover data, 4
  `ScheduleReportJobStandard`, 354
  updating, 129

Ajax-based objects
 artificially triggering campaigns, **127–128**
 description, 38
 overview, **121–124**
 tracking page views vs. actions, **125–126**
Alert Management screen, 169, *169*
alerts, **166**
 handling, 169
 selecting, **166–168**, *167*
 timing and triggers, **168–170**, *169–170*
Alerts function, 166
Alerts report modifier, 140
Alexa vendor
 competitive intelligence, 342
 Related Sites functionality, 343, *344*
All Visits option for Bounce Rate reports, 211
`AllowScriptAccess` setting, 120
alphanumerical segmentation, 192
Amazon.com, 320, *320*
AMOUNT variable
 conversion actions, 37, 40
 currencies, 46–48, 90
 encryption, 51–53
 final revenue amount, 101
 order IDs, 49
 pending sales, 95
 products purchased, 98
 revenue tracking, 46
 units and amounts tracking, **87–89**, *89*
analytics.yahoo.com site, 6, *7*
Anderson, Chris, 326, 334
apostrophes (') in names, 26–27
Application Programming Interfaces (APIs)
 AdWords, 63
 calls, **352–366**
 description, 96
 framework, **350–352**
Apply to Chart option, 332
Area code reports, 203
Areas of the World reports, 203
artificially triggering campaigns, **127–128**
ASK IT Tutor
 Cross-Sell Analysis reports, 265–266, *266*
 report modifier, 140
.asp extension, 30
asterisks (*)
 in cross-reference filters, 150
 in names, 26–27
Asynchronous JavaScript and XML (Ajax)
 artificially triggering campaigns, **127–128**
 description, 38
 overview, **121–124**
 tracking page views vs. actions, **125–126**
attribution filters, **153–154**, *154*
AUD currency code, 47
Automatic PPC Time Zone Adjustment projects, 20
Average option for metrics, **168**
Average Order Value per Search Phrase metric, 156
Average Position metric, 60, 288
Avg. Order Value metric, 216, 221

B

Banner Campaign Activity data source, 129–130
banner campaigns, 58
bar charts, **236–238**, *237–238*
Begins With operator, 150
behavior rates vs. abandonment rates, 261
Between operator, 156
BGN currency code, 47
bid management, 284
Bid Management product, 61
Bookmark Report feature, 139, 186, *186*
bookmarks for custom reports, 183, **185–188**, *186–188*
Bounce Rate by Entry Page Title reports, 212
Bounce Rate by Entry Page URL reports, 212
Bounce Rate over Time reports, 212
Bounce Rate reports, **211–214**, *212–214*
BRL currency code, 47
Broad Match option, 287
Browser Versions reports, 220–221, *220–221*
Browsers reports, 220
Build Custom Reports option, 179
Bulk Campaign Upload screen, 73
bulk campaigns, **72–74**, *72–73*

C

CAD currency code, 47
calendars for reports, 141–142, *142*
 purpose, 138

time comparative reporting, **144–147**, *145–147*
unique visitors, **142–144**, *143–144*
calls, API, **352–366**
Campaign Clicks metric, 60
Campaign Conversion metric, 60
Campaign Cost metric, 60
Campaign ID field in Banner Campaign Activity, 130
campaign_id field in ScheduleReportJobStandard, 354
Campaign Manager category, 65
Campaign Name field in bulk campaigns, 73
campaign object, 350
Campaign Summary reports, 65
customized, 59, *60*
expanded, **268–269**, *268–270*
Campaign Type field in bulk campaigns, 73
campaigns. *See* enterprise campaigns
CANCELLED_SALE action, 34, 86
cancelOrder call
description, 351
working with, **365–366**
Carrabis, Joseph, 299
Carry-Over option, 112–113
Carry-Over Until Any Next Defined Action Occurs option, 113
Carry-Over Until Next Defined Action Occurs option, 113
Carry-Over Until Visit Ends option, 112
CaseSensitive filters, 355
categories
custom fields, 111
enterprise campaigns, **63–67**, *64–66*, 70, *71*
merchandising, **101–105**, *102–104*
causality, 79
CFB (Cipher Feedback) mode, 51–52
.cfm extension, 30
.cgi extension, 30
changeOrder operation, 351
Channel category, 65
Character Encoding projects, 19
Chart Format projects, 19
chart junk, 160
charts
bar, **236–238**, *237–238*
goal, **242–243**, *243*
logarithmic scale, 331–332, *333–334*
pie, **235–236**, *235–236*
reports, 140, *140*
scatter, 339, *339*
trend, **243–245**, *244–245*
CHF currency code, 47
Cipher Feedback (CFB) mode, 51–52
City reports, 203
cleansing ad groups, 287
click-through rate (CTR)
calculating, 96
paid optimization, 293, *293*
Clicks metric, 288
Clifton, Brian, 5
CNY currency code, 47
code validation, **131**
collecting data, **4**, **14–17**, *16–18*
colons (:)
in AMOUNT variable, 52
in names, 26–27
color-coding data, **160–161**, *160–161*, 166
Color-Coding report modifier, 140
Color Palettes reports, 220
comma-separated values (CSV) format
description, 103
exporting data, 163
template, 103–105, *105*
Comparative period option in dashboards, 231
comparative reporting, **144–147**, *145–147*
comparing metrics in competitive intelligence, **345**, *345*
Compete vendor, 342
competing on analytics, **4–6**
competitive intelligence, **341**
funnel ownership, **347**
metric comparisons, **345**, *345*
search engine traffic comparisons, **346**, *347*
tools, **341–345**, *343–344*
upstream and downstream visits, **346**
competitors in upstream and downstream visits, **346**
comScore vendor, 342
Configure External Data Source screen, 130, *130*
Connection Type reports, 220
consolidating costs, **270**
Contains operator, 150
content hierarchy, 111, *111*
content optimization and competitive analysis, **325**
competitive intelligence, **341**
funnel ownership, **347**
metric comparisons, **345**, *345*

search engine traffic comparisons, **346**, *347*
tools, **341–345**, *343–344*
upstream and downstream visits, **346**
internal search query box, **335–339**, *335–339*
long tail
content optimization, **330–334**, *331–334*
keyword optimization, **326–330**, *326–329*
search- and navigation-dominant visitors, **340–341**, *341*
content reports, **207–210**, *207–210*
content sites, paid search optimization for, **296–300**, *297*, *299*
Control Center, 137
conversion action tracking, **34–38**, *35–37*
fixed-system, 34–35, *35*
multiple actions on same web page, **38–42**
multiple sales during same visit, **38**
on-click actions, **42–44**, *43*
visitor conversion count methodology, **44–45**, *45*
conversion reports, **216–219**, *218–219*
Conversion Summary reports, 35, *36*, 38, 217, *218*
conversions
funnel, 257
newsletter, 36, *37*
visit-to-sales, 294
Cookie Support reports, 220
Coordinated Universal Time (UTC), 106
Copy function in dashboards, 228, *229*
Cost field for bulk campaigns, 74
Cost per Action (CPA) metric
campaigns, 70
description, 59–60
gauges, 241
Cost per Click (CPC) metric
campaigns, 70
description, 59
Cost per Thousand (CPM) metric, 59
Cost Type field
bulk campaigns, 74
options, 69–70
counting visitors, **271**
Countries reports, 203
Country field in last visitor reports, 200
CPA (Cost per Action) metric
campaigns, 70
description, 59–60
gauges, 241
CPC (Cost per Click) metric
campaigns, 70
description, 59
CPM (Cost per Thousand) metric, 59
CRC (cyclic redundancy check), **52–53**
CRC currency code, 47
Create Visitor Segments option, 190
`createAccount` operation, 350
`createCampaign` operation, 350
`createITT` function, 39, 123
`createProject` operation, 350
CRM (Customer Relationship Management), 32–33
cross-channel optimization, **283**
cross-reference filters, **147–151**, *148–149*, *151*
metric, **155–156**, *156*
regular expressions, **155**
scope, **152**, *153*
traffic attribution, **153–154**, *154*
Cross-Sell Analysis reports, **265–266**, *265–266*
cross tabulations, 181
CSV (comma-separated values) format
description, 103
exporting data, 163
template, 103–105, *105*
CTR (click-through rate)
calculating, 96
paid optimization, 293, *293*
currencies
bulk campaigns, 74
codes, **47**
enterprise campaigns, 61, *61*
multiple, **89–90**
in reports, 194
revenue tracking, **46–48**, *47*
Currency field, 74
custom fields, tracking, **110–114**, *110–111*, *113–114*
Custom Merchandising Categories page, 103–105, *105*
Custom Report Wizard
Campaign Summary report, 59–60
campaigns, 64
content reports, 208, *208*

custom fields, 114, *114*
product categories, 103
visit reports, 107
working with, 179–184, *181–184*
custom reports, **179–185**, *180–185*
Custom Searches per Search Phrase report, 336, *336*
custom time periods in reports, 142, *142*
custom variables, **23**
Customer Relationship Management (CRM), 32–33
Customize and Schedule Reports for Email Delivery option, 176
Customize Report feature, 139, 179
cyclic redundancy check (CRC), **52–53**
CZK currency code, 47

D

Daily Unique Visitors, 143
Dashboard Item Name option, 231
dashboards, **223**
adding, **227–229**, *227–229*
defining, **224–226**, *225–226*
items
adding, **229–232**, *230–231*
bar and row charts, **236–238**, *237–238*
gauges, **240–242**, *241–242*
goal charts, **242–243**, *243*
KPIs, **238–240**, *239–240*
notes, **245–246**, *246–247*
pie charts, **235–236**, *235–236*
tabular data, **233–234**, *233–235*
trend charts, **243–245**, *244–245*
understanding, **232**
reports, 137
data collection, **4**, **14–17**, *16–18*
data-ink ratio, 229
data sources, external, **128–131**, *128*, *130*
Date field
`cancelOrder` call, 365
events, 172
last visitor reports, 200
Day report periods, 142
Default dashboards, 228
Default No. of Rows projects, 19
Default Report Period projects, 19
Define Product Categories screen, 102, *102*
defining dashboards, **224–226**, *225–226*
Delete option in dashboards, 228, 234
Delivery Options for abandonment rate, 307, *307*
demographic reports
conversion reports, 217
overview, **203–206**, *203–206*
Description field for bulk campaigns, 73
destination URLs in enterprise campaigns, 62
detailed paid search reports, **288–292**, *289–292*
dimensions in reports, 183
Direct attribution model, 153–154, *154*
Direct Traffic information in campaigns, 289
Directories reports, 207
discounts, tracking, **99–101**, *101*
Display Comparative Values as Percentages projects, 19
Display in Reports option, 65, 103
DKK currency code, 47
`.dll` extension, 30
DMA/MSA reports, 203
.do extension, 30
Document Group
filters, 152
reports, 207
DOCUMENTGROUP variable, 23, 28, 86
DOCUMENTNAME variable, 23, 26–27
documents
grouping, **28**
names, **26–27**, *27*
reports, 207
Does Not Begin With operator, 150
Does Not Contain operator, 150
Does Not Equal operator, 150, 156
domains
grouping, **17**, *17*
sales tracking across, **106–107**
DOMAINS variable, 23
double-logarithmic charts, 332, *333–334*
double quotes (") in names, 26–27
Download Data Template option, 130
Download Failed error, 79
downloads
reports, 207
tracking, **28–30**, *29*, 44
Downloads reports, 207
downstream visits in competitive intelligence, **346**

drill-downs and drill-throughs
- description, 147
- path analysis, **254–257**, *255–256*
- working with, **157–158**, *157–158*

Drill_Downs report modifier, 140
drooping tails, 330–333, *333*
duplicate order IDs, **105–106**
Duration field, 130

E

e-commerce sites, paid optimization for, **292–296**, *293–295*
Each Item Individually option, **168**
Edit Alert dialog, 166–168, *167*
Edit Color Coding screen, 160–161, *161*
Edit Dashboard Item screen, 234, *234*
Edit New Event dialog, 172, *172*
Edit option for dashboards, 228
Edit Rights setting, **187**
Edit Your User Profile option, 193
Edition object, 350
EEK currency code, 47
Email Export method, 164
emails
- alerts, 166, 170, *170*
- campaigns, 58
- reports, 177, *178*

Enable Cost Consolidation option, 270
Enable Cost Projection projects, 20
enabling Ajax tracking, 123
encryption, **49–53**, *50*
End Date field in bulk campaigns, 74
`end_date` field in `ScheduleReportJobStandard`, 354
Ends With operator, 150
enterprise campaigns, **57**
- artificially triggering, **127–128**
- bulk campaign management, 72–74, *72–73*
- categories, **63–67**, *64–66*, 70, *71*
- detailed paid search reporting, **288–292**, *289–292*
- fallback, **74–75**, *75*
- identifying, **67–68**
- internal, **79–81**, *80–81*
- paid optimization, 284
- paid search
  - example, **75–79**, *76*, *78*
  - setup, **62–63**, *62–63*
- setting up, **68–72**, *69–71*
- single campaign management, **72**
- types, **58–61**, *59–61*

Entries reports, 211
Entry page field for last visitor reports, 200
equal signs (=) in names, 26–27
Equals/Contains field in bulk campaigns, 74
Equals operator, 150, 156
Estimated Pageview projects, 19
EUR currency code, 47
event management, **170–174**, *171–175*
Events report modifier, 140
Exact Match option, 287
Excel format, 163, 327
exclamation points (!) in names, 26–27
Exclude Browser projects, 19
Executive Dashboards, 225
exit link tracking
- actions for, 44
- competitors, 346
- process, **30–31**, *30*

Exits reports, 211
Export Campaign Settings task, 73
Export Report Data feature, 139
Export Reports dialog, 163, *163*
exporting data, **163–164**, *163*
expressions, regular, **155**
extensions, page view files, 30
external data sources, **128–131**, *128*, *130*
External Data Sources management screen, 128, *128*

F

fallback campaigns
- description, *58*
- setting up, **74–75**, *75*

Few, Stephen, 224
fields
- custom, **110–114**, *113–114*
- types, 130

filters
- Bounce Rate reports, 212–213
- cross-reference
  - metric, **155–156**, *156*
  - regular expressions, **155**
  - scope, **152**, *153*
  - traffic attribution, **153–154**, *154*
  - working with, **147–151**, *148–149*, *151*
- First Time Visitors, 309, *309*

Filters field in `ScheduleReportJobStandard`, *355*
Filters report modifier, 140
First Day of the Week projects, 19
First Time Visitors
  Bounce Rate reports, 211
  filtering, 309, *309*
  First-Time Visitor Resistance segment, 323
  First Time Visits vs. Returning Visits reports, 198–200, *198–200*, 238
five-level-deep campaign classifications, 65
FLA files, 119
Flash-based objects, **116–121**, *120*
Flash Support reports, 220
Flash Version reports, 220
FLASHURL variable, 23
form analysis and optimization, **303**
  abandonment, **312–315**, *312–314*
  form actions, **304–306**, *305*
  funnel optimization, **306–311**, *306–307*, *309–311*
  optimization process, **315–319**, *316–318*
  submit optimization, **319–323**, *319–323*
formats for reports
  exporting data, 163
  scheduled reports, 176
  search phrases, 327
Free Campaign/Other Cost Type option, 70
free campaigns, 58
Full Report function, 234
Full Screen action, 120
functions, **23–24**
funnel analysis scenarios
  ad hoc, **260–263**, *260–262*
  creating, **53–55**, *54–55*
  overview, **257–258**
  predefined, **258–259**, *258–259*
funnels
  abandonment, **312–315**, *312–314*
  optimization
    form optimization, **306–308**
    prequalifying traffic, **308–311**, *309–311*
  ownership, **347**

G

gauges for dashboards, **240–242**, *241–242*
GBP currency code, 47
get operations, 350–351
`getTime` function, 121
`getURL` function, 117–119, 121
.go extension, 30
Go to Full report function, 233
goal charts, **242–243**, *243*
Good portion on gauges, 241
Google
  dashboards, 224, *226*
  paid search, **77**
Google Ad Planner, 342
Google AdWords
  accounts, 61–62
  API, 63
  campaigns, 77
  competitive information, 342
Google Keyword Suggestion tool, 343
Google MCC Accounts, 62–63
Google My Client Center (MMC), 63
greater than signs (>) in names, 26–27
groups
  ad, **286–287**
  data collection, **14–17**, *16–18*
  documents, **28**
  domain, **17**, *17*
  enterprise campaigns, 66
  reports, 181, 183

H

headers in reports, 137, *138*
hexing, 52–53
hits, 196
Hitwise vendor, 342
HKD currency code, 47
horizontal segmentation, 16
HRK currency code, 47
.html extension, 30
HTML format, 163, 176
HTML forms, 304
HUF currency code, 47

I

identifying enterprise campaigns, **67–68**
Impressions metric, 60
in-built fields, 130
IndexTools, 61
indextools.js script, 7, 10

indextools_ssl.js script, 14
Information Dashboard Design: The Effective Visual Communication of Data (Few), 224
information silos, 313
initiated downloads, 29
INR currency code, 47
installation, **10–14**, *11*
Installation tab, 8, 11
Instant Export method, 164
Intelligent model, 153–154
interface for report results, **137–141**, *137–141*
internal campaigns, **79–81**, *80–81*
INTERNAL_SEARCH action, 34, 115
Internal Search Conversion report, 274
Internal Search feature, **114–116**, *116*
  query boxes, **335–339**, *335–339*
  reports, **272–277**, *272–273*, *275–276*
Internal Search Phrase filters, 152
Internal Search Usage report, 274, *275*
internalcamp function, 127
interval scales in trend charts, **244**
IP Filtering projects, 19
IP/Host field, 200
IP lookup, 206
Is Empty operator, 150–151
Is Greater Than operator, 156
Is Greater Than or Equal To operator, 156
Is Less Than operator, 156
Is Less Than or Equal To operator, 156
Is Not Empty operator, 150–151
ISK currency code, 47
ISL currency code, 47
IT Tutor
  Cross-Sell Analysis reports, 265–266, *266*
  report modifier, 140

J

Java Support reports, 220
JavaScript, 8
JavaScript Support reports, 220
JavaScript Version reports, 220
JPY currency code, 47
`.jsp` extension, 30
junk, chart, 160

K

Kaushik, Avinash, 77, 330
Kelkoo site, 50, *50*
key fields, 129
key performance indicators (KPIs), 16
  dashboards, **238–240**, *239–240*
  online video, 120–121
  optimization metric, 300
keys in AES encryption, 51
Keyword identifier field for bulk campaigns, 74
Keyword Identifier Missing error, 79
Keyword Mismatch error, 79
keywords
  bulk campaigns, 74
  competitive intelligence, 347
  long tail optimization, **326–330**, *326–329*
  paid optimization, 284–285
  verification messages, 79
  visit-to-sales conversion, 294
Keywords Retrieved Successfully error, 79
KPIs (key performance indicators), 16
  dashboards, **238–240**, *239–240*
  online video, 120–121
  optimization metric, 300

L

landing pages
  conversion reports, 217
  description, 67
Languages reports, 203
last visitor details
  code for, 32, *33*
  reports, 200–202, *201–202*
LCA (Live Cost Analysis), 78, *78*
lead-generation sites, 298
leading slashes (//) in scripts, 20
leftover data, 4
less than signs (<) in names, 26–27
Lifetime Value of the Visitor metric, 296
Limit field, 354
line graphs, **243–245**, *244–245*
linear funnels toward conversion, 257
Live Cost Analysis (LCA), 78, *78*
logarithmic scale charts, 331–332, *333–334*
login call, 350, **352–354**
Login Failed errors, 78

login page path analysis, 316–318, *316–318*
long tail concept
description, **284**
keyword optimization, **326–330**, *326–329*
lookup table data, 129
loyal customer data, **190–192**, *191*
LTL currency code, 47
LVL currency code, 47

M

Manage Campaign Categories screen, 64, *64*
Manage Campaigns screen, 69, *69*
Manage Custom Fields option, 111
Manage Dashboards screen, 227–228, *227*
Manage External Data Sources option, 128
Manage Internal Campaigns screen, 80, *80*
Market category in enterprise campaigns, 65
market segmentation, 15–16, 188
form conversions, **322–324**, *323*
funnel analysis scenarios, 261
guidelines, **189**
path analysis, 254
in reporting, **188–190**
creating, **190**, *190*
loyal customer data, **190–192**, *191*
setting up, **192–193**, *193*
visit reports, 340–341, *341*
matching options, **287–288**
Max CPC (Bid) metric, 288
MCC Accounts, 62–63
MEMBERID variable
description, 23
external data sources, 129–130
flash-based objects, 117
tracking registered members, 32–33, *34*
merchandising, **83**
basics, **84–85**, *84*
categories, **101–105**, *102–104*
multiple currencies, **89–90**
setting up, **86**
tips, **105–107**
tracking
discount, tax, and shipping, **99–101**, *101*
pending sales and reconciling orders, **93–96**, *95*
products added to cart, **92–93**, *92–93*
products purchased, **96–99**, *97*
products viewed, **90–92**, *91–92*
SKU information, **86–87**
units and amounts, **87–89**, *89*
merchandising reports, **263**
Cross-Sell Analysis, **265–266**, *265–266*
sample, **266–268**, *267*
summary, **263**, *264*
Merchandising Summary reports, **263**, *264*
metrics
alerts, **166**
monitoring, **166–168**, *167*
timing and triggers, 168–170, *169–170*
campaign, 60
comparing, *345*
filters, **155–156**, *156*
Microsoft
dashboards, 224, *226*
paid search, **77**
Microsoft AdCenter
competitive information, 342
paid search, 77
Microsoft Excel format, 163, 327
minus signs (-) in names, 26–27
MMC (My Client Center), 63
modifiers for reports, **140**, *140*
Modify Default Name link, 232
Modify Sale Action, 95, *95*
monitoring metric alerts, **166–170**, *167*, *169–170*
Month report periods, 142
Monthly Unique Visitors, 143
Most Popular Pages report, 254, *255*, 330
Most Requested Pages by Page Title report, 159, *159*, 207, *207*
Most Requested Pages by Page URL report, 252, *252*
Move Dashboard Item function, 233
multiple actions tracking
actions during same visit, **38–42**
sales during same visit, **38**
multiple currencies
merchandising, **89–90**
revenue tracking, **46–48**, *47*
multiple values list segmentation, 192
Mute action, 120
`.mv` extension, 30
MXN currency code, 47
My Client Center (MMC), 63

N

NAICS reports, 203
names
  actions, 35
  bar charts, 237–238
  categories, 103
  custom fields, 112
  documents, **26–27**, *27*
  variables, 23
navigation-dominant visitors, content optimization for, **340–341**, *341*
navigation reports, **211–215**, *212–214*
Negative Match option, 287
newsletter conversions, 36, *37*
Nielsen, Jacob, 336
No Carry-Over scope, 112–113
No Matching Campaigns Found status, 78
No. of visits field, 200
NOK currency code, 47
nominal scales in trend charts, **244**
non-ASCII characters in names, 26–27
nonlinear paths toward conversion, 257
nonsecure domains, tracking sales across, **106–107**
notes, **162**, *162*
Notes dashboard, **245–246**, *246–247*
Number of Visits dimension, 218
Number of Visits Till Conversion reports, 217–219, *219*
number signs (#) in names, 26–27
numerical segmentation, 192
NZD currency code, 47

O

objects in API, **350**
Offset field, 354
on-click actions, **42–44**, *43*
`onClipEvent` function, 121
one-time cost campaigns, 58, 70
One-time Cost option, 70
One Unique Item option, **168**
online video KPIs, 120–121
Online Video Played, Seconds KPI, 121
operations in API, **350–351**
Operator filters, 355
optimization
  content. *See* content optimization and competitive analysis
  form. *See* form analysis and optimization
  paid. *See* paid search
Optional Top Group option, 231
OR function
  cross-reference filters, 149, *149*
  funnel analysis, 259
  regular expressions, 155
order IDs
  duplicate, **105–106**
  tracking, **48–49**
order reconciliation, **93–96**, *95*
Order Reconciliation dialog, 95, *95*
ORDERID variable
  `cancelOrder` call, 365
  conversion actions, 37–40
  description, 23
  duplicate IDs, 105
  merchandising, 86, 88
  order tracking, 48–49
ordinal scales in trend charts, **244**
organic search
  campaigns, 286, 289
  description, 26
  drill-downs, 254, *256*
  paid search balanced with, **300–301**
  phrases, 164
Organic Search Engines reports, 215–216
Organic Search Phrases reports, 215
Organizations reports, 203
Organize Bookmarks screen, 188, *188*
Original attribution model, 153–154, *154*
Other Referrals filter, 254, *255*
out-of-the-box reports, 136
Overture paid search company, 76
ownership of funnels, **347**

P

Page Depth reports, 211
Page Name Contains criteria, 258
Page Name Equals criteria, 258, 262
Page Title filters, 152
Page URL filters, 152
page views
  Ajax, **125–126**
  extensions, 30
  Page View Scope filter, 152
  Page Views filter, 152
  Page Views per Visit reports, 211
  scope segments, 192
Pages reports, 207
paid search
  analysis and optimization, **281**
    ad groups, **286–287**

content sites, **296–300**, *297*, *299*
defining, **282–283**
detailed reporting, **288–292**, *289–292*
e-commerce sites, **292–296**, *293–295*
enterprise campaigns, **62–63**, *62–63*
example, **75–78**, *76*, *78*
matching options, **287**
objectives, **282**
with organic search, **300–301**
search engine content networks, **287–288**
starting, **283–286**, *285–286*
campaigns, 58, 289
cost consolidation from, **270**
Paid Search information, 289
parameters for custom fields, 112
parentheses () in names, 26–27
parking sales, 94
`partner_id` field, 352
partner IDs, 352
`partner_password` field, 352
passwords, 352
path analysis, **250**
drill-down examples, **254–257**, *255–256*
after positive sales conversions, 321, *322*
scenarios for funnel analysis, **257–263**, *258–262*
standalone reports, **250–254**, *251–254*
Path Analysis reports, 211, 230
Path Analysis by Title report, **250–252**, *251*
Pay per Click (PPC)
campaigns, 70
description, 59
Payment and Verification abandonment rate, 307, *307*
PDF format, 163
PENDING_SALE action, 34, 94
Pending Sales
SKU codes, 86
tracking, **93–96**, *95*
percent signs (%) in names, 26–27
percentages in pie charts, 235–236, *236*
periods in reports
calendars for, 141–142, *142*
purpose, 138
time comparative reporting, **144–147**, *145–147*
unique visitors, **142–144**, *143–144*
overview, **138–141**, *139–141*
personal identifiable information (PII), 31
Peterson, Eric, 299
.php3 extension, 30
.php4 extension, 30
.php5 extension, 30
Phrase Match option, 287
pie charts, **235–236**, *235–236*
PII (personal identifiable information), 31
pivot tables, 180
.pl extension, 30
Placement option for dashboards, 231
plain vanilla tagging, 4–5
Play/Pause action, 120
PLN currency code, 47
policies, privacy, 31–32
pound signs (#) in names, 26–27
power law, 326
PPC (Pay per Click)
campaigns, 70
description, 59
PPC Search Engine Name field, 74
predefined funnel analysis scenarios, **258–259**, *258–259*
preinstallation steps, **6–10**, *7–8*
prequalifying
traffic, **308–311**, *309–311*
visitors, 314, *314*
Print Report feature, 139
privacy policies, 31–32
product tracking
added to cart, **92–93**, *92–93*
purchased, **96–99**, *97*
viewed, **90–92**, *91–92*
PRODUCT_VIEW action, 34
product tracking, 90
SKU codes, 86
Project Default Reporting Currency projects, 19
project field, 365
Project Go-Live Date projects, 20
project headers in reports, 137, *138*
`project_id` field, 354
project object, 350
projects
adding and managing, **18–20**, *18*
description, 8, 14
rollup, 16
settings, 18, *18*
purchased products, tracking, **96–99**, *97*

Q

- Quality Assurance (QA), 99
- Quantcast vendor, 342
- Quantity field in bulk campaigns, 74
- Quarter report periods, 142
- Query String field in bulk campaigns, 74
- question marks (?) in names, 26–27
- questions for report results, 136–137
- quotes (‘) in names, 26–27

R

- radio button segmentation, 192
- Read Rights setting, **187**
- reconciling orders, **93–96**, *95*
- `recordaction` function, 41–42
- `recordsale` function, 39–40, 118–119
- red color code, 161
- Referrer field, 200
- referrers reports
  - last visitor, 200
  - search engine, 145, *145*
  - types, **215–217**, *215–217*
- Referring Domains reports, 215
- Referring URLs reports, 215
- Region/State code reports, 203
- registered members, tracking, **31–33**, *33–34*
- regular expressions, **155**
- Related Sites functionality in Alexa, 343, *344*
- Report Cache projects, 20
- Report Chooser, 141, *141*
- report collages vs. dashboards, 224
- `report_id` field, 354
- Report Name field in bar charts, 237–238
- Report Notes feature, **162**, *162*
- Reporting Metric option, 231
- Reporting Period setting
  - bar charts, 237–238
  - dashboards, 231
  - scheduled reports, 176
- `ReportJobId` field, 355
- reports and report results, **135**, **195**, **249**
  - bookmarking, **185–188**, *186–188*
  - Campaign Summary, **268–272**, *268–269*
  - color-coding data, **160–161**, *160–161*, 166
  - content, **207–210**, *207–210*
  - conversion, **216–219**, *218–219*
  - cross-reference, **147–151**, *148–149*, *151*
    - metric, **155–156**, *156*
    - regular expressions, **155**
    - scope, **152**, *153*
    - traffic attribution, **153–154**, *154*
  - custom fields, 114, *114*
  - custom reports, **179–185**, *180–185*
  - customizing, **165**
  - demographic, **203–206**, *203–206*
  - drill-downs and drill-throughs, **157–158**, *157–158*
  - event management, **170–174**, *171–175*
  - expectations, **136–137**
  - exporting data, **163–164**, *163*
  - interface, **137–141**, *137–141*
  - internal search, **272–277**, *272–273*, *275–276*
  - merchandising, **263**
    - Cross-Sell Analysis, **265–266**, *265–266*
    - sample, **266–268**, *267*
    - summary, **263**, *264*
  - metric alerts, **166**
    - monitoring, **166–168**, *167*
    - timing and triggers, 168–170, *169–170*
  - navigation, **211–215**, *212–214*
  - path analysis, **250–257**, *251–256*
  - Report Notes feature, **162**, *162*
  - scheduled, **175–179**, *176–179*
  - search engines and referrers, **215–217**, *215–217*
  - segments, **188–193**, *190–191*, *193*
  - sorting, **158–159**, *159*, 206, *206*
  - surfing, 4
  - system, **219–221**, *220–221*
  - time periods. *See* time periods in reports
  - user rights and role administration, **193–194**, *193*
  - visit, **196–202**, *196–202*
- Request Catalogue action, 36
- return on advertising spending (ROAS) metric
  - dashboard, 238
  - description, 60
  - revenue tracking, 45–46
- return on investment (ROI), 149
- Returning Campaign Clicks metric, 60
- Returning Visitors filtering, 309, *310*
- Returning Visits option for Bounce Rate reports, 211
- Revenue column in visit reports, 197, *197*
- Revenue Participation metric, 141, 208, *208–209*, 335, *335*
- Revenue per Visit metric, 295–296, *295*

Revenue per Visitor metric, 296
revenue tracking, **45–46**
  encryption, **49–53**, *50*
  multiple currencies, **46–48**, *47*
  order IDs, **48–49**
rights for reports, **193–194**, *193*
ROAS (return on advertising spending) metric
  dashboard, 238
  description, 60
  revenue tracking, 45–46
robots.txt file, 214
ROI (return on investment), 149
role administration for reports, **193–194**, *193*
RON currency code, 47
row charts, **236–238**, *237–238*
RSD currency code, 47
RUB currency code, 47

S

`_s_action` function, 43
`_S_AMOUNTS` variable
  currency, 89–90
  description, 23
  final revenue amount, 101
  products purchased, 97–98
  units tracking, 88
`_S_cfxx` variable, 23
`_S_CMPQUERY` variable
  description, 23
  tracking campaigns, 68
  triggering campaigns, 127
`_S_DISCOUNT` variable
  description, 23
  discount tracking, 101
`_s_icmp` variable, 80
`_S_ISK` variable, 115
`_S_ISR` variable, 115
`_S_RUN` variable, 23
`_S_SHIPPING` variable
  description, 23
  shipping tracking, 101
`_S_SKU` variable
  description, 23
  merchandise tracking, 86–87
  products purchased, 98
`_S_TAX` variable
  description, 23
  tax tracking, 101
`_S_UNITS` variable
  description, 23
  products purchased, 98
  units tracking, 88
`_S_URL` variable, 128
SALE action, 34
sales
  multiple
    actions on same web page, **38–42**
    sales during same visit, **38**
  pending
    SKU codes, 86
    tracking, **93–96**, *95*
  tracking across domains, **106–107**
Save Segment Selection setting, **187**
Save Sorting setting, 187
scales
  logarithmic, 331–332
  trend charts, **244**
scatter charts, 339, *339*
Scenario Analysis reports, 211
`scenario_id` field, 355
scenario object, 350
scenarios, funnel analysis
  ad hoc, **260–263**, *260–262*
  creating, **53–55**, *54–55*
  overview, **257–258**
  predefined, **258–259**, *258–259*
scheduled email alerts, 166
Scheduled Report Items screen, 177, *177*
scheduled reports, **175–179**, *176–179*
Scheduled Reports screen, 176, *176*
Scheduled Reports Settings dialog, 176, *177*
`ScheduleReportJobBookmark` call, 351
`ScheduleReportJobStandard` call, 351, **354–365**
scope
  cross-reference filters, **152**, *153*
  custom fields, 112
  events, 172
  filters, 355
Scope setting, 172
Screen Resolutions reports, 220
search-dominant visitors
  characteristics, **275**
  content optimization, **340–341**, *341*
search engine optimization (SEO) activity, 26
Search Engine Optimization Team Ops dashboard, 232
search engine results pages (SERPs)
  description, 214
  internal searches, 114–115

Search Engine Revenue Insight and Referrals report, 234
Search Engine Unavailable error, 79
search engines
bulk campaigns, 74
content networks, **287–288**
referrals, 145, *145*
reports, **215–217**, *215–217*
traffic comparisons, **346**, *347*
Search Engines field, 74
Search Engines reports, 215
Search Listing Avg. Cost per Click metric, 288
Search Listing (Keyword) metric, 288
Search Listing Total Cost metric, 288
Search phrase field, 200
search phrases
custom reports, 184–185, *185*
last visitor reports, 200
paid optimization, 284
Search Phrases reports, 215
custom, 234, *235*
keyword optimization, 327–329, *327–328*
searches
custom, 284–285, *285–286*
internal reports, **272–277**, *272–273*, *275–276*
paid analysis. *See* paid search
path analysis, **254–257**, *255–256*
secure domains, tracking sales across, **106–107**
secure field for login, 352
Secure Sockets Layer (SSL), 13
security
Flash-based objects, 120
login, **352–353**
SSL, 13
Segment Report feature, 139
segmentation, 15–16
form conversions, **322–324**, *323*
funnel analysis scenarios, 261
guidelines, **189**
path analysis, 254
in reporting, **188–190**
creating, **190**, *190*
loyal customer data, **190–192**, *191*
setting up, **192–193**, *193*
visit reports, 340–341, *341*
Segmentation Wizard, 190, *190–191*, 212
SEK currency code, 47
semicolons (;) in names, 26–27
SEO (search engine optimization) activity, 26
SEO & SEM conversion reports, 217
SERPs (search engine results pages)
description, 214
internal searches, 114–115
`session_id` field
login, 353
`ScheduleReportJobStandard`, 355
Session Scope filter, 152
session scope segments, 192
`session_url` field, 353
Set Calendar Events option, 173
`setAction` function, 24
`setAmount` function, 24
`setAmounts` function, 24
`setCF` function, 24
`setCmpQuery` function, 24
`setDiscount` function, 24
`setDocumentGroup` function, 24
`setDocumentName` function, 24
`setDomains` function, 24
`setFlashUrl` function, 24
`setISK` function, 24
`setISR` function, 24
`setMemberId` function, 24
`setOrderId` function, 24
`setShipping` function, 24
`setSKU` function, 24
`setTax` function, 24
`setUnits` function, 24
SGD currency code, 47
shipping, **99–101**, *101*
Shockwave Flash (SWF), 116–117
Show Abandonment Path By Title report, 261
Show All Transit Traffic option, 250, 252–253
`show_description` field, 355
Show Filters icon, 148
`show_help` field, 355
Show Path from Here by Title report, 254
Show Report option, 182
Show Site Entries Only option, 250
Show Site Exits Only option, 253
siloed optimization, 312
simple footer tagging, 4
Simple Object Access Protocol (SOAP), 351–352

single campaign management, **72**
single quotes (‘) in names, 26–27
Site Exits, 316, 318
Site Stays, 316, 318
SKK currency code, 47
SKUs (stock keeping units), 84
  description, 22, 85
  tracking, **85–87**
slashes (/)
  scripts, 20
  variables, 26–27
SOAP (Simple Object Access Protocol), 351–352
sort field, 355
`sort_direction` field, 355
Sorting report modifier, 140
sorting reports
  demographics, 206, *206*
  process, **158–159**, *159*
SSL (Secure Sockets Layer), 13
standalone path analysis reports, **250–254**, *251–254*
Start Date field for bulk campaigns, 74
`start_date` field for `ScheduleReportJobStandard`, 354
Start Time field, 130
Status field for bulk campaigns, 74
status scope for custom fields, 112
stock keeping units (SKUs), 84
  description, 22, 85
  tracking, **85–87**
string cross-reference filters, 151
Subcategory category for enterprise campaigns, 65
submit function, 81, 123
`submit_action` function, 39, 123–124
`submit_icmp` function, 81
submit optimization, **319–323**, *319–323*
SWF (Shockwave Flash), 116–117
system reports, **219–221**, *220–221*

T

tabular data in dashboards, **233–234**, *233–235*
`.taf` extension, 30
tagging, 4
tax tracking, **99–101**, *101*
Test a Scheduled Report screen, 177, *178*
Test Movie function, 118
Thank-You pages
  actions in, 94
  guidelines, **319–322**, *319–322*
THB currency code, 47
tildes (~) in names, 26–27
time comparative reporting, **144–147**, *145–147*
time periods in reports
  calendars for, 141–142, *142*
    purpose, 138
    time comparative reporting, **144–147**, *145–147*
    unique visitors, **142–144**, *143–144*
  overview, **138–141**, *139–141*
Time Spent on Site reports, 211
time stamps in Unix, 105–106
Time Zone projects, 19
time zones, user-specific, 194
Time Zones reports, 203–204, *203–204*
timers for Flash-based objects, 121
timing
  alerts, **168–170**, *169–170*
  bookmarks, **187**
  scheduled reports, **176**
`.tml` extension, 30
Top Entry Pages by Page URL report, 252, *253*
Top Internal Searches report, 115, 272, *272*
`.tpl` extension, 30
tracking
  conversion actions, **34–38**, *35–37*
    multiple actions on same web page, **38–42**
    multiple sales during same visit, **38**
    on-click actions, **42–44**, *43*
    visitor conversion count methodology, **44–45**, *45*
  cost consolidation, **270**
  custom fields, **110–114**, *110–111*, *113–114*
  discount, tax, and shipping, **99–101**, *101*
  downloads, **28–30**, *29*
  exit links, **30–31**, *30*
  Internal Search feature, **114–116**, *116*
  page views vs. actions, **125–126**
  pending sales and reconciling orders, **93–96**, *95*
  products
    added to cart, **92–93**, *92–93*
    purchased, **96–99**, *97*
    viewed, **90–92**, *91–92*
  registered members, **31–33**, *33–34*

revenue, **45–46**
encryption, **49–53**, *50*
multiple currencies, **46–48**, *47*
order IDs, **48–49**
sales across domains, **106–107**
SKU information, **86–87**
units and amounts, **87–89**, *89*
tracking code IDs, 112
tracking scripts
customization, **20–24**
installation, **10–14**, *11*
traffic
acquisition, 58
attribution filters, **153–154**, *154*
prequalifying, **308–311**, *309–311*
search engine comparisons, **346**, *347*
trend charts, **243–245**, *244–245*
triggers for alerts, **168–170**, *169–170*
TRY currency code, 47
Type filters, 355
Type of Event setting, 172

U

UAH currency code, 47
Unique Campaign Clicks metric, 60
unique landing pages, 67
unique visitors, **142–144**, *143–144*
units, tracking, **87–89**, *89*
Unix time stamps, 105–106
Upload Campaign Settings to the System task, 73
Upload CSV File to the System option, 103
Upload Export to FTP Server method, 164
Upload Merchandising Categories option, 102
upstream visits in competitive intelligence, **346**
URL Contains criteria in funnel analysis, 258, 262
URL Equals criteria in funnel analysis, 258
URL/Referrer field for bulk campaigns, 74
URLs
enterprise campaigns, 67–68
vanity, 17
usability studies, **304**, 335
USD currency code, 47–48
user agent strings, 9–10
user-defined fields, 130
User-Level Display Settings dialog, 193–194, *193*
user object, 350
`user_password` field, 352
user rights for reports, **193–194**, *193*
user-specific reporting currency, 194
UTC (Coordinated Universal Time), 106

V

validating code, **131**
Value filters, 355
vanity URLs, 17
variables, 20–22
custom, **23**
merchandising, **86**
Vendor category for enterprise campaigns, 65
verification opportunities in paid search, 78, *78*
vertical segmentation, 15
View Event option, 171
View Events screen, 174, *174*
View Report option, 228
View Visit Path link, 202
Visit path field, 200
Visitor Segment option, 231
Visitor-to-Sales Conversion metric, 294, *295*
visitors
conversion count methodology, **44–45**, *45*
counting, **271**
search-dominant, **275**
visits
reports, **196–202**, *196–202*
Visit Revenue reports, 218, *218–219*
Visit to Sale Conversion metric, 216, 293, *293–294*
Visits filter, 152
Visits per Search Engine report, 182–184
`.vm` extension, 30

W

Web Analytics: An Hour a Day (Kaushik), 77
Web Analytics Association (WAA), **125–126**
web.analytics.yahoo.com site, 6
Web Services Description Language (WSDL), 351
Web Site Title projects, 19
Web Site URL projects, 19
Week report periods, 142

Weekly Unique Visitors reports, 143, *144*
.wem extension, 30
width of search query boxes, 339, *339*
wildcards in cross-reference filters, 150
wrapper functions, 39, 118–119
WSDL (Web Services Description
Language), 351

X

XLS format, 163
XMLHttpRequest objects, 122

Y

Y! OS, 7
Yahoo!
dashboards, 224, *225*
paid search, **76–77**
Yahoo! Buzz Customers, 6
Yahoo! Custom Customers, 7
Yahoo! Japan, 6
Yahoo! Search Marketing, 342
Yahoo! Small Business Merchant Solutions,
6–7, *8*
Yahoo! Web Analytics Partner Networks, 6
Yahoo! Web Analytics Segmentation
Wizard, 16, *16*
Yahoo! Web Analytics site, 8–9, 11–12
Year report periods, 142
yellow color code, 161
YMATracker functions, **23–24**
ypageview function, 123

Z

ZAR currency code, 47
Zero Results Internal Searches reports,
273, *273*
Zip code reports, 203

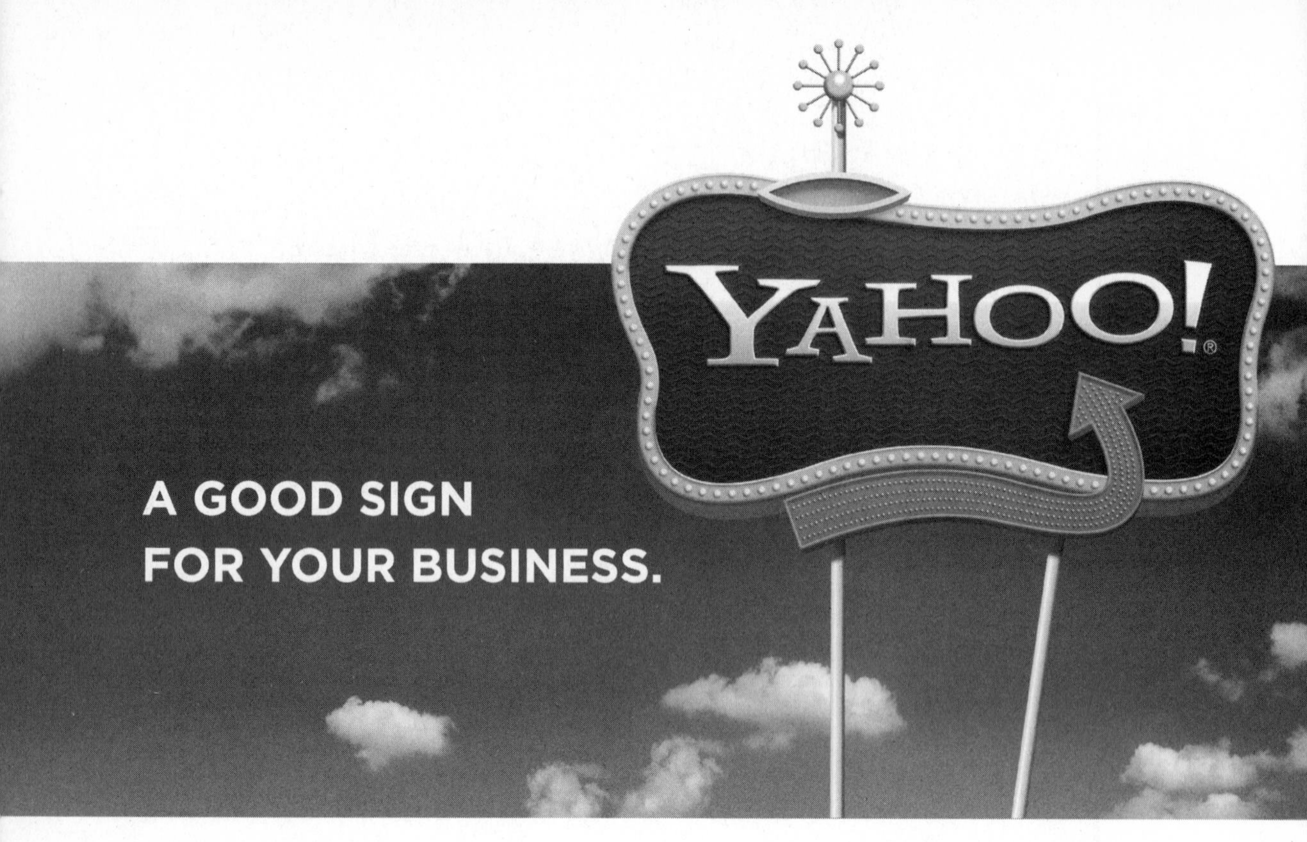
YAHOO!
A GOOD SIGN
FOR YOUR BUSINESS.